SAINTS, SINNERS, AND SOLDIERS

Studies in Canadian Military History

The Canadian War Museum, Canada's national museum of military history, has a three-fold mandate: to remember, to preserve, and to educate. It does so through an interlocking and mutually supporting combination of exhibitions, public programs, and electronic outreach. Military history, military historical scholarship, and the ways in which Canadians see and understand themselves have always been closely intertwined. Studies in Canadian Military History builds on a record of success in forging those links by regular and innovative contributions based on the best modern scholarship. Published by UBC Press in association with the Museum, the series especially encourages the work of new generations of scholars and the investigation of important gaps in the existing historiography, pursuits not always well served by traditional sources of academic support. The results produced feed immediately into future exhibitions, programs, and outreach efforts by the Canadian War Museum. It is a modest goal that they feed into a deeper understanding of our nation's common past as well.

SAINTS, SINNERS, AND SOLDIERS

CANADA'S SECOND WORLD WAR

UBCPress · Vancouver · Toronto

JEFFREY A. KESHEN

09 08 07 06 05 04   5 4 3 2 1

Printed in Canada on acid-free paper

National Library of Canada Cataloguing in Publication

Keshen, Jeff, 1962-
Saints, sinners, and soldiers : Canada's Second World War / Jeffrey A. Keshen.

(Studies in Canadian military history 1499-6251)
Includes bibliographical references and index.
ISBN 0-7748-0923-X

1. World War, 1939-1945 – Canada. 2. Canada – Social conditions – 1939-1945. 3. Canada – Social conditions – 1945-1971. 4. Canada – History – 1939-1945. 5. Canada – History – 1945-1963. I. Title. II. Series.
FC582.K47 2004   971.063   C2003-907124-3

Canadä

UBC Press gratefully acknowledges the financial support for our publishing program of the Government of Canada through the Book Publishing Industry Development Program (BPIDP), and of the Canada Council for the Arts, and the British Columbia Arts Council.

This book has been published with the help of a grant from the Canadian Federation for the Humanities and Social Sciences, through the Aid to Scholarly Publications Programme, using funds provided by the Social Sciences and Humanities Research Council of Canada.

The author and the publisher acknowledge the financial assistance of the Research and Publications Committee of the Faculty of Arts, University of Ottawa. We would also like to thank the Canadian War Museum for its support of this publication.

Printed and bound in Canada by Friesens
Set in Minion and Helvetica Condensed by Artegraphica Design Co. Ltd.
Photo section: Blakeley Design
Copy editor: Sarah Wight
Proofreader: Ian MacKenzie
Indexer: Noeline Bridge

UBC Press
The University of British Columbia
2029 West Mall
Vancouver, BC V6T 1Z2
604-822-5959 / Fax: 604-822-6083
www.ubcpress.ca

Contents

Figures, Tables, Illustrations

Acknowledgments

For as long as I can remember, I have had a keen interest in the Second World War. The reason is simple: I grew up with it. My father was a bombardier with the Royal Canadian Air Force, and my mother became a teenager in Toronto during those years. They are now both deceased, and I am grateful for the opportunity to place some of their memories in this book. I am also grateful for the friendship and professional guidance of Jack Granatstein, who knows more than anyone else about Canadian military history. After I finished a PhD under his direction on information control in Canada during the Great War, Jack suggested the topic of "Canada's Bad War." And despite being busy with several works of his own, he read an earlier, and longer, version of this work, made copious comments, and saved me from many mistakes. Jonathan F. Vance, probably the best of the next generation of Canadian military historians, also waded through an earlier version and offered incisive critiques on both substance and style. I would also like to thank two anonymous reviewers for UBC Press and the Humanities and Social Science Federation of Canada for their very thorough, thoughtful, and constructive commentary.

Many others have read chapters and offered advice. At the University of Alberta, where I spent two years as a Killam postdoctoral fellow, I would like to thank Professors David Mills, Paul Voisey, Rod Macleod, Doug Owram, and the late John Foster. At the University of Ottawa, my appreciation goes out to Eda Kranakis, Chad Gaffield, and particularly to Don Davis, who even came up with the title. Of course, I assume full responsibility for any remaining shortcomings or errors. Also at the University of Ottawa, I benefited from the research assistance of several talented graduate students: Martin Auger, Anne St-Jacques, Melanie Parker, Krista Robertson, Garth Williams, and Cynthia Smurthwaite. Thanks also to Jane McWhinney for improving my style.

Financial support for this research came from the Killam Foundation, the Social Science and Humanities Research Council of Canada, and the University of Ottawa. At the University of British Columbia Press, Emily Andrew expressed interest in this project well before it was written and, when it was finally time, did a wonderful job in shepherding it through the peer review process. As senior editor, she also made a number of suggestions that markedly improved the text. Also at UBC Press, Camilla Jenkins painlessly guided the work through the production process. My copy editor, Sarah Wight, made this a much more readable book. Dr. Dean Oliver, Director, Historical Research and Exhibit Development, at the

Canadian War Museum, spotted this project in its very early stages as a candidate for the Studies in Canadian Military History series that the Museum publishes in association with UBC Press and has been encouraging throughout. My appreciation also goes to the very efficient and helpful staff at the National Archives of Canada, the Archives of Ontario, the Archives of Alberta, and numerous other local archives.

Finally and most important, I would like to thank my wife, Deborah Moynes-Keshen, always unwavering in her support and whose ideas permeate this book. It is to her, as well as to our daughter, Madelaine, that I dedicate this work with love and gratitude.

SAINTS, SINNERS, AND SOLDIERS

Introduction

FOR A WAR, the Second World War has had a good press. For American historian Studs Terkel it was *The Good War* and for Michael Adams, *The Best War Ever.*[1] For Canadian historians J.L. Granatstein and Peter Neary it was *The Good Fight,* and Michael Bliss called it "Canada's Swell War."[2] Although the upbeat mood implied in such titles often belies the substance of these works, these titles pay homage to a long-standing, still widely held, and in many respects understandable view of the Second World War. How could it be otherwise? Did not the Allies save democracy from totalitarian and expansionary powers, and, in the case of the Third Reich, a genocidal one? Did not the war supplant an economic depression with an economic boom? It is no wonder that nostalgia from the Second World War still reverberates strongly: Churchill's defiant *V* for victory sign, Vera Lynn's sentimental ballads, and the uplifting tempos of the big bands. Supposedly it was a better, simpler time, a time when patriotic people, making genuine sacrifices, put defence of country and freedom first. Everyone was a hero, whether he or she carried a rifle, riveted ships, bought or sold war bonds, or collected scrap for munitions. Whenever people lament the "materialism and moral relativism"[3] of the present, or the lack of principled and inspirational leadership, somehow they think of lost innocence and noble purpose. Inherently they refer back to a golden age when people instinctively knew, and were prepared to defend, right from wrong, and when unity behind a great cause prevailed. Apparently, the "good war" was such a time.

Of course, not even the war against Hitler has had universal rave reviews. At moments of remembrance, commentators have recalled the war's horrors, especially those that beg for guilt, like the fire-bombing of Dresden, the atom-bombing of Hiroshima, and the indifference to the Holocaust. Canadian discourse, both academic and popular, has also emphasized such events as the forced evacuation of the Japanese Canadians, the divisions over conscription, and military follies like the raid on Dieppe.[4] The Canadian Broadcasting Corporation, in its now-famous 1992 three-part documentary, *The Valour and the Horror,* chose to focus on the doomed defence of Hong Kong, the "murderous" air raids on Germany, and the waste of Canadian lives in the 1944 Normandy campaign. The fate of the series proved, however, that Canadians wanted to remember the Second World War as a good war, for the CBC took so much flack from military historians, veterans, and politicians that it never gave the sordid mess a second airing. The CBC's coverage of the fiftieth anniversary of D-Day and VE day was, as Canadians wanted, glowingly positive.

The aura of the "good war" pervaded such commemorations. In Parliament, MPs spoke of Canadians being "united in the struggle for a better world" and sacrificing as one for the "liberty and freedom of future generations." Prime Minister Jean Chrétien, speaking at Courseulles-sur-Mer, France, on 6 June 1994, declared that those Canadians who had stormed the beaches where he now stood symbolized a country "united" in a common and "noble" cause, as "on their graves you will find names like McMillan and Cormier and Freedman."[5] Another prominent theme, also found in the work of many professional historians, was that the war "made" Canada: politically into a far more independent country, socially with the rise of the welfare state, and economically as a depression was replaced by an unprecedented, and lengthy, period of prosperity. As one reviewer said in summing up a spate of books in 1995, it was a "good war for Canada."[6]

These pictures contrast with the sombre, often horrifying images typically called to mind by the Great War of 1914-18, images conveyed in the titles of such well-known academic works as *The Broken Years, Death's Men, Dismembering the Male,* and, from Granatstein and Desmond Morton, *Marching to Armageddon.*[7] Recent work on the cultural legacy of the Great War has contested the belief that the carnage of those embattled years discredited romantic conceptions about combat.[8] Still, the Second World War, though lengthier and causing far more death, has enjoyed a far better reputation. While the Great War is often seen to be rooted in shifting and self-serving European alliances, or in rival imperial ambitions, the reason for Allied participation in the Second World War remains clear-cut: saving democracy and freedom from tyrannical dictators.[9] While the Great War is often pictured in terms of static trench warfare and appalling casualties, the Second World War, with its greater reliance on technology, projects as cleaner, and its battles as more fluid.[10] People died, but at least it was for a good cause, and they did not die in the mud, amidst vermin and stench.

Certainly, the trope of the "good war" is not without some truth. The war's cause was just: Hitler was evil, the Japanese often unspeakably cruel, and Germany, Japan, and Italy had expansionist aims against people – the Slavs, the Chinese, and the Albanians – whom they deemed subhuman. At home, many of its consequences were beneficial: the Canada of 1945 was far stronger economically, had earned a greater presence internationally, and, with its welfare state, had become a more compassionate place than it had been in 1939. Moreover, for its size, Canada made a stellar contribution, both on the home front and in providing weapons and men for the fight overseas. The first part of this book will confirm that the myth of the good war has its basis in considerable fact. Here we will encounter passionate army recruits, tireless munitions workers, unflagging war charity volunteers, unsparing Victory Bond purchasers, ardent ARP wardens, and consumers who zealously followed the rationing rules.

But another, less familiar, story shows that just as emphasis on the "good war" comforts, it also clouds. Fifty years after it all started, Charles Lynch, a former war correspondent, felt it necessary to remind his readers that "not everyone was nice ... in Canada's good war."[11] In many ways the popular memory has sanitized and simplified a "complex and problematic" event,[12] whose legacies for Canada were not just profound, but also contradictory.

The not-so-good-war manifested itself in numerous domains. Many asked whether Canadians were working as hard as possible to back the war effort, and to what extent they were profiting illegally from the conflict. Before long the rapidly accelerating demands of the war created much criticism that many Canadians appeared unwilling to make needed sacrifices and were shamelessly placing self-serving and pecuniary interests above national needs. Such attitudes seemed demonstrated by the mixed responses to increased taxation, and by the sometimes hostile reactions from much of the farm belt and organized labour to the extra demands placed upon their services and to Ottawa's implementation of a wage and price freeze in late 1941. Also fostering anxiety was the perception that many ordinary people were exploiting unique wartime conditions to make illegal windfall profits. One manifestation was rent gouging, often for rundown spaces, which was fuelled by extensive wartime migration to centres of war production, mainly from rural areas and small towns. Coupon rationing was implemented in 1942 and 1943 to ensure fair distribution at just prices; but besides obliging people to drive, drink, and eat less, it also precipitated extensive cheating and black market activity.

The war years also saw mounting alarm over perceptions of crumbling social decorum and the spread of debauched sexual conduct. In part, this view was a response to the behaviour of recruits, who attracted from civilians not only warmth and support but also indignation and disgust. Numerous servicemen imbibed and brawled excessively and adopted a predatory attitude toward women when letting loose from the rigours, pressures, and often, the tedium of training. It was also a way to express the bonding process among recruits and the rough masculine characteristics that they thought were expected from men in uniform. Apprehension also developed over the behaviour of women who reacted to the loneliness, strain, and uncertainties of these years by apparently throwing caution to the winds. Worries intensified over marriages undertaken in haste, rising wartime divorce, "loose" young women seeking out men in uniform, growing illegitimacy, and rampant infidelity, the last the subject of often ill-founded rumours that, nonetheless, destroyed relationships.

Prostitution came into public focus. It was seen to be proliferating to serve a military clientele, among whom VD rates rose sharply. Moral and medical concerns sparked raids on red-light districts and brothels in many areas. Action also intensified to control so-called promiscuous good-time girls especially since, at least initially within the military, no lectures, provision of prophylactics, or threat of fines against servicemen who contracted the disease were able to stem VD infection rates. Soon, many women found themselves more carefully scrutinized and often harassed by authorities. Health officials initiated traces to locate the women named as having transmitted VD. They were then compelled to undergo testing and possible treatment. These expedients led not only to successful identifications but also to mistakes, embarrassment, and suffering. Nevertheless, there were other, more positive, reactions: franker discussion of and education about VD and improved treatment facilities, as governments endeavoured to deal with a problem still by and large considered taboo.

The anxiety of many Canadians in wartime was also fed by the large-scale migration of women into the paid workforce, namely into jobs then typically considered "male" in nature, as well as by women's unprecedented inclusion in the military. The received interpretation of these trends in Canada stresses widespread social concern over women's new roles, citing the supposed preponderance of sexist government propaganda and mass media content, the mistreatment of women on job sites and in the military, and, ultimately, their massive dismissal following the conflict. In this version, popular discourse portrays women as offering a short-term patriotic gesture to "back the attack" by releasing men for active service and projecting assurances that women's new, and often "manly," wartime jobs, would not compromise their appearance, femininity, or family-centred role.[13] There is much evidence to back this thesis, but these were not the only messages delivered to or internalized by women. Media content and government propaganda not only influenced but also reflected popular trends and ideas. They lauded women for successfully assuming unconventional and highly skilled roles in the workplace and the military, as well as for running all aspects of the wartime home in the absence of men and managing monumental volunteer activities. Furthermore, both during and after the war, women often stressed their sense of accomplishment, growing confidence, importance, and independence.

The legacy from these years points beyond a traditionalist backlash triggered by anxieties over changing gender roles and their perceived threat to conventional family life. In the context of the times, it also indicates significant and progressive shifts: increased participation rates and growing rights of women in the workplace; greater access to government benefits, particularly to those established by the Department of Veterans Affairs; and a generally growing acceptance of women in new roles, including, relatively soon, the postwar military.

Still, concerns over the stability of Canadian families in wartime, especially over the growing numbers of working mothers, exaggerated negative depictions of Canadian children through an overly attentive scrutiny of child neglect and juvenile delinquency. Contributing to this sense of crisis – though they were not publicized like alarmist assumptions about working mothers – were new pressures on underfunded, understaffed, and easily overwhelmed provincial and local child welfare services. These agencies had the new and onerous obligation to undertake investigations for the federal Dependants' Allowance Board, adjudicating appropriate financial support for women with husbands in uniform. Despite blame for wartime increases in juvenile delinquency being laid at the feet of working mothers, it can be shown that demographic forces were more responsible. The rise in the proportion of adolescent youths among the general population, in combination with the large-scale migration into the military of the most crime-inclined demographic cohort, seems to offer a more convincing explanation. The latter trend provided civilian police forces, even understaffed ones, with the time to prosecute petty crimes perpetrated by youth. Yet wartime discourse remained typified by headlines about latchkey children and street gangs, and the consequent need to reconstitute so-called traditional values and structures as soon as possible after the war. This reaction not only pushed many working women back into the home but also, in several parts of the country, served to bring about initiatives such as more religious instruction in public schools. On the arguably more progressive side, action also intensified to upgrade community recreational services; to create more comprehensive, inclusive, and professionally run schools that could better retain and train youth; and to increase the presence and professionalism of the juvenile justice system.

While the departure of many fathers and older brothers for overseas added to worries over the conduct of the youth left behind, it was among these men and others – those who actually fought the war – that behavioural problems became most evident. Many citizens were aware that those in uniform, in keeping with the sometimes errant conduct they had already demonstrated while in training in Canada, shed inhibitions even more overseas. Those who fought in the Great War, and many family members who welcomed them home, understood that war frequently transformed participants drastically and, all too often, for the worse. But many Great War veterans were silent about their time overseas, or if they did speak, refrained from dwelling on the horrors or suggesting in any way that so much death was in vain. They tended, rather, to recount the amusing anecdotes, to stress the camaraderie of those years, the sacrifices of their comrades, and their participation in a noble cause. Also, by 1939, a generation had elapsed since the Great War. Nearly all the volunteers in this fight against fascism had no direct memories of that event. One study of those joining the Canadian army found their average age to be just nineteen and a half.[14] Although some men enlisting in 1939 sought to escape the Depression, and though many considered themselves realistic about the brutal experiences that might lie ahead, far more prevalent were idealistic notions about patriotism, duty, solidarity with the Empire, and the desire for adventure.

The conditions many confronted would forge attitudes and release conduct that increasingly distanced them from the moral and social norms of their communities in Canada. In contrast to the impression conveyed by morale-raising media accounts and letters home, which generally portrayed a positive picture thanks to censorship regulations and men's desire not to distress loved ones, numerous war participants shamelessly cheated or plundered from desperate civilians; drank excessively at every opportunity; and exploited the loneliness or destitution of women in devastated countries to obtain sex. Among the men overseas, significant numbers succumbed to battle exhaustion and returned home broken in body and spirit – altered, sometimes, forever.

The planning to re-establish these men in civilian life eventually began within weeks of the decision to wage war, to ensure that veterans would be brought back quickly and provided with generous programs to help them thrive in the postwar world. These plans were in large part devised by politicians and mandarins who were Great War veterans. Many recalled only too well the widespread anger among their former comrades and the potentially destabilizing force that numerous veterans came to represent when they lingered overseas while awaiting repatriation or later when provided with what they considered niggardly postwar support programs.

Still, despite their jubilant welcome home, the road back to civvy street and family life was an arduous one for many Second World War veterans. They were often unable to settle down and hold jobs, and were either emotionally distant or overly belligerent. Many felt comfortable only around fellow veterans, considering civilians naïve, parochial, or pampered. Many resented wives or girlfriends who had grown too independent, and others could not reconnect with their children. Divorce rates spiked soon after the conflict and further fuelled anxiety over the moral impact of the war. Indeed, many Canadians even worried about the initial explosion in postwar marriage rates, fearing a continuation of the wartime pattern of quick, ill-conceived unions, a large proportion of which, it was predicted, would end in failure.

Yet the greatest desire of people who by then had lived through a devastating depression and a world war was stability. After years of loneliness, strain, and turmoil, countless Canadians yearned for greater predictability in their lives, a calm and secure future that marriage, home, and traditional family life seemed to promise. Canadian men in large numbers, many with new war brides, quietly eased into this model. For many others, the return to civilian life involved varying degrees of painful readjustment.

A key to the re-establishment of postwar family life was what became known as the Veterans Charter, a program that, like the much-heralded American G.I. Bill of Rights, justifiably contributed to the picture of the Second World War ultimately being a "Good War."[15] Architects of what was arguably the most comprehensive benefit package in Canadian history were motivated by the perception that too many veterans of the Great War had failed to reintegrate. Moreover, there was strong public support to do right by veterans this time around; and bolstering this trend was the demand from most Canadians for more government planning and social security to avoid a repeat of postwar turmoil or a reassertion of the Great Depression. Through programs that included generous cash awards, widely available and free vocational training and university education, and extensive grants to start a farm or business, the Veterans Charter did more than just get men back on their feet. Its legacy was to have provided millions of Canadians who had come of age during the bleakness of the depression and endured a world war with the means of realizing optimistic social mobility, greater financial security, and in many cases a traditional patriarchal family life – though to rather mixed responses from women.

THIS SYNTHESIS SEEKS TO FILL SEVERAL GAPS in the social history of Canada's Second World War.[16] Though some works singling out specific groups – namely, women, organized labour, and servicemen - have addressed fears about wartime immorality and social instability, there is no overall assessment of this troublesome, even sordid, side of Canada's war experience. The political and military story is well known.[17] Not adequately addressed, however, are the multitudes who reacted with alarm, and sometimes panic, over what they perceived as the war's role in unleashing socially and morally destructive trends. Such a story has interested historians elsewhere.[18] But while British and American scholars have written much about war's strains – namely, the suspicions millions had that their countrymen and -women were using the war for personal gain or pleasure – there is relatively little on the subject in Canadian literature. Canadian historians have not reminded us that even a good war can have lots of bad people, or at least people who could be perceived as bad when seen through the prism of wartime anxiety or prudery. Yet this story looms very large in the records of scores of national, provincial, and local government departments and agencies in Canada; in the papers of key national politicians to local social service workers; in both urban and rural newspapers and magazines; in films and radio broadcasts; and, closer to the present, in more than seventy-five personal interviews, covering Canadians from coast to coast, all of which form the foundation for this book.[19] Told from a national perspective, the story that unfolds in these pages will leave some exceptions and nuances unexamined. No doubt, studies homing in on West Toronto, say, or Chicoutimi, Medicine Hat, or Pugwash, would produce slightly different accounts, and in time those local tales must be told and a new synthesis may well emerge.[20] In the meantime, it is crucial to know the national picture, not only because general patterns are more important than anomalies but also because local departures can be properly assessed only by understanding broad trends.

Most notable among historians to assess the implications of the "not-so-good-war" is John Costello, who focuses on Britain and the United States. In two books, *Love, Sex and War* and *Virtue under Fire,* he describes societies being catapulted toward more lenient, or modern, attitudes. Demonstrating this shift, he cites the generally enthusiastic responses given in 1948 to the appearance of Norman Mailer's *The Naked and the Dead* and Irwin Shaw's *The Young Lions,* books by veterans that were "brutally honest ... sexually explicit." Such writers, especially Mailer, made generous use of profanity to elucidate the destructive and cruel as well as to convey the liberating impact of war or military life on those it touched most directly.[21]

Canadian veterans were also soon producing literary accounts of the Second World War. Like those by Mailer, Shaw, and a little later on, James Jones, they cast many of those fighting for the "right side" as ordinary, flawed people, capable of, for example, uttering Nazi-type vitriol against Jews as in Hugh Garner's 1949 novel, *Storm Below,* or giving into carnal temptation, as did Edward Meade's married protagonist, infantryman Bob O'Rourke, in *Remember Me,* published only a year after the war ended.[22] Even more provocative was Earle Birney's *Turvey: A Military Picaresque* (1949). Here, the author used his experiences as an army personnel officer to produce a representational central character: a simple-minded sad-sack private who was always getting into trouble, and whose escapades satirically exposed an often mad military machine that "persecutes" and "buffets around" the lowly. Birney describes, for instance, a full-fledged military court martial to prosecute the trivial, a military psychiatrist more removed from reality than his patients, the heavy involvement of soldiers in black marketing, their insatiable desire for liquor and sex, and their propensity to speak in "raw language."

But did the publication of such works really signify a new and more promiscuous postwar? Meade's book was essentially ignored until 1965, when McClelland and Stewart rediscovered it and made it part of its New Canadian Library Series. *Turvey* initially sold some 7,000 copies, a decent figure but hardly a blockbuster. Also, being the most daring in its use of language – with terms such "lover's nuts" – Birney's book proved problematic for its publisher, McClelland and Stewart. Jack McClelland insisted on changes to accommodate community standards, urging that exclamations of "Jesus Christ" by soldiers be misspelled, and that references to "cunt" or "crunt" be removed. In his defence Birney referred to Meade's use of "horse's arse and dirty bastards," but McClelland called this language gratuitous and said it denigrated *Remember Me.* While many reviewers praised *Turvey* for its realism, others, focusing on the profane and salacious, produced conservative- or even prudish-sounding critiques about an over-reliance on "barrack-room humour" and "bodily functions," and the book was banned in libraries across Canada.[23] Also worth noting is that *The Naked and the Dead,* though remaining on the US best-seller list for two months, was censured in several reviews, including in the *New York Times,* for its "excesses in obscenity and attention to sexual matters." And while words like "bitch" and "ass" punctuate the text, Mailer, after protracted battles with his publisher over the use of "fuck," finally resolved the issue through the creation of a soldiers' dialect that resulted in terms like "fug" and "fugging," which appeared more than 400 times in the book.[24]

But clearly there is far more than misgivings over avant-garde literature to challenge the picture of a more liberal-minded postwar. Indeed, the late 1940s and '50s are often portrayed as projecting the very antithesis to loosening values. Popular images include the stay-at-home wife, the baby boom, clean-cut kids, and a burgeoning middle-class migrating to family-centred suburban neighbourhoods. Such trends are often linked to the yearning for stability after decades of uncertainty and, especially during wartime, to troubling social changes. They are also buttressed by the Cold War, particularly in the United States but also in Canada, which forged a conservative political consensus and the promotion of traditional family life as a source of protection and comfort against the external and internal threats posed by Communism.[25] Yet obviously the postwar years cannot be summed up in terms of ticky-tacky homes, moms in aprons, or *Father Knows Best.* They also saw, for instance, steadily increasing numbers of working mothers, the scandalous Kinsey reports on sexual conduct, and screaming headlines about the juvenile delinquency, or JD, problem.

But how can this period have both these sides? Clearly, the contention here is that much of the explanation lies in the implications of the "bad war," or at least in many of those things that people saw as being bad. In many ways, the war was a social accelerator, quickly thrusting people into situations that boldly challenged their moral and social conventions. On the one hand wartime change charted paths toward greater lenience; on the other it precipitated fear of fragmentation when cohesion was essential, and of a chaotic and morally debased postwar period. As such, it also produced much in the way of reaction and recoil.

Saints, sinners, and soldiers all had their starring roles in "Canada's war" and peacetime reconstruction. Not only the patriotic but also the problematic – the real, the exaggerated, and even, arguably, the imagined – solicited tremendous attention. Through the responses they garnered, they helped produce major legacies in law, society, and culture that echo to this very day. Indeed, one could conclude that in large part this was a "good war" for Canada because so many Canadians fretted over and grew determined to prevent their fellow citizens from going "bad."

1
Patriotism

FOR MONTHS, even years, people had known it was coming. Every effort to appease Hitler had been followed by a fresh crisis. Finally, on 1 September 1939, with Germany's invasion of Poland came the "climax to Europe's long-drawn descent into conflict."[1] Britain and France drew the proverbial line in the sand: withdraw or face war. Desperate negotiations continued – led, so it was widely reported, by Mussolini – but two days later, with German forces still closing in on Warsaw, the Second World War began.

In Canada, no celebratory crowds cheered flashing headlines outside newspaper buildings as they had on 4 August 1914 with the announcement of the Great War. This was in part a result of timing: the news of 3 September reached Canada at 6:18 a.m. EST on a Sunday rather than on a warm summer evening as had occurred a quarter-century earlier. Also, countless people heard the news in the privacy of their homes over radio, a device first produced in Canada only in 1925.[2] Still, in the course of the morning, groups gathered outside newspaper offices and "swarmed" around newsboys to get the latest information. Reporters described these crowds as "sober," "solemn," "tight-lipped," and "grim-faced."[3] Many recalled or still lived with the massive and lingering human cost of the Great War. Margaret Moffatt of Ottawa, for example, then twenty years old, remembered her mother crying "because she had been through the first one and knew what it was like."[4] Also, many Canadians had been affected by the chilling antiwar novels of Lost Generation writers. In the early 1930s, Canadian pacifist groups had enjoyed relatively large followings.[5]

However, Canadians overwhelmingly thought the war was absolutely necessary. Multitudes held the view that when Britain was at war, Canada was too; they were outraged by the Nazi creed and Hitler's intent to dominate the world. If Britain and France fell, many believed Canada, with its vast natural resources, would become a prime target.[6] Across the land, even before Canada officially declared war, thousands of men rushed to recruitment booths. Most, it seems, were not seeking simply to escape the lingering effects of the Great Depression, which in 1939 still saw over 500,000 Canadians unemployed. Terry Copp, in his analysis of the Fifth Infantry Brigade, which was recruited in western Canada, points out that among its first twenty-three volunteers, only one was on relief. Historian Ian Miller contends that most of the volunteers who "besieged" Toronto armouries in September 1939 had jobs and often families to support.[7] That month recruiting stations in several cities remained open on a twenty-four-hour basis to deal with the deluge. Most men simply had their name taken down and were sent home until space and equipment became available several months later. It was as if they were trying to join an exclusive club. Indeed, several regiments stated in their publicity that priority would be given to those with particular experience, such as motor mechanics for Montreal's Black Watch, and cooking and butchering for Winnipeg's Fort Garry Horse. Even the initial response among Québécois appeared encouraging; during the ten days up to 5 September, Montreal's two French-speaking infantry regiments, Les Fusiliers Mont-Royal and Le Régiment de Maisonneuve, received 1,200 and 900 applications respectively, figures that, the *Gazette* insisted, were as good as those of "any English-speaking regiment."[8]

Still, not until 10 September did Canada officially join the fray. Prime Minister Mackenzie King insisted that "parliament would decide" the nature and scope of the country's commitment, and it would take some time to recall the members, who had been on recess since June. This attitude reflected King's long-standing determination to promote Canadian autonomy within the Empire, and also served his more immediate aim of producing a show of unity for such a momentous undertaking. The delay produced little criticism, for on 3 September, King had made clear in a nationwide radio broadcast that his government would seek from Parliament the authority to offer "effective cooperation at the side of Britain."[9]

On 7 September, Lord Tweedsmuir, the governor general, read a brief Throne Speech to a "determined [but] grave-faced" Senate urging a "quick debate" and requesting that "authority" be given to the government to "resist ... aggression."[10] The House of Commons convened the next day. Military leaders, local dignitaries, and foreign representatives packed the galleries. The press reported an atmosphere of "calm and confidence" and a government determined to "quickly get down to business."[11] The debate was scheduled to last just two days; there would be no vote on a formal declaration of war, only approval or disapproval, preferably by voice, of the request made in the Throne Speech. Votes would only delay matters and possibly project a less united front, especially to Quebec, where support for the war was known to be more tenuous. Indeed, just before speeches commenced at 3 p.m., Maxime Raymond, an Independent Liberal representing Beauharnois-Laprairie, delivered to the speaker four paper bags containing "the names of thousands" who had signed a petition "against participation by Canada in any extra-territorial war."[12]

For the proposer and seconder to the Throne Speech, King chose two veterans of the Great War: an English Canadian from Ontario and a French Canadian from Quebec. Representing Algoma West, Lt.-Col. H.S. Hamilton, a former member of the Canadian Expeditionary Force, told the House that Canadians were "confronted with a philosophy that knows nothing of the value of human individuality and human liberty [only] unscrupulous force and violence." The seconder, Joseph

A. Blanchette, representing the riding of Compton just north of Vermont, had served in 1917-18 with the US army. He echoed Hamilton in describing the war as a fight for "human liberty," but also emphasized his opposition – and that of French Canada – to conscription. After the leader of the Opposition, Robert A. Manion, had promised his full cooperation in combating an "anti-Christian ... barbarous and brutal" enemy, it was the prime minister's turn. King spoke for nearly three hours, building a case for war by outlining Hitler's insatiable thirst for expansion and the unsuccessful attempts at appeasement that dated back to the reoccupation of the Rhineland. Things had now reached the stage, the prime minister declared, where the "forces of good and the forces of evil ... [were] locked in mortal combat." But when it came to proposing concrete measures, King was more cautious. He leaned toward Canada fighting a war of "limited liability," emphasizing the need for the country to secure its own borders; for the fight overseas, he favoured the contribution of materiel over military personnel. Moreover, fearing the discord that had engulfed the country and devastated his Liberal party during the Great War, he promised, particularly to Quebec, "no conscription for overseas service."[13]

The outcome was fully expected and rather anticlimactic, especially since King held a huge parliamentary majority. Support for war among MPs, including those from Quebec, was practically unanimous. The only party leader to dissent was J.S. Woodsworth, leader of the tiny Co-operative Commonwealth Federation faction. Yet, in his address, Woodsworth, a former Methodist minister and a committed pacifist, admitted that he spoke only for himself, not for the party. The official CCF position, which came rather close to King's "limited liability" approach, was expressed by M.J. Coldwell, the chairman of the CCF's national council. On 9 September, two more Quebec Liberals, Liguori Lacombe (Laval-Two Mountains) and Wilfrid Lacroix (Quebec-Montmorency), joined Raymond in breaking from their leader, accusing King of slavishly following the British line and predicting that Canada's entry into the war would bring the country crippling debt, conscription, and civil strife. But when the two dissenters demanded a formal vote on participation, they were "drowned out" by a chorus of "nays." At 10:23 p.m., after a few more patriotic speeches, Parliament loudly declared its consent. The next day, following unanimous approval from the Senate, Canada formally declared war.[14]

CANADIANS HUNGERED FOR NEWS about the war, and newspapers and magazines soon enjoyed record circulation.[15] To meet the soaring demand for radios, production increased from 348,507 units in 1939 to 485,010 the next year, though military needs and the shifting of product lines to other war-related requirements soon pre-empted new civilian supplies. One survey in the early 1940s revealed that about three-quarters of Canadian adults listened to a radio broadcast about the war every day.[16] From the outset of hostilities the federal government tried to ensure that information obtained through all communication media would, as far as possible, reflect and reinforce feelings of patriotism, duty, and the resolve to endure for victory. To this end, on 3 September, under the auspices of the War Measures Act, which had been introduced two days earlier, the Defence of Canada Regulations (DOCR) were proclaimed. The DOCR empowered the federal government to suspend jury trials and habeas corpus, to intern enemy aliens, to prohibit organizations deemed subversive, and to censor all media of material "caus[ing] disaffection to His Majesty or ... interfer[ing] with the success of His Majesty's forces" or "prejudicial to the safety of the State or the efficient prosecution of the war."[17]

No time was wasted in establishing a formal structure to manage information. The very day the DOCR appeared, so too did the Ottawa-based Censorship Co-ordinating Committee, composed of six representatives drawn from the Department of National Defence, the Air Force, the Post Office, the Canadian Broadcasting Corporation, and the Canadian Press Association. Their director was Walter Thompson, a "veteran newspaperman" who had been a reporter on Fleet Street, as well as in South Africa, New Zealand, and Australia. Arriving in Canada shortly before the Great War, Thompson became city editor for the Montreal *Witness* and then the *Montreal Herald* before becoming director of publicity for the Canadian National Railway, for which he also managed press relations, including those for the 1939 Royal Tour. *Maclean's* described him as "well liked" and "respected," a man who "probably enjoyed a wider acquaintance among newspapermen, publishers, writers and radio people than any other man in Canada." It also wrote that, given the issues at stake, "publishers, editors and the public accepted the necessity for censorship without a murmur."[18] There were dissenting voices, but they were lonely ones.[19] Typical reactions included that of the conservative *Globe and Mail*, which stressed that there was little "use ... fighting an enemy without if the enemies within [were] given a free hand," and that of its liberal counterpart, the *Toronto Star*, which maintained that it was the duty of everyone to "think and talk confidently and encourage others to think and talk the same way."[20]

Thompson's tenure was short. Given his expertise with publicity, he was reassigned in December to help establish and manage the Bureau of Public Information (BPI), Ottawa's first foray into wartime propaganda. For the next two years, censorship operations were managed by Col. (later Gen.) Maurice A. Pope, the Department of National Defence's designate on the Censorship Committee. In July 1942 Oliver Mowat Biggar, a "distinguished" patent attorney and long-time public servant, member of Canada's short-lived Air Board (1919-22), and most recently the country's chief representative on the Permanent Joint Board of Defence, took over until ill health forced his retirement in January 1944. But during most of Pope's and Biggar's terms, the day-to-day operations fell largely to Wilfrid Eggleston, formerly of the *Toronto Star*. He joined the Censorship Branch (which was eventually directed by National War Services) on 1 November 1939, started managing its English-language operations in April 1940, and, for one year after Biggar's retirement, served as director of censorship. After Eggleston, Fulgence Charpentier, a former reporter whose work had appeared regularly in *Le Droit* and the staunchly Liberal newspapers *La Presse, Le Canada,* and *Le Soleil,* became director. Throughout most of the war he managed the surveillance of French-language newspapers.[21]

Censorship authorities in Ottawa cast themselves and their assistants – in offices located in Montreal, Toronto, Vancouver, Saint John, and Halifax – as advisors to whom journalists, editors, publishers, broadcasters, photographers, and filmmakers could turn to ask about the acceptability of material. Eggleston lauded his former professional colleagues as patriotic Canadians as "anxious as anyone else to win the war."[22] Yet those responsible for disseminating information realized that a gaffe could bring harsh consequences. By late 1941, 325 print sources had been banned in Canada: just over half came from enemy countries, while most of the rest were small-circulation, enemy-language, pacifist, fascist, or socialist tracts from the neutral United States or from Canadian organizations banned under the DOCR.[23] Early in the war, some issues of the *Saturday Evening Post,* then the most widely circulated magazine in America, were held up at the Canadian border for expressing what were judged to be anti-British views.[24] Some mainstream Canadian publications received small fines, usually a few hundred dollars (compared to a possible maximum of $5,000) as warnings. *Le Droit,* for example, was fined $200 in early 1942 for alleging that Allied sorties against occupied France, though targeting industrial enterprises, were also responsible for killing numerous women and children.[25]

Given general knowledge about the Great War, censorship authorities were aware that civilians would react with suspicion to uniformly positive copy. Eggleston maintained that reports depicting a succession of victories could be detrimental to home front morale if they later had to be retracted; defeats, on the other hand, if properly presented, could inspire people toward a greater effort.[26] Accounts of the 19 August 1942 raid on Dieppe, France, are instructive. Whereas fewer than half of Canada's 5,000 troops returned from an ill-conceived and poorly executed attack against fully prepared and well-fortified German troops, the reports, although noting significant losses and some setbacks, assured readers that the "lessons learned" were certain to pave the way for the reconquest of Europe. Reports on Canadians fighting in the Mediterranean and northwest Europe maintained this pattern. The CBC's most famous overseas radio correspondent, Matthew Halton, practised his lines several times like an actor to obtain dramatic effect and reported near the front lines from mobile units so the sound and fury of battle could be conveyed (though sometimes these effects were later added in London studios). Some reports used language that could conceivably worry those at home. Describing the December 1943 battle in Ortona, Italy, Halton told Canadians that "the fighting in the streets resembled the antechamber of Hell." Still, the overall message remained optimistic, stressing incredible heroism in the face of a determined foe. In the same report, Halton continued: "Soaking wet ... against an enemy fighting ... like the devil to hold us, the Canadians attack, attack, attack."[27]

Typically, such material was first vetted overseas; military censors operating near theatres of war and in England examined reports, photographs, films, and radio transcripts before they were cabled, shipped, radio faxed, or transmitted via short- or long-wave to Canada. Most correspondents, it seems, had no major moral qualms about such controls. "I was committed to the war completely and utterly, right from the start," recalled the widely syndicated journalist Ross Munro in later years. "Maybe it was jingoism, chauvinism, and stupidity, but we felt that the Germans were going to wreck this world of ours and that we would have to stop them."[28] Censorship authorities, both at home and abroad, maintained that their primary role was to prevent the leakage of factual information that could be useful to the enemy, but they also heavily excised information or opinions they judged potentially damaging to morale and recruitment.[29] Canadians, already much sheltered by geography, read, heard, and saw relatively little to remind or enlighten them about the grisly aspects of war, or the disturbing and often alarming reactions it aroused in its participants.

To shield Canadians, as well as to bolster their patriotism, dissemination of information was also managed through propaganda. The BPI, formed on 5 December 1939, was initially set up to release press communiqués on Ottawa's war policies. Its activities expanded along with the scope of Canada's war effort. By early 1942, it had, for instance, produced over 18 million booklets and flyers outlining in generally factual but also optimistic tones Canada's many accomplishments relating to the war effort.[30] Still, the BPI was criticized for being unfocused, especially since it failed in the crucial task of rallying Quebec behind the war effort. Quebec's disaffection was demonstrated in the plebiscite on 27 April 1942, which asked Canadians to release the federal government from King's pledge of "no conscription for overseas service." Made in light of German advances in North Africa and Russia, Canada's declaration of war against Japan, and King's belief that a plebiscite would undercut English Canada's support for the pro-conscription Tories, the proposal was accepted by 80 percent of Canadians outside of Quebec but rejected by 72 percent within the province. Restructuring of the BPI was also necessitated by the intensification of the war; not only were more recruits required, but also by mid-1942 other measures were to be promoted to Canadians, including more thorough control of Canada's labour market, steep tax increases, and coupon rationing.

In May 1942 Prime Minister King asked his old friend Charles Vining, then serving as newsprint controller within the Wartime Prices and Trade Board and "a recognized authority on public relations," to analyze Ottawa's propaganda efforts. His recommendations, implemented in September 1942, subsumed the BPI within a new, more comprehensive Wartime Information Board (WIB), which reported directly to the prime minister's office. Initially placed under Vining's direction, the WIB consulted with advertising agencies, journalists, and academics in order to devise its strategy. It also commissioned numerous surveys from the newly created Canadian Institute of Public Opinion (CIPO) to gauge public support for government war policies, identify the most effective propaganda, and point out where more effort or a different approach was advisable. The WIB also became more closely affiliated with the new National Film Board, especially after John Grierson, the NFB's first commissioner, simultaneously held the directorship of the WIB for several months in 1943 (between Vining's departure and his replacement by news-paperman Davidson Dunton). The NFB, established in 1939 with one assistant, two secretaries, and a production supervisor, by the end of the war had a staff of 787 and had produced more than 500 films – most on Canada's war effort – which reached as many as a million viewers every month. They were distributed to over 800 commercial cinemas, as well as to factories, schools, libraries, and town halls, through the NFB's industrial, educational, and rural circuits, for which it provided projectors and projectionists.[31]

The WIB directed much of its effort toward Quebec, though with ultimately disappointing results. Like the BPI, the WIB was unable to counteract growing suspicion and anger toward the federal government as conscription for overseas service came closer to reality. Among its initiatives was the distribution of over 45,000 free copies of a fortnightly magazine, *Nouvelles Catholiques*, which tried to attract support from traditionalist elements, namely the Catholic Church, by par-ticularly stressing the anti-Christian nature of fascism.[32] It also renewed efforts to detect and combat damaging rumours, by enhancing support (originated by the BPI) for a Montreal-based group called the Rumour Clinic, whose directors in-cluded Alfred Charpentier, president of the Confédération des travailleurs catholiques du Canada, and Paul Vaillancourt, honorary secretary of the Quebec Division of the Canadian Red Cross. The clinic printed a "fact sheet" called *Cana-dian Column*, which it sent to newspapers for reprinting, that listed and refuted rumours – typically reported by the RCMP, local police, or military intelligence personnel. Of the thirty-four newspapers regularly sent the *Column* in December 1942, thirty-two were in Quebec (the exceptions being the *Ottawa Citizen* and *Le Droit*), and twenty were printed in French. Attempts to quash such rumours as "things [at Dieppe] were so arranged that the *Fusiliers Mont-Royal* bore the brunt of enemy fire" were geared toward maintaining French Canadian support for the war effort. Other rumours needed to be refuted because of their potential to spread panic about fifth-column activity, sow dissent between capital and labour, or under-mine support for measures like rationing and increased taxation.[33]

WHEN CANADIANS WERE ASKED in mid-1944 if they believed they received generally truthful media accounts about the war, respondents outside Quebec answered in the affirmative by a 62 to 28 percent margin, while in Quebec the responses were weighted 57 to 30 percent in the negative.[34] This discrepancy, highlighting Canada's two solitudes, surfaced in many areas during the war, but in no domain were the consequences potentially more explosive than in regard to military enlistment.

As had been the case with the Great War, Québécois preponderantly saw the Second World War as Europe's – and more particularly Britain's – war. Moreover, and with good reason, they perceived Canada's military as an "Anglo" institution. At the outset of hostilities, only 5 percent of Canadians in uniform were francophones. A unilingual francophone, unlike his anglophone counterpart, could not realistically expect a commission. During the war, training in only ten of more than 200 military trades could be taken entirely in French.[35] Quebec francophones were also less inclined to enlist because they tended to marry younger and had more children.

It was not long before grave concerns over French Canadian recruitment largely eclipsed any initial optimism. In the week leading up to Canada's declaration of war some 1,000 protestors gathered at Montreal's Maisonneuve market to hear Paul Gouin, leader of the Action libérale nationale, rail against Canada's impending participation. Town councils across the province passed resolutions opposing conscription, and Quebec's Union Nationale premier, Maurice Duplessis, condemned the federal government for threatening to gut provincial powers with the War Measures Act.[36] Fearing Duplessis's ability to sabotage the war effort, Quebec's Liberal federal Cabinet members, Postmaster General Charles Power, Public Works Minister P.J. Cardin, and Justice Minister Ernest Lapointe, all said they would resign if the premier was returned to office in the December 1939 provincial election, thereby, it was said, leaving the door open to conscription – a tactic that brought Liberal Adelard Godbout to power.

In June 1940 most of Quebec's political and church leaders accepted conscription for home defence, which initially required just one month's training as stipulated under the National Resources Mobilization Act (NRMA), a measure passed in response to the fall of France and the retreat of British forces from Dunkirk. Still, notable opposition was voiced: *Le Devoir,* for example, maintained that this was the first step toward compulsion to serve overseas, and the populist Montreal mayor, Camillien Houde, was imprisoned for advocating that men not register under the NRMA. Such opposition became more vociferous in February 1941 when NRMA service was extended to four months, and then again in April when, in order to release more men for active service, it was potentially prolonged for the war's duration.[37] Federal authorities were also worried that, after the fall of France, the French-speaking population in Quebec appeared to have more sympathy for the Vichy government than for Gaullist forces. This tendency reflected the great esteem in which many Québécois held Marshal Pétain and the Vichy program, which advocated steering France away from the secularism of the Third Republic and back to a more traditional, corporatist order, based in large part upon the papal encyclicals of Pius XI. One poll taken in July 1942, only four months before Canada broke off relations with the Pétain government, revealed that among French Canadians in Quebec, 66 percent rejected the idea of a war against Vichy. Also disturbing was the finding that only 33 percent believed that "Canada would be fighting this war if she were completely independent and not part of the British Empire."[38]

Not surprisingly, such sentiments translated into dismal recruiting numbers. As of October 1941 voluntary enlistment in Quebec stood at 41.6 percent of Ontario's total, whereas Quebec's population was 85.5 percent of Ontario's. Moreover, about half of Quebec's volunteers were from its English-speaking minority. All told, 25.69 percent of Quebec's male population aged eighteen to forty-five served in the military, either as volunteers or conscripts; in the rest of the country this number ranged from a low of 42.38 percent in Saskatchewan to a high of 50.4 percent in British Columbia, with the remaining provinces falling between 47 and 49 percent.[39] A significant number of Quebeckers – often abetted by their communities – tried to avoid compulsory service for home defence. In parts of rural Quebec, authorities trying to enforce the NRMA were even shot at. There were frequent reports of servicemen being attacked by gangs of civilian youths, particularly in Montreal. "When we went ashore [in Montreal] we'd go in a bunch," said one sailor. "You never went with a buddy or yourself because that way you could wind up in the gutter."[40] Although recruitment of French Canadians outside Quebec more closely approximated rates among the English-speaking population, overall, although approximately 30 percent of Canada's population was francophone, only 19 percent of those in the military fell into this category.[41]

King held out against conscription for overseas service for as long as possible, fearing the issue could divide the nation. In May 1942 his government brought forward Bill 80, in which the prime minister, to reach a compromise out of the plebiscite results, made conscription for overseas service legal, but publicly insisted that it would not be imposed unless absolutely necessary. Bill 80 proved a catalyst for the rise of the Bloc populaire canadien, whose leaders had emerged from the Ligue pour la défense du Canada, organizers of the "non" vote in the plebiscite on conscription for overseas service. Internal divisions between advocates of traditional and more modern and secular *nationalisme* frustrated the Bloc, however; it won just 15 percent of the vote and four seats in the August 1944 provincial election.[42] This result turned out to be small consolation for the federal government, for after nearly five years in opposition, during which Duplessis had denounced Ottawa for decimating provincial powers and warned against impending conscription, the former Quebec premier was returned to power.

Still, hoping to avoid conscription when the end of war seemed in sight, on 1 November 1944 King dismissed his minister of defence. Col. J.L. Ralston was no longer willing to accept delays on compulsory overseas service, especially after his recent trip to Italy and northwest Europe, where commanders had impressed upon him the desperate need for reinforcements. Ralston's replacement, Lt.-Gen. A.G.L. McNaughton, recently returned from Britain where he had commanded the First Canadian Army, expressed confidence that he could convince enough NRMA men to switch to active service voluntarily, but within three weeks admitted failure. Facing high casualty projections from the military and a possible Cabinet revolt within his government, King was finally forced to act, though to the end he remained cautious. On 23 November he authorized the conscription of 16,000 NRMA men for overseas service. This figure corresponded to the bare minimum identified as required by the army, though the government maintained that it represented the number of home defence conscripts considered to be prepared for combat. Ultimately, only 2,463 saw action and just 69 died.

In Parliament, King's compromise was supported by fewer than half of the French Canadian Liberals – only twenty-three – and, according to the CIPO, by just 8 percent of Québécois. The response on the streets was less violent than the reaction to conscription had been in Quebec during the Great War, because King, unlike Borden, was seen to have held out for as long as possible. There were boisterous demonstrations by some 2,000 in Montreal, however, and smaller but still notable numbers of protesters in places that included Quebec City and Chicoutimi. Also, in February 1945 a mob attack on authorities searching for draft dodgers in Drummondville, Quebec, sent scores of people to the hospital for treatment.[43]

This focus on Quebec does not imply the absence of recruitment problems outside that province. The largest occupation-based segment of NRMA personnel, slightly more than 20 percent of the total, came from an agricultural background. Across the country claims by young men, usually justified, that they were needed on the farm resulted in over 170,000 deferments from NRMA service. More than 14,000 university students also obtained deferments and sometimes even resisted their obligation of 110 hours of officer training during the school term and two weeks during the summer, all of which drew considerable criticism. While enlistment rates among Canadians of non-British and non-French background were generally good, Germans, Italians, Poles, Russians, First Peoples, and perhaps most surprisingly, Jews, represented a larger percentage of the NRMA force than their percentage of the population.[44]

Overall, outside of Quebec – whose reactions came as little surprise to most, given its even worse recruitment record and violent opposition to conscription during the Great War – the general pattern proved quite inspiring. The need for conscription for overseas service should not be seen as a failure of voluntarism. Recruitment goals for the major service branches remained exceptionally high for a nation of 11.5 million. The army sought to maintain overseas five divisions and two brigades and even more men – too many, according to some analyses – behind to support them. And according to a 1944 military report, the air force, which was almost exclusively composed of volunteers, recruited far more personnel than necessary.[45]

Although Canada entered the war with just 10,000 full-time military personnel and 50,000 part-time militia, the country ultimately raised 106,522 naval, 249,622 air force, and 708,535 army personnel, over 85 percent of whom were volunteers.[46]

Besides the initial rush of recruits during the opening weeks of the war, the flow was again especially heavy after the fall of France, when the King government abandoned its cautious recruitment policy and within a year authorized five army divisions. Certainly many men understood that a brutalizing experience might await them overseas. They had perhaps encountered Great War veterans with revealing, persistent physical and psychological wounds. Indeed, the army, in which most Great War veterans had served, had the greatest trouble filling its quotas, although in fairness these were far higher than those of the other two services. This pattern was also attributable to the fact that the army remained largely inactive until the Sicilian campaign, which began in July 1943, and thus seemed less exciting to many young men.

Jingoism and even naïveté were very much evident among volunteers. Most were too young to remember the horrors and waste of the Great War. They came of age in a nation that preferred accounts of its "romance and adventure" and the spectacular performance of Canadian troops in helping to secure victory and earning the country international praise and the pride of nationhood.[47] Sometimes these notions were actually reinforced by Great War veterans who chose to stress the valour of the cause for which they fought or the "manly" comradeship they enjoyed, a pattern that helped them cope psychologically by convincing themselves that so much suffering and death was worthwhile. "A lot of the horrors of World War I were not transmitted to us," remembered navy veteran Norm Bowen, whose father and uncle both saw action on the Western Front. "It was given to us in very nice terms ... They talked about the funny things."[48] Indeed, many Great War veterans volunteered for service a second time, often lying about their age, seeking to recapture lost youth or the more appealing aspects of their military past. Also, like countless young men, they were motivated by a sense of duty and patriotism, the desire to stand by Britain and show Canada as a loyal member of the Empire, and the wish to defend freedom and crush Nazism. In a survey taken in mid-1943 by the army's Research and Information Section among 900 soldiers in Canada, 91 percent responded that they were fighting for "democracy," "freedom," and "security."[49]

Many men, particularly the youth, saw war as a heroic, thrilling experience. "It was all an adventure," recalled one man about his decision to enlist in 1940. "War ... was all glory ... You were going to see the world." Young men felt invincible and exuded bravado and confidence that they would come through it all unscathed. As their friends joined up, lads often expressed envy, especially since young women were attracted to men in uniform. Across the country, females began to dominate senior high school classes; boys yet to enlist were pressured and frequently taunted. Teenagers who looked older than their years often hesitated to appear in public for fear of being harassed. Thousands of boys tried to enlist before reaching eighteen – and were often accepted on dubious evidence – while some turned to the merchant marine because, as a civilian employer, it could accept applicants at sixteen. Those of legal age who had been turned down for medical reasons often prominently wore a red maple leaf lapel button to demonstrate their patriotic intentions.[50] Young men throughout English Canada loathed the prospect of being labelled slackers, cowards, or "zombies" on being drafted into the home defence force, a possibility at the age of eighteen and a half. Many promptly shifted to active service if they received notice under the NRMA, especially since civilians quickly learned to distinguish conscripts' uniforms from those of the Canadian Active Service Force, whose members could proudly display their Canada Volunteer Service Medal, Canada flash, and a corps or regimental cap badge. Government propaganda played upon this distinction, especially as reinforcements grew thinner. One advertisement illustrated a soldier admired by a young woman for the "G.S. [General Service] badge on his arm," which singled him out as "a real fighting man," while in another advertising pitch awestruck children remarked, "Gee, he's a G.S. soldier."[51]

SUCH PATRIOTIC RESPONSES by young men were reflected and reinforced by a host of other campaigns to back the war effort. In activities that appeared to involve all Canadians, people from all backgrounds pulled together with a purpose they had not felt before, especially after what had been for many a long period of purposelessness during the Depression.[52] Indeed, despite the obvious pressures of the war, participation brought a greater sense of belonging and direction; with less personal alienation – and the enlistment of some otherwise troubled young men – aggregate suicide rates dropped dramatically, from 978 in 1939 to 758 in 1943 and 731 in 1944, before rising again to 764 in 1945 and then to 1,002 in 1946 – the last figure no doubt linked to readjustment difficulties among veterans.[53]

The range of grassroots patriotic responses and activities was enormous. Some of the most immediate came from individuals eager to demonstrate their patriotism. In November 1939, for example, the Toronto millionaire E.H. Watt donated his seventy-eight-foot motor cruiser to the Royal Canadian Navy Volunteer Reserve to help with training.[54] In the opening months of the war, Finance Minister J.L. Ralston told of ordinary folk simply sending the government money to use for the war effort as it saw fit. One Japanese Canadian resident of British Columbia, most likely later evacuated, donated $100 accompanied by a note stating, "Being a resident of Canada for 32 years, I always have been bearing in my heart to express on behalf of my family and myself our sincere gratitude for the peace, freedom and benefits of Canada which she has rendered me during all these years."[55] Many Canadians soon became involved with campaigns to achieve specific goals. In early 1940, for example, many of Red Deer's 2,500 residents participated in a drive that raised $2,000 to purchase a military ambulance. The same year, the 50,000-strong Imperial Order Daughters of the Empire (IODE), in one of the first of its many wartime undertakings, raised $100,000 to purchase a Bolingbroke bomber, which was unveiled that July at the Rockcliffe air force base just outside Ottawa in a ceremony attended by the newly installed governor general, the Earl of Athlone, and his wife, Princess Alice.[56]

Volunteerism was serious business, but it also had its pleasant social side. In October 1939 the *Vancouver Sun* reported: "A month ago no one felt like giving parties [but] now the war is providing a definite stimulus to the realm of entertaining as hostesses arrange teas and bridges to raise funds for whatever branch of war work they are interesting themselves in."[57] Knitting bees to provide warm clothing to servicemen and British children became popular across the land, including one at the governor general's residence that involved the wives of Ottawa's small diplomatic corps.[58] Ultimately, millions of women became involved in knitting for the war effort, a patriotic activity that, of course, related to stereotyped gender-based roles. Supplies and shipping arrangements were typically provided by groups such as the Red Cross. In one of many workplace initiatives, women employed by the Ontario government formed the Queen's Park War Service Guild, which met, primarily to knit, during lunch hours and after work.[59] Such activities were also organized through churches. The United Church, for example, reported that through its women's committees, in 1940 over 60,000 volunteers had produced for shipment overseas 267,372 pairs of socks, 50,223 sweaters, 18,552 pairs of wristlets, 33,275 scarves, and 22,024 pairs of gloves and mitts.[60]

Women also shouldered the load in preparing packages containing such items as cigarettes, chocolate, candy, tinned food, toiletries, board games, playing cards, and reading material for servicemen overseas. Sometimes goods were targeted on men from a specific church, ship, regiment, or squadron. Other efforts were more general. The IODE concentrated considerable energy on sending reading material to trainees in Canada, overseas combatants, and POWs. Over the course of the war, they collected and distributed 1,404,831 books and 13,364,226 magazines. IODE chapters also led in "adopting" air squadrons and especially naval vessels – over 300 ships during the war – for the purpose of sending men various comforts. Recognizing the appeal of adoption, the Royal Canadian Navy named ships for communities, the larger vessels such as the destroyer *Ottawa* being reserved for major places. It did not matter if people from the community actually served on the ship. Servicemen on the Bangor class minesweeper *Red Deer* received a virtual cornucopia of comforts from that city even though just two central Albertans were among its crew during more than four years of service. Simply having a community's name emblazoned on a ship created considerable local pride; not to have supported it would have brought local shame.[61]

Women's groups also ran enterprises like tea rooms to raise money for war-related charities. Several organizations assisted government-financed auxiliaries such as the YMCA to provide canteens for servicemen, and staffed information kiosks at train stations to direct men on leave to accommodation and entertainment, much of which was reserved for those in uniform and heavily subsidized or offered free. Local social service groups, as well as women's and religious organizations, coordinated with military bases to arrange invitations for men to have a home-cooked dinner, a gesture that, once coupon rationing was implemented, brought the host no extra provisions until a tenth meal was provided.[62]

Far more popular among servicemen, however, were efforts to keep them supplied with cigarettes. As the acclaimed writer and Second World War veteran Paul Fussell recalled, "Anyone in the services who did not smoke ... was looked on as a freak."[63] Cigarettes of good quality were appreciated for two reasons: those supplied in Britain and places closer to action were generally inferior, as they were imported from places such as South Africa; and, largely unbeknown to those at home, servicemen overseas often traded smokes on the black market for food, liquor, and sex. Countless Canadians sent cigarettes to their loved ones in uniform through authorized dealers at the special price of $1.90 per 1,000, which by 1942 was about 30 percent of what civilians paid to feed their habit.[64] Massive donations came from hundreds of tobacco funds started by service groups, religious organizations, women's associations, regimental auxiliaries, and various local groups. For example, over the course of the war, the 50,000-strong Catholic Women's League of Canada sent 7.6 million cigarettes overseas. This number pales when compared with the IODE's contribution of 6.7 million during the twelve months ending in June 1943, and rather ironically, given what is now known about the health hazards of smoking, with the more than 25 million provided by the Red Cross over the first three years of the war.[65]

Millions of Canadians, especially women, became involved both directly and indirectly in the many voluntary activities organized by the Red Cross. Besides having its own volunteers, which included hundreds of thousands of young people who formed Junior Red Cross chapters, the Red Cross coordinated activities with numerous other groups, including the National Council of Women of Canada, the IODE, the Women's Christian Temperance Union, the Catholic Women's League of Canada, the National Council of Jewish Women, and the Federated Women's Institutes. They provided field comforts for servicemen and POWs, bandages and surgical dressings for the wounded, and emergency relief, namely clothing and nonperishable food for, among others, the British victims of German air raids and, eventually, liberated civilians across Europe.[66] Through propaganda stressing the urgency – and safety – of giving blood to sustain the wounded, and by means of clinics in all major communities and mobile services in less populated areas, the Red Cross increased blood donations in Canada from 5,325 units in 1940 to 1,033,701 in 1944.[67]

Starting in 1940, the Canadian Red Cross held a major fundraising drive each March to support its war-related activities. Never did it fail to meet its objective, although $10 million in 1942 was more than triple its goal of two years earlier. During the war the organization collected $90 million from Canadians, some of which was put toward the purchase of 355 ambulances, 41 trailer kitchen canteens, 6 tricycle canteens, 20 station wagons, and 65 trucks (Figure 1.1). The money also played a key role in providing a 600-bed hospital on the Astor estate located fifty kilometres outside of London.[68] Canvassers assigned to specific neighbourhoods provided a Red Cross door sticker to those who gave, a practice that put informal

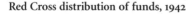

Figure 1.1

Red Cross distribution of funds, 1942

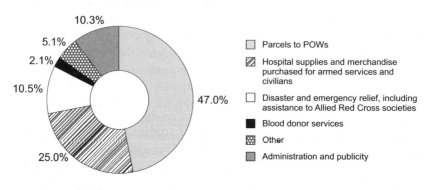

Source: *Saturday Night*, 6 March 1943, 11.

pressure on those who did not and usually led to a follow-up call. Red Cross donation boxes were also carried around to employees at many workplaces.

Fundraising was also often linked to leisure. At Toronto's swank Royal York hotel, for example, funds were raised through a draw that featured such prizes as a hockey stick autographed by members of the Toronto Maple Leafs.[69] Events such as "monster" bingo games to support the Red Cross became increasingly common, though they often drew criticism, especially from religious leaders, for encouraging gambling.[70] Other successful fundraising ventures were second-hand shops, run mostly by women's groups, to which citizens donated all manner of items. Such places included Toronto's Wimodausis Club Shop, Montreal's Nearly-New Shop, and Ottawa's Superfluity Shop, the last of which raised some $100,000 between 1940 and October 1944.[71]

In addition to its annual March campaign, the Red Cross launched supplementary campaigns targeting specific countries for humanitarian relief, the most substantial of which, raising some $4 million between late 1941 and early 1944, was to aid the Soviet Union. While continuing to suppress the Communist Party at home – forcing it to change its name to the Labour Progressive Party in 1943 rather than rescinding a 1940 ban under the DOCR – the federal government, along with numerous business leaders, fully backed Red Cross efforts to help the Soviets in their struggle against the Nazis. Indeed, leading the organization's national campaign in this area were J.S. McLean, president of Canada Packers, and W.R. Ingram, traffic manager for the Swift Canada Company.[72] Canada-Soviet Friendship Leagues were formed and helped the Red Cross organize massive rallies, such as the one at Toronto's Varsity Arena in June 1942 marking the one-year anniversary of the Nazi invasion of the Soviet Union.[73]

The Red Cross's most substantial work, however, consistently claiming about half its budget, was its provision of relief packages to POWs via the International Red Cross in neutral Switzerland. In fact, through a shared-cost agreement whereby it covered just over a third of total costs, the Canadian Red Cross became responsible for providing supplies to most POWs from Commonwealth countries.[74] This undertaking answered a request made in August 1940 from the British Red Cross, which was unable to obtain adequate material or manpower to carry out such a task, especially as Britain was then engaged in a life-and-death struggle against a possible Nazi invasion. To meet this challenge, Red Cross depots in Toronto (1941), Montreal (1942), Hamilton (1942), Windsor (1942), Winnipeg (1943), and London (1944) operated around the clock and adopted assembly-line operations. Each package cost the Red Cross $2 to put together, $1.89 being spent on the contents, which included biscuits, butter, cheese, chocolate, tinned meat, jam, powdered milk, prunes, raisins, sardines, salmon, salt, pepper, sugar, soap, and cigarettes. At its peak, the Canadian Red Cross churned out 40,000 such parcels weekly and its volunteers ultimately provided a remarkable grand total of 16,310,602.[75]

GOVERNMENTS IN CANADA also became increasingly involved in encouraging and directing volunteerism. Perhaps using the Red Cross as a model, the Department of National War Services (NWS) started in mid-1940 to actively promote local efforts to form – and to register with the federal government – "citizen committees" designed to coordinate and thus to optimize the effectiveness of volunteer groups. Such undertakings generated local databases from which volunteers were obtained and, as needed, steered toward campaigns sometimes prioritized by NWS. By the end of 1942 more than sixty such committees had been established across Canada.[76] Their leaders were drawn from local political groups, major religious groups, boards of trade, trade and labour councils, large social service groups, and well-established and respected women's organizations. Such groups provided citizen committees with greater status and better access to an army of volunteers, who, for example, came to number over 3,600 in Edmonton and nearly 7,000 in Winnipeg.[77]

Even so it became evident that more direct government involvement in volunteerism was needed to ensure the well-being of servicemen, a major shift from the way that need had been handled in the Great War, when such efforts were mostly privately financed. In November 1939 Ottawa declared the YMCA, the Salvation Army, the Knights of Columbus, and the Canadian Legion as official auxiliaries for Canada's military.[78] Operating under the Directorate of Auxiliary Services within the Department of National Defence, the YMCA was to focus primarily on providing sporting activities, the Salvation Army on recreational huts, the Knights of Columbus on social functions, and the Legion on educational services – though these were only broad divisions, as on many military bases just one or two of these auxiliary services were present.[79] To carry out their activities in 1941, Ottawa granted the Knights of Columbus $705,000, the Legion $916,000, the Salvation Army $1.46 million, and the YMCA $1.74 million, based upon the scope of their activities and the amount each had raised on its own in 1940, the last year they were permitted to make public appeals for money to help them assist servicemen. By the 1944-45 fiscal year, given their growing activities both in Canada and overseas, funding was increased to $2.38 million for the Salvation Army, $2.57 million for the Knights of Columbus, $4.54 million for the YMCA, and $4.95 million for the Canadian Legion, which, by that point, had become heavily involved in educating and preparing servicemen for their return to civilian life.[80]

In Canada, auxiliary services established dry canteens on military bases and in leave centres where men could obtain free refreshments and stationery, and purchase, for a modest price, items such as cigarettes, chocolate bars, candy, and toiletries superior to or in addition to their standard issue.[81] The Salvation Army, affectionately nicknamed the "Sally Ann" by those in uniform, also became known for providing mobile canteens that followed men on training exercises – and later into combat – to offer items like hot tea and snacks. Recreational huts on bases housed services such as libraries, card and board games and ping-pong tables, and those large enough were used for movies, live shows, and dances (Figure 1.2).[82]

In communities across Canada, auxiliary services opened the doors of their prewar facilities to men on leave and, in larger places, took over buildings to create new recreational centres. Most prominent were the Salvation Army's Red Shield

Figure 1.2

Yearly participation in programs conducted by YWCA war services, 1939-46

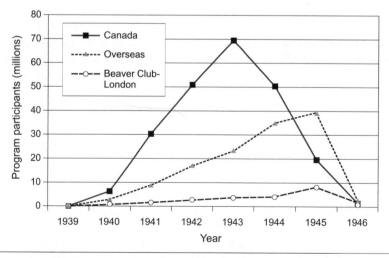

Note: Canadian total = 228,537,910; overseas total = 127,149,805; Beaver Club total = 21,606,822.
Source: Alan M. Hurst, *The Canadian YMCA in World War II* (Toronto: YMCA, 1949), 82.

and the YMCA's Red Triangle Clubs. Here, servicemen could relax and read a newspaper – often from their hometown – write a letter on free stationery, obtain an inexpensive meal, play card or board games, perhaps hear a lecture or learn a craft, and most popularly, attend dances, which some establishments ran nightly. For example, with a major army depot and two air force bases in Ottawa, the Red Triangle Club served some 3 million visitors between its opening in July 1941 and the end of the war.[83] In Halifax, where the population doubled during the war years largely because of a deluge of naval and merchant marine personnel connected to North Atlantic convoy activity, nearly 800 civilians volunteered at the Red Triangle Club, which struggled to cope with nearly a million visitors per year.[84] Also struggling to handle the flow were two recreational centres managed by the Knights of Columbus, two by the Canadian Legion, and a Wings Club for air force personnel. Naval ratings crammed into a revamped, twenty-five-room mansion known as the Ajax Club. Although strident opposition spearheaded by the neighbouring Fort Massey United Church in mostly dry Halifax led to the relocation of this beer-dispensing establishment to the Citadel Hill area in March 1942 – where a small wet canteen was joined by a far more elaborate dry one – there was no denying the desperate need for such clubs in this hopelessly overcrowded community. As one sailor quipped, "You had to be anointed by Christ himself" to find a spot at the Ajax.[85]

Auxiliary services also ran hostels in major communities where, for as little as fifty cents, men on leave could obtain a room, a hot shower or bath, and a decent breakfast. This was welcome not only for being a great deal but also because the influx of war workers into numerous communities severely depleted accommodation at rooming houses and hotels, where many civilians stayed while trying to locate a place to live. Most auxiliaries managed to cope with demand, though sometimes the challenges were formidable. Once again, this was especially evident in Halifax, where as many as 2 million sailors arrived annually. The Navy League, which received some government funding even though it was not named as an official auxiliary, operated thirteen Allied Merchant Seamen's Clubs that were continually jammed.[86] At the city's YMCA hostel, which accommodated 600, queues often stretched out onto the street while servicemen inside, booked in on twelve-hour shifts, "slept in chairs, on canteen tables, on top of old-fashioned radiators ... [or] anywhere there was space."[87]

BESIDES ENCOURAGING greater coordination among volunteer groups and creating official auxiliaries, Ottawa increasingly managed patriotic activities through its War Charities Act, which was passed the day after Canada declared war. Citizens who wished to raise money for the war effort had to apply to the act's chief administrator, who worked within NWS. Each time money was sought, including requests for the annual campaigns of well-established groups such as the Red Cross, the applicant had to supply documentation showing the methods followed in establishing the fund, the total funds expected to be raised, the estimated costs of collecting the money, a list of directors, and the principal objects on which expenditures were to be made. Rules stipulated that a war charity have a minimum of three directors, subject to approval by the minister of NWS; that its financial records always remain accessible to the government; that it undertake an annual audit by a professional accountant if dealing with more than $2,000; and that its administrative costs not exceed 25 percent of the money it raised.[88]

Government records demonstrate that fraud was not widespread, although a different impression was perhaps at times conveyed to the public through warnings issued by the federal government, the media, and institutions like local Better Business Bureaus. Soon after the war started, Toronto's Better Business Bureau told people not to purchase "veteran calendars," which, it alleged, were not being sold to raise money for the Christie Street Veterans Hospital as claimed.[89] Some schemes played upon ethnic groups desperate to help their countrymen flee the Nazis. "Perhaps the sickest, meanest and hardest to pin down of all the charity rackets is the one known as 'the mercy ship,'" reported *Saturday Night* in 1942. "Persons of Norwegian, Greek or Austrian descent are its chief victims ... A letter tells of a 'mercy ship' prepared to carry ... refugees to America and freedom. The ship, however, is in dire need of money for food and supplies [and] a few hundred dollars will suffice."[90] Several sources also mentioned the need for authorities to crack down on what became known as the "concert racket." In one case reported by the *Windsor Star,* a show given on behalf of an unnamed war charity took in $945 in gate receipts, but had only $215 left after expenses and the promoter's fee.[91]

The number of registered war charities grew quickly – from 200 in late 1939 to some 4,000 over the course of the war – and their activities ranged from major undertakings like those of the Red Cross to more modest projects such as an initiative on behalf of the Canadian Ladies' Golf Union War Services Fund.[92] Some applicants were denied the right to raise money; in 1941, for example, a group of Montrealers wanting to collect $45,000 for a third naval canteen were turned down because NWS determined that the city's two existing canteens were not being utilized to full capacity.[93] The next year, the same response was given to a Toronto lawyer who tried to organize a "Dieppe Memorial Cot Fund" to offer special assistance for casualties of the raid. Authorities determined that existing facilities were adequate and that such an initiative might cast doubts upon the government's commitment to Canada's wounded and create jealousy among casualties from other military campaigns.[94]

To minimize overlap and to ensure maximum impact, the War Charities Act allowed the federal government to determine when, where, and for how long appeals could occur. Soon, for example, no other organization was permitted to solicit money during the massive semi-annual three-week-long Victory Bond drives.[95] Without doubt, the most important fundraising campaigns for Ottawa were those designed to pay directly for the war effort. By the end of 1942 the highly mechanized Second World War had already cost Canada more than the Great War. Record taxes on income, corporate profits, and goods and services provided billions, but about half the total bill was ultimately covered by War Savings Certificates and especially by Victory Bonds.

War Savings Certificates began selling in May 1940. They were sometimes sold on city streets or door to door by "Miss Canada" volunteers, but most were purchased at post offices, banks, trust companies, and similar authorized dealers. They matured after seven years and paid back, tax-free, $5 for every $4 invested. Each person could hold a maximum of $600. Certificates could also be obtained by purchasing War Savings Stamps for twenty-five cents each. This program, directed mainly to schoolchildren, involved filling in a special card with sixteen stamps and sending it to the Department of Finance in exchange for a certificate. Although the total of $318 million raised by War Savings Certificates provided only a tiny fraction of what Ottawa needed, the program was a success in getting millions of Canadians financially involved in the war effort. By mid-1941 the War Finance Department was processing as many as 69,000 certificates daily.[96] Government propaganda promoting purchases was supported by a variety of local initiatives. For instance, as part of a 1941 drive in Calgary, Royal Canadian Air Force trainers dropped leaflets, fifty of which were marked for a free $5 certificate.[97]

Of far greater significance were the ten wartime and one postwar Victory Bond drives, for which there were no purchase limits. Bonds were issued on a six- to fourteen-year maturity basis, with interest rates ranging from 1.5 percent for shorter-term to 3 percent for longer-term bonds, and came in denominations ranging from $50 to $100,000. Businesses accounted for about half of total purchases. Besides patriotism, some companies harboured ulterior motives: they may have been looking for ways to avoid the steep Excess Profits Tax; or they may have wanted to advertise their generosity, not only to inspire others but to remind the public of their name in a positive context, as war demands had often diverted them from the civilian market.[98] It was sometimes suggested that civilians too responded in a less than proper spirit to Victory Bond appeals. Concerns over war-weariness prompted the federal government to limit the goal for the sixth bond drive in May 1944, and those that followed, to the same amount as for the fifth, even though people actually had more money to spend. Indeed, after D-Day, the emphasis in government advertising shifted away from a "heavy patriotic, emotional appeal" to one based on self-interest. Publicity emphasized the excellent, tax-free investment opportunity represented by Victory Bonds that would pay off handsomely in building a new postwar life.[99] In early 1945 a CIPO survey showed that only 34 percent of Ontarians and 22 percent of Quebeckers purchased bonds purely out of patriotism, whereas 45 and 62 percent respectively were motivated by the investment opportunity.[100]

Whatever the reasons for purchases or the concerns of authorities, the overall results were indisputably impressive. Canadians bought $12.5 billion worth of Victory Bonds, or some $550 per capita (not including corporate contributions), at a time when the average annual salary stood at around $1,500. The first War Loan in February 1940 met its goal of $200 million within forty-eight hours. Another campaign in September 1940 surpassed its target of $300 million nearly as quickly. But these early drives barely tapped the potential, being largely directed by banks and investment houses working on a commission basis and targeting larger investors. In June 1941, with the demands of the war rapidly mounting and the realization that conflict would continue for years, the drives were reorganized. A central committee was established in Ottawa to direct provincial and local efforts in the now-renamed Victory Bond drive. In December the structure was further honed: the War Bond and Certificate programs were both placed under the new National War Finance Committee (NWFC), first directed by the Bank of Montreal president, George Spinney, and subsequently by the Bank of Canada president, Graham Towers, each of whom reported directly to the minister of finance. Under them was a sixty-member advisory committee composed of representatives from industrial, commercial, financial, labour, agricultural, and women's groups, among others, which helped in the development of strategy, propaganda, and the recruitment of volunteers for Victory Bond drives, whose numbers would soon exceed 100,000.[101]

Approximately every six months intense campaigns were launched during which the public was successfully beseeched to meet substantially higher targets (Figure 1.3). Many Canadians, especially those working in larger companies, took out payroll deductions typically calculated over a six-month period to permit the purchase of at least a $50 bond with each new issue. By autumn 1941, some 10,000 firms had instituted such a scheme.[102] The pressure to give was intense. Volunteers often came to companies to deliver speeches prepared by the NWFC or the WIB, after which sign-up papers were passed around among employees. Many work sites posted lists of those who had purchased bonds or participated in payroll deduction schemes. Among industrial workers, some 97 percent in English Canada, and 93.4 percent in Quebec, had their wages garnished to purchase bonds. One woman, for example, who was earning only $55.80 monthly as a Grade 1 clerk for the federal government – where most departments reported at least a 90 percent participation rate in payroll deduction schemes – recalled, "When a ... drive was on, we were given to understand that we were to buy and if we did not ... we were brought into the chief's office [who] mentioned love of country, duty ... and ... the error of trying to hold out."[103]

Throughout the Victory Bond campaigns, media support was ardent and pervasive. One estimate said that to cover the November 1942 drive, Canadian newspapers provided some 25 million words![104] The federal government spent more than $30 million to promote Victory Bonds, its most extensive propaganda undertaking.[105]

Figure 1.3

Victory Bond purchase goals and results, 1941-45

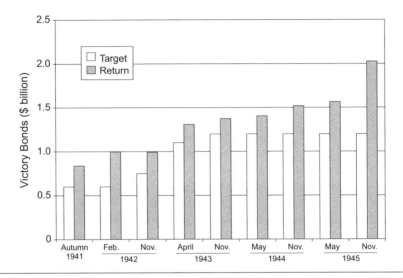

Source: Canada Year Book, 1948-49, 1061.

Posters, direct mailings, movie trailers, and radio spots were all employed, but the greatest expenditures were for large, often full-page, advertisements in virtually every major daily, weekly, business, labour, and ethnic newspaper and magazine. This publicity was supplemented by equally numerous – and tax-deductible – urgent appeals from the private sector to purchase bonds, to the extent that the *Vancouver Sun,* in the midst of the November 1942 drive, commented that for every government plea to purchase a bond there were ten from various companies – an exaggeration to be sure, but a perusal of major newspapers and magazines confirms that the two sources vied for supremacy.[106] The appeals were many and varied. "A drop in the bucket?" asked a government advertisement. "Even one $100 bond will pay for two complete flying outfits or 3,000 bullets ... or ... half a ton of bombs to drop on Berlin!"[107] People were also told that each extra dollar put into Victory Bonds would expedite the return home of loved ones. Among those employing this tactic was the Supertest Petroleum Corporation, which portrayed a teary-eyed young girl pleading on behalf of Victory Bonds so that she could soon be reunited with her daddy.[108]

The NWFC provided communities across Canada with official targets based on population for each Victory Bond drive, goals that became the focus of much local pride. For instance, to ensure that its assigned tally was met, the town of Verdun asked its residents to purchase bonds locally rather than in Montreal where many residents worked. Communities often forged friendly rivalries over Victory Bond purchases with others of similar size. Daily tallies were printed in newspapers, and local Victory Bond committees often employed creative means to inform the public of their progress in attaining their assigned objective. In Halifax, for the seventh loan, a mock guillotine was built so that its blade hovered above a cardboard cut-out of Hitler, ready to fall once the city reached its goal.[109]

Local Victory Bond committees were essential to success. Given the importance and high profile of these campaigns, such committees typically involved prominent individuals and, in larger communities, became quite extensive. In Ottawa, for example, a fourteen-member executive was managed by F.E. Bronson of the city's Board of Control and included members such as Thomas Ahearn, the owner of the Ottawa Electric Railway, and the retailing giant A.J. Frieman. Under them was the "Ottawa Committee" of forty-five members, again involving community leaders, including Mayor Stanley Lewis, who also lent his name to many other war-related causes. The committee in turn directed smaller subcommittees to oversee administration, finance, organization, distribution, publicity, and employees. These subcommittees managed five district committees that directed as many as 2,000 volunteers. Although perhaps overly bureaucratic, the structure was designed to get as many people as possible personally involved.[110]

Campaigns typically kicked off with parades and speeches from local politicians, war heroes, actors, and other celebrities, reminding citizens of their duty to purchase bonds and expressing confidence that the population would exceed its local objective. Volunteers were divided up by district to distribute literature, posters, and other paraphernalia from the NWFC to workplaces and homes. Across Canada, many popular events, typically organized by local committees, added considerable pizzazz and appeal to these campaigns. In early 1942, for example, an old-timers' game between the Montreal Canadiens and the defunct Montreal Maroons drew a sellout crowd of 13,000 to the Forum; proceeds went to the Victory Bond campaign, and numerous bonds were purchased at the event.[111] In November, as part of a Victory Bond rally held at Toronto's Maple Leaf Gardens, the eight-year-old Dionne quintuplets rode in on identical white tricycles to sing "There'll Always Be an England," "O Canada," and a French song.[112]

Perhaps the most dramatic impact was made by staged invasions. In order to raise awareness and shock the complacent into purchasing bonds – and to provide people with a taste of the treatment they would receive under enemy occupation – mock invasions were arranged in conjunction with local training bases. The Toronto local committee and nearby Camp Borden, for instance, collaborated on such an "attack."[113] A similar mock attack in Red Deer was realistically described by the *Edmonton Journal*:

> [It] began at 4:00 p.m. with the laying of fog, mixed with small traces of tear gas, and immediate seizure of the telephone system and its staff, the railroad and the telegraph buildings, city hall, waterworks, and all main streets and highways of importance ...

Citizens were ordered to stop where they were, and those allowed to move had to follow prescribed routes and were "shot" on the slightest hesitation or pretext ... Military trucks with machine-guns also patrolled the streets ... Mayor Hogg, City Clerk Gillespie and other officials and police were seized, tied up with rope, and led by an execution squad to the corner of Ross and Gaetz Ave. and "shot" in full view of the citizens ... The display ended at 5:00 p.m., and traffic was allowed to resume its course ... Within 15 minutes the troops had disappeared ... and the city had settled back to normal with no outward trace of the raid except in the minds of its citizens, who had been given an hour's lesson on: "Buy Victory Bonds."[114]

Large numbers of motivated volunteers were also involved in the Air Raid Protection (ARP) program, an extensive campaign designed to demonstrate to Canadians that they did not live in a "fireproof house." As early as 1931, in the pages of the *Canadian Defence Quarterly,* Flight Lieutenant (later Air Vice-Marshal) G.R. Howsam had pointed out that "aircraft carriers ... could sail to within a few miles of the Canadian coast, then send off attacking forces to bomb major cities."[115] Such fears had spread in the late 1930s, as air power brought about tremendous destruction and mass casualties in such places as Guernica, Shanghai, and Nanking. Newspapers and magazines began carrying stories claiming that Canadian cities were vulnerable. In Parliament, the often hyperbolic Tommy Church declared that enemy aircraft could "be upon us before you could say 'O Canada.'" Ian Mackenzie, then minister of national defence, spoke of bombers being able to fly back and forth across the Atlantic to deliver their payload. Cabinet members in 1938 seriously mulled over a far-fetched report from an unnamed senior air force officer stressing that "the recent ... flight of 7,162 miles by two aircraft of the Royal Air Force is the latest indication of what may be in store for us." Indeed, that March the federal government established an interdepartmental committee to examine the need for air raid precautions. It soon recommended – rather curiously – that the Department of Pensions and National Health, despite its lack of experience in this area, be charged with the responsibility of drawing up guidelines for communities to prepare for such an attack.[116]

On 3 September 1939 municipal officials in Saint John, New Brunswick, acting on their own accord, instituted a voluntary partial blackout focusing upon external business and vestibule lighting; it was directed by local police and 100 special air raid wardens appointed by the mayor. By the end of the week, this exercise had been repeated in Saint John, and also implemented in Halifax and several towns in Cape Breton, including Glace Bay and Waterford. These communities were in part reacting to rumours that a German liner, the *Bremen,* which naval experts claimed could be quickly transformed into an aircraft carrier, had stationed itself off Newfoundland after leaving New York following Britain's declaration of war.[117]

Soon, however, things became more organized. By the end of September, Ottawa had established an umbrella organization to coordinate with provincial governments in the Maritimes, Quebec, and Ontario, which were asked to help organize local ARP committees to prepare for the possibility of an emergency and to conduct more comprehensive blackout drills.[118] After Canada went to war with Japan, its eastern and western coastal areas were designated Category A, meaning they were classified as "most vulnerable" to an air strike, while other areas, with the exception of the Prairies and Ontario west of Toronto, were placed in Category B, meaning they were classified as under "definite risk" of an air strike.[119] In major communities, medical, ambulance, police, firefighting, and public utility employees were registered for possible emergency service. Thousands of ARP volunteers took courses paid for by the federal government and taught principally by the St. John's Ambulance Association, in which they learned first aid and the way to conduct themselves during blackout drills or actual air raids. Ultimately over 200,000 citizens participated in the ARP program, which allowed them to feel actively involved in the defence of their country.[120]

Local ARP committees received orders from provincial directors who, in coordination with the federal government, set dates for blackout drills. Cities were divided into zones managed by district ARP wardens and subdivided into precincts, each under the direction of a block captain who directed ARP volunteers. Many ARP managers on the ground were Great War veterans drawn to this activity by its military dimension, signalled by the ARP "uniform" consisting of a special armband and steel helmet. Through local media, citizens were informed of an air raid drill several days in advance and warned to properly prepare their homes – with blackout curtains, for example. For the earliest exercises, not only were the date and time specified but also a warning siren was sounded a half-hour before the actual event. For later tests, people usually knew the day, but not the precise time. To achieve realism, first aid posts were set up in basements of well-fortified buildings and in fact were often put to use to treat minor injuries sustained during the blackouts. During a drill, drivers were ordered to turn off their headlights and pull over to the side of the road, civilians were advised to stay indoors, and people were instructed to extinguish anything they were smoking outside.[121] ARP volunteers provided any needed assistance to civilians, tested coordination and communication between different districts in the absence of telephone service (which involved using young people as messengers), and carefully watched for rule-breakers.

By late 1941 comprehensive mandatory blackout drills lasting between fifteen and thirty minutes had been undertaken in Sydney, Halifax, Saint John, Quebec City, Montreal, Ottawa-Hull, Kingston, Toronto, Vancouver, Esquimalt-Victoria, New Westminster, and Prince Rupert.[122] These events were initially approached with considerable anticipation and excitement; they brought Canada a taste of the war without the bloodshed. Infractions were rare, considering the scope of the drills and the thousands of often-zealous volunteers searching for violators – though certainly the brevity of these events helped keep down the number of people charged. In Ottawa in June 1941, fewer than ten charges were laid in a blackout drill covering twenty-five square miles and 60,000 people. Another drill in June 1942, covering sixty square miles and 200,000 people in Ottawa and Hull, generated only eighteen infractions.[123] Equally successful blackout drills were held in many other communities.

Toward the end of 1942, however, with the growing recognition that an enemy air raid was at best a remote possibility, signs of complacency became evident. An increased number of violations in a Verdun air raid drill made wake-up measures necessary. To restore a sense of urgency in the population, Liberator bombers, Harvard trainers, and, it was reported, an American B-17 Flying Fortress took part in a fifteen-minute "simulated ... bombing run" in October 1942. They zeroed in on the area surrounding city hall, where "exploding somethings" were detonated, causing "much smoke" and shattering four windows.[124] Meanwhile on the west coast, although some 30,000 British Columbians were counted as ARP volunteers in late 1942, the *Vancouver Sun* charged that "citizens [in the city] stumbled through" an October drill, and were "apt to forget that the Japanese are in the Aleutians ... that their submarines have fired on the shore of Vancouver Island ... [and that] this blackout is no game."[125] Still, when offered the chance to purchase gas masks in early 1943 for just $1.50 each, only 900 Vancouverites responded.[126]

On the opposite side of the country, despite enemy U-boat activity off Canada's east coast and in the St. Lawrence, most locals were convinced that the likelihood of direct enemy action against Canadian soil was virtually nil, a reality that the federal government seemed to tacitly admit by permitting shipyards in Halifax to operate around the clock awash in floodlights. In November 1942, following growing ARP violations, Halifax was also subjected to a mock air attack, but rather than staying inside with their windows covered as advised, thousands gathered in the streets to witness the aerial display. In November 1943 Prime Minister King announced that blackouts would no longer be conducted west of the confluence of the Ottawa and St. Lawrence rivers. The last air raid drills occurred in early 1944. By year-end, ARP committees had officially disbanded in Ontario and Quebec, remaining in coastal areas in name only until the end of the war, as their work too had virtually ceased.[127]

WHILE THE DIMINISHING THREAT of an enemy attack on Canada made ARP committees largely redundant by the end of 1942, another need surfaced. By that time the mushrooming needs of the war had pushed Canada's war output toward 50 percent of internal production,[128] and made salvage operations another activity that demanded widespread volunteerism. Back in November 1940, William Knightley, supervisor of stores and plants for the federal Department of Transport, had been appointed director of salvage operations, answerable to the minister of national war services. Recognizing that people tend to move or undertake major cleanups in the spring, the first national salvage drive, concentrating upon the collection of metal items, was announced for April 1941. From a supply standpoint, the campaign was as yet unnecessary, but as explained by the then minister of national war services J.T. Thorson, it was "inaugurated ... to satisfy the patriotic desire of many of our people who had written ... suggesting that they be permitted to organize voluntary salvage corps as was being done in Great Britain."[129]

However, the situation soon changed, not only because military output had risen but also because the supply of items such as rubber and bauxite was virtually cut off as Japan extended its hold on the South Pacific. In May 1942 Knightley, seen by many as efficient but too quiescent and cautious, was demoted to associate director (he retired in November), and the director's role went to Charles LaFerle, a highly regarded transportation manager for the Robert Simpson Company, who kept his hefty annual salary of $15,000, $10,000 of which was covered by Simpson's as a patriotic gesture.[130] Starting that spring, salvage campaigns became massive undertakings. A new National Salvage Committee issued extensive advertising. For example, in a drive later that year to persuade people to save cooking fat (which was turned into glycerine for making explosives) and bones (to produce industrial glue), $135,000 was spent on appeals in 106 daily newspapers, 804 weekly publications, 35 magazines, 32 radio stations, 4 million leaflets, 35,000 stickers and posters, and 100 prints of movie trailers.[131] Through other publicity, Canadians were informed that old pots and pans made guns and tanks; that newspapers and other paper products produced wadding for cartridges; that old rags were transformed into uniforms; that 250 toothpaste or shaving tubes yielded the tin necessary to construct a Bolingbroke bomber; and that an unusable refrigerator contained enough steel for three machine guns, and an old jalopy enough for a light cannon.[132] Several donations were intended to be in part symbolic, for example, trophies from the Great War such as German field guns, some 40 percent of which were turned into scrap; their donors – typically municipal governments – made the point that they would soon yield new trophies from the present conflict.[133]

By September 1945 from 1,693 local salvage committees across Canada there had come, exclusive of fat and bones, 701,696,906 pounds of reusable material, or about fifty-three pounds for every Canadian. With the exception of Quebec, the highest totals were generally attained in provinces with larger cities, as per capita results were best in Ontario, followed by Manitoba, British Columbia, Alberta, Quebec, Nova Scotia, New Brunswick, Saskatchewan, and Prince Edward Island.[134] Local salvage committees divided communities into districts where block captains directed volunteers to produce as wide an appeal and collection as possible. Salvage programs organized in schools and by groups like the Boy Scouts were encouraged. Links with trade groups were useful, such as plumbers' associations that gathered leftover pieces of metal pipe.[135] Perhaps the most successful local salvage committee was Toronto's: by the end of 1942 it had collected fifteen tons of scrap rubber, or enough for the construction needs of two Tribal class destroyers.[136] This committee ultimately obtained volunteers from eighty-six local organizations to distribute information (on how to separate and pack, and when to leave out, salvageable items) and to help pick up the scrap. On the Wednesday closest to the middle of each month, Toronto's municipal garbage trucks picked up fat left out in pails and bones in specially marked bags for delivery to chemical factories.[137] During wider salvage drives, however, the pickup and transport of other items – those containing large amounts of rubber and metal, as well as newspapers, books, and magazines – was handled by Toronto's Salvage Committee, which used trucks donated by the Salvation Army, the St. Vincent de Paul Society, the Poppy Fund, the Crippled Civilians Fund, and several local businesses.[138]

Junk dealers selected by the federal government to receive scrap were to pay $15 a ton for metal and rubber products, and $8 a ton for paper. The money raised by salvage committees financed their operations and any excess was donated to war charities. In Toronto, a large proportion of the $40,000 raised from the outset of its salvage operations to the spring of 1943 was used "to continue and expand ... activities for men and women in uniform in Military Districts Nos. 1, 2 and 9, Air Force Command No. 1 and at H.M.C.S. *York*."[139] Still, frustration sometimes surfaced because scrap fetched such low prices, so much so that even with mass volunteer labour, salvage committees raised only small sums despite the thousands of tons they collected. Costs regularly reached 80 percent of revenues, and in some cases ate up all the money obtained.[140] The National Salvage Committee, concerned about the possibility of declining commitment, reminded local committee leaders that their most important contribution was the scrap they collected and that donations to other war-related causes were an added, and less critical, bonus.[141]

In several places, small returns produced vicious accusations that Jewish junkyard dealers, stereotyped as money-grubbing, were making exorbitant profits. Such claims derived not only from well-entrenched anti-Semitism but also from the fact that a high proportion of salvage yard owners were Jewish.[142] This was often a natural step up from peddling, the initial occupation of many poor Jewish immigrants, because it required few start-up costs and allowed them – as their own bosses – to observe the Saturday Sabbath.[143] During one of the first national salvage drives, William Knightley was told by the chair of the Fort William salvage committee: "One thing that keeps cropping up every day ... is 'Are the Jews going to get the salvage we, the citizens, are turning in?'" Later that year, the head of the Kitchener-Waterloo salvage committee told Minister of National War Services Thorson that the federal government should go directly into the salvaging business to eliminate excessive profits being taken by the "Jewish middleman." Given many "general comments" of this sort, Thorson assured citizens, through a press release, that all salvage yards operated "on a very small margin of profit" and were "constantly under surveillance by government officials."[144] Still, persistent rumours about crooked Jewish junk dealers, and that Jews were principal black marketeers, were largely responsible for the WIB ending its support for the *Canadian Column* in November 1943; the WIB deemed its directors ineffective in countering such scuttlebutt, and thus perhaps inherently legitimizing it.[145] In January 1944 William Knightley, though no longer connected with the National Salvage Committee, wrote to the *Ottawa Citizen* to denounce what he saw as widespread anti-Semitism based on erroneous assumptions regarding scrap dealers. Among the victims was his friend Alex Betcherman, the owner of Betcherman Iron and Steel, who, he pointed out, besides making minuscule profits from accepting war-related scrap, arranged at his own expense to remove an old iron fence donated by St. Andrew's Church.[146] In fact, many junkyard dealers complained that they made far less than authorized profits because the material delivered by local salvage committees was not separated out as required, thus costing them time and resources; and because up to 20 percent of the scrap received could not be reused by industry, as many people exploited salvage drives to dump a wide range of unwanted goods.[147]

Signs of anti-Semitism, complacency during air raid drills, and charity scams can all be dismissed as aberrations from the positive spirit that typified Canada's home front. True, a comprehensive and rather sophisticated censorship and propaganda apparatus buoyed spirits and helped ensure the success of many volunteer campaigns, but most of the credit still lies with the Canadian people. While they didn't enter the Second World War with the same naïveté or enthusiasm as they did the Great War, nonetheless countless Canadians proved unbounded in the generosity of their contributions of volunteer labour, money, material, and, at least outside of Quebec, willingness to serve militarily. From millions of Canadians determined to do their duty and demonstrate patriotism came exceptional efforts and, as a result, extraordinary numbers with respect to enlistment, Victory Bond purchases, knitted goods produced and sent overseas, contributions to tobacco funds, parcels for POWs, and salvage. Extraordinary too was the small number of charges resulting from recalcitrance in civil defence drills. Such responses provided substance and longevity to the image of the Second World War as a conflict uniting people in a common and noble cause, an image that contrasts sharply with the picture of a directionless and desperate nation during the Great Depression.

Indeed, further bolstering this image of the "good war" was its economic impact, most particularly in Canada and the United States, which suffered no physical devastation. Although the price was huge, the war finally and unequivocally ended the Depression. Copious documentation speaks to a radical economic improvement. Yet, just as pervasive and much-publicized patriotism sometimes concealed displeasing and even shameful conduct, accelerated economic growth also had its darker side. Aside from such trends as improved living standards and pride over Canada's massive contribution to the war effort, growth was also a source of increasing social strain that engendered mounting concern over whether, at home, the war ultimately forged greater selflessness or behaviour that threatened the country's very moral fibre.

2
Growth, Opportunity, and Strain

BY THE EARLY 1940s some Canadian companies were already looking ahead to the end of the war. They were taking out advertisements, not only to urge Victory Bond purchases or contributions to other war charities but to let people know about their war-related production. Many were proud, others perhaps concerned about a postwar backlash if they were not seen to have pitched in; some were attempting to keep their name before the public as their products were deflected from consumer markets.[1] Toronto's Tip Top Tailors, for instance, in 1943 proclaimed to civilians who were facing significant shortages of new clothing that it was producing part of a military uniform every eight seconds.[2] Some firms, foreseeing a postwar boom, endeavoured to secure their share of the future peacetime market by advertising the superior performance of their products in wartime. Gypsum, Lime and Alabastine, Limited, of Paris, Ontario, told prospective builders of homes or commercial establishments that its durable, fire-resistant gyproc had been the product of choice in constructing buildings for the British Commonwealth Air Training Plan. The Alemite Company of Belleville, Ontario, declared that its "lubrication systems" never let down Allied military vehicles, even in the hot, sandy conditions of North Africa. And General Electric boasted about its new Lampa, a germicidal lamp developed for military hospitals, which "bombard[ed]" bacteria with "special ultra-violet rays," an invention that it promised would ensure better health in postwar homes.[3]

WHILE THE LAMPA did not win the war on germs, the conflict that gave it life did rapidly cure an ailing economy. The key was military spending. Canada's military had been starved for funds in the interwar years. Between 1937 and 1939, even as war clouds gathered over Europe, defence appropriations rose from $32.7 million to just $34.4 million per fiscal year, or roughly the equivalent of what Canada had spent every month to fight the Great War.[4] To make matters worse, the one major prewar arms contract the federal government signed in 1938 with the John Inglis Company to furnish 7,000 Bren guns sparked charges of corruption and the appointment of a royal commission after it was discovered that no other tenders had been solicited – a scenario that recalled the scandals in Canada's Shell Committee during the First World War.

In 1939 the Royal Canadian Navy had just 2,000 personnel and 8 outdated vessels; the air force 3,000 personnel and 37 "remotely combat-worthy" aircraft; and the permanent army 5,000 personnel and just 2 light tanks and 4 anti-aircraft guns.[5]

With the outbreak of war, wishing to see how matters would unfold, the King government maintained caution about an all-out arms buildup. In December 1939 King expressed the hope that the $350 million that Canada had finally agreed to spend on the Canadian-based Commonwealth Air Training Plan would serve as the country's major contribution to the war effort.[6]

Canadian industrialists and manufacturers often complained that excessive bureaucratization was undermining the possibility of an effective and timely transition to a war footing. In July 1939 the federal government established the Defence Purchasing Board and structured its procedures in response to recommendations made earlier that year by the royal commission report on the Bren gun controversy. The report had not uncovered corruption, but it did make the government determined to avoid even the appearance of impropriety.[7] The purchasing board was therefore to remain separate from the Ministry of National Defence and was to enforce strict profit caps. To prevent graft, it instituted a complex approval procedure for firms involved in military contracts worth over $5,000, complicated enough that some prospective government suppliers questioned the value of seeking out this business. As of 31 October 1939, by which time excessive backlogs had discredited the board, it had arranged only $43.7 million worth of war contracts. It was replaced by the War Supply Board, which projected a more businesslike appearance under the direction of Wallace Campbell, president of the Ford Motor Company of Canada. In practice, however, it was no more effective. Apparently, King's "limited liability" philosophy guided Wallace's masters in the finance department to the extent that they blocked or delayed several proposed contracts for committing funds beyond the current fiscal year.[8]

The basis for dramatic change was established just as the phony war ended, with the creation of the Department of Munitions and Supply. Although legislation authorizing its inception was passed on 12 September 1939, and its minister, Clarence Decatur (C.D.) Howe, was appointed in November, the department remained confined to paper until 9 April 1940, a month after the Liberals were re-elected with a huge majority. With the Nazi blitzkrieg proceeding through Scandinavia, the Low Countries, and France, and with Britain the next logical target, Canada launched a massive rearmament program. Howe, an engineer who had run a heavy construction company before entering politics, had a reputation for efficiency and results, and for not being timid about using government to achieve his ends. This was a trait he had demonstrated by merging his first two Cabinet posts – Railways and Canals, and Marine – into a new Transportation ministry where he cleaned out "patronage and pork barrelling" and successfully pushed ahead to create a new national airline.[9]

With the sweeping powers conferred on him under the Munitions and Supply Act, Howe became, as Michael Hennessy wrote, the "absolute monarch of Canadian war production." The billions that came from Victory Bonds for rearmament were augmented by new taxes, as the federal government obtained control over income and corporate tax fields, according to recommendations in the 1940 Royal Commission Report on Dominion-Provincial Relations. Another critical measure was the 20 April 1941 Hyde Park Declaration, in which the United States agreed to buy far more Canadian goods and help finance British defence purchases in Canada, and which, given Canada's growing American trade deficit, saved the country from a potentially crippling liquidity crisis.[10]

Howe and his assistants cut through red tape, sending letters of intent to firms so they could get moving on war production, and quickly followed up with formal contracts. "Dollar-a-year" men, experts from large companies that often continued paying their salaries, were brought into Munitions and Supply to ensure that operations ran efficiently and in a business-friendly manner. Through the new War Industries Control Board operated by Munitions and Supply, essential raw materials were obtained for firms engaged in war production. Profits on war contracts were limited to 10 percent, and scandals involving Munitions and Supply, or war contracts in general, were virtually nonexistent during the Second World War.[11] Unlike its predecessors, Munitions and Supply actively helped with the mass transformation of industry and manufacturing to war production. Among other forms of support, it facilitated discounted loans and grants, the purchase of licences to enable Canadian production of foreign-designed weapons, and assistance in securing technical experts from Britain and the United States; and it permitted claims of double depreciation against taxes for plant renovations, machinery acquisition, and other necessary expenses.

There is no doubt that Canada, still very much a country geared to the export of raw materials in 1939, transformed itself into an industrial giant, with military production leading the way (Figure 2.1). The war effort claimed virtually all federal government expenditures (Figure 2.2). Canada produced 400 naval and 391 cargo ships, 50,000 tanks, 16,000 military aircraft, 850,000 military vehicles, 1.5 million rifles and machine guns, 72 million artillery and mortar shells, and 4.4 billion rounds of small arms ammunition. With the addition of spinoff activities from war production, unemployment evaporated. Between 1939 and 1944 the number of jobless Canadians plunged from 523,000 to 62,000. Countless factories that during the Depression had operated considerably under capacity struggled in wartime to keep up with demand, and where private industry was unable to respond as required, the federal government filled the void. Munitions and Supply created twenty-eight Crown corporations, which employed 189,976 as of 1 July 1943, including 55 percent of Canada's 104,620 aircraft workers and 79 percent of the 19,718 who made machine guns and small arms.[12]

With Munitions and Supply understandably targeting its huge orders on larger firms with proven track records and known managerial competence, industrial consolidation intensified (Table 2.1). Several smaller firms unable to obtain needed supplies or labour went under during the war, though those regarded as more efficient benefited through subcontracting. Given the tendency of Munitions and

Figure 2.1

Trends in manufacturing output, 1938-45

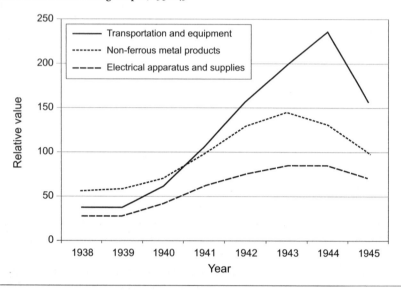

Note: 1949 = 100

Source: K.A.H. Buckley and M.C. Urquhart, *Historical Statistics of Canada* (Toronto: Macmillan, 1965), 476.

Figure 2.2

War-related expenditures and total federal government spending, 1940-45

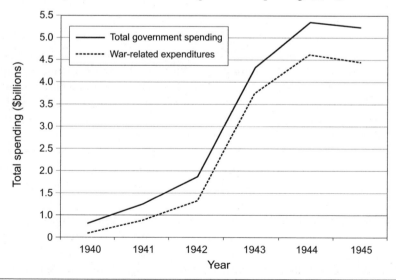

Source: Canada Year Book, 1948-49, 973.

Table 2.1

Canadian manufacturing: Consolidation trends, 1929-44

Value of production ($)	Establishments	Establishments (%)	Total production ($millions)	Total production (%)
1929				
Less than $25,000	14,024	59.4	59.4	1.5
25,001-50,000	2,802	11.9	99.5	2.5
50,001-100,000	2,209	9.4	156.4	3.9
100,001-200,000	1,688	7.1	237.5	5.9
200,001-500,000	1,519	6.4	504.2	12.6
500,001-1,000,000	636	2.7	443.6	11.0
1,000,001-5,000,000	601	2.5	1,217.9	30.3
$5,000,001 +	118	0.5	1,298.2	32.3
Total	23,597	99.9	4,016.7	100.0
1939				
Less than $25,000	15,623	63.0	120.9	3.5
25,001-50,000	2,808	11.3	99.6	2.9
50,001-100,000	2,215	8.9	156.4	4.5
100,001-200,000	1,584	6.4	225.6	6.5
200,001-500,000	1,285	5.2	390.6	11.2
500,001-1,000,000	689	2.8	466.4	13.4
1,000,001-5,000,000	520	2.1	1,091.3	31.4
$5,000,001 +	81	0.3	923.7	26.6
Total	24,805	100	3,474.5	100.0
1944				
Less than $25,000	13,942	48.9	128.8	1.4
25,001-50,000	4,011	14.1	143.0	1.6
50,001-100,000	3,442	12.1	245.3	2.7
100,001-200,000	2,513	8.8	355.2	3.9
200,001-500,000	2,256	7.9	714.5	7.9
500,001-1,000,000	943	3.3	661.7	7.3
1,000,001-5,000,000	1,089	3.8	2,294.5	25.3
$5,000,001 +	287	1.0	4,530.6	49.9
Total	28,483	99.9	9,073.6	100.0

Note: Rounding of figures will sometimes produce slight deviations from 100 percent.
Source: Canada Year Book, 1947, 563.

Supply to favour larger firms, wartime economic growth was most intense in Ontario and Quebec, Canada's industrial heartland. Between 1939 and 1944 the gross value of manufactured goods in Ontario rose from $1.7 billion to $4.4 billion, while in Quebec the corresponding figures were $1.0 billion and $2.9 billion.

In Montreal, then Canada's largest city with just over a million people, the gross value of industrial and manufacturing production rose from $483 million in 1939 to $1.2 billion in 1944, and the number of employees in these sectors increased from 105,315 to 185,708.[13] The Vickers shipyard built corvettes and minesweepers, and United Shipyards built scores of freighters, tugs, and diesel barges.[14] From the Canada Car and Foundry plant came propellers and wings for Avro Ansons and Hawker Hurricanes; from Pratt & Whitney, engines for Harvard trainers and Catalina flying boats; from Noorduyn Aviation, Mosquito and Norseman fighters; and from Fairchild Aircraft, Bristol and Bolingbroke bombers.[15]

Toronto closely followed Montreal, with the gross value of its industrial and manufacturing output rising from $482 million in 1939 to $1 billion in 1944, while the total number of employees in these sectors increased from 98,702 to 154,538.[16] By 1943 eighty-seven industrial and manufacturing plants in Toronto and environs were geared to war production. Among the best known were de Havilland, which made the Mosquito and other aircraft, and National Steel Car in Malton, whose facilities were taken over by the federal government in 1942 to become Victory Aircraft, makers of Lancaster bombers.[17] Hamilton, nicknamed the "Birmingham of Canada" for its steel production, saw the value of its industrial and manufacturing output grow from $153 million in 1939 to $363 million in 1944.[18] A little further west, Kitchener-Waterloo experienced what the local chamber of commerce called an "industrial revolution," as over the first four years of the war, its blue-collar workforce increased by some 60 percent to just over 18,000.[19]

Even in remote parts of central Canada, the economic impact of the war was enormous in many cases. In Iroquois Falls, a lumbering centre about 300 miles north of Toronto, for example, timber companies could not hire enough people to keep up with demand.[20] In the mining sector, to conserve labour for the extraction of minerals critical to industrial production, the federal government placed a cap on gold mining. While gold-mining towns like Kirkland Lake were hurt, others such as Sudbury and Arvida benefited from the record demand for metals such as nickel and aluminum respectively. Even these growth areas also struggled to retain adequate labour, as large numbers of relatively low-paid workers migrated to better opportunities in urban manufacturing.[21]

IN FEBRUARY 1945 Nova Scotia's Ministry of Industry and Publicity, seeking to promote the province to investors as peace came into view, boasted in a full-page *Maclean's* advertisement of its massive shipbuilding sector, a "thriving commercial weaving industry," and steel and coal companies that had smashed all previous records.[22] However, some historians argue that in the Maritimes wartime prosperity had little long-term impact, and that outside of Moncton, Saint John, and Halifax, the region fared poorly during the conflict, experiencing significant population loss both from military enlistment and from emigration to better opportunities in Quebec and Ontario.[23] Precise figures are problematic because the census was done decennially, in 1941 and 1951. A comparison between the June 1941 census and the number of ration books distributed in September 1943 does reveal that Prince Edward Island lost 9.8 percent of its population (95,047 to 85,767), Nova Scotia 1.6 percent (577,962 to 568,531), and New Brunswick 5.5 percent (from 457,401 to 432,386). This trend was most pronounced in rural areas and small towns. In Nova Scotia, outside the counties containing Halifax, Sydney, and New Glasgow, the population declined from 303,814 to 280,447, or by 7.7 percent, while in New Brunswick, outside the counties containing Saint John and Moncton, the loss was from 324,088 to 296,948, or by 8.4 percent.[24] With leaders like C.D. Howe convinced that the Maritimes were far less appropriate than central Canada for manufacturing and industry, not one wartime Crown corporation was based in the region; of the $1.6 billion provided by Munitions and Supply by the end of 1943 to help with the expansion of industry, only $27 million was earmarked for the Maritimes.[25]

Of Maritimers asked in 1943 whether Ottawa was treating all parts of the country fairly, 37 percent replied affirmatively, 38 percent negatively, and 25 percent said they were unsure. This result did not compare badly with other parts of Canada. While respondents in Ontario split 52, 25, and 23 percent respectively, Quebeckers produced returns of 35, 34, and 31 percent, the Prairies 38, 39, and 23 percent, and British Columbia 29, 45, and 26 percent.[26] Moreover, wartime and initial postwar regional sentiment in the Maritimes was mild in comparison to the 1880s or 1920s. Certainly such sentiment was contained by the fact that the war mobilized Maritimers as Canadians. But it is also reasonable to assume that wartime economic growth, even if more short-lived and less intense than in central Canada, still proceeded quickly and widely enough to prompt many Maritimers, who had been among the hardest hit in Canada during the Depression, to share the optimism expressed by Nova Scotia's Ministry of Industry and Publicity.

Not long after hostilities started, the Maritime steel sector was booming, coal orders skyrocketed, the cotton and clothing sectors revived, and the timber companies struggled to keep up with demand.[27] Over the first two years of the war, employment in Maritime shipbuilding doubled.[28] To assist the movement of military personnel and commerce, the federal government helped fund improvements to the region's railway network and significantly upgraded ports in Saint John, Moncton, Sydney, and especially Halifax. In 1939 the Halifax dockyard still retained, as local historian Thomas Randal wrote, an "eighteenth-century" air with its many dilapidated wooden structures, but by war's end it was dominated by "multifarious stores and workshops" and a "brick block of administration offices" to manage most of Nova Scotia's 15,000 wartime shipyard workers.[29]

THE CANADIAN WEST, where, as in the Maritimes, regionalism had deep roots, also had its share of complaints over the distribution of economic benefits generated by the war. However, also as in the Maritimes, complaints were muted by the fact that many areas did prosper. In Regina, hardly known for industry, the General Motors assembly plant was employing a record 1,600 people within a few years.[30] In Edmonton, Aircraft Repair Limited, which entered the war with 100 employees, grew to over 3,000 from business generated by the British Commonwealth Air Training Plan (BCATP) and the Northwest Staging Route.[31] Across British Columbia, some 39,000 obtained jobs in the shipbuilding sector, and, while in September 1939 industrial employment in Vancouver and Victoria stood at 39,205 and 3,571 respectively, by July 1944 those figures had reached 88,938 and 13,332.[32]

Construction connected to military training had its most profound economic impact in the Prairies, where the greatest number of BCATP bases were concentrated. Large numbers of army recruits could be trained at places such as Camp Borden and Camp Valcartier in Ontario and Quebec, which had been built during the Great War, although they required upgrading and new construction. But for air training, two-thirds of wartime facilities had to be built from scratch, as Canada possessed relatively few – and generally small – airfields before the conflict.

According to the terms of the BCATP, signed in December 1939 after much financial haggling among Canada, Britain, Australia, and New Zealand, Canada would cover $353 million of the initial bill of $607.2 million, as all training facilities were located within the country.[33] The first agreement was to run until 31 March 1943. However, spiralling costs necessitated a new one on 5 June 1942 that extended until 31 March 1945. The total bill reached $1,757,367,389, of which Canada paid $1,589,954,609 in return for being granted management over the program. Ultimately, Canadians made up 72,835 of the BCATP's 131,553 graduates.[34] Across Canada, 137 BCATP schools trained pilots, navigators, bombardiers, gunners, and wireless operators. Scores of small and often isolated communities were opened up to – and sometimes deluged by – men arriving from all over the country and indeed from around the world: the BCATP trained 42,000 airmen from Great Britain, 7,606 from Australia, 7,002 from New Zealand, and smaller numbers from the United States, Poland, France, Belgium, Czechoslovakia, and the Netherlands.[35]

Communities competed with each other for bases, sometimes sending delegations to Ottawa to make their case. When Yorkton, Saskatchewan, received news of its success in securing a base, its local newspaper, the *Enterprise,* beamed, "It will bring about 1,000 men here with an average pay of about $100 a month. [Also] airmen have clothing to buy, suits to be cleaned, shoes to be purchased, yes, and shoes to shine ... Yorkton will be in for one of the greatest booms in its long history."[36]

With riches in the offing, allegations were sometimes heard that the federal Liberals chose locations for the bases to reward areas loyal to the party. However, no such correlation was proven; it was simply a matter of mathematics that most bases were located in Liberal ridings since, after the March 1940 federal election, the party held nearly three-quarters of the parliamentary seats. Indeed, realizing the crucial importance of establishing bases and graduating air force personnel quickly – and the likelihood of political catastrophe if it were concluded that patronage compromised these goals or the lives of trainees – the Liberals made a point of separating the process of base selection from the political level. This task was handed over to technical experts, primarily at the Ministry of Transport. They sought out locales with topography best suited for good-quality airfields and with large expanses of surrounding space free from potentially dangerous obstacles.

Indeed, even though Prince Albert, Saskatchewan, was represented by Prime Minister King, and though its local leaders were among the most active in lobbying for benefits under the BCATP, it was not among the first places approved for a base. Moreover, because of problems in acquiring adequate space for emergency landing fields around Prince Albert, it received a smaller elementary flying school and an observer training school rather than the larger service flying training school it desired, and, despite its strong opposition, both its schools were among the first to be closed.[37] Meanwhile, British Columbian politicians argued that despite its mountainous terrain, the province's milder climate provided more good flying days than any other part of the country.[38] Gripes were also heard from northern Alberta over the fact that virtually all the province's BCATP bases were south of Red Deer. But southern Alberta and Saskatchewan provided land best suited to air training: lightly populated, lightly forested, flat, and remote from the possibility of an enemy air attack launched from an aircraft carrier. In Saskatchewan, the province hardest hit by the Depression, fifty flight schools were set up, the greatest single concentration. However, bases ultimately appeared in all parts of Canada, both near such major communities as Calgary, Saskatoon, Toronto, and Montreal, and in places few Canadians knew existed: Bowen, Alberta; Caron, Saskatchewan; Virden, Manitoba; Ancienne Lorette, Quebec; Penfield Ridge, New Brunswick; and Mount Pleasant, Prince Edward Island.[39]

Before the war, military construction had been the responsibility of the Royal Canadian Engineers, but to rapidly meet the huge requirements of the BCATP, Ottawa created a new directorate under R.R. Collard, vice-president and general manager of the Carter-Hall-Aldinger Construction Company of Winnipeg, who was well experienced with large contracting projects. Collard, assigned the rank of air marshal, recruited engineers and draftsmen from civilian construction firms to prepare designs for hangars, drill halls, and barrack blocks, and many of these companies were awarded building contracts by Munitions and Supply. For speed and efficiency, standardization was implemented, parts often arrived pre-cut, and buildings were put up in as little as a day.

Contractors and labourers were imported into less populated areas, thus precipitating boom conditions. To build the $800,000 aerodrome in Yorkton, Saskatchewan, companies and crew came from Winnipeg and Saskatoon.[40] The

BCATP also provided civilian employment beyond construction needs. With initial shortages of skilled air force pilots in Canada, and wartime demands that prevented the release of British personnel, civilian air clubs were hired until the plan could produce its own instructors. Bases frequently offered employment for civilian mechanics, janitors, cooks, and stenographers.[41] Also of tremendous significance was the business generated by airmen on leave. Advertisements in BCATP base newspapers give a taste of local desire to capitalize on this new resource. In the *Slipstream*, printed for the No. 7 Service Flying Training School in Fort Macleod, Alberta, the Macleod Photo Studio publicized its "special RCAF frames"; the Java Shop billed itself as the most "swinging joint" in town; and Al's Billiard Hall, with its new air conditioning system, said it was the "coolest."[42]

Although discontent was felt in northern Alberta over the distribution of BCATP bases, it soon dissipated. By the end of 1940, three separate delegations of local politicians and businessmen from Edmonton had visited Ottawa, and arrangements were made to transform the city's exhibition grounds into an air force manning depot. An air observer school, an elementary flying school, and an initial training school soon followed in Edmonton.[43]

Of far greater significance, both to Edmonton and areas further north, was the creation of the Northwest Staging Route, which in late 1941 started supplying the Soviet Union with military hardware, including aircraft. Edmonton served as its base of operations, and for a short period in early 1942, with additional activity relating to the construction of the Alaska Highway, the city's airport, Blatchford Field, was the busiest in North America.[44] The Americans, who directed both the staging route and the highway, provided Blatchford with $3.5 million for buildings and $6 million to upgrade and increase the number of runways, thus ensuring its status as Edmonton's main airport for years after the war. The next year, to ease pressure on Blatchford, the Americans spent another $7 million to construct the Namao airfield, with two 7,000-foot runways, eight miles north of Edmonton's then-current city limits.[45]

The staging route, which ended in Fairbanks, Alaska, consisted of a line of thirteen small airports, built at the cost of $58.5 million, eleven of which were on Canadian soil. Between 1941 and 1944 the route accommodated some 9,000 flights by fighter and bomber aircraft.[46] Usually to mixed responses, the airfields opened up small, often isolated, communities, some with a high percentage of Aboriginal peoples. There was plenty of work to help construct, maintain, and supply the airfields and accompanying facilities, especially in the "principal staging points" of Grand Prairie, Alberta, Fort St. John and Fort Nelson, British Columbia, and Watson Lake and Whitehorse in the Yukon. Each of these airports was equipped with a 4,000-foot runway with lighting for night landings. Also, because atmospheric conditions often interfered with radio signals, the Americans installed 2,400 miles of landlines, which tremendously upgraded communication facilities in Canada's northwest and far north.[47]

Links to the northwest and the far north were also reinforced by the Alaska Highway, which was rapidly constructed, at least in rough form, between February and November 1942, against the possibility of an attack from the two outer Aleutian islands Japan had occupied.[48] The road stretched just over 1,600 miles from Dawson Creek, British Columbia – already connected by road to Edmonton, the administrative headquarters of the highway – to Fairbanks, with all but 250 miles located in Canada. Despite some bad feelings toward the arriving Americans for their generally higher pay and, it was often said, their pushy and arrogant nature, the majority of people spoke of the project as a bonanza. Such was the case in Edmonton, then a city of some 100,000 through which nearly 50,000 Americans passed and in several cases lived for a considerable period of time. To attract US greenbacks, several Edmonton businesses placed the term "American" in their name. Moreover, the Americans, to accommodate their personnel and administrative needs, leased more than fifty downtown sites in Edmonton, and at some places made extensive renovations; an example was the city's Jesuit College, to which the construction company Bechtel-Price-Callahan added sixteen residences and a new cafeteria for 500.[49]

The construction of the Alaska Highway involved 14,000 military personnel from the US Army Corps of Engineers, 77 civilian contractors, and 6,000 civilian employees, and cost some $130 million. The military cut the initial path, and civilian contractors and workers followed behind to grade and gravel, a process that continued until October 1943, when the road was judged to have passed the "pioneer stage."[50] Most heavy equipment came from America's Public Roads Administration. However, Canadians were very much involved. Toronto's R. Melville Smith Company served as one of four civilian project managers. Thousands of Canadians were hired as construction workers, though at Ottawa's request those employed by American firms were paid lower Canadian rates to stem migration from Canadian to US companies and to protect the integrity of the federal government's new wage and price freeze. Resentment was evident but was often tempered by the unprecedented opportunities. Given the frenzied pace of construction, it was not uncommon for men to work eighty-hour weeks. One Canadian truck driver, for example, received $0.75 an hour and paid out $1.25 a day for food and lodging, thus earning $222.65 free and clear each month at a time when a decent yearly income was $1,500 (though undoubtedly it still rankled that his American counterpart received $1.40 an hour and overtime pay of $2.10 for anything beyond a forty-eight hour work week).[51]

Media accounts often emphasized that the new economic opportunities extended to Native peoples as well. Those who were not working on the highway were portrayed, rather condescendingly, as being "swamped with orders for souvenir moccasins" and other such items.[52] In fact, their involvement in better-paying construction jobs was minimal; typically Natives served as guides and packers. Moreover, hardly noted in popular discourse was the spread of disease to groups like the Teslin band in the Yukon, who before the arrival of the highway had had virtually no contact with white society.[53] Natives obtained alcohol from whites, and within several bands unaccustomed to liquor there occurred rising levels of alcohol-related crime and other signs of social disintegration. Increasing numbers of prostitutes moved to the north to take advantage of the lack of women, and there were many sexual liaisons with Natives, among whom the venereal disease rate rose – a plague that also spread among men working on the highway.[54] The "invasion" from the south also had major ecological consequences, namely large-scale clear-cutting, toxic spills, forest fires, overhunting and overfishing, and significant interference with the natural migratory patterns of animals.

But given its apparent military necessity and the fact that the site of construction was generally considered a backward area, nearly everything Canadians read about the highway, regarding both its immediate impact and its role in the future development of an increasingly romanticized north, was upbeat. In late 1942, when the highway was little more than a dirt trail, the *Edmonton Journal,* in a series on the road, described the newly accessed area as a "vacation paradise ... filled with game and lakes ... teeming with fighting trout and grayling." The next year, *Maclean's* wrote of the "applications ... being received in Ottawa for hamburger, barbeque and filling station concessions" along the route. *Saturday Night,* though skeptical, reported on "speeches ... made in Eastern cities, prophesying that at a not too distant day, a motorist in Toronto or Montreal would be able to drive to Moscow, via the Alaska Highway, a ferry across the Bering Strait, and another great highway across Siberia."[55]

Along the construction route many communities boomed as never before, enjoying incredible economic benefits but also desperately trying to cope. Hotels and restaurants were jammed around the clock. The population of Dawson Creek, British Columbia, grew from 728 before the coming of the highway to 9,000. There, and in several other northern communities, the Americans built water mains, sewage facilities, telephone lines, roads, and other infrastructure then beyond the financial reach of such locales. Into Whitehorse, which the Americans made their northern headquarters for highway construction, there came over 8,000 newcomers and more than $9 million in US investment to provide, among other things, gigantic storage facilities that often were left empty and became decayed after the Americans left. During the war Whitehorse eclipsed Dawson City, which the highway bypassed, as the Yukon's most important urban centre, a change in fortune confirmed in 1953 when it assumed from Dawson City the role of the territory's capital.[56]

The withdrawal of military personnel and construction crews from the far north, virtually completed by the end of 1943, left the highway far from ready to accept civilian traffic. With the disappearance of the Japanese threat, the Americans departed rapidly, selling off heavy equipment – often badly worn – at deep discounts, or sometimes abandoning it along the roadway. The boom quickly fizzled, yet much of the north remained significantly and forever altered. To a remote region that had been largely isolated in 1939, there were now new links via road, airfields, telegraphs, and telephones. Many small communities inherited important facilities such as pumping stations, weather monitoring facilities, storage buildings, and radio broadcast centres. Permanent communities, though remaining small, generally stabilized at numbers appreciably higher than their prewar levels. More government employees remained in the north to manage the new facilities and the upgrading of the highway for civilian use. In 1946 Ottawa completed financial arrangements with the United States to give Canada control over the highway within its borders. Despite the federal government's initial reluctance to spend the funds to improve and keep the road in good repair, by 1948 enough had been accomplished to open the route to civilian traffic – thus also opening a new chapter in the history of Canada's northwest and far north.[57]

THE PROBLEMS RELATED to accelerated wartime growth in Canada's far north were, to use a geographically appropriate cliché, only the tip of the iceberg. Along with war-generated boom conditions came a seemingly alarming number of Canadians who, rather than making sacrifices as expected, put their own narrow, often pecuniary, interests first: those who complained about rising taxes, workers who hit the bricks to protest the wage freeze and to settle old scores, and farmers who grew angry over extra hardships and unsatisfactory remuneration.

Throughout the war, corporate taxes, when averaged out among all contributors, stood at around 12 percent, but strict caps were placed on the amount assessed at this, or lower, levels. This was because the Excess Profits Tax introduced in 1941 grabbed all declared earnings at a 50 percent rate above a firm's 1936-39 average profits. The next year, the tax was increased to 75 percent, and by 1942 took all profits above the 1936-39 norm, measures that, with the promise of a 20 percent rebate after the war and benefits such as higher depreciation allowances, prompted criticism from organized labour and little regard for firms that griped.[58] Many companies chose to bury their profits in Victory Bonds, the purchase of new machinery, or plant expansions. Nevertheless, the Excess Profits Tax, which in its first year yielded the federal government $23.99 million, with expanded production brought in $465.8 million by 1945. Total annual corporate taxes in Canada rose from $85 million in 1938-39 to $850 million in 1943-44.[59] Companies also faced a maximum 10 percent profit on government war orders, despite frequent extra costs from shifting assembly lines to a war footing and training new employees. Under the banner "A FACT OR TWO ABOUT WAR PROFITS!" an advertisement from Dominion Textiles of Montreal declared with some exasperation, "From 1939 to 1942, our wage bill increased from $4,511,433 to $9,379,203 ... In the same period our taxes rose from $244,000 to $8,000,000. The tax load is now 32 times what it was in 1939."[60]

Although most firms accepted the reasons for high taxes, and often expressed pride in their financial support of the war effort, a number claimed that they were being prevented from building up any reserves and would emerge from the conflict terribly weakened. This point was angrily driven home by the owner of one Toronto industrial establishment, who maintained that over a six-month period in 1942 his profits were slashed from $136,000 to $20,000, and doubted his ability to survive the "very difficult period of post-war readjustment."[61] Formal charges for tax evasion were rather rare, although several firms, especially those dealing with goods in short supply, were fined by the Wartime Prices and Trade Board (WPTB) for engaging in black-market cash sales, typically above the legal price ceiling. For example, in 1944 the Caledonia Farms Corporation was charged with some $40,000 worth of such transactions involving rationed canned meat.[62]

In a country that before the war had enjoyed minimal levies on incomes or on goods and services, Canadians suddenly found themselves paying unprecedentedly high taxes. Between 1939 and 1945 income taxes collected by the federal government soared from $142 million to $977.7 million. The rates were steeply progressive. At one point, assuming no deductions, a taxpayer with a declared annual income of $500,000 would lose $433,682.[63]

The taxes of June 1940 gave a foretaste. A new National Defence Tax was added to rising income taxes, starting at 2 percent on $600 a year for a single person and $1,200 for a married couple. On a net income of $1,000 a single person paid $83.00 in tax, whereas five years earlier someone earning three or four times that amount had paid only $42.41.[64] Canadians also faced new taxes on a variety of purchases: 10 percent on most imports; 10 percent on phonographs, cameras, radios, and radio tubes; and five cents per pound on tires and tubes. "Sin" taxes also increased: a ten-cent-per-pound levy was placed on raw tobacco; the tax on manufactured tobacco rose from twenty-five to thirty-five cents a pound; and on cigarettes, which became a notable black-market item, the tax went up from $5 to $6 per 1,000 on sales to civilians.[65] Among the highlights in the 1941 budget was a 20 percent luxury tax on tickets to movies, live theatre, sporting events, and other forms of entertainment.[66] Income taxes also continued rising. In June 1942 a single person with no dependants and earning $1,750 annually was taxed $471, over 20 percent more than the previous year – though $140 of that sum was in the form of new compulsory savings, which were to be paid back after the war with 2 percent interest.[67]

Most Canadians publicly maintained their unswerving commitment to pay whatever the federal government asked. In December 1942, when surveyed as to whether they would be willing pay "more taxes to help win the war," 60 percent answered affirmatively, 14 percent said no, and 22 percent claimed they were unable. The strongest support was registered in Ontario (72 percent), the Prairies (68 percent), and British Columbia (65 percent), and among those identified as upper and middle class (72 percent and 70 percent respectively). However, in Quebec, only 36 percent expressed a willingness to pay higher taxes, compared to 29 percent who were unwilling and 27 percent who claimed they were unable, while among those identified as "lower class," the numbers were 50, 15, and 29 percent respectively.[68]

By 1942, the finance department felt it necessary to step up propaganda criticizing those who seemed ready to balk. One appeal in newspapers and magazines soon after the Dieppe raid carried in small print the names of some of those killed, while superimposed was an image of civilians shamelessly griping that "taxes are awful."[69] Canadians were told that the British paid heavier taxes without complaint, although the fact that Americans paid less, doubtless realized by some, was conveniently ignored. Ottawa also stressed that compulsory saving, besides being necessary to help fund the war effort and dampen demand to control inflation, was a "good deal" at 2 percent interest, considering that "on treasury notes ... the [federal] government ... secure[d] money ... as low as one-half of one percent."[70]

Income tax evasion was difficult to assess because employers usually deducted taxes at source and there were few write-offs. Still, high taxes, especially on each extra dollar earned, apparently added significantly to absenteeism, even though Ottawa also targeted workers in its propaganda by stressing that progressive taxation meant that the rich were sacrificing more.[71] In September 1942 *Saturday Night* wrote disdainfully of Canada's many "well-paid" labourers regularly "taking off a day or two" because taxes did not make it worth their while to show up.[72] In a national poll the following December inquiring about reasons for absenteeism, 39 percent of "working-class" respondents cited "too many taxes," the most common answer.[73] At a 1944 Ottawa-based conference sponsored by the federal government to examine absenteeism, Earl R. Jarvis, the general manager of Canada Bread, told his audience that many "men [who] work overtime ... take the next day off because they know that a large proportion of the overtime pay is taken away ... in the form of income tax."[74] Meanwhile, in reporting on Ottawa's June 1944 decision to stop deducting compulsory savings, the *Canadian Unionist,* the newspaper of the Canadian Congress of Labour (CCL), underlined working-class tax complaints by claiming that this change was more than a response to the D-Day landings and the growing prospect of victory; it was an antidote to "absenteeism" because "Canadian[s] ... did not ... distinguish ... between refundable and non-refundable taxes."[75]

CERTAINLY, MOST EMPLOYEES did not deliberately skip work or express anger over their situation in wartime. More than ever, people were getting better jobs and arguably moving toward middle-class status after a dismal depression. Between 1938 and 1943 the average annual pre-tax salary rose from $956 to $1,525. Moreover, while the consumer price index (CPI) rose from 101.5 in 1939 to 118.9 in 1944 (with the 1935-39 average equalling 100), wages during the same period rose from 103.1 to 141.1. Even with record taxes, Victory Bond purchases, and war-related donations, Canadian households, which in wartime often had more than one wage earner, had far more available cash. Between 1939 and 1943 total grocery sales rose by 48 percent, and despite shortages of many consumer goods, retail sales went up by 58.1 percent, rates that were two and a half to three times greater than cumulative inflation.[76]

Besides being better off, countless workers were determined not to let down the country – or their loved ones in uniform – during this crisis. Patriotic commentary was common in union newspapers. For example, in the *Canadian Congress Journal*, the official organ of the Trades and Labour Congress (TLC), Fred Milineaux, general organizer for the Painters, Decorators, and Paperhangers Union of America, lyrically asked: "Did you do anything to-day / To help us win the war / And hold together all those things / Brave men are fighting for?"[77] Without complaint over high taxes, wage controls or, as of 1940, a decrease in the number of statutory holidays from eight to six, millions of workers produced to their absolute limit.[78] Whereas in 1939, 46,165 people laboured between fifty-one and fifty-five hours per week, by 1943 that figure had risen to 151,231, and the number of workers clocking up fifty-six to sixty-four hours per week increased from 61,067 to 176,730.[79]

Both the TLC and CCL leadership officially discouraged strikes. CCL president A.R. Mosher declared, "It is more important ... to defeat Hitler and his gangsters than to bring the most tyrannical and reactionary employer in Canada to his knees."[80] Of course, union leaders also realized that support for strikes among the rank and file was more difficult to achieve in wartime, and that such action risked strong public condemnation and government repression. This response had already been demonstrated by the arrest, relatively early in the war, of Communist labour leaders Pat Sullivan of the Canadian Seaman's Union, C.S. Jackson of the United Electrical Workers, and Kent Rowley of the United Textile Workers, all of whom led strikes judged detrimental to the war effort. Still, the TLC executive, though representing what was generally considered the more moderate of Canada's two labour congresses, emphasized that workers had "a right ... to be assured that [their] patriotism would not be exploited."[81]

Recalling the social strains involving labour during the Great War, Prime Minister King at the outset of hostilities said it was crucial that "responsible" workers be kept fully committed to the cause. Having made his mark as an industrial relations expert by the end of the First World War, King was open to compromise, but in this area – as seemingly in all others – he proceeded with great caution, seeking out the middle ground. He maintained that in labour-management struggles a truly successful solution could not be imposed or legislated; the parties had to be convinced and wholeheartedly accept what was just and right. King first displayed this ideal when, as deputy minister of labour, he played a key role in devising the 1907 Industrial Disputes Investigation Act (IDIA), which initially covered public utilities and mines. The act did not compel union recognition, the key demand of organized labour, only a "cooling off" period before a strike while compulsory conciliation took place under a tripartite board representing labour, capital, and government. His belief – promptly exposed as unrealistic – was that the unbiased judgments of investigators, or the force of public opinion, would generate a fair settlement.[82]

Early in the Second World War, King ignored union demands to overhaul the IDIA. Instead, on 7 November 1939 its scope was enlarged under the War Measures Act to cover all industries related to the conflict. This expansion was viewed by much of organized labour as a retrograde step; the IDIA was criticized as a tool to delay strike action. Reacting to labour's grievance that Canada had no legislation compelling employers to recognize unions, King's government initially passed a bill prohibiting employers from firing employees "favouring a union," a rule that was easily circumvented. This was followed in June 1940 by PC 2685, which declared that fair wages and standards "should" apply in the workplace and that employers "should" respect the right of workers to form unions. Unions dismissed this as an empty gesture, since it was ignored by most businesses. For example, in 1941 Dominion Steel and Coal in Montreal disregarded it even though 93 percent of its employees had signed union cards.[83]

Despite the rising incomes of many workers, another major issue that emerged within the labour movement was mandatory wage controls. This matter traced back to 3 September 1939, when Ottawa created the WPTB to control inflation, which had spiralled by an estimated 77 percent during the Great War and was blamed for precipitating considerable economic and social instability. By the end of 1940 inflation hovered annually at near double digits and threatened to worsen as war production intensified and growing numbers of workers chased fewer consumer goods. In December 1940, following hefty wage settlements in several large aircraft and machine shops – where labour peace was deemed essential – and with the likelihood of more such agreements also threatening to raise inflation, the federal government responded with PC 7440. This order appointed boards under the IDIA to try to limit wage increases to the "highest rate established during 1926-29" within the sector or company. However, the system was not compulsory and still allowed for sizeable pay hikes in two ways: salary levels in the late 1920s had been relatively high before their downturn during the Depression, and an additional weekly $1.25 cost of living bonus was permitted.[84]

Inflation did not abate, reaching a total of nearly 18 percent during the first two years of the war. The definitive solution came on 18 October 1941 when the federal government imposed a comprehensive, compulsory price and wage freeze. The order, which became effective on 1 December, pegged wages to rates prevailing on 15 November and fixed prices at the highest level charged during a four-week "base period" between 15 September and 11 October. A twelve-member National War Labour Board (NWLB) was established in Ottawa, with representatives in nine regional centres, to correct wage anomalies and other "gross injustices." Nearly all workers, as outlined in government legislation, would be limited to a raise of 1 percent up to a maximum of twenty-five cents weekly for each one-point rise in the CPI.[85]

Many labour leaders, often seeking to legitimize their newly formed unions, denounced Ottawa for arbitrarily and completely removing wage negotiations from the bargaining table. TLC leader Tom Moore went so far as to classify the freeze as the "longest step yet taken by any democracy toward the establishment of a totalitarian state."[86] It was often asserted that wages had been given little chance to rise from Depression levels, or had in fact fallen behind early wartime inflation. To those who highlighted statistics indicating that workers were earning and purchasing more than ever, several union leaders responded that these seeming gains came from having multiple wage-earners in the same household and many people who worked overtime – often, it was added, to the point of exhaustion, which threatened to bring about higher workplace accident and fatality rates. The government was also accused of drawing up this plan, and others affecting labour, without union input. In this respect, labour leaders further charged that dollar-a-year men not only came from business but were commonly put in charge of regulating sectors in which they had vested interests; they cited, for example, an executive with Hollinger Mines, a staunchly anti-union company, who was made metal controller for the War Industries Control Board.[87]

Also rankling to much of organized labour was the fact that, while Ottawa seemed determined to persist with a hands-off approach toward guaranteeing collective bargaining rights to unions that enjoyed majority support among employees, it seemed increasingly prepared to intervene to deny workers freedom of movement and job choice.[88] The federal government, faced with the rapidly growing demand for military recruits and resulting shortage of workers for the war economy, on 24 March 1942 established National Selective Service (NSS) within the Department of Labour.[89] Its first director, Elliot M. Little, formerly an executive with the Anglo-Canadian Pulp and Paper Mill and director of the Wartime Bureau of Technical Personnel, was charged with estimating the need for men and women in war-related industry, and ensuring, through compulsion if necessary, the availability of adequate numbers.

NSS improved labour supply problems, but by no means eliminated them. It could and sometimes did order striking workers back to certain sectors such as the Vancouver shipyards. It became illegal for healthy males between seventeen and forty-five to work in a number of occupations deemed nonessential: real estate agent, messenger, bartender, sales clerk, and taxi driver, for example. NSS classified civilian work as "very high," "high," "low," or "no priority," with war jobs and those providing resources for heavy manufacturing and industry dominating the "very high" category. Theoretically, one could not transfer from a higher to a lower job category, but in January 1943, PC 246 permitted NSS to transfer male workers – women were exempt – from lower- to higher-priority employment.[90]

Besides precipitating the need for NSS, however, labour shortages also proved a key factor in helping the cause of unionization, since people became less fearful about losing their jobs if they supported a union. The growing number of union members in wartime Canada was unprecedented, rising from 358,967 in 1939 to 724,188 by 1944.[91] This growth also largely explains why NSS rules were not strictly enforced. According to historian Michael Stevenson in his study of wartime industrial mobilization, NSS was compelled to "follow tactics of conciliation and compromise" because the federal government feared further deteriorating relations with an increasingly powerful and apparently more militant union movement, some portions of which accused NSS of trying to establish an "industrial autocracy." NSS officers often issued permits allowing those in high-priority jobs to seek different employment. It was not unusual for 5 to 10 percent of Canada's workforce to change jobs in a single month.[92]

As serious labour supply problems persisted, Little, who was not inclined toward compromise, proposed that large sections of nonessential civilian production be shut down, a suggestion that the federal Cabinet rejected as far too extreme and certain to exacerbate already significant black markets. Frustrated at being unable to structure the labour market to the degree that he thought necessary, Little resigned in November 1942. His replacement was Arthur MacNamara, formerly Manitoba's deputy minister of labour, then acting chair of the Unemployment Insurance Commission and a known advocate of compromise. Although labour shortages continued to worsen in several essential sectors, MacNamara initiated few compulsory transfers. Prior to November 1943 NSS undertook seven investigations, which identified 104,000 men working in nonessential areas who it believed should be shifted to more important jobs; however, action proceeded in only 17 percent of cases. When it came to maintaining people in employment classified as essential and understaffed – such as coal production, logging, and the steel sector – NSS did not begin acting until late 1942 and continued to provide permits to people working in such areas to transfer to other domains of similar priority. Consequently, although arming itself with considerable power to direct labour, the King government, as Stevenson wrote, "muddled through." Although it ultimately managed to get by, "the margin for error was razor-thin ... and any significant Allied setback in ... 1943 or 1944 could have precipitated a ... crisis."[93]

In another overture to labour, starting in 1942 the King government strongly encouraged the creation of labour-management production committees (LMPCs), basing its actions on apparently successful initiatives taken the previous year in some aircraft factories. King hoped that this structure would enable labour and management to simply sit down and iron out differences, solve matters such as absenteeism, and secure maximum output. By war's end, the country had more than 1,000 LMPCs involving nearly 300,000 workers, particularly those in war-related industry. Many workers welcomed these committees for giving them access to corporate boardrooms and because they too, out of patriotism, sought increased war production. But to many, the committees were yet another demonstration of King's cautious gradualism – perhaps a step in the right direction, but by no means an acceptable substitute for unequivocal collective bargaining rights.[94]

Ottawa also continued strong on the propaganda front. A monthly newsletter, *Teamwork for Victory*, which often focused on successful LMPCs, was distributed to major workplaces by the new Industrial Production Cooperation Board, and early in 1943 the Wartime Information Board established an Industrial Morale Committee (IMC).[95] Among its initiatives was a speakers' section that arranged for volunteers to visit war-related job sites to rally workers with patriotic addresses, often supplied by the IMC. Newspaper advertisements and posters drew analogies between the production line and the firing line, comparing, for example, "factory smokestacks with the gun barrels of artillery." In conjunction with the CBC, the IMC produced twenty episodes of the radio show *Production Front,* highlighting important war efforts by workers in different sectors. By linking up with the National Film Board, the IMC helped develop "industrial circuits" to show movies, such as 1943's *Coal Face – Canada,* which aimed at bolstering morale and production in a sector beset with labour emigration and disturbances due to unfavourable pay and working conditions.[96] Both the Industrial Production Cooperation Board and the IMC also stressed the success of the comprehensive freeze, as confirmed by an almost static consumer price index. However, many members of organized labour remained skeptical. Unions pointed out that the index failed to take into account the virtual elimination of store sales; the disappearance of many low-priced items as a result of the streamlining of product lines; the declining quality of many consumer durables, necessitating their more frequent replacement; the increased price of many goods ignored by a CPI that tracked only forty-three items; and the adverse impact on income from wartime black markets, increased taxation, compulsory savings, and Victory Bond purchases.[97] A September 1943 poll revealed that only 62 percent of Canadians believed the CPI accurately reflected prices, and among those identified as "working class," the figure was just 56 percent.[98]

Members of the labour movement were also increasingly angered by Ottawa's ongoing reluctance to pass strong collective bargaining legislation. In Hamilton, Stelco's "self-made" president, H.G. Hilton, ignored a union slate overwhelmingly elected from the Steel Workers Organizing Committee, while in British Columbia, where the International Woodworkers Association claimed 10,000 members, not one local was certified and several union organizers were run out of logging camps.[99]

Despite pledges from many of Canada's union leaders to avoid wartime strikes, labour troubles mounted. In 1939 the country experienced 120 strikes at a cost of 224,588 workdays. By 1941 the numbers reached 231 strikes and 433,914 lost days, and the following year, 354 strikes and 450,202 days. The CCL cast these figures as low, considering Canada's rapidly expanding wartime workforce and the number of new union locals seeking recognition. But in 1943 there were 401 strikes and 1,041,198 days lost, with many stoppages occurring in areas considered essential to the war effort.[100] In January and February, steel workers in Sault Ste. Marie and Sydney, pointing to substantially higher wages among their American counterparts, took to the pavement for a fifty-cent an hour minimum wage, which represented an average 15 percent raise.[101] The federal government threatened hefty fines and jail terms but backed down in the face of the numbers on strike, and the NWLB in fact approved the minimum rate and time-and-a-half for the seventh consecutive day worked. Later that year, among other stoppages, were a ten-day walkout by 9,000 coal miners in Alberta and British Columbia; a two-week strike by 21,000 Montreal workers at Canadair, Fairchild Aircraft, and Noorduyn Aviation; and strikes among freight handlers in Halifax, shipyard workers in Montreal and Kingston, and tramway workers in Montreal.[102]

In 1943 wage disputes accounted for a third of strikes, and union recognition struggles for almost that many. A disgruntled CCL concluded that employers emerged victorious in 37 percent of cases and labour in 27 percent, while 36 percent of disputes did not produce a clear-cut winner.[103] Far less equivocal, however, was public reaction to wartime strikes. In one of its first national surveys, taken in late 1941, the newly created Canadian Institute of Public Opinion found that 78 percent of respondents supported outlawing strikes in any company involved in war production.[104] That year, the press strongly supported the federal government's decision to dispatch the RCMP to St. Catharines to protect strikebreakers at the General Motors plant that produced military vehicles. The same response was evident later that year when Ottawa sent troops to Arvida after workers who belonged to a Catholic union striking for higher pay took over the Aluminum Company of Canada plant, turned off the blast furnaces, and let the molten metal freeze. This strategy generated rumours that the workers were being led by German agents. Implausible as it sounds, even a year after the strike the *Canadian Column* believed it necessary to refute rumours that Arvida was "planned and laid out to read 'Arvida' from the air so that it w[ould] not be bombed by Axis planes."[105]

No matter their reasons, those who went on strike were regularly condemned for being unpatriotic and for placing their personal goals above the survival of democracy. Canadian media often pointed out that servicemen overseas who read accounts of strikes at home suffered lowered morale because they perceived a lack of support for their sacrifices. Addressing this point in 1943 in light of rising strike activity, Minister of Labour Humphrey Mitchell commented, "I sometimes wonder when people go 'on the street' ... whether they ever think of those youngsters in Tunisia and men on the seas and under the seas, and what would happen if they acted the same way."[106]

However, as demonstrated by initiatives like the LMPCs, the King government continued to follow the path of conciliation. In early 1943 it also cut the size of the NWLB in Ottawa from twelve to three members to make it less "clumsy" and had the revamped board undertake a comprehensive investigation of labour relations under its chair, Mr. Justice C.P. McTague, formerly of the Ontario Supreme Court, and the prominent labour lawyer J.L. Cohen. Hearings in April and May generated over 120 submissions by representatives of business, provincial governments, and unions. The unions consistently demanded federal legislation to compel employers to bargain collectively with the clearly chosen representatives of workers, to lift the wage freeze for those on low pay, and to create a national minimum hourly wage, with fifty cents usually the suggested level. For unions, frustration persisted. During the hearings, McTague emphasized the need to hold the line against inflation; indeed, though he did not state so publicly, he thought that family allowances, then under consideration by the federal government, could substitute for any broad movement away from the wage freeze. In August a majority report authored by McTague and a separate one from Cohen, which was far more labour-friendly, were submitted, but they were not made public until early 1944. Both agreed that improvements in collective bargaining rights for labour were justified and played a significant role in framing PC 1003, Ottawa's eventual response.[107]

While Ottawa apparently stalled, the desire for political survival prompted quicker action at the provincial level. When Mitchell Hepburn resigned as Ontario's premier in 1942, he was loathed by organized labour.[108] The Ontario Liberals immediately tried to win back working-class support for the approaching provincial election by passing an act guaranteeing unions collective bargaining rights. By this point, however, both the Conservatives and, of course, the Co-operative Commonwealth Federation supported similar legislation. Labour's vote almost decided the outcome. In the election of August 1943, George Drew's Conservatives, saved by the rural and small-town vote, squeaked in with thirty-seven seats, three more than the CCF, which the CCL officially endorsed and which elected nineteen trade unionists. The same year in British Columbia, where the CCF had two years earlier become the official opposition, the Conciliation and Arbitration Act was amended to require an employer to enter collective bargaining with a union when the provincial minister of labour was satisfied that the union held majority support among workers. The next year the Godbout government in Quebec, in an unsuccessful bid to stave off electoral defeat to Duplessis, passed the Loi des relations ouvrières, which soon facilitated successful unionization drives among thousands of Montreal tobacco, shoe, and electrical workers.[109]

Five days after the Ontario vote, the federal Liberals, who were also being stung by pressing demands for more extensive planning to prevent an expected postwar economic downturn, lost four by-elections, two to the CCF and one each to the Tories and the Labour Progressive Party. In September 1943 a national public opinion poll showed that the CCF had the support of 29 percent of decided voters, compared to 28 percent each for the other two national parties. Prior to 1944 the King government could come up with little of substance to satisfy organized labour. In 1941 it had introduced unemployment insurance, but unions criticized the scheme as too limited in terms of who was covered and the individual level of monetary support. Moreover, with full employment the fund soon built up a huge surplus, leading some to interpret the payroll deduction for unemployment insurance as yet another form of taxation. At the end of 1943, responding to continuing anger over the wage freeze, the federal powers promised that "if the cost of living rises more than 3% and remains at that level for two consecutive months, the government will review the whole program of price control and wage control." However, low inflation, at least as officially measured, prevented the need for action.[110]

Yet in 1943 the groundwork for substantive change was indeed being laid, not only by the NWLB investigation but also by a major government inquiry into social security under Professor Leonard Marsh of McGill University. This initiative derived in part from the growing threat posed by Canada's political left, including the labour movement. It was also inspired by the rhetoric of Roosevelt and Churchill's 1941 Atlantic Charter, promising a postwar world based upon "four freedoms" including "freedom from want." Moreover, Britain's well-publicized 1942 Beveridge Report had recommended vast improvements to the UK's social welfare system. There was growing support among key federal mandarins and the Canadian public for a Keynesian-style planned economy in which, it was thought, an improved level of social welfare would create a spending stream to initially soften and then offset an expected postwar downturn.[111]

Much of Marsh's *Report on Social Security* was geared, both directly and indirectly, toward improving the lot of labour. He stressed that too many workers fell below an appropriate minimum annual salary, which he calculated out to be $1,134.[112] Among other measures, Marsh called for better unemployment insurance, postwar retraining for the unemployed, government health insurance, and family allowances of $5 to $8 per month for each dependant child up to the age of sixteen. Even if perceived by some, including many businesses, as a substitute for across-the-board wage increases, family allowances still constituted a major benefit for numerous workers with dependants, often adding the equivalent of one to two months' salary to their annual income.

King's intention to move boldly toward greater social security was made clear in the January 1944 Speech from the Throne, when he committed his government to paying family allowances the following year. Then on 17 February, in a direct overture to labour, the federal government introduced PC 1003, which finally provided "compulsory recognition of trade unions with majority support." A new national Wartime Labour Relations Board and nine provincial boards were established to administer the measure, and every province except Alberta and Prince Edward Island soon passed enabling legislation to include nearly all sectors under PC 1003. The *Canadian Unionist* "heartily welcomed" Ottawa's initiative. However, like other such sources, it was quick to add that "in some details ... the Order is open to criticism," namely that it could not compel workers to take out membership or pay dues to a union even if it was officially recognized as their bargaining agent.[113] But the impact of PC 1003 was indisputable: between 17 February 1944 and 31 March 1945, the Wartime Labour Relations Board certified 133 new union locals and rejected just twenty-eight applications.[114]

PC 1003 helped secure King's re-election in June 1945, as a large proportion of labour voted Liberal or at least turned away from the CCF. Still, after the war, many Canadians continued to see organized labour as a threat, or at least considered its conduct irresponsible and selfish. In 1945 days lost to strikes again topped a million, and in 1946 they reached an all-time record of 4.5 million. Despite government entreaties to hold the line against postwar inflation and maintain statutory wage and price controls, unions battled hard for significant salary hikes, often to make up for ground seen as lost during the war with the wage freeze. There also remained the issue of compulsory deduction of union dues, or check-offs, especially since many unions feared that returning servicemen, in reaction to wartime strikes, would prove hostile to members and help employers to decertify locals. Starting in September 1945, a bitter ninety-nine-day strike occurred at the Ford plant in Windsor to obtain compulsory check-offs as well as over pay levels. To settle the dispute, the Ontario government dispatched an arbitrator, Mr. Justice Ivan Rand. Although he did not compel union membership, Rand required that everyone covered by a collective agreement pay union dues because all shared in any benefits won.

Several other provincial laws and the 1948 federal Industrial Relations and Disputes Investigation Act further improved labour's collective bargaining rights. A "peace formula" was cobbled together "mitigat[ing] class conflict" by allowing labour to consolidate wartime gains. After years of struggle and want, unions and their members chose legal legitimacy and steady workplace improvements over broader, class-based campaigns to gain shop-floor control or effect major socioeconomic change. They cast their lot with the prevailing – though now more regulated and welfarist – capitalist system, even, in the case of most unions, to the point of becoming fully fledged allies in the Cold War campaign to flush out and ban communists from their ranks.[115]

Although ultimately contained – or even, as some critics would say, co-opted – in the war years, the labour movement was initially feared to be yet another basis for, or symbol of, increasing social disorder and moral failure during a time of crisis. In fact, the dissenters probably attracted greater attention than their numbers warranted. Even at its peak of union membership in wartime, only about 15 percent of Canadian workers were unionized, and just a minority of them went on strike. Many realized they were doing better than they ever had; they laboured enthusiastically to the point of exhaustion to support the war effort and remained steadfast in their opposition to wartime work stoppages. Still, by generating accelerated economic growth, labour shortages, high taxes, and wage controls, the Second World War provided workers with more leverage, and often greater determination, to redress grievances. A more powerful and militant union movement caused considerable apprehension, and its complaints and protests produced much condemnation of – and sometimes armed government intervention against – the seemingly worrisome numbers of Canadians who were seen to value the materialistic over the survival of freedom.

The story in rural Canada was broadly similar. Like labour, during the war many farmers experienced a dramatic upturn in fortunes as compared to the dismal 1930s. With rapidly expanding demand for numerous commodities from burgeoning Canadian cities, the military, and Britain, aggregate sales of farm products soared from $766 million in 1940 to $1.7 billion in 1945.[116] But other statistics point to a different, more chequered, story. A comparison between the June 1941 census and the number of ration books distributed in September 1943 shows that in Quebec, Ontario, and British Columbia, populations in counties that can be classified as mostly rural declined by 5 to 6 percent.[117] In the Prairies, where the relatively new settlement patterns still necessitated a census every five years, the portion of Manitoba's population classified as rural declined between 1941 and 1946 from 56.1 to 53.6 percent, that of Saskatchewan from 67.1 to 62 percent, and that of Alberta from 61.5 to 55.9 percent. Wartime conditions, namely serious shortages of agricultural labour and new implements, and what many farmers cast as the artificially low levels at which commodity prices had been frozen, squeezed out many smaller and less efficient operations. Of course, it could be argued that such a process built a stronger, more competitive agricultural sector. Between 1941 and 1946 average holdings per farmer in Manitoba climbed from 291.1 to 306.2 acres, in Saskatchewan from 432.3 to 473.0 acres, and in Alberta from 433.9 to 462.9 acres, while average indebtedness among farmers in these provinces decreased by 51.5, 55.9, and 50.3 percent respectively.[118] But along the way many farmers suffered much hardship and felt considerable resentment. They loudly assailed the federal government for ignoring their plight and clamoured for more assistance, and as will be discussed in Chapter 4, provided a major source for black markets in several areas where commodity shortages developed.

Much of the growing demand for Canadian food came from Britain, which was cut off from its suppliers in continental Europe early in the war and had to feed its burgeoning industrial workforce and men in uniform, many of whom arrived from across the Commonwealth and the United States. Canadian exports to Britain expanded tremendously in commodities that included canned meat and fish, dehydrated milk and eggs, beef and cheese, and most particularly pork.

In the spring of 1940 Britain lost its pork trade with Denmark, which in 1938 had provided 49 percent of British pork imports. While Canada in 1938 supplied 18.5 percent of Britain's pork imports, by 1944 that figure had reached 83 percent. In meeting, and typically exceeding, targets established in pork contracts between Canada's new Bacon Board and Britain's Ministry of Agriculture, Canadian pork farmers took pride in their patriotism and concern for the UK.[119] Many welcomed the assured market after the unstable years of the Depression, but a number of farmers groused over prices. Even with the first contract in late 1939 their dissatisfaction was sufficiently evident that, to ensure necessary supplies for Britain, the Canadian government imposed strict controls over pork exports to America, where prices were higher.[120] One farmer pointed out in the *Family Herald and Weekly Star* – the closest thing to a national rural publication, since it produced both eastern and western editions in Montreal and Winnipeg – that the current contract with Britain paying just 7.5 cents per pound for hogs was 25 percent lower than the average 1929 price, resulting in a loss of $2.40 on the sale of a 180-pound pig. This was refuted in a subsequent letter to the *Weekly Star* by an official with the Bacon Board who accused the farmer of grossly inflating the costs of raising such a pig.[121] Still, to retain production levels and contain demands that more pork be allowed for export to the United States, the federal government was soon paying pork farmers subsidies exceeding $25 million annually.[122]

Angered and embarrassed over what they saw as the distasteful image of rural Canada projected by disgruntled farmers, others wrote to agricultural publications to denounce their "whining" colleagues for being unpatriotic or, as one contributor put it, "as worthy of contempt as the soldiers who won't fight because they don't like the Sergeant Major."[123] But there was no denying that numerous farmers were bitter, and not only about pork prices. For instance, problems in the wheat sector were often cited as a key factor in rural depopulation, and the federal government was often accused of showing indifference to them.

After a disastrous Depression, wheat farmers had anticipated good wartime incomes, as they recalled that the First World War had brought sharply increased demand from much of Europe. During the opening week of the war, wheat futures shot up rapidly on commodity markets. Also, a record wheat crop in 1939, along with strong exports, accounted for $40 million in sales above the previous year. But in 1940 things took a dramatic turn for the worse: the German blitzkrieg across continental Europe eliminated an export market estimated at nearly 20 million bushels annually. Increased demand from Britain was not nearly enough to compensate. Further aggravating matters was the fact that the 1940 crop was larger than that of 1939. Grain silos and elevators filled to capacity, and prices tumbled from $1.00 to $0.70 per bushel.[124] In response, the Canada Wheat Board announced a plan to reduce the amount of wheat it would market in 1941 by 35 percent. It also rejected calls from the Canadian Federation of Agriculture to set a floor price of $1.00 per bushel, a demand the Federation considered modest since the 1929 price had been $1.20. Instead, Ottawa encouraged farmers to cut back on wheat production, paying them $4 an acre per year for land left fallow, and $2 an acre for land reallocated to other coarse grains. For wheat farmers, the bottom line was not good: while their total net income was $182 million in 1940, the next year it was $168 million, and in 1942 it bottomed out at $137 million.[125]

Among those expressing empathy was James G. Gardiner, the federal minister of agriculture and a native of Saskatchewan, the province hardest hit by low wheat prices. Known as a strong advocate for farmers, Gardiner, the most powerful minister from the Prairies, pushed in Cabinet for higher wheat prices, stating that no group "in Canada has felt the impact of the war as severely." Yet despite his status, a majority in Cabinet agreed with Finance Minister J.L. Ilsley on the absolute need to control inflation in wartime. Ilsley also emphasized that with silos and elevators jammed, it would be irresponsible to do anything to encourage higher wheat production, especially with so many other pressing wartime needs.[126] Many farmers were left frustrated – and sometimes seething – until 1945, when with the liberation of Europe and the desperate need to feed millions of civilians a strong market and rising prices for Canadian wheat re-emerged.[127]

Farmers grumbled over commodity prices in many other regions as well. Generally, prices had been low as Canada entered the war, a legacy of the Depression. Reacting to talk of a freeze, many farmers claimed that commodity prices had not yet had enough of a chance to rise. One Nova Scotia farmer, in a letter to the *Family Herald and Weekly Star,* asked angrily, "Why should we be expected to give the stuff away?" The Canadian Federation of Agriculture determined that before any freeze was implemented, there had to be "an immediate and substantial increase in farm income in relation to national income."[128] Rural Canadians assumed that the booming war industry meant that corporate profits and workers' wages were climbing at a far quicker rate than returns from crops and livestock.[129] When the freeze was implemented, farmers said most commodity prices remained at "depression levels."[130] Prime Minister King admitted that some food prices were abnormally low, but rather than letting them rise, possibly produce inflation, and discredit the freeze in its infancy, his government paid subsidies through the new Commodities Prices Stabilization Board. This response in turn prompted some criticism from urban Canada that farmers were receiving special treatment. This criticism, along with Ottawa's desire to control costs, explained the federal government's reluctance to respond more fully to rural Canadians' complaints that subsidies were not applied widely enough, were far too low, and did not begin to compensate for what farmers could have earned in a fair and open market.[131]

There was also the matter of farm machinery. Many farms required updating, as major purchases had been put off during the Depression, but many farmers felt thwarted in their attempts to meet demands for increased production. As early as 1940, advertisements from agricultural implement firms urged farmers to buy new equipment before military needs slashed supplies. By mid-1940 sales of farm implements had risen 10 percent over the previous year, but supply problems emerged long before needs were filled.[132] In September 1941 American companies, from which Canadians obtained about half their farm implements, were ordered to cut production of new machinery to 80 percent of the 1940 level, though they were allowed to manufacture 50 percent more repair and spare parts. In Canada, in areas where the federal government thought new machinery was indispensable to meet increased demand, more production was authorized; between 1940 and 1942, for example, the output of cream separators doubled. Other items fared poorly. During those same two years, the production of potato planters was cut by 50 percent, disc ploughs by 70 percent, and tractors by 75 percent. Overall, by the end of 1942

Canadian output of new farm machinery was only one-third its 1940 level, though as in the United States this decrease was offset to some extent by an authorized 50 percent increase in the production of repair and spare parts.[133] Prospective purchasers of new equipment or, more often, spare parts, had to demonstrate their need to a local WPTB official. Nearly all applications were approved, though the great majority of repairs served to keep older, often less-efficient, equipment operational, which often complicated the job of compensating for labour shortages.[134]

In 1939 farm labour had been easily obtained and cheap, typically costing about $15.00 a month plus room and board. But in wartime, even a private could earn $1.30 a day, and soon hundreds of thousands of decently paying industrial and manufacturing jobs became available in cities. By 1944 some 500,000 Canadians from farms and small towns had donned a military uniform, and 300,000 had migrated to cities for work.[135] Farmers asked to no avail that military recruiters ease off in agricultural districts, or that Ottawa allow commodity prices to rise so they could afford the wages necessary to retain experienced labourers, who by 1942 were commanding about $3.50 a day plus room and board.[136] Many farmers talked of eighteen-hour days becoming the norm, of wives being forced to make housework a "secondary matter," and of pulling children out of school.[137] Following the 1942 harvest, the United Farmers of Alberta wrote angrily to Agriculture Minister Gardiner of operations that had lost up to 40 percent of their crop because of labour shortages, a situation that it insisted the government had been "warned about from the early stages of the war."[138]

Numerous sources of labour were mined in what often became a desperate attempt to deal with deficiencies. In western Canada, Native reserves were solicited and ultimately provided 1,400 agricultural workers. Conscientious objectors were enlisted – principally Doukhobors in Alberta and British Columbia and Mennonites in Ontario – as the federal government, under an April 1943 Order-in-Council, could demand of them "alternative service" that included farm work. Some 2,000 German POWs whom authorities classified as not being ardent Nazis, or as anti-Nazi, were employed on farms, primarily in eastern Ontario, western Quebec, and southern Alberta. Farmers were compelled to pay conscientious objectors and POWs a standard rate for agricultural labour, though most of that money was remitted to the federal Department of Labour. Moreover, about 1,000 Japanese evacuees, desperate for work, laboured on Manitoba and Alberta sugar-beet fields, undertaking a job so unpleasant and arduous that many German POWs refused it.[139]

Although farmers often remained dissatisfied and disgruntled, the government initiated extensive agricultural labour programs. Starting in the summer of 1940, military trainees from rural areas who proved their need on farms could receive up to eight weeks' leave without pay. Another measure in March 1942 allowed men to postpone volunteer or NRMA (National Resources Mobilization Act) service for up to six months in order to perform essential farm work. Still, as one farmer argued, "Most spirited young fellows abhor the idea of appealing for exemption. The government should make it mandatory."[140] Moreover, leaves and deferments usually provided labour for only one season. The 1942 Farm Duty Plan allowed military trainees and servicemen stationed in Canada, most of whom were NRMA personnel, to work as agricultural labourers. But they did not come cheap: $3 per day in the Maritimes and $4 in the rest of the country. At the plan's peak, some 20,000 men participated, often volunteering because they received the difference between their military pay and the standard farm labour rate.[141] The program helped, especially at seed and harvest time, but many farmers said the assistance was too short-term – often lasting for only a few days – and could not be relied on, as military duties always took precedence. From NSS, almost immediately after its creation, came the Stabilization of Employment in Agriculture Regulations, but the measure was criticized for permitting the free movement of farm labour among different types of agricultural work. And farmers complained that NSS officials virtually never turned down a request from a farm worker to switch to an entirely different sector.[142]

In its most substantial initiative to provide agricultural workers, starting in mid-1941 Ottawa signed a number of shared-cost agreements with the provinces to recruit, transport, and place farm labour. Generally, participants came from areas in the Maritimes, northeastern Ontario, and eastern Quebec where the war had had less economic impact, and from groups that had time available during the summer, such as teachers (many of whom welcomed the opportunity to supplement generally poor pay), university students, and over 100,000 high school students.[143] Despite their need for labour, numerous farmers hesitated to accept such help because they thought the participants were capable of performing only the simplest tasks and were not up to the rigours of agricultural life. Necessity convinced many to temper their opposition, as did, when it came to student workers, the bargain-basement wage of $15-$25 monthly plus room and board. Even when the newcomers worked out well, farmers often remained resentful toward Ottawa for what they saw as an ad hoc approach to the critical issue of farm labour. Even the passage of PC 2551 in March 1943, which fixed full-time male agricultural labourers in their existing positions, failed to abate the anger in much of agricultural Canada. Besides being criticized for coming too late, the order allowed farm labour to enlist as well to shift to jobs of equal priority if permission was secured from a NSS officer – permission which, many farmers complained, was granted all too often.[144]

Most farmers ultimately accepted the need for substantial wartime sacrifices and, despite their grievances, worked harder than ever to meet demands for increased production. But in the June 1945 federal election, the Liberals declined to 127 seats from 178 in 1940, and a high proportion of that decrease derived from rural Canada. Many farmers no doubt voted against the King government because their sense of patriotism convinced them that the prime minister had delayed for too long before accepting conscription for overseas service. Also, some slippage from the massive Liberal landslide in 1940 was inevitable, especially with a re-named and somewhat invigorated Progressive Conservative party under John Bracken in contrast to Robert Manion's disastrous leadership, and with the CCF becoming a more formidable force. Yet anger over Liberal policies, namely the price freeze and the perceived mismanagement of agricultural labour, also con-tributed to the party's decline. In the Prairies, government pricing policies, espe-cially for wheat and beef (as will be addressed in Chapter 4), had brought much suffering. The Liberals dropped from fourteen to ten seats in Manitoba between the 1940 and 1945 elections, from twelve to three in Saskatchewan, and from seven to two in Alberta.[145]

Similar disaffection also becomes evident from an analysis of more than fifty ridings in English Canada in which the rural vote played a major role.[146] On the basis of population, six such ridings were selected from Nova Scotia, five from New Brunswick, two from Prince Edward Island, eighteen from Ontario, five from Manitoba, five from Saskatchewan, five from Alberta, and six from British Colum-bia. In 1940 the Liberals won thirty-six of these ridings, but in 1945 only twenty, in relative terms a worse performance than in urban areas. Also revealing is the aver-age popular vote received by the Liberals in those ridings: in Nova Scotia, it de-clined from 58.8 to 48.9 percent; in New Brunswick from 57.1 to 52.5 percent; in Prince Edward Island from 57.6 to 49.2 percent; in Ontario from 52.9 to 44.6 percent; in Manitoba from 48.8 to 35.8 percent; in Saskatchewan from 48.5 to 37.1 percent; in Alberta from 33.9 to 20.3 percent; and in British Columbia from 37.5 to 28.5 per-cent.[147] Clearly, in rural Canada, the war, and specifically the sacrifices it demanded, yielded not only record output but also a considerable harvest of bitterness.

ACCOMPANYING PATRIOTISM and self-sacrifice, stupendous economic growth, and an accelerated drive toward modernization in several industries and locales, and despite the achievement of greater social security and enhanced workplace rights for ordinary folks, the war saw evidence of considerable social strain and what numerous Canadians saw, with alarm, as extensive grasping and unpatriotic con-duct. Citizens from all walks of life complained about being overtaxed, while among organized labour and farmers in particular a sizeable number fumed over – and sometimes actively protested against – what they saw as neglect and other forms of mistreatment from Ottawa. Whether these reactions were justified or not, they did spark concern about the moral qualities of Canadians as a whole. Were too many members of the population too sheltered, too complacent, too self-serving, and morally unresponsive during a time of crisis? The potential of an affirmative response to such questions was significantly bolstered by evidence that during the war many Canadians rapaciously pursued their personal appetites and ambitions, often by ruthlessly exploiting their fellow citizens in what became large and lucra-tive black markets.

3
The Wartime Prices and Trade Board and the Accommodation Crisis

"I SAY, SIR, that to-day I know of no more important ... policy for this government to adopt than to insist that there is no profiteering during this war." So declared the leader of the opposition, Robert Manion, the day Germany invaded Poland. Addressing the topic a week later during the emergency debate to approve Canada's entry into the war, Prime Minister King assured Parliament, "I do not care who the individual may be ... if he seeks to profiteer in this crisis he belongs to the underworld and should be treated as one of those who menace all that is sacred in human relations." Yet almost in the next breath, King admitted, "Sometimes it is very difficult to cope effectively with this underworld and its methods."[1]

Although the government avoided major scandals with war contracts, King no doubt realized there were many illegal channels through which businesses and individuals could pursue nefarious aims. Canadians obeyed the rules, at least for the most part. Given the small sacrifices asked of them compared to those overseas, many portrayed any lawbreaking as unforgivable. Black markets in Europe and Britain were viewed as more understandable in light of the severity of the deprivations faced, and when it came to the "stalwart British," the inspirational message carried in the media often bore little resemblance to the widespread extent of such cheating.[2] Moreover, it often seemed that in the absence of an imminent threat to Canada's survival, many Canadians became preoccupied with – and hence prone to exaggerate – the perceived moral and social failings of fellow citizens in regard to the war. Still, there is no doubt that people carried out transactions on black markets for virtually every item that became scarce and swindled their fellow Canadians, including those in uniform. This was most evident in major cities, with Montreal apparently leading the way – no surprise, given its status as Canada's largest urban and commercial centre and the strong antiwar sentiment in Quebec. Beyond periodic comments to this effect in such documents as the papers of the Wartime Prices and Trade Board (WPTB), however, available evidence makes this portrayal of the city impossible to prove statistically. Nationwide, however, black markets became extensive enough that F.A. McGregor, chief of the WPTB's Enforcement Branch, suggested that the federal government drastically reduce its printing of $50 and $100 bills because they were the favourite currency of major black marketeers.[3]

CREATED A WEEK BEFORE CANADA declared war, the WPTB was given the power to set prices and wages, license firms selling consumer goods, prosecute hoarders, and manage the distribution of scarce items.[4] Its first chairman, H.B. McKinnon, formerly Canada's commissioner of tariffs, answered to the minister of labour. Initially, with McKinnon and two other senior civil servants from the departments of finance and national revenue managing affairs, the WPTB was relatively nonintrusive. But the need for the WPTB to exert greater control over cheaters became evident in the first week of the war as people, fearing a repeat of the shortages and high prices of the Great War, were already hoarding potatoes, flour, butter, tinned goods, coffee, tea, and especially sugar.[5] The WPTB responded with communiqués stressing that supplies were healthy; for instance, unlike the case in 1914, Britain did not rely on Germany, Austria, and Hungary for a high proportion of its sugar, but now imported it from the West Indies and the Far East. The WPTB sternly reminded people that hoarding was a crime, and storeowners were encouraged to limit purchases of several commodities. Prices remained stable, and panic buying quickly subsided. However, on 10 September, several hundred pounds of sugar valued at $75 were stolen from Montreal's Arctic Cream Company, as were "many large bags" of flour from bakeries across the city.[6] In hindsight, these were disturbing signs of things to come.

Commodity supplies, and hence prices, remained at satisfactory levels throughout the phony war, so black markets and similar criminal activity did not present a problem. But by mid-1940, with the sharply rising demand from war industry and the military, the WPTB found it necessary to set maximum prices for several goods, including coal, wool, butter, and sugar. In addition, migration to cities for war jobs necessitated the creation of the Rental Division. In April and May 1940 alone, rents across Canada as measured by the consumer price index rose 2.5 basis points; in centres of war production, the trend was of course worse.[7] A yet more hands-on approach to controlling inflation was signalled in August 1941 when direction of the WPTB passed from the Ministry of Labour to Finance. Three months later, the low-key McKinnon was replaced by Donald Gordon, deputy governor of the Bank of Canada, who was known in government circles to be more outspoken and forceful. A comprehensive freeze on wages and prices followed almost immediately.

In managing the freeze and a growing array of other regulations that soon included coupon rationing, the WPTB developed into one of the most prominent government war agencies. At its peak, its head office in Ottawa employed more than 600 to run some 30 administrative divisions; more than 100 WPTB offices were established across Canada, and the agency had some 6,000 people on its payroll.[8] Volunteers were also crucial to its operations, the most conspicuous being the approximately 16,000 women who became associated with the Consumers' Branch, created on 18 December 1941. Under the direction of *Chatelaine* editor Byrne Hope Saunders – who, for her efforts, was later named a commander of the Order of the British Empire[9] – Consumers' Branch members reported price increases in violation of the freeze or profiteering through sales of lower-quality goods at unreduced prices.[10] These women also provided feedback to the WPTB on reactions to and the success of its initiatives. To increase feedback the WPTB also established an Information Branch, which surveyed thirty-eight daily and twenty-one weekly newspapers. On its own and in conjunction with the Wartime Information Board, it commissioned polls from the Canadian Institute of Public Opinion and released massive propaganda, some $750,000 worth in 1943, for instance. Its media appeals depicted grave consequences for the country should WPTB rules be ignored; in one illustration a runaway train symbolizing inflation rushes headlong toward a cliff, while a spur track labelled "price controls" leads the locomotive back to safety.[11]

At Gordon's first press conference, he enlisted media support by extolling the "tremendous part the press can play in this campaign – namely the education of Mr. John Public to a realization that he and his family are soldiers in this battle." Media backing for controls was generally strong. In a typical article, the Brantford *Expositor* condemned black marketeers as "selfish, foolish and unpatriotic." Public opinion polls also indicated solid support: in December 1941, 75 percent endorsed the price freeze.[12]

As the war dragged on, however, support waned. Between April and September 1943, public approval for wage and price controls declined from 80 to 69 percent, and in mid-1943, with rationing in full swing, only 45 percent endorsed further WPTB restrictions.[13] Canadians began to think they were making enough sacrifices – record taxation, compulsory savings, long work hours, an income freeze, and the siphoning of their salary to Victory Bonds and war charities – and they grew more disposed toward skirting the rules in compensation. Many thought their behaviour would make no difference to the outcome of the war as news reports highlighted mass bombing campaigns against German cities, the surrender of the Nazis at Stalingrad, the defeat of Rommel in North Africa, and the successful invasion of Sicily. In October 1943 a sampling of 309 Torontonians revealed that 84 percent expected Japan, and 57 percent Germany, to surrender within a year.[14]

Some citizens who had supported controls came to view the WPTB as too overbearing. Detractors in Quebec complained that its regulations interfered excessively in provincial affairs. The influential former (but soon to be re-elected) premier, Maurice Duplessis, portrayed the WPTB as part of a general wartime thrust by the federal government to replace democracy with bureaucratic dictatorship.[15] Meanwhile, despite having offices across Canada, the WPTB was perceived in many parts of the country as an Ottawa-run show whose bureaucrats were ignorant of, or disregarded, local conditions, and who often acted officiously by prosecuting honest mistakes and thus branding patriotic Canadians as criminals. "Almost Gestapo-like ... in trying to catch ordinary people" was the way one Nova Scotian described local WPTB personnel.[16] And then there was Gordon himself, nicknamed the "price czar" by the press. Many admired his candour and thought him charismatic and unbounded in his dedication to his job – some even touted him as a successor to King. But others found him brash, unfeeling, and power-hungry, intent on building the WPTB into a personal fiefdom.[17]

Some WPTB officials were indeed relentless and Gordon was at times brusque, but under his chairmanship the WPTB actually promoted a strategic and often cautious approach to enforcement. Too unbending a process, Gordon thought, would "completely jam the nations' courts" and create "public resentment."[18] He also realized that, given the many other mounting demands of the war, a massive enforcement apparatus would not be an effective government strategy. Directives from his office recommended pursuing only major offences and cases for which convictions would be clear-cut. Because its legal staff was small, the WPTB avoided long and difficult court proceedings, on the theory that too many failed prosecutions would incur public animosity for supposedly hassling the innocent.[19] Also to avoid negative publicity, Gordon suggested that "persons over 75 years of age" and those who were "bedridden or suffering from a chronic illness" not be prosecuted.[20]

Some media sources, on the other hand, realizing that the WPTB's characterization as an overbearing organization was much exaggerated, demanded a more vigorous approach. "Call it a Gestapo if you will," wrote *Canadian Business*, "but the honest citizen and businessman should be protected." The *Lethbridge Herald* predicted that if large numbers of infractions continued to go unpunished, "respect for the law would disappear."[21] Penalties imposed for breaking WPTB regulations were criticized for being too small: some 75 percent of convicted violators incurred fines of less than $100. As one member of the agency's Enforcement Branch indignantly exclaimed, "We have had cases where a manufacturer may have been fined $50 respecting sales which gave him excess profits of hundreds or even thousands of dollars." Some sources demanded that individuals convicted more than once of breaking WPTB rules be jailed, and that recalcitrant businesses lose their licence to operate, but Gordon rejected this approach as too "rigid."[22]

As restrictions proliferated and people became war-weary, convictions increased for breaking WPTB rules: 31 between September 1939 and December 1941; 1,201 in 1942; 3,663 in 1943; 4,170 in 1944; 5,425 in 1945; and over the next two years, even as operations wound down, 9,027. In 253 cases jail terms resulted, though nearly all were for less than one year. Fines totalled $1,780,000, the steepest being $25,000 against a large Montreal clothing manufacturer that continued to produce large quantities of prohibited apparel, ignoring laws designed to save cloth.[23] However, the number of infractions could well have been much higher. Responding to a survey in May 1943 asking if they knew of someone who purchased or sold goods on black markets, an average of 25 percent of Canadians said yes (the fewest in the Prairies at 16 percent, and the most in Quebec at 32 percent).[24] Internal estimates by the WPTB concluded that a more rigid enforcement of the rules could have led to as many as 400,000 charges per year.[25] Although Canadians told pollsters that they supported WPTB measures – up to 90 percent in the case of rationing – Gordon became apprehensive. In departmental correspondence in late 1942, he wrote about "citizens ... beginning to tolerate illegal purchases." Indeed, he refused to give interviews about black markets for fear that they would send the message that few people were obeying the rules.[26]

ONE OF THE FIRST AREAS OF CONCERN continued to consume much of the WPTB's attention into the postwar period, namely rental rates. In many places the amount of available accommodation shrank alarmingly as people flocked to cities for war-related jobs. The war in fact highlighted a problem that reached back a generation, as housing shortages had existed in Canada before the end of the Great War. However, the federal government was strongly committed to the free market, especially in this key sector, and had intervened little even to help house veterans. Provincial schemes were minimal, the most notable being the 1919 Ontario Housing Act, which provided some subsidized loans to municipalities and facilitated the construction of a mere few hundred small units.

Unlike in Europe or Britain, where strong unions or socialist movements had successfully pressured governments for sizeable amounts of public housing, in Canada governments expected private enterprise to remedy any shortages.[27] During the buoyant last years of the 1920s, as many as 75,000 units per year were built. But this surge in the housing market dropped dramatically during the Depression. Between 1928 and 1933 contracts for residential construction in Canada fell from an annual total of $139 million to $24 million. From 1932 to 1939 home construction in Montreal amounted to less than that of 1928 alone, and in Toronto, fewer homes were built between 1930 and 1939 than during the last three years of the 1920s. Also, as local surveys taken between 1932 and 1935 revealed, much of the existing housing stock in Hamilton, Toronto, Winnipeg, Montreal, and Ottawa was in poor condition.[28]

The federal government's response was formulated primarily by the highly influential deputy minister of finance, W. Clifford Clark, who clearly favoured private enterprise over publicly assisted housing, reflecting his background as vice-president of the American-owned real estate investment firm S.W. Straus and Company. His strong belief, shared by many in government, was that ownership of private property was a social good because its acquisition forced people to work hard and save, whereas subsidized public accommodation encouraged lethargy.[29] Clark contended that the solution to the housing problem was to create conditions that would spur growth in the private sector. This approach was articulated in the 1935 National Housing Act (NHA). In helping to draft the legislation, Clark dismissed the conclusions of a previous House of Commons committee, chaired by Conservative Arthur Ganong, that private developers were uninterested in building low-cost housing.

Clark maintained that if Ottawa became heavily engaged in subsidizing accommodation, it would initiate an inexorable trend toward across-the-board public housing, possibly delivering a mortal blow to a key component of the private sector, as he perceived Franklin Roosevelt's New Deal to have done. Consequently, the 1935 NHA made provision for the federal government to work with the Dominion Mortgage Insurance Association to reduce home down-payment requirements from 40 percent to as low as 20 percent by providing funds to lending institutions at discounted rates. Mortgages could also be amortized over periods of up to twenty years, whereas before the act they had often been short-term loans for up to five years with no vested right of renewal. Still, with unemployment hovering near 30 percent in the 1930s, depressed wages, and little job security, a 20 percent down payment and regular mortgage instalments often proved out of the question for those who were not already homeowners, especially since lending companies retained the right to charge higher interest rates to people whom they considered greater risks. While the legislation defused calls for public housing in the short term, it had little effect in encouraging construction; in its nearly four-year lifespan, it was credited with facilitating the purchase of only 7,500 homes when hundreds of thousands were needed across the land.[30]

In 1938 a second NHA was passed, partly in response to another sharp economic downturn in 1937 that followed two years of modest recovery. Once again, through subsidies to lending institutions, the federal government lowered down-payment requirements, this time to as little as 10 percent on homes costing less than $3,000, though between 1938 and 1941, only 20 percent of new homes fell into this category. The new legislation made funds for public housing available to municipalities until 1 March 1940, but since they were provided on a shared-cost basis, most cities could not take up the offer, as the Depression had depleted local budgets often to the point of near-bankruptcy. Many also criticized the act because it set the maximum federal funding per unit of public housing so low as to make construction virtually impossible.[31]

IN SEPTEMBER 1939 Canadians started migrating to accommodation-starved cities for war jobs. At a 1940 meeting of Canadian mayors in Ottawa, the situation in many communities was already being described as an "emergency," and the mayors pleaded with the federal government to provide at least $30 million for the immediate construction of low-cost housing. Private developers could not respond. With worsening shortages of building supplies and construction workers for civilian needs, house construction in 1941 stood at just 24,900 units, and then dipped to 18,000 in 1942 and 15,000 in 1943.[32]

The limited amount of decent and affordable accommodation was quickly scooped up. In 1941, with Canadians earning on average about $1,200 per year, the 25 percent of pay accepted by most welfare agencies as an appropriate threshold for rent translated into a monthly figure of roughly $25. The proportion of rental units within that price range was then approximately 60 percent in Halifax, 75 percent in Montreal, 50 percent in Ottawa, 55 percent in Toronto, 65 percent in Winnipeg, and 70 percent in Vancouver.[33] And many of those rentals were single rooms in homes. Although wartime brought better jobs and more than one wage earner into a greater number of families, deductions for taxes, compulsory savings, Victory Bonds, and war charities meant it was often difficult for people to spend more. Families were especially hard hit: many tried to come up with the money for more space, assuming they could find it, but all too often they squeezed into shelter that was far too small or dilapidated.

Soon after the war started, new housing registries appeared in most major cities, run primarily by the YMCA and the YWCA, groups long involved in providing emergency shelter. By the end of 1942, the YWCA reported that it had placed over 61,000 people.[34] Countless homeowners generously opened their doors to newcomers, often out of patriotism, since many of the new tenants were war workers. But others, including those with extra space created by military enlistment within the family, put a high premium on their privacy. Moreover, in several exclusive areas, such as Ottawa's Rockcliffe Park and Vancouver's Shaughnessy Heights, local ordinances prohibiting tenants remained in effect.[35] Some homeowners resented tenants for not paying local taxes and blamed them for the overuse of municipal services, the physical deterioration of neighbourhoods and, they claimed, decreasing property values.

ACROSS THE COUNTRY, communities were bursting at the seams. In Halifax, by January 1940, before the major influx of sailors, merchant marines, and shipyard workers, the WPTB considered accommodation shortages serious enough to justify rent controls, its first such initiative. Since many Halifax homes had not been rebuilt after the 1917 explosion, the city entered the war with an accommodation shortfall already estimated at 4,100 people. By 1941, while the average family in Halifax contained 3.69 people, the average household contained 4.67.[36] The situation deteriorated as Halifax assumed its full role as the western hub of North Atlantic convoy traffic. By September 1943, according to one estimate, some 18 million servicemen had visited the city, many of whom had to be temporarily billeted in the community because of inadequate military accommodation. Moreover, the expansion of dockyard activity was key in attracting just over 19,000 more civilians to the city between 1 September 1939 and mid-1944. Overall, Halifax's population approximately doubled during the war to some 130,000. Constant queuing, sharing restaurant tables with strangers, and other such inconveniences became a way of life. And foolish was the person who did not plan ahead for a place to stay: one landlord advertising a flat for rent was quickly swamped with over 200 requests.[37]

Things seemed no better at the other end of the country as people in search of war jobs poured into Vancouver and Victoria from the BC interior and the Prairies. Between 1940 and 1942 Vancouver's vacancy rate dropped from 1 percent to just 0.257 percent.[38] In some prairie cities, housing shortages were not severe; Regina and Saskatoon, for example, coped relatively well with the extra 2,000 people each received during the war. But in other places the story was very different. In the first three years of the war, Calgary's population increased by nearly 20 percent to top 100,000, thus producing an official vacancy rate of just 0.09 percent at one point.[39] Edmonton's permanent population climbed from 91,000 in 1940 to approximately 119,000 in 1943. With the arrival of the Americans in 1942, the city's housing registry received as many as 100 applications per day, most of which just piled up on desks. Even in mid-1943 after the Americans had left, things continued to be difficult, for with thousands of new employees at such establishments as Aircraft Repair Limited, the Great Western Garment Company, and the Canada Packers plant, the local housing registry still had a waiting list of 1,350 people who had nowhere to live, or who needed more affordable or less run-down accommodation.[40]

Montreal, then Canada's largest city and home to the country's most substantial war industry, "welcomed" more than 250,000 people over the course of the war, a growth in population that, fortunately, military enlistment effectively halved. More than any other place in Canada, Montreal was a city of tenants, a fact largely attributable to the relatively poor pay received by French Canadian workers. During the mid-1930s, when 46 percent of Torontonians rented their accommodation, the figure in Montreal was a remarkable 85 percent.[41] Consequently, though Montreal had far more rental units per capita than the norm, it also had, especially in wartime, far more people searching for space. In 1942 the city's Planning Department estimated Montreal's vacancy rate at 0.81 percent, a situation most critical in lower-cost accommodations. The next year a survey by the Canadian Welfare Council revealed that in Montreal 919 families lived in stores, thirteen in shops, seven in garages, seven in sheds, six in huts, and four in factories.[42]

Toronto received some 100,000 migrants during the war. Its housing crunch was not as serious as Montreal's: it had fewer newcomers and higher enlistment rates, and a lot of Toronto's major war-production firms were located in outlying areas such as Downsview (de Havilland), Malton (Victory Aircraft), Scarborough (the General Engineering Company), and Ajax (Research Enterprises). Still, between 1940 and 1941 Toronto's vacancy rate dropped from 3.2 to 1.79 percent, and the following year it reached a fifty-year low of just over 1 percent. One result was that in early 1942 an impromptu trailer park was formed behind the Toronto General Hospital by out-of-towners frustrated in their search for affordable and decent accommodation. Local authorities soon dispersed the community because its size had become a traffic hazard.[43]

In Ottawa, some 24,000 extra civil servants were added to a prewar number of 12,000. New war departments and agencies accounted for most of these newcomers, who were typically single women recruited for entry-level administrative jobs. Besides seeking lodging in a city that had entered the war with an accommodation shortfall of around 1,200 people, these women also had to deal with the fact that Ottawa was one of Canada's more expensive communities, with monthly rents averaging about $25. Many women were forced to double or triple up in small flats, and sometimes even to share beds.[44] Most rejected the option of living in

Hull, according to Miss M.C. Williams of Ottawa's room registry, because of Hull's many drinking establishments and nightclubs, a legacy of the fact that Quebec had ended prohibition eight years before Ontario. However, necessity often overcame prejudices, and accommodation shortages soon became severe in Hull also, even though according to the 1941 census 54 percent of its homes had no bath or shower, 11 percent no flush toilet, and 16 percent no refrigeration facilities.[45]

Many smaller communities also confronted accommodation crises. These included industrial towns such as Kitchener and Peterborough, which obtained substantial war contracts; mining and logging communities such as Arvida and Prince Rupert; remote locales connected to projects like the Northwest Staging Route and the Alaska Highway; and places near army or air force bases, such as Aldershot, Nova Scotia, and Vulcan, Alberta. Near British Commonwealth Air Training Plan bases on the Prairies, to which family members, fiancées, or girlfriends of trainees sometimes relocated to remain close to their loved ones for as long as possible, people were known to pay to live in barns or large storage bins.[46] Shantytowns also grew up around many military bases, with small shacks cobbled together from whatever material could be scrounged. Even this type of accommodation was often scarce because of shortages of scrap. Therefore, contrasting with commentary about the communal atmosphere in these mostly female settings, there were many occurrences like those outside the bombing and gunnery school in Dafoe, Saskatchewan, where the owners of such hovels charged newcomers up to $25 a month to share their premises. Some permanent residents assisted the newcomers by furnishing needed supplies, but many others seized the opportunity to price gouge. Also, many denounced the migrants for blighting the countryside: aside from the shacks, open sewers often ran through these communities, thus risking the spread of disease. These places were further condemned for leading to moral decline, as many of the women were assumed to be prostitutes or "good-time girls" trying to pick up business from sex-starved servicemen.[47]

WHAT WAS OTTAWA DOING to alleviate the accommodation crisis? Not nearly enough, many concluded. Clifford Clark, still the federal government's point man on housing policy, had established its approach to the question early in the war. In response to the Canadian mayors' 1940 request for $30 million for emergency low-cost housing, Clark had said that "war demands" necessitated that people accept "an increasing amount of 'doubling up' and overcrowding."[48] However, several key figures in King's government, including Munitions Minister Howe, realized inaction was not feasible, given the mounting crisis, the need to house war workers, and the fact that large-scale public housing projects existed in Britain, the United States, and even Nazi Germany. Some people complained Germany was doing a better job of decently sheltering its citizens than Canada.[49]

The answer was Wartime Housing Incorporated, a Crown corporation created on 24 February 1941 to build prefabricated temporary structures, principally for those who relocated to work in essential war industry. By the time the corporation ceased operations in 1947, it had produced just over 27,000 housing units and spent $253.7 million. Although its intervention was an unprecedented foray into the housing market on the part of the federal government, this financial contribution was minimal in light of the need. By comparison, Ottawa had by late 1944 spent $1.7 billion on military construction projects in Canada. From several quarters, Wartime Housing was denounced as a grossly inadequate response.[50]

Its headquarters was in Toronto and it was run by Joseph M. Pigott, president of Pigott Construction of Hamilton. Under him were six directors: Charles David, vice-president of the Quebec Architects' Association; William Somerville, a prominent Toronto architect; Ernest Ingles, vice-president of the International Brotherhood of Electrical Workers; William Tibbs, secretary of the Halifax Relief Commission; Robert Gourley, general manager of the Beaver Lumber Company; and Hedley Wilson, manager of the Maritime Trust Company.[51] Despite disparate backgrounds, they all – including Pigott, who was an exception within his industry – strongly advocated that Wartime Housing play a major role in supplying accommodation. But this group answered to Finance Minister Ilsley who, like his deputy minister Clark, sought to prevent Wartime Housing from establishing for the government a major and, he feared, permanent role in house construction.

On the surface, obtaining funding from Wartime Housing seemed straightforward. A municipal government applied to the Crown corporation outlining its needs. For $1 each, the city would sell to Wartime Housing building lots free from encumbrances and situated on public streets. Wartime Housing would then build the homes and install hot water tanks, bathtubs, sinks, toilets, light fixtures, blinds, and hookups to municipal services. To speed up construction and save on labour and material, a few standard and simple styles and prefabricated parts were employed. The homes were small, 800 to 1,100 square feet, and typically built on four-foot foundations without basements.[52] Although housing shortages meant that applicants for these places always well exceeded supply, the homes were no bargain, largely because the federal government did not want to make public housing too attractive. Four-room homes rented for $300-$330 a year, and six-room homes for as much as $384, in other words, from $25 to $32 per month. This initially matched or exceeded the 25 percent rent threshold for most single wage earners, especially since these tenants were also responsible for paying for water and heat. Municipalities had the option of purchasing the homes for $1,000 each after fourteen years; if they did not, then the tenants could buy them.[53] However, many of them were disassembled long before that point, as they had purposely been constructed as temporary dwellings in order to minimize public housing.

With Clark and Ilsley keeping close tabs, Wartime Housing fell far short of the need. By the time hostilities ceased, it had completed only 18,300 structures, about half of what had been widely considered appropriate for its first year of operations alone.[54] Despite some municipal officials' complaints about giving up building lots for $1 and opposition from some homeowners who thought the temporary structures ruined their neighbourhoods, virtually all major communities asked for much more wartime housing than the Crown corporation offered. Edmonton mayor John Fry thought he was being conservative in requesting 500 units in 1942, but he obtained only 200. Halifax, the most generously supplied city, had received some 1,000 units for shipyard workers by 1942, only about half the minimum demanded by the local government. Local officials in Vancouver clamoured for several thousand homes, but by 1943 had obtained only 600 or so.[55] In Ottawa, soon after Wartime Housing was established, Mayor Stanley Lewis expressed the hope that the Crown corporation would alleviate a crisis that, he emphasized, was attributable to the expansion of the federal government itself. But he met only with frustration, because Wartime Housing refused to classify civil servants as "war workers."[56] After more than a year of wrangling, a deal was finally struck in October 1942 for the construction of 300 homes. Disputes over their location persisted for yet another year, and when these were finally settled, the number had dropped to 200.[57]

Despite the federal government's reluctance to build accommodation, it aggressively pressured homeowners to make space available for tenants. By late 1942 the WPTB had begun supplementing the resources of room registries in more than thirty communities with both advertising money and administrative support. As the year drew to a close, rumours were circulating that the WPTB might even impose compulsory billeting; in a much publicized comment, Finance Minister Ilsley, when asked about billeting, had cryptically replied, "Ownership of property is a responsibility as well as a privilege."[58] In several communities – including Windsor, Kingston, St. Catharines, and Ottawa – the WPTB arranged compulsory surveys by having homeowners send back information cards. Although many homeowners certainly lied about the space they had available, depending upon the size of the community, between 100 and 500 rooms were usually located. But owners were not compelled to rent them out, and the space available often lacked cooking or laundry facilities, or even indoor plumbing.[59] Despite stepped-up efforts, the situation remained critical in many places. At the end of 1943, for instance, the ratio of people seeking housing to available places on Vancouver's housing registry was 2,371 to 15, in Victoria 470 to 14, and in Ottawa 1,850 to 25. Between April and June 1944 the Toronto housing registry managed to locate 377 places, but only half of them would accept children, and 1,100 families with children were on the waiting list. That year registries in Halifax and Quebec City decided to stop advertising to locate space, realizing that further efforts would be futile.[60]

WHILE SOME HOMEOWNERS WERE COMPLACENT about desperate conditions, others saw a golden opportunity to line their pockets. People who did not need to be in cities could sell their homes for huge profits. In Victoria a municipal government report noted examples such as a house that had been bought for $2,500 in 1941 fetching $5,000 in 1945 "with no alterations." In Toronto, where housing stock was more plentiful, prices commonly increased by 50 percent over the first three war years. In Edmonton the influx of Americans pushed up home prices to as much as triple their 1939 values.[61] Such prices reflected a combination of record demand and abnormally scant supply. Most homeowners worked in the city and feared they would be unable to find a replacement property if they sold. And after April 1942 gasoline and tire rationing made it problematic to move to cheaper housing outside the city. Real estate companies offered rewards for leads to listings, and prospective buyers advertised their willingness to immediately pay the full purchase price in cash for houses that met their specifications.[62]

Column after column of classified ads in big city dailies testified to the public's need for rental accommodation: "Reliable, childless couple," "Well-behaved child," "Naval officer, wife, baby, urgently require small apt.," "Reward for information leading to an apartment."[63] To get the jump on available space, some wily people checked obituary columns or bribed undertakers; some went knocking on doors, no doubt thinking it would be harder for a homeowner to turn down a person face to face. Some went further: on a "cold and rainy" Ottawa night toward the end of 1943, the wife of a wounded veteran took to the streets with her four-month-old baby, carrying a sign pleading: "Who will rent a flat or rooms to Daddy and us?"[64]

The WPTB devoted considerable resources to preventing landlords from exploiting such situations. Fifty-one of its first sixty-four orders preceding the general price freeze of October 1941 concerned rents.[65] Following on double-digit rent increases, rates were frozen in Halifax in January 1940, and in Kingston, Calgary, and Ottawa soon afterward. In each case, responding to requests from municipal officials, the WPTB established a rental board to set rates and adjudicate landlord-tenant disputes, an initiative that in these centres and several others also led to rental courts. By 30 September 1940 thirty more communities had joined the rent control list, and with the general freeze, rent control went nationwide.[66] Each area's rates were to be set according to the average for the accommodation type in its neighbourhood as of 2 January 1940. Rooms let for the first time were to be registered with the WPTB, with a description of their amenities and proposed rent, to ensure that they met the rent control guidelines. Rent hikes were permitted only if a property faced substantially increased local taxation or if a landlord had made significant renovations. However, with material and labour shortages, local governments kept infrastructure projects to a bare minimum, a measure that often actually lowered municipal taxes.[67] And to preserve resources, homeowners required a special permit from the WPTB to proceed with repairs worth more than $500.[68]

Complaints from landlords soon poured in. Many claimed that rents had only begun to recover from their abnormally low Depression levels, and that with war work the salaries of tenants had risen at twice the rate of rents.[69] Several landlords also pointed out that with space shortages more tenants were subletting parts of their premises to cover their own rent and passing on extra costs in increased utility bills and greater wear on the property.[70]

By referring to official statistics, the federal government insisted that rent control was a great success. Using the 1935-39 average as a base, it pointed out that while rates across the country rose by 11.3 percent over the first three years of the war, for the remainder of the conflict the increase was only 0.72 percent.[71] However, those statistics included areas that experienced significant out-migration and low demand for accommodation – and they reflected only recorded transactions. Many landlords stretched or ignored WPTB rules, feeling justified that their grievances were legitimate, and lured by the opportunity for significant and, perhaps as important, tax-free returns.

The WPTB was also besieged by complaints from tenants. Several trotted out the anti-Semitic Shylock analogy when it was known or thought that the landlord was Jewish.[72] In its first year, Calgary's rental court heard 500 cases, but another 500 waited in the queue.[73] During the war, more than 2,000 landlords, besides being compelled to lower what they charged, were fined for deliberately breaking rent control guidelines. As in other domains governed by the WPTB, this figure could have easily been far higher had Enforcement Branch personnel been more numerous and aggressive. It had been concluded that too harsh an approach could drive many landlords out of the rental business, thus exacerbating an already difficult situation. Even if found guilty of intentionally flouting the law, most first-time offenders faced a small fine, typically in the $50 range, an amount that for some was no deterrent.

Some tenants were hesitant to complain, as the low numbers of charges may also have testified. "Conscious of the shortage of shelter," a number "were more anxious to retain possession of the space they occupied than to argue the rate," read a WPTB report. An intimidated elderly woman in Edmonton, for example, stopped taking public transit so that she could pay extra to a landlord who threatened to give her place to an American.[74] The reluctance of some tenants to complain also related to the fact that most rental investigators were former real estate agents who needed work after the collapse of home sales. The WPTB considered these men ideal for the job because of their knowledge of the residential market, but tenants often distrusted them, believing that they would naturally side with property owners.[75] Moreover, though the WPTB promised it would protect tenants from reprisals if they brought forward their grievances, many were unwilling to take the chance. Indeed, authorities sometimes appeared not to keep their word. In one such case an Edmonton tenant whose monthly rent had been lowered by the rental court from $35 to $32 soon complained about his landlord's mistreatment. Unable to obtain satisfaction from the WPTB, he turned to the mayor in desperation. Ever since the court victory, he wrote, the landlord had made his family's life unbearable: "Use of the washing machine which was part of the agreement was stopped by not supplying sufficient hot water facilities ... Having his children stand in hallways shouting insulting remarks is another trick. But the dirtiest trick of all is going to the City Police complaining of unbearable noises made by us when none exist ... Now he has made application to the Rental Authorities to have us evicted."[76]

Many tenants endured scandalously high rents. In Halifax in late 1940 the press reported on the plight of a woman who paid $60 a month for a one-bedroom apartment with an untiled bathroom and a windowless kitchenette.[77] The next year, in Vancouver, where rent guidelines classified a two-storey, seven-room home near the major shipyards and in "good repair" at $44 per month, single rooms in the area fetched as much as $60, and small houses $90.[78] In Edmonton, one man arriving from the countryside to take a job at Aircraft Repair Limited angrily wrote to the city commissioner, "I looked over a small house on Saturday last. I could have it but the landlord stated frankly: 'I am raising the rent $5.00 and have lots of people who are willing to pay.'" Soon, knowing that they could extort higher prices from Americans, some Edmonton homeowners simply refused to rent to Canadians. "I blush deeply for my fellow Canadians," wrote an embarrassed resident to the *Edmonton Journal.* "Because of [their] unashamed greed many Americans will return home with empty purses [and] bitter tales of crawling in and out of dark, hastily converted attic and basement quarters rented to them for prices that would secure an elegant apartment in the best district of their own war-congested home city."[79]

To maximize profits, some homeowners divided their premises into minuscule living quarters. One Ottawa woman remembered her grandmother, the widow of a prominent doctor who lived in a 4,500-square-foot home, making a "fortune" during the war by renting out the attic, four rooms on the second floor, the main floor sunroom, dining, and living rooms, and the basement, leaving herself with just the parlour.[80] In the vicinity of war plants that operated around the clock, some rooms were rented out on a twelve-hour basis. In Montreal, one gouging landlord collected $113 a month for a small flat shared by four women who alternated between day and night shifts. It was not uncommon to charge key money of a month's rent to new tenants. Sometimes tenants were compelled to purchase old furniture at grossly inflated prices. *La Presse* reported in 1944, for instance, that a seven-room house in Montreal was rented for $30 monthly in accordance with WPTB guidelines – but with well-worn furniture thrust upon the tenant for several hundred dollars.[81] Writing soon after the war about a situation that continued for some time, a disgusted B.K. Sandwell, a columnist with *Saturday Night,* contended that "there seems to be very little doubt that some illicit consideration ... is given in connection with about half of the new leases." This, he claimed, spoke to a moral breakdown among both landlords and tenants, because it was "extremely difficult ... to retain scruples to get any kind of accommodation."[82]

THE FEDERAL GOVERNMENT did step up legislative efforts to control the rental market more effectively. In October 1942 it introduced Order 204. In an overture to landlords, the law permitted them to charge twice the total cost of local property taxes and utilities on a rental unit. It was claimed that this level would guarantee a fair return; however, it actually justified few rent increases. To provide greater security to tenants, Order 204 doubled to six months the required notice to vacate for those who had lived in a place more than three months, prohibited winter evictions (between 30 September and 30 April), and stipulated that the sale of a property did not change these rights. It also outlawed key money, forced purchases of furniture, and any other form of tribute to obtain accommodation.[83]

Landlords reacted bitterly: Order 204, they said, was an attack upon property rights certain to deter homeowners from renting space.[84] Yet the legislation also left many tenants disappointed. They feared that provisions to evict the badly behaved could be abused with trumped-up charges. Even good tenants could be evicted with three months' notice in the event that their space was required to house an immediate family member, another loophole that could be used in a fraudulent manner. Moreover, as one angry Montrealer wrote to Donald Gordon, all Order 204 did for tenants was shift the crisis day to 1 May.[85]

Indeed, in mid-1943, rallied by the demand for an indefinite freeze on rental agreements, a Montreal tenants' association representing seven badly overcrowded districts was formed, and by December it claimed nearly 2,000 members.[86] Newspapers gave it considerable coverage, especially as 1 May 1944 approached, for with 1,300 eviction notices pending, as many as 5,000 extra homeless people were predicted in Montreal. Sit-down strikes to protect tenant association members facing eviction were mentioned. However, the anticipated crisis did not materialize, because most renters managed to secure alternative accommodation, though emergency shelters strained to cope with the additional demand. Still, many worried about the potential for trouble – even violence – and not only in Montreal. Toronto and Vancouver tenants also formed new associations in 1944, and in Vancouver, the *Daily Province* reported, talk circulated about establishing "human barricades" outside homes where tenants faced eviction.[87]

WARTIME HOUSING and controls over rent and evictions were not the only measures being taken by Ottawa to address the accommodation crisis. In 1941 the King government had appointed an Advisory Committee on Postwar Reconstruction; one of its several subcommittees was to make recommendations on housing needs. The report of this subcommittee, chaired by Dr. C.A. Curtis of Queen's University, was released in March 1944 and did not sugar-coat the situation. It cited a shortfall of 600,000 urban and 125,000 rural homes, and another 335,000 in need of extensive repairs. The report recommended that as soon as building materials became available, incentives be used to stimulate private-sector construction, and also that the federal government provide 92,000 subsidized public housing units. Justifying the latter, Curtis pointed out, for instance, that "only 7.7 percent of the lower third of Montreal families paid 20 percent or less [of their income] for rent," while in the same income bracket "even fewer, 6.4 percent, could afford the rents they were paying in Toronto."[88]

The federal government accepted Curtis's numbers and did enact legislation to enable the achievement of his goal, but almost exclusively through the private sector. Wartime Housing ultimately played a minor role in solving the postwar supply crisis, constructing only 8,902 units for veterans between 1944 and 1946.[89] Still, in March 1944 the prime minister announced Ottawa's aim to have 750,000 dwelling units built within a decade after the war ending. To make this possible, a new National Housing Act was passed that same year. Under the provisions of the new act, Canadians could buy a home costing up to $4,000 for 10 percent down (requirements were slightly higher for a more expensive house) and on a twenty-year fixed-term mortgage.[90] With mortgages hovering around the 5 percent range, monthly payments worked out to about $23 on a $4,000 home. Helping to maintain those numbers was the creation, in 1945, of the Central Mortgage and Housing Corporation (CMHC), which made necessary funds available to private lending institutions at a discounted interest rate.[91]

Among those who strongly endorsed the government's approach were the Ontario Association of Real Estate Boards, the National House Builders' Association, and the Canadian Manufacturers' Association, each of which agreed that these initiatives would strengthen private enterprise and spark considerable postwar growth. The CMA estimated that, based upon an average annual salary that it reasonably calculated at $1,680, 85 percent of Canadian families could afford a home costing $4,000.[92] However, not everyone was impressed. The Citizens' Rehabilitation Committee in Edmonton asserted that if the government truly wanted to democratize home ownership, it would fix interest rates at 3.5 percent, amortize mortgages over forty years, and allow a 10 percent down payment on homes costing up to $7,000. The Royal Canadian Legion, stressing the strong desire among men overseas to purchase a home soon after they returned, pointed out that most places cost between $5,000 and $6,000, and that to carry such a property, a $2,000 annual income was necessary.[93] But many Canadians had been able to sock away money during the war, especially with record numbers of working women. Moreover, in 1945 family allowances were begun, and hundreds of thousands of veterans began receiving cash rewards amounting to several hundred dollars – often more than $1,000 – for their service. One poll taken shortly after the war showed that among those who planned to purchase a house the median expected expenditure was $5,000.[94]

The most formidable obstacle to postwar home ownership was not price but supply. Housing could not come fast enough for Canadians. Results from a July 1944 poll led the federal government to conclude that 500,000 families wanted to buy a home as soon as possible after the war. Compounding the problem, Canadian homeowners who had put off making substantial repairs or renovations during the war (36 percent according to the poll) would be looking for building materials.[95] Thus, though Ottawa remained determined that the private sector would ultimately fill the housing gap, the potential for catastrophe in the short term, especially with the repatriation of servicemen on the horizon, necessitated even more comprehensive government controls.

In late 1944 and early 1945, the WPTB established Emergency Shelter Administrations in several cities to help find temporary accommodation for those without a place to stay. In Ottawa, for example, an old fire hall and a detention home were conscripted into service. Although they did not apply it, emergency shelter administrators were given the power to force homeowners to rent out spare space. Prospective tenants could no longer be refused accommodation because they had children, though it was difficult to prove that this influenced a landlord's decision, given the fact that most landlords solicited multiple applicants.[96] Far more drastically, however, the WPTB responded to requests made by local officials by introducing regulations between December 1944 and February 1945 that prohibited civilians from migrating to designated cities unless they had a formal job offer and a permit from an emergency shelter administrator.[97] In major newspapers and national magazines, large advertisements from the federal government warned those without permits that it was illegal for them to move to Vancouver, Victoria, New Westminster, Hamilton, Toronto, Ottawa, Hull, or Winnipeg, and in some cases, to their surrounding suburbs.[98]

Despite protests from several municipal governments, the permit system was abandoned in late August 1945. The federal government claimed that an initial postwar production slowdown had reduced civilian migration and it dared not interfere with veterans' choice of where to settle. It also quietly admitted that the system was too difficult to enforce. However, a month earlier, with nearly 8,400 eviction notices pending in congested areas, it did issue Order 537, which froze leases indefinitely in communities where the permit system applied (although provisions remained for evicting the "destructive, abusive and unruly" and for landlords to repossess, with three months' notice, space needed for immediate family members, presumably those returning from military service). While the freeze provided many tenants with greater security, for others it underscored the difficulty of obtaining alternative accommodation, a problem that convinced some renters to continue paying usurious rates.[99]

In addition to applying legal coercion, Ottawa stepped up its appeals to the patriotism and generosity of Canadians. Beginning in late 1944, and continuing well into the postwar period, the new Department of Veterans Affairs (DVA) urged citizen rehabilitation committees to create special veterans' housing registries, and supplied such organizations with sample speeches, press submissions, and advertising copy. Newspapers could be given, for instance, an illustration of a blind veteran walking the streets with his wife and daughter desperately searching for a place to live. A sample speech read: "We have numerous veterans who, after being away from their wives and children, three, four and five years, return to Canada and find themselves unable to resume normal home life [which would make] the adjustment period much shorter and easier. We feel there are a number of people [...] who have space in their homes ... We realize that this may mean some inconvenience ... but it is nothing compared to the sacrifice these men just went through."[100] The results of such appeals typically proved disappointing, as people either did not have space or remained unmoved. They may also have feared WPTB rules that suggested it might be a very long time before they could regain full control over their property. Two-day publicity campaigns in Ottawa, Calgary, and Winnipeg produced just two, three, and six rooms respectively.[101]

In a survey taken at the end of the war asking Canadians to name the most significant problem facing postwar Canada, 63 percent identified "slum clearance and housing." Among respondents in Montreal, Halifax, Ottawa, Toronto, Hamilton, Winnipeg, and Vancouver, that response averaged out to 83 percent.[102] In regard to supply deficits, the Canadian Lumbermen's Association predicted another two years of wood shortages for house construction. Contractors often had to leave homes uncompleted because of difficulties securing piping, electrical material, tiles, basins, tubs, sinks, furnaces, and even nails. Labour remained scarce: in July 1945, one builder who had obtained approval to construct 120 homes in Edmonton reported to the local National Selective Service office that he required fifty carpenters but could obtain only sixteen.[103] Under the Industrial Selection and Release Plan introduced by Ottawa on 24 May 1945, the repatriation from overseas of some 5,000 former construction workers was fast-tracked, and although peacetime industrial conscription was not implemented, it was seriously considered for this sector. In August 1945 the federal government ordered the registration of "either skilled or unskilled building construction tradesmen or labourers ... not now engaged in building construction work, who have had a total of at least two years experience ... in the construction industry since December 31st, 1936, and have passed their 16th birthday but have not yet reached their 65th."[104]

In such circumstances, builders frequently cut corners. Shortly after the war, *Saturday Night* charged that "bungalows hurriedly thrown together with green lumber and cheap stucco ... have been sold for $5,000 and up, which are not worth more than $3,000." Even in such homes, many new owners no doubt considered themselves fortunate. One survey of soldiers who had returned to Montreal found more than a third living with their parents or in-laws; about half of them reported overcrowded conditions that engendered arguments and, among those who were married, presented a "serious obstacle" to good conjugal relations.[105] Also in Montreal, 192 people, 152 of them children, were forced into temporary living quarters that included padlocked gambling establishments. In Ottawa 300 people were housed at the Rockcliffe air force barracks and the Hopewell hospital.[106] In Edmonton, veterans and their families were placed in American army barracks abandoned after the construction of the Alaska Highway and shipped down from Dawson Creek. They measured 20 by 120 feet and were converted into four tiny family "suites" with paper-thin walls and poor plumbing, but were probably preferable to the tents that other veterans pitched in various parts of the city in the spring of 1946.[107]

Many veterans were furious that their overseas sacrifices failed to protect them from countrymen who were exploiting shortages to make huge illegal profits, despite stricter WPTB rules. As a former private with the 3rd Division complained soon after returning to Toronto: "Soldiers cannot find houses or apartments unless they have a lot of money or get it through the black market."[108] In fact, some greedy landlords sought out veterans because they qualified for at least several hundred dollars in DVA gratuity payments. In Halifax and Montreal, ex-soldiers reported being charged $70 a month for one-room flats – about four times the rate when they had enlisted.[109]

Some feared violence from veterans over the housing situation. In July 1945 Canadian newspapers reported on "house commandos" being formed among British veterans who, in overcrowded cities like London, Portsmouth, and Liverpool, raided and took over properties known to be vacant for their homeless comrades, which the *Ottawa Citizen* saw as "a warning that should not go unheeded."[110] Indeed, veterans in Vancouver came to dominate a new Anti-Eviction Committee that, authorities noted with concern, drew significant trade union, CCF, and communist support. As well as lobbying for more low-cost housing and stronger legislation to protect tenants, the group arranged for round-the-clock pickets outside places where veterans faced eviction.

In January 1946, tensions escalated considerably when 300 veterans, led by the sergeant-at-arms for the British Columbia Command of the Canadian Legion, occupied the Hotel Vancouver. Although slated for demolition before the war because it had gone bankrupt, it had been kept standing during the conflict to house troops. After the war, the Legion, the Canadian Corps Association, and the Army and Navy League lobbied to have the hotel turned into a hostel for veterans. Once the request was denied, the offensive was launched. Within days, the hotel was filled and a waiting list of more than 1,000 veterans and their families was generated. Some condemned the occupiers as communists, though it seems more people sympathized with these veterans who had fought for Canada and now faced homelessness. A standoff ensued for nearly a month, but ultimately the federal and municipal governments agreed to temporarily turn the hotel into a hostel. Ottawa even coughed up $15,000 toward basic renovations. The arrangement lasted until 1948, by which time most veterans in Vancouver, including those who had occupied the hotel, had found decent accommodation, thus permitting its demolition in 1949.[111]

Similar incidents occurred elsewhere. In May 1946 fifty veterans converged in front of a Verdun flat to protect a former comrade and his family from bailiffs serving eviction papers. A Union Jack was symbolically strung across the porch. For two days veterans stood guard until new accommodation was secured for the tenants, and violence was averted only because the police were under orders not to intervene.[112] In nearby Montreal, postwar housing shortages produced the Ligue des vétérans sans logis. Led by Henri Gagnon, a veteran and the French-language organizer for the Labour Progressive Party, the group occupied several local government buildings to press home its demands for a moratorium on evictions and for the provision of low-cost housing.[113]

In September 1946 a Veterans' Housing League in Ottawa occupied an abandoned military building on the Lansdowne Park fairgrounds. Mayor Stanley Lewis, who viewed homelessness among veterans as a national tragedy, refused to have the twenty-five adults and thirty-five children forcibly removed, even though the building had no running water, a leaky roof and, according to the fire department, faulty and potentially dangerous electrical wiring. However, in October Lewis stationed police outside Lansdowne's horticultural building because of rumours that the Housing League planned another such operation. When another attempt at occupation did occur, during the wee hours of the fifteenth, it was thwarted. Still, the occupation at the fairgrounds persisted into early 1947, when an agreement was finally reached for the remaining members of the group to move into barracks at the Rockcliffe airport.[114]

THE FEDERAL GOVERNMENT maintained rent controls after the war, initially under the National Emergency Transition Powers Act.[115] Its strategy was to back away steadily, decontrolling in stages while also encouraging the construction of new units, so that soaring rates would not add significantly to inflation and to pressures for public housing. Clark and Ilsley contended that initial rent increases would spark new construction and improvements to existing premises, and that with rates stabilizing at a decent level reflecting the laws of supply and demand, black markets would soon disappear. This strategy was also buoyed by the fact that across the country, wartime rental rates, at least as officially measured, had climbed only 20 percent as quickly as family income. Therefore people could supposedly afford to pay more, especially with planned postwar income tax cuts, the new family allowances, and DVA benefits.

Rent decontrol began shortly before the end of the war. Rate increases were permitted on units constructed after 1941, but these were only a tiny proportion of properties.[116] In December 1946, all landlords could *apply* for a 10 percent increase, 15 percent if they provided the tenant with fuel, and up to 21 percent if the tenant sublet. In November 1947 new leases and renewals were released from federal rent control and a year later, eviction for any number of reasons again became allowable with six months' notice. Despite continuing evidence of overcrowding in several cities, and polls indicating that most Canadians living in communities of 100,000 or more still classified accommodation shortages as "very serious," Ottawa maintained that the situation was quickly returning to normal, that its foray into rent control had essentially been a wartime measure, and that where conditions still warranted, such legislation could now be imposed by the provinces, which actually held constitutional jurisdiction in this area.[117] Indeed, between 1949 and 1951 every provincial government except Ontario's, which held off until 1953, established some system of rent control. These measures varied considerably and were often short-lived: typically they allowed for some, sometimes notable, increases, and they usually relied upon municipalities to enforce the regulations despite sometimes inadequate resources.[118]

A successful conclusion to the accommodation crisis would only come through the mass construction of affordable housing by the private sector. Reiterating the federal government's commitment to this approach in a 1947 speech in Montreal, then justice minister and future prime minister Louis St. Laurent declared, "No government of which I am a part will ever pass legislation for subsidized housing."[119] By this time, such resistance was bolstered by Cold War ideology, which saw public housing as uncomfortably close to the communist model. That year Wartime Housing was merged with the CMHC and its properties were sold off. In 1949 the federal government passed its new National Housing Act. On the surface, this act appeared to deviate from St. Laurent's position, as Ottawa offered to fund up to 25 percent of the costs for public housing. However, this gesture was immediately criticized by public housing advocates – as well as by interested provincial and municipal governments – for being grossly inadequate, especially in light of continuing federal control over income and corporate tax fields. Humphrey Carver, the CMHC's director of research and one of its few supporters of public housing, labelled the 1949 legislation a "shabby trick" because, even though Ottawa's financial offer was clearly insufficient, it still managed to deflect much of the pressure for public housing to other levels of government. Moreover, public housing initiatives had to go through some eighty steps before being approved. As housing historian John Bacher observes, "only where political demands were strongest" did construction result. Between 1949 and 1963 a mere 11,000 subsidized units were built with federal assistance.[120]

Incentives were instead continued for private-sector construction. In 1947 the CMHC was authorized to make loans directly when the presence or liquidity of local private lending institutions was deemed insufficient. Interest rates continued to hover at around 5 percent and amortization periods were extended to as long as thirty-five years. It took time to clear the backlog – especially with the onset of the baby boom and high levels of immigration from wartorn Europe – but such intervention certainly helped alleviate pent-up demand, especially when supported by a strong postwar job market, significant wartime savings, veterans' benefits, family allowances, and eventually the maturation of War Savings Certificates and Victory Bonds. In 1946, 67,200 dwelling units were completed, over 75 percent of which were single-family homes, a total that exceeded the federal government's stated target of 50,000 for that year by more than a third. Yet, as demonstrated in Table 3.1, this figure was soon dwarfed as more building supplies

Table 3.1

Dwelling units in Canada, 1945-55

Year	New single dwelling units ('000s)	Dwelling units completed ('000s)	Dwelling units abandoned and destroyed ('000s)	Net increase ('000s)
1945	33.4	48.5	7.4	41.1
1946	51.4	67.2	8.4	58.8
1947	58.8	79.3	8.4	70.9
1948	61.8	81.2	8.5	72.7
1949	69.0	91.7	8.8	82.9
1950	68.7	91.8	10.2	81.6
1951	60.4	84.8	11.0	73.8
1952	56.0	76.3	7.1	69.2
1953	68.9	100.7	7.8	92.9
1954	71.7	106.3	8.3	98.0
1955	90.5	132.3	9.3	123.0
Total	690.6	960.1	95.2	864.9

Source: KA.H. Buckley and M.C. Urqahart, *Historical Statistics of Canada* (Toronto: Macmillan, 1965), 520.

and construction labour became available. The numbers of new rental units also rose at an accelerating rate; in 1949 they exceeded the total for the three preceding years. Despite a dip in construction during the 1950-53 Korean War, when more resources went to defence, the increase in accommodation still significantly surpassed the decade-long goal set by the federal government following the Second World War.

Construction concentrated in suburban areas where large tracts of inexpensive land beckoned. Between 1945 and 1960, over a million Canadians flooded into new subdivisions in satellite communities such as Scarborough, North York, and Etobicoke outside Toronto; Burnaby and Coquitlam outside Vancouver; Pointe-Claire and Beaconsfield outside Montreal; and Gloucester and Nepean outside Ottawa.[121] More and more construction was being done by large firms, which, for speed and cost-effectiveness, increasingly used tract-building techniques and pre-fabricated parts. Clearly the CMHC also thought in terms of speed as well as simplicity and affordability when it came to housing Canadians. In 1947 it issued a public challenge and offered cash prizes to architects to provide appealing and functional house designs that could be built swiftly for less than $6,000. Some 60 percent of homes constructed during the initial postwar years were 1,000- to 1,300-square-foot bungalows, or slightly larger single-storey or storey-and-a-half ranch-style dwellings.[122]

Although often later criticized for their blandness and for supposedly symbolizing the conservatism and conformity of the 1950s, these homes, the large suburban lots on which they sat, and the relative openness of suburbia itself all represented the fulfilment of a dream to millions of Canadians long crammed into tiny and dingy flats in overcrowded cities. Even acknowledging the approximately one-third of Canadians who in the mid-1950s, according to some studies, lived in poverty and for whom the dream of home ownership remained elusive, generally housing had become far more accessible.[123] Home ownership grew at an unprecedented rate, rising between 1941 and 1951 from 57 to 65 percent of Canadian households.[124] Moreover, a detailed study of Hamilton shows that, during the fifteen years following 1941, the percentage of "common labourers" who made the leap into home ownership nearly doubled, from 28.9 to 57.1 percent.[125] By 1953, when Canadians were polled during the federal election campaign as to what they considered the most pressing problem for the next parliament, only 79 of 2,021 respondents identified housing shortages.[126]

DURING THE PERIOD when accommodation shortages persisted, many Canadians clearly did not rise patriotically to the occasion. Rather than considering the common weal or assisting those in uniform during the war and afterwards, such people created the impression that a worrying, if not scandalously high, number of Canadians prioritized their privacy, the value of their property, and their personal income. Although severe wartime housing shortages spurred important, and arguably generous and successful, legislation – namely the 1944 NHA and the creation of the CMHC the next year – government wartime housing policies also exacerbated suffering and fuelled the black market in rental accommodations. Even if the ardent opposition of those like Clark and Ilsley toward public housing was eventually vindicated by the strong postwar performance of the private sector in supplying homes, their policies certainly worsened shortages of accommodation during the war and provided more opportunities for the unscrupulous. Finally, to many Canadians, the self-serving and often illegal behaviour of homeowners and landlords was a sign of a deeper social and moral malaise. This malaise was also seen in the seemingly unpatriotic protests by many workers, farmers, and taxpayers, and undoubtedly verified by the manifestations of greed and cheating on Canada's other black markets.

4

Black Market Profiteering: "More than a fair share"

MOST CANADIANS INSISTED that the WPTB rules made hardly any difference in their lives and that their sacrifices were trivial compared to those endured by civilians and servicemen overseas. Millions took pride in growing victory gardens to save food. In markets they searched out items labelled with victory tags testifying to their more plentiful supply and diligently used those ingredients to make the recipes for "patriotic dishes" printed in newspapers and magazines.[1] They learned tricks such as mixing rationed butter with gelatin and milk to make it last longer.[2] To save gasoline and tires, they walked rather than drove to work, and to preserve coal they dressed warmly instead of stoking up the furnace. They embraced such initiatives as opportunities to demonstrate their patriotism and their solidarity with those battling to defeat fascism and save democracy. But just as with rental accommodation, there was another less inspiring story that, even if sometimes exaggerated by worried government officials or in sensationalist newspaper accounts, had good reason to become a notable part of public discourse.

DURING THE FIRST THREE YEARS of the war, Canadians accumulated some $400 million in spending power but found fewer consumer goods to spend it on as manufacturers turned their attention to the war effort.[3] The federal government ordered drastic production cuts to myriad goods deemed nonessential, including such household items as irons, pots, pans, coffee percolators, kettles, toasters, sewing machines, vacuum cleaners, and lawnmowers. Between 1940 and 1943 furniture production plunged by 50 percent.[4] In November 1940 appliance companies were prohibited from introducing new lines, and the following year the Department of Munitions and Supply ordered production cuts of 25 to 49 percent. With appliance companies soon retooling for war production, the actual cuts were far deeper. For example, between 1940 and 1941 the output of household refrigerators plummeted from 53,161 to 2,137, and of washing machines from 117,512 to 13,200.

Compounding matters was the fact that by the Second World War, major appliances in Canadian homes were, on average, more than five years old, as people had postponed new purchases during the Depression. Exchange controls prohibited large-scale imports from the United States, and in any case by late 1941 American appliance manufacturers were turning to war production and within a year virtually stopped producing for the civilian market.[5] Support services such as commercial laundries were soon swamped by military contracts. Repairmen became harder to find, as many enlisted or took war jobs. Those available often charged exorbitant rates or, if employed by companies, asked customers for an under-the-table cash bonus.[6]

Many people got to know their neighbours better as the sharing of utensils became more common. Others scrambled to find a hotplate or pull an old washboard out of storage. Soon the classified section of daily newspapers looked like a swap meet as people sought out goods in short supply. A typical day saw entries such as "Fur coat ... for bed" or "Radio, 7-tube ... for car accessories."[7] Many realized that the war had turned some household items, even those that under normal circumstances would have been thrown out, into tax-free gold. In a sign of the times, newspapers solicited this new source of advertising revenue. For instance, a headline above the classified section of the *Ottawa Journal* declared, "Wartime Shortages Make Used Articles Valuable – Insert a ... Want Ad and Dispose of Toys, Clothing, Equipment at a Nice Cash Profit."[8] Columns of entries under the category of "Wanted Misc." offered cash for appliances, furniture, radios, bicycles, and baby carriages. These were joined by appeals from businesses seeking stock. Increasingly common were notices such as, "Washing machines and ironers wanted, any condition ... Will pay the highest price." By mid-1942, it was virtually impossible for businesses to purchase metal furniture or filing cabinets. Typewriters also ran short because that year Ottawa ordered that their production be cut to 65 percent of the 1941 level. Moreover, virtually all new typewriters were taken by the military and a rapidly expanding federal government, which also advertised its willingness to purchase used typewriters at a "fair" price, unlike many businesses that made a point of publicizing their willingness to pay the "highest" price.[9]

Countless advertisements offered used merchandise for sale without quoting a price. Many items were sold as if new, thus ignoring early WPTB guidelines in 1942 that suggested 60 percent of the original cost as a maximum price. So widespread did abuses become that in 1943 the WPTB issued a regulation specifying price schedules as a percentage of an item's original cost, based upon its age and condition.[10] However, given the millions of deals, the small amount of cash usually involved, the subjectivity of judging a used article, and the limited numbers of WPTB Enforcement Branch personnel, Canadians were by and large left to their own devices in this area.

Used automobiles were an exception because of the sizeable prices paid for them. By the end of 1939, with more people working, demand for cars began rising. Dealers with foresight acquired as many cars as possible. In June 1940, with plans to rapidly step up military production, the federal government tried to soften demand for new cars by introducing a tax schedule. The flat tax of 5 percent on the portion of the purchase price above $650 was replaced by a graduated levy ranging from 10 percent on the entire purchase price up to $700, to 80 percent on any part of the price exceeding $1,200. Nationwide, car sales dropped from 15,730 in June to 6,849 in July.[11] But many buyers would have coughed up the money if they had known how difficult it would become to obtain a car later in the war.

In September 1941, production of passenger cars was ordered cut to 40 percent of the 1940 level, which was already less than two-thirds that of 1929, the last year of healthy car production for more than a decade as demand for automobiles dropped off dramatically during the Depression. Imports from the United States could not compensate. Besides the impediment presented by exchange controls, in July 1941 the US Office of Price Administration had ordered a 50 percent decrease in civilian car production for the 1941-42 season in preparation for the possibility of entering the war.[12] By mid-1941, even second-hand vehicles were becoming scarce. As the *Ottawa Journal* reported that August, "On used car markets ... vehicles bought in the morning are being sold in the afternoon with the mud and the dirt of the previous day's driving still on them."[13]

In early 1942 Munitions and Supply ordered a halt in the production of vehicles for general civilian use. Although 102,664 units had rolled off the assembly lines in 1940, two years later only 11,966 were put out, over half of which were to serve as ambulances, police cars, fire trucks, and vehicles for rural physicians. In 1943 and 1944, the sale of new vehicles to civilians was prohibited and only 4,480 were produced for essential services. Another regulation specified that civilians could purchase only one used vehicle a year – assuming they could find one.[14]

Following the price freeze, the WPTB introduced a formula for the sale of used automobiles. As for other second-hand goods, it linked age and general condition to price but factored in car accessories. What buyers actually paid for used cars often bore little relationship to the price reported to the WPTB, however. One man in Edmonton recalled selling his eight-year-old Pontiac: "He gives me six one-hundred dollar bills and the rest in tens and we go down to the garage ... and pick up one of those forms, and he fills in 325 bucks as the buying price... A crazy time ... and everyone laughing his head off at all the government regulations."[15] Also, car thefts began increasing more quickly than theft in general, rising by some 30 percent between 1939 and 1942.[16]

Many dealers searching for stock pleaded to owners in advertisements not to "sell your car in the black market." However, they themselves often led the way in illegal transactions. Many stolen cars were fenced through dealerships trying to compensate for plunging revenues due to declining stock.[17] Also, besides transacting cash sales in excess of the price ceiling, a common ploy by dealers was to charge the legal price and throw in an automobile rug or some other such accessory for several hundred dollars. According to an exposé in *Maclean's,* another scheme was for the customer to "pay perhaps $600 for a jalopy, drive around the block, return with his 'trade in' and be allowed $25 on the ceiling price of the car he wanted in the first place."[18]

Stiff penalties sometimes resulted. In Montreal, the owners of an automobile dealership and a service station were each fined $1,000 for their part in selling a second-hand car for $3,000, which was double the official ceiling price. It was a hefty fine, but others seemed ready to take the risk for the sake of the potential profits. One WPTB report said that in major centres, particularly Montreal and Toronto, auto dealers conspired to stymie the efforts of authorities: "An investigator who has been spotted by one ... will be known to every other dealer in the city in a matter of hours ... Each yard is equipped with outside bells and you can hear them ringing all along the street when a warning is being issued."[19]

IT BECAME HARDER not only to find cars but also to keep them running. With Japan's expansion throughout Asia, particularly into Malaya, rubber shipments dried up. By mid-1942, 91.1 percent of the world's rubber supply was controlled by the Axis powers.[20] Canadians found it difficult to buy garden hoses, rubber boots, fly swatters and, of course, tires. Between 1939 and 1942 Canadian output of standard balloon tires for civilian use collapsed from 1,397,901 to 56,608.[21]

Control over tire purchases was put into effect almost immediately after Canada went to war with Japan. In January 1942 a WPTB Essentiality Certificate became necessary for the purchase of new tires and inner tubes. The rules were toughened on 15 May 1942, when three civilian classifications established eligibility to buy new, retreaded, or used tires and inner tubes.[22] Most drivers had somehow to make do with what they had for the duration of the war. Even for those who had permits, the limited options made for creative experimentation. For example, Halifax's Garden Taxi Company, unable to obtain adequate supplies, tried using tires made from birch.[23] Tire shops urged people to come in more frequently for rotations and realignments and to have their tires vulcanized to seal small cuts and pores – services also designed to compensate for reduced sales.[24] In 1942, to conserve both tires and gasoline, Ottawa ordered that speed limits be reduced from fifty to forty miles per hour on "open roads," a measure that mostly accounted for a 36.5 percent increase in number of traffic violations compared to 1939.[25]

Black market tire sales also led to prosecutions: 1,623 between January 1942 and the lifting of controls on New Year's Day 1946. As in other areas monitored by the WPTB, this number could easily have been much higher had there been more WPTB Enforcement Branch personnel and a more vigorous implementation of the rules.[26] In the summer of 1940, a new tire had cost about $7, and the WPTB ceiling price averaged $9, but reports told of black market sales fetching up to $70 each for new and $40 each for good used tires.[27] Across the country, tire thefts multiplied. In Vancouver, where figures rose from 27 instances in May 1942 to as high as 400 a month by the end of the year, the police department warned of an organized ring that used juveniles to strip cars and paid them as much as $20 for each tire.[28] In an effort to thwart thieves and create more business for themselves, several tire dealerships and garages offered customers a new service of having initials vulcanized on their tires.

Tire vendors were also targeted by thieves. In Toronto, the Universal Ignition Garage found itself missing 100 tires one morning. In Vancouver, thieves at the Butler Tire Company were more brazen, cutting a padlock on the back gate one evening and stealing tires out of the rear of the shop while several employees were working at the front.[29] While speculation about an inside job at Butler turned up no concrete evidence, in other cases crooked employees were implicated. A manager at Ottawa's Goodrich Tire Company, who had in fact formerly served as a regional tire representative for the WPTB, was fired and fined $400 for pocketing cash bonuses on tire sales. Tires were also obtained with counterfeit permits. One RCMP report in early 1945 traced 200 such sales to a few dealerships in eastern Canada, though no charges were laid against the owners.[30]

Cheating relating to gasoline consumption was much more widespread, leading to 5,169 successful prosecutions.[31] Between 1940 and 1944 the annual production of crude petroleum in Canada rose from 8.5 to 10.1 million barrels, most of which went to meet the skyrocketing demand from war industries and the military.[32] Moreover, both eastern and central Canada still depended heavily upon supplies from Texas, Colombia, and Venezuela, while British Columbia obtained much of its oil from California. Importing proved increasingly difficult as the U-boat threat made shipping hazardous and oil tankers were seconded to help supply Britain. Also, when the United States joined the war, it required more of its own stock.

In June 1940 Ottawa appointed G.R. Cottrelle as oil controller within Munitions and Supply. That August he prohibited the opening of new gasoline stations, as well as new pumps and storage tanks for retail purposes. By July 1941 gasoline could no longer be purchased on credit, and motorists were allowed to fill only the tank used to power their own vehicle, as people were starting to hoard. Hours of sale at gas stations were restricted to 7 a.m. to 7 p.m. Monday through Saturday.[33] Canadians were asked to cut back voluntarily, but it soon became evident that too few were willing to change their ways. Shortly after an appeal by Cottrelle for people to carpool, for instance, a survey taken in Ottawa on a working day showed that only about 40 percent of cars arriving downtown carried passengers, a figure that the *Citizen* claimed was virtually unchanged from the usual pattern.[34] Government officials came to realize that many of those who did cut back were becoming discouraged, wondering if their efforts were fruitless and, in the absence of compulsion, whether shortages were really as serious as claimed.[35] This perception, coupled with mounting fuel requirements for the war effort, brought about rationing on 1 April 1942 that remained in effect until VJ day.

To obtain gasoline ration booklets drivers had to register their cars with the oil controller's office. They had to write their name and licence plate number on the cover as well as on each coupon, which gas station attendants were to detach and verify as the property of the driver. To control theft, loose coupons would not be accepted. Motorists were divided into several categories: the majority, nonessential drivers, were entitled to 120 gallons a year, which provided for about 2,000 miles.[36] Within this category, additional coloured gasoline was allotted to farmers, commercial fishermen, tourist outfitters, and licensed guides, but strictly for business operations.[37]

When introducing gasoline rationing, the federal government emphasized not only necessity but also the good fortune of Canadians in comparison to civilians elsewhere; in Britain and Australia, for example, motorists were then limited to about 1,000 miles per year. Public support appeared strong: the *Vancouver Sun* reported that 60 percent of its readers endorsed a ban on pleasure driving.[38] Some sources publicized the health benefits of rationing gas because it encouraged walking and the use of bicycles, though by 1943 steel restrictions meant that children's bicycles were no longer produced and adult bicycles were reserved primarily for those who needed one for their work.[39] Countless Canadians made the necessary adjustments and planned each car excursion carefully. "When ... go[ing] out now the great thing is to make the trip count," wrote a woman in Toronto to her husband overseas. "So I visited the hair dresser, the grocery store, shoe repair shop ... and mother's."[40] In several communities carpooling committees were started. With store delivery services curtailed, neighbours pooled purchases to reach minimum order requirements; several businesses went back to horse and buggy for deliveries.[41]

Gasoline rationing also encouraged greater use of public carriers, though these services often presented quite a challenge. To conserve fuel and tires, the federal government ordered the elimination of many duplicate intercity bus routes offered by different companies.[42] Moreover, much of the available bus space was reserved for military personnel and the transport of war workers to out-of-town plants.[43] Bus companies such as Greyhound asked civilians to avoid long-distance travel unless it was absolutely essential, to purchase tickets well in advance and for off-peak hours, and always to carry minimal luggage. Civilians were not allowed to book a bus trip exceeding fifty miles if a train went to the same destination.[44] Yet people were also told to minimize train travel since railways carried hundreds of thousands of servicemen and contended with record cargo shipments.[45] Sometimes the system could not cope. For instance, at Christmas 1942 some 400 Ottawa civilians with tickets to Toronto "were left standing in the station ... as the rule 'armed services personnel first' was strictly applied."[46]

Overtaxed ground transportation, along with rising levels of disposable income, the need for government and military officials to reach places more rapidly in wartime, the increased use of airmail, and the demonstration of aircraft sophistication in battle all contributed to an unprecedented "take off" in commercial air traffic. Both the newly established Canadian Pacific Airlines and Trans-Canada Airlines added carriers and routes, the latter expanding into the Maritimes and finally living up to its name. The number of Canadians who took flights increased from 149,025 in 1940 to 229,047 in 1942, and following gasoline rationing reached 314,642 in 1943 and 403,938 in 1944.[47]

Urban mass transit systems, however, underwent by far the greatest increase in demand. Between 1939 and 1944 the number of passengers carried per year rose in Vancouver from 62.0 to 118.7 million, in Winnipeg from 41.6 to 82.3 million, in Hamilton from 15.6 to 37.3 million, in Ottawa from 19.6 to 55.4 million, in Toronto from 154.1 to 293.8 million, and in Montreal from 208.9 to 361.0 million. Meanwhile, material and labour shortages prevented any significant upgrading of systems that had already failed to meet local needs at the beginning of the war because of depleted municipal budgets and Depression spending freezes.[48] To keep vehicles moving at a decent clip, numerous bus and tram stops were eliminated. Responding to requests from Dominion Transit Controller Gordon S. Gray, many large companies and schools in Halifax, Ottawa, Montreal, Toronto, and Vancouver instigated staggered shifts.[49] Appeals went out to shoppers not to use public transit during the morning or afternoon peaks. Hostility was often directed toward those who took up space with shopping bags. Overcrowding also produced complaints from women that men took advantage of packed vehicles to fondle them.[50]

Whether or not they were motivated by difficulties with public transit, many car drivers tried to obtain more than their legal ration of gasoline. "Cynical fellows look upon the driver who puts his car away when he exhausts his ... coupons as a good deal of a sap," angrily editorialized one newspaper. "We all talk about the 'brave new world' we are to set up when Germany and Japan are licked ... We talk about Utopia, and then we – or many of us, far too many – join up in a mean racket to get more than a fair share of gasoline."[51] Clearly, many were dissatisfied with their allotment. Farmers often said they should receive more because of their distance from towns, and no doubt it was only the dearth of WPTB inspectors that limited the numbers charged with using coloured gasoline for nonbusiness purposes.[52]

Considerable resentment was expressed by those whose livelihood depended upon gasoline. Leonard Brent, president of the Vancouver Taxicab Owners' Association, said that in the course of their jobs drivers could easily log 4,000 miles per month, or double their allotment. Many cabbies quit because rationing limited their income. This fact, along with the ruling from National Selective Service (NSS) barring healthy men between seventeen and forty-five from this job, forced several cab companies to close down – three in Ottawa between April and November 1942 – or to hire women for the first time.[53] Taxis still on the road were highly in demand to the extent that cab companies took out advertisements urging people not to request a ride unless absolutely necessary. In November 1942 the federal government decreed that cab rides be limited to a fifteen-mile maximum and that taxis double up on passengers headed in the same direction. Cabbies complained because the procedure stipulated that the flag be pulled down on arrival at the first destination, after which the remaining party would pay the rate for the distance from the first to second drop-off point. Several cab drivers were fined for attempting to charge longer-distance passengers the full fare.[54]

More substantial violations were not uncommon. In Montreal in April 1944, Sylvia Berman, the owner of twelve cabs, was given the option of paying a $1,000 fine or spending three months in jail for illegally acquiring over 3,000 gallons of gasoline, and in September two taxi drivers were sentenced to a $3,000 fine or nine months in jail for using "illegal coupons" to obtain an extra 17,000 gallons of gasoline over a one-year period.[55] Commercial travellers and truckers, despite receiving 2,500 gallons a year, were notorious for trying to obtain more. The black market was a godsend to some, such as two brothers who owned a small freighting company. One of them recalled the big break that came their way after a poker game at which they had complained about how difficult it was to make a decent living with gas rationing in effect:

> About half an hour later there's a knock, and I let this fellow in, and his friend with him, and they've got a suitcase. He put it on the bed and opens it and there it is, full, with gasoline ration books. I guess you could say my eyes bugged out, and my brother ... let out a war whoop like he'd found the lost goldmine ... Upshot was ... that I'd give those two fellows a quarter of my gross take ... and they'd give me the books I wanted.[56]

Drivers were warned to keep an eye on their gasoline ration books. "Locking it in your glove compartment is not safeguard enough – thieves always look there first," warned a government advertisement. "Carry your book carefully on your person ... [or] keep it under lock and key at home."[57] There were also many instances of gasoline being siphoned at night from parked cars, which was only petty theft. In Montreal in 1943, the arrest of several men caught in an attempted heist of a service station led the RCMP to a crime ring that, it said, could have sold up to 750,000 stolen and counterfeit gasoline ration coupons.[58]

Service stations were in the game also. Many accepted loose coupons, or none at all, especially if they were offered a high enough cash bonus. Some were reacting to the obligatory reduction in hours of operation and resulting lower legal sales.[59] Starting in March 1943, stations that did more than $5,000 in business a year, like other companies dealing with rationed goods, were required to participate in ration banking. This meant that they had to open up a bank account into which they deposited the coupons they collected, both to confirm their need and as a check against illegal sales. Fines levied against gas station owners for breaking WPTB rules were comparatively stiff – typically ranging from $100 to $500 – because it was assumed that their involvement in black markets signalled a larger-scale diversion of scarce resources and high illegal profits. On top of such penalties gas station pumps were padlocked, usually for a few weeks on a first offence, though repetition of the crime could result in the revocation of a licence. In August 1942, thirty-three pumps in Vancouver were padlocked, and in September fifty-nine in Toronto. For its actions the WPTB was both cheered and censured. It was often accused of overzealousness and of punishing station owners for honest mistakes perhaps made by their attendants, a reaction that no doubt reflected in part the condoning attitude of drivers who were also inclined to cheat. An RCMP officer who surveyed a Windsor filling station for a few hours noted, for instance, that "30 cars drove up for service and only four presented proper credentials."[60]

ANOTHER FUEL on which illegal transactions thrived was coal. In October 1939 Ottawa appointed a coal administrator to balance military, industrial, and civilian needs. Between 1939 and 1944 Canadian production of bituminous and anthracite coal rose 5.3 percent, but demand increased even faster, as over those five years the proportion of domestic requirements met by domestic production went down from 50.6 to 35.7 percent.[61] Canada was also vulnerable because before the war it had imported considerable quantities of coal from Great Britain, Belgium, the Netherlands, Indochina, Russia, Morocco, and even Germany. Although Canada began to obtain increasing amounts of coal from the United States, America's own rapidly mounting needs often limited supplies.[62]

Electricity was not a realistic alternative. Much of rural Canada was not serviced, and in centres of war production, utility companies struggled to cope with increased industrial demand. In September 1942, after machinery slowed down in war plants across the Niagara peninsula over a two-day period because of an electricity shortage, rumours circulated that coupon-type rationing was coming. Things did not go that far, but in Ontario the energy allotted for civilian purposes was cut by 10 percent, and in some parts of Quebec by up to 20 percent.[63] For nearly two years this meant darker cities, as the federal government mandated that most external business lighting, all floodlighting outside homes, and every other streetlight be turned off. Moreover, between late 1942 and early 1945 Canada kept to year-round daylight saving time to allow natural light to extend into the evening when more people were at home, though the change also had them trudging to work or school in darkness during the winter.[64]

By early 1942 difficulties in obtaining adequate coal supplies from the United States threatened to temporarily shut down nonessential industries. Additional problems were caused by transportation bottlenecks in Canada resulting from a lack of railway cars and reduced cargo space on Great Lakes vessels. In the Maritimes, miners worked only a three-day week during the autumn of 1942 because railways could not cope with the growing piles of coal. When materials began moving, labour shortages became a problem. Thousands of coal miners enlisted or opted for other jobs in the war economy – nearly 14,000 from the Maritimes alone – seeking better pay or less difficult working conditions than mining offered.[65] An increasing percentage of the miners still in the pits were older and presumably less productive. Whereas before the war only a third of Nova Scotia's miners were over forty, by 1942 that figure was 41 percent.[66]

To address this problem, NSS declared in October 1942 that coal miners would be frozen in their jobs along with those working in base metals and the aircraft sector. They could still enlist in the armed forces, however, and with permission from a NSS officer could shift to a different civilian job with the same priority classification, permission that mine owners claimed was too often granted. In late 1942 the Alberta legislature began issuing special four-month mining licences under which inexperienced workers were permitted to perform a number of surface jobs, thus releasing more men to work in the pits.[67] The next year Ottawa introduced a scheme allowing some experienced miners serving overseas to return home to work, but of 500 volunteers from Nova Scotia the military released only 59. However, coal miners in uniform but still in Canada could apply for a three-month leave of absence under the provisions of a scheme that at one point supplied some 1,200 workers.[68]

The federal government implored citizens to heat their houses to a maximum of sixty-eight degrees Fahrenheit, to clean their furnace regularly, to seal windows properly and keep them closed on cold days, and to close the doors of rooms not being used.[69] By the winter of 1942-43, some nonessential buildings such as theatres were temporarily shut down during cold snaps to save energy. The following winter, Canadian households were obliged to accept half their coal order in grades B and C, which did not burn as long or give off as much heat.[70] Also, coal companies warned their customers to give them plenty of time to fill orders because of shortages of trucks and personnel. Several municipal governments reassigned sanitation services to help out with deliveries. As the winter of 1943 approached and numerous households were in danger of not getting their coal supply, the federal government postponed until 1 February 1944 the start of military training for all coal-delivery men who worked in cities of 50,000 or more.[71]

Some people hoarded coal. In 1943, Toronto's Labour-Progressive alderman J.B. Salsberg demanded that city council order the police to crack down on people who "had extra bins built and now have them crammed."[72] Several coal companies broke the price ceiling, in the belief that customers would not tell authorities and risk jeopardizing their source of supply. In fact, some customers, seeking to ensure the delivery of their order or a higher percentage of grade A coal, went in person to coal companies and offered a bribe. Delivery men, determined not to lose out, were known to imply to customers that their order might go somewhere else if a bonus was not paid.[73] Not even the military escaped rackets involving coal. In 1943 the owner of Ottawa's Bruce Coal Company was arrested after it was discovered that shipments to the Rockcliffe air force base were consistently underweight. In his defence Bruce claimed that he could not obtain a scale to weigh loads exceeding 1,500 pounds, but authorities pointed out that each shipment carried a label guaranteeing its accuracy.[74]

Wood fuel also came at a premium because of increased industrial and military demand, transportation bottlenecks, and labour deficiencies.[75] By the end of 1942, over 1,000 women had been recruited to work in logging and sawmill operations in British Columbia, although they were usually given comparatively light jobs and were paid about half the amounts men earned. The federal government recruited and transported several hundred lumbermen from Newfoundland.[76] In 1943 it faced criticism from the state government of Maine and from many Quebec lumber workers for reducing the number of men allowed to cross the border to fill better-paying US timber jobs. That summer, some 700,000 Canadian farmers and farm labourers received circulars from NSS asking them to consider work in the timber sector following the harvest. In September nearly 600 men with the army's Canadian Forestry Corps were temporarily repatriated from overseas to help fell trees.[77]

Fences, park benches, and street signs were destroyed for wood fuel. A man who had grown up in Toronto recalled his father even cutting up an old Heintzman piano for firewood one cold February day.[78] In the Ottawa-Hull area, to avoid a catastrophe during the upcoming winter of 1943, the Federal District Commission permitted people to cut up to five cords of wood in Gatineau National Park, an offer taken up by some 1,000 "amateur axemen," some of whom had no doubt previously been among those fined for cutting wood illegally in the park or for selling it above the ceiling price.[79] Indeed, "for the protection of homeowners," several newspapers listed the ceiling price for various types of wood fuel and sawdust. Besides breaking the price ceiling, some wood dealers cheated both on quantity and quality: one major supplier was jailed for six months for passing off "inferior hemlock and fir sawdust" for "first-class fir."[80]

IN WARTIME CANADA, it also became more difficult to secure adequate quantities and decent qualities of clothing and footwear. Before the war Canada had raised only 10 percent of its domestic wool needs internally, and wartime shortages of shipping space cut deeply into imports of wool and cloth from Britain, Australia, and New Zealand. Seeking to exploit the situation, the Lechasseur clothing company of Montreal advertised the day after Canada declared war that it had secured extra woollen products and that people should rush to one of its three outlets before supplies ran out permanently.[81] Matters never became that serious, though the situation did grow more severe. By the autumn of 1940, 80 percent of Canada's woollen and worsted industrial plant capacity and 75 percent of its footwear production capacity were geared toward supplying the military.[82] Also, as higher-paying jobs lured women away from clothing factories, the industry suffered significant labour deficits. Between 1942 and 1944, 24 percent of workers left Quebec's textile sector, the country's largest, for other jobs.[83]

In 1942 manufacturers were instructed to emphasize practical items such as work clothes and winter undergarments for the civilian market. Among the items deemed frivolous and prohibited for production that year were bloomers, lounging pyjamas, teddies, parkas, ski suits, evening dresses, skirts longer than thirty inches, cloth-on-cloth designs, double-breasted suits, tuxedos, full-length dinner jackets, suit vests, long topcoats, dresses with more than nine buttons, pleats, pant cuffs, epaulets, shoulder pads, and extra pockets. To facilitate maximum output, clothing and footwear were standardized to fewer and simpler styles.[84] To save dyes, functionality rather than taste was also stressed: thread colours were reduced from over a hundred to thirty-seven, women's shoes were restricted to seven colours, and men's to five. With rubber shortages, girdles, corsets, elasticized pants, and bathing caps disappeared from the stores. Silk stockings were replaced by nylon and lisle, though they too became difficult to find. To replace them, some women bought products such as Velva Leg Film or used tan makeup and drew a thin black line up the backs of their calves.[85]

Propaganda reinforced these economies by informing Canadians of the many ways in which their small sacrifices with clothing added up to major contributions to the war. "The yardage saving on cuffs [can] make 110,000 pairs of RCAF pants," went one appeal, while another claimed that restrictions on the use of buttons saved enough thread to "stretch from Bedford Basin to Berlin." To quell grumbling, references were made to the situation in Britain. There, stated one WPTB advertisement, civilians had "to get along on 51 clothing coupons a year," of which "a woman's woolen dress takes 11 [and] a man's suit 26 ... But in Britain they would rather be free than fashionable."[86] The WPTB considered implementing rationing of clothing and footwear, but decided that shortages were not severe enough. Still, people were forced to become less choosy not only with style but also with fit. "What he wore last year wouldn't even go over his shoulder," wrote one woman to her husband overseas in recounting her efforts to locate undershirts for their adolescent son. "I asked for a size 34, they only had 36 ... I said I would take three," to which the salesman replied, "Only two to a customer."[87]

Retailers drew praise for trying to fairly apportion scarce supply, but at the same time they, along with manufacturers, elicited condemnation from many shoppers. They were accused of exploiting the standardization of product lines to make extra money. Standardization, it was said, should have lowered prices, but all clothing and footwear seemed to be priced at the ceiling. Consumers also complained that manufacturers provided shoddier goods as a means of obtaining extra profits. The WPTB reminded people about the difficulties that producers often faced in securing supplies such as strong glues for footwear, and assured them that the Excess Profits Tax prohibited large profit margins. Still, the WPTB responded to brewing dissatisfaction and suspicion in mid-1943 by establishing a Standards Branch to license clothing and shoe lines, and to periodically check quality. This gesture was disingenuous. With so many stores and items to check on, the WPTB considered such surveillance too massive a task, to which it consequently committed few resources, thereby making few arrests. Sometimes the WPTB turned to the Consumers' Branch for help, but many of its members' accusations against firms were not pursued, being interpreted as overreactions by overzealous volunteers.[88]

Despite accusations directed at retailers and manufacturers, Canada's black market in clothing also fed on the demands of unscrupulous consumers. In mid-1942, upon receiving their first ration coupon books for food, nervous consumers ignored antihoarding laws and scooped up as much extra clothing and footwear as possible because they imagined that the extra unassigned coupons at the back of booklets would be used to limit such purchases.[89] Rumours that a store had silk stockings typically started a stampede, and queues often stretching for blocks. In

1943 the RCMP uncovered a Montreal-based "stocking racket" doing "brisk business" as far away as Ottawa, preying upon the vanity, selfishness, or naïveté of buyers. According to the *Ottawa Citizen,* "the operators ... produce order blanks bearing the name of the non-existent company ... and sample cases with several pairs of precious stockings neatly displayed." Patrons were also shown an official-looking document stating that government regulations demanded a 25 percent deposit, which, of course, was never again seen.[90] Meanwhile, for the right cash price, several tailors continued to make double-breasted suits, pants with cuffs and pleats, full-length dresses, and other illegal items, often from pilfered supplies. In most port cities there were organizations that "acted as receivers of cloth stolen by longshoremen." In Montreal in 1946, authorities uncovered one clothing store that over the previous four years had sold as much as $50,000 worth of items made from stolen textiles.[91]

THE WPTB HAD GOOD REASON FOR CONCERN as the prospect of food rationing loomed. In contrast to positive attitudes toward victory gardens and victory tags, a November 1941 poll showed that 18 percent of those surveyed admitted to accumulating some food as a precaution against future shortages, and when asked about others, 56.5 percent said they were aware of "quite a few" who hoarded.[92] Canadians had already been asked that year to reduce their consumption of butter to help the country meet Britain's needs. The list of products in short supply soon included several imported goods limited by a lack of shipping space, the Nazi U-boat menace, and Japan's occupation of places such as Java and the Philippines. In January 1942 Canadians were urged to reduce their sugar intake to three-quarters of a pound per week per person, and in May to half a pound, along with cutting their coffee and tea consumption by 25 and 50 percent respectively.[93] However, not all proved honourable enough for the honour system. The day after voluntary rationing of sugar was introduced, several stores reported panic buying. By February 1942 only 29 percent of Canadians surveyed said that they believed voluntary rationing could work.[94]

On 1 July 1942 sugar became rationed by coupons on the basis of half a pound per person per week. As of 3 August people over twelve were permitted just four ounces of coffee or one-third of an ounce of tea per week. In September 1943, as shipping conditions improved, however, these allotments rose by 40 percent, and the limits were removed the following September.[95] On 21 December 1942 butter was added to the ration list, initially at half a pound per person per week, an 18 percent cut to the current consumption level. Between January and March 1943 that ration dropped to six ounces; in March 1944 it was set at seven; and in December 1944, with millions of liberated and starving Europeans to feed, it was again pegged at six.[96] As of 27 May 1943, meat was rationed at one to two and a half pounds per person per week, depending upon the type and cut.[97] Finally, starting in September 1943 Canadians were limited to one quart of molasses or two pounds of honey or twenty fluid ounces of canned fruit or twelve fluid ounces of jam every two weeks, hardly a sacrifice to most; in February 1944 these quantities were doubled.[98]

At restaurants, diners faced "Meatless Tuesdays" and found themselves entitled to just two teaspoons of sugar, one cup of coffee or tea, and a third of an ounce of butter. Theatre-goers watched movies without buttered popcorn, and in most stores purchases of chocolate bars or bottles of soda pop were limited to one per person, if they were available.[99] People began sweetening their food with juices, added a pinch of salt to remove a sour taste, saved coffee by letting the percolator run longer, and kept butter out of the refrigerator so that thin amounts could be spread easily.[100]

Polls consistently showed that three-quarters of Canadians or more supported rationing, and most newspapers printed strong endorsements. The *Calgary Herald* wrote, "Death and wounds are a sacrifice [but] rationing is just a pinprick," while the *Vancouver Sun* said, "To call a slight shortage of sugar, tea and coffee [a] sacrifice ... is a mockery of the word and an insult to the people who are really sacrificing."[101] The federal government assured Canadians that ration levels were devised with advice from medical experts and would not compromise their health, and reminded them of their good fortune compared to civilians elsewhere: in Britain in 1943 people were entitled to only one-third as much butter and one-tenth as much meat.[102]

Still, to lessen their hardships, numerous consumers bent or ignored the rules. Many simply refused to believe that food shortages could exist in Canada.[103] For example, despite record butter exports to Britain and shipments of nearly 100,000 pounds a week to Commonwealth POWs via the International Red Cross, only 43 percent of Canadians polled in early 1943 thought the level of butter rationing appropriate. (By comparison 14 percent thought it too severe, 36 percent believed it altogether unnecessary, and 7 percent were undecided.) Moreover, because rationing was in force during a period when news about the war was steadily improving, a little cheating conjured up less guilt for a growing number of people who saw victory as a foregone conclusion. Black markets also added excitement to some people's war experience, reflecting what many perceived – or worried about – as a heightened tempo of life during this period when moral standards seemed to be loosening.[104]

One of the most common activities was trading ration coupons or commodities. Many thought this harmless since the aggregate quota offered through coupons was not exceeded. But the WPTB stressed that its ration levels had been based upon "normal consumption patterns" and thus assumed that some people would not use all their coupons. In September 1943 the WPTB found it necessary to formally outlaw the trading of coupons or rationed goods with anyone not living in the same household.[105]

Ration coupons had to be detached by storekeepers or their employees, who were to verify their validity and, at their discretion, make sure that they were the property of the bearer. Should a cardholder die, leave Canada, or join the military, that person's coupon book was to be surrendered immediately to the WPTB. Cases were uncovered, usually by the local postman, of applications for ration books being filled in for dead family members. In December 1943 Ottawa made it a responsibility of undertakers to collect and turn in the ration books of the deceased. If a ration book was lost, the owner had to swear out a legal statement testifying to that fact before obtaining a replacement, and the finder was to turn it in immediately as it was "against the law to have in your possession a ration book ... not belonging to a person in your household."[106]

Establishments that used or sold rationed goods had their allotment determined by the WPTB according to previous sales and available supplies and, as of March 1943, if they transacted more than $5,000 per annum, they were required to participate in ration banking. As well as grumbling over lowered profits and excessive regulations, several storekeepers, especially in communities overrun with newcomers, groused over "not getting a fair share of ... consumer goods" and had less compunction about skirting the rules to supplement their income.[107] The fact that people traded coupons meant that many storekeepers were accepting loose ducats. Many retailers made substantial cash on the side, often with regular clientele whom they knew would pay a premium for, say, a superior cut of meat, or even for the convenience of knowing that their legal share of a rationed item would in fact be available.[108]

Strong public demand continued to fuel numerous such rackets. Many people purchased butter directly at an inflated price from dairy farmers dissatisfied with the commodity price ceiling. And whereas before the war coffee had been an unlikely enticement to thieves, with black-market sales fetching as much as $2 a pound – about four times the official ceiling – events such as the theft of 800 pounds of coffee from the warehouse of Larsen's Grocery in Vancouver in October 1942 were not uncommon. At one point, so many trucks on the London-Windsor run arrived with crates of tea pried open that some companies hired detectives to watch their drivers.[109] In Casselman, Ontario, about fifty miles southeast of Ottawa, a hotel owner reported that "a truck load [of sugar was] driven up ... and offered to any person" willing to pay the price. In late 1944 six Montrealers were fined a total of $10,600 for what authorities said could have resulted in the distribution of a million pounds of sugar through stolen and counterfeit coupons. Perhaps some of that cache reached William Bloomberg, the owner of Peer's Beverage of Montreal, who early the next year was fined $4,000 for obtaining sugar illegally.[110]

Among food products, however, the most extensive cheating involved meat. One reason meat was in high demand was that harder-working civilians were hungrier, and servicemen on average consumed 50 percent more meat than civilians. In addition, escalating exports of Canadian pork and beef to Britain sharply reduced supplies: 15 percent of total Canadian beef production went to that market.[111] Labour deficiencies, particularly in the meat-packing sector, worsened matters.[112] By early

1942, though meat shortages were evident in several Canadian cities, many people – including cheaters who thus justified their actions – thought the problem had been artificially created. They blamed the failure of distribution to adapt to the shifting wartime population, and prices having been set too low, especially after a very public fight between the WPTB and beef producers.

Many producers argued that the general freeze was imposed before prices had been given adequate time to recover from their record lows during the Depression. A factor in this dispute was the fact that American meat prices were significantly higher than Canada's.[113] Agriculture Minister Gardiner supported higher prices, or at least increased subsidies, for beef producers as he had for wheat farmers. However, he was once again blocked in Cabinet by Finance Minister Ilsley, whose position on the need to control inflation won King's support, especially since Donald Gordon threatened to resign from the WPTB if the government buckled to beef producers.[114] Another development saw the federal government impose strict controls on exports to America to secure Canadian and British supplies. While in 1941 61 percent of Canadian beef exports went to the United Kingdom and 21 percent to the United States, by 1943 those numbers stood at 80 percent and 9 percent respectively. With access to their more lucrative markets cut off, some cattle producers protested by holding back stock. Whereas 1,340,000 head were sold in 1941, this figure dropped to 1,288,000 in 1942 and to 1,243,000 in 1943. Gordon maintained that the WPTB would not be blackmailed; however, in October 1942 a modest increase of $1.50 per 100 pounds of carcass weight was allowed in a measure that impressed few ranchers.[115] Brian Chance, president of the Nicola (BC) Beef Cattle Growers' Association, told the press, "There is no beef shortage, there is a price shortage."[116]

Some frustrated producers turned to black marketeering. A number slaughtered animals in excess of family need (the amount permitted under the law) and then sold the meat above the legal ceiling directly to consumers or, along with live cattle, to unlicensed meat dealers. Cattle rustling saw a revival, often, it was claimed, by organized rings. "Here's how they operate," wrote the *Ottawa Citizen* about activities in nearby Carleton County. "The head of the gang travels along the highways, concessions and side roads, and spots cattle at pasture ... That night the black market slaughtering truck steals out of the city. A gun with a silencer does the killing. Then the animal is strung up and dressed, sometimes right in the pasture."[117] The meat dealers and rustlers often sold their product to slaughterhouses or direct to retailers, and all the illegal profits were eventually paid by consumers hungry for more than their legal share. In January 1943 the *Montreal Standard* suggested that as much as half of the meat sold in the city came through black market sources.[118] The WPTB did lay charges but could not adequately police livestock producers scattered throughout rural Canada and some 9,000 places licensed to slaughter or sell meat, especially since so many consumers were complicit in illegal transactions.

By early 1943 black market meat had become so widespread that some shops and restaurants claimed they could not obtain even minimal supplies unless they paid premiums. Meanwhile, with shortages persisting, queues outside meat shops sometimes became so long that police were brought in to keep order. On 27 March 1943 the federal government announced its intention to extend coupon rationing to this area to ensure order and fairness in the distribution of meat. The measure, which would cover beef, veal, mutton, lamb, and pork, was to take effect within three months, and its aim was to cut aggregate consumption by 20 percent. Despite strong press agreement and apparent public support, some people responded by trying to hoard before the coupons were distributed.[119]

Coupon rationing no doubt helped, but it did not come close to solving the problems related to the sale and consumption of meat. Sellers reportedly tried to pass off inferior cuts as meat in a better ration category. The WPTB tried to stop this practice by supplying charts that shops were required to post, illustrating the different cuts and the ration category under which they fell. Consumer attitudes were also problematic. When asked in mid-1943 what rationed product they found most difficult to cut back on, most Canadians identified meat.[120] This response was not surprising, considering that when the ration order was enacted, meat consumption was 29 percent higher than the 1935-39 average. Of course, many limited their intake as required and cooked the "patriotic dishes" that minimized meat or used none at all, such as brainburgers, which actually used sweetbreads, and tamale pie, which relied heavily on cornmeal. People not only consumed more chicken and fish but, more adventurously, ate more moose, bear, whale, and horse, though a number of butchers tried to sell the last as beef and priced it accordingly.[121]

Another factor affecting meat consumption was that Canadians, with their greater wartime income, bought meat to the full ration limit of each family member. Thus under rationing people ironically *increased* the amount of meat they ate from 63.6 pounds of beef and 57.3 pounds of pork per capita in 1942 to 72.5 and 66.0 pounds respectively the next year.[122] They also dined out more often, clearly to supplement their meat intake. Between 1942 and 1945 expenditures at restaurants rose from $157 million to $211 million, and in 1943 Canadians actually consumed approximately 25 pounds more meat per capita than they were permitted through coupon rationing.[123] Some complaints about meat rationing took on a gendered aspect as several unions claimed that the allotment failed to supply "hard-working men" with adequate energy and nutrition. Indeed, advocates for miners in both western and eastern Canada demanded a doubling of the official ration and predicted increased illness or absenteeism should the government not comply.[124]

In March 1944 several factors brought about the suspension of meat rationing. Large herds born in the early 1940s were now ready for market, and ranchers could no longer afford to hold back such high numbers. Also, transportation bottlenecks and shortages of cold-storage space in Canada made nearly 25 percent more meat available for the Canadian market. In suspending coupon rationing, Ottawa stressed its likely return once the transportation and storage problems were ironed out. However, many took the suspension as confirmation that the war was winding down and that rationing would soon be completely ended, a supposition reinforced by the lifting of coffee and tea rationing in September 1944. That year Canadians ate more meat than ever, with weekly consumption reaching just over three pounds per person, a pattern strongly suggesting that the reintroduction of controls would be difficult, even if they were presented as measures to save the lives of millions of starving Europeans.[125]

THE WAR WAS A TENSION-FILLED PERIOD, and substances that could relieve stress were hot-ticket items on the black market. Among these were legal and illegal narcotics. Supplies of certain drugs were severely limited by such factors as the war in the Far East, shipping limitations, and demand from the military. Between 1939 and 1940 the amount of cocaine legally imported into Canada dropped from 12,333 ounces to 819, crude opium from 34,262 ounces to 310, and morphine from 30,087 ounces to 6,241.[126] At the end of 1940 the RCMP reported that the street price of opium had jumped as much as tenfold in the short time since the beginning of the war, while during the first four years of the conflict the street price of a quarter-gram tablet of morphine rose from a few cents to as much as $5.[127]

Many addicts turned to the softer barbiturates, but these usually failed to satisfy. To maximize their limited supplies, vendors raised adulteration levels to as high as 90 percent. Some people expressed the hope that shortages would force junkies to break their dependency, but criminal activity increased instead. Convictions under the Opium and Narcotics Act rose from 102 in 1936, to 150 in 1939, to 176 in 1941, and peaked at 190 in 1942.[128] Frequent drugstore robberies meant that pharmacies often faced climbing insurance rates. When Frederick Fullerton, manager of the Pharmaceutical Association of British Columbia, asked Vancouver's mayor to supply extra police protection for drugstores, he claimed that the "life of every druggist ... in this city is continually in danger."[129] Doctors were also at greater risk. In 1943 the cars of sixty physicians across Canada were robbed for drugs, and of the 230 drug thefts for the year ending 31 March 1945, the greatest number (93) were from doctor's offices (with 92 from pharmacies, 30 from civilian hospitals, 9 from wholesalers, and 6 from military hospitals). Some suggested that doctors always carry sought-after drugs on their person, but this proposal prompted strong objections from physicians who feared assault or worse. However, about 25 percent of the charges laid under the Opium and Narcotics Act were against doctors, pharmacists, and veterinarians who had been tempted by the potential for extraordinary profits.[130]

Far more significant were the black markets that took advantage of legal vices. Between 1939 and 1944 the number of cigarettes purchased in Canada rose from 6.9 billion to 11.4 billion, a result of greater civilian affluence and the fact that almost all servicemen seemed to be smokers.[131] The supply of tobacco was not a problem – as of late 1942, 131 million pounds were in storage in Canada – but shortages of labour and cigarette-making machines continued throughout the war. Ottawa attempted to reduce civilian consumption and at the same time obtain extra money by raising taxes; the levy on cigarettes rose from $4.00 per 1,000 in 1939 to $10.50 by 1943. During those years the federal government's revenue from this source rose from $32.8 million to $75.6 million, but illegal transactions proliferated among those hoping to escape the tax. The availability of cheaper cigarettes in the United States also encouraged smuggling; a 1945 RCMP report revealed that charges "reached the highest total since 1934 with 3,226 seizures."[132] Trying to discourage such transactions, the federal government appealed to patriotic citizens that black market purchases deprived servicemen of cigarettes. In fact servicemen in Canada were themselves a major source of black market smokes, because they received large quantities from their family, friends, or various tobacco funds, and could buy their own supplies at special cut-rate prices. As early as 1940 servicemen in several regiments were warned that complaints from cigarette companies about such illegal sales were so frequent that the "generous privilege" of receiving price-subsidized cigarettes might be discontinued.[133]

Still more profitable black markets revolved around bootlegging and alcohol sales. Between 1939 and 1942, recorded purchases of spirits in Canada rose from 3.4 to 4.3 million gallons, malt liquor from 63.3 to 97.6 million gallons, and wine from 3.5 to 4.2 million gallons – patterns that resulted in a 15 percent rise in convictions for drunkenness among civilians. Once again the federal government increased taxes to conserve resources and labour, reduce consumption, and raise money. In the same three years, the taxes it collected on liquor sales more than tripled from $99.2 million to $316.6 million.[134]

From the outset of the war, groups such as the Sons of Temperance, the Canadian Temperance Federation, and the Women's Christian Temperance Union stepped up their campaigns for prohibition, a measure Ottawa had implemented as a wartime precaution in 1917.[135] As the conflict widened, so too did support for this crusade, or at least for serious curbs on the production of booze. Many argued that it was reprehensible during the present emergency to use grains and valuable labour to make beer. Increasingly heard were exhortations that alcohol could be more useful as an ingredient in such items as smokeless powder for shells, synthetic rubber and plastics, de-icing chemicals for planes, and disinfectants to treat the wounded. Liquor consumption was blamed for increasing absenteeism and dangerously compromising the need for "complete mental clarity" in the modern war factory. Supporters of prohibition also stressed that much of the money currently "wasted on drink" could be better directed toward Victory Bond purchases and donations to war charities.[136]

But opposition was formidable. Breweries publicized the information that it took only fifty men to produce a million gallons of beer, and that none of the ingredients were in short supply. With drinking establishments often attached to hotels, the Hotel Association of Canada was strongly averse to prohibition. More significant to the King government was the opposition of the Canadian Legion and the Army and Navy Veterans in Canada, whose gatherings typically involved a convivial round or two.[137] But the prime minister listened most to the protestations of the working classes, especially with regard to restrictions on beer, referred to as the "workingman's drink" because it was cheap. It was argued that beer's low alcohol content actually induced little drunkenness and that a "social glass" in fact helped increase wartime production by "easing tension" and raising morale after "long hours" on the job. This need was recognized in Britain, many contended, where pubs continued operating with few restrictions – although few mentioned or even realized that most establishments in the old country at that time served watered-down beer.[138]

Still, the trend toward greater government control of alcohol consumption gained momentum with the growing recognition that large-scale alcohol production was unacceptable in light of soaring demand for munitions and labour shortages in areas critical to the war effort. Also, Ottawa's decision in mid-1942 to ration sugar was a convincing indication that the use of some 22 million pounds of sugar by distilleries was untenable. When Prime Minister King proposed alcohol restrictions to his caucus in August 1942, he found the members divided. Besides those who worried about large-scale bootlegging, a contingent of MPs from Quebec pointed out that newspapers in that province earned a larger-than-average share of their advertising revenue from liquor companies and that press reaction also had to be considered. But the prime minister's options narrowed on 31 August when Washington announced that as of 1 November, America's 128 distilleries would convert entirely to war-related production, and that stockpiles of alcohol would be rationed.[139] King was not prepared to let Canada become a base for bootlegging, as it had during the late 1920s and early 1930s, especially in wartime. He was unwilling to risk the political consequences of giving the impression that Canada, more than the United States, prioritized liquor over military production.

On 23 October 1942 the WPTB announced that as of 1 November the supply of malt to breweries would be limited to the amount used in the preceding twelve months and that all Canadian distilleries were to convert to the manufacture of industrial alcohol. At the time, it was estimated that the existing stock of spirits could last up to five years if properly rationed. On 16 December, in a radio address introducing liquor rationing, King declared that "if the military might of Germany and Japan are ultimately to be crushed [then] self-denial and self-discipline" were necessary from all. Many media sources were in accord: the *Victoria Times*, for example, reasoned that "no fair-minded person could disagree with the measure."[140] However, the morning after King's address people jammed into liquor stores to stock up on extra supplies. Polls that month showed that support for prohibition, a measure that many suspected would soon follow rationing, was just 37 percent. Yet King's plan displayed his customary caution. Its goal was to reduce purchases of spirits by 30 percent, wine by 20 percent, and beer by just 10 percent. Liquor advertising would be outlawed after a six-week adjustment period, but breweries, distilleries, and wineries would still be allowed to keep their names before the public by publicizing their wartime activities.[141]

Responsibility for imposing cuts was initially delegated to provincial governments, which applied varying quotas and typically reduced hours of sale at liquor stores and taverns to eight per day. In British Columbia, for example, beer parlours were open from 2 to 6 p.m. and 7 to 11 p.m. These restriction generated complaints, especially from daytime workers who found little left by the time they arrived. Patrons accused establishments of putting extra ice into drinks or watering them down, using smaller glasses to serve draft beer, and pouring the beer so that the foam filled more than half the glass.[142] Supplies were often quickly exhausted in places that had experienced rapid population growth and a large-scale influx of military personnel. Such shortages created rumours that for political reasons the government was distributing alcohol unevenly – stories that the Rumour Clinic tried to counteract, fearing that such talk would incline more people toward cheating.[143] Another more confrontational reaction took place in March 1943. As one of the periodic Victory Bond drives got under way, Vancouver shipyard workers set up signs and donned lapel pins warning "No Beer, No Bonds." Although their ultimatum was denounced by many, including numerous union leaders, they were soon followed by factory labour elsewhere in Canada. *Maclean's* reported that "some Members [of Parliament] were loathe to go home at Easter recess without more beer for thirsty war workers," while *Saturday Night* urged, "Whatever is done about the situation should be done promptly."[144]

What Ottawa did about the situation was to introduce liquor rationing by coupons in May 1943 in an effort to bring about fairer and more orderly distribution, as it had done with other products. Canadians twenty-one and older were allowed to buy forty ounces of spirits, four bottles of wine, and thirty bottles of beer per month, although often it was difficult to obtain anything near this amount. Ten months later, on 13 March 1944, the King government ended coupon rationing of beer, handing back responsibility for cutbacks to the provinces. This retraction, along with the introduction of PC 1003, may have helped the prime minister woo labour support, but it made little difference to the actual supply of beer, since production remained legally capped at 90 percent of the 1942 level.[145]

With each new issue of liquor coupons, Canadians rushed to stores to beat the long line-ups, determined to get their promised allotment. Some feared this reaction would bring about heavier consumption, but in fact between 1942 and 1944 convictions of civilians for drunkenness dropped by 7 percent. Still, alarmist press accounts told of mothers carrying their babies so as to leave their baby carriages free for beer and liquor, and of boys who hung around stores with wagons or sleighs to ferry bottles for a small fee. This practice was condemned for contributing to the corruption of youth, especially since rumours circulated that these children were sometimes "offered a drink as a tip."[146] Many nondrinkers obtained liquor for family, friends, or employers, and employees, especially women, were often pressured to contribute their allotment for the entertainment of company clients.

The black market in liquor was extremely lucrative. Many individuals sold their liquor permits or their bottles, as a $4 forty-ouncer of spirits could command $25.[147] Organized liquor rings operated on a larger scale: police in Vancouver reported rings that acquired up to 1,500 bottles of spirits monthly, mainly through purchases from consumers. Near Chatham, Ontario, another ring was suspected of robbing trucks of some 250 cases of liquor with an estimated street value of $30,000.[148] Taxi drivers, often trying to supplement their reduced wartime earnings, helped guide buyers to illegal supplies. Black market booze was also sometimes available from sailors and merchant marines who could obtain cheap liquor, particularly rum, in places such as Newfoundland, St. Pierre and Miquelon, and various Caribbean and South American ports. Demand was especially strong in dry Halifax, where bootleggers and blind pigs had long done a brisk business because partial prohibition had been in effect before the war. (The exception was private social clubs whose members had to supply their own cache from government liquor stores, stores whose supplies ran short in wartime.) Longshoremen also became involved as suppliers, to the extent that by mid-1943 the RCMP were assigned to guard crates of liquor. Moonshine enjoyed a revival because it was cheaper, often the only thing available, and frequently more potent than the legal stuff. But it was a case of "buyer beware," as some confiscated hooch was discovered to contain ingredients such as shaving cream, hair tonic, and shoe polish. In May 1945, the de-icing fluid in one batch killed three women and an airman.[149]

On 7 August 1945 alcohol coupon rationing ended, but provincial liquor outlets usually continued to apply quotas, in some cases until early 1947.[150] Allotments were more generous than in wartime, as in the final months of the conflict Ottawa had permitted distilleries and breweries to return to civilian production. However, it wasn't only temperance groups who wrung their hands in despair. When citizens were asked in September 1945 whether they supported the continuation of liquor rationing, women – some of whom had undoubtedly experienced drink as a threat to family stability if not their own safety – responded 51 to 35 percent in favour; men, on the other hand, were 52 to 34 percent opposed.[151] As the first postwar Christmas approached, police were on hand at liquor outlets in several cities, including those in Toronto, which were visited by as many as 30,000 people daily. But according to press reports all remained orderly and even festive as for the first time in years people came away with enough stock to ensure good holiday cheer.[152]

WHILE POSTWAR SUPPLIES OF LIQUOR moved relatively quickly toward meeting demand, supplies of many other commodities did not. Continued shortages posed the threat of runaway inflation, especially since Canadians held some $6.5 billion in purchasing power by the end of the war, on top of which they were receiving veterans' benefits, family allowances, and extra funds from tax cuts, which in 1946 averaged 16 percent.[153] Also, after years of doing without, first during the Depression and then in wartime, people were keen to spend. One survey taken shortly before hostilities ended showed that 21 percent of respondents planned to buy a new car at the first opportunity, and 22 percent a major appliance.[154] The federal government implored Canadians to be patient when it came to such purchases, and to accept the prolongation of wage and price controls. People were reminded that the absence of government controls after the Great War had permitted a buying frenzy that produced rapid inflation and social instability, trends that would be far worse this time around, it was contended, because "the accumulated store of purchasing power is relatively much larger."[155]

Under the National Emergency Transition Powers Act, the WPTB retained control over the prices of certain items until their supply reached levels at which removing the ceiling did not in its view risk generating significant inflation. Of Canadians surveyed in July 1945, 77 percent indicated their support for continued price controls. Some in fact suggested that businesses and industry were trying to move too quickly toward decontrol so that they could reap windfall profits from shortages. In early 1946 another poll tallied some three-quarters of citizens in agreement with the statement, "Some price controls are a good thing."[156] Although the statement indicated a rather tepid endorsement, Canadians were indeed impressed by the fact that during 1945 the consumer price index indicated only a 0.83 percent rise in the price of food, 0.07 percent for clothes, and 0.1 percent for furniture. The WPTB also publicized the fact that in the United States, where wage and price controls were removed sooner, inflation was more than triple the Canadian rate.[157] But with the return of peace the federal government felt it was important to decontrol relatively quickly so as to stimulate production and maintain public support. Some officials with the Wartime Information Board predicted that as early as ninety days after Germany's surrender, "C-Day – Complacency Day" would arrive, even among many who had diligently followed WPTB regulations in wartime.[158]

By February 1946 about 300 items had been decontrolled, though not until early 1948 was the process virtually complete. Significant shortages, and hence controls, persisted for some time on items containing large quantities of steel, wood, rubber, copper, and several chemical alloys. Consumers who wanted new appliances had to make a reservation at stores and in many cases waited more than a year for delivery. A 1945 poll found that demand for washing machines was seven times higher – and for refrigerators thirteen times higher – than in the greatest single production year in Canadian history.[159] Another war-end study estimated that Canadians required some 750,000 cars, a major challenge considering that the greatest annual output of vehicles in Canada to that point had been 209,000 in 1929. To stimulate car production, the WPTB permitted a 20 percent price increase between 1946 and 1948. Also, to maximize production numbers, car manufacturers eliminated frills such as sunroofs and rear-window wipers until the late 1940s. In 1947 sales hit 159,205 units, but only in 1950, when the figure reached 324,903, was the backlog of demand cleared.[160]

Many Canadians continued to exploit such shortages. Veterans were shamelessly targeted since they had the greatest need for civilian goods and were thought to have money. The Department of Veterans Affairs warned those awaiting demobilization about civilians lying in wait to cheat them, and took measures to safeguard their funds. Veteran gratuity payments were distributed in monthly instalments equivalent to the recipient's gross monthly military pay, not only to control inflation and government expenditures but also "to help protect" returning servicemen from the unscrupulous and from squandering their money.[161] In Toronto, the Better Business Bureau sponsored a fifteen-minute weekly radio show outlining various swindles veterans might encounter. In one of many such scams, WPTB authorities in Vancouver charged a civilian with selling a 1939 Studebaker to a veteran at 50 percent above the ceiling price. Stories circulated about items like used tables, worth perhaps fifty cents before the war, being resold to veterans for as much as $10.[162]

Postwar shortages also persisted with several food items, as Canada contributed generously to overseas regeneration. In rallying support, WPTB press releases pointed out that Belgians were forced to live on one ounce of meat per day, and the Dutch on three ounces per week. The WPTB also drew attention to Canada's international obligations as part of the "United Nations," a term the Allies increasingly used to describe themselves, and particularly to the new Relief and Rehabilitation Administration, which was created in November 1943 to provide food, shelter, medical supplies, and eventually basic infrastructure and machinery to war-devastated areas. Besides the humanitarian angle, government publicity cited practical considerations for future business. The WPTB told Canadians, not without exaggeration, that "the people of Western Europe have always been our best customers for the produce of our farms, fisheries, mines and forests. We must do all we can to get Europe back on its economic feet ... [to] have a firm basis for prosperity here."[163] Several media sources further advised Canadians to keep in mind the "importance in consolidating ... military victory through averting the unrest and possible chaos which might spread through Europe ... if tens of millions are left to starve and freeze."[164]

When asked near the end of the war if "for a year or two" after the conflict they would "continue to put up with shortages ... to give food to people who need it in Europe," 70 percent of Canadians surveyed responded that they would.[165] And they did get that opportunity. Butter rationing continued until early 1947, with allotments set at six ounces per week (although for a few months in late 1946 this dropped to four ounces). Between June 1945 and January 1946 the sugar ration was cut a further 10 percent to compensate for devastated crops in the Philippines and Java.[166] Undoubtedly most Canadians respected these levels. Indeed, by the end of 1945 some 250 organizations in Canada were raising money and sending millions of pounds of food and second-hand clothing to Europe. Yet in January 1946, to take one month at random, 176 people were convicted of breaking sugar and butter rationing rules, a figure that no doubt represented only a small fraction of actual violators, especially given the 20 percent reduction in WPTB Enforcement Branch personnel during the second half of 1945. Most infractions were minor, but not long after the war, authorities in Quebec City discovered a printing press being used to produce thousands of forged sugar ration coupons.[167]

An even greater challenge for the federal government was to secure compliance with meat rationing, which was reimplemented between September 1945 and early 1947, following record consumption during its suspension.[168] Only after winning another parliamentary majority in the June 1945 election was King ready to act on this issue. On 5 July his government announced plans to reintroduce meat rationing to help feed Europe. The next month, meatless Tuesdays and Fridays were applied to restaurants, the latter to minimize prejudice and to respond to earlier complaints from Catholics. However, a temporary shortage of cold-storage space delayed implementation of more general rationing until 9 September. The aim was to reduce annual per capita meat consumption to 130 pounds, a level comparable to that of the May 1943 ration order. A new token system was introduced to minimize waste. Coupons were issued for the value of one to three pounds of meat, depending upon the type purchased, but people did not have to buy the full amount because tokens worth between one and three ounces (again depending upon the meat involved) could be given as change.[169]

Many advocated even tighter meat rationing, considering the desperate situation overseas. A September 1945 poll showed 68 percent favouring or accepting meat rationing, whereas 23 percent were opposed and 9 percent expressed indecision. By the spring of 1946 some 88,000 coupons were voluntarily returned by citizens to the WPTB so that more meat could be sent to Europe.[170] However, it was clear from the millions of coupons distributed that nearly everyone was claiming a full allotment. Indeed, a substantial number of Canadians were tired of cutbacks or had become used to freedom from meat rationing. Many felt that Canada was already doing its part to help Europe, and may have heard the rumours that there was plenty of meat in cold storage.[171] Although the leadership of the Trades and Labour Congress and the Canadian Congress of Labour endorsed meat rationing, many workers in the labour movement did not. In late September, 9,000 coal miners in Alberta and British Columbia took a "holiday" and threatened to take more unless they received a "double ration of red meat." Compounding the situation for Ottawa was the fact that in October the American government, which considered peacetime meat rationing "unworkable," had initiated rapid decontrol to encourage production and quickly normalize supplies. Even though American prices immediately rose, Washington's decision led many Canadians to question Ottawa's approach.[172]

Purchasing War Savings Stamps from a "Miss Canada" volunteer, Ottawa, August 1942.
A.E. Armstrong, NAC PA-116109.

Demonizing the enemy to raise funds for the autumn 1943 Victory Bond campaign.
Harold V. Shaw, NAC C-091547.

Results from a more modest salvage drive pile up outside the Indian residential school at Kuper Island, British Columbia, June 1942. James Coleman, NAC PA-123244.

A cry from a lonely US Army engineer working on the Alaska Highway. Nicolas Morant, NAC PA-113213.

A sign above the production lines at the John Inglis plant in Montreal urges against absenteeism, November 1942. A. Armstrong, NAC PA-169532.

Servicemen and their wives searching for accommodation in wartime Halifax. National Film Board of Canada, NAC PA-116116.

Preparing a sidewalk at a Wartime Housing project in Vancouver, July 1943.
National Film Board of Canada. NAC PA-116150.

A WPTB poster urges Canadians to conserve. NAC C-074141.

The beginnings of coupon rationing, 1942. Montreal Gazette, NAC PA-198300. *Reprinted with permission of the* Montreal Gazette.

A Canadian sergeant in France examines photographs received from home. The always welcome cigarettes are nearby, also probably sent in the package. NAC C-042450.

Military personnel and civilians crowd a dance floor in Halifax, 1942. Malak, NAC PA-192943.

An army poster warns against pickups as a source of venereal disease. NAC PA-141001.

One of five female crane operators helping to produce anti-aircraft guns at the Westinghouse factory, Hamilton, Ontario, April 1942. National Film Board of Canada, NAC PA-116929.

A woman volunteer helps children wash their hands at a government-subsidized day nursery, Toronto, February 1943. National Film Board of Canada, NAC PA-112750.

Happy to be a housewife again? An unidentified woman and child, Montreal, February 1946. Andy Graetz, NAC PA-115226.

Members of the CWAC Laundry Unit, Carshalton, Surrey, England, August 1943. Jane Armstrong, NAC PA-129090.

CWAC personnel working as vehicle mechanics, Montreal, April 1942. Montreal Gazette, NAC PA-108273.

Trainees enter a gas hut at the No. 2 CWAC (Basic) Training Centre, Vermillion, Alberta. Ken Bell, NAC PA-141008.

A six-year-old British child evacuee holds up an ice cream cone and smiles for the camera soon after arriving in Canada, summer 1940. Montreal Gazette, NAC PA-167949. *Reprinted with permission of the* Montreal Gazette.

The "Little Happy Gang" in Moose Jaw, Saskatchewan, knits for the Canadian Red Cross Society, May 1940. Victor Bull, NAC C-053880.

*"Wait for me, Daddy." Five-year-old Warren chases after his father, Pte. Jack Bernard of the
Duke of Connaught's Own Rifles, who marches through the streets of New Westminster,
British Columbia, to board a ship to Nanaimo for further training. Warren remembered those
years as "pretty tramautic." The same was true for Jack who, in Normandy, was the sole
survivor among a tank crew hit by a German shell.* Claude P. Dettloff, NAC C-038723.
Reproduced with permission of Mrs. Joan Macpherson. Ottawa Citizen, 2 Sept. 1939, B6.

Children playing on the streets in the Moss Park district of Toronto, 1941. Gordon W. Powley, Archives of Ontario, C 5-1-32-0-1 (10002623).

A Canadian sergeant stocks up on wine in San Leonardo, Italy, December 1943. Frederick G. Whitcombe, NAC PA-131642.

The road to Caen, 15 July 1944. H/Captain Robert L. Seaborn, chaplain of the Canadian Scottish Regiment, prays over a casualty of the 3rd Canadian Infantry Division. Harold G. Aikman, NAC PA-142245.

A corporal with the No. 2 Canadian Provost Company warns about dangers other than those posed by the enemy, Normandy, August 1944. Michael M. Dean, NAC PA-131272.

Canadian soldiers and a Dutch woman, April 1945. Daniel Guravich, NAC PA-130965.

British troops clearing streets of debris following riots by Canadian soldiers in Aldershot, 6 July 1945. Harold D. Robinson, NAC PA-147117.

A French Canadian soldier reunites with his family at Lansdowne Park, Ottawa, 8 May 1945.
Department of National Defence, NAC PA-128248.

A war bride saws logs in the northern Ontario hamlet of Manitowaning, 1946.
Gordon W. Powley, Archives of Ontario, C 5-2-2-16-1 (10002897).

Veterans cram into a chemistry class at the University of Toronto, February 1947.
J.F. Miller, NAC C-049426.

Training as a welder with DVA assistance, April 1946. Jack Long, NAC PA-157252.

Meat producers protested. The Ontario Beef Cattle Producers' Association, for example, demanded that prices be allowed to rise more quickly or that export controls to the United States be lifted. Meat shop owners griped over the prolongation of low profits in peacetime, and found the new token system confusing and time-consuming.[173] In late September many meat shops closed down to protest rationing, often for several days, in major centres such as Victoria, Vancouver, Edmonton, Lethbridge, Calgary, Hamilton, Toronto, Saint John, and Halifax. This action was precipitated by a series of intense and widely publicized events in Montreal. On 24 September the owners of some hundred meat shops, several hundred of their employees, and other supporters, such as longshoremen who wanted greater meat allotments, marched through city streets demanding an end to rationing. The protestors "visited" several butcher shops and grocery stores to convince their owners to join this cause and destroyed the stocks of some who refused. On 27 September the protestors attempted to close down the downtown Eaton's store, one of the city's citadels of business, an offensive that resulted in fifty-five arrests. Although Eaton's remained open, the protestors did manage to deflate the tires of ten Canada Packers trucks to prevent meat from reaching consumers. On the next day, in a mêlée after another protest march, demonstrators overturned several meat trucks. Seventy-three people were arrested and three were sent to the hospital, including a policeman with a fractured skull.[174]

Meat shop owners and butchers were hardly immune to the widespread tendency to disregard the ration rules. They earned extra cash by reselling tokens, since tokens were not assigned to a specific ration book. This practice was encouraged by the general knowledge that overworked WPTB investigators did not bother pursuing small discrepancies between coupons and tokens collected and recorded meat sales.[175] The Toronto Retail Grocers' Association, at its May 1946 meeting, described the meat black market as "still assuming alarming proportions."[176] Around the same time, a report in the Montreal *Gazette* confirmed what countless consumers already knew: three of four butchers offered to sell rationed meat at illegal prices to a reporter posing as a shopper. Also in mid-1946 an exasperated manager with Montreal's Canada Packers plant complained to the WPTB that 75 percent of the meat sold in the city came through black markets. Fuming over the impossibility of acquiring adequate stock through legal means, and at the prospect of being forced to implement a shorter workweek for his employees, the manager asked indignantly, "Are we just going to sit back and wait until the situation has been straightened out by heavier volume eventually coming on the market?"[177]

Although it was not publicly acknowledged, the federal government's inaction strongly suggested that this was indeed its strategy. Ottawa seemed prepared to ride out the storm, satisfied that most people were obeying the law and that existing enforcement efforts still served as a deterrent. Since supply problems would certainly soon dissipate, a crackdown in peacetime seemed unwarranted and risked generating a political backlash.

To MANY AMONG THE MAJORITY of the population who supported and respected the rules, and to numerous authorities, especially those within the WPTB who devised and enforced them, the degree of dissent and cheating in wartime Canada appeared alarming. To numerous Canadians the war remained distant, not just logistically but also psychologically, and critics charged that as such it was not being approached with the appropriate sense of urgency. Despite overall compliance, after 1942 a growing proportion of Canadians quietly condoned or participated in bending or breaking the rules to obtain a little extra luxury, especially as they grew increasingly confident of victory overseas. By the time rationing was imposed, many people felt that they had already sacrificed plenty by way of record taxes and Victory Bond purchases. Many Canadians bristled against the creation of a vast WPTB enforcement network, in large part because they thought it would label otherwise patriotic citizens – perhaps even themselves – as criminals for breaking what were perceived to be petty regulations. In fact the WPTB did not seek to prosecute violators en masse precisely in order to secure public support. Meanwhile, having become embedded in wartime Canada, black markets continued after hostilities ceased, sometimes with veterans as prime targets, and despite calls to help combat starvation overseas.

Ultimately, real concerns about moral decline were fuelled by more than the black marketeering, rent gouging, charity scams, strikes, and complaints from Canadians over the sacrifices they were asked or compelled to make. To many, these patterns were just one facet of a wide-ranging threat to community standards apparently related to wartime conditions – a conclusion derived from concurrent perceptions of rampant promiscuity, women abandoning femininity and family life, and ill-governed youth turning to delinquency.

5
(Im)moral Matters

"OUR ILLEGITIMACY, our promiscuity, our venereal disease, our separation ... are all at new highs. We have to take the responsibility ... for the whirlwind we have sown." So declared Charlotte Whitton, the conservative-minded social policy analyst for the Canadian Welfare Council, at the group's 1944 annual conference in Niagara Falls.[1] Hers was by no means a lone voice in wartime Canada. Many Canadians had begun to decry the evidence that the war had proven a "great releaser" insofar as morality was concerned.[2] While there was some substance to these apprehensions, it is also true that the Canada of those years was a milieu where current attitudes easily led to talk of moral crisis. It was a place where, in the strongly French Canadian town of Eastview just outside Ottawa, the police chief could be roundly criticized for opposing a bylaw prohibiting women over fourteen from wearing shorts in public. It was a place where after some "solemn" debate in 1939 the city council of "Toronto the Good" declared it permissible to kiss in public following complaints about displays of affection between couples as servicemen prepared to ship out.[3] It was a place where divorce was scandalous. In Quebec and Prince Edward Island there were no divorce courts; couples who wanted to end their marriage were forced to petition for a private member's bill in Parliament. Since grounds for divorce were excruciatingly narrow – only bigamy, desertion, and adultery – many couples were forced to have a private detective photograph a staged extramarital affair. In Quebec, where the Catholic Church held tremendous sway, only men had the right to pursue a divorce, even when their own adultery was involved.[4] As the war went on, however, Canadians had to revise their attitudes to the reality of new standards of behaviour.

WARTIME MARRIAGES were considered risky. As soon as war broke out, the marriage rate in Canada almost doubled; while the aggregate number of marriages in July and August 1939 was 16,879, in September and October it shot up to 31,103. In the days immediately following Britain's declaration of war, Toronto's *Globe and Mail* reported: "So great was the rush that [the] City Clerk ... was forced to post a guard on the door leading to the [marriage] bureau." In Winnipeg the *Free Press* told of officials having to make an emergency trip to the Vital Statistics Branch to obtain extra marriage licences.[5] That trend continued throughout most of the war, although at a less frantic pace. While the marriage rate per 1,000 people averaged 7.9 over 1937 and 1938, it reached 10.2 per 1,000 between 1939 and 1943 before dropping to 8.75 during the final two years of the war. The birth rate followed suit, rising from 20.6 to 24.2 per 1,000 women between 1939 and 1943 before dipping slightly to 24.15 over 1944 and 1945.[6]

Many couples who had put off marrying during the Depression because of financial difficulties found their situation improved. Both partners perhaps had better-paying and steady war jobs, and the enlistment of men also often gave a couple a new source of income through the dependants' allowance program. Passed in August 1939, this government grant was initially pro-rated up to the level of a wife and three children, and paid between $35 and $69 monthly to the spouses of noncommissioned personnel. Because the rates of these grants were substantially lower than those paid to officers' wives, and because noncommissioned personnel were assumed to come from a lower economic class, enlisted men were also required – while officers were only "encouraged"– to assign half their pay to their wives, usually about $20 to $25 monthly.[7]

On a psychological or emotional level, marriage gave couples a tangible sign of commitment that they hoped would sustain them through what could be a long and lonely separation. Some men heading into action said that having a wife awaiting their return home helped strengthen their determination to prevail through whatever lay ahead. There were also women who married on the spur of the moment, fearing that they might be too old to find a mate by the time the war ended. Many young people felt that in these uncertain times they should grab at any chance for happiness and therefore grew more disposed, or according to critics, susceptible, to being carried away by the intense feelings generated by whirlwind wartime romances.[8]

The escalation of wartime marriages soon sparked considerable concern over the stability and sanctity of unions cemented by such quick trips to the altar. As early as December 1939 there were reports of clerics refusing to conduct ceremonies for what they saw as hasty, ill-conceived marriages certain to end in divorce. George Antheil, advice columnist for the *Halifax Chronicle,* admonished his readers, "Marriage is too serious a step to be taken on as a sort of farewell gesture between a boy and girl who have merely indulged in a light flirtation."[9] Some couples defended themselves, claiming that in wartime, pressures of an impending departure stripped away "superficial social barriers," thus allowing people to get to know each other better in a "six week engagement" than, as one writer sneeringly put it, "Great-aunt Maria did after a six year courtship with Great-uncle Albert arriving Sundays to sit primarily on the horsehair sofa for the conventional number of hours." Many empathized, but to many more such claims rang hollow. The publicly voiced consensus was that, with time and separation, the feelings generated by brief and passionate romances would soon wane. Also, such actions cheapened marriage. How could people who had acted so impulsively stay loyal to each other during years apart? Even if such relationships endured the war, many of them were predicted to fail once couples tested their compatibility in day-to-day routines where character flaws would not be so easily overlooked. Eleanor Dare, in her column for the *Canadian Home Journal,* advised her single female readers that if a serviceman's love were genuine, he would put off marriage until the war ended and conduct himself "honourably in the interim" – a comment reflecting the observation that some men used the promise of marriage just as a means to obtain sex.[10]

Skepticism arose about other motives for matrimony as well. Early in the war some marriages were undertaken to avoid military service, as the rules initially stipulated that men who were married by 15 July 1940 were exempt from conscription for home defence. In Sherbrooke, Quebec, for instance, so many weddings took place on the final weekend before the cut-off date that jewellers ran out of wedding rings![11] Women were criticized for being driven by superficial considerations such as the "excitement of a hurry up, furlough wedding" or the "enjoyment in having the spotlight that is turned on a war bride."[12] Some judged women to be motivated by financial self-interest, marrying only for the dependant's allowance or even marrying several times under different names in order to collect multiple cheques. *Maclean's* reported that Irene Murial Vivian Hornby was sentenced to four years in jail for marrying four different soldiers.[13]

MANY OBSERVERS OF THE TIMES linked hasty wartime unions to another worrying trend: increased wartime divorce. Despite narrowly defined grounds for divorce and difficult administrative procedures, the divorce numbers rose from 14.4 per 100,000 in 1936 to 20.8 in 1940 and to 27.7 in 1943. In aggregate terms, the numbers remained modest, rising from 2,068 in 1939 to 3,089 in 1942 and to 3,778 in 1944. Nevertheless, as early as 1941 *Saturday Night* felt it appropriate to characterize divorce as an "infant industry," reflecting concerns over the apparently declining respect for marriage and the institution's growing instability.[14]

A related trend was the notable wartime increase in spousal and family desertion, as measured by charges for "non-support of family and neglecting children," which increased from 1,547 to 2,546 between 1938 and 1941 and then stabilized around that higher level for the remainder of the war.[15] Trying to put a positive spin on the picture, some said that the war gave people in bad marriages an excuse to obtain a "respectful" separation.[16] But not all separations were mutual. Husbands sometimes enlisted to escape family responsibilities, although their numbers do not show up in statistics, but most of the women they left behind were then at least provided with a dependant's allowance. Canada's burgeoning war economy also made it easier for men to desert their wives and families to take work in another part of the country. Provincial governments provided inadequate resources to track down marital deserters and, at best, had rudimentary structures in place for sharing information on such men.[17] Deserted women with children could, like widows with dependants, apply for a provincial mother's allowance, though it took up to two years after the initial desertion to qualify for the money. Although compensation differed among the provinces, the common denominator was inadequate support. In 1941 the mother's allowance in Ontario, which corresponded to the national average, was $480 per year, or 44 percent of what the Toronto Welfare Council then identified as the minimum level to support an "average family."[18]

ATTRACTING FAR MORE ATTENTION than desertion as a cause of increased wartime divorce was the view that fidelity might not withstand the strain of loneliness and long separations. A whole industry grew up around keeping people in touch with each other. Realizing that some spouses and sweethearts were even worried about forgetting what their loved ones looked like, companies like Kodak encouraged couples to send each other photographs. At some leave centres in England, servicemen could make a phonograph recording to send home. To do its bit, the CBC in early 1941 started to produce weekly half-hour radio broadcasts called *With the Troops in England.* In another program of the time entitled *Comrades in Arms,* men could line up to state their name and hometown and send a brief encouraging message to loved ones they hoped would be listening when the show was rebroadcast in Canada.[19]

For almost everyone, however, letters remained the sole means of international communication. Given the importance of mail to morale both at home and abroad, the federal government hired thousands of civilians in Canada and Britain to cope with the deluge of transatlantic correspondence and packages. To speed up delivery, airmail service was introduced in 1941 along with the new airgraph: for six cents, a writer could compose a letter on a letter-sized page that was then microfilmed for transport and enlarged to 4.5 by 5.5 inches upon arrival in England or Canada.[20] To minimize the disruption in long-distance dialogue that resulted from letters arriving out of order, couples frequently numbered their correspondence. However, a lost ship or a plane, a misdirected letter, poor weather, or mechanical difficulties could disrupt the flow, sometimes for months.[21] Men overseas commonly told those at home not to fret over gaps in their correspondence. "I was very relieved to hear that you are finally getting my letters because I could tell that you were becoming very worried," an army captain fighting in northwest Europe wrote to his wife. "However, darling, if and when it happens again, I hope you won't be too alarmed ... Even if you don't hear from me you'll know I'm alright because if anything did happen ... you would be immediately notified."[22]

Even a postal system operating at peak efficiency could never make up for the absence of loved ones. "How can you make love through the mail," complained one wife who had been left behind for only three months.[23] Sometimes letters worsened matters, especially since delays were known to aggravate misunderstandings and suspicions. "Things are bound to happen sometimes ... when an ocean divides us and letters are misinterpreted," wrote a woman to her husband, in suggesting that they choose their words with care. "What one writes down is not always what one intends to say and a written sentence can often suggest a different meaning to one spoken, where the inflection of the voice and perhaps the smile alters the meaning."[24] Women were told that it was their duty to write cheerful letters to keep up the morale of Canada's fighting men. *Chatelaine* gave the following advice to readers who felt moved to express their despair: Write the letter and then "tear it into dozens of small shreds [because] you'll get the same sense of relief you would have if you sent it and you'll be in a better mood tomorrow ... to sit down and write a perfectly swell letter." An advertisement in the *Toronto Star* offered women a booklet containing over twenty model letters designed to entertain and lift the spirits of a husband or boyfriend in the military – and, it ominously added, to prevent them from turning elsewhere for comfort.[25]

In trying to emphasize the positive, several columnists recounted stories of couples in relationships that had grown stale or sour before the war who had, after being separated, rediscovered in each other their "heart's desire."[26] But it was also true that many wives and girlfriends became lonely, irritable and depressed. Many took on volunteer or paid work to keep themselves busy. For companionship, some moved back home with their parents or listened to the radio every evening. Of her first weekend home alone, one woman sadly wrote to her husband, "This is the first Saturday night, and I am afraid the beginning of many ... that I find myself ... with not so much as a dickybird to talk to." Another admitted to her husband that some of her friends with spouses overseas "drowned their sorrows in liquor."[27] One analysis of 100 servicemen's wives undertaken by researchers at the University of Chicago found that two-thirds experienced "moderate to severe loneliness," while 29 percent reported "symptoms of nervousness, irritability, restlessness, insomnia, loss of interest, feeling subdued or feeling older."[28]

Suspicion aggravated matters for Canadian women. Returning servicemen or men who were sent home wounded often told stories about Canadians screwing around overseas.[29] Potential confirmation was provided by the more than 8,000 Canadians who had taken a British war bride by the end of 1942. Grace Craig, for example, though married nearly twenty years when her husband went overseas to serve as a staff officer in England, feared her inability to "hold him" and thus reacted strongly to any hint of unfaithfulness. "You speak of a nation 'in a state of adolescence' and another 'in a state of adultery.' Please expound," she demanded. "One hears such tales about the women over there ... One woman told me she believed that half the married men with the Canadian Army were no longer corresponding with their wives. Surely the English women aren't as fascinating as all that!"[30]

Several groups, including the YWCA, the Victorian Order of Nurses, the Catholic Women's League of Canada, the Federation of Jewish Philanthropies, and military groups such as the Naval Wives' Auxiliary undertook to help the spouses of servicemen experiencing emotional and family problems, and, in some cases, financial difficulties. One of the most active was the Montreal Soldiers' Wives' League (MSWL), which had been founded in 1899 to perform this role during the Boer

War. In the Second World War it was involved in such activities as lectures, concerts, cooking lessons, and beauty sessions, as well as offering a place where women whose men were in uniform could commiserate with each other and do patriotic work. By June 1943 its volunteers had also made 191,452 home visits. Besides lending a sympathetic ear, they sometimes arranged for emergency financial assistance in cases of family illness, when a woman was left with large debts, and particularly during the one-month period when wives waited for their first dependant's allowance cheque. In publicizing its efforts, the MSWL quoted letters from servicemen, such as a private with the Signals Corps who wrote, "Since I received your letter letting me know how well you have been helping my wife ... I have felt much better and I want you to know how much I appreciate it."[31]

MSWL visits also had other purposes. In many cases they and other such groups made home visits because of accusations, rumours, or suspicions that a wife was not behaving herself in her husband's absence. Certainly the war encouraged adultery and permitted many to escape intolerable marriages. Some women felt perfectly justified in straying. "I knew what he was doing over there," said a woman from Winnipeg about her husband in England. "I'd have been a fool if I didn't, so I had a right to live my own life too."[32] As the memory of those overseas grew hazy, many women turned to servicemen still in Canada, to the more exotic men who came over as part of the British Commonwealth Air Training Plan (BCATP), or to civilians too old or unfit to fight. Enough "Dear John" letters were dispatched to prompt the men on board one destroyer to start a "TS [tough shit] club."[33] In most cases, the signs were more subtle. "The ... letters just kept coming, but they weren't like they had been," recalled one soldier. "They were friendly letters ... Before she had been writing love letters ... [Then] she described a wonderful party she'd been at and ... there was a couple of references to a guy she'd met ... When I looked back at it later, that was the first of the friendly letters."[34]

Although wartime infidelity is impossible to quantify, as historian Magda Fahrni writes, it is "safe to assume that anxiety [over women straying] was more common than actual instances of adultery." Nonetheless, such concern fed "a larger discourse of disloyalty" and inflicted considerable and often unjustified pain upon Canadian women.[35] Investigations were frequently launched after accusations reached servicemen from family, friends, and neighbours in Canada. A request for an investigation into a wife's conduct proceeded through a serviceman's commanding officer. If it emanated from overseas, it was first filed with Canadian Military Headquarters in London, then relayed to the Department of National Defence in Ottawa, which sent it on to the Dependants' Allowance Board (DAB), which in turn paid a small fee to a local social service agency to look into the matter. Among those interviewed were family members, neighbours, relatives, and friends, as deemed appropriate. Even if such inquiries uncovered nothing salacious, they undoubtedly caused many a woman a great deal of embarrassment and a besmirched reputation.[36]

While husbands and boyfriends in uniform liberally sowed their wild oats without consequence, women realized that they had to keep their behaviour beyond reproach. Many went out in public only with female friends and never accepted male callers. Several marriages were destroyed because of the slightest transgressions. "My husband was away in the Signals Corps," recalled one woman. "I went to a dance once in a while at the Y. My dad always objected, and I could see why later on ... Things went wrong when someone wrote to tell my husband about me. There was no need ... I just loved to dance ... We split up after a while."[37] One army chaplain, distraught by the number of marriages he saw being maliciously sabotaged, claimed, "At least half the tittle-tattle in letters to soldiers ... is groundless." For instance, one soldier's mother-in-law tried to end her daughter's marriage to a man she herself detested by maligning her own daughter's reputation.[38]

Many servicemen were inclined to jump to conclusions and believe the worst about what was transpiring back home, no doubt in part because they had witnessed so much cheating amongst their comrades. A 1945 survey of American troops overseas with "a girl at home" revealed that approximately one-third doubted her faithfulness.[39] If an investigation launched for a Canadian serviceman discovered anything inappropriate, he would frequently ignore advice from military chaplains and instruct that his wife's dependant's allowance be cut off immediately, without waiting for her explanation. Several divorces were initiated by servicemen through lawyers assigned by the judge advocate general's office. In an effort to preserve marriages, George Davidson, the executive director of the Canadian Welfare Council, advised R.G. Bennett, the chair of the DAB, that damaging information should not be sent to a serviceman until his wife had been given a chance to explain to him what happened and, if necessary, to ask for his forgiveness. Davidson also recommended a three-month cooling-off period before a serviceman be permitted to cut off his wife's dependant's allowance, claiming that such retributive action irreparably damaged many marriages.[40] But Bennett maintained that men who were making sacrifices for home and country had the right to be informed promptly of any conjugal deception and, in light of that information, to direct their money as they saw fit. Some investigators, mostly women, also concluded that full disclosure was not always the best approach – when the wife was "truly repentant" for a brief fling, for example. However, those running the DAB in Ottawa, nearly all of whom were men and often Great War veterans, tended to approach their task as advocates for servicemen and as protectors of taxpayers' funds, with which they didn't want to support the deceitful.[41]

When the allowance of a wife with children was cut off, she was often further penalized by having the portion of the grant designated for the children placed under the administrative control of a person named by the serviceman or an organization such as the Children's Aid Society. Moreover, even though the allowance for the children was raised in compensation, the overall monetary support received by the family declined – for instance, a mother with two children lost 10 percent – thus forcing many women into the workforce and often compounding their problems with accusations of child neglect. In some cases, especially when a woman's illicit relationship continued, her children were removed by authorities.

When investigators discovered an illegitimate child, the serviceman was given three months to decide whether he was prepared to stay married, accept the child as his own, and request a supplemental dependant's allowance – though approval of the extra payment was by no means guaranteed.[42] When a baby's delivery date indicated that a woman had conceived after her husband's departure, investigators were sometimes begged not to inform the husband because the wife planned to put the child up for adoption. Some investigators were sympathetic, especially since they feared that a woman might otherwise have recourse to an illegal abortion. But these transgressions were almost always reported to the DAB, which maintained that a husband had the right to know, even when the investigator disagreed. Such was the case with a wife found to be "providing good care" to her legitimate child, while an illegitimate child conceived during a brief fling had died shortly after birth. The investigator maintained that little good would come from disclosing all the facts to the husband overseas, but the board stuck by its policy, and as things turned out, the woman's allowance was discontinued and the soldier soon filed for a divorce.[43]

ANXIETY OVER WARTIME ILLEGITIMACY was not confined to the wives of servicemen. Certainly the aggregate statistics appeared worrisome. The number of recorded cases of illegitimacy rose from the 1930-32 average of 8,295 to a 1940-42 average of 10,266, and then climbed to 11,944 in 1943 and 12,409 in 1944. Illegitimate births actually peaked in 1945 and 1946 at 12,937 and 13,595 respectively, perhaps because veterans continued to play the field once back home or because many intense postwar reunions did not lead to marriage. Comparing 1930-32 to 1940-42, the rate rose fastest among those aged twenty-five to twenty-nine (from 13.5 to 17.1 percent of the total), and those aged thirty to thirty-four (from 5.9 to 7.4 percent), a pattern suggesting that war-related separations were indeed the cause of infidelity within many war marriages. However, when considered as a ratio of total live births, wartime illegitimacy appears less alarming. It rose from an average of 3.95 percent between 1936 and 1940 to 3.96 percent in 1941, and to a wartime high of 4.07 percent in 1942.[44] These figures were dampened by rising fertility rates, and they do not take into account illegal and unrecorded abortions, which were said to have risen during the war years. Still, as a number of social workers pointed out, many illegitimate children were born to women who insisted that a wedding would have occurred had the father known about the baby before his departure.[45]

Whatever the circumstances of illegitimacy, they typically made no difference to the portrayal and treatment of the mothers, who were regarded as "fallen women." Unless they were widowed, or divorced as a result of desertion or an adulterous or bigamous husband, they were refused a mother's allowance because it was believed that financial support would condone and reward their immoral conduct. Most commentary on illegitimacy, stemming from attitudes typical of the double standard, blamed the woman. Men, socially constructed as aggressors, were expected to pursue women; women, portrayed as more virtuous, were expected to maintain restraint and decorum. The mother of an illegitimate child had the right to launch a legal suit for child support against the alleged father, but the success rate was low, especially since paternity tests did not exist. When it came to taking action against military personnel, the complainant had to indicate where the man was likely to be found and the circumstances of their relationship, to demonstrate the likelihood of paternity. Such information was furnished to the appropriate military authorities, but precious few claims led to any monetary support. Typically, the man's denial sufficed to have the matter dropped, as the military wanted men to focus on their duties and appeared to share the view that mothers of illegitimate children had only themselves to blame.[46]

INFIDELITY AND ILLEGITIMACY were but one social consequence of the large numbers of military personnel in Canadian society. Countless Canadians wished to demonstrate their patriotic support for those in uniform. When soldiers from 331 units stationed across Canada were canvassed in May 1944, only 12 percent said that civilians had failed to do something "substantial" to increase their comfort.[47] The benefits were mutual. Military camps generated significant economic activity, and bases in outlying areas became social centres, especially for young women. (In larger communities, places such as the Red Triangle and Red Shield clubs to some extent served the same function.) The military drew in top-flight entertainers for morale-raising concerts to which civilians were often invited. People flocked to watch parades and war games, military tattoos, track and field meets, and boxing and wrestling tournaments.[48] Military athletic teams often took the place of professional squads, as by the early 1940s both the Canadian Football and the Canadian-American Baseball Leagues had suspended operations for the duration of the war. Among professional sports, only the National Hockey League continued. The federal government believed that keeping "Canada's game" going would serve to boost morale, though many citizens criticized the players for trying to evade military service. Soon, however, many fans concluded that the best hockey was not being played in the NHL, but rather by military teams across Canada, which ultimately were manned by more than 200 top-flight amateurs and 130 former professionals.[49]

The relationship between civilians and the military also had less positive aspects. Air base commanders often received complaints about daredevil pilots buzzing low over farms and frightening animals or testing their skills in urban areas by flying under bridges, among other feats. In 1941, of the 170 fatal training accidents in the BCATP, 40 were attributed to "low acrobatics and low flying."[50] Civilians also protested about the reckless driving of servicemen showing off in heavy military vehicles.[51] Even when such vehicles travelled at low speeds, they tended to tear up city streets at a time when available material and labour were inadequate to make repairs in a timely manner. Some people also found the loud, round-the-clock clatter of military traffic nerve-racking. In several communities, the presence of servicemen aggravated the strain on local facilities. Not all citizens gracefully accepted the fact that it often became virtually impossible to find a seat at a restaurant or movie theatre; with public transportation at full capacity, car drivers often became impatient with servicemen haranguing them for rides.[52]

The crowding was probably most extreme in Halifax. One former member of the Royal Canadian Navy recalled that many of his comrades used their four-day passes on the twenty-hour rail journey to Montreal rather than stay in Halifax where everything was jammed, "even the sidewalks." Exacerbating matters was the fact that in this long-time garrison town, servicemen were such a familiar sight that they were not greeted with the same outward enthusiasm as in many other places; there were numerous remarks about "stand-offish" civilians and "shop-keepers interested solely in ... earnings."[53] Access to alcohol was another source of friction. Although some sailors sold booze on the black market if the price was right, many more fumed over the absence of public drinking establishments, and their exclusion from private civilian clubs whose members they accused of hoarding stock. The 1942 closing of the Ajax Club further poisoned the atmosphere, especially with the few remaining wet canteens continually jammed and often running short of supplies. By 1944 Halifax's mayor, Joe Lloyd, had to admit that antagonism between numerous civilians and service personnel was "strong and mutual." Indeed there can be little doubt that the VE day riot in Halifax, when more than 1,000 naval personnel led the looting of some 500 stores and the theft of 65,000 quarts of booze, was not triggered simply by the 8:00 p.m. closing times that hampered their ability to obtain a celebratory drink or meal. Rather, it derived largely from the desire for revenge on a community toward which resentment had been building for years.[54]

Well before that event, however, many civilians had realized that the tough military training regimen produced more than a desirable esprit de corps. The minimum four months of training in Canada unfortunately also produced many men with a pent-up need to cut loose from drills, route marches, inspections, picayune regulations, shouting NCOs, spartan living conditions and, in some cases, isolated bases.[55] Many men had been drafted under the National Resources Mobilization Act. Besides loathing their compulsory service, after mid-1941 these conscripts were forced to train alongside volunteers who sometimes subjected them to verbal and even physical attacks, and with superiors who gave them an especially rough ride to pressure them to switch to active service.[56] In any case, as one soldier described the leaves of trainees in general, it was like "tying up a dog and then letting him loose; he'll run all over the place."[57] Sailors were particularly eager for release in coastal communities after patrolling in cramped vessels for weeks, or returning from unnerving convoys across the rough, frigid, and U-boat-infested waters of the North

Atlantic. Montreal and various east coast cities received air force pilots on leave after the hazardous task of ferrying airplanes across the Atlantic or conducting antisubmarine warfare as part of Eastern Air Command; in Edmonton, pilots needed to relax after their harrowing flights to and from Alaska. No doubt many BCATP trainees also felt the same, particularly new pilots, whose courses included tasks like night flying and formation flying in "tricky, unforgiving Harvards." Casualty rates were high for training, and washout rates were higher, especially as the need to speed up the graduation of pilots resulted in shorter and more intense courses.[58]

Recreational services at military bases helped men get exercise and vent tension and frustration, but many servicemen needed other outlets for their energies. Indeed, a 1943 survey taken by the Army Research and Information Section among 900 men stationed at five advanced training centres in Canada revealed that 39 percent of them thought "much" or "most" of the free time spent on bases was "boring."[59] In addition, since most servicemen were young, single, and away from home for the first time, they were apt to be adventuresome and have few responsibilities. Even many of those who were married with families revelled in the chance to relive their bachelorhood or lost youth when they were on leave. Almost like tourists, many servicemen changed into different personalities when visiting new places, doing wild things they would not do under normal circumstances and believing that they could leave all the consequences behind.

The tendency toward intense activity was also heightened by the shortness – typically forty-eight hours – of most leaves. Men commonly blew whatever money they had accumulated, being assured of food and shelter by the military. Moreover, the masculine conduct often encouraged by military culture linked the tough and domineering "manliness" expected of servicemen to hard drinking, brawling, and womanizing. This behaviour was a means of establishing a reputation among fellow servicemen and bonding with them. The habit of those in uniform of peppering their language with excessive profanity, in which sexual innuendoes were prominent, was more than simply a tension reliever; it was also means of demonstrating strength, virility, and freedom from the restraints of civilian life.[60] Such patterns were further encouraged in wartime by men thinking it appropriate to live for the moment, or feeling a need to demonstrate their toughness and their readiness for the challenges that lay ahead – including, if need be, killing.

In throwing caution to the winds, numerous servicemen gambled excessively and often quite publicly, their favourite games typically being poker, craps, and Crown and Anchor. But a far more significant concern for a public worried about the corrupting influence of alcohol was the high number of offences for drunk and disorderly conduct. Under military law, this offence could cost a serviceman a maximum of three months' pay and a month's incarceration with hard labour. However, given the prevalence of such behaviour, the need to maintain manpower, and the adverse effects on morale that would result from punishing large numbers of men, the general practice was only to issue warnings, to take away privileges, or, for repeat offenders, to issue small fines. These responses naturally limited the deterrent effect of the regulations.[61] Many young men, often below the legal drinking age of twenty-one, were initiated to alcohol in the military and, typical of inexperienced drinkers, imbibed excessively in what they saw as a rite of passage into manhood. Base newspapers often joked admiringly about the ability of tough military men to consume vast quantities of alcohol no matter its strength. As an entry in the *Foothills' Fliers,* distributed at the No. 3 Service Flying Training School in Airdrie, Alberta, quipped, "Liquor is said to be over proof if it contains enough alcohol to: a. Dissolve silver; b. Burst into flames; c. Measure at least 50% by volume; d. Remain liquid down to 60° below Fahrenheit." Military personnel expressed anger at civilian groups who opposed wet canteens, and surveys showed that military morale was lower where only dry canteens were available.[62]

According to an August 1943 army report, the combined monthly incidence of drunk and disorderly conduct among troops in Ottawa and Hull stood at 13.5 per 1,000. In a twelve-day period in January 1942 selected at random from the War Diary of the Canadian Provost Corps in Ottawa, the following entries relating to drunkenness appear:

Two drunken soldiers arrested in St. Charles Hotel

Four drunken soldiers arrested by the Hull Police Department for smashing windows, etc. at the Frontenac Hotel

One drunken soldier removed from the Belle Claire Hotel

British Café called that a drunken soldier had broken water glasses

Called to stop a fight at the Cdn. Tea Room in Lower Town. Two arrests for drunkenness and fighting and resisting arrest

The Station Patrol arrested a drunken soldier in Union Station

Called by neighbours to arrest a drunk soldier at an address on Gladstone Avenue

A soldier who was AWL and drunk was arrested in the Vendome Hotel

One drunken man was arrested in Lafayette Hotel

Ottawa Police reported a soldier drunk on Margrove St. Wagon Patrol arrested this soldier

Wagon Patrol called to arrest a drunken soldier in Chez Lee Restaurant

One drunken soldier arrested in Dunkerque Hotel

One drunken soldier arrested in Victoria Hotel

The Bank Street Patrol arrested a drunken soldier carousing in the street.[63]

Yet servicemen in Ottawa and Hull were by no means the worst offenders. In Sherbrooke, where men complained about inadequate recreational facilities, the rate for drunk and disorderly conduct was 24.6 per 1,000. Until it was closed down, the Ajax Club in Halifax was the subject of numerous complaints from civilians, especially women, who were hassled or propositioned by sailors sloshed on beer that sold for ten cents a pint.[64]

In virtually every community where servicemen regularly spent leave time, taverns were temporarily declared "off limits" after drunken brawls. These stemmed from men blowing off steam, showing off their personal prowess, or boasting about the fighting spirit of their regiment, service branch, or even country. Canadians in uniform not only picked fights with each other but also took on visitors from other Allied nations. Brawling was often caused by competition for women. Air force personnel were resented for their reputation among women as the most dashing of the military. Scraps involving rivalry also occurred with civilians. The fact that civilians, unlike servicemen, did not have special clubs where they could take women put them at a double disadvantage, since women generally found servicemen more sexually appealing as well.[65]

Perhaps the most serious single incident of male rivalry occurred in 1944 in Moose Jaw, Saskatchewan. Local civilian men, some of whom were too young to fight or were desperately needed on farms, had come to loathe airmen at the No. 32 Service Flying Training School; not only did they appear condescending, but they lured young women away to dances from which civilians were excluded. The airmen, many of whom were British, openly questioned the manliness of the civilians, laying themselves open to being taunted as "limey bastards." On 9 September, fighting broke out between the two sides and continued sporadically for five nights. During the worst of them, on 12 September, some 200 airmen left a dance and combed city streets and parks following rumours that eight of their comrades had been beaten up by a mob of civilians. Fortunately, fights that erupted in various parts of the community were promptly broken up by military and civilian authorities, as it was discovered that several participants on both sides carried such weapons as homemade billies, chains, lead pipes, and in one case a "large jack-knife."[66]

The inundation of towns and cities with military personnel also raised public apprehension over sexual impropriety. Inexperienced adolescents desperately sought to lose their virginity to affirm their manhood, to shed embarrassment, or to experience sex before going off to face the uncertainties of war. To them, women were often solely sex objects. And many servicemen, subscribing to the image of the tough, virile military man, thought themselves not only protectors of women, but also their conquerors and predators.[67] One air force recruit, writing from Winnipeg to a civilian friend in Toronto, boasted, "I've already got my steady piece here. The bitch says she loves me ... She's really solid." A couple of weeks later, after running into a mutual acquaintance, he wrote, "We got pissed two nights in a row. Next, Bob got his joint kopped by an old whore about 40 years old and also got laid by another one and threw her out of the hotel room after he was through with her about 4 a.m. I had quite a few workouts, but with different women. We really gave that hotel room bed hell."[68]

Public anxiety was also aroused by the not unfounded belief that young women desperately wanted to date men in uniform, who seemed more handsome, courageous, noble, and manly. To attract the attention of such a man was an ego boost for many women; adolescents especially became the envy of their friends if they had such a relationship. Alarmist accounts abounded that portrayed women as camp followers hanging around military bases and relentlessly pursuing service-men, or even rationalizing sex with those in uniform as a patriotic gift to men facing a hazardous future. Parents were admonished to keep a close watch over potentially wayward daughters. Most often, however, women seemed to need pro-tection from servicemen. For example, one Ottawa father frantically phoned the police because two drunken soldiers who had been rebuffed by his daughters, one of whom was just fifteen, stood outside the house shouting that the girls were "cocksuckers."[69] In Edmonton, teachers at both the Victoria and Commercial High Schools complained about "troops molesting and annoying girls." Routine orders also warned soldiers in Edmonton of "severe disciplinary action" following re-ports about men on "main thoroughfares ... physically impeding the way of women, grabbing them by the arm," and harassing them for dates.[70] Not surprisingly, dances arranged for men on bases by service groups were highly "controlled affairs." Be-fore one dance sponsored by the YMCA for those at the army training facility in Debert, Nova Scotia, the young women – daughters of service club men who were "thoroughly vouched for" – gathered at the club's building in town to board buses for the camp. Once at the site of the dance, "no young ladies were permitted to leave the building" until the event ended and the "motor buses call[ed] for them."[71] At other dances, servicemen were permitted to walk women home, but were clocked out and given a specified time to return. Also at such affairs, while popular tunes like Glen Miller's "Moonlight Serenade" no doubt stoked romantic fires among many couples swaying cheek to cheek, dance organizers seeking to contain pas-sions sometimes banned jitterbugging because many of the moves were thought to demonstrate "disregard for modesty."[72]

INCREASED PROSTITUTION was another side effect of the large numbers of service-men in Canadian towns. The battle to retain moral standards in wartime Canada and, as many emphasized, to protect servicemen from "diseased women" was also waged on this front. Venereal disease was a huge problem for the military; at its peak in 1940, one man in eighteen was infected. Through much of the war, VD cost the Canadian military stationed in Canada more absentee days than any other ailment, including influenza (Figure 5.1).[73] To control VD, some Canadians argued in favour of legal, regulated brothels where "employees" would be medically examined at regular intervals and certified to be disease-free. This idea was over-whelmingly condemned as such establishments were viewed as a moral and medi-cal scourge. The Canadian Council on Social Development claimed that in France, where regulated brothels existed, doctors did not have time to examine women frequently enough and, reflecting the criminal activity bred by bawdy houses, often accepted bribes to furnish medical certificates testifying to a prostitute's good health.[74]

Figure 5.1

Leading causes of medical noneffectiveness in the Canadian army domestically, 1941

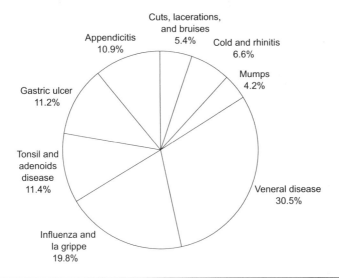

Note: Data based on total days lost.

Source: National Archives of Canada, RG24, Department of National Defence records, Vol. 6617, File 8994-6, pt. 1, The Canadian Army Venereal Disease Problem, n.d.

Canada's first Criminal Code in 1892 specified that women and men could be arrested for inhabiting a "bawdy house" or "disorderly house" – which could also refer to a place where gambling and drinking occurred – and also made it illegal to "live off the avails" of prostitution. During the Great War, fears over rising VD among servicemen resulted in a 1917 federal Order-in-Council prohibiting a woman with venereal disease from soliciting or having sex with a member of the armed forces. Women charged were subjected to a compulsory physical examination and, if infected, were detained until cured. In 1919 this measure was modified and incorporated into the Criminal Code to regulate sex among civilians. Provincial vagrancy laws were also enacted in order to control streetwalkers. Ontario's 1897 Female Refuges Act, for example, made provision for a woman thirty-five or younger to be incarcerated for up to two years if she was out at night and could not give a satisfactory account of her intentions, or was seen as a "habitual drunkard or by reasons of other vices as leading an idle and dissolute life."

Soon after the war started, raids were launched against brothels and streetwalkers in several communities. In Toronto, between 1938 and 1939, charges against those working in bawdy houses jumped from 42 to 172, while the number of women picked up for vagrancy rose from 158 in 1938 to 212 in 1941. Some younger women arrested – those considered still reformable – were sent to places like the Mercer Institution in Toronto or the Oakalla Prison Farm in British Columbia, where moral and religious instruction and "honest labour," usually domestic work, were applied to facilitate rehabilitation.[75] Other women who were arrested for prostitution but not infected with VD were fined, usually a maximum of $20; if they worked in a bawdy house this tab was almost always picked up by management.

With strong demand for prostitutes from military personnel, such raids often proved just a hiccup in operations. Some women arrested in brothels took their business to the streets, though typically their places of employment reopened in a short time, often at the same location. In several places, the military complained that local authorities quickly grew lax in their battle against prostitution. Indeed, police did sometimes ease off to prevent women from turning to streetwalking, which was more difficult to monitor, and to keep prostitution confined to informal red light districts and out of residential areas considered more respectable.[76]

VD rates continued higher than normal for the military in several communities. In Halifax the incidence of VD among naval personnel hit 86 per 1,000 in 1941. Reports told of streetwalkers arriving from Montreal who announced their presence to customers by wearing white galoshes. One brothel in the city was said to have sailors lining up for more than a block. Perhaps as a result, a large new establishment appeared in an old Barrington Street home conveniently located near the docks. Raids were launched, and on one occasion, eleven employees from Montreal were told to leave Halifax or face jail terms. Still, this brothel and others continued to operate, especially since local authorities preferred them to large numbers of streetwalkers. Many stores near the docks also opposed drastic action because military personnel drawn to the area by brothels spent money, and because the brothels themselves provided business: the Barrington Street establishment purchased $400 worth of groceries every month.[77]

The most serious VD problem was in Quebec. It was an open secret that police took bribes from brothel managers in Montreal, including an establishment employing seventy-five women located "just down the street" from the No. 4 police station. In 1940 the VD rate per 1,000 army personnel in Montreal rose to 116, while in Quebec City the rate hit an astonishing 202. (It was a popular leave destination for those training at the large Valcartier army base, and brothels and prostitutes congregated in the Palais district.) Pressure from the military led to raids, but these were typically carried out only for appearance's sake. Brothel managers were often tipped off in advance by corrupt law enforcement authorities, the fines levied on the few women who were left behind were paid for by management, and operations continued virtually without interruption. If the police went through the charade of padlocking the front door, customers simply used a rear door that was often plainly marked by a sign.[78]

In the summer of 1943, with VD rates among servicemen stationed in Quebec by far the highest in the country, exasperated military authorities, who also faced decreasing recruitment and the prospect of mounting casualties with the start of the Mediterranean campaign, upped the ante. Pressure was also building to clear the Quebec City downtown of brothels before the September conference between Roosevelt, Churchill, and King. The army actually threatened to declare much of downtown – namely the Palais area – "out of bounds" if officials did not take some meaningful action. By the time of the conference on 17 September, forty-seven arrests had been made at twelve brothels; it was known, however, that far more women actually remained on the job. The army next targeted Montreal, where it made similar threats in early 1944. That February police took action to close down, at least temporarily, a number of larger well-known bawdy houses. However, as local officials predicted, and as had also occurred in Quebec City, many women simply moved to the streets. Soon after the February raids, a memo from a military investigator reported that on Montreal's Dumarais Street, which was only one block long, "active solicitation of passers-by was being made from several buildings by female voices through shutters at the windows."[79]

Greater education and action on the part of both military and civilian authorities did help bring down the incidence of VD among military personnel in Canada. In the army the rate dropped from 55 per 1,000 in 1940 to 38 in 1942, and to 26 in 1944.[80] Lectures, literature, posters, and films warned men about the dangers of VD and instructed them how to avoid it. Much emphasis was placed on the avoidance of "pickups" willing to have sex, because, while most men may have suspected prostitutes of carrying VD, it was felt that they usually held no such presumption about other women. In the army training film *Three Cadets,* the narrator cautioned, "If she will have intercourse with you ... you know she has had it before with other men. If such is the case ... you must regard her as a source of VD." Other movies tried to shock men into restraining their behaviour by graphically displaying the physical effects of VD in full colour.[81] Adopting a similar strategy, one army publication described syphilis: "In the final stage the heart, brain and skin may show destruction of tissue, and tumour-like growths may appear quickly. General paralysis ... insanity, progressive loss of muscular control and heart disease are among the tragic results." The possible transmission of VD to loved ones, including one's future children, was also stressed. Appealing to a man's fidelity to his comrades was another tactic, as the man who contracted VD and made "himself unfit for duty" was portrayed as "let[ting] the whole team down ... and betray[ing] the unit just as though he had deserted."[82]

Although their policy was that sexual abstinence was the best way to control VD, Canadian military officials recognized that this expectation was unrealistic. Despite some concerns about being seen to encourage promiscuity, service branches increasingly distributed condoms to servicemen, as well as personal prophylactic kits containing a soap-impregnated cloth and tubes of nitrate jelly and calomel ointment to be applied to the genitals and surrounding areas following intercourse.[83] As an additional safeguard, men were told to visit an early prevention treatment

(EPT) station as soon as possible after intercourse to avoid the penalties they would be subject to if VD manifested. These centres were open around the clock on military bases, in armouries, in hospitals, and in most cities, in discreet locations made known to men heading out on leave and identified by a blue light. Still, many men were recalcitrant. One survey of 200 men who had contracted VD, for example, revealed that 137 had not worn a condom. When asked why, 56 percent said they were sure the woman was clean, 17 percent cited the condom's "pleasure-impairing effects," 13 percent claimed they were too drunk to remember to use it, and 12 percent said they had not been given one.[84] Many men did not bother to visit an EPT station – being inclined to live dangerously in light of their job – choosing instead to spend the night with their sexual partner or continue with other leave-time festivities; some admitted they feared the EPT treatment, which included an 8 percent protargol solution being injected into the urethra and being held there firmly for five minutes to prevent any discharge.[85]

Despite educational programs, many men did not recognize or tried to deny the early signs of VD, thus making their treatment more difficult and lengthy. Others who had not visited an EPT station hid their ailment to avoid repercussions. One report on infected air force personnel in Canada indicated that nearly 25 percent waited four or more days after noticing the first symptoms before reporting to a medical officer.[86] Some would have waited longer had their VD not been discovered through a "short arm" inspection, usually held weekly, though sometimes with greater frequency if rumours were circulating about heavy use of brothels.[87]

Early in the war men who contracted VD were segregated from other hospital patients in order to stigmatize and humiliate them. They were denied privileges such as going to base canteens or attending entertainment for military personnel. They also faced fines, though not large enough to prevent them from topping up the dependant's allowance as required, thus helping to shield those at home from any knowledge of their transgression. However, medical staff eventually concluded that the punitive approach did not work. Rather than reforming behaviour, it prompted men to try to hide the disease and further lowered the morale of those being penalized. Although many officers continued to portray VD as a self-inflicted wound that deserved to be punished, by mid-1942 penalties had generally been discarded in favour of simple medical treatment.[88]

Another response to the problem of venereal disease in the Canadian military was the creation of the position of VD control officer, whose role was to plan and implement more comprehensive preventive education, to increase efforts at distributing condoms and prophylactic kits, and to convince men to use EPT stations. This office also strengthened links with civilian authorities in their efforts to locate and take action against women and establishments that servicemen named as sources of VD.[89] Indeed, throughout the war men who had contracted VD were interviewed to determine where, and with whom, they had made the fateful contact. This information was forwarded to provincial health officials. At a minimum, the alleged source would have a letter delivered to her home – or to her place of employment if that was all that was known – demanding, under threat of a heavy fine, that she "present [her]self before a duly licensed and qualified physician ... to procure ... a report or certificate ... as to whether or not [she was] suffering from venereal disease." Even though these letters were sent in plain envelopes with no return address, they undoubtedly raised suspicions and queries.[90] When a serviceman could supply only a first name and perhaps a description of the woman and a location where she might be found, local health officials or the police made a personal visit. This often led to scandalous rumours, ostracism, breakdown of relationships and, too often, a mistaken accusation.[91]

Servicemen being interviewed were pressured to provide answers about the source of their infection. Brig. G.B. Chisholm of the Army Medical Corps ordered investigating officers, "Don't accept an answer about 'being too drunk to remember.' Repeated sincere questioning will produce the truth." Many men fingered brothels and streetwalkers, but by no means were these the only or even the major source. One 1942 study in Alberta reported that, incredibly, only 1 percent of servicemen with VD had identified a professional prostitute as the source, compared to 23 percent who pointed to a waitress. Many men were embarrassed to admit they had used professional services; they also sometimes thought that visiting a prostitute would be interpreted as a gross disregard for the threat posed by VD.[92] In the same survey, 23 percent maintained they could not remember from whom they contracted the disease. Some were trying to protect the reputation of their sexual partner, realizing that she would be contacted by authorities and be compelled to take a test for VD. According to historian Paul Jackson, in other circumstances men were trying to cover up VD contracted through homosexual encounters, for if such encounters were discovered, men could be sentenced to penal servitude with hard labour or a dishonourable discharge, which entailed the forfeiture of veterans' benefits.[93] Such deceptions could lead to the implication of someone else other than the true carrier of the disease. Indeed, one survey indicated that of the 2,354 women named by air force personnel as a source of VD in 1944 and 1945, 858 were located – with the help of often sketchy information – but of that figure, only 420 tested positive.[94]

Efforts to locate infected women and better control the promiscuous often curtailed women's freedom. This occurred in part because the crusade against VD targeted certain businesses. A place named as a "contact point" by more than one infected serviceman was threatened with being declared "out of bounds" to military personnel or with being closed down by civilian authorities if the frequency of VD cases suggested that it was serving as a base of operations for prostitutes or "good-time girls." At one point, orders issued to trainees at Camp Borden identified sixty-seven places – principally cafés, hotels, and dance halls in Toronto, Hamilton, North Bay, Brantford, and Barrie – as "off limits," because they were either the site of frequent brawls or suspected venues for the transmission of VD.[95]

Several proprietors, seeking to protect themselves, reacted by excluding women who seemed flirtatious. Increasingly, commercial dance halls and beer parlours – places long identified with immoral conduct and rising VD rates – barred their doors to unescorted women on the basis that many were either prostitutes or sex-obsessed pickups.[96] Taxi drivers operating at night sometimes refused rides to women whose demeanour or circumstances seemed suspect, because they feared being accused of abetting prostitution and the spread of VD and thereby jeopardizing their operating licences. This left some women stranded late at night and susceptible to arrest under vagrancy laws.[97]

In a breakthrough of sorts for women, several police forces hired female officers to facilitate the search for suspected carriers of VD, to help handle female prisoners, and to fill positions left vacant by the enlistment of men.[98] In Toronto, which had hired its first "police matron" in 1913 to help process female prisoners and offer "maternal guidance" to promote their moral reform, the number of police-women grew over the first four years of the war from three to ten.[99] Similar changes were evident in other cities, including Halifax, Montreal, Ottawa, Barrie, Hamilton, Winnipeg, Calgary, Edmonton, Vancouver, and Victoria.[100] Much trepidation accompanied these advances. In Halifax, the one woman hired during the war was always to be accompanied by a male officer. Winnipeg's sole female officer was kept to a daytime shift.

In Regina, however, Police Chief Martin resisted the trend, insisting that "police work is ... a man's job." Discrimination also showed up in the matter of pay, as women typically received between half and two-thirds of men's salaries, though their annual income of $1,000-$1,200 in most urban departments compared well to what women earned in other positions. In addition to continuing to serve as matrons, female police officers assumed more public and active roles in wartime, although their assignments remained true to gender-based stereotypes and even reinforced restrictive moral standards governing women's conduct. As their primary responsibility was to identify and maintain control over suspected prostitutes and pickups, it was their task to check up on and often interrogate women, especially at commercial dance halls, pool halls, taverns, bowling alleys and, depending on the hour, on streets and in parks.[101]

DESPITE ITS REACTIONARY QUALITIES, the wartime civilian campaign against VD did succeed in providing Canadians with more candid information about and better treatment facilities for this often-fatal disease. Organized efforts to control VD in Canada dated back to the Great War era, the result of fears that high rates among servicemen overseas would result in a postwar epidemic. The Canadian National Council for Combatting Venereal Disease had been founded in May 1919 to disseminate information on how to avoid and recognize VD, and to advise the infected to promptly seek out treatment. During the interwar years, this organization, which changed its name first to the Canadian Social Hygiene Council and then in 1935 to the Health League of Canada, also presented lectures and films. Its most widely shown movie, obtained from the American Social Hygiene Association, was *The End of the Road,* which stressed the need for abstinence outside marriage. Indeed, purity and prudery were the dominant characteristics of early anti-VD efforts. For example, the Health League excluded those under eighteen from its talks because lecturers used diagrams of the human body indicating the sex organs. Meanwhile, budget cuts caused the federal government in 1932 to end the modest funding it had been giving the provinces since 1919 to help establish VD clinics and produce educational material. A start had been made in "shatter[ing] the silence" surrounding VD, but in 1939 widespread ignorance persisted, as public discussion of the topic was still largely taboo. Even the term "venereal disease" was commonly avoided in public discourse in favour of such euphemisms as "social hygiene."[102]

Change accelerated during the Second World War. In addition to rapidly rising rates of VD among the military, these years also brought mounting civilian rates, the latter moving from 97.6 per 100,000 in 1939 to 155.3 in 1941, 211.2 in 1943, 325.0 in 1944, and 336.2 in 1945.[103] Not only were more people sexually active but more accurate statistics had become available, raising the numbers of documented cases. Concerted government campaigns were in place to trace carriers, educate people on how to recognize VD, and pressure them to get tested if the possibility of the disease existed. New rules also made it mandatory for civilian doctors to report all cases to health officials in order to generate reliable statistics.

British Columbia led the Canadian provinces in this reinvigorated anti-VD campaign, thanks largely to the crusading efforts of Dr. Donald H. Williams, who in 1938 became the director of the provincial Department of Venereal Disease Control. Four years later Williams's activist approach earned him the rank of lieutenant-colonel and the job of managing the Army Medical Corps' anti-VD program. Soon after taking the post of provincial director, Williams set his sights on Vancouver's beer parlours, characterizing them as magnets for prostitutes and the promiscuous, especially since such establishments were often attached to hotels. He advocated physical barriers to separate male and female patrons and threatened to have operating licences promptly revoked when VD contacts were traced back to these locales.[104] He also maintained pressure on law-enforcement authorities to target brothels and streetwalkers, and directed considerable efforts to the search for disease facilitators. In addition Williams substantially intensified efforts on the publicity front to educate people about a disease that, he contended, was the object of far too much ignorance, deceit, and denial. He always insisted on using the term "venereal disease" in public, believing that frankness was essential to education and to removing the shame that steered people away from obtaining treatment.[105]

With increased, though still modest, funding from the provincial government, operations under Williams expanded considerably. While BC's Venereal Disease Control department had provided just 34 lectures and distributed 8,385 pieces of literature in 1938, by 1941 those figures had reached 171 and 135,228 respectively. New VD clinics opened up in New Westminster, Prince Rupert, and Trail. Williams also persisted with the tough approach. In part thanks to his unrelenting pressure, British Columbia's Liquor Board in April 1942 made it mandatory for beer parlours to set up partitions at least six feet high to separate the sexes.[106] VD clinics in the province redoubled their efforts to obtain all possible information to enable the tracking of carriers. Moreover, in BC and in several other provinces not only were private doctors compelled to report to provincial health officials all the VD cases that they treated but they were also urged to obtain and pass on information about the likely carrier of the disease; many physicians refused to pursue this information, however, seeing this requirement as too great a departure from the principle of doctor-patient confidentiality.[107]

By the early 1940s other provinces were noticeably stepping up efforts to battle VD by tracking down suspected carriers, issuing stern warnings to businesses thought to be facilitation points, and improving public education and treatment facilities. In Alberta between 1939 and 1942, the number of audience members reached by VD lectures sponsored by the province's Board of Health rose from 7,000 to 25,000. In Ontario, where over 200,000 pieces of literature on VD were distributed by the provincial government in 1942, Health Minister Dr. R.P. Vivian pressed home the need for yet more action: "There is ample reason to believe that for every reported case of syphilitic infection, there are two more people in the Ontario population who have syphilis [and] for every case of gonorrhoeal infection ... as many as four or five other people have this disease."[108] Noting the more vigorous and forthright approach to VD prevention that was developing across the country, a 1943 *Chatelaine* editorial remarked that the "taboos, ignorance and fear" that had long supported venereal disease were "losing [their] strength," while the *Canadian Home Journal* observed, "Venereal disease is no longer a hush-hush topic."[109]

Indeed, the more direct, though often harsh, approach to VD prevention was also gathering support in the federal government. Spurred into action by recent provincial initiatives, by the need to retain as many healthy recruits and war workers as possible, and by the well-publicized appointment in 1942 of the famous FBI agent Elliot Ness as director of the new Division of Social Protection in the United States, in 1943 Ottawa reassigned Williams to head a newly formed Venereal Disease Control Division within the Department of Pensions and National Health. During Williams's tenure federal funding to the provinces for VD prevention, although still not overly generous, was renewed to provide annual monies that exceeded the prewar peak of $150,000 by more than a third.[110] Williams worked with provincial governments and the military to better coordinate anti-VD programs, including efforts to track down suspected facilitators. In December 1943 the new federal division organized a national venereal disease control conference in Ottawa, which was attended by 105 delegates from federal and provincial health departments, university medical faculties, nursing schools, the National Research Council, the Canadian Medical Association, the Canadian Hospital Council, the Health League of Canada, and the American Social Hygiene Association. By no means were its recommendations revolutionary – increase public education, implement pre-matrimonial blood tests, suppress prostitution, and trace alleged facilitators – but considerable press coverage further raised the public profile of the campaign against VD.[111] Moreover, at this conference and another in 1945, delegates from nursing schools and medical faculties revealed plans or measures already undertaken to increase the amount of training time devoted to the detection and treatment of VD.[112]

The new federal department also helped furnish more educational material. In 1944 it generated over 700,000 pieces of literature for civilians and military personnel in Canada, and advertised in print media and over the radio. In both 1944 and 1945 it earmarked an extra $25,000 to raise public awareness about VD prevention through a conservatively named new National Social Hygiene Day declared for 7 February.[113] With federal money, provincial governments continued to enlarge their anti-VD campaigns, providing in 1944 more than 600 lectures and distributing nearly a million pieces of literature. In Ontario, Manitoba, and Saskatchewan, programs were introduced to supply sulpha drugs and later penicillin to remote areas, while in Alberta, federal funds were used to help create new VD clinics in Peace River, High River, and McLennan.[114]

THE RISING INCIDENCE OF VD, as well as the increasing need for healthy servicemen and wartime labour, certainly necessitated a more intense campaign against the disease. However, anti-VD strategies were frequently clumsy, repressive, and destructive. If women's conduct did not conform to current notions of female decorum, or if they frequented establishments to which cases of VD were traced, they were often presumed to be prostitutes or promiscuous pickups responsible for spreading VD and undermining Canada's war effort. As such, they were often turned away from establishments that themselves were trying to avoid being penalized by authorities. On the basis of flimsy and dubious evidence, many women were named as contacts and compelled to get tested, often in a public and humiliating manner and sometimes at great cost to their personal lives. Clearly, the social stigma surrounding VD had by no means disappeared by war's end. On the medical front as well, there was much room for progress. In 1945 provincial VD clinics across Canada had only thirteen doctors on staff, six of whom worked part-time.[115]

Mounting concern over VD did generate franker public discussion, more education, and better treatment facilities, and played a significant role in helping to increase the number of female constables – though with rather mixed implications for the advancement of women. Yet these trends were driven in part by the belief that the rising incidence of VD was further proof of a brewing moral crisis in wartime Canada that had to be reversed. Behind this belief also lay the perception of too many dubious wartime marriages, rising divorce rates, rampant infidelity, increasing rates of illegitimacy, pervasive prostitution, and masses of loose women lusting after servicemen, whose behaviour too often seemed out of control. Hand-in-hand with Canadians' pride over their wartime accomplishments was an increasing apprehension about what type of nation would emerge from the conflict. Would VD remain epidemic? Would marriage endure as a respected institution? Would the nuclear family maintain its role as the moral backbone of society? For many, such anxieties were also fed by the notion that the Second World War, far more than any previous conflict, was bringing about dangerous and perhaps permanent changes to long-established gender roles.

6

Civilian Women: "Two steps forward and one step back"

IN THE SUMMER OF 1943, Mary Etta Macpherson, who had taken over from Byrne Hope Saunders as editor of *Chatelaine*, Canada's most widely circulated women's magazine, wrote, "We hope some of those bright college girls, soon to troop back for the fall term, will write a thesis on 'What War Has Done to Improve the Lot of Canadian Women.'"[1] For many Canadian women the war had brought relatively little change in daily routine, but Macpherson was referring to the quarter-million women, including many wives and mothers, who in the first four years of the war had joined the paid workforce, demonstrating their competence to perform physically demanding work and jobs typically assigned to males.

Although it is unknown whether any college women took up Macpherson's challenge back in 1943, with the rise of the field of women's history in more recent years her question has attracted scholarly interest. However, the dominant interpretation in academic research has been quite different from the optimism implied by Macpherson's proposed thesis topic. The title of Ruth Pierson's 1986 book, *They're Still Women after All,* aptly summarizes the now-received version of what the war ultimately meant for Canadian women.[2] Pierson argues that the persistence of gender-based stereotypes and discriminatory government policies in fact permitted only relatively minor breakthroughs for women during the war, and that these advances were by and large reversed once the troops came home. She shows, for instance, that women faced condescending characterizations and sometimes scurrilous accusations as they migrated into civilian jobs and military auxiliaries; mistreatment from many male colleagues; concentration in low-status job ghettoes; and at the end of the conflict a concerted push back into the domestic sphere or the narrow range of poorly paid tasks traditionally deemed suitable for females.

Like all historical questions involving numerous issues and actors, the patterns here are not neat and tidy but as chaotic and at times contradictory as the complex society in which they occurred. Indeed, wartime mass media and government propaganda also defy easy generalization. Much publicly directed material, in aiming to recruit female labour and encourage maximum output, emphasized the ability of women to perform competently and expertly in radically new domains. Working women interviewed during the war often described expanded horizons and ambitions, while their postwar oral testimony underlines the fact that their new experiences contributed to greater self-reliance and confidence and helped to build a legacy of broadened opportunities. Along with noteworthy acceptance of working women and their right to better treatment on the job site, however, contemporary public opinion polls revealed apprehension over changing gender roles. Bold wartime challenges to constructed gender roles triggered not only anxiety but ultimately a postwar backlash stressing the need to reconstitute so-called traditional family life. Still, soon after the conflict it became clear that too much had changed for too many women to permit a return to the antebellum status quo.

CANADIAN WOMEN were initially asked to contribute to the war effort through volunteer work. Their responses were heartening and often beyond expectation. Three months into the war the *Canadian Home Journal* reported that at least 100,000 women were already busy knitting clothes for British children evacuated to the countryside.[3] This volunteerism was rarely perceived as a challenge to male authority, for it was unpaid, tapped into the supposedly self-sacrificing nature of women, and mainly involved projects that reflected their traditional domestic tasks or mothering duties. For example, besides knitting, they rolled bandages, packed bundles for servicemen and POWs, and prepared and served food in canteens for men on leave. By contrast, male volunteers were given jobs that had a military or managerial dimension, as air raid wardens, auxiliary police and firemen, or organizers of key campaigns such as Victory Bond drives.

Still, recognizing the indispensable role played by females in the voluntary sector, in the autumn of 1940, only months after creating the Department of National War Services, the federal government added a Women's Voluntary Services Division to it. While some local organizations run by women resisted being subsumed under a government department directed by men, many others saw Ottawa's initiative as a validation of their importance. Ultimately the division established forty-four female-run branches across Canada to better promote and coordinate the wide variety of patriotic efforts undertaken by women's groups.[4] Because of the prestige of these Women's Voluntary Service Offices, as well as their appeal to patriotism, WVSOs invariably attracted women of stature to run their affairs, in particular the leaders of local branches of the National Council of Women of Canada, the Imperial Order Daughters of the Empire, the Business and Professional Women's Association, and in rural areas, the Federated Women's Institutes.[5]

The many women who worked within these sometimes extensive operations also derived pride and a sense of importance from activities heralded as being critical to the war effort. Praise issued from influential sources such as political platforms and church pulpits, radio and film, and newspapers and magazines, many of which introduced a special page detailing voluntary service and singling out those who achieved stupendous results. One publication claimed that in the recent years, through volunteerism, many women had "proven [themselves] leader[s]," and were "ready ... to shoulder greater responsibilities" – a statement impossible to verify with any precision, given the millions of participants whose names have been lost to the historical record.[6] Account after account lauded the dedication and strength of women volunteers, many of whom donated their time to multiple campaigns or performed physically taxing tasks, such as the thousands of young women who participated in farm labour programs either full- or part-time.[7] Government propaganda and media accounts also praised the women who volunteered with the Consumers' Branch of the Wartime Prices and Trade Board, portraying their work as crucial in the fight against inflation, which had caused significant social strain during the Great War. Although the role of Consumers' Branch members was linked to the stereotypical depiction of women as shoppers for the family, these volunteers spoke out with confidence as purchasers. As an informal police force they developed a degree of power over male retailers, a trend that some historians link to postwar female consumer activism such as that conducted through the Housewives' Consumer Association and Consumers' Association of Canada.[8]

IMPORTANT CHANGES were also occurring in the wartime household, an even more traditional sphere for women than the voluntary sector. In this realm, women assumed greater responsibility and, if their husbands enlisted, became the chief authority figures. With some concern, an American psychologist wrote that as women became "accustomed to making all decisions," they would prove "less willing to give up authority when the family [was] united again." Meanwhile, a female Canadian social worker writing in *Chatelaine* expressed the hope that such decision-making patterns would in peacetime allow a greater number of housewives to enjoy a "more equal partnership in marriage."[9]

Whether or not the men in a family were away, the wartime household presented women with many new challenges. Even the pampered and privileged had to fend far more for themselves, since large numbers of the domestic workers who had been cheap and plentiful during the Depression moved on to better jobs.[10] Rationing and shortages of materials made shopping a trying experience, often akin, said one source, to a "strategic campaign."[11] Women found themselves on crammed buses and streetcars, on bicycles, or trudging on foot from store to store in search of scarce goods; they had to lug home items in paper bags thinner than usual due to wartime restrictions, and plan carefully and creatively to make reduced food allotments last longer. One advertisement from Benson's Corn Starch praised women as "Canada's Housesoldiers," consumers who bought its product in order to stretch out meals, illustrated by a wife standing at attention, saluting and carrying a kitchen spoon as a rifle. Although perhaps demeaning in hindsight, at the time such an advertisement could be interpreted as symbolizing the growing importance of women within many wartime households, as well as, *Chatelaine* noted, the rising status of what many women had regarded as the "rather dreary" position of housewife.[12]

Women in wartime obtained more, and often complete, control over domestic responsibilities typically falling within the male purview, including family finances.

financial power

|Many women whose husbands were in uniform were given power of attorney so that they could sign cheques, make investments, or sell property. This was a significant shift since, under normal circumstances, women were then excluded by common and civil law from any control over joint property. Long after the war, Mary Turner of Toronto recalled the "sense of importance" she felt from "going into the bank myself" to do the family finances.[13] Moreover, with the skills of most repairmen redirected toward war production, and many new consumer durables disappearing by 1942, many women learned basic maintenance and repair techniques for their appliances and cars, as well as for household heating, plumbing, electricity, and minor structural matters.[14]

DESPITE THE SIGNIFICANT and much-heralded efforts of women volunteers and their proficiency in overcoming new obstacles in the home, the volunteer and household settings are rarely cited by scholars as origins for major and lasting challenges to the traditional gendered order, perhaps because they meshed naturally with patriarchal constructions (and in the case of the wartime household mainly involved unrecorded private negotiations). Rather, nearly all contemporary and subsequent analyses, whatever their conclusions, suggest that the most meaningful advances for women were achieved within male-dominated domains from which substantial economic and social mobility, status, and power derive: higher education and the paid workforce.|

change

Certainly, sexism was rife on wartime college campuses. Most universities were denominational, and women faced considerable moral regulation, such as strictly enforced curfews at female residences.[15] At the University of Toronto – where, as at other campuses, women were required to provide three hours each week of war-related voluntary service – the administration refused to endorse a separate officer-training detachment for women, viewing this type of training as unfeminine and claiming that females were ill-suited to such regimentation. Instead, a Women's War Service Committee was established to direct university women toward activities such as knitting. Some young women gravitated instead to the Red Cross, partly because it gave them the opportunity to drive ambulances, participate in simulated military drill, and learn such skills as automobile repair. However, the university administration expressed concern over the organization's paramilitary nature. With some reluctance it provided the group with rooms on campus, though it also obtained a commitment that emphasis would be placed upon "training hospital nursing aides [and] volunteers for child-care facilities," sewing, knitting, and packing articles for servicemen and needy civilians overseas.[16]

Meanwhile quite different trends were taking hold on wartime university campuses. With the departure of enlisted men, women came to constitute a larger proportion of the student body: in 1945 28.6 percent of all undergraduate degrees in Canada were conferred upon women, up from 21.3 percent in 1939. The media began focusing greater attention on female students. For instance, between 1941 and 1943 in the *Gateway,* the student newspaper at the University of Alberta, the number of stories on women almost doubled to eighty-two. Several *Gateway* articles indicated that as the ratio of women students rose, so too did their opportunities; a 1942 issue, for example, reported on the University of Alberta's first female engineering student and the election of a woman as student vice-president.[17]

Studies in the arts continued to attract most women, but the number of BSc degrees granted to women increased nationally from fifty-one in 1941 to ninety in 1945, or from 14.9 to 20.6 percent of the number of degrees granted to students. While twenty-five women graduated as physicians in 1941, representing 4.4 percent of the total, by 1946 their number had reached forty-five or 7.9 percent. Such trends resulted not only from the higher percentage of women at universities, but also from the decision of some program directors to select highly qualified or "very serious" women over "mediocre men."[18] Female university graduates also had greater opportunities to secure rewarding employment during the war. "Marriage still claims many," wrote the *Ottawa Journal,* but in the nation's capital arts graduates were being scooped up by an expanding civil service – and not only for entry-level positions. Those with scientific or technical knowledge frequently received offers from such institutions as the National Research Council or, as in communities across the land, from numerous industries involved in war production.[19]

THE MOVEMENT OF UNIVERSITY GRADUATES into higher-level jobs was but one aspect of the mass migration of women into the paid labour market and an unprecedented array of employment (Table 6.1). Women working in low-paid areas such as domestic service, retailing, and the textile sector were often able to obtain far better posts. Many women began working outside the home for the first time. Others who had had jobs before settling down to a life revolving around home and family returned to paid employment. Not only were record numbers of women working, but also a greater variety of women than ever before were taking jobs, including many who before the war would likely not have seen paid employment as part of their future.

Whereas only 6,000 women were working in manufacturing outside the textile sector before the war, by the autumn of 1943 this number was 261,000. Between June 1939 and the beginning of 1944 some 370,000 women obtained employment in domains directly connected to the war effort, and the number of women with jobs outside the home totalled nearly 1.4 million growing from 22.7 to 33.1 percent of the female noninstitutional population, 14 and older.[20] Record numbers of working women were married and had children. By mid-1942 the need for wartime labour prompted the federal government to institute income tax breaks for working couples – doubling the basic exemption for husbands to $1,200 – and legislation was passed promising state-run and subsidized child care.[21]

To help manage female recruitment into the job market, a Women's Division was created within National Selective Service (NSS) in May 1942. Its director was

Table 6.1

Female noninstitutional labour force, 14 and over, 1939-50

Year	Total labour force ('000s)	Total in non-agricultural jobs ('000s)	Total not in labour force ('000s)	Total participation rate (%)	Participation rate in non-agricultural jobs (%)
1939	873	686	2,967	22.7	18.8
1940	911	733	3,010	23.2	19.6
1941	958	800	3,049	23.9	20.8
1942	1,070	874	3,012	26.2	22.5
1943	1,355	1,184	2,772	32.8	29.9
1944	1,387	1,199	2,798	33.1	30.0
1945	1,394	1,193	2,858	32.7	29.4
1946	1,089	889	3,264	25.0	21.4
1947	1,069	898	3,366	24.1	21.1
1948	1,074	914	3,427	23.8	21.1
1949	1,099	967	3,484	24.0	21.7
1950	1,112	1019	3,650	23.3	21.8

Source: K.A.H. Buckley and M.C. Urquhart, *Historical Statistics of Canada* (Toronto: Macmillan, 1965), 62.

Mrs. Rex (Fraudena) Eaton who, among her other qualifications, was the only woman to have served on British Columbia's Board of Industrial Relations. One magazine profile insisted that Eaton, despite her new position, remained "essentially [a] domestic" woman, a trait apparently demonstrated by her decision upon taking up her job in Ottawa to rent an apartment rather than a house so that she could clean it herself.[22] The implication in this observation about the virtues of domesticity gives an insight into wider concerns over the direction in which wartime migration of women into the paid workforce was leading, especially when it came to wives and mothers. Despite the growing need for female labour, the government approached the recruitment of women with caution. Seeking to demonstrate its preference that, as far as possible, women maintain their primary roles as wives and mothers, NSS made its first national registration of women in September 1942 voluntary and sought to identify only women aged twenty to twenty-four in order to target the "single [and] mobile." Moreover, though Ottawa introduced child-care services and tax breaks advantageous to working wives, not until July 1943, with the Sicilian campaign under way and an invasion of northwest Europe anticipated – thus necessitating more men overseas and still greater war production at home – did NSS extend its registration to wives and mothers.[23]

State-supported training programs to prepare workers for the war economy showed deference toward a gendered hierarchy in the workplace, where male dominance was well established. An initiative that extended into the early months of the war was the 1937 Dominion-Provincial Youth Training Programme, which had been designed to counteract Depression unemployment by teaching marketable skills to sixteen- to thirty-year-olds – though typically it limited women to such options as "handicrafts and homecraft." This program was replaced in 1940 by the much more comprehensive Dominion-Provincial War Emergency Training Programme, which used new facilities established by the federal government, as well as technical schools and on-the-job training, to prepare labour for war production. Courses lasted from a few weeks to a few months, during which trainees received an allowance, normally $7 a week if they were single and $10 if married.[24] By the time the program ended on 31 July 1944, some 235,000 civilian men and women had obtained qualifications, as had 115,000 service personnel in military trades, training that undoubtedly continued to benefit many after the war.

Priority placement in these training programs was offered to Great War veterans, men honourably discharged from the current conflict, and unemployed men over forty, but labour shortages soon opened the doors to women. Indeed, between April and December 1942 the 11,579 women who entered the program constituted 48 percent of its total registrants. Despite these numbers, the training women received was usually quite minimal. While the average course for men lasted two to three months, it often took just a couple of weeks to prepare women for lower-rung, less-skilled, and of course, more poorly paid jobs. But in the context of the times, progress was evident. Noteworthy numbers of women demonstrated the aptitude and the determination to qualify for higher-status and unconventional trades for females, including such jobs as fine instrument mechanic, power machine operator, welder, woodworker, bench fitter, industrial chemist, laboratory technician, and draftsman.[25]

As women moved into new social roles, much public discourse attempted to reassure people that very little was in fact changing. This message was delivered by numerous sources, including companies that saw new business opportunities in the needs of working women. Playing upon the theme of women's ornamental qualities, the makers of cosmetics and other personal hygiene products advertised that no matter the roughness of the job being performed, they would help maintain a woman's beauty and femininity. "No mechanics' hands" was the pledge made by the makers of Campana's Balm Cream, while the Palmolive Soap Company promoted its products' ability to quickly restore a fresh, beautiful complexion to women working "in a man's world."[26]

Such messages could certainly be viewed as trivializing women's work by suggesting that women's feminine traits were more important than their abilities. However, they could also be interpreted as reassuring a woman that she need not sacrifice her sexual appeal by taking on physically demanding, typically male jobs; in other words, this was not an "either-or" proposition. Several other appeals expressed more directly the view that women could balance new and often unconventional workplace behaviour with so-called traditional feminine roles. The Modess company let women know about its smaller, more comfortable sanitary napkin for the new "busy girl," while the makers of the new Wonder Bra emphasized its capacity not only to provide a "more youthful appearance" but also to "yield to every movement for the active woman of today."[27]

Mixed messages were also conveyed in other non-news print media. The short, typically melodramatic romance stories that were geared toward women and serialized in several newspapers and magazines, including the nationally distributed Maclean-Hunter publications *Chatelaine* and *Maclean's*, indicated the attitudes of the day. Before the war, married women who worked outside the home had been portrayed in such short stories as "arch villains," and this message still resonated during the early war years.[28] In "This Is Corda," a short story by Leonora Walker that appeared in the January 1941 issue of *Chatelaine*, a young wife who takes over her uncle's remodelling business after he develops high blood pressure is taught the error of her ambition. "For four of the happiest months of her life, she ... sketched corner cupboards on shingles [and] fought with the electrician." However, her sister warned her that her husband might resent a working wife, especially if she earned more money than he did, thus depriving him of his "birthright" as a "breadwinner." Corda remained unswayed – that is, until she ran into a former acquaintance, an ambitious, wealthy career woman who had paid the price of her freedom with a divorce.[29]

In wartime literature, female protagonists moved steadily away from being "passive, weak and naturally inferior."[30] Some displayed heroism. The plot of Dorothy Eden's "Café Encounter," which appeared in *Chatelaine* shortly before D-Day, revolves around an Englishwoman running a café in occupied France, who hides Allied soldiers as they scout out sites for an invasion of the Continent.[31] Other stories set on the home front placed women in positions of responsibility and illustrated their competence with difficult tasks. In John Delgado's "Safe at Last," a young woman not only finds true love among her co-workers at a Vancouver shipyard but also, as safety inspector, earns the respect of the "big and burly men."[32] In Ann Hall's "On the Job," a Canadian sailor home on leave comes to accept the fact that his wife has taken a job as a steelworker. Although the implication is that his wife's job is temporary, by the end of the story the sailor is helping out with the shopping and housework while she is "on the job."[33]

Press commentary was more likely to take the reassuring stance that women workers had taken jobs solely out of patriotism – to "back the attack" – in order to release men for action, and that they would happily return home once victory was attained. "Work after the war? Not if she doesn't have to. [She]'d ... like to get married," was the message of one article in the December 1942 *Saturday Night*.[34] Some stories trying to show women's labour in a positive light played on the stereotype of women's virtue to suggest that in factories they would have an uplifting effect on the conduct of "gruff men." On the other hand, concern was voiced that such settings could be morally corrupting through exposing women to excessive profanity or tempting them into sexual relationships or adultery if their husbands were away. While many women recalled in later years that their male co-workers had been polite and even "chivalrous," some also remembered lewd comments or ogling. Women were themselves at times reprimanded and sent home for wearing clothing that was considered too bright or tight. There was also talk of women workers, including married ones left on their own, going out for drinks or to dance halls after clocking out, even very late at night after the swing shift.[35]

Would the physical stature of women allow them to do the same job as men? Would the demands of industrial work turn them into unattractive females with hard biceps or, conversely, cause physical collapse or nervous exhaustion? One account insisted that over the longer term, the employment of women in heavy industry was impractical because their inferior strength made them about 40 percent less productive than men.[36] To make industrial jobs seem more natural and less threatening to women, or to make such work more palatable, several articles compared their new factory tasks to housework. For example, large lathes were likened to sewing machines. Other common clichés cast women as well-suited to jobs working with fine instruments because of their so-called delicate touch and fastidious attention to detail. Women were also said to be good at various assembly-line jobs because, habituated to repetitive and mundane household tasks, they were less likely than men to become bored and distracted.[37] Indeed, in October 1942 *Saturday Night* columnist Anne Fromer, citing a recent American study, wrote, "Of the 623 operations required in today's war plants, women can perform all but 57," abilities she attributed to "generations spent at the monotonous tasks of the housewife" which gave women "more patience in handling repetitious machines." But such stereotypes could also have the ironic effect of creating, as historian William Chafe asserts, "a framework within which women could begin to do work that would ultimately shatter traditional images."[38]

As well as conveying restrictive stereotypes about women, many news stories and editorials gave inspirational accounts of female strength and skill in numerous unprecedented roles outside the domestic sphere. Interestingly, such accounts were often set outside Canada. Some of the earliest focused on British women, who were portrayed as heroically enduring the Blitz and performing all manner of work to ensure their country's survival. H. Napier Moore, the influential long-time editor of *Maclean's* and a past president of the Canadian Authors Association, declared to *Chatelaine's* female audience, "If a [British] woman is capable of doing what used to be considered a man's job, she does it ... You see them in the factories and on the land. You see them handling cranes, operating machines, and pushing heavy ingots around."[39] After June 1941 considerable positive attention focused on Russian women, nearly half of whom worked outside the home, often in jobs to help defend their homeland from the Nazis. "To give some idea of the tremendous change in women's life and work here, consider domestic service," wrote *Saturday Night* columnist Nils Bergen. "Twenty years ago or so eighty percent of the working women in Russia were employed in that capacity. Today, the figure is about one in fifty. The remainder have become engineers, tram drivers, air pilots and so on."[40] Dini Aldridge further pointed out in *Chatelaine*, "Women do as much heavy work as the men. In an armament factory ... which I saw outside Moscow, seventy percent of the staff are women. In a foundry ... giant cranes suspended over hot furnaces carrying loads of hot metal are worked by women."[41]

Readers encountered approximately twice as many stories about Canadian women in their newspapers and magazines in 1944 as they had in 1939.[42] Many celebrated women's contributions and accomplishments in new workplace domains. Some women read about themselves. Dorothy Hendsbee was just sixteen when she left the isolated northeastern Nova Scotia fishing village of Half Island Cove to take a job as a welder in the Halifax shipyards – a job title she first had to look up in the dictionary to understand what it entailed. She was soon beaming with pride after reading and rereading a newspaper article about "pioneer women" – citing her by name – performing a job crucial to the war effort and just as skilfully as their male counterparts.[43] Such a spin was especially evident in accounts written by female journalists; not only did their interests lead them in that direction but they were most often assigned to cover subjects of particular interest to women readers. In any case, a noticeable shift was occurring in many widely circulated publications that before the war had confined their stories on females mainly to a "women's page" that focused on fashion, cooking, and family life. For instance, Thelma Lecocq, in a major 1942 *Maclean's* feature on women aircraft workers – who at their peak numbers made up 30 percent of the national total – stressed these women's pride in the positions they held and the efficiency and skill with which they performed their tasks. "Ask them what they were doing six months or a year ago," she wrote. "Fifty percent of them reply that they were doing housework ... Now they're making ... wings for the planes that are going to help win this war ... and they're turning them out faster and getting fewer rejections than the men who were previously making them."[44]

Another account on women aircraft workers appeared in *Mayfair,* a Maclean-Hunter publication traditionally devoted to covering fashion trends and the society scene for middle- and upper-class women. It hailed those who "perform[ed] with the skill of master-craftsmen," with expertise that would "be available to make planes for a world of peace.[45] Perhaps most optimistic with respect to the consequences of women's new wartime work was Lotta Dempsey, *Chatelaine*'s future editor-in-chief, then probably its most prominent columnist and certainly one of the most outspoken feminists among wartime journalists. In a 1943 article she declared, "This was the time and the place it really started, the honest-to-goodness equality of Canadian women. It began to happen that hour when Canadian girls left desks and kitchens ... stepped into overalls and took their places in the lines of workers at lathes and drills."[46]

In early 1943 the widely syndicated American writer Clare Booth Luce went even further in an article carried in *Chatelaine:* "Today ... the woman war worker ... is ... glorified ... and has replaced the glamour girl and the movie star on magazine covers."[47] The most striking example of this trend was Norman Rockwell's illustration of "Rosie the Riveter," which appeared on the cover of the 23 May 1943 edition of the *Saturday Evening Post,* then the most widely circulating magazine in the United States and among the top sellers in Canada. The "long-lashed" and "buxom" Rosie, by no means stripped of feminine charm despite wearing coveralls and a bandanna wrapped around her head, was portrayed as physically powerful, rolling up the sleeves of her shirt to reveal rather muscular arms ready to do the work needed by her country.[48] Several covers of *Chatelaine, Maclean's,* and the nationally distributed *Star Weekly* also showed, either through illustration or photographs, women performing industrial jobs critical to the war effort.[49]

Women workers were the subject of several multipage newspaper and magazine features that included photographs of them operating heavy, sometimes massive, machinery. The most impressive magazine commentary was *Women at War,* a special 1943 edition of *Maclean's* made in cooperation with the Department of Munitions and Supply, which, through NSS, was then stepping up efforts to recruit female labour. Here, it was pointed out that the idea of women as weak or prone to nervous breakdown bore little resemblance to the profile of women who handled TNT and nitroglycerine in their work for chemical companies. "There is no picking of 'soft' jobs or shifts for women," read another account, paraphrasing a "grizzled foreman" at an unnamed shipyard. In making his point, the foreman directed attention to a woman operating a massive crane to lower a large gun on to a ship. "She does the job as well as he does and with less fuss and swearing," he remarked. "If they want to stay after the war I don't see why they shouldn't."[50]

Ambivalent messages about working women were also projected on cinema screens. With more people earning money and being attracted to movies about the war, these images reached a massive audience, one that was increasingly female as more men departed for overseas.[51] Popular full-length motion pictures – preponderantly from Britain and the United States – commonly reinforced notions of female dependence and objectified women as sex objects. Among these was the 1944 RKO production *Something for the Boys* starring Carmen Miranda and Vivian Blaine, which, as promised in its publicity, presented viewers with a cavalcade of "tall girls, small girls, fair girls, red-heads and raven brunettes, all in lovely Technicolor." These were the years of "blonde bombshell" Dorothy Lamour, the "cover girl" Rita Hayworth, and the "pin-up" Betty Grable.[52] But women in particular were attracted to wartime films with strong female leads. Certainly among the most popular was *Mrs. Miniver,* the winner of six Academy Awards in 1942, including the award for Best Motion Picture. Greer Garson portrays Kay Miniver, a middle-class British mother who before the war had been a quintessential consumer. But during the Blitz she comes to discover an inner strength that to many moviegoers was symbolic of Britain's resolve to resist the Nazis, a strength that empowers her to call the authorities and courageously deal with a wounded German who parachutes from a damaged aircraft and breaks into her home. Although her strength was born from necessity and it is suggested that Mrs. Miniver's life would return to a more traditional form after the war, as film historian Andrea Walsh writes, this homebody wartime heroine projected "personality traits encouraged by contemporary feminists: power, courage, physical stamina, and perseverance."[53] Among the top-grossing films in 1944 was *Since You Went Away,* which starred Claudette Colbert as Anne Hilton, a middle-class mother of two daughters forced out of a life of complacency and dependency after her husband enlists in the US navy. In fact, he does not appear in the movie except in a mantelpiece photograph. Anne confronts new challenges such as dealing with a brusque male boarder and taking a job as a welder. While this movie also implies an eventual return to domestic life, it portrays a woman growing in self-assurance, a quality also conveyed in the tone and content of Anne Hilton's voice-over of the film.[54]

Several shorter newsreels and documentaries from Canada's National Film Board – shown either at cinemas before feature presentations or in travelling NFB circuits – featured the working lives of civilian women. Some reiterated the theme that women had entered wartime jobs solely out of patriotism and were anticipating men's eventual return home. In making the point that rough jobs would not subvert femininity, one film recorded a beauty contest among female munitions workers.[55] But many other movies detailed and celebrated women's workplace contributions, in part as propaganda to encourage yet greater participation and output. Shorter clips included *Canadian Women Help to Build Giant Tanks* and *Eastern Port: Canadian Women Do Big War Job Building Ships,* both of which showed women deftly working with various manual and power tools.[56] In 1942 the NFB made *Women Are Warriors,* directed by Jane Marsh, one of the few women the NFB hired in this capacity. For fourteen minutes, it reviews the many new and impressive civilian jobs performed by females in various Allied countries. At a British airplane factory, for example, the male narrator describes women "adapt[ing] themselves easily" to tasks that include "working on electrical circuits, soldering iron ... working with drills and lathes [and] rivetting sheet metal." He singles out Margaret Crawley, who had been unemployed before the war but is now proving herself as an "accomplished mechanic."[57]

WHAT MOTIVATED WOMEN themselves to join the wartime workforce? Many were indeed patriotic and accepted wartime work as a temporary undertaking. Polls showed that about 70 percent of women supported giving veterans the first crack at postwar jobs, though such surveys never broke down the results between women who were employed and those who stayed at home.[58] Still, it is unmistakable that over the course of the war, as more women moved into the workforce and especially into decent jobs, they increasingly came to desire or seek greater opportunities, including continued employment after repatriation. Many found personal fulfillment and respect through their work. Financial need, however, was the primary motive for women to pursue paid work and undoubtedly disposed many to clamour for more rights and benefits including the continuation of their relatively well-paid, traditionally male jobs after the war. According to a March 1943 survey of female war workers in Toronto, only 9 percent were motivated by "patriotism" to enter the job market, whereas 32 percent cited "personal reasons," including loneliness and boredom, and 59 percent identified financial considerations.[59] According to the NSS, about two-thirds of married women with children joined the workforce "to supplement the family income."[60]

Among the new double-income families were many in which the husband was in the military. Numerous servicemen's wives were trying to accumulate money for the future, but many took jobs out of very basic, sometimes desperate, financial need. These included women in cities where rents were high, or those whose husbands had enlisted and left them to cope with considerable debts. Many found the dependants' allowance insufficient. Propaganda assured every potential recruit that his family would not suffer financially in his absence, and that Canada's program was more generous than those of other Allied countries – a claim that was in fact true.[61] However, a private's wife with three children received about 80 percent of the average male industrial wage. A June 1941 report from Montreal's Family Welfare Association said that the city's social service agencies saw about 120 women a month who were in financial need, some three-quarters of whom already received support from the dependants' allowance program.[62]

Although Finance Minister J.L. Ilsley publicly maintained that allowances were generous, he conceded in November 1941 that some adjustments were in order, especially since he realized that heavy bad publicity could adversely affect recruitment. Besides increasing the marginal rate to provide, for example, an extra $5 monthly for a wife with two children, Ilsley widened the scheme to cover as many as six children (though at only $6 monthly after the third child), and support was extended from age sixteen to nineteen if the child was a full-time student.[63] Still, in 1942 Toronto's Welfare Council calculated that a mother of four required a minimum of $110 monthly, excluding medical bills. For a private who left behind such a family, the allowance exceeded this amount by only $6 even after half his pay was added to the pot.[64]

In January 1942 the federal government responded to numerous emergency cases by creating the Dependants' Board of Trustees, which could approve a maximum 25 percent supplement to the dependants' allowance. This allowance helped avert many personal catastrophes, especially since most claims related to medical emergencies.[65] But to obtain extra funds applicants had to go through a rather humiliating process of proving their poverty to a local board, which sometimes denied requests if it concluded that the applicant "did not appear to be making the maximum effort ... toward self-support." Even when money was approved, applicants

vay embittered by the attitudes of stingy boards, such as the one that
.50 to help pay for a funeral but refused any money for flowers, con-
a frivolous expense.[66]

Whatever their motivation for taking jobs, women, and especially wives and
mothers, often met with strong opposition to their large-scale and possibly long-
term presence in the paid workforce. In mid-1942, when NSS officials were recruiting more women for Quebec's textile sector, Catholic unions warned of
"ill-fated consequences" for family life. In this conservative and religious society,
priests denounced women's work outside the home as "contrary to the principles
of the church." A 1943 petition in Quebec gathered 122,283 names demanding that
"female labour at night be prohibited" as well as work for mothers with children
under sixteen.[67] Such sentiments, although expressed more often and loudly in
Catholic Quebec, were by no means confined to that province, although the percentage of married women and mothers in Quebec's labour force remained below
the Canadian average. Ontario's labour minister in 1943 suggested that Ottawa do
everything possible once hostilities wound down to ensure that working wives
and mothers be channelled back to their homes. Many employers nationwide demanded that mothers provide a letter from a "reputable source" proving that adequate child care was being provided while they worked.[68]

Even so the problem of high female absentee rates resulting from inadequate
child-care services became pressing. By the end of 1941, for example, Toronto's
West End Crèche had a waiting list of some 700 for 150 spots.[69] To address this
matter, Ottawa introduced a plan in June 1942 for a jointly funded Dominion-
Provincial Wartime Day Nursery Program to provide full-time care for children
aged two to five – the message being that women with children under two should
not work – and lunchtime and after-school supervision for children six to fifteen.

According to some sources, this initiative helped save families during this extraordinary time, and such child-care facilities, in being developed by experts, would
enrich the upbringing of children.[70] Still, strong public apprehension was a factor
in limiting the program; many women feared they would be seen as neglectful if
they entrusted their children to daycare. The Catholic Women's League of Canada
resolved that "any movement ... which tends to separate parents from children ... is
to be deplored." In Quebec, many French Canadians suspected government nurs-
eries of drawing children away from their faith. Rumours that in such places children would be confiscated and put up for adoption were widespread enough to
generate reassuring press communiqués from the Rumour Clinic.[71]

It soon became evident that government-run daycare would be a small-scale
venture, not only because of public opposition but also due to costs and the policy
that such services were strictly an emergency wartime measure. In this spirit, Ottawa stipulated that 75 percent of the spaces be reserved for the children of war
workers. Ontario and Quebec, both being centres of war production, were the
only provincial governments to participate in the scheme, signing the agreement

on 29 July and 3 August 1942, respectively. Ontario opened twenty-eight da
facilities, though the 1,085 spaces provided met only perhaps 20 percent of
need among mothers in war industry. In Quebec only six facilities opened, offering just under 200 spots in Montreal.[72] When it came to government-assisted lunchtime and after-school supervision, which also stipulated that 75 percent of spaces
be reserved for the children of war workers, the number of places was also inadequate. In Toronto, the waiting list for participation topped 3,500, prompting
various initiatives from social service groups, recreational associations, and parents. At Montreal's Rosemount school, the demand was such that the janitor's
wife began selling bread, soup, and milk for a dime, ultimately to 150 children.[73]

Not only did working mothers have to deal with inadequate child care, but they
sometimes also had to face the assumption that their working constituted criminal neglect of their youngsters. Working parents were blamed for the delinquency
of older children (whose experiences will be detailed in Chapter 8), and sensationalist press accounts talked about "car babies" abandoned all day in workplace park-
ing lots.[74] Feeding this sense of crisis was the fact that many child welfare agencies
became easily overwhelmed with the slightest extra demand. Most received about
two-thirds of their typically meagre funding from local governments operating
on modest budgets, and drew the rest from community chests and other philan-
thropic sources. During the war, they earned extra money by undertaking investigations for the Dependants' Allowance Board, but this revenue was more than
offset by the additional expense of performing this work, and by the strain on
limited personnel.[75] In making their case for more government support, child welfare agencies pointed out the extra demands they faced: periodic checks on British
child evacuees who had come to Canada in the summer of 1940, requests from
parents arriving in severely overcrowded cities to temporarily shelter their children, and the needs of neglected and delinquent youth. Moreover, given the poor
pay of social work compared to war jobs, it became increasingly difficult to retain
good staff. The Montreal-based Society for the Protection of Women and Children spoke of a "crisis" after receiving only twenty additional children at its facility, while the same message came from the Children's Aid Society of Vancouver,
even though the number of its child neglect cases grew by just thirty between 1939
and 1943.[76]

Some mothers left on their own had trouble coping with children even if they
weren't doing paid work. In a letter to the *Canadian Home Journal,* one desperate
woman said, "My husband is a private in the army. We have four children from
two to six years ... Looking after the[m] ... has grown to an intolerable burden ... I
am getting afraid of the way I am slipping; losing my self-control and therefore
losing control of the children."[77] In Toronto, of the 1,530 families dealt with by the
Children's Aid Society in 1942, 339 were those of servicemen. There were also cases
of criminal neglect by working mothers, some of which led to tragedy. A Montreal
woman was jailed in 1943 after her preschool son, whom she often left on his own

malnutrition.[78] Happily, such cases were rare in light of the
...orking mothers and the paucity of government support for
...r care providers pitched in to look after children. An Octo-
...working mothers with 118 preschool children in London,
...8.4 percent of youngsters stayed with fathers, siblings, or
...ent were in private daycare or homecare, 15 percent were
left with neighbours, 13.3 stayed with relatives, and 3.6 percent were left with
babysitters.[80]

AT THE WARTIME WORKPLACE, women generally found that men dominated the
higher-prestige and higher-paid jobs and virtually monopolized positions of authority. Ella Gilfouy, who was among thousands of women hired at the Leaside,
Ontario, branch of the Crown corporation Research Enterprises Limited, could
not recall a single female engineer or manager.[81] During the war, the average annual salary for men increased from $1,055 to $1,761, as more high-paying jobs opened
up and the average work week increased from forty-seven to forty-nine hours.
Although some women did very well financially – in the aircraft sector they averaged nearly $1,500 in 1944 – the average annual pay among women rose from $594
to $1,051 during the war, a marginal improvement from 56.3 to 59.7 percent of the
male rate.[82] Canada's National War Labour Board promised to implement the principle of "equal pay for equal work" when government war contracts were being
filled. However, this attempt at equity was easily circumvented by employers who
claimed that they had to reduce their expectations from women, watering down
tasks to compensate for women's lack of strength. Most women accepted a pay
differential or at least considered it unpatriotic to complain. The role of breadwinner was still assigned to the male, and most war jobs were significantly more
lucrative than typical female employment. In the Maritimes, northern Ontario,
and the Prairies, from which thousands of women migrated to centres of war production, annual salaries for females were commonly below $300.[83]

Many men feared that the large-scale presence of women in the workforce would
drive down wages. To demonstrate the inability of females to perform their jobs,
some men did things such as overtighten screws before a woman took over. Meanwhile, many people expressed dismay at seeing women not only wearing coveralls
and carrying lunch pails but also sitting behind the wheel of the buses or streetcars transporting workers to formerly male-dominated factories. Some people refused to board such vehicles. The Toronto Transit Commission's initiative of hiring
women as "passenger guides" to sell tickets and speed the transport process along
was considered more appropriate; women's "sunny" disposition, said TTC publicity, would help people cope better with overcrowding and delays. Yet even in
Toronto, labour shortages led to the hiring of some 100 women as TTC drivers. In
total, 333 women in twelve Canadian cities drove buses and streetcars, a job that
displayed female competence on a broad public stage and, with time and low acci-

dent rates, achieved at least a grudging acceptance among many of its opponents. "Not a word, mind you, about the 'woman driver,'" commented an article in *Saturday Night*. "Within a half-dozen blocks the old tradition had given place to the new, and thirty or forty citizens had settled back, tired and relaxed, and quite content to accept the change-over as right and proper."[84] Clara Clifford, who became a TTC streetcar conductor, remembered the snide comments from male co-workers fading as she proved she "could cut it" in dealing with unruly customers or reaffixing the large overhead rod when it became dislodged from the electrical wire.[85]

Indeed, both during and after the war women workers commonly spoke of their growing pride and confidence in coping with long hours and physically demanding tasks, in successfully performing "men's" jobs, and in earning the respect of many male co-workers. More than three decades after the war ended, Irene Wheeler recounted, for example, that her workplace performance at the Canadian National Railway upholstery shop in Winnipeg "brought around" most male co-workers who had at first even refused to lend her scissors to cut the heavy material.[86] Joan Bailin said that her work at the Montreal Crown corporation Defence Industries Limited precipitated a "whole social and emotional evolution" that made her more "ambitious [and] worldly-wise."[87] Her assessment was also no doubt influenced by the fact that Bailin was among the thousands of young women who set out on their own from more sedate and close-knit rural communities and small towns to find work in urban centres. Many women, especially those with spouses, emphasized the satisfaction they gained from feeling more self-sufficient. "It was a tremendous thing to earn your own money," said a married woman who had worked in the Vancouver shipyards; another, formerly with the Ottawa Car Manufacturing Company, which had converted to aircraft production, spoke of her job in terms of "buying self-respect."[88]

Some women may have unconsciously reinterpreted their personal development in light of later events such as the flowering of second-wave feminism in the 1960s and 1970s. Still, their comments are also representative of a great deal of wartime commentary from working women, a number of whom contended that their job performance entitled them to equal treatment with men. "Our foreman says that we are doing the job more accurately and faster than the men, therefore we are entitled to the same pay," was the attitude of several Toronto women surveyed in 1943 by the Canadian Youth Commission, an investigating body established in 1941 by the YMCA to survey the opinions of older adolescents and young adults.[89] Moreover, in commending women for their contributions to the war effort, a notable amount of press coverage expressed the view that "to cling to the ... notion that a woman is somehow inferior to a man in her ability ... is to fly in the face of demonstrated proof."[90] Columnist William Haig exclaimed in the *Winnipeg Free Press*, "The cold fact is that [in numerous jobs] women ... are quite as good as the men. Why, then, are they not being paid the same wages?" Evidently, many Canadians agreed.

In late 1942 the Canadian Institute of Public Opinion reported that 86 percent of women and 73 percent of men supported the concept of equal pay for equal work, although many added their opinion that employers had been forced to make jobs less physically demanding for women.[91]

In some settings such as plants whose workers were organized by the United Automobile Workers of America (UAW), the United Electrical Workers, the Boilermakers and Shipbuilders' Union, and the United Steel Workers of America, women did often receive the same pay as men.[92] But few male-directed union locals stressed or even addressed this issue, or the fact that females were congregated in lower-status jobs that were more poorly paid. "Women have to be trained more slowly than men to do a specific job [and are] not worth the same pay," was the unequivocal conclusion of one union official.[93] When unions endorsed equal pay for equal work, this policy was often seen as a necessary evil, to avoid the possibility of women driving down men's wages. This view was partly responsible for a short strike in 1942 by the UAW at the Ford plant in Windsor after thirty-seven women had been hired at a lower wage for exactly the same job performed by men.[94] Another factor detrimental to females was that, despite paying union dues, women were typically denied seniority, so that their eventual dismissal was easier. Although this injustice was recognized by the Women's League of the Canadian Congress of Labour, formed in 1944, the league's efforts to change this practice were without effect.[95]

The battle to improve women's rights and prospects within the workforce was also being waged on other fronts. In early 1943, after nearly two years of lobbying by women's groups, a ten-woman subcommittee was established within the federal government's Advisory Committee on Postwar Reconstruction to examine employment issues of particular concern to women.[96] It was placed under the direction of Margaret Stovel McWilliams, a former journalist and Winnipeg alderman. Most of the submissions it received from women's groups, though conceding to veterans the first priority in the postwar job market, made clear their desire that wartime gains not be erased. Mrs. Edgar D. Hardy, president of the often cautious and conservative National Council of Women of Canada, maintained, "We have definitely proved our capability and our adaptability to undertake any job which is given us ... Is it logical to expect that when the war is over all ... this should go for naught?"[97]

In November 1943, as per its deadline, the subcommittee delivered its report. Despite insufficient time for adequate research, McWilliams stated, the report's conclusions were nevertheless definitive: "Whatever field of employment women have entered they have proved themselves competent, conscientious workers." If these women were dismissed after the war to make room for veterans – a possibility the report did not oppose – it predicted many of them would seek other jobs, especially since they had "grown accustomed" to greater "economic independence." For these and other women, the subcommittee strongly endorsed equal pay for equal work and, where necessary, retraining programs – not only for trad female positions like nursing, teaching, and domestic service (which it advocated raising to the status of a semiskilled, diploma-backed occupation) but also for a variety of technical and commercial jobs, and even the running of a small business. Support was also expressed for government-subsidized daycare in peacetime and for a fourteen-week maternity leave, both of which spoke to a mother's right to work.[98]

The report was not well received in Parliament when tabled in January 1944. Most members, including the prime minister, did not even acknowledge its existence. Only Dorise Nielsen, who was elected in 1940 as a Communist to represent North Battleford, Saskatchewan, and a long-time advocate for women's rights, quoted passages into Hansard.[99] This inattention did not negate the significance of what had transpired, for neither the creation of the subcommittee nor its recommendations had emerged in a vacuum. They reflected women's growing conviction that they were making substantial contributions in the workplace, were proving themselves equal to men in numerous previously exclusively male domains, and as such deserved greater workplace rights, including the right to decent employment in peacetime, no matter their marital status.

Numerous media accounts, especially those written by women, reflected these attitudes: "Grown accustomed to economic independence at a wage higher than she has ever before been permitted to enjoy, will she in future be content to live on the average man's salary?" rhetorically inquired *Saturday Night* columnist Dorothy Norwich in December 1942. "Many [have proven] handier with the machine that puts brass bands on shells than ... with the cook stove and the vacuum cleaner." As the prospect of victory approached, *Maclean's* contributor Janet Tupper wrote that although most working women would step aside, at least temporarily, to allow veterans to re-establish themselves, many were adamant that "postwar reconversion not include reconversion of the Woman Worker into the Little Woman."[100] Indeed, a 1945 survey taken by a "large" but unnamed trade union of approximately 1,000 female industrial workers revealed that if given the choice, 80 percent of the married, 95 percent of the single, and 100 percent of the widowed women would continue working at their jobs after the war.[101]

As THE AXIS POWERS COLLAPSED, however, public commentary intensified its recommendation that women prepare to leave the job market. In mid-1944, C.D. Howe, then in the midst of shifting Cabinet portfolios from Munitions and Supply to Reconstruction, insisted that most women "would prefer to stay at home once the war [was] over."[102] Advertisements reflected this notion as several firms, in preparing to shift back to civilian production, linked their products to the re-establishment of a traditional and idealized gendered order. Appliance manufacturers, for example, illustrated women dreaming about what one company called the postwar "Victory Kitchen."[103] Juxtaposed with articles expressing hope for the

continued progress of women in the paid workforce were those advising them, on the contrary, to "come out from behind ... the welder's mask and to swap ... overalls for aprons."[104] Married women were told to put the needs of veterans first and show unyielding "support and patience" in order to speed their reintegration into civilian and family life, a responsibility often presented as being incompatible with full-time work, especially if it threatened the self-esteem that men gained from being the breadwinner.[105]

Another threat to the economic status of men and, according to many, one that made the prompt minimization of the participation of women in the workforce even more imperative, was the prospect of high unemployment during the process of peacetime reconversion. Among Canadians polled in January 1944, 58 percent thought that a period of serious joblessness would follow the war. This pessimism was based on the economic difficulties and social turmoil that followed the Great War, to which unemployed and thus angry veterans had significantly contributed.[106] The fact that unemployment did show signs of rising as Canada moved away from war production soon fed this anxiety. In the first six months of 1945 the unemployment rate increased from 0.7 to 3.0 percent. Just before VJ day, with some 600,000 servicemen yet to return to civilian life, 61 percent of Canadians expressed apprehension at the prospect of high unemployment.[107] Until those men were reintegrated, it would be necessary for women to step aside. One report released by the Labour Ministry shortly after the war encouraged women "only to enter the labour market when economic activity [was] at such a level that their employment [would] not prevent men from obtaining positions."[108]

Several government initiatives encouraged women to leave the job market, one of which was the family allowance program, a facet of the federal government's newly adopted Keynesian strategy of pump-priming the economy to offset the anticipated postwar downturn. Although principally geared toward developing healthier children and a better postwar life for youth, this program was also an attempt to reduce organized labour's pressure to end the wage freeze, help the Liberals to siphon off CCF support, and encourage a domestic role for women. Monthly payments started in July 1945 and were scaled from $5 to $8 for each child up to age fifteen inclusive for a maximum of four dependants, after which the amount for each extra child was reduced.[109] One historian has called family allowances an "indirect salary" for women to accept motherhood as a career.[110] Although this description considerably distorts the principal aim of the program, the subsidy did made it financially easier to have families and for women to stay at home. A family with four children, for example, could bring in an extra $250 to $300 per year, the equivalent of about two months' salary for a male industrial worker.[111]

Veterans' programs also contributed to women's relinquishment of their jobs. Generous cash payments to men, amounting to as much as a year's salary, and retraining and education programs did much to re-establish men as breadwinners. The 1942 Reinstatement in Civil Employment Act had a more direct effect; it guaranteed that veterans could return to their pre-enlistment jobs, many of which had been assumed by women in their absence. The federal government also ended its wartime hiatus from the 1921 regulation prohibiting the employment of married women in the civil service. A former employee of the National Research Council recalled that shortly after the war a woman was fired after arriving at work wearing an engagement ring.[112] On 30 June 1946, Ottawa ended its financial support for the Dominion-Provincial Day Nursery Program, and by the end of the year had phased out the wartime tax breaks that had helped attract wives into the workforce. The application of the new federal unemployment insurance program also pushed women into domestic roles or low-paying and typically female jobs. Married women who were fired were commonly denied benefits on the basis that their husband earned enough money to support them. A woman's funding was also often cut off if she rejected what she considered to be an unacceptable alternative in lieu of her wartime job, an approach rarely taken with men. In Parliament, Stanley Knowles, the CCF member from Winnipeg, spoke of one married woman who was fired from her $90-a-month job as a Grade 2 clerk in the federal civil service and was then denied unemployment insurance because she refused a job in a commercial laundry that paid about half that amount.[113]

No protection was extended to women as large sections of the private sector returned the gender composition of their workforce to prewar proportions. Irene Wheeler, who felt that her job performance in the Canadian National Railway upholstery shop had earned her considerable respect, bitterly recalled a foreman who, soon after the war, approached her and commented sarcastically, "You look like a good-looking man," before firing her.[114] Union newspapers made practically no mention of the massive dismissal of women, demonstrating either indifference or quiescent acceptance. One of the few articles on women workers in mid-1945 in the *Canadian Unionist* simply cited a 1942 British study claiming that women were more prone than men to fatigue and illness. Overall, the results were telling: Canada's female participation rate in the paid employment market plunged from a 1944 peak of 33.1 percent to 25.0 percent in 1946 (see Table 6.1, p. 150).[115]

IT WOULD CERTAINLY BE A GROSS MISREPRESENTATION to imply that all working women who returned to domesticity were forced back home. Many accepted the message that their employment had been an emergency wartime measure and that they consequently had "no right to kick" when let go. In fact, some women had come to loathe their wartime jobs. One female worker at Dominion Rubber in Montreal remembered the dust, dirt, and stench that pervaded the plant from the Molson brewery across the street and insisted that "anyone in their right mind" would have wanted to leave. Many were exhausted after years of the "double day" and yearned for an easier and, they hoped, more stable and tranquil life. They had often endured dreadful living conditions in overcrowded cities, started and ended their work day on packed public transit vehicles, and had to scramble for child care."[Many who were married had saved hard during the war to help buy a house and finally settle down. Women with children felt guilty – or were made to feel guilty – for not spending more time at home. "I almost feel as if I've lost my baby," was the comment of one worker at Peterborough's General Electric plant when interviewed by the Canadian Youth Commission. Others dreamed of marrying and starting a family. Among the single women interviewed at the Peterborough plant, only 4.4 percent said they did not want children.[118] After nearly six years of war, many such women worried that time was of the essence if they wanted to avoid spinsterhood. This impulse to home and family – which was also the desire of countless servicemen after years away – was indicated by a marriage rate that rose from 9.0 per 1,000 in 1945 to 10.9 the following year, and by a fertility rate per 1,000 women that climbed from 24.3 in 1945 to a postwar peak of 28.9 in 1947.[119]

The popular view of the initial postwar years is that things by and large settled down into a traditional, patriarchal order. This trend was helped considerably by a buoyant job market and low inflation, which made it easier for single-income families to be economically comfortable. Industrial wages doubled during the first postwar decade, and unemployment remained below 6 percent until 1957. The picture that still prevails from those times, with reason, is of mass migration to suburbia, into new communities filled with affordable housing, then viewed as ideal for raising families because of their wide-open space, serene atmosphere, and neighbourhoods brimming with young couples and children.[120] This image also includes the stay-at-home wife who devoted herself to supporting her husband's career and raising her family, a woman whose "extracurricular" activities seemed to revolve around visiting neighbours, playing mah-jong and bridge, and participating in the local parent-teacher association. Women who did not have children were often portrayed, in one way or another, as "deviant, selfish, and pitiable." In this world, even new home designs seemed to reinforce women's domestic, family-centred role. Large kitchens attached to most other rooms in a free-flowing, open design not only maximized available space in small bungalows, but also made it easier for a woman to supervise children while she went about her other household responsibilities.[121]

In the postwar media, family-oriented women assumed considerable prominence. One analysis of Canadian magazine advertising observed that portrayals of women in the role of housewife rose from a 40 percent average between 1939 and 1943 to a figure close to 70 percent in 1950.[122] Newspaper and magazine stories carried such titles as "I Quit My Job to Save My Marriage."[123] Postwar fashion, in reacting against wartime functionalism, emphasized ornamental femininity. Christian Dior's 1947 New Look, which made the biggest splash, projected the "flower-like woman" through clothes that presented "rounded shoulders, full feminine busts, and willowy waists above enormous spreading skirts." Many women buyers resisted – especially given the use of corsets and wired brassieres – but ultimately the new trend took hold.[124] Similar messages were projected on the big screen. In

Hollywood, independent women were often portrayed as "socially dangerous," and men who hooked up with them were "ruined" – sometimes even committing murder for these "unnatural women," as in *Double Indemnity* (1944) and *The Postman Always Rings Twice* (1946).[125] Strong and resourceful wartime heroines were gradually replaced by virtuous and pretty women like Doris Day and Audrey Hepburn, or by sex symbols such as Jayne Mansfield, Rosalind Russell, and Marilyn Monroe. Among the National Film Board documentaries of 1947 was the instructional film on maternal and child care *Mother and Child,* which told viewers the story "of a young suburban couple" from the time they learned of their pregnancy until their baby turned one.[126]

Manuals and how-to books proliferated across North America, further glorifying the domestic role for women. Doctors, psychiatrists, psychologists, and other "experts" on child-rearing also disseminated their advice through the mass media to mothers of the emerging baby-boom generation. By far the most widely sold work was Dr. Benjamin Spock's *Common Sense Book of Baby and Child Care,* which first appeared in 1946 and, as one of the first mass-marketed paperbacks sold in supermarkets and pharmacies, quickly went through several editions. Spock's emphasis on the need for a "steady, loving person" – whom most assumed to be the mother – as a continual presence and "promise of security" for the baby and child was especially well received after a period of great instability for children.[127] Also widely circulated in North America was the 1947 work by American psychoanalyst Marynia Farnham and her husband Ferdinand Lundberg, *Modern Woman: The Lost Sex.* Using, and perhaps abusing, Freud's comment that "anatomy is destiny," they argued that good mental health for women was possible only when women "accept[ed] with deep inwardness and readiness ... the ... goal [of] impregnation" and embraced a life revolving around family.[128] Several Canadians joined this group of public and quasi-celebrity experts, the most prominent being William Blatz of the University of Toronto's Institute of Child Study; Karl S. Bernhardt, chief of the Parent Division at the same institute; and Samuel R. Laycock, professor of child psychology at the University of Saskatchewan. In print and over the airwaves, they espoused an essentially conservative vision of what constituted "normal" and successful family life, placing, as historian Mona Gleason writes, great emphasis upon the "entrenchment of traditional gender roles."[129] Polls reflected the power, or popularity, of such ideas. Two-thirds of Canadian respondents to a 1950 poll (not broken down by sex) agreed with the notion that men should have the first chance at jobs, while another survey taken late in the decade found that 80 percent still thought it "best" that women with preschool children not work outside the home.[130]

BUT DID ACCEPTANCE OF TRADITIONAL GENDER ROLES – whether enthusiastic or tacit – constitute the dominant postwar legacy for Canadian women? The works of such historians as Americans Joanne Meyerowitz, Leila Rupp, and Verta Taylor, and Canadians Veronica Strong-Boag, Valerie Korinek, Joan Sangster, Franca Iacovetta, and Frances Swyripa all caution, in one way or another, against "reducing ... the multidimensional complexity" of these years "to a snapshot of middle class women in suburban homes."[131]

Millions of Canadian women did not live in suburbia, were not middle class, and needed to work for a living. Indeed, many women whose lives outwardly conformed to the popular, patriarchal constructions of the 1950s actually chafed against being homebound. High rates of depression were reported among suburban women who, in notable numbers, turned to psychoanalysis to combat this disease and often ended up riding the roller coaster of "uppers" to give them energy for the day and barbiturates to bring them down at night.[132] Several sociological studies of married women reported their strong desire to get far more out of life. Most controversial in this regard was the two volume work coordinated by Alfred C. Kinsey of the University of Indiana entitled *Sexual Behavior in the Human Male* (1948) and *Sexual Behavior in the Human Female* (1953). Both books received extensive coverage in major Canadian publications, including *Saturday Night* and *Chatelaine,* though several other sources called for the suppression of Kinsey's work. Although Kinsey's methodology came under fire – he used volunteers for interviews, for example, rather than seeking out a representative cross-section of the population, thereby perhaps attracting sexual extroverts – nonetheless the 5,300 men and 5,940 women contacted by his research team provided the basis for some disturbing, if not scandalous, conclusions.[133] In the case of women, these included claims that numerous suburban housewives felt great emotional and sexual disappointment with their married lives, that they resented the authority usually enjoyed by their husbands, and that about 25 percent had had an affair.[134] Not nearly as titillating, but also instructive, was a 1956 investigation by three Canadian academics entitled *Crestwood Heights,* which focused on an outlying upper-middle class section of Toronto. Many housewives expressed satisfaction with their lives, though the authors also noted words such as "humdrum" and "monotony" figuring prominently in several interviews. One woman said she was "slowly going out of [her] mind" from boredom, while another commented that she had the "brains" to do much more than serve as the "cook and floor-waxer."[135]

When it came to the postwar job market, many women, just as they had before the war, were compelled to work to support themselves or their families. Others worked because they were left as war widows, had husbands who came out of the military physically or psychologically incapable of working, or found their marriage no longer workable after years apart from their spouses and set out on their own. But even beyond such cases, after the economic reintegration of veterans, a steadily increasing number of women joined the paid workforce. This is not to dismiss widespread resistance toward this trend; it is important to remember that it took a generation after the end of the Second World War for Canada's female job-participation rate to reach its 1944 peak. But throughout the late 1940s, the average aggregate number of women in the paid workforce remained higher than pre-1943 levels, and the participation rate, especially outside agriculture, was slightly greater than at the outset of the decade (see Table 6.1, p. 150). While some historians use 1944 as a benchmark to largely dismiss the lasting impact of the war on women's workplace participation, 1940 is a far more appropriate reference point. That year the Depression had essentially ended, and massive government recruitment of women into the workplace had not yet commenced; exceptional highs and lows therefore do not figure in the equation. Once such factors are taken into account, it does indeed appear the Second World War did leave a legacy of greater numbers of women working outside the home.[136]

Probably more telling is that set against the image of the postwar stay-at-home wife is the contrasting fact that the total number of married women in Canada's employment market rose from 85,600 in 1941 to 349,000 in 1951. During the 1950s married women who worked outside the home, as a ratio of all working women, rose by nearly one-third to just over 30 percent.[137] Admittedly, several qualifications must be kept in mind. Some of the increase derived from postwar European immigrants; within this group, work by wives, typically in low-paid areas like the textile sector and domestic service, was essential for the family's economic survival.[138] Among many more affluent Canadians, the employment of wives was simply a means of supplementing family income to enable fuller participation in postwar consumer society, not a stepping stone to a career or a challenge to the husband's breadwinner status. Mothers frequently delayed participating in the paid workforce until their children were in school, and then, to accommodate their children's schedule, they worked part-time, receiving fewer benefits and opportunities for advancement.[139] Low-paid female job ghettoes persisted. In 1951, 96.4 percent of stenographers and typists were women, 98.2 percent of nurses, 96.5 percent of telephone operators, 88.9 percent of sewing machine operators, and 72.1 percent of schoolteachers. That year male labourers earned approximately $2,500 annually, while about half of women in the clerical sector earned less than $1,500. Men still typically made more for doing the same job; male sewing machine operators, for instance, earned an hourly wage of $1.20, approximately 50 percent more than women received.[140]

These ongoing inequities do not negate the reality of the changes that, in the context of the times, were regarded as constituting significant progress for women, and that several sources traced to breakthroughs achieved during the Second World War. These advances were even emphasized in usually cautious official government publications. Commenting in 1950 on the increasing number of women in the paid workforce, the federal government's *Labour Gazette* referred particularly to the "Second World War ... when they came through with flying colours." Four years later, the same source asserted that "the employment situation for women today is very much different ... Marital status alone is apparently no longer sufficient to prevent them from entering employment as it was in most instances in

1939."[141] The postwar mass media conveyed messages, particularly from female columnists, that brought forward the more liberal opinions expressed in wartime regarding "women's place." Tanis Lee, writing in *Saturday Night* in 1947, argued that women had proven their "strength" during the war and that the time had come "to stop pushing them in and out" of jobs and to "give them the freedom ... to work from choice or necessity."[142] Two years later, CBC radio began broadcasting an interview program entitled *Why Do Women Work?* In the first episode, host Ann Francis, who also worked as a columnist for *Chatelaine,* referred to the Second World War, when "women proved they could do jobs which had always been considered too difficult for female brains."[143] Indeed, in her detailed analysis of *Chatelaine* during the initial postwar generation, historian Valerie Korinek presents a magazine that, in seeking to maximize readership, tried to capture the main currents of women's lives and views, and during the 1950s published articles in which the topics "ranged from the stay-at-home mother with children, through to the working wife, the childless couple, [and] the single career girl."[144]

The steadily increasing employment of women also energized the ongoing struggle for greater workplace equity. When it came to the postwar campaign to secure legislation requiring equal pay for equal work, polls showed that despite a powerful conservative discourse, many Canadians retained the sympathetic attitudes expressed during the Second World War, views also no doubt derived in part from husbands coming to depend on their wife's income. One survey in the early 1950s showed that 69 percent of females and 57 percent of males supported the equal pay principle.[145] Spearheaded by prominent and indefatigable trade-unionists Eileen Tallman and Margaret Lazarus, and with active support from groups including the National Council of Women of Canada and the Business and Professional Women's Association, this campaign first achieved success with the 1951 Ontario Female Employees Fair Remuneration Act, which symbolically became law on 8 March, the United Nations' International Women's Day. By the end of the decade, eight other provinces had followed suit, as had the federal government in 1956 with its Female Employees Equal Pay Act. Moreover, the rapidly expanding presence of married women in the paid workforce undoubtedly helped account for the fact that by 1955 barriers to their employment had been removed by the federal civil service and most school boards.[146]

MANY BATTLES LAY AHEAD for Canadian women in the 1950s, probably more than had been won. Equal pay provisions were poorly enforced and were replete with loopholes – reflecting the still widely held belief that women's work had to be watered down – and the matter of low-paid job ghettoes remained virtually unaddressed. Women were still regularly fired for getting pregnant. Social constructions of gender still deterred young women from pursuing certain careers. For example, a new introductory text adopted in the early 1950s for Ontario high school home economics classes said that motherhood remained a woman's most important job. Yet, reflecting recent change, it also made the point that "the notion of male superiority is obsolete," adding that with increasing mechanization the "jobs reserved for men are becoming fewer."[147]

Both during and after the war, such dichotomies prevailed, reflecting what was a controversial, complex, and often contradictory process of historical change. Employment restrictions based on traditional notions of the woman's role remained entrenched, especially since many people saw in women's decision to work the signs of intensified moral decline that had begun during the war, including greater problems with children. But just as such fears helped fuel a postwar backlash against social conservatism, different and more progressive legacies flowed from other wartime trends. Among these were the widespread and laudatory coverage given to women's capacities and accomplishments as part of the wartime workplace; their growing self-esteem from having successfully performed typically male roles both inside and outside the home; and their knowledge – for better or for worse – that they were capable of managing in their daily lives both the household and paid work. Even if the changes encouraged by the Second World War proved small compared to the gender-based inequities that persisted after the war, a half-century ago, transformations such as the growing permanent presence of working wives and weak legislation mandating equal pay for equal work represented notable breakthroughs for females. In assessing the impact of the war upon her generation, a former woman war worker turned to cliché: "Two steps forward and one step back."[148] As the next chapter will illustrate, this aphorism is equally applicable to the 50,000 women who donned military uniforms.

7
Women Warriors: "Exactly on a par with the men"

AMONG THE WOMEN who donned a military uniform during the Second World War, only Canadian nurses did so without generating controversy. Their presence in the military had long been established, comfortably extending the social role of women as nurturers. Propaganda regularly presented the nurse as self-sacrificing and saintly, a glowing example of virtuous Christian womanhood. Her uniform – ankle-length dress, frontal apron, long sleeves, high collar, and headdress – projected both the maternal and the religious, and testified to a limited acceptance of women within a military world seen as far too brutal, and likely too morally debasing, for female delicacy and higher virtue.[1]

But from the beginnings of their association with the military, Canadian nurses actually faced assignments that demanded great physical and mental stamina. They made their debut in rudimentary frontier field hospitals during the northwest campaign against Louis Riel in 1885. Those who accompanied Canadian forces in South Africa during the Boer War, which claimed more military lives from disease than battlefield deaths, often worked without antiseptics or even decent sanitation facilities. During the Great War, 2,504 Canadian nurses and roughly 2,000 less-trained members of Voluntary Aid Detachments served in Britain, France, and the eastern Mediterranean in Gallipoli, Alexandria, and Salonika. Many worked at casualty clearing stations performing triage and administering basic care, sometimes within range of enemy artillery. Thirty-six Canadian nursing sisters died during the Great War while serving overseas: fifteen at sea (fourteen of whom were on the *Llandovery Castle,* which was torpedoed on 27 June 1918), fifteen from disease, and six from enemy fire. Historian Linda Quiney notes that many Great War nurses significantly honed their skills and developed self-assurance as they coped with tremendous pressures. She links this experience to the intensified lobbying by such women for the formal accreditation of nurses, a step that, between 1916 and 1922, seven provinces joined Nova Scotia (1910) and Manitoba (1913) in implementing.[2]

Within a month of the outbreak of the Second World War, 81 nurses were made part of Canada's Army Medical Corps, and 227 were on their way to England by April 1940. Indicative of recent strides toward professionalization, Voluntary Aid Detachment members were not used during the Second World War, and military nurses, all of whom were commissioned as officers, were required to have graduated from a school accredited by the Canadian Nurses' Association and to be registered in a provincial nurses' association. By the end of the war, 3,656 nurses had served with the Royal Canadian Army Medical Corps, 481 with the Royal Canadian Air Force Nursing Service (created in November 1940), and 343 with the Royal Canadian Navy Nursing Service (begun in autumn 1941).[3]

Nurses were still often publicly portrayed in terms that effectively denied their professionalism. At one extreme was what historian Kathryn McPherson dubs the "asexual saint," whose image shone forth from the cover of the October 1940 edition of the *Canadian Home Journal* in the guise of an army nurse in "double-breasted tunic, white square-cut apron, and white nun-like dress." At the other end of the spectrum, and just as trivializing, was the depiction of the nurse as an object of servicemen's lust. One cartoon drawn by an army sergeant, which appeared in the *Halifax Chronicle,* depicted an older heavy-set, stern, asexual head nurse at a base hospital instructing her young, blonde, and buxom female assistant "to kindly leave for a few moments" because the smiling and ogling male patient's temperature was being raised by her presence.[4]

Several media accounts began to note – to varying degrees – the skills, stamina, and mental strength required of nurses, a trend that was more pronounced than during the Great War, when Victorian mores still exerted a repressive influence over public discourse about women. Following visits to hospitals in England, *Maclean's* writer Dorothy Norwich lauded Canadian nurses for having "brains, initiative and courage [and for having] won ... a respected place among the modern company of the followers of Hippocrates." Reporting from Sicily in autumn 1943, war correspondent Wallace Reyburn not only played upon stereotypes by writing about nurses who used "feminine initiative" to rustle up a delectable meal from army rations but also described those who, like soldiers, endured without complaint lengthy marches and spartan living conditions, such as accommodation in a badly damaged former jail.[5] Such notions were reinforced by what Canadians saw on film. In the 1943 Paramount epic *So Proudly We Hail,* for example, Claudette Colbert leads a group of tireless American army nurses in tending the wounded while intense fighting rages nearby in Bataan. The *Montreal Star*'s film review told readers that they would see "our fearless girls at the fighting front" capable of "marching side by side with their men."[6]

As in previous wars, however, the actual experiences of nurses diverged fundamentally from the stereotypes. Approximately 28 percent of military nurses remained in Canada, where they also frequently faced intense and horrible situations, such as when dealing with the mutilated victims of crashes that occurred under the Commonwealth Air Training Plan or treating the coal-black frostbitten survivors of sunken naval or cargo vessels.[7] Most nurses serving outside Canada were stationed in Britain.[8] The first to arrive, attached to the No. 15 Canadian General Hospital, were soon dealing with as many as 150 operations a week as a result of the German blitz. By mid-1942 Canadian nurses in England were working in seven British and fifteen Canadian hospitals, including the No. 1 Canadian Neurological Hospital, which dealt with some of the worst cases of battle exhaustion. On several occasions, work stretched around the clock. "You just couldn't believe how much and what we operated on," said Patricia Moll of the deluge of patients received at the Basingstoke facility following the Dieppe raid – over 600 wounded in a nineteen-hour period.[9] In addition, far more than any other group of women who served in the military, Canadian nurses got close to the action. Although only one was killed during the Second World War – on a ferry torpedoed off Newfoundland – nurses were often found in hazardous settings.[10] Those assigned to the No. 1 Canadian General Hospital landed in Sicily only five days after its invasion and initially remained within enemy artillery range, experiencing daily air raid warnings. Nurses followed I Canadian Corps up the Italian peninsula. Like soldiers, they lived in tents or abandoned and dilapidated buildings, traversed rough terrain, and on many occasions slept in full battle gear. This was the experience of the nurses sent in December 1943 to the casualty clearing station in San Vito, which was sometimes shelled as a major battle was raging in nearby Ortona. Nurses attached to the Nos. 2 and 3 Casualty Clearing Stations in France in July 1944 first settled just outside Secqueville-en-Bessin, less than twelve kilometres from Caen, where heavy fighting persisted. In October 1944 nurses with the Nos. 6 and 8 Canadian General Hospitals established operations in Antwerp, but were forced by Christmas to move forty kilometres southwest because of V-1 rocket attacks.

Demands upon nurses near the firing line often severely taxed their physical and mental resources. In late August 1944, following attacks by Canadian soldiers on Germany's Gothic Line near Rimini, Italy, nurses at the Nos. 4 and 5 Casualty Clearing Stations worked up to thirty-six hours straight. One Canadian nurse in Belgium recalled many soldiers among the flood of wounded from the Scheldt campaign in November 1944 languishing on stretchers, while nurses were obliged to perform surgical procedures because not enough doctors were available.[11]

In later years it was common to hear the refrain that such experiences had built self-esteem and confidence. "For me [it] was wonderful [and] valuable," commented one nurse about her years in England. "I think it makes a person stronger and teaches [her] how to stand up to any situation." Gaetane Kerr of Montreal, who was assigned to a British hospital for two and a half years, observed that the demands of wartime nursing made her every bit a "real soldier."[12] Another recalled her time in Italy not only in terms of the "sweet and sickening smell of decaying bodies" but also as a period that was "immensely challenging and satisfying." Like servicemen, many nurses forged meaningful ties with the comrades with whom they shared and overcame tremendous hardships, and developed a strong esprit de corps. At the end of the war, many expressed a "keen sense of regret" at leaving behind close friends and resuming a civilian life in which, some feared, they would never again enjoy the same sense of belonging, purpose, excitement, and prestige. One nurse credited the self-reliance and skills she acquired overseas with giving her the determination and professionalism to carve out a high-profile postwar career in her field and even, she insisted, an egalitarian marriage. Yet many also said it was "very hard to settle down." For one former army nurse, this restlessness translated into a haphazard home life and a constant shifting between jobs in Canada and the United States. Also, as historian Olga Gruhzit-Hoyt writes, many military nurses who had been forced into making "life and death decisions" were disillusioned to find themselves as civilians with far fewer important responsibilities, and re-established firmly in the role of "handmaiden to doctors."[13]

ALTHOUGH CANADIAN MILITARY NURSES confronted highly stressful and harrowing situations and often functioned close to the line of fire, they received comparatively little attention in Canadian government propaganda and the mass media. This was largely because their presence raised few concerns. Despite some recognition of their stalwartness and professionalism, the perception of nurses remained comfortably ensconced within conventional gender constructions. Although the personal development that many nurses experienced would later challenge restrictive stereotypes, media attention to women in the military was primarily focused on the fact that the Canadian government had for the first time sanctioned women warriors. To many, these military women symbolized a bold and threatening challenge to the "proper" gendered order, to supposedly higher female codes of conduct, and indeed to the moral state of Canada in time of war.

The creation of female soldiers can be traced back to British Columbia. There, in 1938, the "intelligent [and] scrappy" Joan Kennedy, who was convinced by the Munich crisis that war was coming, was inspired by women's military detachments formed in Britain during the Great War to start her own Women's Service Corps.[14] Its volunteers, who bore the cost of uniforms and other equipment themselves, were trained in drill, first aid, map reading, basic motor mechanics, and the handling of small arms. When British women were once again called into action for auxiliary military service on 9 September 1939, Kennedy began lobbying the federal government for a similar program. By that point her corps had already topped 400 members, and with the war, others emulated her initiative. Indeed, by early 1941 over forty women's units of a military nature had been formed across Canada, containing some 7,000 volunteers.[15] In her continuing campaign for official recognition, Kennedy pointed out that South Africa, New Zealand, and Australia had joined Britain in accepting women into auxiliary military roles. Yet by May 1941 she was able to secure from the government only a willingness to hire a few female personnel for clerical duty at National Defence Headquarters. Canada's director of army recruiting insisted that women were unsuited for military duties because they possessed inadequate physical strength and had "more delicate feelings, more spiritual values and more romantic attitudes."[16]

Refusing to relent, Kennedy moved to amalgamate her Women's Service Corps with the province's Canadian Red Cross Corps, some of whose female members also engaged in drill, took first aid courses, and drove heavy trucks. In fact, the formidable Kennedy was soon named BC commandant of the Canadian Red Cross

Corps. This appointment put pressure on the federal government to re-evaluate its opposition, as concern grew that Kennedy and her followers were becoming too powerful, too autonomous, and too ambitious, just when the demands of the war made it imperative that Ottawa have an unchallenged say in how to deploy women if necessary to release men for action overseas. Another event that helped to alter government policy was the arrival that spring of members of Britain's Women's Auxiliary Air Force to assist with the Commonwealth Air Training Plan. Perhaps affected by their example, in June 1941 Ottawa acceded to a request from the British Mechanical Transport Corps to recruit Canadian women for auxiliary service overseas.[17]

On 27 June 1941 the federal government also announced the creation of the Canadian Women's Army Corps (CWAC). Within six weeks it began recruiting, initially to a cautious cap of 3,000 personnel over the first six months. As more men were required overseas and as women proved themselves competent in their assigned military tasks, CWAC numbers ultimately reached 21,624. Still, not until March 1942 was the CWAC fully integrated into the Canadian army; before then, for example, its insignia and rank designations deviated from standard army practice. Also, as Ruth Pierson argues in *They're Still Women after All*, by refusing to import an existing command structure from any of the women's volunteer corps into the CWAC, the federal government underlined its intention to control female recruits completely and channel them into lower-rung secondary roles based on gender stereotypes. At the time, the government maintained that to transfer any command structure was to invite charges of favouritism among different women's volunteer corps and thus possibly to hurt recruitment. More basic, understandable, and also applicable to male recruits was the contention that it was up to the military, not any autonomous civilian organization, to determine who was in charge and how things ran. Kennedy accepted this, and like most women who had long pushed for the official involvement of females in the military, enthusiastically greeted the establishment of the CWAC. While the first officer administering the CWAC was Elizabeth Smellie, formerly matron-in-chief for Canada's nursing sisters in the Army Medical Corps, one of her early appointments was Kennedy, who eventually became a lieutenant-colonel and succeeded Smellie in autumn 1942.[18]

On 2 July 1941, less than a week after the CWAC was created, Charles Power, Canada's air minister, announced the formation of a Canadian Women's Auxiliary Air Service. The following February it was renamed the Royal Canadian Air Force Women's Division, or RCAF(WD). On being reorganized, its role expanded and, like the CWAC, it became more fully integrated into the military; its numbers eventually reached 17,018. Finally, as the German navy had become a major presence in the northwestern Atlantic by January 1942, thus necessitating a greater military presence and administrative staff at major Canadian ports, the Women's Royal Canadian Naval Service (Wrens) was established on 31 July 1942. Like the navy in general, its numbers remained the smallest of Canada's three military services, ultimately reaching 6,781.[19]

Government propaganda strongly emphasized that the employment of women in the military was a temporary emergency measure. Such publicity material also assured Canadians that precautions were in place to prevent femininity from being compromised in the rough military world, in terms of either women's appearance or the supposedly higher moral standards that governed their conduct. Initially, women who enlisted earned two-thirds the male pay rate, the principal justification being that they were kept out of combat (indeed, of the more than 45,000 women in the three auxiliaries, only three members of the RCAF(WD) were killed). Servicewomen were not allowed to participate in the dependants' allowance program. As keepers of the domestic sphere, women with children were barred from military service whether or not their husbands were at home.[20] Unlike the volunteer units created by Kennedy, women recruited by the government were more limited to nonmilitary tasks, mainly related to administration and duties of a housekeeping nature.

Of these and other similar trends, Pierson emphatically states, "The cautious and carefully circumscribed extent to which women were admitted into the military ... precluded any fundamental change in gender relations." She further contends that because women were excluded from "combat duty and official arms bearing ... the male sex retained exclusive access to positions of high command ... as well as the symbolic power and authority of the 'protector' within society as a whole."[21] While much evidence supports Pierson's interpretation, nonetheless she sets the bar too high in identifying what needed to be changed or be dismantled to constitute "real progress." Her standard is unrealistic given widespread contemporary apprehension over the unprecedented move by Canadian women into the military, and more specifically into an institution then entirely male-run and populated (and which, moreover, deemed essential for battlefield success the notion of tough, domineering men protecting women on the home front). As a standard it also has several other drawbacks: it inherently places too narrow a focus upon restrictions and disappointments to explain continuing inequities; it too easily dismisses important and progressive shifts with respect to the images, attitudes, and treatment of servicewomen; and it fails to address the expansive and positive ways in which these women viewed themselves.

WHEN ASKED IN 1942 how women could best help the war effort, just 7 percent of the Canadians polled identified military service.[22] The following year, another national survey showed that acceptance of women serving in noncombat military roles as an emergency measure was approved by a margin of only 4 percent (43 to 39 percent). However, if one subtracts the results from Quebec, where enthusiasm for the war was lukewarm and strong disapproval from the Catholic church of women in uniform produced an approval rating of just 22 percent, support from the rest of the nation shows up at 52 percent.[23] A March 1943 poll revealed that only 58 percent of Canadians, and just 43 percent of Quebeckers, thought that a woman who wore a military uniform would not "restrict [her] chances of marriage." Many believed that such women would be considered too masculine and unattractive for marriage, were sexually loose because they were drawn to an overwhelmingly male environment or, worse yet, were lesbians seeking out trysts among their comrades.[24]

Simply by enlisting, numerous young women demonstrated considerable independence and courage. "I didn't tell my parents ... I had a fight with my boyfriend," remembered one who joined the CWAC. A twenty-one-year-old from Alberta said that her mother threatened her with a "thrashing" after discovering that she had enlisted in the army. In St. Stephen's, New Brunswick, a former member of the RCAF(WD) remembered waiting until a couple of weeks after Christmas to break the news in order not to spoil her family's holiday celebration. After she told her father, who insisted that the military was "no place for women," he threatened to go down to the local recruiting station to have her decision reversed; however, he ultimately reconsidered.[25]

To attract recruits and to reassure their loved ones, government propaganda tried to counteract the assumption that women in uniform would become masculine in appearance or temperament, as well as what became known as the "whispering campaign" that such women were "man-hungry, prostitutes, or lesbians." Among recruitment material released by the RCAF(WD) was the reassuring message that "Canadian mothers can cease worrying about their daughters the moment they enlist ... The reason being that [their] sergeant ... acts as a second mother."[26] The Wrens tried to cultivate an image as the most feminine and high-class of the three auxiliaries. "A Wren is a lady before she's in the Navy, so she conducts herself as one, rather than like a sailor," read one alluring advertisement.[27] Still, a 1943 survey of 7,300 Canadians undertaken for the Joint Committee on Combined Recruiting Promotion for the three women's services, by the Montreal-based commercial research firm Elliot-Haynes Limited, revealed that a not insignificant number of Canadians believed many women recruits came from red-light districts.[28] To offset such rumours and to boost sagging recruitment at a moment when men were particularly needed overseas – the Allies were preparing to invade Sicily and Italy – the dissemination of reassuring material was intensified. From the Wartime Information Board came press communiqués telling, for example, of servicewomen who always happily attended church parade. Moreover, in May 1943 after investigations disclosed that servicemen had probably initiated the whispering campaign, the army's Adjutant-General's Office issued warnings that scandalmongers could face prosecution under the Defence of Canada Regulations.[29]

Besides reassuring worried citizens that women would be little altered by military service, government propaganda also directly targeted potential recruits, who had many other choices in the civilian job market. Although most women would have rejected the prospect of sacrificing conventional notions of femininity in military service, propagandists clearly thought it necessary to project bolder images in order to make enlistment enticing. One advertisement, though making the point that women in uniform "relieve men for front-line duty," also depicted two CWACs confidently marching and declaring, "This is our battle too!" while the caption appealed to patriotism by reminding women, "Not since the historic and gallant days of Madeleine de Verchères have Canadian women been offered such an opportunity to serve their country."[30] Recruiting material typically downplayed jobs such as clerking, cleaning, and cooking, and instead showed women undertaking glamorous assignments such as, in the case of the RCAF(WD), logging air force flights and "despatch[ing] secret teletype messages."[31] Some publicity further suggested that military service could strengthen the peacetime employment potential of women, as did this appeal from the RCAF(WD): "Many [airwomen] are taking vocational courses which will fit them for more useful work now – and for better positions in the post-war world – for the RCAF conducts the largest vocational training school in Canada."[32]

Contrasting messages about women in uniform also emanated from National Film Board propaganda. Most crude in addressing this subject was the National Film Board's first major effort, the 1942 entry *Proudest Girl in the World.* A chorus line of CWAC personnel sings answers to potential recruits who ask, for instance, whether "the sergeants are nice or rude" (admittedly, some lyrics highlight prestigious jobs performed by women, such as radiographic and X-ray technician).[33] The next year, the NFB released two major documentaries on women in the military. *Proudly She Marches,* which also focuses on the CWAC, opens with the comment, "Women may be flowers and ornaments all right, but they are a whole lot more." The "whole lot more," contrasting with the narrator's sexist joke that "all girls like to have a good cry once in a while" when recruits are shown running out of a gas hut, is suggested by such images as a determined-looking CWAC completing an army transport course requiring her to skilfully manoeuvre a Jeep over exceptionally rough terrain. The narrator emphasizes that "never before in their day-to-day work" have women felt "a greater sense of personal fulfilment and a fuller sense of participation and pride in the very destiny of Canada" – a comment of the type that NFB historian Gary Evans contends could well have "raised hopes" among many women that "changes in [their] status might be[come] permanent."[34]

A similar pattern is evident in 1943's *Wings on Her Shoulders,* which looks at the RCAF(WD). Pictures of bombs loaded on planes for another massive raid on Germany open the NFB film, while the voice of the male narrator booms, "As the Allied air offensive gains in strength, the demand goes out for ever more men. To perform those thousands of necessary tasks to release the men to fly –" and Canada's answer dramatically marches across the screen, "the RCAF(WD)." Besides emphasizing that women's most essential role was to "back the attack," the film pays much attention to their "attractive" uniforms "altered and re-altered for a perfect fit." It also celebrates airwomen for "shaping the nation's destiny" and suggests that the new skills that many of them learned could be useful in the postwar job market where, for example, people would be required to send messages to and track aircraft, and otherwise contribute to "expand[ing] civil aviation."

Mixed messages also appeared in major newspapers and magazines. Certainly, much of the press coverage had as its reference point concerns that military service would imperil femininity. The *Winnipeg Free Press,* in reassuring readers that this was not the case, reported that when the public was invited to an open house at the women's barracks and recreational centre at Fort Osborne, all came away pleased to have seen buildings displaying a "feminine touch" and to have been treated to a "display of handicraft work" that included "doilies, fancy work, [and] petit point." A story in *Maclean's* disclosed that practically all servicewomen took advantage of regulations allowing them to wear a little rouge and lipstick.[35] Much ink was also spilled over their military uniforms. Whereas *Saturday Night* described the first version of the airwomen's uniform as "chic as well as practical," it said the 1943 edition of the uniform was even more sure to please because it was "planned and executed with the aid of Canada's foremost designers."[36]

Like government propaganda, such image-making did not constitute the whole story. As well as hearing about the preservation of femininity in the military, Canadians were also told about groundbreaking military contributions made by women, including overseas. In a feature on Britain's female air ferry pilots, who sometimes crossed the Atlantic, the *Family Herald and Weekly Star* predicted that their achievements would "figure one day ... side by side with the daring exploits of the RAF."[37] Several accounts highlighted the military contributions of Russian women. For instance, in September 1942 the *Toronto Star* profiled Lyudmila Pavlichenko, a twenty-six-year-old sharpshooter then visiting the city and fêted before a crowd of 20,000 at city hall, who had "picked off" over 300 Germans.[38]

As more Canadian women enlisted and proved their competence in military service, more press copy adopted a liberal, often inspirational, tone. As with similar coverage of civilian women workers, this pattern was particularly marked among, though not exclusive to, female journalists. The *Vancouver Sun's* Doris Milligan, after visits to five air bases in southern Alberta, said, "New types of work are constantly being taken over by aircraftwomen ... A girl may sign on for general duties and end up anywhere her capabilities, energy and ambition will take her ... Take the case of AW1 Freda Dixon ... Just the other day she was a messwoman. Now she's in charge of the station's [female] personnel." In April 1943 the Brantford *Expositor* printed a special twenty-five-page supplement on women in the military, emphasizing their stellar performance in high-profile jobs such as wireless operator, mechanic, laboratory assistant, and X-ray technician.[39]

Articles often suggested – and to varying degrees endorsed – longer-term progress that could result from women's military service. As part of its series entitled "Women in the Services," the *Halifax Chronicle* wrote that though this group might ultimately provide the "best wives" because they were conditioned to "fac[ing] unpleasant ... tasks and getting them done without excuses," their experiences might also "actually complete the process of emancipation" because, in possessing greater "strength and confidence ... they [would] likely ... take a fuller and far more important part in every phase of public and private business."[40] In the government publication *Canadian Affairs* (distributed mostly to military personnel abroad to keep them abreast of events at home), columnist Irene Baird, whose writing skills had landed her jobs with both the *Vancouver Sun* and the NFB, maintained that by "shatter[ing] precedents," women in the military had "raise[d] questions that [would] one day have to be answered" because many would neither "settle for the old order [nor] be put off by being told that such and such a thing is impossible."[41]

WHAT OF THE WOMEN THEMSELVES? Why did they join up? What treatment did they encounter? How did they come to regard their military service? Surveys taken in 1943 by Elliot-Haynes Limited found that about 40 percent of those who enlisted were inspired by "patriotism," which for most could be translated as the desire, in the words of one former CWAC, to do "more to defeat Hitler than help with the metal drive, knit for servicemen ... or assist in a canteen." A number of women sought to emulate a male family member in uniform; others enlisted because there was no man to uphold the family name; and yet others sought in some way to avenge the death of a loved one at the hands of the enemy. About one-third of respondents indicated their desire for adventure, greater independence, and escape from civilian routines, which for many had meant a narrow range of generally low-paid and dreary jobs or living at home under the direction of parents. The survey also revealed that the "prestige" associated with a military uniform motivated 13 percent to enlist, while just 12 percent specified the goal of releasing more men for active service.[42]

Although some women hoped to perform the same wartime duties as men, they constituted a minority. One was Molly Beale, an expert civilian pilot from Edmonton who was eventually inducted into Canada's Aviation Hall of Fame but as a member of the RCAF(WD) was denied her request to take to the sky like her brother.[43] Ultimately airwomen gained access to 65 of 102 possible air force trades, but these did not include pilot, navigator, gunner, or bombardier. In January 1943 Air Minister Power proposed to the Cabinet War Committee that women be given "light flying duties," but the decision was continually deferred on the basis that shortages of male pilots were not serious enough. Meanwhile, as of March 1945, 62 percent of CWAC personnel were clerks, 8 percent were cooks, and the addition of other assignments reflecting traditional female civilian jobs – such as storewoman, switchboard operator, postal sorter, and dental assistant – brings the total to 87 percent.[44] Some disenchantment was noted in morale reports, such as one in 1944 that concluded, "Those employed as GD [general duties], batwomen and waitresses

[are] becoming bored with their work or dissatisfied because they are not up-graded." Although CWAC propaganda often highlighted women mechanics, only 2 percent of its recruits actually ended up performing this job.[45] Moreover, in all the auxiliary services, women commissioned as officers had to defer to men at the same rank. Men outranked by a woman were not required to follow her directives unless they were specifically placed under her command, and men saluted women officers as a courtesy rather than as an obligation.[46]

At military bases, servicewomen encountered positive, though clearly sexist, comments that their presence helped to raise the moral conduct of servicemen, although they also met reactions such as "Why aren't you home?" and "You're old enough to be married and have a baby."[47] An August 1944 survey by the army's Research and Information Section of sixty-four CWAC units in Canada reported that 31 percent of women had "some trouble" with male soldiers accepting their presence, 24 percent described their relationship with the men as "excellent," and, significantly, 45 percent expressed no opinion.[48] Some may have been fearful of complaining, wanting to avoid the label of "whiner" and thus lend credence to the notion that females were too sensitive and weak for military service. Also indicative of male attitudes was the beauty contests among servicewomen organized on several bases and the pin-up photographs of them often carried in military newspapers. These servicewomen were always dressed in full uniform and never posed in an overtly sexual manner, so as to retain a sense of professional decorum and to counter the supposition that women in the military were loose.[49]

Most women who yearned for a posting overseas were disappointed. Only one in nine servicewomen was selected: 1,984 CWACs, 1,340 members of the RCAF(WD), and 503 Wrens, most of whom were stationed in Britain. With some 22 percent of their personnel receiving assignments outside Canada, Wrens were by far the most widely travelled; for example, 568 also served in Newfoundland, primarily to help administratively with North Atlantic convoy activity. In general, women overseas were assigned to a limited selection of tasks, namely clerks, cooks, and laundry workers. As of spring 1944, of the 853 noncommissioned CWAC personnel in Britain, just four were cipher clerks and two were driver mechanics, jobs considered to be higher prestige.[50]

Constructions of gender not only determined the jobs to which most servicewomen were assigned but they also governed the expectations of women's off-duty conduct; servicewomen were expected always to project an image of exceptional moral stature. Servicewomen were not provided with wet canteens, were told that public drunkenness would not be tolerated, and were reminded that they should not be seen in bars and taverns. They were lectured not to swear, smoke, or act in a familiar manner with men in public – which, to many military authorities, included holding hands.[51]

Controlling the sexual behaviour of servicewomen, especially conduct considered deviant, assumed a high priority. The official line on lesbianism – though not publicized lest people think it widespread – was that "it must be watched for, always," and not in the least tolerated. Those judged guilty were quietly and dishonourably discharged. Typically, they were not given the opportunity to defend themselves in a military court for fear that the exposure could create too much publicity and reinforce the idea that the military was no place for women.[52] Servicewomen who got pregnant were also not given a second chance. Once her pregnancy was discovered, a woman was immediately transferred to light duties and soon after discharged. This was largely understandable since there were no facilities for children on military bases. However, authorities acted with haste because they believed that the sight of pregnant women in uniform would reinforce the often-assumed link between military service for females and moral corruption. Starting in basic training, women were made to sign for each issue of sanitary towels and, according to one former CWAC, anyone who did not claim her allotment at the prescribed time was "called up on the red carpet to explain why." During 1944 the pregnancy rate within the CWAC, at 32.01 per 1,000, actually exceeded that among civilian women by approximately one-third. Unlike servicemen, however, servicewomen had absolutely no access to contraceptives; it was thought such acknowledgment of their sexuality would endorse promiscuity and undermine the higher code of moral conduct demanded of them. However, contradicting the presumption that pregnant servicewomen were "fallen" was the fact that over half were married, typically to servicemen.[53]

Meanwhile, despite rumours of high VD rates among servicewomen, the statistics demonstrated that they were less frequently infected than men. During the first half of 1943, the incidence among CWACs stationed in Canada stood at 25.8 per 1,000, compared to the army's average of 32. Higher male rates derived in part from consorting with prostitutes. In addition, servicewomen feared pregnancy, some internalized the expectation that they demonstrate higher virtue to earn respect, and a number were dissuaded from sex by the threat of punishment if the disease manifested. Most women who contracted VD were treated and retained in the service, though in cases where "other indications ... ma[d]e it advisable," such as repetition of the disease or the belief that the woman was a "sexual incorrigible," a discharge was issued.[54] Lower infection rates were probably not linked in any substantive way to the quantity and quality of education about VD prevention, as frank discussion of sexual matters was generally considered inappropriate for female ears. Before mid-1943, most servicewomen received just one lecture on VD prevention during basic training. A January 1945 survey reported that only about half of the CWAC units in Canada provided VD lectures at "regular intervals." As for the talks themselves, many servicewomen said they were too "technical." Also typical were lectures that simplistically stressed the advantages of chastity and warned that "there [were] no contraceptives which [were] foolproof against venereal disease."[55] The more graphic anti-VD films shown to men were thought too shocking for female eyes. One of the few movies made specifically for servicewomen was *For Your Information*. It features a male officer sitting behind a desk lecturing on the need for restraint, including admonitions against the consumption of alcohol, because "under its influence, without your knowing it, you may expose yourself to venereal disease." He reminds his female audience that after the war they "will want to get married and have a home and family of your own," a dream that venereal disease would surely destroy. Summing up against a background of uplifting music, the officer gets to his feet, walks in front of the desk, looks directly into the camera and, as if addressing each viewer personally, states, "You can play your part best in the present crisis and for your future if you are free from disease and in perfect health."[56]

SERVICEWOMEN certainly did experience a great deal of harassment and discrimination. But it is unreasonable to expect momentous change to result from this first foray into the military beyond nursing, and it is unrealistic to think that military service was intended to advance the status of women: it was meant to help win the war. Nearly all women who volunteered – they were never conscripted – believed it was their duty to replace men so that more of them could go overseas to defeat the Nazis. If some were left unfulfilled by their military service, they were in large company, but at least, unlike Private John Smith, they were not forced to face direct enemy fire. Moreover, it was not surprising that within the circumscribed job options to which they had access, most women ended up in lower-echelon tasks, or what the CWAC labelled "Class C" postings. Within the world of servicemen, things were not very different. Most male army personnel did not have glamorous jobs; for every air force pilot there were scores who tried and failed to become pilots; and countless sailors came to loathe their lives in cramped and damp quarters and on patrols that sometimes lasted weeks.

Nonetheless, female recruits did have the chance to demonstrate their potential to perform higher-status jobs. Upon enlistment they were given an "M Test" in mathematical, verbal, and mechanical skills to gauge their aptitude. On the basis of their results, as well as their pre-enlistment experience, CWAC recruits, for instance, were grouped into six categories indicating whether they were suitable to train for more complex trades or to become an officer. Those with average or below-average scores were assigned to posts – such as laundry worker, canteen helper, cook, and clerk – that essentially made them the female equivalent of the infantry grunt.[57] Like any system, this one was far from perfect, and no doubt many intelligent women, just like many men tested for proficiency, did not perform well or were left frustrated in their assigned tasks. Still, many talented women, and those with appropriate prewar experience, did have opportunities to obtain posts requiring considerable skill or carrying significant responsibilities, chances that many women would not have enjoyed in civilian life.

Surveys among servicewomen indicated that the least-preferred jobs were as cooks and laundry workers, postings to which only about 20 percent were assigned.

Administrative positions, most commonly given to women, were viewed much more positively, as in civilian life, as white-collar work of higher prestige. In one survey of CWAC recruits about one-third indicated this type of work as their first preference; many had performed such jobs before the war and realized they could provide valuable experience in preparation for postwar employment.

Government propaganda and press accounts undoubtedly inflated the numbers of women performing high-prestige jobs, though this exaggeration likely raised the public's perception of servicewomen. But as more men went overseas, a greater array of opportunities did open up to women. When the CWAC started some thirty trades were listed for women, and by the end of the war that number had reached fifty-five, including posts such as draftsman, mechanic, and technician.[58] Several of the sixty-five trades that opened up to members of the RCAF(WD) – which initially assigned women to just eight – required considerable preparation that gave graduates valuable skills, as in the case of a three-month course to qualify as a photographic technician, a job requiring extensive knowledge of cameras, the developing process, and "how to interpret reconnaissance and bombing photographs." Airwomen dominated the "information-handling trades," which often involved coded and top-secret material and which enjoyed considerable status, since it often required a superior M-Test score and training that, depending upon the scope of the job, might last up to twenty-four weeks. In Canadian coastal areas, Newfoundland, and Britain, airwomen were assigned to chart flight paths and to the often stressful job of air traffic controller.[59] "We had to be very quick because the pilots that were asking for a bearing were sometimes running out of fuel and not sure where they were," remembered a former airwoman who worked on Canada's east coast. "It was quite demanding because you could tell from their voices that they were pretty scared ... So it was essential that you were not only fast, but accurate."[60] Wrens accessed some thirty trades, by no means always mundane. Many stationed in the Maritimes, Newfoundland, and Londonderry, Ireland – the eastern terminus of North Atlantic convoy traffic – became involved in operational and naval intelligence, helping to plot the course of ships and working with coded material and mathematical equations to try to locate enemy vessels. Wrens staffed "wireless interception and direction-finding stations" that relayed information about, and sometimes detected transmissions from, enemy submarines. The work, though frequently tedious – Wrens often simply sat for hours wearing headsets – was still portrayed by military and civilian sources as critical to Canadian security. The job also demanded considerable fortitude, as several stations were located in rough and isolated settings where Wrens, sometimes left on their own, had access to weapons in case of undetected enemy activity.[61]

Besides widening the parameters of their participation, servicewomen also gradually acquired a better financial deal. Nearly all servicewomen accepted some pay differential with men largely on the basis that, as one former CWAC said, "They were required to kill and we weren't."[62] Still, soon after the auxiliary services were established and servicewomen demonstrated their competence in several domains, support grew, both among women in uniform and in organizations like the National Council of Women of Canada, for equal pay when women performed exactly the same job as men. More significant in seizing the attention of military and government authorities was the increasing difficulty in recruiting women, given the availability of decently paid civilian jobs. One survey conducted for the CWAC in the summer of 1942 concluded that "the greatest deterrent to enlistment appears to be the smallness of the basic and trades pay."[63]

To bolster female recruitment, especially with the Mediterranean ground campaign under way, servicewomen were granted significant concessions on 24 July 1943. They were allowed to assign a dependants' allowance to parents or siblings (husbands or children remained excluded because to name them as beneficiaries would suggest that the woman had abandoned family life). A woman in uniform married to a Canadian serviceman became entitled to his dependant's allowance as long as their combined annual income did not exceed $2,100. The basic pay for females was raised to 80 percent of the male rate, while raises for qualifying for a military trade were provided on an equal basis with men. Although these measures were implemented primarily to enhance recruitment, they were interpreted by the CWAC's chief personnel officer, Capt. Olive Russell, and undoubtedly by many servicewomen, as "further evidence of our country's growing recognition of the importance of the part played by Canadian women of the Armed Forces."[64] Among those echoing this theme was Canada's navy minister, Angus MacDonald, who said that numerous "women [were] doing work fully up to the standard of any done by men." Air Vice-Marshal John A. Sully justified the improvements by pointing to the many Canadian servicewomen in England who faced greater dangers than more highly paid men of the same rank whose duties kept them in Canada.[65]

DESPITE DISCRIMINATION and disappointments, most servicewomen said that they found military life "agreeable." Unit morale reports show expressions of disenchantment being overshadowed by the satisfaction gained from "broadened perspectives," "learn[ing] to cope" with difficult tasks, developing "greater self-discipline," and making "lifelong friends." One poll among CWAC personnel taken in early 1945 found that fewer than 15 percent expressed regret about their decision to have enlisted.[66] This result accords with an American study taken soon after the war, in which servicewomen, when asked to rate the personal importance of, and feelings they held toward, their time in the military, came up with an average score of 8.6 out of 10.[67]

Like servicemen, servicewomen later spoke fondly of the comradeship they had experienced. Sara Johnson, a former member of the RCAF(WD) who had grown up in an isolated rural setting, wrote that to be "surrounded by girls my own age, doing the same things ... was sheer paradise." Of the friends she made during her time with the CWAC, one woman said in later years, "They became closer to me than my mother and sisters back there in Ottawa."[68] Women who described themselves as "shy" or "self-conscious" prior to enlistment often talked of gaining "security" and confidence from the sense of belonging to a close-knit female family.[69] In building and expressing that comradeship – as well as in letting loose when off-duty – servicewomen, though more closely monitored than men, often managed to liberate themselves significantly from gender-based constructions of proper feminine conduct. Former CWAC Valerie Lowry recalled being shocked, but only at first, by the amount of swearing she heard in barracks.[70] Also doubtless initially shocking, but also liberating, to many were open discussions of sexual matters. Besides women who confined their activities to shopping, sightseeing, and the like while on leave, were others who, as a group, "played hard [because they] worked hard." With some despair, Olive Russell wrote, "A great many young [women] who never drank before have learned to do so since joining one of the armed services."[71] Moreover, both in Canada and overseas, servicewomen were known to fight members of rival Canadian female auxiliaries and British servicewomen, both over men and also over "who was tougher."[72]

Many women derived pride simply from being accepted into the services, since some 25 percent of applicants were rejected; but such feelings became especially evident after volunteers had completed their four weeks' basic training. Although their regimen was briefer and less rigorous than that endured by men, female recruits persevered through what must have often seemed endless drills and inspections, callisthenics, route marches, and many other challenges designed to build cohesion and counteract the softness of civilian and especially, many thought, feminine life. A CWAC from Quebec's Eastern Townships remembered "being yelled at all the time" by women drill instructors who, she asserted, were "more merciless than the men" in order to prove they were adequately tough and that their supposedly weak female charges were "capable of taking it."[73] Russell agreed that this was often the case, but she supported harsh training in order to bring out the "latent potential" of female recruits, a large percentage of whom, she claimed, lacked "self-discipline and confidence."[74] After basic training, many women did indeed feel ready to take on anything. A former Wren said, "That's where they either made or broke you, so I guess most of us were made," while an ex-CWAC boasted that basic training "weeded out the weaklings" because it was designed "to see whether or not you had the guts for life in the service."[75]

Even though most women who completed the training process did not end up performing high-status jobs, they did not necessarily feel resentment or disappointment at having made an insignificant contribution. On the contrary, with surveys showing that patriotism and the desire to help defeat the enemy guided some 40 percent to recruitment booths, and that more than 20 percent were drawn into the military by the "prestige" of the uniform and the desire to release more men for action, numerous women, no matter what task they were assigned, felt they had never before performed such valuable work.[76] One CWAC concluded that since the government was willing to feed, clothe, and pay her, clearly the "general duties" she was assigned were "critical to the war effort." Another insisted that it was wrong to equate domestic work performed for the army with such a job in civilian life, because in the military, this same task was "helping to save democracy."[77]

Such positive feelings were even more evident among the servicewomen assigned to jobs outside of Canada. Even if selected for work as a cook rather than wireless operator, laundry worker rather than instrument mechanic, clerk rather than truck driver, or telephone operator rather than air traffic controller, merely having been chosen to serve abroad was greeted with excitement. Overseas assignments were in themselves considered an accomplishment that validated one's "high proficiency" and, besides offering adventure, brought the feeling of contributing more directly to the war effort.[78] Without giving any thought to the type of job she might be assigned, an airwoman in Dartmouth, Nova Scotia, when told that she and several of her comrades were heading overseas, wrote in her diary that "there certainly have never been prouder, happier girls ... The fact that Canada thinks we're useful enough to send to England really thrills me."[79] One CWAC asserted that she could not "think of a single person who wouldn't have given her eye teeth to get over there [Britain]." Indeed, to obtain such a posting, some noncommissioned officers dropped rank to fit into the distribution of personnel that military planners intended to send overseas.[80]

Adding to the prestige of such postings and further enhancing the public perception of servicewomen, those sent overseas, because of their novelty, became the focus of numerous positive news reports. In one segment of the radio show *Comrades in Arms,* Canadian servicewomen in England were described by a senior male officer as "serious [and] committed," the type of personnel of which the country "needs more."[81] Press dispatches from Britain also told of servicewomen enduring without complaint the same demanding conditions as servicemen, living in poorly insulated corrugated-metal Nissen huts, for example, where "the utter cold and damp" was barely "assuaged by feeding the ... single pot-bellied stove with scraps of wood and coal." Women were also praised for "carr[ying] on with their duties" through "some of the worst blitzkrieg" from V-1 and V-2 rocket attacks.[82] During the later stages of the war, considerable attention was focused on the 43 CWACs who served in Italy and the 156 in northwest Europe, principally in administrative posts. Although they were kept well to the rear, several articles highlighted their ability to shoulder burdens just as well as the men. "No fancy uniforms here," read a Canadian Press dispatch quoting a CWAC in Italy. "Battledress and bush shirts are the order of the day. We are treated exactly on a par with the men ... Discipline, rations, quarters, clothing, working hours are all for one and one for all."[83]

YET BY THE TIME CANADIAN WOMEN set foot on continental Europe, plans were already under way to disband the three female military auxiliaries. This process was initiated in early 1945 but not completed until the end of 1946, as some women were retained to help administratively with the demobilization process. Only the nursing corps was kept in peacetime, though in drastically reduced numbers.[84] Both the federal government and the military rejected the idea of maintaining a skeleton crew of CWACs, RAF(WD)s and Wrens. The only concession was made by the army, which offered CWACs the option of placing their name on a supplementary reserve list in case of a future war.[85] Reflecting much of the popular discourse, one article in the *Ottawa Journal* assured readers that servicewomen looked forward to marriage and "lots of babies."[86]

However, just as the popular image of civilian working women heading back to the domestic sphere had its ambivalence, the return to peacetime was also not so straightforward for servicewomen. As the conflict drew to a close several stories, particularly from female journalists, spoke of the hope, or even the expectation, of progressive legacies. *Chatelaine*'s Lotta Dempsey, expressing what were for the time strong feminist beliefs, contended that "the average girl coming out of the services is twice the girl she went in," and as for their potential impact, she commented, "Forty thousand may not seem like a lot of women ... but maybe you remember that little group of long ago who were called suffragettes?" Rita McLean Farquharson, the *Canadian Home Journal*'s associate editor, said that though many servicewomen being discharged dreamed of "a man ... a home [and] a baby," they also had become more independent and would "not wait" with bated breath "for a Prince Charming to come riding by." She also warned families that they may not "get the same girl back" because their "daughters had grown" as a result of "serving in all parts of Canada, Newfoundland, France, Belgium, Holland, [and] Italy [and] performing men's work."[87]

Some military reports indicated that women in uniform would not easily accept the role of the demure and dependent spouse. This was strongly suggested, for example, in a May 1945 survey by the army's Research and Information Section of 800 CWACs in Canada and 200 in Britain as to their intentions following demobilization. Among those who were single, 31 percent wanted to get married as soon as possible. However, 21 percent either wanted to or would consider joining the peacetime military, 15 percent talked of attending university, and 33 percent put paid work or vocational training as their top priority. Some army psychiatrists even predicted that servicewomen would have a tougher time readapting to civvy street than servicemen because the "change in their pattern of life was more radical."[88] A Wren lieutenant quoted in the *Halifax Morning Chronicle* shortly before the war ended suggested that women be given the option of staying in the military for a "period of time" following hostilities to help ease their transition to civilian life.[89] In June 1945 the YWCA felt it necessary to establish a counselling service for ex-servicewomen having trouble readapting.[90] Many women lamented the separation from their comrades. Some talked about missing the discipline and highly directed nature of military life. Several said that they had felt important while in uniform and, as civilians, were having trouble coping with "being treated like nobody again." Compounding such difficulties was the widespread supposition among civilians that servicewomen would quietly and contentedly slip back into domestic life on the basis that their military service had been a mere aberration in their life plan that, many sources stressed, had changed them little. Many female veterans remembered growing exasperated with parents, husbands, or suitors who thought they would be pleased with a "a semi-dutiful life" revolving around "babies, coffee parties and bridge."[91]

Rather than taking advantage of retraining or education programs offered by the Department of Veterans Affairs (DVA), about 70 percent of women veterans claimed, in addition to a military gratuity based upon their length of service, a re-establishment credit roughly equivalent to that gratuity. Among permissible expenditures for the re-establishment credit was the purchase, repair, renovation, or furnishing of a home. A woman who had served in the Western Hemisphere for two years could collect a total payout of about $400, which approximately equalled the required down payment for a small house. While some servicewomen pursued this option to help settle into domestic life, many others joined the job market as self-supporting single women. Their prospects were often brightened by the skills they had learned or enhanced while in uniform. For example, Jean Geldart's wartime job with the Royal Canadian Air Force fingerprinting section landed her postwar employment with the RCMP and a life that, she pointed out, contrasted sharply with that of most of the young women she left behind in St. Stephen's, New Brunswick, who spent the war and many years afterwards working for a "pittance" at the local cotton mill.[92] But many ex-servicewomen found themselves stymied as better-paying and higher-prestige jobs went to male veterans who were considered to have made greater sacrifices and for whom, as current or future breadwinners, good salaries were deemed more essential. Like civilian women workers who were fired when male workers returned, ex-servicewomen were frequently denied unemployment insurance benefits if their husband earned enough money to support them, or if they refused a job that bore no relationship to their skill set or was woefully underpaid.[93]

In many cases, however, government policies intentionally avoided sending ex-servicewomen down a path to the household kitchen. In January 1942, under the auspices of the Advisory Subcommittee on Demobilization and Rehabilitation, Ottawa had established another committee to examine the special problems of discharged women. Its recommendations, designed in large part to attract more female recruits, served as the basis for steady improvements for women in accessing veterans' benefits. By the time the DVA was created in March 1944, females enjoyed, at least on paper, pretty much the same treatment as men under the various veterans' programs. The DVA's deputy minister, Walter Woods, insisted that this stood as "testimony to the value of their services and the esteem in which they [were] held."[94]

When it came to the actual administration of these programs, however, the DVA counsellors – mostly male – typically tried to steer married servicewomen into domestic life, and most of the others into the set of job options widely perceived as female. As of March 1945, by which time 10,000 women had been discharged, the DVA had only two female counsellors. After many complaints from, among others, Olive Russell – who in December 1944 was named executive assistant to the DVA's general director of rehabilitation – in July 1945 Mary Salter, a CWAC officer, was finally appointed superintendent of women's rehabilitation and, over the following year, came to supervise a staff that grew to twenty-one female counsellors and nineteen female interviewers.[95] But discrimination remained evident. Some DVA programs were considered unsuitable for "weaker" females. By the end of 1948 only 147 women, or 0.5 percent of the total number approved, had received the grants and low-interest loans available under the Veterans Land Act to start farming operations. Moreover, though the slightly more than 7,000 servicewomen who took advantage of DVA retraining opportunities by the end of 1947 represented a participation rate higher than that of male veterans – who, however, had a far easier time obtaining good civilian jobs – most courses in which they enrolled were comparatively short and channelled them into less lucrative and traditionally female fields. For example, 3,059 ex-servicewomen qualified as stenographers and typists, 1,459 as hairdressers and beauticians, and 1,021 as textile workers.[96]

It would be misleading to suggest that women veterans were simply victims of DVA counsellors and administrators determined to ensure male dominance in the workforce. When women veterans were asked about their preferences for vocational training before meeting with a DVA counsellor, in a 1945 survey taken among personnel with more than 100 CWAC units in Canada and Britain, 85 percent of them identified commercial courses, hairdressing, dressmaking, and nursing. Many women made a practical and strategic choice in selecting such options, believing that employment prospects for females in nontraditional fields were not as bright, especially when they would be competing for work against male veterans. Certainly a number felt most comfortable doing such jobs, especially since they had often performed them in the military. These vocational courses sometimes trained women to a quite high standard, as in clothing schools where they could learn dress design and management techniques for both larger and smaller establishments. It is also significant that, despite the strong recommendations of several DVA counsellors, virtually no servicewomen agreed to take a "home aide" course to prepare for what was being billed as semiskilled, decently paid domestic work. Furthermore, with thousands of women taking advantage of government retraining programs, the number of exceptions to the typical gendered pattern grew, thus making female participation in a wider spectrum of jobs less unusual and presumably providing more inspiration to other women. All told, ex-servicewomen took training for eighty-five occupations, including journalism, printing, bookbinding, linotype operation, commercial art, and photography, as well as various mechanical, laboratory, and technical posts.[97]

By the end of 1947, again courtesy of the DVA, some 3,000 ex-servicewomen were attending university, at percentages comparable to the rates among male veterans. Just under half entered arts programs, and when other domains traditionally accessed by women, namely social work and household science, are factored in, the total rises to about 80 percent. For numerous ex-servicewomen, university education represented, in the words of a former airwoman, "a chance most of us would never have dreamed of in those depression pre-war years."[98] Moreover, as historian Susan Hartmann writes, any movement further opening the doors of higher education to women created a larger pool of women with a "vision of life beyond domesticity and ... the ... subordinate."[99] Increased numbers of women at university also meant small but noteworthy gains and hence a greater foothold in areas of study leading to higher-profile professions. While the number of Canadian women graduating as doctors in 1944 was thirty-five, or 4.8 percent of all graduating doctors, by 1948 that number was fifty-four, or 8.3 percent. Also attributable in part to vocational and university training in DVA programs was the rising number of women actually working in professional roles: between 1941 and 1951 women chemists and metallurgists climbed from 3.5 to 10.2 percent of the total number in the civilian job market; architects from 1.3 to 2.5 percent; veterinarians from less than 0.1 to 2.2 percent; and draftsmen and designers from 2.7 to 4.9 percent.[100]

Growing recognition of the success, rather than the masculinization and moral corruption, of women in uniform was further demonstrated five years after the three female services disbanded. In 1951 women were again recruited into military auxiliaries during the early phases of the Cold War and Canada's participation in the United Nations' "police action" in Korea in 1950. By 1952 the air force had 3,133 females in uniform, while the army and navy peaked in 1954 at 1,307 and 349 respectively. Opposition was again apparent, though far less strongly expressed than a decade earlier. Canadians who were asked in August 1951 about these female auxiliaries indicated their approval by 53 to 27 percent. Resistance remained strongest in Quebec, where only 31 percent approved, but this proportion was up significantly from 22 percent in 1943; in the rest of the country 61 percent approved, up from 52 percent in 1943.[101]

Consistent with the times, however, servicewomen continued to confront demeaning stereotypes and much discrimination. In seeking recruits, the navy stressed its "stylish" uniforms, which, having been designed by a fashion expert, were "more feminine and smarter" than those used during the Second World War. Married women were prohibited from enlisting. Most women were still limited to low-level and low-paying trades such as clerk, typist, and supply technician. But building on earlier precedents, women continued to have access to higher-status jobs that included aircraft control assistant, radar operator, and mechanic, and they received the same trades pay as men for the same jobs. Ongoing discomfort with women in the military played a considerable part in the near-termination of their service again during the late 1950s and early 1960s when Canada began scaling back its military expenditures. Significantly, this time around the female presence endured, maintaining the breakthroughs into a male realm that many had thought inconceivable a generation earlier, and soon afterwards, with the impact of second-wave feminism, their numbers grew along with the scope of their activities.[102]

DESPITE MANY GROUNDBREAKING EXPERIENCES and signs of heightened self-confidence among servicewomen, their growing acceptance by society at large, and considerable evidence that, in the context of the times, military service translated into noteworthy and lasting progress for females, nevertheless much remained unchanged at war's end. To numerous Canadians, women in uniform, with the exception of nurses, were still viewed as a moral threat because their service was feared to subvert femininity, and because the military supposedly attracted the promiscuous and the perverse, including prostitutes and lesbians. Like civilian working women, particularly wives and mothers, women warriors – beyond the nonthreatening and deceptively maternal image of the nurse – were perceived by many to constitute a dangerous challenge to male dominance and to the primacy of the domestic role for females. With these attitudes as a backdrop, new military roles for women, while helping to advance gender equity, also played a part in reinforcing a strong though incomplete postwar backlash against social conservatism.

Overall, servicewomen were seen as yet another menace to the health of the nuclear family, already considered to be under siege during the war by such factors as quick, supposedly ill-conceived wartime marriages, rising divorce, widespread infidelity and illegitimacy, and the perception of mothers prioritizing their desire for money above their maternal responsibilities. Indeed, contrasting with the celebration of young people who pitched in patriotically en masse were mounting fears over the rising numbers of ill-governed youth who were going astray and turning to a life of crime. Yet like the wartime experiences of civilian and military women, the wartime situation of Canadian youth was exceedingly complex, blending conservative reactions based upon moral panic with responses that encouraged important, long overdue, and arguably progressive social change.

8
The Children's War: "Youth Run Wild"

CHILDREN IN WARTIME CANADA elicited both tremendous praise and deep concern. Among the first objects of admiration were the nearly 6,000 British "guest children" who joined Canadian families to escape the Blitz and a potential invasion. The way these children were portrayed was heavily influenced by the need to raise spirits during the bleak early days of the war. Their story whitewashed wartime problems by deflecting public attention onto the Canadians who became wartime foster parents and, it was said, displayed the dominion's solidarity with the mother country. Also, brave and unflinching British youth were held up as symbols of a nation that would never surrender. When it came to Canadian children, however, other considerations led to a very different, equally distorted scenario. While they were praised for their myriad patriotic contributions, social anxiety over general moral decline and family instability did much to feed into panicked – yet ill-supported – assumptions about masses of Canadian youth turning toward delinquency.

As A PRECAUTION against anticipated German air raids, some 1.5 million urban British children were evacuated to the countryside between 1 and 11 September 1939.[1] Although most soon went back home, this event prompted the National Council of Women of Canada – which since mid-1938 had been lobbying the federal government to form a reception plan for evacuated British children – to establish the National Committee for the Voluntary Registration of Women. Their aim was to raise money and clothing for the care of these children and to generate a list of Canadian households willing to offer them a safe haven.[2]

In 1939 Canada received only 253 British children, nearly all of whom were housed by relatives.[3] But Germany's sweep through western Europe and Britain's clear position as the next target changed the situation dramatically. Talk of mass child migration exploded, initially from continental Europe. Leading the crusade for a compassionate response was the Canadian National Committee on Refugees and Victims of Political Repression, which was led by Canada's first female senator, Cairine Wilson. In early June with the fall of France imminent, this group pleaded with the federal government to "act now" in a coast-to-coast newspaper advertising blitz, stressing that "this week the lives of hundreds of thousands of children are in our hands. Next week the deaths of thousands may be on our heads." This was no exaggeration: a large percentage of the children were Jewish. But as when

German Jews searched for a safe haven during the Depression, Mackenzie King balked, fearing a political backlash in a nation where anti-Semitism was still widespread and even fashionable, especially in the Liberal stronghold of Catholic Quebec.[4]

Regarding British youth, no such concerns were voiced, at least not publicly. This was a matter of Empire solidarity, and these were desirable migrants. "What a privilege for Canada" proclaimed the *Montreal Herald,* while the *Charlottetown Patriot* said that in future, these children would help "cement the ties of Empire."[5] Their numbers ultimately included virtually no Jews (even though thousands of Jewish child refugees had managed to reach Britain, and Canadian Jewish groups had solicited large numbers of potential sponsors) and, as things turned out, comparatively few Catholics.[6]

Overseas, Prime Minister Churchill was on record as opposing such migration, fearing it would send the message that Britain was "abandoning ship." But the iron leader had to bend; it was politically untenable to deny parents the chance to find a refuge for their children, especially with widespread talk – fuelled by the opposition Labour party – that only the rich were obtaining an escape route for their young.[7] On 20 June 1940 Britain's Parliament approved the creation of the Children's Overseas Reception Board (CORB) to arrange for the evacuation of children aged five to sixteen from cities heavily targeted by German bombers. Within a month of its opening, CORB's staff of 620 were trying to cope with over 200,000 applications. Rumours that New Zealand had agreed to accept 25,000 children, and Australia far more, prompted several Canadian newspapers to warn that great shame would befall Canada if it did not respond promptly and with equal generosity. Across the land, people sent in their names to child welfare agencies, to hastily appointed local committees, and to the National Council of Women of Canada. By mid-July over 50,000 offers of space had been received and newspapers congratulated Canadians on their loyal response, which, as one headline put it, "Revealed the Soul" of the country. They confidently predicted that the figure would soon top 100,000, and in fact, it did.[8]

To keep costs down in Canada and minimize adjustment problems in Canadian households, CORB children had to be of "normal health" and at least "normal intelligence." The excluded included the "feeble minded," epileptics, the blind and deaf, the physically challenged, and those with tuberculosis, congenital syphilis, heart disease, trachoma, favus, ringworm, scabies, "seriously defective teeth" and, if identifiable, chronic bedwetters.[9] For transport purposes, children were divided into "A" and "B" categories. Category A children, to make up at least 75 percent of the total, were to come from families of modest means, largely to offset complaints that only children of the elite were escaping under private arrangements. Category A children would receive free passage to their destination, but their parents were required to make weekly payments of six shillings for their upkeep (although the money actually went to support CORB operations and not to the host families). Parents of children who fell into Category B were obliged to pay for ocean transport. Families who accepted CORB children could write off from one income up to $400 per child for tax purposes as long as their annual household revenue did not exceed $5,000, and free hospital care was promised for the children. Legal guardianship of the CORB children rested with the governor general in Canada, and British parents had to agree to free authorities in both countries from all legal liabilities. British parents were promised that their children would be placed in a "suitable home or homes," with foster parents of the same religion, and be "suitably educated."[10]

Once shipping was located in England, the children selected were given only days, and in some cases just hours, to prepare. Some bubbled with anticipation about a great adventure: a trip to a land of Mounties, cowboys, Indians, and Eskimos. But for the many who were unsure, who were crying, who desperately clung to their often weeping parents, CORB officials were on hand to offer encouragement, to lead them in rousing songs like "There'll Always Be an England," and to tell them it was "unBritish" to cry. To reduce the trauma, parents were actually requested not to accompany their children to the docks.[11]

Britain bore the costs of ocean transport. The Canadian federal government, beyond helping the provinces with any hospital care required for the children, limited its financial responsibility to medical examinations at the receiving port and rail transportation within Canada, expenses estimated at $215,000 for 10,000 children.[12] Needing to control its financial commitments in the face of massive pending war-related expenditures, Ottawa delegated other responsibilities to the provinces, including the provision of temporary shelter for dispersion purposes and the arrangements for the permanent placement of the children.[13] The federal powers refused requests for extra funds for these services, ignoring the sorry state of most provincial and local child welfare agencies. Although British Columbia, Ontario, and Manitoba were the leaders in this field, they too lacked adequate numbers of staff, particularly professionally trained ones. New Brunswick did not even possess a provincial child care service.[14]

With the exception of Quebec, where only the anglophone minority was interested in housing British children, CORB evacuees were to be divided up among the provinces in accordance with their share of the national population. Within provinces, investigators sought to place most children in cities in accordance with their urban background, not to mix religious groups, and to try to ensure that they were housed in a "spiritually warm" and "morally appropriate" environment. Typically excluded were "unmarried [household] heads," who were thought to convey an inappropriate image of family life, though it is unclear whether this always applied to widow(er)s.

Parents who could not have children, whose children had left home, or who had had the tragedy of losing a child, were especially eager to take in an evacuee. Some

Canadians, however, seemed to have less noble intentions: for instance, to be the first on their block, or within their social group, to obtain a British child as a sort of status symbol. This motivation may not have been the basis for the soundest commitment, but it did attract a number of wealthier applicants and provided several CORB evacuees with rather posh accommodation. Other families wanted someone to help out around the house. Although the number of Canadian homes registered far exceeded British evacuees, many Canadians were fussy. Older and less attractive children often lingered for some time in placement depots. One welfare official in Halifax was moved to implore citizens in the press not to deny a child a home should he or she not have "blond hair or blue eyes." Also problematic was the fact that that staff shortages in local child welfare agencies often meant that untrained volunteers checked on the suitability of foster homes. Investigations were often cursory, and decisions were frequently based on technical considerations such as the amount of space available, the age of the adults, and the family's financial status. Follow-up investigations were at best haphazard. Unless a problem was reported, the CORB children were typically left on their own.[15]

The situation was even more lax with privately arranged and financed child migrations from Britain, which ultimately numbered more than twice those sent to Canada by CORB. In these cases, governments in Canada had no involvement beyond registering the children (e.g., for schooling) and verifying that they had no communicable diseases.[16] Many children within this group were younger than five, because with private migrations mothers or long-serving nannies were allowed to accompany children – although the currency restrictions that until 1943 limited each emigrant to bringing only £10 from Britain meant that virtually no nannies were brought along. Guest arrangements were also made by religious and social service groups such as the Kiwanis Club, which had branches in both Canada and Britain. Wallace Campbell, president of the Ford Motor Company of Canada, was instrumental in the migration of 102 children of UK Ford employees.[17] A number of British university professors sent their children to Canadian colleagues. Several British public schools partially relocated to Canada, in one case involving twenty children, including a niece and nephew of Queen Elizabeth, from the Parents' National Education Union School, which set up shop in a large "white-painted dormer-windowed house" in the Laurentian ski resort of St-Sauveur. Very often, however, these ventures foundered because of the impossibility of getting money out of the United Kingdom. For example, Lady Eden, the sister-in-law of the future British prime minister Anthony Eden, failed for this reason to establish a school in Vernon, Quebec. Many children from such ventures ended up in private Canadian institutions.[18]

Most British children came to Canada during the summer of 1940, though shortages of shipping space kept their number well below expectations. The flow of CORB children was cut off after 77 were lost in September 1940 when the *City of Benares* was torpedoed 800 kilometres off the coast of Ireland, and the British government ordered CORB to suspend operations. In 1941 only 458 children made the voyage, through private arrangements. All told, 5,954 British children came to Canada, which actually topped any other destination: 1,532 came through CORB, while among the privately arranged transports 2,350 children came with their mothers, 236 with another relative, and 1,836 on their own.[19]

During the summer and winter of 1940 these children received glowing press coverage in Canada. Reflecting Canada's confidence in Britain's ability to win the war, and the warmth of their welcome in this "loyal dominion," the newcomers were officially called "guest children" rather than refugees. Press reports painted an inspiring picture of cheering and gift-bearing crowds of Canadians greeting courageous, excited, and happy children at docks and train stations. For many children the trip was an adventure at first. One child wrote in her diary about the thrill of being greeted by newsreel cameramen when arriving in Halifax in August 1940.[20] What moviegoers and newspaper readers did not encounter, however, were private complaints from CORB officials throughout that summer over poor organization: children waited on boats in Halifax harbour for several days because trains were not ready, and then were herded onto old colonist coach cars where they often had to sleep two to a bed without enough pillows or blankets.[21] Press accounts were instead typically heartwarming and rather cute. The local paper in Dauphin, Manitoba, for example, went on about how the community gave a trainload of delighted guest children on their way to points further west their first-ever taste of hot dogs. All types of generous contributions were highlighted: in November a benefit concert by the Winnipeg Orchestra and Philharmonic Choir raised $3,000 to help defray emergency costs foster parents might face, and in December the Alberta Dental Association offered to provide a free examination for each guest child. In these cases the press deftly underplayed the extent to which such initiatives were needed.[22]

In one of many accounts about the bravery of the guest children, the *Edmonton Journal* wrote of nine-year-old Marcia Middleton of Scarborough who glibly referred to air raid sirens overseas as being like "Canadian train whistles," and then went on to state with a maturity suspiciously beyond her years, "We like Canada very much ... We want to be in your schools and learn about your country." *Ottawa Citizen* columnist Reg Hardy wrote of "our brave little Miss," Daphne Carroll, also nine years old, whom he addressed rhetorically after her arrival on Canadian shores. "Your face lighted up and your little chin went out and we knew you were made of the stuff which has made the British people what they are," gushed Hardy. "It was just the kind of reassurance ... that we in Canada need ... a reassurance born out of the realization that if little English girls can show this kind of pluck ... then English men and women are still made of the same dauntless stuff as Alfred the Great and Richard-Coeur-de-Lion!"[23]

Some articles did acknowledge homesickness, lest the impression be created that the children did not care about their real families, though such admissions were more than offset by upbeat accounts about their new lives. The children were described as being taken with Canada's physical beauty, quickly adapting to Canadian games and sports, preferring North American fare, and growing more quickly because they were now better fed than in Britain where severe rationing was in force.[24] In schools, they were supposedly the most popular students because of their direct contact with the war and the attention garnered by their accent.[25] The newcomers were presented as preferring Canadian schools because they were coed, did not require uniforms, and were characterized by more relaxed relationships between teacher and pupil. They were also said to excel academically, although it was rarely mentioned that many found the Canadian curriculum far easier than the British system.[26] Also not part of public discourse was the fact that the generally superior academic performance of the guest children often brought scorn from Canadian classmates, and not admiration as typically reported. If the British accent attracted curiosity it also attracted teasing; many newcomers tried to lose it as soon as possible. Many British boys also quickly ditched their public school dress of shorts, blazers, and caps because such attire exposed them to ridicule and got them into fights.[27]

Guest children sometimes grew exceptionally close to their foster parents, many of whom made tremendous sacrifices and extended great love. John Hutton, a seven-year-old CORB evacuee, insisted on calling them "mummy and daddy" despite their suggestion of "auntie and uncle." Betty Heeley, whose foster parents had long tried to adopt, recalled always being fussed over. A woman who came from Glasgow later described her adoptive parents as epitomizing the "height of generosity" since they paid for her to join her new "sister" – with whom she became best friends – at the privately run Ottawa Ladies' Academy.[28]

To their credit, many Canadians stuck it out with very difficult children. But the public rarely heard the less pleasant stories. As early as autumn 1940, Charles Blair, the chief civil servant in the Immigration Branch, complained to his minister, T.A. Crerar, about the many Canadians who had issued invitations in a rush of patriotism or sympathy for the children, but "didn't realize ... the financial commitment" and were now "figuratively washing their hands of it." With rising taxes and early wartime inflation, with currency controls that prevented British parents from sending over money and, in some cases, with the enlistment of the Canadian foster-father or a wage-earning older child, the guest children often became a serious financial strain. The Canadian Welfare Council estimated the yearly cost for a guest child at $250. Added to that could be medical expenses; for some reason, a relatively high proportion of guest children – about 5 percent from CORB within a year of arriving in Ontario – required a tonsillectomy or adenoidectomy. A number of families who had taken in children through private arrangements unsuccessfully lobbied the federal government to have the youngsters reclassified as CORB evacuees so that they could qualify for the tax break and hospital coverage. Guest children were sometimes made to feel ashamed of their "freeloading" parents overseas.

Thirteen-year-old Fred was given so many chores on his uncle's Manitoba farm as "repayment" that school officials soon made inquiries because the lad was absent so often. By 1941 some 150 privately arranged child placements in Ontario were transferred to the care of the Children's Aid Society, with financial difficulties – sometimes considerably exaggerated – leading the list of reasons. CORB parents also grew increasingly bitter about not receiving the six-shilling payment. In 1940-41, 11 percent of CORB children were moved to new homes. Compounding matters was that as publicity about the guest child program was overwhelmed by other war news, and as Canadians could demonstrate their patriotism through many other venues, accepting a war guest became less fashionable, thus making it more difficult for officials to find alternative accommodation.[29]

Also adding to difficulties was that British families and siblings were often unexpectedly split up soon after their arrival because of lack of money or household space among their host families. A former guest child who came to Ottawa at the age of ten with her mother and two younger sisters with the help of an evangelical group called Moral Rearmament recalled that her mother was "shattered" when she learned that only her youngest child, then aged two, would be able to stay with her. While the eldest adapted well to her new home, her eight-year-old sister, whom she described as "nervous," would often "lock herself in the toilet and howl and our mother would have to be fetched by telephone ... to come and get her."[30]

Many guest children suffered from more than just normal homesickness. Although formal studies were not undertaken on children sent to Canada, British psychologists did note high levels of anxiety, depression, and "infantile behaviour" among children who had been placed in foster homes in the English countryside.[31] Similar symptoms appeared evident in one Toronto home where the twelve-year-old son of a British university professor took to walking around naked.[32] Guest children often worried that their parents might be killed in an air raid. Some Canadian parents insisted that the children write home regularly, but many evacuees felt forgotten, rejected, or punished by being sent abroad. In a sort of sibling rivalry, some Canadian children – often never asked if they wanted a new brother or sister – resented their new family members' competition for their parents' love. Many children did not even know what to call their foster parents, feeling it a betrayal of their real parents to use terms like "mother" and "father." Some used "aunt" and "uncle," but others could not get beyond "Mr." and "Mrs." A number of war guests rejected the authority of their foster parents. In August 1941 B.W. Heise, who managed child welfare services in Ontario, reported that Children's Aid Society branches had been forced to remove war guests from homes because parents could no longer cope with their behaviour. The CAS then frequently had difficulty locating alternative accommodation, especially for adolescents, who were perceived to be more defiant and to be expensive to house and feed. Indeed, as early as November 1940, officials with child welfare agencies in Ontario, British Columbia, and Saskatchewan suggested that if the CORB program was to be renewed the following spring, no child older than thirteen should be included.[33] Tragic as it was, the sinking of the *Benares,* by ending the flow of British child evacuees, likely saved Canada from a major embarrassment.

The guest children began returning to Britain in late 1943, and by February 1945 only 205 remained in Canada. Projecting a positive picture to the end, press reports typically romanticized reunions in Britain: invariably, after some natural initial awkwardness, they proved joyous. Of course, such accounts often rang true. Echoing the feelings of many others, one thirteen-year-old girl recalled her "sheer delight" in feeling part of a "real family" again, which to her meant that she no longer needed to ask permission to take food or a drink.[34] But different experiences were not publicized. Because a number of children had grown close to their foster families and new friends, they did not want to return to a former life with which they no longer felt any connection, or from which they perceived themselves as having been banished. Many younger evacuees did not remember their biological parents. Those who recalled life in Britain were often shocked at just how much their parents had aged, and those who had come to idealize their former life during their long absence also experienced disillusionment. Many guest children had lost their British accent, which upset their parents and led to taunting from other children, some of whom also called them cowards or traitors for having left. After having shone in Canadian classrooms, they often faced a rough readjustment to British schools in which they had now fallen behind. Many came to detest life in devastated cities under severe rationing, in generally smaller British houses, and carried on about how much better things were in Canada – especially the CORB children from lower-income families. Such behaviour frequently aroused angry responses, including suggestions that they should return to Canada if they so disliked their homeland. Many eventually did, though not necessarily because they were enamoured with Canadian life. Rather, even despite difficult times in Canada, they decided to emigrate permanently after coming to the painful realization that they could not reconnect to an environment from which they had been torn at such a tender age.[35]

AMONG CANADIANS who grew up during the war, memories of the thrills and adventure of those years, rather than the difficulties or fears, typically stood out most strongly. Budge Wilson of Nova Scotia remembered that she "longed to be one of those Wrens in their snappy little hats," or, better yet, "a spy" foiling German plans.[36] The war permeated playtime activities. Baseball and hockey teams took on military nomenclature such as "Corvettes" and "Brigades." Young boys dreamed of "flipping through the skies in ... agile fighter planes" and organized mock war games. The popular Quebec author Roch Carrier remembered, "We had our ... wooden rifles ... We would die, moaning. And when we'd finished dying, we would start another war." For many, blackout drills were a time of excitement, not fear; toy companies marketed special-glow-in-the-dark kits for the occasion.[37] Young

Canada lapped up radio shows such as *L is for Lankey*, which portrayed the death-defying but always victorious exploits of Allied bomber crews. In newspaper comic strips, Superman and the Green Hornet crushed the enemy abroad as well as spies and saboteurs at home. Although the 1941 War Exchange Conservation Act denied Canadians American comic books, which unlike American magazines and newspapers were deemed nonessential imports and thus banned to control Canada's growing trade deficit, they turned to homegrown substitutes. The most popular was *Johnny Canuck*, the leotard-clad "answer to Nazi oppression," even though he appeared in black and white to conserve scarce dyes.[38]

Patriotic behaviour was cultivated in schools, particularly those attended by English-speaking Canadians. Saluting the flag, singing "God Save the King," and swearing allegiance to the Crown usually became mandatory, a demand that sometimes led to suspension of students who refused to conform, as did twenty-seven Mennonite children from Kitchener schools in 1940.[39] Schoolchildren were often gathered into assemblies to hear rousing speeches and sing patriotic songs. Without "touching on gruesome details or depressing features," a portion of class time was devoted to discussing the war. Students heard about the threat to freedom posed by the Axis, the importance of pitching in patriotically, and the heroic sacrifices and dauntless progress achieved by Allied forces. In June 1940, for example, even as the Nazis were completing their occupation of continental Europe, Ontario's Department of Education advised teachers to stress such themes as the "brilliant rearguard action" by the British.[40] The impact of the war on every school subject – spelling lessons that used military terms, for example, and mathematical problems "drawn from aviation, navigation [and] mechanized warfare" – no doubt gave them greater appeal to many children.[41]

No matter how small the patriotic task they took on, Canadian youth were praised and made to feel important. They often gained a "sense of purpose" as they left the relatively carefree activities of childhood to undertake new responsibilities and contribute to the war effort, which for many also provided great excitement and fun.[42] A full-page newspaper advertisement from Canada's Department of Munitions and Supply addressed youth directly: "When you boys go out and cut lawns ... you are doing a man's work [which] releases one more man for the armed forces ... When you girls ... help with the housework ... that means more hands to work in munition plants."[43] In innumerable areas, children achieved impressive and often, it was reported, spectacular results. By the end of 1944 Ontario students had raised $792,287 for the Red Cross and $596,566 for other war charities by door-to-door canvassing, rummage and bake sales, movie and dance nights, plays and carnivals, and by tapping their parents.

Youths were major contributors to the War Savings Certificate program. In Edmonton, for instance, their annual tally rose from $1,783 in 1940 to $41,926 in 1945.[44] The success of salvage campaigns depended a great deal upon children. With gusto they foraged through attics, garages, and barns, and then transported items by wagon or in six-quart fruit baskets to depots that were often located on school grounds. The zealousness of some children caused headaches for parents when items like kitchen pots and pans went missing, but far more children were lauded for donating their old metal toys. Several schemes capitalized upon the enthusiasm of youth. In late 1942 Rotarians in Yarmouth, Nova Scotia, working in conjunction with elementary schools, turned the salvaging effort into a war game, moving students up in rank for every fifty pounds they collected. Those who received promotions had their names announced over the local radio station, and the highest-ranking students were feted at a special Rotary luncheon.[45]

In Junior Red Cross chapters organized in schools across Canada, some 875,000 girls rolled bandages, practised first aid, and packed up clothing and nonperishable food for overseas servicemen and child victims of the war.[46] In industrial arts classes, boys made wooden splints and test-tube holders for medical staff, cribbage boards and ping-pong paddles for servicemen's recreation centres, and model aircraft for Commonwealth Air Training Plan recognition classes.[47] Hundreds of thousands of boys from twelve to seventeen enthusiastically enlisted in the Air Cadets, Sea Cadets, or Royal Canadian Army Cadets well before cadet training became mandatory in large parts of the country in 1943 and 1944. This involvement gave them a "greater sense of connection with the drama unfolding overseas." Like real regiments, cadet units had their own distinctive colours, presented in elaborate ceremonies, and like real soldiers, cadets learned military drill, paraded in public, fired .22 calibre rifles or old First World War guns, and learned skills that included wireless operation, map reading, and Morse code.[48] Members of groups like the Boy Scouts assisted with Air Raid Protection drills by running messages and watching for violators during blackouts; they also delivered handpowered water pumps to designated points and distributed sand to the homes of the elderly and the infirm when a bucketful became mandatory in every house. Girl Guides and their older counterparts, the Rangers, also pitched in as nurses' aides, for which they received a special badge.[49]

Starting in spring 1941, schoolchildren took paid work on farms to compensate for the loss of agricultural labour. The youngest joined the Children's Brigade, which enrolled boys twelve to fourteen and girls fourteen to sixteen for lighter and less-skilled tasks on nearby farms from which they returned home each day. More significant initiatives were the Farm Cadet Brigade, which sent away boys fifteen to eighteen for up to three and a half months, and the Farmerette Brigade, which did the same for young women sixteen or older who were still in school.[50] Despite the reluctance of some farmers to accept such inexperienced help, this work was considered important enough that, depending upon the agricultural activity, high school students with passing grades could end their classes without academic penalty as early as Easter or return as late as mid-October. Seeking to attract volunteers to these programs, one advertisement from the federal government struck a military theme: it declared that those "wearing the insignia of the Farm Cadet or

Farmerette Brigade" were, like those in uniform, providing "honourable service to their country."[51]

THE LAUDATORY CONDUCT of Canadian youth was not the only reason they received attention, however. There was great concern over the impact of the war on young minds. As early as 1940 Canada's National Federation of Kindergarten, Nursery School and Kindergarten-Primary Teachers reported that a noticeable number of children with family members in uniform were displaying "evidence of strain which shows itself in nervous habits, usually fidgeting, loud harsh voices, and very often an amazing display of impatience."[52] Debate swirled over whether parents should try to shield children, especially younger ones, from upsetting news reports or their anxieties about the war. Dr. Samuel Laycock, a director with the National Committee on National Hygiene, advised parents to always maintain an optimistic disposition. Others disagreed, including Dr. Karl Bernhardt, the director of child psychology at the University of Toronto, who maintained that even when parents "tried to shelter children," children still detected worries that magnified their fears. Roch Carrier, for one, remembered "day after day" his parents "disappearing behind the newspaper" and talking in hushed tones, causing him to lie awake at night for fear that "some type of monster" was coming.[53]

Concern over what information to share with children was certainly fuelled by the belief that the war had a bearing on errant conduct. Moral reformers, who in every age seemed to fret over influences on children, once again sounded the sirens. Charlotte Whitton of the Canadian Welfare Council spoke with alarm and doubtless some embellishment about the "loss of respect for life and limb" among children who, "with a glint in their eye, looked at [movie] scenes of obliterated cities."[54] Some claimed that mock war games were becoming too rough and children too fascinated with destruction, death, and killing. Dr. Kenneth Rogers, secretary of the Toronto Big Brothers, whose voice became more prominent with mounting wartime concerns over youth, wrote about two thirteen-year-old boys who used air rifles to make their war game more realistic, from which one lad suffered a deep leg wound and the other a severe cut above the eyebrow.[55]

Predictions of trouble with youth were voiced early on. In an address to the Big Brothers, whose members often served as parole officers for delinquents, Toronto juvenile court judge H.S. Mott warned in late 1939 of more difficult times ahead, referring back to the Great War, during which prosecutions in Canada of children under sixteen rose from 2,628 to 4,104.[56] A perceived connection between delinquency and the war was reinforced by newspaper reports on youth gangs in Britain who roamed city streets during blackouts looting shops and homes damaged by enemy bombs. By early 1941 *Canadian Welfare* wrote of "an unprecedented juvenile crime wave" in England, which it attributed to a live-for-the-day attitude created by the bombings and to the disarray in family life caused by war work that took mothers out of the home. Although Canada still remained "on the backwash of war disruptions," this source warned that with an expanding war effort "similar trends must be expected" among Canadian youth.[57]

Fears were also inflamed by reports from the United States about young people who, left by working parents to fend for themselves, turned to crime. The FBI reported that during the first nine months of 1943, arrests of those seventeen and younger were 19.9 percent higher than in the same period the previous year. Also in 1943, a well-publicized report by the Senate Sub-Committee on Wartime Health and Education called juvenile crime the "number one social problem in America."[58] In major US magazines, most of which circulated widely in Canada, stories on delinquency more than doubled once the United States entered the war.[59] Hollywood reflected and reinforced concern about delinquency in films like the 1944 production *Where Are Your Children?*, in which "a luckless little waitress falls into the clutches of sin via the dance hall, strange boys, liquor, joy rides, and jam sessions." At Ottawa's Elgin theatre, this movie was held over for several days to accommodate the large audiences attracted by the timeliness of the subject as well as publicity material that used unnerving fictional headlines like "Youth Run Wild" and "Boys Sought for Murder."[60]

Many Canadians observed that the war had brought about a crisis with delinquency in Canada, too. Court appearances by juveniles rose from 9,497 in 1939 to 13,802 three years later (see Figure 8.1). With accelerated wartime urban population growth, this trend was most evident in major cities. Between 1938 and 1943 juvenile arrests in Halifax rose by 60 percent, while between 1939 and 1942 increases in Toronto, Hamilton, and Ottawa were 45, 27, and 25 percent respectively.[61] The concentration of the mass media in such large centres, and the publicity they gave to such behaviour patterns, pushed the issue of delinquency to the forefront. As revealed in the *Canadian Periodical Index*, in the period 1939-46 there were nearly twice the number of published accounts of youth crime than in the period 1927-37.[62] Not noted, however, was that in areas where population decreased, juvenile crime also declined, as in the Ontario counties of Essex, Grey, and Haldimand where, between 1939 and 1942, arrests of minors dropped by 22, 44, and 33 percent respectively.[63]

Among those who urged against jumping to alarmist conclusions was the executive director of the Vancouver Council of Social Agencies, who noted that overall, Canada's youth "have made a magnificent response to the war effort and ... have maintained their balance extremely well in a world that has toppled about their ears."[64] But comments implying that legions of young people were turning bad increasingly competed with such praise. Rising anxiety over delinquency triggered investigations by social agencies in London and Toronto in 1942, in Winnipeg and Ottawa in 1944, and in Vancouver in 1945. Unless thoroughly addressed, these agencies emphasized, delinquency would get worse, especially during the postwar transition to civilian production when high unemployment was anticipated. Moreover, it was widely held that a large proportion of those responsible for social unrest in

Figure 8.1

Juvenile court appearances, 1939-60

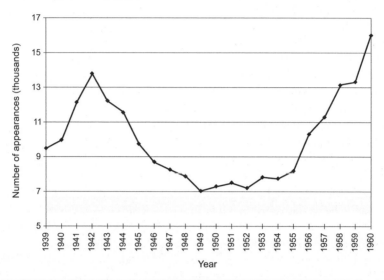

Source: K.A.H. Buckley and M.C. Urquhart, *Historical Statistics of Canada* (Toronto: Macmillan, 1965), 653.

Canada following the Great War had been younger workers, and that, in the economic and social chaos of prewar Germany, the Nazis had garnered their most fanatical supporters from among alienated youth.[65]

To explain rising delinquency, some observers conjectured that, as adolescent males saw more of their acquaintances enlist, they grew "restless" and in order to prove their readiness for action sometimes struck out in a "spectacular" manner. They also noted, conversely, that some young men were apprehensive about what lay ahead. A 1943 report by the Ontario Department of Education asserted that while "most ... carried on exceedingly well, feelings of unrest, uncertainty and anxiety" were also evident, a trend that with some produced "less self-discipline."[66] On a more general level, it was often said that young people, just like adults, were influenced by an "increased tempo of life" in wartime which "loosen[ed] social restraints," a circumstance almost always seen to be most evident in major cities.[67]

Shortages of living space, particularly in large cities, were also related to wartime problems with youth. When families were forced to split up temporarily while searching for lodging, parents sometimes placed their children in the care of foster homes or agencies like the Children's Aid Society, a stratagem that according to many experts made children increasingly insecure, resentful, unable to develop normal friendships, and antisocial. Marriages were said to suffer, and family squabbles to intensify, under the strain of looking for housing or enduring cramped

and rundown accommodation. Overcrowded, noisy homes increased the numbers of children having difficulty in school. Although not publicly discussed, no
doubt the combination of tired and tense war workers, packed homes, and ram-
bunctious youth produced instances of child abuse.[68] What some sources did mention was that lack of living space was a dubious moral environment for youth.
Sometimes only a partition separated parents from their children, a situation that
according to the president of the Ottawa and Carleton County CAS provided "no
opportunity for ordinary decency."[69] Overcrowded homes also meant that children were often sent outside to play so that "tired workers" could get some sleep or
"a little peace." This fact, or the desire of children to spend as little time as possible
in unpleasant living conditions, was frequently given as the reason behind excessive unsupervised "street dawdling" and also, for adolescents, too much time spent
at the "hamburger stand, seedy café and the juke joint."[70]

Communities began tightening curfew bylaws. Young people under sixteen generally had to be accompanied in public by a parent or "guardian of full age" after 9
or 10 p.m.[71] Police increased their surveillance of parks, cheap eating establishments, pool halls, bowling alleys, and any place where a jukebox was located. Juke-
boxes and juke joints were seen as magnets for delinquents, particularly the "zoot
suiters" who, considering their small numbers, received extraordinary press coverage. This limelight resulted largely from their outlandish costumes: wide-
brimmed gangsterish-looking fedoras, long and loose-fitting jackets with padded
shoulders, high-waisted baggy trousers pegged at the ankles, and brightly coloured
shirts with huge bow ties. Their outfits, which young people considered "hep," to
the broader public symbolized a threat to social order and a lack of patriotism in
light of government restrictions to save dyes and fabric.

Even minor crimes committed by zoot suiters in Canada were transformed in
press accounts to sound like serious infractions. This picture was also based on
sensationalist coverage of the June 1943 zoot suit riot in Los Angeles. Sailors from
the Chavez Ravine naval base, responding to alleged attacks on their comrades by
Chicano zoot suiters, roamed the city for two days, stripping the youth of their
costumes and administering severe beatings. Shore patrols and the city police
turned a blind eye, and newspapers, led by the Hearst chain – a "trumpet of white
supremacy" – blamed the victims. In Canada, newspapers emphasized the supposed obsession of zoot suiters with jitterbugging (and by implication, sex) and
also their periodic clashes with servicemen, whom some zoot suiters were known
to call "suckers."[72] Many fights involved competition for young women. In the spring
of 1943, for instance, there was a large fight outside Biggart's Refreshment Booth at
Toronto's Sunnyside Beach, to which many young people were drawn by a jukebox
until police confiscated it under the auspices of the Lord's Day Act because coins
were being deposited on Sundays.[73] The problem of zoot suiters was most serious
in Montreal, where it was linked to gangs made up of working-class French Canadian, Italian, and also some Anglo youths. Feeding on antiwar and anticonscription

sentiment, violence often erupted not only among gangs, but also against service-men, especially when French Canadians were involved. Media coverage of such events exploded between 27 and 31 May 1944 when fifty-three arrests in the district of St-Lambert resulted from brawls between soldiers and civilian youth, whom the English-speaking press in particular identified as zoot suiters. Then on 3 June, to avenge the beating of some comrades, approximately 400 sailors patrolled down-town Montreal in search of zoot suiters. Being unsuccessful, they turned their attention to the working-class community of Verdun, where a mêlée ensued with some sixty civilian youths at the Dance Pavilion, a favourite haunt for zoot suiters. The local French-language newspaper, *Le Messager,* accused the sailors of "Ge-stapo methods," but the *Verdun Guardian* called the civilians zoot suiters who had it coming to them because of their "insolence, [military] evasion [and] frivolity in wartime."[74]

Mounting delinquency statistics were persuasive that, quite apart from the skir-mishes involving zoot suiters, gang activity in general was on the rise. Prompted by this concern, in the summer of 1944 the Toronto Big Brothers sponsored a field study by two high school teachers, which was subsequently written up and published by Kenneth Rogers under the ominous-sounding title *Street Gangs in Toronto: A Study of the Forgotten Boy.* By focusing on downtown working-class neighbourhoods, the work identified twenty-six "youth gangs." Its definition of a gang was fairly wide, since it noted that none of the groups wore gang markings or defended specific turf, and that, in several cases, members came together prima-rily for the purposes of play. Still, the study stressed that in such settings youth tended more toward smoking, swearing, and various illegal acts ranging from minor violations such as stealing empty milk bottles from home doorsteps for the de-posit money to more serious offences that included smashing school windows and robbing street vendors.[75]

THERE WAS ALSO GROWING ANXIETY about increased moral corruption among ado-lescent girls in wartime. Between 1939 and 1943 the number of girls brought annu-ally before Canadian juvenile courts rose from 983 to 1,430. The fact that the majority of the charges were for breaking curfew, vagrancy, indecency, and incorrigibility suggests that police were making a concerted effort to crack down on the inci-dence of sexual misconduct. Judges commonly lectured girls about how they were cheapening themselves and heading for a life of ruin; indeed, even if the alleged crime had nothing to do with sexual misconduct, questioning by juvenile court judges often headed in that direction. This moral dimension consistently resulted in a higher proportion of girls than boys being institutionalized, whereupon much emphasis was placed upon teaching them domestic skills and sexually demure behaviour. They were also commonly tested for VD when admitted into institu-tions. In wartime, this panic over sexual propriety intensified. Whereas in 1941,

2 percent of boys and 7 percent of girls arrested in Toronto were sent to training schools, by 1945, the figures were 6 and 17 percent respectively.[76]

Indeed, during these years, adolescent girls in general were thought to be disturbingly open about their interest in sex and the teen idols who excited them. They seemed obsessed with "The Voice," Frank Sinatra. Canadian newspapers used the term "riot" to describe the reaction of "25,000 bobby sockers" in New York who tried to get a glimpse of the blue-eyed heartthrob. The press even made rather a large issue out of assuming that adolescent girls in Montreal had caused the disappearance of posters announcing a 1944 Sinatra concert.[77] Far more serious, however, were allegations that teenaged girls aggressively pursued servicemen. They were accused of using makeup and dressing to make themselves look older. With their parents busier than ever with work and volunteer activity at night, many adolescent girls were thought to be secretly dating servicemen and experimenting sexually. *Maclean's* wrote about fifteen-year-old "Betty," whose father was overseas and whose mother worked evenings in a munitions factory. When she was "found by health authorities to be a source of gonorrhoeal infection," she admitted that "since she was fourteen she had been having contact with soldiers."[78]

Adolescent girls were also cast as putting themselves at increased risk of contracting VD or getting pregnant by running away from home, usually from small towns and farms – and no doubt sometimes from abusive home situations – to seek out work and adventure in thriving centres of war production. "If they're under sixteen, they'll still get jobs by the simple expedient of lying about their age," wrote *Chatelaine* columnist Adele Saunders. "After work they roam the streets looking for excitement ... and have very little judgment ... when it comes to deciding when fun ends and trouble begins."[79] Taking a different tack, a representative of Vancouver's John Howard Society claimed that many girls, unable to secure decent jobs, "form acquaintances at lunch counters, dance halls or picture shows until necessity forces them to accept meals ... or articles of clothing from their new friends." From there, "it is but a short step to inviting the man to come to their room."[80]

The Ligue de la jeunesse féminine, an adult-run Catholic youth organization in Quebec, claimed that promiscuous teenaged girls were the primary source of rising wartime VD rates.[81] Most comments were less extreme, but many agreed that there was reason for considerable concern, and with some justification. The Manitoba Department of Health, for example, in 1942 reported fifty-six girls between fourteen and seventeen with VD. Hardly an epidemic, this number was likely boosted by more diligent wartime reporting on the part of physicians, but it was approximately double the annual cases in this age group recorded in the immediate prewar years.[82] Then there was matter of illegitimacy. Among women under twenty (the only appropriate age group cited in government statistics), recorded illegitimate births moved from an annual average of 2,648 in 1930-32 to 2,866 in

1940-42, and then reached 3,573 in 1945. Distressing as such figures might have been, the young actually held up well compared to older women. Among those under twenty, illegitimacy as a percentage of total such births declined from 31.9 to 27.9 to 27.6 during those same years, though in part this may have reflected a rush to the altar among young people before men shipped out, another trend that generated considerable public concern.[83]

IN ADDITION TO RUNNING AWAY from home, unprecedented numbers were dropping out of school before the legal leaving age to take the "dead-end" jobs that became available when their former occupants migrated to better-paid positions or were forced by National Selective Service into more essential employment. Many employers preferred child workers because they were more pliable and cheaper than adults. Four years into the war one *Saturday Night* columnist was moved to write, "Canada has almost reached the stage where ... another Charles Dickens is needed to rouse the nation out of a wholesale reversion to child labour."[84] Others worried that young people with considerable money in their pockets, still living at home and with few responsibilities, would adopt reckless and destructive spending habits. Critics spoke of boys spending lavishly to impress and entice girls, and of adolescents losing respect for their parents because they sometimes earned salaries comparable to their father's Depression-era wage. Many also worried about the economic and social consequences of having so many more unskilled, and eventually, it was presumed, dissatisfied workers. In the minds of many, these trends linked to increased delinquency, both because of poor attitudes being encouraged among youth and because truancy was a "forerunner of other, more serious problems."[85]

Among the provinces there was a real hodgepodge of legal school-leaving ages during the war. In English Canada, it ranged from fourteen to sixteen. In Quebec, education became compulsory only in 1943, after a long period of lobbying mostly in urban areas, where wayward youth seemed more numerous and were considered a greater social threat. The provincial Liberals, who came to power in 1940 with their strongest support from the cities, had indicated their approval of compulsory education, but many thought the timing of the initiative was linked to heightened concern over rising child labour.[86] Still, enforcement of school attendance remained weak across the country, especially in rural areas. Indeed, during the war, many more parents obtained permits to pull their children out of school to undertake full-time work. In Ontario between 1939 and 1942 the number of such permits issued per year soared from 2,146 to 12,792. While most were obtained in rural areas to compensate for the loss of agricultural labour, a number of cases involved mothers left on their own, sometimes too ill to work, who found the dependants' allowance inadequate.[87]

While parents who arranged permits to get their children out of school were criticized for "placing ... greed" above their children's future, greater censure was directed at those assumed to be allowing their underage children to work full time without a permit. For example, fifteen-year-old "Peggy" of Toronto dropped out of school with her mother's permission after her father's enlistment halved the family income, thus forcing Peggy, her working mother, and three younger sisters to move from a "comfortable home to three rooms."[88] In September 1943 the Toronto School Board requested that police step up efforts to "stop and question children of apparent school age seen on the streets during school hours."[89] The Ontario Department of Education reported that the total number of absences from public schools had climbed from 8,403,000 days during the 1939-40 academic year to 9,962,000 in 1942-43. The proportion that could be conclusively attributed to "parental neglect and truancy," while by no means exploding, did rise from 7.3 to 7.8 percent, or by nearly 164,000 days.[90]

Far more common than children with work permits or truants with full-time jobs were students who had jobs outside of school hours. As long as such part-time work was performed in a decent environment and did not involve excessive hours, most adults considered that it instilled a sense of responsibility. Many part-time jobs provided important services in wartime, such as the delivery of groceries by wagons after the introduction of gas rationing. But war made many more options available. There were reports of girls babysitting up to forty hours weekly for working parents. Other jobs were thought to carry significant moral risks. *Chatelaine* wrote of fifteen-year-old "Annabelle" of Toronto, who worked as a waitress weekdays from 5 to 9 p.m. and all day Saturday at an establishment where there were "plenty of fights and all kinds of men hanging around."[91]

Billiard halls and bowling alleys, which provided work opportunities for many boys, were cast as havens for unsavoury characters, a perception that had prompted Alberta's government before the war to ban those under eighteen from working in such establishments. In wartime Vancouver, press reports told of children as young as thirteen being employed as bowling-pin setters almost every night until the 9 p.m. curfew. In London, Ontario, one fourteen-year-old lad worked "part-time" as a pin setter up to 48.5 hours a week. In response to such reports, the Ontario government in 1944 amended the Factory and Shop Building Act to prohibit those under sixteen from working in pool halls and bowling alleys past 6:30 p.m.[92] Also that year, responding to concerns over excessive part-time employment, school administrators in London sent out questionnaires to over 4,500 pupils aged thirteen to eighteen. Just over half (52.7 percent) said they worked outside the home, though usually fewer than twenty hours a week. However, 291 worked more than twenty-four hours per week, and 1,165 often past 8 p.m., after which, they admitted, they were sometimes too tired to do their homework.[93]

MOST CANADIANS AGREED that as well as better housing, what was needed to address problems among youth was the stronger application of curfews and compulsory school attendance laws. But the fundamental source of delinquency was seen to be the instability of the wartime family. *Saturday Night* columnist A.M. Finlayson, though stressing his full support for fathers who enlisted, noted that many boys badly needed a father's "sound guidance" and "sterner direction." Another source claimed that with the "chief disciplinarian" gone, many children took advantage of the supposedly "kind-hearted" mother.[94]

Of course, fathers or older brothers who were servicemen or breadwinners were seen to be justifiably absent. But working mothers were considered problematic. While generally accepted as a needed emergency measure, women's absence from the home generated talk about "eight-hour orphans" and "latch-key children."[95] With distress, Nora Lee of the Canadian Welfare Council wrote of children, even in kindergarten, who "let themselves into their homes at all sorts of hours, and snatch what food they can."[96] An account in *Saturday Night* told of a "gaunt" seven-year-old boy who regularly sneaked out of his house at night when his mother was at work to collect scrap to sell to junk dealers so that he could buy pop and see movies. In giving "concrete meaning [to] juvenile delinquency," another article in the magazine wrote about two Toronto boys who, while their mother worked, broke into a neighbour's house and, for no apparent reason, "smashed all the glass jars" in sight.[97] A *Toronto Star* editorial concluded that if the father was away, delinquency "increased," but if the mother also worked outside the home, "it doubled." A Catholic group in Quebec went so far as to claim that "three quarters of juvenile delinquents come from the homes of working mothers." Stories from America continued to bolster such notions, including one widely syndicated piece written by FBI chief J. Edgar Hoover in 1944 entitled "Mothers ... Our Only Hope" in which working women were blamed for increased "perversion" and crime among juveniles.[98]

The consistent presence and guidance of a parent at home could indeed have helped some children cope better with war-related strains and stay on the right side of the law. But greater parental guidance could certainly not have eliminated increases in wartime delinquency. The fact is that between 1943 and 1945, just as the number of working mothers peaked, annual juvenile court appearances followed a downward pattern of 12,225, 11,554, and 9,756 respectively.[99] In explanation, some sources cited the increased attention paid to delinquency and the greater efforts therefore undertaken to provide youth with organized recreation. These were important developments that will be addressed shortly, but because they remained ad hoc and limited at war's end, they do not provide a satisfactory answer.

Far stronger evidence points to broader demographic trends being answerable for the rise and fall in delinquency numbers among the teenaged population, the age group consistently responsible for about two-thirds of juvenile crime.[100] The number of teenagers peaked in the early 1940s because the 1920s had seen relatively high birth rates as well as heavy migration into Canada.[101] The decline in delinquency during the mid-to-late 1940s can be attributed to drastic cuts to immigration and a declining birth rate during the Depression as much as to the postwar return of fathers from overseas and the renewed presence of women in the home.[102] It also makes perfect sense that by the early 1950s, and especially after 1952, juvenile court appearances started climbing again, because of the renewed rise in birth rates after 1940. Indeed, in 1958, when the first baby boomers reached their teenaged years, juvenile court appearances rose to 13,134, basically comparable to their wartime peak (see Figure 8.1, p. 206).[103]

Wartime delinquency trends were also affected by changes in arrest patterns on the part of the police. While some serious charges such as "theft and receiving stolen goods" and "wilful damage" were more frequent, most of the total increase came from minor infractions such as "breaking curfew" and "disorderly conduct."[104] Overall, between 1939 and 1942 minor offences committed by youth increased nearly twice as fast as major crimes.[105] Some talked about a lower threshold of tolerance during the war toward young people who broke rules. Vancouver's chief city prosecutor said in 1943 that many charges brought against children "would otherwise have gone unreported" before the war.[106] Probably more significant, however, was the ability of police to respond to youth crime. Although military enlistment of eighteen- to thirty-year-old males had drained police forces, it also reduced the numbers of people in the most criminally inclined demographic group, thereby allowing remaining officers to direct more energy to minor crimes committed by youth.[107]

EVEN IF EXAGGERATED or misinterpreted, reports of high incidence of child neglect and delinquency did lead to action on several progressive initiatives, specifically in the areas of organized recreation, public education, and the juvenile justice system. Most such initiatives had long been advocated, but were now propelled to greater prominence by the intense focus on problems relating to youth and the fact that systemic deficiencies, significantly worsened by wartime conditions, were more blatantly exposed. Motivated both by idealism and social conservatism, which were not mutually exclusive, the overarching aim of these programs was to steer the young more effectively toward conformity to, and success within, widely accepted social norms. It was hoped that young people would emerge from the war as generally content, loyal, and productive citizens, not as a group that harboured large numbers of disillusioned and alienated youths perhaps liable to cause a postwar crime wave or dangerous political instability.[108]

For some time, urban reformers had stressed the importance of organized recreation in building physical health, promoting healthy social interaction, steering idle youth away from delinquency, and moulding good citizens. During the Great War, Toronto's Local Council of Women had colourfully described recreational opportunities as a "regulated pleasure," a "moral prophylactic against crime and immorality." While all participants were directed toward sports – to counteract softer urban lives and drain surplus adolescent energy – other activities, in keeping with gender constructions, saw boys engaged in manual arts and girls in handicrafts and domestic activities like sewing.[109] However, with the decline of urban progressivism after the Great War and severe cost-cutting during the Depression, municipal governments, which funded most public recreational facilities, largely neglected them.[110] During the Second World War the situation initially worsened, as nearly all cities announced their intention to run frugal skeleton administrations to save human and material resources. Also, many recreational workers enlisted or obtained better-paying war jobs, as did the unemployed who, to be eligible for relief during the Depression, had often been assigned to clean up and maintain recreational facilities. While such facilities in Calgary received 433,190 hours of labour from the unemployed in 1933, by 1939 that figure had dropped to 193,691. In Ottawa, in the first winter of the war several public ice-skating rinks had to be closed, and in the summer the grass grew so high in parks that children's baseball league games had to be cancelled.[111] Parks in many cities were pre-empted for military drill and war games; in Halifax's north end, military needs left children without a park until 1942.[112]

Rising delinquency and declining recreational opportunities in wartime combined to highlight the need for recreational programs for youth. Among those who warned about the consequences was Kenneth Rogers, who observed that "idle" children and those "with no club connections" were at increased risk of turning to "immoral" conduct. Claiming that "youth ... in these times of stress are no less in need [than servicemen] of recreation," Rogers vigorously but unsuccessfully tried to persuade the federal government to fix recreational workers in their jobs and to strongly discourage their enlistment in the military. "Their total would make but little difference in the strength of our ... forces," he argued, "whereas their function ... is indispensable to the welfare of Canadian youth."[113] The *Toronto Star* went further, pointing out that in 1943 Britain had released 500 men from less essential military jobs to serve as recreational workers in order to "prevent ... youth from falling into an aimless existence." Similarly *Maclean's* observed that delinquency had increased in Britain when cuts were made to recreational programs during the first two years of the war, but once authorities there "reversed the policy ... substantial improvement" occurred.[114]

Several groups with a history of working with youth managed to step up their efforts with recreation. Looking back near the end of the war, George Tuttle, associate director of the Canadian Youth Commission (CYC), concluded that "during these war years" recreational programs had been "mushroom-like and various"; the CYC alone became involved with some thirty initiatives.[115] The YMCA, trying to broaden its appeal to young people of high-school age through its Hi-Y program, set up teen clubs to provide games, sports, music, and adult-supervised dances where, it was said, adolescents were taught to "get along ... in a wholesome and acceptable way" with the opposite sex.[116] In late 1942 Rotarians in Calgary, emulating efforts by several other branches of their organization, supplied a building for boys that contained an old lathe, electric jigsaw, car motor, work benches, ping-pong tables, and basketballs. The next year, the Junior League of Montreal purchased an eleven-room house for its new Jabberwocky Club for those of high-school age. For a twenty-five-cent annual fee, participants were directed into activities such as "carpentry, painting, sewing, sketching [and] dress designing," depending on their sex. To instill responsible attitudes, elected youth representatives ran a "club court" that could expel "troublemakers." Within a week of the club's opening, 600 young people had joined and nearly as many were placed on its waiting list, thus leading one local newspaper to comment that many more such venues were needed "as an answer to idleness and delinquency."[117]

Governments did start to become more involved with recreation, although at the municipal level the desire to conserve resources delayed most concrete action until after the war. Perhaps the most significant wartime initiative occurred in Toronto. After council debates on delinquency in late 1943, the city sent its commissioner of public welfare to assess "area projects" that had been started in poorer districts of Detroit, Chicago, and Cleveland, in which municipal officials helped channel more money into local recreational services and coordinate volunteer groups working with youth. Toronto's first proposed target was Moss Park, an overcrowded downtown working-class district long plagued by gang activity. In mid-1944 after a positive report from the commissioner, the city government established a committee that included representatives from its parks and police departments, the Toronto Board of Education, and several social service groups. Basing its recommendations on studies commissioned from field workers – who conducted some 200 interviews with local religious leaders, teachers, parents, students, and even gang members – the committee advocated hiring more full-time workers to organize and coordinate local groups working with youth and to initiate more recreational programs. These plans were, however, not implemented until 1945.[118]

Although the federal government refused to freeze recreational workers in place, the 1943 National Physical Fitness Act did help modestly. It made available to the nine provincial governments a total of up to $225,000 per year, apportioned by population and on a matching-fund basis, to develop recreational programs to counteract delinquency as well as reduce high absentee rates in industry and the large numbers of men rejected as unfit for military service.[119] Monetary support was lean since, given its other war-related demands, Ottawa was reluctant to commit massive funding, especially to an area under provincial jurisdiction. However, considerable publicity was generated thanks to the unbounded enthusiasm with which the program was promoted by its director, Ian Eisenhardt, a former Danish star athlete who, before the war, had managed British Columbia's modest public recreational program.[120] Ultimately, seven provinces participated; Ontario and Quebec declined, claiming that not enough money was forthcoming to make it worthwhile to accept Ottawa's incursion in their constitutional domain. Young Ontarians arguably ended up with a better deal, for, to compensate, Premier Gordon Conant added $250,000 to the province's education budget to promote physical fitness. Still, the federal government supplied to participating provinces some $100,000 per year, a large portion of which went to support local recreational initiatives and to fund training courses for physical fitness instructors and community recreational leaders.[121]

By war's end, much work was still needed to provide decent recreational services for youth. Most programs were small and relied extensively on volunteers. In 1945 only 42 percent of Canada's 316 municipal governments had a full-time recreational leader on staff. That year, the CYC reported that while America's National Recreation Association had set $3 per capita annually as the bare minimum to maintain adequate services, no major Canadian city met this standard, and the mean was just seventy cents.[122] But change from the prewar period was unmistakable. In early 1945 *Maclean's* wrote, "One of the healthy developments of recent years has been the renewed recognition ... that society has been at fault in not providing enough recreational services at which the youngsters can divert their energies into socially-useful channels." Later that year, in light of recent trends, *Chatelaine* printed a guide on how to set up a youth club, illustrating how easy and affordable it was. Also in 1945, the University of British Columbia created the Community Centres Institute, which offered courses on matters such as locating and modifying appropriate buildings for recreational use, fundraising, staff recruitment, and program development.[123]

The campaign for recreational facilities benefited greatly after the war from the fact that, rather than building new war memorials, most communities decided to modify monuments constructed after the Great War to commemorate those killed in the latest struggle. Money was thereby made available to pay tribute to Canada's fallen servicemen in other ways that could also help build a better postwar society. Of the $10.1 million raised in various communities by 1 February 1947 under the war memorial funds, $3.5 million was used to build twenty-nine recreational centres and $850,200 to provide thirty-eight public ice-skating rinks or swimming pools, all of which, either by way of their name or a commemorative plaque, were dedicated to Canada's war dead.[124]

Several municipal governments made improvements in recreational services a high postwar priority. Soon after hiring additional recreational workers for Moss Park, the Toronto municipal government did the same for its Beaches district and talked about dividing the city into a dozen zones for the purposes of more comprehensive recreational planning.[125] Ottawa's municipal government increased its recreational budget by 25 percent in 1945 to nearly $71,000, and then by another 31 percent in 1946 to $93,000.[126] The government of George Drew in Ontario created a Community Programs Branch in 1945, placing it under the direction of J.K. Tett, a former competitive swimmer. It could authorize a maximum grant of $3,500 to a municipality to cover up to a third of the costs of hiring recreational workers and a quarter of operating expenses. In its first three years, the branch helped fund 100 programs. Behind this initiative was the desire not only to check idleness and delinquency but also to bring together people from different backgrounds, particularly to help promote the quick assimilation of European refugees and to defuse any class tensions. Such aims began to take on considerable importance in the context of the emerging Cold War. Indeed, in selling the new branch to the public, Premier Drew said it would serve as a "means to combat [the] reds."[127]

THE CHALLENGE WITH YOUNG PEOPLE during the war was not only to keep them constructively occupied while outside the classroom, avoid problems with truancy, and discourage their opting for dead-end jobs, all of which were viewed as contributing to delinquency. Significant changes were also needed within school systems to keep youth in school and on track.

Several responses in the educational arena took on a strong conservative moral tone. Some seventy schools across the Prairies implemented courses in religious instruction in 1942 and 1943.[128] In Ontario, soon after his 1943 election, Drew established twice-weekly compulsory religious classes in public schools, specifically in response to rising delinquency statistics. The government maintained that virtually no one could object to the program since it stressed widely accepted principles such as "the brotherhood of all men under ... one God, charity and the golden rule," and since students could be excused from the classes with a note from their parents. However, the *Canadian Forum,* one of few voices of dissent, argued that those who chose not to attend often faced "mental cruelty" from fellow classmates and even sometimes from teachers.[129]

Another response by numerous school boards was to intensify education in citizenship and civics. "Weakness in citizenship," asserted one Ontario educator, had "manifested itself in attempts to hoard, to set up or patronize black markets," and among youth in "increased delinquency." Another supporter of the programs, Dr. H.R. Kingston, president of the Ontario Educational Association's Collegiate and Secondary School Department, said that since "Hitler demonstrated that fascism could be taught," it was crucial that greater efforts be made to "do the same with democracy."[130] Of course, civics education was further encouraged by wartime patriotism and the desire to keep youth staunchly committed to the war effort; but it also aimed to ensure that the conduct of young people not exacerbate the difficult times anticipated after the conflict. A 1943 report from Ontario's Department of Education brought the reminder that the immediate postwar period might "very well be beset by economic decline ... bitterness and hysteria as in 1919," and added, "Education in the responsibilities of citizenship [is] one of the best guarantees against any drift to totalitarian forms of government."[131]

The Canadian Council for Education in Citizenship was very helpful in this area. Its mission was to promote greater knowledge of and respect for Canada's democratic institutions, the responsibilities of citizenship, and a sense of Canadian identity, albeit one based upon its Anglo-Saxon heritage. Formed in 1940, it developed strong links to the Wartime Information Board and the National Film

Board. Moreover, its board membership connected it to each provincial department of education as well as to the Canadian Teachers' Federation and the Canada and Newfoundland Education Association (CNEA). To schools across Canada, it sent reams of literature such as the booklet *How We Hold Elections,* and arranged for showings of stirring films like *Churchill's Island,* which in 1941 won the Academy Award for Best Documentary.[132]

In another trend, cautious moves were made toward implementing sex education to "prevent mishaps and sex delinquency" and to "direct young people into having a successful marriage and good family life."[133] Prewar initiatives in this area had been exceptionally rare and typically did not extend beyond a single lecture given to high school students by groups like the Canadian Social Hygiene Council. In attempts to relieve the "mental anguish" of youth, their talks focused on matters like bodily changes during adolescence and the need to maintain personal cleanliness and always adhere to a healthy, Christian lifestyle. Calls for more comprehensive sex education became more urgent during the Second World War in response to rising illegitimacy and VD rates. One supporter was Dr. John Leroux, Ontario's director of venereal disease control, who, during the war, pointed out that the province's syphilis rate had reached as high as 176 per 100,000, whereas in Sweden, where sex education was well established, the corresponding proportion was just 14.[134] Canadians learned from the press about the extension of sex education in British high schools and in some American states with the assistance of groups bearing such conservative-sounding names as the American Association for Family Living. A 1943 poll showed that 76 percent of Canadian adults favoured sex education for high school students.[135]

But the devil lay in the details. Despite evident public support, sex education remained an explosive issue. Although most of the young people the CYC surveyed approved of sex education, the organization refrained from any official endorsement to prevent its director of operations in Quebec from resigning. In 1945 provincial education authorities in Alberta considered a sex education program for secondary school students but ultimately rejected it because of especially strong opposition in rural areas, upon which the Social Credit government relied for support. Many Social Credit members of the legislature with evangelical Christian connections believed that such programs would undermine morality.[136]

The changes that did occur were therefore cautiously implemented. In 1942 British Columbia's Venereal Disease Control Division launched a program that brought sex education lectures to thirty-eight high schools under the discreet title of "Health and Human Relations." Attendance was optional and talks encouraged the development of "healthy diversions" as the most effective means of avoiding VD. By the end of 1943 similar initiatives had been adopted in several – though by no means all – high schools in Winnipeg, Regina, Saskatoon, and London. The Toronto Board of Education seemed ready in 1944 to implement a program to educate high school students in VD prevention, but then balked because the city's superintendent of schools, Dr. C.C. Goldring, feared a public backlash. Only after another two years were the board and Goldring ready to act, tentatively. Medical personnel or experts on VD were to deliver lectures to students in grade ten, to keep the program within high schools yet also ensure that youth received some instruction before they reached the legal school-leaving age. Students needed parental permission in order to attend, classes were gender-segregated, and no mention was made of birth control beyond premarital abstinence. Moreover, to ensure that younger children not have access to the material, there were no textbooks, homework, or tests, and students were instructed not to take notes.[137]

Another significant wartime reaction toward order and discipline was a backlash against "progressive education." By the Second World War, this approach, which de-emphasized memory work and lock-step grade divisions in favour of a more child-centred strategy that encouraged students to explore and develop their natural interests and talents, had made only very modest forays into Canadian schools. Ontario's 1937 revised education program, which came as close as any in the country to progressive education, went only so far as to encourage more play for elementary students, and had begun experimenting with group work in upper grades. But the progressive approach, though barely initiated, became a lightning rod for mounting concerns over delinquency. It was vehemently denounced from several quarters for its potential to turn out slack and undisciplined youth because of its supposed denial of standards, and its alleged suggestion that it was fine for students to abandon things they found difficult or uninteresting.[138] In Alberta, which had shown signs of accepting progressive education before the war, it was during the war "consciously purged" from Department of Education literature.[139] Ontario's Premier Drew, who had also taken over the education portfolio, shelved progressive education, claiming that it turned out young people with substandard academic skills, "little discipline," and a propensity for delinquency.[140]

Along with the reaction against the supposed impracticality of progressive education came the growing consensus that for schools to reverse disturbing trends among young people and to more effectively mould them into productive and law-abiding citizens, all secondary institutions, not just commercial ones, should do more to produce "useful and successful workers." Basing its remarks upon "contacts" with nearly 31,000 people who had left secondary schools and collegiates at the age of sixteen, the Ontario Department of Education reported in 1943 that strikingly high numbers of them saw little point in attending institutions that were "geared solely for the 5 percent who were going on to university."[141]

Support grew within political and educational circles for establishing, as soon as circumstances allowed, more comprehensive high schools in which students could experiment with both academic and vocational streams. This was a direction that the public seemed to endorse. When surveyed in mid-1945 as to what they considered the most significant failing in schools, most Canadians cited a "lack of practical training." Reflecting the new trend, Duncan McArthur, Ontario's deputy minister of education, suggested that high school French and Latin be removed as compulsory courses. Ultimately, this was considered too radical. However, that year Ontario did establish what turned out to be a $300,000, five-year royal commission on education under Justice John Andrew Hope. One of his principal aims was to create schools that would produce "persons of general experience, and not merely scholars or workers efficient in technical skills."[142]

The goal of establishing more comprehensive, functional, and it was hoped, more appealing schools was also pursued by expanding vocational guidance services. Some advocated that guidance counsellors be trained to provide psychological help for problem youth, especially given the few psychiatrists on retainer to school boards. However, the counsellor's role generally remained limited and – a factor critically important to most school boards – financially modest, a job that could be filled by less-trained staff who could help students choose an appropriate career path and possibly link them with prospective employers.

A crude form of this service had appeared after the Great War in a few schools, courtesy of volunteers from agencies such as the YMCA. The Ontario Vocational Guidance Association, in trying to build support for more action, argued with considerable exaggeration in 1940 that significant guidance programs had emerged in the United States, Australia, South Africa, England, Scotland, and the Soviet Union. It also stressed the waste of resources to the nation during the war as a result of students dropping by the wayside, and warned of postwar instability from "frustrated youth" not being properly directed into "opportunities for suitable employment."[143]

A few years later, a different tune was heard. George M. Weir, a professor of education at the University of British Columbia, observed, for example, that "the war has added new emphasis to this guidance movement." To keep things in perspective, many new programs were offered only on a part-time basis, sometimes because they were shared between schools or because the counsellor was a teacher instructing in other subjects. The person assigned to the post frequently had no formal training in guidance. A 1943 report from the CNEA said that in high schools across Canada, more than 1,000 guidance counsellors were still needed. Still, enough change had occurred to prompt the CNEA to comment optimistically: "The trend toward guidance has recently become more ... marked [and] must now be ranked as an innovation of major importance."[144] Among other initiatives, between 1943 and 1945 high schools in Halifax, Fredericton, Saint John, and Summerside all hired vocational guidance counsellors.[145] During the war years seven Toronto collegiates did the same, and in 1944 the Ontario government established a Guidance Branch. In January 1946 even the federal government got involved by establishing the Council for Youth Guidance and Placement, which, in part, assisted school guidance services by providing information on job trends drawn up by the National Employment Service.[146]

It had long been realized that to upgrade education significantly, far more funding was needed. Since most education funding derived from local property taxes, many districts, especially in more sparsely populated rural areas, were habitually starved for funds. This matter assumed greater urgency during the war because of a mass exodus of underpaid teachers from the classroom to more lucrative employment. In 1940, when the average annual salary in Canada was approximately $1,200, the mean for teachers was $860, and female teachers in New Brunswick averaged only $391. In 1942 fifty Catholic school boards in Quebec also paid their female teachers less than $400 per year.[147] By 1943 teacher shortages, which were most extreme in rural areas, had climbed to 600 in Nova Scotia, 250 in Manitoba, and 1,000 in Saskatchewan. That April, after a long period of intense pressure from school boards and provincial education departments, National Selective Service assigned teachers an "A" priority job classification, thus theoretically preventing their movement to lower-rated, although higher-paid, employment. By that time, however, the wartime departure of teachers was already to blame for the closure of 449 Alberta schools and 295 in Ontario, among others.[148]

School boards faced tremendous pressure to hire new staff quickly. Many suspended the rule against employing married women.[149] Retired teachers were called back into action and the partially qualified were rushed before students. Several provinces created six-week summer courses that granted a special interim teaching certificate, with the stipulation that graduates would finish off the program the following year. By the 1942-43 school year, some 250 such teachers were in Alberta classrooms, 300 in Nova Scotia, and 500 in Ontario.[150] This situation, especially in the context of heightened anxieties over the conduct of youth, further publicized the need for improvements. In a 1943 feature headlined "Give Teachers the Respect They Deserve," *Saturday Night* linked the problem of poor pay and the resulting departure of teachers to substandard instruction, greater disinterest among students, and higher truancy and dropout rates. The next year *Maclean's* ran a story making the provocative analogy that 17,000 teachers in Canada were paid less per year than it cost to keep a person in prison.[151]

In rural areas, poor funding had also been manifested in small, run-down institutions and lack of basic equipment. One study made shortly after the war found that 15 percent of Canada's "small rural schools" lacked safe drinking water, and 40 percent had no indoor toilet. One Alberta critic sarcastically commented, "If one finds even a baseball and a bat, he will probably discover that some pupil or the teacher supplied it."[152] To many teachers and school officials these conditions reflected the prevailing view among rural parents and children that education beyond the rudiments was of little use. Yet growing numbers of rural youths who dropped out of school did not end up in farming but moved to cities, often into low-paying and dead-end jobs. The answer, frequently heard before the war but clearly gaining momentum during the conflict, was school district consolidation, particularly in rural areas. It was anticipated that with more extensive areas from which to draw taxes, such districts would have the means to hire better teachers and build larger and more comprehensive institutions providing a range of both academic and vocational courses to prepare students for a wider array of options.[153] Also, because larger districts could support high schools, fewer rural youth would be served only by a one-room schoolhouse and forced to leave home to proceed beyond grade eight, an obstacle that often curtailed further education.

As during the prewar years, opposition to consolidation continued, largely for fear of steeper taxes and loss of local control. Nonetheless, in every province outside Quebec (where heavy church involvement in education kept a large percentage of schools tied to parishes) and especially in rural areas, pressure intensified to create larger school districts to set the stage for composite schools to be built after the war. Between 1943 and 1948, for example, 3,070 Ontario school districts were reduced to 484 Township School Areas, while in New Brunswick during that period 1,350 school districts were reduced to just 37.[154]

To help carry out programs to improve schools, the share of expenditures for public education assumed by provincial governments nearly doubled from 15.9 to 29.1 percent between 1939 and 1946. This pattern was evident in every part of Canada except Prince Edward Island (where both before and after the war the provincial government already carried more than half the costs of education).[155] School consolidation continued. Between 1945 and 1947 the British Columbia government reduced the number of its school boards from 696 to 89. In boosting the vocational, or "practical," side of education, school boards scooped up items from Ottawa's War Assets Corporation, namely laboratory and industrial arts equipment, typewriters, adding machines, and drafting tables.[156]

Several provinces introduced measures to enhance professionalization among teachers, although the process proceeded slowly because the exploding postwar school population required the rapid hiring of many partially trained instructors, thus contributing to continued low salaries. Still, signs of progress were evident. In 1945, partly as a symbolic gesture to encourage professionalization, the Alberta government made the staff at the province's two normal schools part of the Education Faculty at the University of Alberta. The next year, the University of Saskatchewan expanded its small College of Education to offer a new four-year program in which expertise could be gained in fine arts, agricultural science, commerce, household science, industrial arts, and physical education. Soon after the war, most provincial governments were funding a record number of specialized courses in subjects such as drama, sociology, civics, industrial arts, and vocational guidance to provide staff for the more comprehensive schools that were in the works.[157]

CANADA'S JUVENILE JUSTICE SYSTEM, particularly its shortcomings and poor results in achieving rehabilitation, was of course implicated in wartime discourse over rising delinquency. Back in 1908 the federal government had introduced some structure and standards to the trial and treatment of young offenders by passing the Juvenile Delinquents Act. The initiative had sprung from the desire, typical of progressive-era reforms, to promote both social uplift and social order. The act defined a legally responsible minor (seven to sixteen inclusive), stated what constituted "delinquency" (breaking a federal, provincial, or local statute), and specified that provinces or municipalities declaring the act in force were to provide a separate court and pretrial detention facility for youth, an industrial school or reformatory for both boys and girls, and an adequate staff of probation officers.[158] By no means did the new system lose its authoritarian quality; it was arguably more intrusive than other courts, as juvenile court judges, in deciding upon matters like whether or not to institutionalize a young offender, could probe into the affairs of their parents to determine if they were providing a suitable home life. But juvenile courts were presented and widely interpreted as progressive, a place where a "family-like" atmosphere supposedly prevailed, where the judge did not sit behind a desk that towered above the proceedings, and where liberal use was made of "empathetic" experts, namely social workers, psychologists, and psychiatrists.[159]

In the early twentieth century, juvenile courts were established in Halifax, Charlottetown, Montreal, Ottawa, Toronto, Winnipeg, Vancouver, and Victoria. However, the trend had dissipated by the 1920s with the waning of the progressive impulse in the years after the Great War, and the impetus continued weak during the Depression, principally because of budgetary restraints. By the Second World War, with many jurisdictions yet to declare the Juvenile Delinquents Act in force, about half of Canadian minors were theoretically susceptible to being tried and punished as adults, a situation that the Canadian Bar Association cast as "inconsistent with modern thought."[160] Even when the act was declared in force, its spirit, and often its provisions, were ignored. Most juvenile courts lacked professionally trained parole officers, turning instead to volunteers from social service groups like the Big Brothers and Big Sisters. In rural areas and small towns, social services were often unavailable. Psychiatric staff were regularly used only by juvenile courts in Montreal, Toronto, and Vancouver. And juvenile court judges were often chosen more on the basis of social stature, moral reputation, or involvement in "child saving" than for their legal qualifications. Because one did not have to be a lawyer to serve as a juvenile court judge, some women had the opportunity to perform the job because of their supposed nurturing qualities, though there is no evidence that they acted more leniently than men.[161] Stipendiary magistrates, also not necessarily trained lawyers by background, also served part-time as juvenile court judges; however, they had spent most of their time with adult defendants and were not always successful in making the "considerable adjustments" needed to deal effectively with youth. At the outset of the Second World War, only two juvenile courts in Ontario heard cases in a building separate from adult court – the usual setting was a room or the judge's chamber in the same place as adult courts. Children awaiting trial were often held in a "youth section" close to, and in some cases actually beside, cells containing adult criminals.[162]

During the war, facilities appeared inadequate to keep delinquents presumed to be dangerous off the streets. Organizations such as the Children's Aid Society, to which juvenile courts often turned to temporarily house delinquents, found it more difficult to perform this role in wartime given their overburdened staff and facilities. Worsening matters in Ontario was the fact that in 1941, before delinquency came to the forefront as an issue, the federal government had convinced Queen's Park to make available a major boys' reformatory in Bowmanville for housing German POWs sent from Britain. A temporary structure was built nearby to accommodate thirty residents, some boys were paroled to work on nearby farms, and more serious cases were transferred to reformatories in Guelph and Mimico.[163] The next year, a facility for delinquent girls located in Galt was transferred to the Women's Royal Canadian Naval Service to serve as a training centre. Most of the serious cases were sent to the Ontario Training School in Cobourg, a facility that, however, lacked adequate dormitory space. Protests soon resulted; the Canadian Welfare Council, for instance, stressed the "disturbing potentialities in wartime [for] serious delinquency among girls." There were also sensationalist press reports that juvenile court judges had refused to consider institutionalization except in the most serious cases because of a lack of reformatory space, thereby feeding panic over rising delinquency and bolstering assumptions that the current system was not working.[164]

By no means did the war years witness an overhaul of Canada's juvenile justice system. Indeed, the pace and scope of change – which in some provinces was non-existent – aroused demands that the federal government take over constitutional control of all matters relating to the treatment of juveniles in order to ensure decent and uniform services across the country.[165] But in comparison to the prewar period, more public discussion and action were evident. In early 1943 Alberta's Social Credit government struck a legislative committee to examine the treatment of juvenile offenders. Its June report recommended financial assistance for communities to create juvenile courts, separate pretrial detention facilities for youth, greater use of psychologists and psychiatrists, and the appointment of more and better-trained parole officers. Despite delays, by 1946 part-time psychologists were assigned to youth courts in Edmonton and Calgary, matching funds had been provided to Edmonton's municipal government to build a new pretrial detention facility for boys, and under the new provincial Child Welfare Act, committees were established to recommend on the recruitment and training of parole officers.[166] In Ontario between 1943 and 1945, juvenile courts were created in Kenora, Dryden, Sioux Lookout, Cornwall, and the Keewatin district. Toward the end of the war, the British Columbia government provided extra funds to enable stipendiary magistrates to hold part-time juvenile courts covering several interior and northern districts. This was hardly an ideal solution, but money was also made available so that the magistrates could travel and confer on a regular basis with full-time juvenile court judges.[167]

Moves were also made toward improving reformatories, as the trend strengthened away from the usually urban industrial school model, which was increasingly criticized by childcare experts for being too similar to adult penitentiaries in emphasizing punishment rather than advice from professionally trained experts, and thus too often making delinquents "more hardened in their ways."[168] Certainly, the need for improvements was glaringly evident. Many institutions were old, overcrowded, and decrepit. Lack of professional input was no doubt the reason many youths with serious mental illnesses were housed with those who had committed relatively minor crimes. The new path, as charted out in legislation such as the 1931 and amended 1939 Ontario Training School Act, was to move to cottage-type structures in rural settings. Here, in calmer, pastoral surroundings, youth would be placed under the direction of a "parent" who was a childcare expert, with the intention being to nurture a sense of belonging and the ability to function within a family-like structure. Typically, the extent of reforms proved less dramatic than the rhetoric. In both the old and new reformatories, the emphasis remained on moulding youth to accept a narrowly defined vision of appropriate conduct. While both sexes received basic academic instruction, boys were also trained in manual arts and girls in domestic chores and proper, restrained, feminine etiquette. Few inmates, even long-term ones, finished the equivalent of high school. They were given very limited free time; religious instruction was included in the curriculum; and a system of privileges and punishments, including beatings and solitary confinement, was still practised. Nonetheless, as more discussion focused on the problem of wartime delinquency, the cottage system was increasingly praised as being more progressive, benevolent, and effective, improvements portrayed as long overdue and as contributing to the building of a better and more stable postwar society.

Such discourse was evident when plans were unveiled in 1943 to revamp the Boys' Farm and Training School in Shawbridge, Quebec, which mainly served the province's English-speaking population. Administrators there also took inspiration from the Borstal system that had been widely adopted in Britain during the 1920s, albeit usually for offenders between sixteen and twenty-one years old. It advanced a flexible approach to privileges and jail time, depending upon the behaviour of the inmate, which was sometimes identified by methods such as having prisoners wear different coloured uniforms.[169] Although billed as both compassionate and highly efficient in achieving behavioural modification, the Borstal method became associated with many abuses and during the 1950s was largely abandoned in both Britain and Canada. However, in the context of wartime and immediate postwar Canada, the Borstal, like rural, cottage-type facilities, was generally perceived as kindly and enlightened.[170] This conviction was projected by the

Ontario government when, in 1945, it resumed control over its facility in Bowmanville. Moreover, the 1943 Alberta inquiry into the treatment of delinquents singled out Shawbridge as a model, and soon after the war the provincial government moved toward cottage-type facilities and the Borstal system, such as at its major reformatory for boys in Bowden.[171]

ALTHOUGH CHILDREN AND ADOLESCENTS were a source of inspiration and the focus of admiration, particularly early on in the war, wartime anxiety and worries about delinquency led to distorted interpretations of their actual experience. British war guests emerged as inspiring symbols of the United Kingdom's resolve to resist the Nazis and Canada's determination to stand by the mother country to an extent that resulted in an almost exclusive focus on heartwarming and successful experiences, with virtually no attention being paid to significant failings in the program and much suffering. The message conveyed about Canadian youth was in some ways the antithesis. Despite their many patriotic contributions, their behaviour was often cast in a negative light because of widespread concern over their moral and social degradation and over the stability of families in wartime. Yet despite the assumptions behind these negative distortions, delinquency in fact declined as mothers moved in record numbers into the wartime workforce. The statistical pattern shows that the increased incidence of juvenile crime is most effectively explained by demographic shifts: namely the changing size of the teenaged population, which predetermined a delinquency peak in the early 1940s; and the massive exodus from Canada of eighteen- to thirty-year-old males, which allowed police to charge more youths with minor offences.

Attempts to improve the behaviour of young people by clamping down on wayward conduct and reasserting a traditional moral order led to numerous reactionary responses: tougher curfew laws, more religious and civics training, the retraction of progressive education, and, of course, intensified pressure upon working mothers to return to the hearth. However, exaggerated concerns about youth also brought attention to the need for several other, and arguably more progressive, initiatives to improve conditions and opportunities for young people and encourage them to live within social norms. Action was taken to increase and to upgrade recreational services so that youth would be constructively occupied in their free hours; to improve schools that in wartime appeared especially beleaguered and unable to hold students in the classroom; and to expand, professionalize, and improve a still rudimentary juvenile justice system.

Rising fears over moral decline and social instability in wartime Canada derived from many trends. Whether these trends were bona fide or exaggerated, they led to initiatives that affected, often profoundly, countless Canadians – children, working women and servicewomen, wives and girlfriends, labourers and farmers, tenants and landlords, and shoppers and shopkeepers. But what about the men in uniform who left Canada? While in training, their behaviour often gave cause for concern, yet little was heard on the home front about their untoward conduct overseas – conduct that, even if comprehensible in light of what servicemen confronted, would undoubtedly have been far more shocking to those at home than any moral failings they perceived among their fellow civilians.

The Men Who Marched Away: "Everyone here is optimistic"

WHILE SERVICEMEN WERE OVERSEAS, they of course hungered for news about home. Canadian authorities, the press, and the media did what they could to keep them in touch with their civilian lives. The first edition of *Canadian Press News,* a four-page summary of major stories about the home front, came out soon after the 1st Division began arriving in England in late 1939. The next year the CBC started regular short-wave radio broadcasts for servicemen in Britain. These initiatives were soon followed by *Canadian Affairs,* a fortnightly magazine supplied by the federal government, and *Canada Digest,* a monthly publication similar to *Reader's Digest.*[1] Military newspapers were more effective in maintaining morale because they were prepared by servicemen – typically with pre-enlistment experience in journalism – and more clearly reflected soldiers' views. The highly popular *Maple Leaf* debuted in January 1944 for Canadians fighting in Italy, who wanted their own newspaper comparable to the British *Eighth Army News* and the US *Stars and Stripes.* Besides focusing on Canadian soldiers overseas and events at home, the *Maple Leaf* often had a cynically humorous take on military life, which most senior officers understood helped men vent frustrations and tensions in a safe and controlled way. The most endearing and enduring of its features was the sad-sack cartoon character Herbie the private, who poked fun at military authorities and the vagaries of military life.[2]

Important as these publications were, men overseas were always most keen to keep up on hometown and neighbourhood events, and particularly news of friends and family. Many Canadian newspapers started special columns summarizing the week's local news for readers to clip out and send abroad. Of course letters and packages from home were especially coveted. Mail call was a time of either great jubilation or sorrow depending upon whether one's name was called. To men who had not been able to return to Canada for years and felt increasingly cut off, the mail never seemed to move fast enough, even though letters often reached Britain within a week.

In 1942 several chaplains with Canadian troops in Britain began lobbying for a system of home leaves to buoy morale and "prevent the disintegration of ... matrimonial ties."[3] When the campaigns in Italy and northwest Europe got under way, lobbying continued, but the Army Council continued to resist, claiming that its manpower needs were too critical. It rankled Canadian soldiers that other services seemed capable of implementing a leave system, including the Royal Canadian Air Force (RCAF) in September 1943 – though its prerequisite of thirty ops (tours of duty) and six months' instructional duty was beyond the reach of the vast majority. Not until September 1944, with Germany clearly heading toward defeat, did Canada's army begin to relent; eighty-three soldiers who had been wounded in action on three separate occasions qualified for home leave under a "tri-wound" system. After the hostile reaction to this scheme, it was quickly revised to provide a six-month tour of duty in Canada for twice-wounded three-year veterans, and one month's home leave for those stationed outside Canada for five years. However, manpower shortages allowed an initial quota of just three men per battalion per month. In early 1945 the numbers rose, but the grand total of 626 officers and 9,063 from other ranks allowed leave represented only a tiny fraction of those who had not seen their loved ones for years.[4]

Front and home front often grew increasingly estranged as personal correspondence inclined toward omission and distortion. Certainly, many marriages and relationships were able to survive the war precisely because writers excised information. However, this pattern added to difficulties in adjustment when people came together again, by heightening the shock of the significant changes that had transpired during years apart. Even if families had realized in the abstract that men could be profoundly transformed by combat, both physically and psychologically, countless civilians were still unprepared for the problems they encountered themselves, since their letters, just like news reports, had typically been upbeat. Most men did not want to worry or upset their loved ones and felt they had to project an image of strength. For example, following the December 1943 bloodbath at Ortona, Italy, which produced some 2,000 Canadian casualties, one soldier, in a typical understatement, assured his wife, "Everyone here is optimistic ... and think[s] it will not be long [for] the Hun."[5]

The troops were also aware that their letters were read by censors and that penalties could ensue from providing information considered useful to the enemy. This included not only technical matters such as troop location, strength, and movements – the direct focus of censors – but theoretically anything that could compromise the "recruiting, training, discipline or administration of any of His Majesty's Forces." This wider definition cost one private in England with the 1st Division several days' pay for writing about widespread drunkenness among his comrades.[6] It is also significant that the men in action commonly knew who the censors were, as within each army company and air force squadron, and on board every naval vessel, an officer was assigned to this task. For some writers, this personal connection generated trust and a willingness to open up. But others became inhibited in writing and held back their feelings, perhaps because of a personality clash with the censor, and hence a greater fear of reprisal, or embarrassment that someone they knew would be privy to their innermost thoughts.[7]

THE PSYCHOLOGICAL DISTANCE between Canadians at home and the men who marched away was first manifested in England, where within three months of its arrival Canada's 1st Division numbered 23,000. On 12 June 1940, several thousand were rushed to Brest, France, as part of the 2nd British Expeditionary Force, in a desperate attempt to retain a portion of northwest Europe. However, after only two days, and before encountering the enemy, the plan was abandoned as suicidal. Canadian soldiers then settled in Britain to protect the island from a possible Nazi invasion. By 1943, as the First Canadian Army, their presence had grown to three infantry and two armoured divisions, as well as two armoured brigades, with over 250,000 men. With the addition of air force and naval personnel, Canadian forces in Britain peaked that year at 494,000. While members of the RCAF and Royal Canadian Navy saw regular action, most of the army just continued training. Except for the 645 men from the 1st Division who in September 1941 launched an unopposed raid against the Norwegian Arctic archipelago of Spitzbergen, the 350 who served for three months with British forces in North Africa,[8] and the almost 5,000 from the 2nd Division who in August 1942 participated in a disastrous raid on Dieppe, Canadian soldiers in Britain were not heavily involved in combat until the Sicilian campaign of July 1943.

Many had a great time. They found their hosts warm and generous, often willing to share their meagre rations and buy them rounds of drinks. Positive feelings were reinforced by the great respect that Canadians developed for British civilians, who endured strict rationing, blackouts, and the horror of the Blitz.[9] Canadians in turn endeared themselves to locals by sharing their provisions when on leave, and helping to harvest crops, mine coal, fell trees, douse fires, and dig people out of the rubble after bombing raids.

In trying to keep Canadians in good spirits, many recreational opportunities were made available. By the time the 1st Division began arriving, Mrs. Vincent Massey, the wife of the Canadian high commissioner, had already played a key role in establishing a Canadian officers' club in London. In February 1940, also with help from the Masseys, the Beaver Club was formed, where, to recreate a sense of home, men could obtain hot dogs, waffles, and pancakes with maple syrup, and read Canadian newspapers and magazines. Canada's four official auxiliaries opened up some twenty facilities, providing canteens, recreational, reading, and writing rooms, movie and dance evenings, and offices where men could book a show or tour (many of which were free to those in uniform) or arrange a room for the night, as the auxiliary services also ran over twenty hostels.[10]

However, as Canadian soldiers stayed on in England for several years, morale reports described them as increasingly restless, bored, and "browned off." Some felt they were just languishing in Britain, especially after June 1941, when the Blitz had ended and Hitler's attack on the Soviet Union appeared to confirm that Germany had abandoned the idea of invading England. Their patience and their nerves wore thin. They groused over a diet that many said was too skimpy and dominated by porridge, imitation sausages, dehydrated eggs, and mutton. They were often angered by British instructors who, they said, treated them as incompetent colonials. The charge, while often legitimate, also reflected the ill-preparedness of the Canadians; several senior officers were sent home as a consequence of poor performance.[11] Also demoralizing were Britain's damp and cold climate and the rather spartan accommodations to which many men were assigned. These factors accounted for high influenza rates, particularly during the abnormally cold winter of 1939-40, which, although the harshest on record since 1894-95, was exceeded in severity the following year. During those two years, most of the 1st Division was stationed fifty kilometres southwest of London in Aldershot, Sussex, where they were lodged in drafty century-old buildings with no central heating and too few fireplaces to compensate. Fuel shortages meant that wood or coal could not be burned in the evening, and complaints from the Canadians incensed many locals because their fuel allotment was even lower.[12]

Tensions also derived from the fact that Aldershot had long served as a garrison town. Its residents, like those of Halifax, were used to the presence of troops, and since they therefore made little fuss over the Canadians, many soldiers regarded them as aloof and unappreciative of the protection they were being provided. During those two brutal winters, morale plummeted and relations with civilians deteriorated to the extent that soldiers arriving in later years derided the 1st Division for the horrible reputation it had made for Canadians. Vandalism and theft were frequent as soldiers scrounged for extra food and fuel, and men often released their frustrations, tensions, and boredom by drinking heavily. Things became so bad by late 1941 that Lt.-Gen. A.G.L. McNaughton – soon to be promoted to general officer commanding-in-chief of the First Canadian Army – threatened to proceed with a widespread replacement of officers throughout Sussex should things not be brought under greater control.[13]

Indeed, civilians further afield than Aldershot began to look askance at the Canadians. Tabloids in London and England's southwest, where most Canadian soldiers were stationed, reflected and reinforced such feelings. By highlighting cases of robbery, assault, and even murder committed by Canadians, they gave the impression of wild men freshly arrived from an untamed frontier. For the sake of maintaining good relations among the Allies, Canadian military headquarters pleaded that such accounts be toned down. It also released statistics showing that, at least when it came to such major crimes, Canadian soldiers were no worse than among British civilians.[14] But the Canadians' dismal reputation was also directly affected by the mayhem they created in numerous communities by taking too great an advantage of the ubiquitous British pub and Britons' looser approach toward social drinking. As of late 1941 arrests of Canadian troops for drunk and disorderly conduct had reached 500 monthly.[15] This behaviour can be traced to boredom, but also to the desire to prove toughness, since Canadian soldiers were sometimes chided for having seen no real action, particularly by their British counterparts.[16]

British women, who were sometimes the cause of "disorderly conduct," were certainly a big factor in the lives of Canadians overseas – far more than during the

Great War, when Canadians had spent much less time in Britain. Many English women found Canadian men refreshingly less reserved than British men, and because Canadians were paid about twice as much as English soldiers, they could show these women a good time. Given the uncertainties of the times and the always-looming departure of men for action, relationships moved along quickly. As early as 1940 Canada's military had to face the issue of British war brides, marriages the brass tried to discourage for distracting men from their duties, for being undertaken far too impulsively, and it was charged, because the women involved were sometimes simply out to get a dependant's allowance. Servicemen under nineteen and British women under twenty wishing to marry had to show "written consent" from their parents or legal guardians, and the bride was also required to provide reference letters from respected citizens testifying to her "good moral character." Also customary was a waiting period of at least two months after the serviceman's commanding officer granted the initial permission to marry, to give the parties time to reconsider. Despite such precautions, 1,221 such unions occurred in 1940, 3,011 in 1941, 4,160 in 1942, and 5,897 in 1943. By the time Canadians returned home, an enormous total of 44,886 marriages to British women had taken place (which involved 21,358 children), a figure that far exceeded marriages involving servicemen from any other Allied nation.[17]

The war brides, however, represented only a tiny fraction of Canadian relationships with British women. For numerous men, the closer they got to action and the prospect of death, the greater became their need for sex, and the craving was easily satisfied in wartime Britain.[18] In London's Piccadilly Circus and all major parks, prostitutes plied their trade openly. Also, many British women were lonely and frightened, needful of some comfort and pleasure no matter how fleeting, or had been led to adopt a carpe diem attitude by the general air of excitement and insecurity. Meanwhile, for many Canadian servicemen the girl or wife back home became an abstraction, an image that could not satisfy their immediate longing for female companionship. They saw "no apparent correlation between their faithfulness" and the woman awaiting their return, the rationale being that their sexual encounters overseas were based solely on physical need, and that since no love was involved, they were not actually cheating.[19] Such "logic" was noted by a Canadian nurse in England, who remembered a patient with a wife and four children in Vancouver. "He used to talk about how he missed them," she said. "One night he went out on leave and he was late getting back to the hospital ... When he got in he said, 'I've been over to see my girl in East Grinstead.' I said I didn't understand how he could, and he was furious, because in his mind he didn't connect this girl with his family back home."[20]

Among Canadian soldiers in Britain, VD was a major problem. Although lower than in Canada, rates hovering around 35 per 1,000 totted up, as in Canada, more hospital days than any other ailment. This was despite the fact that as of December 1939 – to prevent a repeat of the high VD rates among Canadians overseas during the Great War – condoms and prophylactic kits were widely distributed, and early prevention treatment (EPT) centres were set up on all bases and in every major community frequented by men on leave.[21] Canadian, and eventually American, military authorities also lodged complaints over rampant prostitution, primarily to Britain's Home Office. Initially, however, there was little response. Understaffed civilian law enforcement authorities were badly overworked, and many preferred activity to be centred in red light districts or places like Piccadilly Circus rather than fanning out. Moreover, a number of British politicians expressed concern that, with such high numbers of women working night shifts in the war economy, a crackdown would result in "many of good character" being mistakenly arrested, thus producing "a great outcry" and possibly even compromising production. Canadian military authorities insisted on action to control not only prostitutes but also loose "good-time girls," because medical interviews with Canadian troops with VD revealed that some 80 percent believed they had contracted the disease from a person to whom no money was paid.[22] Finally, in December 1942, with VD rates among British civilians nearly double their prewar levels, Regulation 33B was added to the 1916 Venereal Diseases Act, authorizing the tracing of alleged carriers and their mandatory testing. But this response failed to satisfy Canada's military because British civilian authorities required two references against an alleged source before they would initiate a trace.[23]

While British authorities were slow to react, many British servicemen were not. Violence often resulted when they saw Canadians moving in on their women. Indeed, as far away as North Africa, among men recruited primarily from south England who learned in letters from family and friends about relationships Canadians were having with their wives and girlfriends, rumblings of threatened revenge were heard.[24] Only after 1942 did this tension abate noticeably, largely because both groups were distracted by the newly arrived Americans whom they considered brash and pampered and who, with their superior pay and exclusive recreational clubs, were doing even better with the women.[25]

Still, the Canadians remained active and popular, and the results of their conduct lived on not only in the form of tens of thousands of war brides but also an estimated 30,000 illegitimate children.[26] As of August 1945 only 414 English women, operating through civil courts, had managed to obtain a child maintenance order against a Canadian, though these orders were unenforceable once the man left Britain. Following the war, British organizations, principally the National Council for the Unmarried Mother and Her Child, sometimes asked Canadian welfare agencies to contact an alleged father, but usually little assistance was provided. "Our personal feeling is ... that the man's own family responsibilities must take first place," contended Mary Livesay, executive director of the Calgary Family Welfare Bureau. "In so many cases the domestic relationship between a husband and wife has been somewhat strained through years of separation [and] we are most anxious to cement it at all costs." It was also Livesay's belief, one shared by countless others, that it was not worth complicating the successful re-establishment of men for these women who, she stressed, "some of our better-type ... war brides say ... encouraged the men to such an extent that they are hardly to be pitied." By autumn 1946, Canada's military would no longer cooperate in helping to locate discharged men in response to paternity claims, insisting that by that time all legitimate cases had been launched and veterans were "once more private citizens ... entitled to protection."[27]

WHILE BOREDOM MAY GO FAR to explain problematic conduct among Canadian ground troops in England, when it came to air force and naval personnel such behaviour derived mostly from the stress of combat, which had been encountered quite early. Pent-up tension and raised endorphins after aircrew returned from nerve-racking missions often led them to take every opportunity for pleasure while they had the chance. The VD rates for RCAF personnel in England were some 50 percent higher than among Canadian soldiers training there. Of the 249,622 men who served with the RCAF, 93,844 went overseas, and of that figure, 17,101 died, almost all of whom were aircrew, the highest fatality level among the three main service branches.[28]

Canadian pilots were in England by 1940, though relatively few participated in the Battle of Britain because of an inadequate aircraft supply and because the British, with reason, saw them as lacking skill.[29] But with nervous exhaustion taking its toll among the British, the RCAF's No. 1 Squadron and the 242nd (Canadian) RAF Squadron soon became engaged. Over fifty-three days, No. 1 Squadron lost sixteen Hawker Hurricanes, but was credited with between thirty and thirty-eight kills. By the end of October, after some two months' action, forty-seven Canadian fighter pilots had been killed, while among many survivors, in the words of a squadron medical officer, "there [was] a definite air of constant tension ... forced enthusiasm ... and general tiredness."[30]

Although Canadian fighter pilots remained heavily engaged for the remainder of the war, principally in the Mediterranean and northwest Europe, the country's main contribution to the air war was with Bomber Command.[31] Canada ultimately supplied fifteen squadrons and 25 percent of the personnel to Bomber Command for its massive night raids on German cities starting in spring 1942 and involving up to 1,000 planes – namely the newly developed Handley-Page Halifax and Avro Lancaster. Their mission was to destroy heavy industry, communication centres, transportation systems, refineries, port facilities, and military installations, to break the will of civilian populations, to provide something of a second front, and, of course, to reap revenge for the Battle of Britain. Of the war dead suffered by the RCAF, 9,919 had been part of Bomber Command.[32]

These missions left many survivors psychologically devastated. Men often loaded up on caffeine pills to keep them alert throughout the night. Unpressurized cabins were so cold that condensation from an oxygen mask could freeze in a flyer's windpipe, causing him to black out. Gunners who sat in partially open turrets risked frostbite if they sweated. When planes flew in formation toward Europe at night, everyone was aware that bad turbulence or even a strong tailwind could cause a collision. A moonlit night made it easier for them to see, but also easier for the more nimble enemy fighter aircraft to pick them off. Once over Europe, crews knew they were being detected by German radar and that their jamming equipment had, at best, mixed results.[33] Throughout the heavily industrialized Ruhr Valley, where Allied bombers targeted cities such as Cologne, Hamburg, and Essen, powerful searchlights pierced the night sky to guide German anti-aircraft fire and fighter pilots. Berlin was ringed by 3,000 searchlights. Bombers could do little to avoid these lights lest they collide with another plane. Realizing this fact, German anti-aircraft gunners put up a "box barrage" of flak to fill a section of the air through which some planes had to fly. In many ways, survival was a matter of chance. One pilot described the prudent and common tactic that in part explains why more than half of the bombs dropped missed their target: "Get there, drop them, and get the hell out."[34]

With exhausted and frazzled pilots at the helm, bombers arrived back at daybreak, just when British airfields were most likely to be covered in fog. Crash landings were common, especially among damaged bombers, though ditching early in the water gave only a one-in-three chance of survival. Planes with the RCAF No. 6 Group, which began operations on 1 January 1943 with the goal of becoming a Canadian-commanded and staffed section within Bomber Command, had an extra hour's flying time added to their missions because their base was located to the north in Yorkshire. Incoming pilots were also often hampered by dense factory smoke blowing in from the nearby industrial centres of Leeds-Bradford and Middlesborough.[35] In 1942 and 1943 an average of almost 5 percent of planes were lost in every raid launched by Bomber Command. In the case of No. 6 Group the challenges were further compounded by trying to quickly integrate large numbers of inexperienced Canadians from different sections of Bomber Command at a time when increasingly complex "electronic measures and countermeasures" were being adopted for night fighting. Saddled mainly with Wellingtons and Halifaxes rather than, as hoped, the superior Canadian-built Lancaster X, their loss rate in 1943 and 1944 averaged 5.4 percent, and in all, No. 6 Group suffered 4,272 dead as a result of some 41,000 ops.[36]

Typically, morale went through cycles during a tour of duty – which fewer than a third of those with No. 6 Group completed. Following the exaltation of surviving the first couple of ops, air crews, seeing more and more of their comrades perish, increasingly questioned how much longer they could survive. After flying five ops in eight days, one Canadian pilot said that he wanted to be shot down to get the "inevitable over and done with." Men were known to scream in their sleep, vomit after each meal, and become consumed with fear and foreboding as their next mission approached. Not only did they see planes around them being shot down but they watched fellow crew members, particularly gunners, blown to bits by enemy fire or sometimes shredded in the propellers of attacking aircraft after bailing out. Many became callous or cynical, laughing gleefully about taking out enemy planes, civilians on the ground, or even Germans who tried to parachute to safety. Still, most did not crack outwardly. At Bomber Command's peak, only 0.4 percent of its aircrew were relieved of duty for psychological reasons. However, in order to keep men in line, most commanders had adopted the policy of labelling those who refused to fly as LMF – lacking moral fibre – an offence that brought not only personal shame but also demotion to the lowest air force ground rank, possible reassignment to the army or British coal mines, or up to 180 days' imprisonment with hard labour. Former RCAF pilot Murray Peden was among those who thought the tough approach was absolutely essential "because the strain was so great. If there had been an easy ... way to abandon operational flying," he said, "many crews would have found the temptation hard to resist." But many, like pilot Jack Western, saw the policy as a "load of crap" for forcing men to go on mission after mission even though "some literally couldn't put a cigarette in their mouth [because] they were shaking so much."[37]

THE ROYAL CANADIAN NAVY also saw action early in the conflict. By war's end the RCN, ultimately the Allies' fourth largest, had destroyed twenty-seven U-boats and forty-two enemy surface vessels. Canadian sailors served on armed yachts, patrol boats, cruisers, minesweepers, frigates, destroyers, aircraft carriers, and most commonly corvettes. The RCN lost twenty-four vessels and 2,024 personnel, numbers that, while small when compared to those the air force and the army lost, fail to convey the dangers and the distress faced by those at sea.[38] Indeed, by June 1941, the RCN had established a psychiatric service in its main hospital in Halifax, which within eighteen months treated some 900 patients, over 80 percent of whom suffered from psychoneuroses related to nervous exhaustion.[39]

The RCN patrolled in the St. Lawrence, along Canadian and British coastlines, off India and Africa, and in the Caribbean and Mediterranean. But after the American fleet focused its operations in the Pacific to compensate for vessels destroyed at Pearl Harbor, the most prominent Canadian naval activity soon became the protection of Atlantic merchant ship convoys. All told, the RCN successfully escorted 25,343 cargo vessels to Britain across the Atlantic's rough northern waters, where U-boats had more difficulty operating. Convoys of as many as 100 cargo ships and their military escorts gathered in Bedford Basin, Halifax's massive ice-free natural harbour, and on a smaller scale outside Sydney, Nova Scotia, and St. John's, Newfoundland, for journeys that went as far north as Cape Farewell, the southern tip of Greenland.[40]

The mainstay of these convoys was the corvette, a midsized naval vessel first built in 1938 in England, and two years later in Canada. While there were later and larger versions, the basic design was 205 feet long, with a beam of 33 feet and a draft of 15 feet. It carried a crew of about sixty. It was relatively simple, quick, and inexpensive to construct and repair, important considerations given Canada's tiny navy at the start of the war and the initially limited capacity of its shipyards. Patterned after whaling ships because of their ability to cope with rough waters, the corvette rode low and bobbed much like a cork.[41] It offered little by way of comfort: most men lived like sardines in quarters on the lower deck measuring about 33 by 22 feet. Never was there a moment's privacy. The space was dimly lit and often cold and damp, with water dripping off steel walls and exposed pipes. A foul odour pervaded, as the ventilation was poor, portholes were kept shut during voyages, and men vomited from seasickness. Nerves frayed under such conditions, which were typical of almost all naval vessels, and strict discipline was needed to ensure that cohesion and battle-readiness were maintained.

To keep supplies flowing, layovers in port were usually short, often with just enough time for repairs and refitting before a ship embarked on another ten- to fourteen-day trip usually between Halifax and Londonderry, Ireland. Convoys were forced to travel at the speed of the slowest ship, and all kinds of decrepit vessels had been called into service to carry supplies. Increasing the danger was the fact that many cargo ships burned coal, which puffed out highly visible plumes of black smoke. Especially during winter, the weather was a potentially deadly foe. Between December 1942 and March 1943, only ten days in the North Atlantic failed to see gale force winds. Waves often crashed over the main deck and semi-submerged vessels, immobilizing many men not only with seasickness but also, as noted by the RCN's surgeon commander, with fear and sometimes psychoneuroses. Alan Easton, who commanded the corvette *Sackville,* remembered sometimes being consumed by "vivid pictures of the ship breaking up under stress of weather." Frigid conditions also presented the threat of icing. No matter how high the swells, sailors were often forced on deck and sometimes precariously up on masts with steam hoses, picks, and axes to remove the ice that could capsize a vessel within an hour. Those performing such work realized that if they fell into the frigid North Atlantic they would survive only a few minutes, a fact graphically illustrated from time to time by bodies that were pulled out "coal black with frostbite."[42]

At all hours, a portion of the crew stood watch for enemy subs, sometimes "holding on for dear life, hoping not to be swept overboard with the next wave." But smooth seas also invited anxiety because they made it far easier for the enemy to spot convoys and for torpedoes to stay on course. Some sections of the voyage were particularly hazardous, especially a several hundred kilometre strip in the mid-Atlantic known as the Greenland Gap, over which long-range aircraft could not provide cover for convoys. Nor, since air support lumbered along far too slowly – with the Douglas Digby, Lockheed Hudson, and Consolidated Catalina making up the majority of air support for much of the war – could it surprise U-boats. When attacked, naval vessels played a tense cat-and-mouse game with the enemy, which often went on for days. The asdic apparatus, which used sound waves to locate U-boats so that depth charges could be dropped, was unreliable in rough water and was often thrown off by underwater currents, temperature changes, rock formations, and even schools of fish.[43]

By the time more powerful RCN ships – second-generation River-class destroyers and new River-class frigates – made their debut in 1943, many other vessels were being equipped with better radar, bigger guns, and more powerful depth charges. The British also introduced frigates designed for antisubmarine warfare. Besides serving in defensive convoy escort duty, new, faster, and more sophisticated Allied vessels were deployed to hunt down Nazi U-boats to clear the way for an invasion of Europe. The British, and particularly the Americans, built more vessels with flight decks – for Avenger torpedo bombers and Wildcat fighters – which considerably enhanced air support throughout convoy routes. The new, faster, land-based and extra-long-range Liberator bombers from the United States also helped shrink the Greenland Gap. Operating from Yarmouth, Nova Scotia, in 1943 and Iceland the next year with Canso patrol bombers, No. 162 RCAF Squadron also enjoyed considerable success, sinking six U-boats and damaging one. Once Allied code-breaking became more effective at locating where German U-boats refuelled, their record was even better. While the enemy sank 1.7 million tonnes of Allied shipping during the first half of 1943, that figure dropped to 0.5 million tonnes during the second half. Still, the threat remained significant until the end of the war. In September 1943 the Germans introduced an acoustic homing torpedo, the Gnat, which was far more accurate than air-driven models; that month, it was responsible for sinking the RCN destroyer *St. Croix,* leaving just one survivor from a crew of 147. In February 1944, the schnorkel U-boat came into action in the Atlantic. Capable of remaining submerged far longer than other submarines, it destroyed several merchant vessels off Canada's east coast and, on 16 April 1945, just weeks before Germany surrendered, sank the HMCS *Esquimalt* as it patrolled near the mouth of Halifax harbour.[44]

Whatever their circumstances, nearly all naval personnel hungered for shore leave as a result of living in cramped quarters under tight discipline, and after facing the tedium of long patrols, severe and potentially deadly weather, or enemy attack. Some needed only the relief of a comfortable room, a hot bath, a good meal, and a rest, but others itched for far more.[45] One sailor recalled that no matter the port, men would always "hit the first bar, get blind drunk, and then head to the nearest whorehouse."[46] Despite the condoms distributed to those heading out on shore leave, VD rates in the RCN regularly stood near 40 per 1,000.[47] On patrols up Canada's Pacific coastline, one of the few highlights for many sailors was the brief stop in Prince Rupert where they made a beeline for the area known as "Over the Hump," where moonshine and the local whorehouse were found. Sailors patrolling to the south, who docked in Panama as they headed through the canal, flocked to a red light district that one Canadian described as marked by "tiny wooden cribs" where there sat "half-naked little Indian females." By contrast, probably the most detested stop for those who endured the North Atlantic run was Iceland; in this rather closed society, the women wanted little to do with sailors. As Joseph Schull poetically relates in his official history of the RCN, "On a rare and gala night, the lissom, blonde, Icelandic girls danced with you, light as a feather, cold as an icicle, silent as a tomb, and left you without a word when the dance was ended."[48]

THE CANADIAN ARMY was the last of the major service branches to see continuous action in large numbers. Two of its early and limited engagements ended in disaster. On 8 December 1941, only hours after the attack on Pearl Harbor, Japanese forces attacked Hong Kong, where ninety-six officers and 1,877 men belonging to the Royal Rifles of Canada and the Winnipeg Grenadiers, along with two Canadian nursing sisters, had arrived on 16 November in response to a British request. Ottawa's reluctance to accept this assignment was overcome by political considerations: if word leaked out that it had turned down this apparently modest and, the British insisted, safe mission, King's government risked political disaster, given the small amount of fighting done by Canada's army until then. Assigned to Hong Kong island, the Canadians did not encounter the Japanese until 18 December. Although they demonstrated considerable tenacity for green troops and were assisted in their defence by the hilly terrain, the 1,689 surviving Canadians, 483 of whom were wounded, surrendered on Christmas Day.[49]

The army's next major engagement, the raid on Dieppe, was designed to test combined operations' procedures and German defences in Europe to see whether a defended port could be taken in an amphibious assault. The Americans, and especially the Soviets, were pressuring for the creation of a western European front, and the Canadians were eager to help make this a reality. Lt.-Gen. Harry Crerar, acting commander of the Canadian Corps in England, led in giving the message that involving Canadian troops in such a mission would raise their morale, especially since many were becoming frustrated as they saw American soldiers already playing a more active part in the war. Meanwhile, the King government saw Canada's taking a leading role in this limited, though important, offensive as a means to calm demands from English Canada that the country's ground troops assume a heavier load. With just under 5,000 Canadians actually to be involved, casualties would be controlled and not necessitate further steps toward conscription for overseas service.

Nearly all the men selected were from Canada's 2nd Infantry Division. Crerar lobbied for its participation, and Britain's Gen. Bernard Montgomery, who helped plan the Dieppe raid, considered the 2nd the country's best trained and its commander, Maj.-Gen. Hamilton Roberts, to be most "able." Initially the raid was slated for July, but was cancelled because of bad weather, thus perhaps allowing dangerous leaks from among those selected to participate. Despite continuing pressure from Canadian commanders to get involved, a number of historians lay much of blame for what transpired next on Admiral Lord Louis Mountbatten, the British chief of combined operations. A poor tactician and unrelenting self-publicist who was determined to push ahead with what he saw as a high-profile venture, Mountbatten brushed aside growing concerns from subordinates and apparently made sure that the raid was remounted.[50]

At Dieppe, the Germans had a formidable defensive network. Even if they had not expected the raid, they were given time to prepare after an attacking flotilla ran into a German coastal patrol, which opened fire in the English Channel. During the raid, Allied naval and air support was inadequate. Heavy bombers were not used because, it was said, they could not provide adequate precision. The navy supplied only eight small destroyers to soften up enemy defences – not nearly enough, but the Admiralty judged that larger and more valuable ships would be at too great a risk in the narrow Channel waters, especially with the Luftwaffe nearby. Many troops were taken to the wrong landing spot, and late. They stormed ashore in full day-light along three long and steep stony beaches with no cover from nearby cliffs and difficult footing. Few got very far. Of the 4,963 Canadians who participated in the raid, 907 were killed, 586 were wounded, and 1,946 were taken prisoner.[51]

Though the Canadian army had seen little action, it had supplied about two-thirds of Canadian POWs by the end of the Dieppe raid. Over the next three years, especially in 1943 and 1944 as bombing raids intensified and Canadian soldiers pushed up Italy and across northwest Europe, another 4,706 fell into Nazi hands: 1,681 airmen, 2,939 soldiers, and 86 sailors. Of the 7,973 Canadian POWs held by the Germans, 390 died: 171 killed by the enemy (usually very soon after their capture),[52] 133 from battle wounds, 21 accidentally killed by Allied aircraft, 29 from disease, 3 from other injuries, and 23 from unknown causes. Of the 1,733 Canadians captured by the Japanese, 290 died in captivity: 256 from disease, 10 from battle wounds, 6 killed by their captors, 13 from injuries, and 5 from unknown causes.[53]

For most of the war, the Germans generally respected the Geneva Convention, which specified, among other matters, minimal living standards and prisoners' freedom from cruelty and forced labour. Also guiding the Germans was the principle of reciprocity: they would treat POWs as they wanted the enemy to treat their men. This policy sometimes brought unfortunate results, however, as following the Dieppe raid, when Canadian POWs remained shackled for a "lengthy period" because Germans had captured orders directing Allied soldiers "whenever possible" to tie the hands of those they took prisoner.[54]

In German stalags, Canadian POWs tried to carve out a tolerable existence. The YMCA's War Prisoners' Aid Association helped considerably by supplying, through neutral parties, items such as sporting equipment and musical instruments. POWs performed concerts, plays, and vaudeville shows, and organized sporting competitions that drew hundreds of spectators including German guards.[55] The parcels POWs received as often as weekly from the International Red Cross were the most welcome. Their contents (see Chapter 1) were developed by University of Toronto professor of pediatrics Dr. Frederick Tisdall, who analyzed typical fare served to POWs in Germany and then provided supplements to ensure adequate vitamins and minerals, along with some morale-boosting treats. Also, prisoners used the cigarettes received from the Red Cross as "camp money" to make secret deals with German guards for extra helpings of more tolerable rations, particularly bread and potatoes.[56]

News received on the home front suggested that POWs were adapting well and being decently treated. Of course, stalag censors excised negative reports in letters home, and prisoners realized that complaints could invite retaliation. The news-letter of the Canadian Prisoners of War Relatives' Association, which sought to obtain information on POWs, generally had an encouraging tone to keep up the morale of readers who had loved ones in captivity.[57]

For some men, being captured actually brought a sense of relief because it meant they would likely survive the war. Few risked death by trying to escape. However, after years behind barbed wire, many became despondent and severely changed as people. Some felt shame, guilt, and self-loathing, believing that they had failed in their military role and were considered cowards for having surrendered. Reacting to overwhelming boredom and their captors' micromanagement of their lives, some developed infantile behaviour, deriving great amusement, for instance, from ac-tions like farting. Others became increasingly irritable or brooded continually, sometimes contemplating suicide. They obsessed over mail and easily convinced themselves that any delay in correspondence meant they had been forgotten or cast aside by a wife or girlfriend. Many thought constantly about women, though after being in an all-male environment for so long, it was common that, once released, POWs felt crippling awkwardness when in female company. To compensate for the absence of women, prisoners often held dances amongst themselves. More than any other military setting, the POW environment led a number of hitherto straight men toward sexual experimentation or brought to the fore previously suppressed homosexuality, a situation that, though liberating for some, often pro-duced violent, vigilante-type responses from fellow prisoners.[58]

Despite the Geneva Convention and periodic visits by Red Cross representa-tives, some POWs in Germany were forced to perform hazardous work that on occasion produced fatalities. Harsh justice was sometimes applied, such as the case of a Canadian lance-corporal who was executed without trial after being charged with plundering. Brutal treatment became the norm as defeat loomed for Germany. In January 1945, despite inadequate winter clothing and footwear, thou-sands of POWs were ordered on a forced march from eastern Germany to stay ahead of advancing Soviet forces. Because they were allowed just five minutes rest per hour, they covered some thirty kilometres each day. Food transported by make-shift sleighs sometimes froze solid. One Canadian survivor remembered eating snow and "bits of turnips" picked out of fields. Some POWs were killed for breaking regulations, often petty ones, as the patience of relatively older and exhausted guards – younger men having been sent to the front – was strained past tolerance. Other POWs simply collapsed and froze to death.[59]

On balance, despite the brutality they endured and the difficulties POWs in Germany eventually had in readapting to civilian life, their suffering paled in comparison to the experiences of those who were held by the Japanese. Tokyo had never signed the Geneva Convention. Its attitude was that surrender was contemptible; during the fall of Hong Kong, among other atrocities, Japanese soldiers sometimes killed and then mutilated the corpses of those who had surrendered. Rarely and only for brief periods were Red Cross inspectors allowed into Japanese POW camps. They were permitted to speak only with specific prisoners and always in the presence of guards, and for these occasions POWs were given clean clothes and extra blankets that were promptly confiscated once the inspectors left. Not until September 1942 did the Japanese agree to accept Red Cross shipments to POWs, and even then not on a regular basis; their contents were often confiscated or heavily pilfered before they reached the inmates.[60]

The treatment of Canadian POWs would eventually result in forty-eight convictions against the Japanese for war crimes, including four that led to the death sentence (three of which, however, were commuted to life imprisonment).[61] By early 1942 Canada's federal government believed that the Japanese were committing widespread violations of the Geneva Convention. However, they did not make their fears public to avoid further hardening the attitudes and conduct of the Japanese – who for eighteen months after the fall of Hong Kong would not even reveal the names of their prisoners – and to avoid adding to the worries of the families of POWs. The Canadian Prisoners of War Relatives' Association maintained its relatively optimistic outlook. In its February 1942 newsletter, it assured readers, "So much pressure has been brought to bear upon the Japanese ... it would seem fairly well established that these prisoners of war are to receive treatment ... equal to that accorded other allied prisoners of war."[62] Letters from POWs were uniformly positive. Only when analyzed on a broad basis did they signal that something was wrong. That conclusion was confidentially conveyed to the federal government by the Bureau of Public Information in early 1942 after its examination of some 500 pieces of correspondence from Canadian POWs in Japan. They practically all said the same thing: the writer felt fine, was well treated, and had plenty of recreation and good food. Cleverly, some men conveyed a more truthful message, such as by mentioning their weight to indicate malnourishment. POW George Soper, in "helping" the Japanese make a radio propaganda broadcast, said he longed to join his father – who, unknown to his captors, was dead.[63]

Such surreptitiously conveyed snippets of truth could hardly make Canadians at home aware of what these men endured. On entering a POW camp, they were warned that "severe punishment" would be applied against those who "attempt bad acts," "influence others to bad acts," "dislike work," or "[are] not obedient."[64] At

Camp 5B in Niigata, Japan, where seventy-five Canadians died, commandant Masato Yoshida – who committed suicide to avoid trial for war crimes – used punishment methods such as tying lightly clothed men to stakes for long periods in winter, which sometimes produced death either from exposure or from frostbite-initiated gangrene. In some cases, men were destroyed psychologically as the Japanese proceeded with all the formal steps to an execution but gave a reprieve at the very last moment. Men dealt daily with sadistic guards who, for the slightest infraction, real or concocted, pummelled them with bamboo poles, clubs, whips, hammers, rifle butts, or shovels.

Slave labour was imposed. In mines, steel mills, shipyards, and in building airport landing strips with pick and shovel, men put in fourteen-hour days for fourteen days straight before being allowed a day of rest – and then only if they had filled their work quota.[65] The sick were required to work, and if they were unable, their skimpy rations were further reduced or cut off. Meals were a rotation of items such as "green horror," a soup made from "weeds, flowers and other unidentifiable greens"; rice that often reeked of gasoline because of the barrels in which it was cooked; and seaweed and fish heads. Yet the spectre of starvation not only drove men to desperately grasp at these rations, but in some cases virtually dehumanized them. As one former POW recounted, "We all had diarrhoea or dysentery ... a good deal of the time and ... the rice and barley could go through you practically untouched. One day I was in such bad shape that ... I cupped my hands under a man squatting with diarrhoea, caught the barley coming through, washed it off as best I could and ate it." Malnutrition produced swelling and burning of the feet and left POWs highly susceptible to diphtheria, beriberi, pellagra, parasitic worms, dysentery and what they nicknamed "Hong Kong balls," which caused their testicles to enlarge sometimes to the point that they could no longer walk.[66]

POWs were but a small segment of those "on the ground" whose wartime experiences would eventually, and often significantly, compromise their ability to function effectively as civilians. Throughout late 1942 and early 1943, pressure again built up in English Canada, and among Canadian soldiers and commanders in England, for the army to become more engaged. The exception was General McNaughton. A fierce nationalist, he wanted to keep the First Canadian Army intact and under Canadian command, preferably his, for an invasion of Europe. But his influence was fading, and he was sent back to Canada in early 1944 as a consequence of several botched training exercises, particularly "Spartan" in March 1943, a dress rehearsal for an invasion of Europe. Prime Minister King remained circumspect. He again sought a ground operation sufficiently high in profile to satisfy those who clamoured for action, but unlikely to decimate the ranks enough to force him to go back on his "not necessarily conscription" policy. The answer appeared in the summer of 1943. Following Allied victories in North Africa, plans were made to invade Sicily and then Italy, domains comparatively less fortified than northwest Europe and defended largely by nationals known to have lost much of their fighting spirit.[67]

On 10 July 1943 some 30,000 Canadians with the 1st Infantry Division and the 1st Army Tank Brigade stormed ashore near the town of Pachino, Sicily, as part of an invasion force numbering over 180,000. The great majority of Sicilians were uninterested in fighting; to them, Mussolini and Hitler had long ago drained the limited resources out of their poverty-stricken island. The reluctantly conscripted Italian soldiers with the 6th Army were quick to surrender, symptomatic of the disintegration of Italy's Fascist party and Mussolini's imminent fall from power after a series of military defeats, mounting economic problems, and the likelihood of an Allied invasion. Only seven Canadians were killed during the landing and consolidation of a bridgehead.[68]

But Sicily turned out to be a "tough nut." Advancing Canadians had to cross mountains via steep, narrow, and winding goat paths often blocked or booby-trapped by the enemy – obstacles also present in Italy, as were deep ravines and many waterways that favoured defending forces. Moreover, there was Sicily's often desert-like terrain and excruciating summer heat to contend with. When marching, commonly with some sixty pounds of equipment, men tried not to lift their feet so as to avoid kicking up clouds of limestone dust that formed into a hard crust when mixed with sweat. Disease posed a serious threat: some 1,200 Canadians in Sicily contracted malaria, and diphtheria, dysentery, jaundice, and hepatitis also left their mark.

The troops had little leave time during this intense thirty-eight-day campaign.[69] The Canadians soon confronted battle-seasoned German troops with the 15th Panzer Division and the Hermann Göring Division. The enemy, fighting a well-executed rearguard action before retreating into Italy, inflicted more than 19,000 Allied casualties, of which 2,310 were Canadian, including 522 dead. Although green, most Canadians acquitted themselves professionally, even according to the frequently hypercritical Montgomery, who led the Eighth Army under which they fought.[70] Over the course of this campaign, as in others, padres reported that whereas some men turned to religion for comfort, others abandoned hope, compassion, and ethics.[71] They were overcome with anxiety and despair as a result of the suffering they witnessed, the randomness, butchery and putrid smell of battle-field death, the deafening cacophony of artillery barrages and bombing raids, and the killing that they themselves were compelled to inflict. Some who saw their comrades killed, or who feared more intensely for their own survival, became consumed with hate for the enemy, including the civilian population. Men in action felt themselves more and more dehumanized. For weeks, tired and often without washing, many lived in the same uniform, in which they might have urinated or defecated out of fear in battle. To cope, many buried their emotions, grew callous toward death and suffering, and built a psychological barrier around themselves. Many more succumbed to "battle exhaustion," the manifestations of which were screaming, uncontrollable weeping, shaking, hallucinating, becoming consumed by "morbid fears" – including that they would kill one of their own – or, perhaps most common, shutting down and becoming virtually comatose, simply staring vacantly off into the horizon, even in the midst of mortal danger. In Sicily, battle exhaustion accounted for about 11 percent of Canadian casualties.[72]

Few people back in Canada realized the extent or the impact of battle exhaustion, or the many other disturbing ways in which life at the front hardened and changed men. In Sicily, this also manifested in the interchange between Canadian soldiers and the local civilian population. Many encounters were cordial, even warm, as the Canadians were often greeted as liberators, though understandably many troops doubted the sincerity of such displays. Some men, however, repelled by the squalid conditions in which the Sicilians lived, were contemptuous of them; others, acting on long-held stereotypes, saw all Sicilian men as members of the "Black Hand Society" and the population in general as thieves.[73] A lot of mutually beneficial bartering went on, with Sicilians typically supplying produce and wine in exchange for army compo rations, fuel, clothing, and especially cigarettes, which became a medium of exchange in lieu of the decimated lira. But many soldiers also felt entitled to take what they wanted from people they regarded as defeated, pathetic, and crooked. Scrounging was legal, in that goods needed by the military for its campaigns could be confiscated in return for fair payment, but Canadian soldiers, if not actually stealing, often compelled Sicilians to accept promissory notes bearing signatures of Hollywood stars or cartoon characters.[74] Many civilians complained that the Canadians swiped not just food but also items like jewellery, sometimes even at gunpoint. Certainly, some claims of poverty-stricken Sicilians who sought compensation from the military were fraudulent. Yet, on the other hand, the well-known novelist Farley Mowat, who fought in Sicily as a member of the Hastings and Prince Edward Regiment, commented in later years that "there was brutal contempt" for these civilians whose "meagre possessions seemed fair game."[75]

The harsh and precarious environment of even this brief a campaign undoubtedly was the cause of much drinking and cavorting. Some men claimed that they turned to locally produced wine, marsala, and other alcoholic drinks because of the poor quality of drinking water in Sicily – and later Italy – to which chlorine tablets had to be added to prevent illness. But of course alcohol also allured with its promise to relieve tension and help drown out horrors. Military officials issued warnings that much homemade wine and other liquor contained dysentery-causing bacteria or worse, but they seemed to have no impact. In addition to trading for drink, men often looted civilian wine cellars when taking over areas, and were known to empty unfermented wine still in presses on farms into demijohns.[76] On occasion, drunkenness produced tragic results. In Valguarnera, Sicily, members of the Hastings and Prince Edward Regiment broke into wine shops that were declared "off limits" and were soon "wandering up and down the streets firing their rifles" into the air and sometimes into houses. One Canadian soldier, believing this to be enemy fire, shot at some civilians and killed a child.[77]

Canadians in Sicily also committed sexual assaults and rape. After seven reported rapes by the end of July, Captain A.T. Sesia, war diarist for the 1st Infantry Division, commented in the official record, "Unless serious measures are taken to check this, Gabby Goebbels will get wind of it and have a field day."[78] Of course, this behaviour was only one extreme of the contacts between Canadian soldiers and local women, though the spectrum of encounters rarely included lasting relationships. Men were on the move, few spoke Italian, and many rejected the women for being "too dark." No war brides came from Sicily, and only twenty-six from the eighteen-month long Italian campaign.[79] But it was a very different story when sex alone was sought. In Sicily, where prostitution was legal, brothels were declared "out of bounds" to the troops. This prohibition meant little since the military was unwilling to post guards outside such establishments; the signs that were posted were regularly torn down. For morale purposes, many officers turned a blind eye when it came to the use of brothels, which they themselves often patronized.

Besides the "professionals," many women in this poverty-stricken land, some barely into their teens, sold themselves to survive or to support their families. Sesia wrote of "soldiers having women ... in Sicily for a few cigarettes or a tin of bully beef" and of "boys of not more than 8 or 9 years" pimping for their sisters.[80] Despite a short stay, very limited time off, and easy access by soldiers to protective devices, VD still managed to account for 10 percent of hospital visits by Canadians in Sicily. The situation was considered serious enough by Maj.-Gen. Chris Vokes, commander of the 2nd Brigade, that he suggested the creation of a "brigade brothel" to follow troops, in which the women would be regularly tested for VD, a measure also considered by Patton. This suggestion, besides infuriating padres, was quickly nixed by nearly all commanders in the Eight Army for its potential to outrage the home front should word of such a novel initiative leak out.[81]

On 3 September 1943 Canadian troops, with the 3rd Brigade in the lead, joined the Eighth Army in crossing the Strait of Messina into Italy for what turned out to be a long, tough, and costly campaign that produced just over 300,000 Allied casualties by early 1945. Of the 92,757 Canadians assigned to Italy, 5,764 were killed, 19,486 were wounded, and 1,004 were captured. This loss rate of 28.3 percent was especially high considering that about half the men remained behind the front lines.[82]

Only the beginning was easy. The Germans had moved inland and the Canadians landing near Réggio di Calábria suffered just nine wounded as they faced virtually no opposition from Italian defenders. That first month, the Canadians advanced over 500 kilometres at the cost of just 42 dead and 146 wounded.[83] Initially, the Allies hoped to take Rome before the winter set in. However, after Italy's surrender on 7 September, Germany beefed up its forces in the country, ultimately to thirteen divisions. In October the 1st Canadian Infantry Division met stiff opposition some

100 kilometres northeast of Naples at Campobasso. The next month, it moved northeast to cross the Sangro River, advancing in cold and sleet through mud-soaked terrain, and on 6 December encountered heavy German resistance at the Moro River, which many came to call the "river of blood." This was the stepping stone to San Leonardo, taken on 9 December, also at a considerable contribution to the butcher's bill.[84]

At this point, Farley Mowat wrote to his father, a Great War veteran who he knew had seen and understood much about combat, "Things have changed so much since Sicily. Too many pals gone west. Too many things that go wump in the night ... Pray God we get a decent break."[85] Many soldiers were sent over the edge by the next major clash at Ortona, a city of some 17,000, where, between 20 and 28 December, the Canadians battled two well-seasoned and well-entrenched German paratroop battalions. Fighting often proceeded room by room as the Canadians blasted their way through adjoining row houses, some of which were booby-trapped. All told, in December 1943, the 1st Canadian Infantry Division lost 2,339 men killed and wounded, with some rifle companies suffering a 50 percent casualty rate, and battle exhaustion cases, at some 500, totalling nearly a third of the nonfatal casualties.[86]

Still greater challenges awaited, as to the north lay the major German defences, starting with the Gustav Line. Although not yet complete despite five months' preparation, it nevertheless presented a forbidding objective, as it consisted of mine belts up to one hundred metres deep, "concrete and steel machine-gun emplacements," pillboxes, tank turrets embedded into concrete, and antitank ditches. Starting on 14 May 1944, I Canadian Corps battled for three days to break through its section. On 16 May, the Germans fell back to the even more formidable Hitler Line. The Canadians attacked on 23 May and their breakthrough by the end of the month was critical in opening the road to Rome, which the US Fifth Army captured on 4 June. Although a triumph for I Canadian Corps and testimony to its increasing professionalism, the toll of the battle was huge. On the first day of the attack, Canada's 2nd Infantry Brigade took 543 casualties, a record for such a formation during the Italian campaign, and during the three weeks it took to breach both lines, Canada's army suffered nearly 3,300 casualties, of which neuropsychiatric cases accounted for about a quarter.[87]

The invasion of northwest Europe on 6 June 1944 brought mixed reactions among those battling in Italy. Initial celebrations over the prospect of a more imminent victory often turned to bitterness because it seemed that all attention had shifted away from the Mediterranean. Morale declined as Allied soldiers who faced a determined and powerful foe perceived themselves to be fighting and possibly dying in a sideshow.[88] Spirits also sank because of dwindling reinforcements and Prime Minister King's persistence in avoiding conscription for overseas service. It became increasingly necessary to remuster men to the infantry from other areas and rush them into battle with what many considered minimal preparation. Nonetheless, on

25 August 1944 the Canadians launched a major offensive, ultimately across six waterways, with the coastal town of Rimini as its goal. This objective required them to break through the eastern flank of Germany's daunting Gothic Line, undoubtedly among the finest achievements by Canadian soldiers during the Second World War. However, this operation, which was largely conducted in miserable weather and lasted until 22 September when Rimini finally fell, saw the 1st Infantry Division lose 2,511 men, including 626 dead, while the 5th Armoured Division suffered 1,315 casualties, including 390 dead, rates that, in total, exceeded losses during any equivalent period throughout the Mediterranean campaign.

To the very end of their service in Italy, the Canadians encountered formidable opposition. In December 1944 they endured some 2,500 casualties in crossing the Lamone River, the Fosso Vecchi, and the Naviglio Canal. Even in early 1945, with the Germans reeling, opposition still remained such that battle exhaustion figures, while declining on an aggregate basis along with total casualties, accounted for up to one-third of the men removed.[89]

DURING THIS LENGTHY CAMPAIGN, Canada's military kept up substantial efforts to maintain morale. As far as possible, regular rotations were provided out of the firing line. Auxiliary services assumed a prominent presence. They brought food, candy, tea, cigarettes, reading material, and sporting equipment to points near the front. They arranged movies in settings such as abandoned barns, and constructed makeshift stages for live entertainment, including the rather elaborate Number 1 Canadian Army Show, which played before more than 25,000 soldiers in Italy between May and August 1944.[90] Leave centres were established throughout Italy, the first in October 1943 in Campobasso. There, for instance, the YMCA provided, at its Canada Club for officers and Aldershot Club for other ranks, canteen service as well as rooms for reading and writing, games, dances, and shows. The Salvation Army managed lodging capable of handling up to 4,000 visitors.[91]

Such services were not as effective as military authorities hoped in diverting men from the coarse conduct paralleling their raw and perilous existence. Early in the Italian campaign, no doubt due in part to experiences in Sicily, the Canadian army provided a handbook to soldiers containing not only basic information about the country and useful phrases in Italian but also advice on appropriate behaviour. Although describing Italy as a "wine-drinking country," the booklet insisted that drunkenness was "rare and [considered] disgraceful." As for women, it said, "the less you have to do with them the better." Italian men were described as "jealous," their "code of morals strict," and thus, it stressed, even the "most harmless behaviour on your part will arouse suspicion."[92]

Many Canadians spoke warmly of the Italians. "They had never wanted war," said one, "nor had the majority of them ever borne any hatred of Britain." As in Sicily, there were many reciprocal exchanges between soldiers and civilians. But some Canadians considered the Italians, or "Iyties" as they called them, in the same light as they saw the Sicilians: chameleon-like in allegiance, crooked, and thus deserving of little consideration. Shopkeepers were accused of exploiting short-ages to overcharge soldiers. It is true that early in the campaign the Allies felt it necessary to post official prices for some 100 items and threatened to confiscate stock or jail storeowners who broke the rules.[93] However, it is also true that only days after Italy was invaded, reports flowed in about Canadians committing armed robbery. Indeed, theft by Canadian soldiers was serious enough to warrant regular examination of parcels sent home to ensure that stolen items, particularly jewellery, were not among the "souvenirs" being sent to family and friends. As late as August 1944, as its troops prepared to assault Rimini, those commanding the Princess Patricia's Canadian Light Infantry still thought it necessary to stress, "Looting is strictly against ... regulations."[94]

In fact, just outside Rimini, at the 100-room Villa des Vergers, which the Germans had used as a local headquarters, there occurred the worst recorded incident of looting by Canadians, involving the Seaforth Highlanders. Because the Germans had not looted the hilltop mansion, the Canadians were mistakenly convinced that its Italian owner, Prince Mario Ruspoli, was a Fascist, and proceeded to mete out a most self-serving form of revenge. Army trucks pulled up like moving vans and removed dining services and silver cutlery, rare books, antique clocks, pianos, chandeliers, and dozens of original paintings, including a portrait of the French king Henri III attributed to Titian. Some items were bartered to locals, typically for valuables that could be mailed home. Paintings, ripped from their frames and concealed in sleeping rolls, also certainly found their way back to Canada. One of two pilfered pianos was voluntarily returned, but the other, along with fine china, was discovered at an officers' mess in Rimini.[95]

Wine and other locally produced liquor could still be obtained through purchase, trade, or theft. Some army transport drivers were discovered to be involved in black market schemes to supply troops. In early 1944, after several "departures from discipline" – such as when drunken Canadians on leave in the coastal community of Bari staggered through streets, pounded on doors, and threatened locals who did not provide liquor – Maj.-Gen. E.L.M. Burns, who commanded I Canadian Corps, ordered wine shops in leave centres to restrict sales "so that men [would] not become drunk." Most Italian storeowners were unwilling to try to enforce this order.[96]

Not long after landing in Italy, the Canadian army stepped up its campaign against VD. New venereal disease control officers were appointed here, and later in northwest Europe, to give lectures and distribute printed material advising against sexual contact with local women, to ensure widespread access to condoms and prophylactic kits, and to urge men who had intercourse to visit medical personnel or one of the EPT stations that were soon available in every leave centre.[97] But VD continued to reduce the ranks. Legal brothels abounded and, as in Sicily, destitute women turned to prostitution to obtain food, clothing, cigarettes, or cash that even for a private amounted to pocket change. In Naples, a major leave centre for Canadians, one estimate placed the number of prostitutes, professional or not, at 50,000. When large numbers of men were at rest or on leave, VD rates always soared. A July 1944 study of I Canadian Corps showed that among men sent on leave after a month of steady fighting, weekly VD totals increased tenfold. Among Canadians stationed in Rome from mid-1944 onward, the VD rate, when extrapolated over a yearly basis, peaked at an astonishing 217 per 1,000 men. Indeed, during the latter half of 1944, for reasons Canada's military did not attempt to explain, VD rates among its troops in Italy topped all others from the Commonwealth.[98]

IN FEBRUARY 1945, under Operation Goldflake, I Canadian Corps left Italy to join II Corps in northwest Europe. Starting with the D-Day invasion on 6 June 1944, the northwest European campaign ultimately involved some 237,000 Canadians, 44,339 of whom became casualties, including 11,336 killed in action.[99] On D-Day, some 15,000 extremely untested Canadian troops, principally from the 3rd Infantry Division and the 2nd Armoured Brigade, stormed ashore at Juno Beach as part of the largest-ever amphibious assault. D-Day brought the Canadians 914 casualties, including 340 dead, though preinvasion estimates had predicted double that number. That first day, to their credit, Canadian forces actually advanced farther than other Allied armies, but the Germans soon regrouped and consolidated near the villages of Buron and Authie near Caen. House-to-house fighting ensued, and within five days, Canadian losses reached 1,017 dead and 1,814 wounded, rates that corresponded to some of the worst fighting on the western front during the Great War. Ultimately, it took thirty-three days for Canadian and British forces to capture Caen, a port city that Montgomery had thought could be taken by the end of D-Day.[100]

Canadian troops next moved along the Caen-Falaise road to help cut off and capture the bulk of German forces in Normandy. On 20 July, five kilometres south of Falaise, they encountered the gently sloping eighty-eight-metre-high Verrières Ridge, upon which the Germans had perched plenty of tanks, large guns, and infantry. By 24 July, the Essex Scottish had endured 244 casualties and the South Saskatchewan Regiment 215. The next day, one of the war's worst for Canada, nearly 1,500 casualties, including 450 dead, were suffered. Medical officer Jack Leddy recalled men arriving at his casualty clearing station "crying hysterically ... shaking uncontrollably [or] just sitting and staring into space."[101] At many other dots on the map in Normandy, death reaped a rich harvest, including Tilly-la-Campagne, May-sur-Orne, Rocquancourt, Quesnay Wood, and Falaise, which fell on 17 August following a brutal week-long battle. With morale in some Canadian units disintegrating, battle exhaustion cases reached as high as 35 percent of the casualties.[102] Yet despite inadequately prepared troops, charges of poor Canadian leadership throughout the Normandy campaign, and, in fact, the sacking of several commanders, the newly operational First Canadian Army under Crerar's command ultimately played a key role in closing the twenty-five-kilometre Falaise-Argentan Gap by 21 August. They confronted tough terrain and crack SS formations – namely the 12th Division directed by the brutal Kurt Meyer – to help end German resistance in Normandy. But a horrible toll was exacted: in Normandy, Canada took 18,444 casualties, including 5,021 dead, losses that almost matched those suffered during the entire eighteen-month Italian campaign.[103]

In September, Canadian troops assumed the left flank of the Allied advance and were assigned the capture of the French channel ports. By 1 October Le Havre, Boulogne, Calais, and – most symbolically for the Canadians – Dieppe, were in Allied hands. However, the facilities at each port were badly damaged; in any case, they were too small and soon too distant to handle the magnitude of supplies required by the hundreds of thousands of advancing Allied troops and millions of liberated, and often starving, Europeans. Only the Belgian port of Antwerp, the largest in Europe and located eighty kilometres inland from the North Sea along the Scheldt River, could fill the bill. It had been captured undamaged by Britain's Second Army on 5 September. The task of the Canadians was to clear the Germans from the series of waterways and islands that formed the Scheldt estuary to the north, an initiative that was launched on 6 October.

Realizing the strategic importance of the Scheldt, Hitler ordered that it be held to the last man. The terrain strongly favoured the defenders. Advancing Canadians had to traverse rivers, canals, water-filled ditches, and badly exposed roadways and fields. Throughout the campaign, the weather was cold and rainy. With much of the land situated below sea level, it was easily churned into a morass of mud, and some areas were waist-deep in frigid water. Making matters worse, advance intelligence had underestimated the enemy's strength in some sectors by as much as half, and the Canadians often faced "first-class formations" such as Germany's 64th Division. Not until 8 November did the Canadians prevail – with help from one British and one American division – though at the cost of 6,367 casualties, just over 1,800 of which were fatal. Official battle exhaustion figures stood at only 15 percent of total casualties, but it was known that acute troop shortages had commanders sending only the most extreme cases to the rear. Indeed, while psychiatrists warned that men could retain "good efficiency" in combat for perhaps three weeks, some 90 percent of those evacuated from the Scheldt with battle exhaustion had seen three months of near-continual front-line service.[104]

The next major offensive, Operation Véritable, was launched on 8 February 1945. The First Canadian Army moved west to take Nijmegen in the south-central Netherlands, and south to neutralize the enemy between the Maas and Rhine rivers in Germany, in preparation for crossing the Rhine itself. They confronted three major German defensive lines: an "outpost of trenches, anti-tank ditches, minefields, and fortified strongpoints"; the Siegfried Line in the forested Reichswald, which included numerous "dugouts and concrete bunkers"; and a defensive network in the heavily wooded Hochwald area that from its high ground allowed the Germans to guard the Rhine crossings. Much of the land was flooded, as the Germans had destroyed several dikes; only by following tree lines could Canadian armoured vehicles locate roads. While German outpost divisions, which contained large numbers of older and more poorly trained soldiers, were dispatched relatively easily, those situated behind, which included many SS and Gestapo, put up stiff resistance; indeed, in defending their homeland, they often "fought like ... demons." Some 1,000 of the more than 8,500 Canadian casualties in February resulted from battle exhaustion, though by this point, as in the later stages of the Italian campaign, this included men not only in urgent need of relief, but also desperate to survive a war that clearly would soon be won.[105] On 26 February, in a new operation codenamed Blockbuster, II Canadian Corps drove east to take the ancient Rhine town of Xanten, some fifty kilometres northwest of Essen. Twelve days of heavy fighting produced 3,638 casualties, 700 from battle exhaustion. However, Xanten's capture did finally end Operation Véritable, and on 24 March, both I and II Canadian Corps drove north to liberate the Netherlands and advance into northwestern Germany. As the enemy forces crumbled, the Canadians moved forward rapidly, although in several areas tough pockets of resistance remained, not only from the Germans, but also from the Dutch SS who, fearing retribution from their countrymen, thought they had "nothing to lose." In Apeldoorn, for instance, between 11 and 17 April street-to-street fighting claimed many of Canada's 506 casualties, while on 1 May, the day Hitler committed suicide, twenty members of the Cape Breton Highlanders were killed during the liberation of the heavily defended Dutch port of Delfzijl. Indeed, during the last phase of operations extending from 24 March to 5 May, the First Canadian Army, though having evolved into a "superb fighting machine," still suffered 6,298 casualties, 1,482 of which were fatal.[106]

IN NORTHWESTERN EUROPE, as in Italy, rather elaborate recreational facilities were set up to rejuvenate men during their time off.[107] But also as in the Mediterranean campaign, men still pursued other, more basic recreation. There was French wine, champagne, cognac, and, most preferred, calvados, an apple-based liquor affectionately nicknamed "liquid dynamite" because it was usually 15 to 20 percent stronger than brandy or scotch.[108]

Along with sampling wine, numerous Canadians, true to the saying, took every opportunity to enjoy women. Soldiers arriving in Amiens, France, for example, had at least two dozen legal brothels to choose from in the city's red light district.[109] These establishments were legally required to arrange regular medical examinations for their employees, while prostitutes working the streets had to carry a card proving that they too had maintained an examination schedule and were free from VD. Compliance had never been complete, however, and during the war there was even less certainty of disease-free sex, because more women turned to prostitution to survive economically, and civilian doctors and law enforcement authorities were consumed with so many other matters. In September 1944, following the Normandy campaign, the VD rate in several Canadian units, at more than 170 per 1,000 when extrapolated over a yearly basis, was nearly twenty times greater than during the previous month.[110] As Canadian troops moved, so did the VD problem. Between October 1944 and March 1945, 75 percent of cases were traced to Antwerp, Ghent, and Brussels. In fact, in Belgium, legalized prostitution was more difficult to regulate than in France, for rather than having large brothels, it was the custom to have smaller operations located above cafés. In Ghent, for example, there were more than 100 such establishments. Moreover, according to a British military report, soldiers visiting Brussels could choose among some 1,000 card-carrying prostitutes or an estimated 10,000 others who did not bother with this formality.[111]

SOME 170,000 CANADIAN TROOPS ended the war in the Netherlands. They were greeted with jubilation, having liberated a population that had probably suffered under the Nazis more than any other in Europe. The Dutch SS was substantial and vicious, and both they and the Germans dealt brutally with the larger population, who proved uncooperative even when it came to identifying Jews and included an underground that was arguably the Continent's most active and effective. Ruthlessness became especially intense after 5 September 1944, the day the Dutch came to call "mad Tuesday." Responding to rumours that the Allies had entered the Netherlands from Belgium and that their liberation was imminent, thousands of Dutch took to the streets to celebrate wildly. It was a tragic, fatal mistake. Meting out revenge, the Nazis rounded up and summarily executed large numbers of civilians whom they suspected of belonging to the Dutch underground, and practically cut off the flow of food and fuel to all civilians. In the densely populated area around Arnhem, nearly 18,000 people had starved to death by the end of the war.[112]

The Dutch threw parties and receptions for their Canadian liberators, and opened up their homes to billet soldiers, especially since their guests often brought food. Besides distributing food and fuel, the troops cleaned city streets, removed rubble, repaired buildings, constructed temporary bridges, and even ran the Dutch railway and local public transportation systems. Gratitude was widely and deeply felt, forging a special bond between Canada and the Netherlands that survives to this day (poignantly demonstrated in anniversary celebrations of the liberation every five years between 1985 and 2000, when tens of thousands of Dutch, most of whom were born after the war, came out to cheer aged Canadian veterans who paraded through places like Apeldoorn).[113]

But such feelings were also attributable to the fact that in 1945 Canadian military authorities realized that the soldiers were impatient to return home and could easily transform into a dangerously disruptive force, especially if they became bored. This had been demonstrated after the Great War when Canadian soldiers became involved in at least fourteen serious disturbances at military bases across Britain, most notably a riot at Kimnel Park that left five dead, twenty-five wounded, and fifty-nine under arrest.[114] To avoid such troubles in the Netherlands, auxiliary services "went all out" by establishing substantial recreational facilities in twenty-nine locations, and men were given plenty of time off to avail themselves of these amenities. The overall friendliness and mutual affection that continued to characterize relationships between Canadian soldiers and Dutch civilians was also the result of the momentum toward demobilization, which by the end of the summer was rapidly depleting the number of soldiers left overseas. Indeed, as early as July 1945, Queen Wilhelmina diplomatically suggested that it was best for all concerned if Canadian and British troops were quickly repatriated. Some Canadians resented her remarks, as they did the appearance of graffiti pleading, "Free us from our liberators." But by that point many also realized it was time to go because, as one soldier put it, "We had grown slack and we were wearing out our welcome. The smart, well-disciplined troops that had waved and smiled their way into Dutch hearts and homes in the delirious days following VE day had become just another occupation army, not hated yet, but standing in the way of a return to normal family life."[115]

Some Dutch accused the Canadians of exploiting their desperation as they would an enemy, using cigarettes, food, fuel, and countless other goods in short supply to drive hard bargains to obtain items such as family jewellery.[116] Relations between Canadian soldiers and Dutch women reflected both closeness and controversy. Romantic liaisons were quite easy to establish since the Dutch were as a rule so competent in English. Compared to Dutch men, many of whom had endured years of slave labour in Germany, Canadian soldiers appeared more physically and psychologically robust. Canadians also had money and access to exclusive clubs and restaurants; after years of suffering poverty, Dutch women understandably jumped at the opportunity for a good meal and some fun. Romances quickly blossomed, and with demobilization to Canada in the offing, 1,886 became marriages. As elsewhere, military authorities and chaplains tried to discourage such unions for being too hasty and, it was often said, motivated by women's urge to escape the Netherlands. Many Dutch men accused Canadians of stealing their women, and brawls did result, even near-riots in Zwolle in mid-August and in Utrecht the next month.[117] Dutch women who dated Canadians were sometimes cast as prostitutes or even traitors, and a few had their heads shaved as if they were collaborators. They were often warned that they were being used by the Canadians and might find themselves left in a very difficult situation. This in fact was frequently true, for besides the 428 children that Dutch war brides brought along to Canada, more than 7,000 illegitimate Dutch children were born in 1946, double the number in the previous year.[118]

Canadians also provided a strong market for prostitution, which they were often accused of exacerbating. The Amsterdam newspaper *De Ochtendpost* charged the Canadians with spreading VD to at least 2,000 professional and amateur prostitutes. Although generally a religious country, the Netherlands had not outlawed prostitution; however, a prostitute who knowingly spread VD or ignored legislation requiring regular examinations faced a maximum fine of 3,000 guilders or up to three years' imprisonment (by contrast, in Belgium, the maximum penalty was twenty-five francs or a week in jail). Postwar civil authority in the Netherlands was weak, and the country's limited medical personnel were overwhelmed by caring for a population that had recently faced collective near-starvation. Moreover, as in other parts of Europe, economic desperation sharply augmented the number of women willing to sell their bodies. As early as May 1945 the VD rate within the 2nd Canadian Infantry Division in the Netherlands reached 130 per 1,000.[119] Soldiers with VD were questioned so that Dutch police could trace facilitators, but by the end of June 1945 only 15 percent of those interviewed had provided "information sufficient to permit a definite tracing." Most troops claimed that they did not know or could not recall the names of prostitutes or the location where the contact was made – deficiencies for which language barriers were perhaps to some extent to blame, if, for example, men tried to cite the name of a street or an establishment.[120]

IN PLANNING FOR THE POSTWAR OCCUPATION of Germany, Canada initially promised eleven RCAF squadrons and a total of 25,000 men for the zone that would fall under British control. However, the King government, leery about being drawn into too lengthy and expensive an undertaking after six years of war, said that Canadians would be made available only to the end of the "period of adjustment and disarmament immediately following the operational occupation of Germany." Even in fulfilling this limited commitment, Canada came up short. The Canadian Army Occupation Force (CAOF) stationed in northwest Germany peaked at 853 officers and 16,983 other ranks, some 10,000 of whom were volunteers and the rest recent arrivals overseas who were at the bottom of the heap for returning to Canada. By the end of 1945 RCAF personnel had been repatriated, and in early 1946 ground forces began departing. The British lobbied Ottawa to maintain the CAOF until the spring of 1947, but the federal government kept to its original stance, and by July 1946, save for a skeleton administrative staff, Canada's last major military commitment to the Second World War had ended.[121]

Nearly everyone was happy to leave. Postwar Germany was devastated and its people were generally sullen or quietly hostile. Despite a lavish lakeside leave centre established for the CAOF near Oldenburg, most men with a few days off travelled to the Netherlands or Belgium. There at least they were allowed – or had the desire – to talk to civilians. Allied forces were prohibited from fraternizing with Germans except to secure their compliance with military edicts. A first offence could cost a soldier two weeks' pay, a second four weeks, and a third jail time.[122] For many, such rules posed no problem. The challenge was often to prevent not fraternization but violent retribution. Although discipline was generally maintained, and nothing approaching the postwar rampage by Soviet forces against

Berliners occurred among Canadians, there were some vicious outbursts. For example, in late May 1945, Canadian soldiers in Oldenburg ransacked and looted several homes and physically attacked their occupants; a Canadian sergeant who tried to reimpose order was killed when one of the culprits accidentally discharged his Tommy gun as he was physically restrained.[123]

Hatred of the Germans by no means consumed all the members of the occupying force. Well before the "no fraternization" rule was officially lifted in August 1945, transgressions were so widespread that most officers turned a blind eye rather than issue huge numbers of fines. Some Canadians distinguished the Nazi leadership and the SS from ordinary Germans, whom they perceived as having been forced into the war. They felt sympathy for civilians left in such a wretched state, or they simply softened their attitude with the passing of time and growing ennui.[124] There were also more self-serving reasons for fraternization. Many Canadians were eager to exploit the economic desperation of their enemy, and some made a small fortune doing so; for instance, some Germans were selling family heirlooms for as little as a pack of cigarettes.[125] The sex drive of servicemen also broke down many barriers. While numerous Canadians refused to have anything to do with German women, in January 1946 after what one medical report identified as "abnormal drinking ... associated with the Christmas and New Year season," the CAOF VD rate, extrapolated over a yearly basis, hit an astounding 383 per 1,000.[126] Although brothels were declared "off limits" to soldiers, enforcement and compliance remained lax, and with so many impoverished and desperate civilians, sources for sex were ubiquitous. Indeed, of 752 members of the CAOF interviewed in January 1946 with VD, 420 said that they had met the alleged carrier on the street and in 522 cases the intercourse had taken place "in the open."[127]

OVER 40 PERCENT of Canada's male population aged eighteen to forty-five donned a military uniform in the Second World War. Of that total only about 6 percent had any prewar military experience, the vast majority of which had been just as weekend warriors with the militia. But ultimately the professionalism, sacrifices, and courage of Canadian servicemen, among other feats, kept supply lines moving in the North Atlantic, sapped enemy strength from the air, and resulted in the defeat of many of Germany's finest troops. In the process of becoming such soldiers, sailors, and airmen, many men were transformed. They lived a life far removed from civilian norms, one that induced, or further encouraged, scrounging, looting, hard drinking, and womanizing, activities that were often first displayed during training in Canada. Also, in addition to 42,042 war dead, 54,234 Canadians were wounded in action, often horribly and permanently, and thousands more carried home deep psychological injuries, unable to shake off the effects of too many unnerving land campaigns, sea voyages, ops, or tortured years behind barbed wire as POWs.[128]

Eventually, most readapted to civvy street and family life. For the half of all veterans who never directly engaged with the enemy, readjustment was relatively smooth. Many others had to will themselves to psychologically compartmentalize their unsettling experiences and get on with life. Still, in legions of households, long-anticipated and initially joyous reunions soon descended into painful and sometimes nightmarish situations. To minimize such scenarios, many recommended the postwar prescription of reinforcing conservative trends: namely, to reconstitute traditional family life with the woman at home to provide a stable and supportive environment, and to open up more decent jobs for veterans and thus re-establish them as breadwinners. However, some veterans had changed too much for this vision to be realized, or too much had changed among women who had been forced by wartime conditions out of a dependent role. There was far more at work in helping men to readjust and thrive than the assertion of social conservatism or government measures to remove women from the postwar job market. There was also Canada's Veterans Charter, which for thousands of Canadians ultimately and fortunately had an impact arguably as deep and long-lasting as the war itself.

10

A New Beginning: "A very clear tendency to improve upon pre-enlistment status"

BARELY HAD THE SECOND WORLD WAR begun than planning for its end was put in motion. One month into the war, Canada's minister of pensions and national health, Ian Mackenzie, a former vice-president of the Great War Veterans' Association, was already advising Prime Minister King to begin planning for demobilization and rehabilitation. It had to be done differently this time. Mackenzie and the many key players who came together to devise and manage the series of programs that in 1946 became known collectively as the Veterans Charter were of the opinion that the paltry support that government programs offered Canadians who had fought in the Great War had significantly magnified their problems in readjusting to civilian life, leading disgruntled and angry veterans to aggravate postwar social instability. Informal estimates made in Winnipeg in May 1919, for example, suggested that as many as half of the veterans sided with organized labour in the general strike that authorities saw as a Communist conspiracy to seize power.[1] Others, too, were worried. *Maclean's* magazine was moved to write as early as December 1939, "Without definite, well-worked out plans for the post-war employment of men who ... have served the country we shall be faced with a repetition of the upheaval which followed the last war."[2]

Indeed, early that month, while Canada's 1st Division was still preparing to depart for England, the planning commenced. The passage of PC 4068.5 created, under Mackenzie's direction, the Cabinet Committee on Demobilization and Re-establishment to identify problems relating to the eventual discharge of men and to determine how they might best be minimized.[3] However, most of the real work was handed over to an advisory subcommittee composed of deputy ministers and experts drawn from the civil service, the military, and the private sector.[4] Instrumental in setting direction was its executive secretary, Robert England, a twice-wounded Great War veteran and a former director of the Canadian Legion Educational Service. England maintained that the government had to "learn some ... lessons ... in regard to the thoroughness ... of [previous] rehabilitation plans," which he described as "meagre."[5] The other key figure on the subcommittee was the associate deputy minister of pensions and national health, Walter S. Woods. A former member of the Canadian Expeditionary Force who had been wounded in 1915, Woods had served after the war as president of the Calgary branch of the Great War Veterans' Association, and as a director with the federal government's Soldier Settlement Board (which placed veterans on farms). In 1930 he became the first chairman of the War Veterans' Allowance Board, which, under his direction, moved toward greater compassion, especially in awarding pensions for long-term burnout cases.[6]

The work of these two committees was primarily responsible for the Post-Discharge Re-establishment Order on 1 October 1941, which significantly appeared just when the federal government was stepping up efforts to attract recruits. Men were promised on honourable discharge a tax-exempt gratuity of $7.50 per month for time they had served in the Western Hemisphere, and $15 per month for time overseas (a scale triple that paid to British servicemen).[7] They also received a tax-exempt rehabilitation grant of one month's pay and a clothing allowance voucher initially set at $35 ($100 by war's end) for those with at least six months' military service. For veterans who did not claim other benefits, such as retraining, more cash was available, up to a level matching the gratuity, in the form of a tax-free re-establishment credit intended to help them purchase, furnish, or equip a home or business.

Several other pieces of legislation soon flowed from the Re-establishment Order, which was also designed to guarantee veterans the right to: "(I) re-enter their former employment ... (II) find new employment ... (III) train for new work ... or (IV) finish their education."[8] The 1942 Reinstatement in Civil Employment Act affirmed healthy veterans' right to resume their premilitary jobs, or comparable posts with their former employers, at a rate of pay equivalent to what they would have earned had they not enlisted.[9] Veterans could claim new federal unemployment insurance benefits for up to one year during the first eighteen months after discharge. Grants and subsidized loans were made available to those who wished to start up a business, to enter commercial fishing, or, under the 1942 Veterans Land Act, to farm full-time or start a maximum two-acre hobby farm. Self-employed veterans who struggled financially before revenue started flowing in could apply for an awaiting returns allowance, which paid, for up to one year, from $44.20 monthly to a single veteran with no dependants to a maximum of $120.40 monthly to a married man with six dependent children under seventeen years old. The 1942 Vocational Training Co-ordination Act provided such allowances to any veteran who decided to retool at the government's expense, an opportunity that, after the Great War, had been available only to those whose injuries significantly compromised their likelihood of finding work. Qualified veterans could obtain free university education with the same living allowance for a period equivalent to their time spent in the military, and provision was made for others to participate by obtaining a high school diploma in as little as six months under a special accelerated program.[10]

In March 1944 the Department of Veterans Affairs (DVA) was created to better coordinate these and other programs, including pensions and medical care, which had formerly involved several government ministries. Under Mackenzie's direction, the DVA quickly grew to mammoth proportions, with over 12,000 employees by the end of 1946. Even with the availability of unemployment insurance and

Figure 10.1

Veterans' benefits and other federal social welfare expenditures, 1943-45

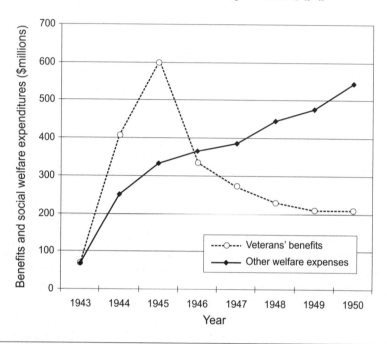

Source: K.A.H. Buckley and M.C. Urquhart, *Historical Statistics of Canada* (Toronto: Macmillan, 1965), 207.

family allowances, DVA benefits and pensions dwarfed all other federal social welfare costs, accounting for expenditures of $1.842 billion out of $3.621 billion between 1944 and 1948 inclusive (Figure 10.1).[11]

PUBLIC OPINION STRONGLY SUPPORTED such generosity. Two-thirds of those polled in mid-1942 agreed, for example, that veterans of this war should receive better treatment than their counterparts had a generation earlier.[12] The generous approach to veterans' benefits was also linked to the expanding influence of the new bureaucrats and advisors recruited by the federal government to help direct the war effort and peacetime reconversion. Many subscribed to the Keynesian strategy of priming the economy to generate spending that would offset the economic trough anticipated after the war.[13] Keynesian economics also drew strong public support, as surveys made it clear that Canadians feared the return of Depression-level unemployment and the emergence of social unrest after the war. Many indicated their intention to turn to the CCF if the Liberals did not introduce more comprehensive peacetime planning and social security – of which veterans' benefits were part – to ensure postwar stability and opportunities.

The King government was also concerned by the attitude among servicemen that the prime minister was antimilitary and even a coward for not serving in the Great War himself, despite having been nearly forty in 1914 and in no shape for military service. Many accused him further of abandoning Canada's fighting men by his determined resistance to conscription for overseas duty. Military morale reports also showed dissatisfaction over the paucity of information servicemen had received about veterans' programs, a situation that generated much cynicism and pessimism. A survey of 900 soldiers in May 1943 revealed that only 21 percent were optimistic about their postwar prospects, and 30 percent foresaw hard times, while the rest refrained from speculating.[14] Another poll taken early the following year by the Canadian Youth Commission among 159 servicemen in Canada from all three service branches showed that 40 percent backed the CCF, 37 percent the Conservatives, and just 12 percent the Liberals.[15]

During the final two years of the war, not only did the federal government improve several programs for veterans – increasing, for instance, living and awaiting returns allowances by $15 to $18 monthly, depending on the number of dependants involved[16] – but it also intensified efforts to publicize DVA benefits throughout the ranks. The air force and navy were most inclined to support this effort, believing it would raise morale. In 1944 each of these services appointed over 100 counsellors to meet with men and familiarize them with their postwar options. The army was more cautious, as several high-ranking officers believed that such information would distract men from the still formidable task of defeating the enemy, or perhaps make them hold back in battle to ensure that they would live to enjoy DVA benefits.[17] Still, from around D-Day onward, military publications such as the *Maple Leaf* printed stories detailing in generally positive tones the different programs being instituted. By the end of 1944 all service branches were distributing DVA literature such as the pocket-sized sixty-page booklet *Back to Civil Life* – of which over a million copies were printed – which outlined in laymen's terms the essentials of all the benefits to which veterans were entitled.[18]

The National Film Board helped out with several short, upbeat instructional clips such as the 1945 three-minute entry *Getting Re-established: School and University Opportunities.* Its most substantial entry, *Welcome Soldier,* a fifteen-minute film that appeared in late 1944, opens with a scene of men being transported home on a railway passenger car. Amid singing and good-natured ribbing, a few ponder their prospects after discharge. The film then cuts to a boardroom of "experts" ready to implement many "carefully constructed" DVA plans, after which men are shown proceeding smoothly through the demobilization machinery, quickly obtaining the cash rewards to which they are entitled and then receiving sage advice from counsellors.[19] Assistance also came from the CBC. Among its radio shows broadcast overseas was the eight-part series *Honourable Discharge,* in which DVA personnel answered letters sent in by servicemen as a means of further explaining the particulars of the various programs.[20]

The DVA was indeed getting its message across. A survey taken in December 1944 among 7,000 army personnel overseas indicated that 52 percent considered themselves "adequately informed" about veterans' programs compared to 32 percent who still wanted more information.[21] More men were giving thought to how they would take advantage of DVA benefits. Another survey taken that month among 12,000 soldiers both overseas and in Canada revealed that 4 percent wanted to finish high school, 11 percent favoured university education, 26 percent thought of vocational training, and 11 percent hoped to start a farm – figures that the Department of National Defence interpreted to show a "very clear tendency ... to improve ... upon pre-enlistment status."[22] The general outlook among men regarding their postwar plans was growing more positive as yet another poll taken among soldiers in late 1944 showed that 54 percent believed "things [would] be better" or "comparable" for them following the conflict, as opposed to just 15 percent who were pessimistic.[23] Meanwhile, although the June 1945 federal election revealed continuing anger among servicemen toward Mackenzie King, the promotion of veterans' benefits no doubt helped the Liberals avert a political catastrophe among this group who, according to one straw poll, ended up giving the party a narrow margin of support: 35 percent, compared to 32 percent for the CCF, 26 percent for the Conservatives, and 7 percent for other parties.[24]

ALTHOUGH THE LIBERALS SURVIVED at the ballot box, the government still faced the daunting responsibility of reintegrating about 7 percent of the country's population into civilian life. Their first task was to bring home the half-million servicemen stationed outside of Canada in a timely manner. For this too Ottawa began planning early, to avoid the problems that followed the Great War. Then, shortages of transatlantic shipping space and railway cars in Canada, along with inadequate recreational facilities established overseas, had resulted in delays and boredom, and greatly contributed to several violent outbursts among those awaiting repatriation. It was also predicted that greater efforts would be needed to convince men that the demobilization process was fair. After the Great War, the method had not been clearly articulated, and bitter rumours of favouritism arose, especially since such tasks as maintaining supply flows and administering repatriation sometimes created the need to keep certain types of personnel overseas, and led to the seeming inequity of less-essential battalions being sent home before many longer-serving troops.

Back in early 1941 the Canadian government had begun reserving shipping space to transport men home as soon as the shooting stopped. Also, the Advisory Committee on Demobilization and Rehabilitation proposed that repatriation be conducted according to a point system closely conforming to the "first in first out" principle. In February 1944, with the war clearly turning against Germany, each of Canada's three service branches set up a Demobilization Directorate to work with the new Directorate of Reorganization and Demobilization, whose job was to apportion transatlantic shipping space. Arrangements were also made with Canada's railway companies to reserve nearly all existing sleeper cars and to convert an additional 100 cars to the role of transporting veterans back to their homes.[25]

However, the destructive impact of Germany's U-boat campaign had made shipping space difficult to acquire. Britain's War Office announced in March 1944 that during the first six months after the conflict Canada could expect to transport home 90,000 men, just 60 percent of its goal. Ottawa lobbied hard to raise that number, but at war's end, with most of the US navy still occupied in the Pacific and the United States also wanting to move its troops out of Europe, estimates for the summer of 1945 remained pegged at 15,000 Canadians per month. Japan's surrender in August then freed up much of the US fleet, so that by the fall Canadians were being repatriated at the rate of some 1,000 per day. By March 1946 the process was essentially complete, with fewer than 25,000 troops remaining overseas.[26]

After years away, men were extremely impatient to return home. While they waited, they needed to be kept active and content. Military duties were reduced to a minimum, and leave facilities were abundant. Thousands heeded the advice of the Legion's Educational Service to use their time taking correspondence courses to prepare themselves for civilian life. Still, military censors reported that men complained bitterly in letters home that some of their compatriots had already departed for Canada despite having fewer points and were likely snapping up the best jobs. On the surface, the process governing demobilization seemed straightforward: two points for each month of service in the Western Hemisphere and three points for each month further afield. However, there were several exceptions. Priority was given to repatriating the wounded, POWs, and men with family emergencies. A 20 percent bonus was added to the score of married men, widowers, and those with dependent children. Thousands with the skills critically needed in the postwar economy, such as experienced construction workers, moved up in the queue. Between May and August 1945, those in Europe who had volunteered to fight against Japan were first given a month's leave to Canada, which became permanent after the dropping of the atomic bomb.[27]

Men were assured that delays caused by loopholes in the point system that allowed exceptions to the "first in first out" principle were minimal. Yet, as the mouthpiece for servicemen, the *Maple Leaf* became so vociferous in its criticisms of such exceptions that Lt.-Gen. G.G. Simonds, then general officer commanding Canadian forces in the Netherlands, fired its editor, J.D. McFarlane.[28] Impatience over repatriation played a role in a July 1945 uprising among Canadian troops in Aldershot, although other contributing factors were bad food, overcrowded barracks, and a history of strained relations between locals and Canadian soldiers. Some 800 windows in town were smashed and eight Canadians were arrested, ultimately receiving jail sentences ranging from twenty-eight days to seven years.[29]

This harsh response, and also the ensuing improvements in the pace of demobilization, helped prevent other such incidents. Still, authorities were sometimes reminded of the potential for trouble, as when in January 1946, RCAF ground crew in Odiham, England, staged a brief sit-down strike to protest meagre rations and "their retention overseas." The threat of fines and the loss of gratuity payments quickly ended the demonstration.[30]

WHEN FINALLY ON THEIR WAY back to Canada, nearly all veterans approached their homecoming with relief, excitement and, it seems, considerable optimism. One survey among army personnel about to be repatriated showed that 64 percent believed that through military service they had "gained greatly or a good deal" in confidence and 48 percent felt they had acquired superior leadership qualities. These traits were often subsequently verified, as many veterans who had overcome obstacles during the war ultimately became less self-doubting and more successful in civilian life. Among this group was Eddie Goodman, who went on to become a prominent lawyer and political organizer for the Conservative party and who maintained that much of his confidence derived from the knowledge that he had been "tried in battle and not found wanting."[31]

However, some had misgivings as they prepared to return home, admitting to their loved ones that difficult times might lie ahead. Even a Protestant chaplain thought it advisable to tell his family to expect some "rough edges" because he had "lived with a lot of rough and ready fellows" and had "seen ruined towns by the score ... and hundreds of poor, dirty children, dozens of dead bodies and many sorrowful things."[32]

Wishing to avoid replicating the problems experienced by many Great War veterans, the government made personnel available to prepare men for their return to civilian life. Over the first ten months of 1945, some 700 new army education officers joined the counsellors appointed earlier by the air force and navy to give lectures not only on veterans' benefits but also on topics such as "Canadian Civics" and "Canada since 1939."[33] Their talks, as well as sermons from padres, also often warned men not to idealize home and family life, for they realized that such pipe dreams could lead to a profound sense of letdown and disillusionment. Men were advised, for instance, to "allow" for the fact that "for three, four or five years," their wives or girlfriends had had to "make decisions and live ... life without [their] daily help and presence."[34] The clear implication was that many wives would not easily accept the submissive homebound role anticipated by numerous men longing for tradition and tranquility after so much strain and suffering, and who, while in the military, had often developed an even more dominant attitude toward females.

Advice was also offered to Canadian civilians, particularly women, on how best to deal with returning servicemen. Contrasting with the wartime pattern in the mass media that generally ignored the disturbing ways in which the war might have affected the outlook and conduct of men, more columns began cautioning civilians that those they were preparing to welcome home were often not the same people they remembered, nor would they live up to the cheery correspondence they had typically sent. *Chatelaine* warned its female readership: men "who ha[ve] faced death and danger ... will return wounded in soul, if not body."[35] Parents were advised that though "he may look like a kid ... he'll be very adult ... with years of responsibilities behind him," and might react against coddling. Still, to build the confidence of veterans, wives and future wives were urged to "cultivate patience" and to offer a "secure [and] reassuring environment."[36] Several accounts stressed the need for women to vacate traditional male jobs to make room for veterans so they could more easily re-establish their "natural role" as breadwinner.[37]

Local groups stood ready to assist veterans. They included more than 700 Citizen Repatriation and Rehabilitation Committees, which were managed by local political, religious, business, labour, and other community leaders, and which attracted over 25,000 volunteers. Besides organizing official welcome home ceremonies, these committees helped veterans to better understand and access DVA programs, to find acceptable employment, and to locate decent accommodation in overcrowded cities.[38] For instance, the Edmonton committee advertised in newspapers and over the radio its "work-pile," for which employers were asked to list jobs suitable for the "more seriously disabled veteran." The Vancouver committee arranged for volunteers from the Board of Trade to give a sixteen-session course for veterans on how best to utilize the money made available by the DVA to start a business.[39]

Official homecomings were typically joyous and often spectacular events. Even with a point system in effect, for administrative convenience large groups of men usually returned home at the same time; also, despite casualties and remusterings, a notable number from the same battalion, squadron, or ship had usually served for a comparable length of time. Although the shifting of personnel over the years meant that most regiments had lost their territorial base, this never seemed to dampen the enthusiasm or size of welcoming crowds. In Windsor, for example, such a throng turned out to see the returning Essex Scottish Regiment that the troops could hardly march up Ouellette Avenue.[40] Inside large train stations or auditoriums, family and friends, many of whom had travelled considerable distances to be present, were organized alphabetically according to the man for whom they waited so as to be more easily found. Sometimes barricades were toppled in the excitement as long-separated loved ones spotted each other. Initially, veterans were treated like celebrities. He had "never been [so] drunk ... never eaten so much food ... never danced so much and never [been] kissed by so many pretty local girls," recalled one man of his first night home.[41]

Ultimately, most veterans reintegrated in their communities. Many silences speak for those who easily or through force of will put the war behind them; there were hundreds of thousands like Bill Irvine of Winnipeg, who said that within two weeks of returning home he "simply got a job and moved on."[42] But for many the reintegration process was difficult, and sometimes traumatic. Even some whose military career had never taken them outside of Canada had difficulties. As noted by the army's Pacific Command, "These soldiers have been subjected to several years of propaganda glorifying their ... comrades [overseas] ... [and] this has left its mark in many places, resulting in a form of inferiority ... and creating a sense of futility."[43] Numerous veterans found their former home community disturbingly alien. It was one thing to read or hear about places being radically transformed during the war, but quite another to confront first-hand a city whose population had as much as doubled, or a rural area or small town that had experienced huge out-migration. Severe shortages of living space frequently forced veterans, often with new families, to live with parents or accept overpriced and tiny hovels, situations that often led to bickering at home and much resentment toward the community at large.

A sense of deflation often followed the initial euphoria of reunions as people returned to their everyday routines.[44] Some veterans became despondent, feeling a lack of importance, direction, and comradeship. They had left behind buddies with whom they had gone through hellish experiences, shared every secret, and entrusted their lives. Trying to recapture those feelings and bonds, several came to spend inordinate amounts of time conversing and drinking, often excessively, in Legion halls.[45] Such places beckoned because many veterans could not reconnect with civilians, who had been sheltered by geography and sanitized information. Moreover, after having lived in close quarters with people from different regions and social and ethnic backgrounds, and after having seen and experienced so much, veterans were known to dismiss civilians, sometimes curtly, as self-serving and parochial. Their complaints over things such as high taxes or rationing were considered trivial, and their willingness to gouge and grasp in postwar black markets "grotesque."[46] This perception of pampered and selfish civilians had also been cultivated during the war by news reports of labour strikes, which many servicemen condemned as resulting "in more of us dying so that they can make good wages."[47] Indeed, by war's end, organized labour felt it essential to stress to those being demobilized that, during the conflict, civilians had worked record hours and that strikes had been declared only as a last resort and had rarely affected war production. Labour leaders realized that some companies eagerly courted veterans because they hoped they would rally against unions and work toward their decertification, though it quickly became apparent that few veterans, despite possible resentment, were inclined to do anything to jeopardize decent wages and benefits.[48]

The DVA also found it necessary to beseech employers to show compassion and patience toward those who had sacrificed and had been through so much. A number of employers avoided hiring veterans, regarding them as having too many problems, such as difficulty settling down into workplace routines or a lack of initiative because they had taken orders all the time. Meanwhile many veterans grew frustrated and angry because they returned to their former jobs expecting more than the junior positions they had left years earlier, or a raise far greater than the amount that reflected the wage freeze that had been in effect since late 1941. Following such a momentous time in their life, many veterans had trouble accepting jobs that they found meaningless or stultifying. It was particularly hard for officers and NCOs who had led men into battle to stomach such disappointments, especially when they found themselves taking orders from civilians who had not fought.[49]

Of course, reintegration also involved reassuming family life. In countless cases, the lack of commentary reflected successful reunions or people who managed in varying degrees to work through their difficulties. Eager to make up for lost time, veterans and women were soon marrying and producing children in record numbers. Interviews with unmarried servicemen showed that they linked marriage with the process of re-establishing themselves as civilians and with the sense of "home" and "security" after such perilous times.[50] Moreover, many Canadian women, in light of the thousands of young men killed overseas and the thousands returning with war brides, became more eager to avert spinsterhood, and hence less choosy.[51]

Although about 70 percent of veterans were single, tremendous attention and concern still focused on the reconstitution of spousal relations and stable nuclear families. Marriage and family were both perceived as having been under siege in recent years, and things seemed to grow worse after the war as long-separated couples often had trouble reuniting. In 1946 divorces in Canada stood at 7,683 and the next year they reached 8,199, in comparison to just 2,068 in 1939. Spousal and family desertion also increased sharply, as indicated by the rise in charges of "non-support of families and neglecting children" from 2,442 cases in 1944 to 3,148 in 1945. Some men returning from combat were apparently unprepared to resume family responsibilities.[52] Convinced that many divorces and desertions had resulted from ill-conceived "quickie" wartime marriages, some worried that the postwar rush to the altar would exacerbate these problems. Shortly after the conflict, *Saturday Night* columnist Anne Fromer wrote that many people were putting less thought into their marriage than they would into "raising hogs [or] growing roses."[53]

Social service agencies and churches began marriage counselling programs. Starting in mid-1945, the University of British Columbia's Extension Department offered a Marriage and Family Life course to help "iron out the wrinkles in the lives of newlyweds, and smooth the path ahead for the husbands, wives and children who have to face the rocky days of the postwar era."[54] Others, however, responded to the greater incidence of marital difficulties following the war by proposing less restrictive grounds for divorce; the Canadian Legion, for example, said it was wrong to force veterans to stay in bad marriages. Some small changes did occur. In 1945 Prince Edward Island created its first divorce court, a measure that related to increasing applications for divorce and growing anger, especially among veterans, over the time and money it took to obtain a parliamentary decree to annul a marriage. In

February 1946 the Toronto Liberal MP Col. David Croll argued in Parliament that the prevailing rules governing divorce forced too many couples into choosing between ongoing unhappiness or committing fraud by hiring a private detective to take pictures of a staged extramarital affair. Although Croll's resolution for "amendments to ... enlarge the grounds for divorce" was defeated, the Ontario provincial government, seeking to unclog the higher courts, that year passed a measure permitting more accessible and less intimidating county and divisional courts to handle divorces.[55]

Throughout the first postwar decade, the annual divorce rate remained two-and-a-half to three times higher than in 1939.[56] But divorce only slowly became a more accepted part of Canada's social landscape; undoubtedly the postwar rate would have been far higher if, as one veteran said, divorce had not remained "such a dirty word." After years apart, many couples found themselves estranged. They had lived very different lives; had been transformed, sometimes radically, both physically and psychologically; and with the passage of time had often felt their love fade or had become habituated to the absence of the other. Many men, grown accustomed to doing what they wanted on leave time, found it difficult to consider the feelings of a wife or family. If there had been an exciting extramarital wartime affair, postwar disappointment in the marriage would likely have been more keenly felt. A number of couples, perhaps most commonly those who had married after a quick wartime romance, even had trouble recognizing one another at first. Far more problematic with such unions, however, was the difficulty of settling into a more mundane routine with a person who, under day-to-day scrutiny, did not appear nearly as dashing or exciting as remembered, and, as was often discovered, still remained very much a stranger.[57]

In this regard, much concern was expressed over Canada's 47,783 war brides, most of whom arrived in 1945 and 1946. Some were shocked to see their husband out of uniform for the first time. Some, however, never saw their husbands at all because they were abandoned. One woman in Halifax remembered meeting a war bride in tears because her husband had telegraphed from Vancouver to say he had changed his mind.[58] Many war brides were distraught by Canada's frigid climate, or life on isolated farms or in dismal flats in overcrowded cities that, with the possible exception of Montreal and Toronto, seemed small and culturally barren. They also had other challenges: adapting to strange food and often to a strange language, living with in-laws, and sometimes, as well as meeting locals eager to help, confronting those who accused them of stealing Canadian men.[59] Most of these women toughed things out and, contrary to many dire predictions, their marriages actually had a high success rate. What kept them in Canada? Besides loving their spouse and expecting some hardships in their new life, it was not financially easy to leave – and home would hardly have seemed enticing, considering the devastation they had left behind overseas. Moreover, many did not want to admit a mistake and run back home, especially since most had been warned against these marriages in the first place. At the end of 1945, by which point nearly 10,000 war brides had arrived in Canada, only twenty-nine had applied to return home, and in January 1947 the assistant national commissioner of the Canadian Red Cross, a group much involved in the transport of war brides to their new homes, stated, "Our impression [is] that the percentage of shattered romances among these couples is negligible."[60]

The tendency to idealize did make things difficult for many postwar couples. The serviceman who "remember[ed] his wife as a beautiful dream girl," or the wife who thought of the "dashing man in uniform" was quite often disappointed. It took time to adjust to a person who was "older [and] tired ... with a most unusual vocabulary and strange attitudes toward some of life's values."[61] Friction frequently developed after many men came back looking far more grizzled and often with a shocking propensity for profanity, cigarettes, and liquor. One woman remembered that only two weeks after her husband returned home – during which he got drunk every night – she threw him out, adding, "It didn't matter to the kids, because by this time their hearts were like stone to him."[62]

Some women felt worn out after having been left with children during the war, having had difficulties coping financially with the dependants' allowance, or juggling home life, the workplace, and volunteer labour. They sometimes resented their husbands because their letters had given such a positive impression of the grand old time they had had while in uniform.[63] A number of women had grown in confidence and become far more self-sufficient, and now resisted a subservient role within the so-called traditional family structure. However, one survey of nearly 200 Canadian soldiers taken shortly before their demobilization showed that by a margin of 56 to 21 percent, they agreed with the statement, "A woman's place is in the home."[64] Consequently, soon after the war a number of veterans talked resentfully about wives or sweethearts having "grown too independent." One former soldier angrily berated his wife because after "earning good money ... she didn't like doing kitchen work any more."[65]

Another complicating factor was that wartime infidelity, or signs of it, sometimes came to light: one veteran returned home to find books on the shelf inscribed, "To my darling May, from John."[66] Many marriages survived only because people purposefully avoided probing about behaviour during their separation. To men returning home, one syndicated advice columnist urged, "If you have a secret that would make one who loves you unhappy to know, bury it in your soul ... The war ended one phase of your life. You are starting another."[67] But such information was not always so easy to conceal. Sometimes news of a paternity suit launched overseas reached the alleged father in Canada. Men treated for VD shortly before their discharge had their names sent to provincial boards of health for a follow-up examination; even though the notice was sent in the proverbial plain envelope with no return address, the contents no doubt still became known to some spouses.[68] Some people unfortunately learned that their loved one had strayed only because they too contracted VD. With the return home of servicemen, aggregate recorded cases of VD in Canada rose from 38,772 in 1944 to 40,528 in 1945 and to 41,556 in 1946.[69]

The challenge of re-establishing relationships with children became a major cause of family strain in a number of cases. For many children, their father's return was a joyful day indelibly etched into their memory. André Bernard, only three-and-a-half years old when his father – a man he knew only from a mantelpiece photograph – came home, remembered leaping into his arms at first sight, thrilled to no longer have just a "cardboard daddy." But many children were unsure about how to greet a man so long absent from their lives, and with whom, typically, they had exchanged few letters during the war. They had often grown used to a father's absence and upon his return saw him as a competitor for a mother's love and attention. "He always felt like a stranger [who] had come and taken over my life and my mother's house," said one man who for some time after the war called his father "Mr. Palmer."[70] Children who had engaged in hero worship had to adjust to the reality that few returning fathers could meet their expectations. Bitterness was known to develop when a veteran attempted to re-establish fatherly authority, sometimes in a military manner. "I didn't like the way my dad ran our home like an army barracks," said one woman whose diagnosis was that her father never shook off his former role as a sergeant-major. There were also those such as Jean Little, who did not understand why her father regularly "blew up" for little or no apparent reason.[71]

What Little's father displayed was a classic symptom of the lasting effects of battle neurosis, which has since become known as post-traumatic stress disorder (PTSD). Such men had an especially tough time reintegrating. Their numbers were substantial, though precise figures are impossible to arrive at since most cases went undiagnosed.[72] Compared to the general population, victims of PTSD showed a greater propensity toward irritability, argumentativeness, and violent outbursts. More often, they were plagued by restlessness, insomnia, and nightmares.[73] They were more easily startled and unsettled by loud noises and had trouble concentrating, sustaining conversations, and coping with pressures and responsibilities. Many complained about debilitating physical pain. A 1945 study by Canada's Army Medical Corps of 740 men discharged with severe battle exhaustion said that 19 percent claimed recurrent stomach troubles, 14 percent problems with their legs or feet, 11 percent respiratory ailments, and 8 percent heart troubles. However, doctors could find no physical evidence to explain – nor prescribe effective medicine to treat – such problems, which led to growing frustration and anger among such veterans, and often to resentment from families who began to suspect malingering. Compounding the situation, and constituting one of the most glaring shortcomings of DVA programs, was the decision, effective until 1959, to deny a pension for "neuropsychiatric ailments." The rationalization that there was no visible disability to assess further stigmatized, infuriated, and alienated these men.[74]

Readaptation problems were also particularly marked among former POWs, especially those liberated from the Japanese. POWs in captivity for at least six months were placed at the front of the queue for repatriation to Canada. Once judged physically able, they were moved to reception camps such as the No. 4 Canadian General Hospital in Aldershot. There, back pay and medical examinations were attended to, and staff were on hand to help explain DVA programs and bring men up to speed on key events that had transpired in Canada during their absence. However, such staff often later observed that many of these men should have been held back longer before returning to a country and a life from which they had been so completely cut off. Moreover, to fulfill promises to get POWs home as soon as possible, medical examinations were sometimes cursory, and POWs themselves frequently concealed or dismissed what they thought were minor ailments. These complicities led to much bitterness later on: men judged healthy on discharge were refused pensions for conditions that showed up subsequently. Indeed, this policy was maintained until 1969 toward those who had been held by the Japanese, despite abnormally high instances among this group of debilitating disorders such as crippling pains in the feet and legs.[75]

Disaster also fell on many households because POWs had had endless time to dwell upon and unrealistically romanticize home life. Many who had obsessed about women but had not seen one for years seemed to have forgotten how to act in their presence, even if they were their spouses. One POW greeted his wife with a timid handshake. Civilians were also jolted to find once-robust men mere shells of their former selves, both physically and spiritually. Like victims of PTSD, POWs often suffered from recurring nightmares, "shot nerves," and an inability to hold down steady work. Having been so controlled by and dependent on their captors, they often proved unable to deal with responsibilities or make decisions. In reflecting why, like so many other POWs, he had come back so "cold-hearted" and drained of emotion, one former captive of the Japanese simply explained, "I saw a man sit on a can for five days and just drop dead – [he] shit himself to death."[76]

Despite notable difficulties in reintegrating, Canadian Second World War veterans were generally perceived to be less embittered or alienated than Great War veterans had been, nor were they considered as great a risk to social stability. This difference can be largely attributed to the fact that the challenges and pains associated with reintegration were not generally made worse by stingy government support, as they had so often been after the First World War. Of course, the Veterans Charter could not guarantee that all couples separated by the war would successfully reunite, that the minds of the battle-fatigued would be soothed, that POWs would return to full physical and psychological health, or that children would gravitate to their returned fathers. With DVA programs, "as with everything else in life," remarked one veteran, "there were winners and losers."[77] On balance, and with good reason, the Veterans Charter came to be seen as a key factor in accounting for far more happy endings.

Upon formal discharge, veterans turned in their kit (except for one full uniform), had a final medical and dental examination, registered with the federal government's National Employment Service, had a preliminary discussion of their options with a DVA counsellor, and received their discharge pay (any back pay, the rehabilitation grant, the first monthly installment of their gratuity, and the clothing allowance voucher). By late 1945 the DVA was contending with the discharge of up to 70,000 veterans per month.[78] Such a record, Mackenzie told the press, was the result not only of careful planning but also of the dedication of DVA employees, just over half of whom were Second World War veterans themselves. Such men, he stressed, regularly worked extra hours without complaint to process their former comrades as quickly as possible.[79]

As a politician and head of the DVA, Mackenzie understandably minimized snags and complaints. Other sources told a different story. A September 1945 account in *Maclean's*, for instance, compared the DVA's main office in Montreal to a Depression-era "soup kitchen" with men waiting on wooden benches for hours to register, and then waiting again while their files were retrieved. Those who applied for pensions were promised a decision within a month, but it often took three.[80] However, much was forgiven because overall a compassionate approach was in evidence. DVA counsellors, in both preliminary and more in-depth interviews if requested, were instructed to make it clear that veterans had the right to pursue any program they qualified for. Departmental guidelines said that counsellors were to "advise" on choices. Although some decisions were no doubt made under pressure, they were ideally to be reached in a "cooperative" spirit considering the best interests of the veteran in light of individual qualifications, physical condition, interests and aptitudes (which were sometimes gauged through testing), and the likely demands of the job market.[81]

Approximately two-thirds of veterans chose to forgo free vocational retraining or university education, or the chance to start a farm or business with DVA assistance, and opted instead for maximum cash payouts. A Canadian private returning home after two years' service in the Western Hemisphere and three years overseas qualified for a $720 gratuity – roughly 40 percent of a year's pre-tax salary for a civilian male worker – and a re-establishment credit equal to that amount to acquire, repair, modernize, or furnish a home or business. By 31 March 1951, the DVA had approved 98.2 percent of requested re-establishment credits, worth $267.8 million. With such cash at their disposal, veterans had by 1947 committed themselves to purchasing some $200 million in new accommodation. Low required down payments as specified under the 1944 National Housing Act were helpful, as was the assistance of the Central Mortgage and Housing Corporation in obtaining buyer-friendly mortgage rates.[82]

According to a September 1945 analysis, 27 percent of veterans returned to pre-enlistment employers and 6 percent to farms or businesses that they or their families owned or managed, while 24 percent sought out new jobs.[83] Unlike the period immediately after the Great War, the employment market was favourable. The release of women workers created many vacancies, but more significant was the buoyant postwar economy. Pent-up consumer demand was strong, and the money available from wartime savings, postwar income tax cuts, and the new social programs – namely family allowances and veterans' benefits – created an invigorated spending stream. Moreover, with the Department of Reconstruction arranging for corporate tax breaks, low-interest loans, and other incentives to help business and industry retool, reconversion to peacetime production moved ahead expeditiously. Between 1945 and 1947 inclusive, Canada's civilian labour force increased from 4,447,000 to 4,862,000. Even with a flood of some 600,000 servicemen entering the civilian job market in the first year after the war, some 86 percent had obtained jobs within two months after their discharge.[84] Moreover, the government took a stance in stark contrast to its prewar position, when it had derided the unemployed for opting for the dole, and encouraged veterans to take advantage of "out of work" benefits if they weren't satisfied with resuming their prewar employment or had difficulty finding a job.[85]

Under what became known as Canadian Vocational Training (CVT), the DVA spent $75,260,723 by 31 March 1951 to prepare 81,418 former service personnel for over 100 occupations.[86] Entry into CVT could be pursued any time within eighteen months after discharge, though the deadline was flexible for those with a war-related injury. Veterans who had partially used their re-establishment credit could still take a shorter course, for depending on the vocation, training lasted between a month and a year. Classes were held evenings and weekends in public schools or technical institutes, during the day at centres established under the War Emergency Training Programme, or on the job where companies were required to pay a minimum of 80 percent of the normal wage for the job. If necessary, the DVA made up the difference to the allowance received by those in training facilities, which by 1944 ranged from $60 a month for single trainees to $138 for those with a spouse and six dependent children under seventeen. Such support could be further supplemented by a spouse earning up to $75 per month, as well as by the trainee obtaining an extra $40 per month through part-time work, thus allowing the more industrious to secure quite an acceptable income.[87]

About 90 percent of those who started CVT courses completed them successfully. By late 1946 their unemployment rate was about half that of veterans in general.[88] Assessing the program six years after the war ended, a DVA study produced 80,110 names, or approximately 96 percent of the participants. Of those it could trace, only 10.2 percent were classed as having had "unsatisfactory results," a figure composed of those who had not finished their program, had left the country, or were deceased. Otherwise, 59.4 percent were employed, and 7.3 percent were self-employed in a position for which they had trained; 15 percent were employed in a job unrelated to their training but still indicated job satisfaction; 1.3 percent were taking further training; 2.8 percent were classed as "awaiting placement" because they had recently finished further courses; 1.8 percent had rejoined the military; and 2.2 percent were unemployed or, especially in the case of women, at home.[89]

Among veterans who wanted to work for themselves, 16,685 had received an awaiting returns allowance by 1947 to help them start a business. Moreover, under the 1947 Veterans Business and Professional Loans Act, the federal government earmarked $25 million to help protect banks against financial loss by making low-interest and high-risk loans to veterans.[90] Still more extensive was the assistance directed toward those who desired to farm. Under the Veterans Land Act (VLA), applicants could qualify for a loan of up to $4,800 to buy land and buildings, and up to $1,200 to obtain livestock, feed, seed, and equipment. The veteran was required to make a 10 percent down payment, but payments to the government were to be based on two-thirds of the amount loaned under the VLA. The rate was fixed for twenty-five years at just 3.5 percent interest, thus requiring a monthly government payment of only $16 on a property worth $4,800. Once the veteran made payments for ten years and demonstrated that the farm was profitable, the balance of the debt to the government would be waived. Moreover, after complaints from veterans that in several parts of the country $4,800 was inadequate to purchase good-quality property, the federal government on 13 April 1945 amended the rules to allow some or all of the $1,200 designated for supplies and equipment to be used for land and buildings.[91]

The VLA was not only more generous, but also far more successful, than the Soldier Settlement scheme created for Great War veterans. That scheme had essentially been a pure loan program under which the federal government selected the vast majority of the land, which was designated only for full-time farming. Much of the property was badly isolated and of poor quality, and not surprisingly the failure rate was high. By contrast, under the VLA most veterans picked out their own property, though the DVA hired agricultural experts to inspect the land to ensure that it was worth the price and was of suitable quality for the type of farming being proposed. Also, prospective full-time farmers were screened to ensure that they were in good physical shape and had adequate experience for such work. The physically disabled were often not able to avail themselves of this opportunity, but veterans who were judged to simply require greater knowledge of farming could qualify at the government's expense by taking a course (usually for six weeks) offered at a number of institutions across the country, or by spending a specified amount of time working on a farm approved by a VLA official. A veteran who chose to do neither could still start a hobby farm for which no experience was necessary, an option that was also successfully pursued by a number of physically handicapped veterans.[92] Despite some complaints about the interference of VLA bureaucrats, about two-thirds of farm applications were approved by the end of

1946: 14,366 full-time farms, 9,468 hobby farms, and 343 commercial fishing operations, which were also administered under this program. By November 1947, expenditures under the VLA, at some $400 million, approximately quadrupled the amount spent by the Soldier Settlement Board.[93] Ultimately, VLA farms topped 60,000, and most seem to have done quite well, as by 1955 their average worth was judged to have doubled (not to mention that many of these farms later became part of housing subdivisions, making their owners – or their heirs – quite a windfall).[94]

Probably the most high-profile DVA program, in that it opened up a world still generally seen as being for the privileged, was free university education. In 1918 the National Conference on Canadian Universities had proposed a modest "loan-grant program" to help veterans enter academe, but Prime Minister Robert Borden rejected it as too expensive. By contrast, between September 1942 and March 1951, Ottawa spent $137,801,657 to provide 53,788 veterans with a university education. Just over half took a degree in general arts, though the number of Canadians with professional degrees also dramatically increased as 18.5 percent of veterans went into engineering, 10.2 percent into commerce, 6.9 percent into medicine and dentistry, and 2.8 percent into law.[95]

As with CVT, a veteran could access this program if he or she qualified within eighteen months after discharge. Universities helped out by admitting veterans with a junior or senior matriculation. Because the school year lasted eight months, veterans obtained government support for 1.5 years of academic study for each year of military service. However, as Mackenzie emphasized, even if a veteran had not been in uniform long enough to qualify for the full program, "a good student" would receive funding to complete a degree and, if "outstanding," could get support to pursue postgraduate study.[96]

At the peak implementation of this program, veterans constituted some 40 percent of Canada's university population. Every institution received veterans, though numbers varied according to size, offerings, reputation, and location.[97] Canadian universities, which had hitherto been rather quaint and cloistered institutions, were propelled toward "reinvent[ing] themselves" into larger, more comprehensive, and accessible places. Increased federal and provincial funding was provided to rapidly expand classroom space and to hire more faculty. As of 30 June 1950, for example, in addition to covering the tuition costs of veterans, Ottawa had provided $3.86 million to the University of Toronto and $2.51 million to the University of British Columbia. With additional millions from the provincial government, UBC built new science and agriculture buildings and a new library wing, and established faculties of medicine, pharmacy, and law to cope with the needs and demands – as well as the space requirements – of a student body that rose to nearly three times the university's recommended capacity of 1,500.[98]

The university program may have been the DVA's most prestigious, but the conditions for students at many schools were anything but glamorous. To deal with the flood of students, many institutions adopted a trimester system – starting courses in January, April, and September – and scheduled classes from 8 a.m. to 10 p.m.[99] At McGill University, Principal F. Cyril James's economics class ballooned from 52 students in 1944 to 295 in the fall of 1945. Makeshift arrangements often became necessary. That year, McGill established Sir William Dawson College in what was formerly the RCAF's No. 9 Observer Training School, and the University of Toronto, in order to teach some 3,000 engineering students, began renting from the federal government a series of buildings formerly used as a shell-filling plant in Ajax, twenty-five miles from its main campus. Army Nissen huts were built on campus at several universities to serve as classrooms and student housing. The University of Alberta temporarily housed veterans in the city's main ice-skating rink.[100] Moreover, veterans often complained they could not get by on the monthly government living allowance, which was meant to cover room, board, books, and other educational supplies. Some emphasized that lack of money, more than short-age of living space, forced student veterans, often with families, to jam into small flats and even to double up with other families, thus making it exceptionally diffi-cult to study and introducing great marital strain.

Such issues figured prominently at the inaugural convention of the National Conference of Student Veterans held in Montreal on 27 and 28 December 1945. Attending in Mackenzie's place, Maj.-Gen. E.L.M. Burns, the DVA's director-general of rehabilitation, rejected resolutions for a higher allowance and for free books. Government support, Burns argued, could be supplemented by spousal income, by part-time work, and by special low-interest loans for up to $500 a year.[101] He also pointed out that if preferential treatment was given to veteran uni-versity students, other veterans would be resentful or force the government to similarly augment support for all DVA recipients, which he insisted Ottawa could not afford.[102] Not articulated to the delegates was the belief of many DVA officials that if allowances were kept relatively modest, only serious, hard-working veter-ans would seek university education. Indeed, those who failed a course and a supple-mentary examination were cut off from government support, although it was decided in 1947 that such students could requalify if they funded themselves for an academic year and passed all their subjects.[103] Ultimately, most veterans coped fi-nancially, though the situation was more serious than the DVA acknowledged. For instance, in an October 1946 press release the department stressed that only nine veterans had dropped out claiming poverty; however, 841 others had discontinued their studies because they said they wanted to find a job, a notable proportion of whom undoubtedly had financial difficulties.[104]

Other challenges for student veterans involved adapting to the classroom setting and to the solitude and self-discipline required for studying and essay writing. A February 1945 DVA analysis of thirty-two veterans attending the University of Toron-to with an average of twenty months' military service reported that twenty-two often "felt restless," eighteen had "trouble concentrating," and seven experienced "difficulty ... remembering."[105] That year the university established a psychiatric service for veterans having trouble coping. Indeed, many university administrators and professors were reluctant to accept large numbers of veterans, believing that far too many would prove ill-prepared, too agitated, battle-hardened, hard-drinking, disruptive, and inclined to "swinging the lead." Yet, although there was some suggestion that professors were reluctant to be hard on or fail veterans, the results from ex-servicemen surprised and in some cases astonished the skeptics. Most veterans were determined to make the most of this golden opportunity. Desiring to finish as quickly as possible, many avoided paid work during the summer so they could squeeze in an extra term. Professors often came to praise the keenness of this group; one at McGill said that "twenty in a class of 200 would set tone." At the University of Toronto, the failure rate for veterans in the 1945-46 academic year, at 12 percent, was half that of the general student body. That same year, seventeen of twenty Canadian Rhodes Scholarships were awarded to veterans, and in universities across Canada twice as many veterans as nonveterans passed with honours.[106] The following year, 77 percent of veterans passed unconditionally, and only 13 percent lost their funding. About half of those who failed repeated their courses at their own expense, and between 1948 and 1952, of 2,962 such cases, 2,604, or 87.9 percent, managed to requalify for DVA funding.[107]

University education also meant better incomes. By 1949 the average salary of a veteran graduate was $2,400, about 20 percent higher than the norm for male workers, and with time this differential likely increased. While some veterans were returning to university studies that had been interrupted by the war, for many, given their social background, the DVA opened the door to opportunities that had not seemed possible before their enlistment. An October 1945 survey by the Department of National Defence revealed that some two-thirds of those entering university with the help of the DVA had never before attended such an institution.[108] Of course, a number had enlisted straight out of high school, but there were many examples like the Manitoba veteran who returned home with a grade-five education, and yet in 1951, after completing an accelerated high school course and university studies, graduated as an engineer. "Where would I have been if there hadn't been a war?" remarked another veteran who went on to become a lawyer. "[Maybe] riding the boxcars looking for work ... or ... a two-bit clerk ... with no future."[109] In 1951, as it had done with the CVT program, the DVA followed up those whose university studies it had supported. Of the 44,063 identified (approximately 81 percent of participants), only 8.5 percent fell into the "unsatisfactory" category, compared to 57.8 percent who were employed, and 6.7 percent who were self-employed, in their field of study; 10.2 percent who were in another but still – according to the respondents – satisfactory line of work; 11.4 percent who were still in school; 3.3 percent who were in the military; and 2.1 percent who were either unemployed or at home.[110]

PERHAPS THE DVA'S GREATEST CHALLENGE was to re-establish those who returned home with debilitating injuries. For Great War veterans in this group, ongoing disputes and bitterness over pensions considerably compounded their difficulties. Pension commissioners, few of whom were veterans, had acted in accordance with their cost-conscious superiors and commonly denied compensation unless an injury was incontestably related to military service. Moreover, only about 5 percent of claimants had been awarded the highest possible annual rate – which for non-commissioned personnel ranged from $600 to $900, depending on marital status and the number of dependants. By contrast, 80 percent received less than half of the maximum, largely because it was reasoned that a modest pension would encourage a man to triumph over his handicaps and not become a permanent public charge.[111]

This is not to suggest that pensions were not a source of discontent in the Second World War. Those discharged during training were typically denied support for an injury because it was claimed that it predated their enlistment. Although this was often the case, clearly an exceedingly stringent approach was applied, for by July 1941, only 687 of 12,786 applications had been approved.[112] Following the war, many veterans who had hidden what they mistakenly thought to be small ailments in order to expedite their discharge, or whose injuries were missed by doctors performing examinations during the demobilization process, were denied support. Many pension recipients, as well as the Canadian Legion, complained that average awards were too low, as was the scale paid for different types of injuries, such as 40 percent of the maximum rate for the loss of an eye or 70 percent for a leg.

Still, compared to the pensions paid to Great War veterans, or even to the average annual male salary of some $1,750 in 1945, post-Second World War pensions do not come across that badly. Annual amounts ranged from, at the 10 percent disability level, $756 for a single to $1,574 for a married veteran with six dependent children under seventeen, up to, at the 100 percent level, from $1,260 to $2,364.[113] And compared to the treatment of their Great War counterparts, the handling of Second World War pensioners was far less adversarial. Veterans could obtain free advice from the DVA's Pension Advocate's Office when making a claim or when appealing an award. By the end of 1945, pension boards, which were increasingly staffed by veterans, provided some support in 86.3 percent of cases. Ottawa also raised the award level for several categories of injury shortly after the war and allowed more cases of maximum coverage by adding together, rather than averaging out, claims for multiple injuries thought to overlap.[114] Moreover, as long as an injury remained evident, the pension was paid, whether or not the veteran worked or even earned a lucrative salary.[115]

To treat such veterans medically, the DVA was by 1948 running thirty-four new hospitals or wings of existing institutions, seven occupational health centres, four facilities for paraplegics, three for those with tuberculosis, and nine to provide long-term care. The department recruited doctors who had served with the military and were thus familiar with battlefield injuries, and it linked its facilities with university medical faculties so as to turn them into teaching and research centres. In several areas, veterans reaped the benefits of recent and dramatically improved procedures, such as new ways of treating spinal cord injuries, for which the mortality rate plunged to 10 percent as compared to 80 percent following the Great War.[116]

Key to the economic and, in many cases, the psychological rehabilitation of the wounded was the DVA's Casualty Rehabilitation Section. It arranged for retraining, assisted with the acquisition of benefits and, when the veteran was ready, help in finding employment and often a place to live. Created in January 1945, its first director was the blinded veteran Maj. Edward A. Dunlop; many, including Mackenzie, thought he would serve as an "inspiration" to the injured. Dunlop strongly opposed directing the disabled into simple, sheltered jobs, a policy largely applied after the Great War and which, he said, led to low pay and disillusionment. A tireless and impressive campaigner, Dunlop often spoke before business and industrial associations, stressing, for example, that only 5 percent of jobs "require[d] all a man's physical capacity." His department sent employers, among other materials, literature containing plenty of photographs of rehabilitated veterans performing a wide array of workplace tasks.[117] Whenever possible, press releases from the Casualty Rehabilitation Section cited studies to reinforce this message. A survey of 125 "large companies" that hired disabled workers, conducted in 1945 by the American Society of Safety Engineers, found that 66 percent indicated that the disabled worker's productivity was as high as, and 24 percent that it was higher than, that of the able-bodied, results that Dunlop attributed to employees being more grateful for, and hence more dedicated to, their jobs.[118]

Dunlop's approach of aggressively emphasizing that veterans like himself could always triumph over disabilities undoubtedly pushed some men into the workplace before they were ready and exaggerated the expectations of some employers. Of course, men who were no longer in DVA medical facilities represented a cost saving to the government. But more important to those like Dunlop was that a veteran's successful rehabilitation and ultimate happiness required that he achieve a strong sense of self-worth, a key ingredient of which, Dunlop insisted, was the ability to hold down a job and, if married, to perform to some extent the breadwinner role. In attaining this goal, and in providing higher incomes to the injured and their families, Dunlop and the various others involved from the DVA were remarkably successful. As of 1948, 65.3 percent of the 29,361 veterans who had returned home with "serious wounds" were employed, while 24.8 percent were still retraining. Another study completed two years later observed that of Canada's 5,093 veterans with a pensionable disability rated between 1 and 24 percent of the maximum award, 89.5 percent were employed; of the 9,912 rated between 25 and 49 percent, 87 percent had jobs; of the 6,312 rated between 50 and 74 percent, 83.7

percent worked; and of the 7,328 rated between 75 and 100 percent, 61.4 percent were gainfully employed.[119]

OVER THE YEARS, the DVA certainly found itself the target of grievances. The Canadian Legion persevered with its campaign for higher pensions. Not until 1992 did the federal government respond to persistent lobbying and change its position about former merchant marines being nonmilitary personnel with no right to compensation for their exclusion from veterans' benefits. At the time of writing, Canada's Native veterans are still seeking redress for what they claim was prejudicial treatment by the DVA.[120] Yet overall, Canada's Second World War veterans have expressed satisfaction and gratitude more strongly than anger and protest. Servicemen may have distrusted and even despised Mackenzie King, but his government provided what likely still stands as the most generous welfare and benefit package in Canadian history. While the Veterans Charter could not cure the heartache that came into many homes after the conflict, it is no understatement that it provided millions of Canadians with a new beginning and, at least in financial terms, a better life. Moreover, by enacting legislation such as the Reinstatement in Civil Employment Act, and by furnishing valuable skills, education, first-rate medical care, and a variety of special grants and loans, the government did much to reinstate veterans as breadwinners. In many cases, this meant a return to the traditional gendered order that many deemed essential, particularly after a period seen to be plagued by family instability and moral decline.

Such programs were inspired by the desire to do better for veterans than in 1918, a desire in part stimulated by the fear of disgruntled ex-servicemen emerging as a destabilizing social force, and further supported by a widespread determination that the postwar period not see the type of instability that had followed the Great War or the reassertion of Depression-like conditions. In this light, the Veterans Charter can be viewed as a part of an overarching campaign by Canadians to realize greater progress and stability out of the Second World War, a resolve that encouraged several other social initiatives and ultimately contributed greatly to the lasting impression of the Second World War as the "good war."

WHILE HISTORIANS STILL DEBATE the degree of societal disillusionment flowing from the Great War, at least in North America there seems to be no similar contention with respect to the Second World War. In Canada, despite well-known and now widely criticized events such as the evacuation of Japanese Canadians, the dominant and still popular images are of people, at least in English Canada, pulling together in a common and unquestionably just cause to defeat the greatest tyrants known to modern history. Canada is seen as a still-young country that made a remarkable contribution of men and matériel, a nation emerging triumphant in 1945, not just from the war but also from a crippling economic depression and a self-serving isolationist foreign policy, to become a modern, prosperous, respected, and engaged middle power. While the First World War remains in popular discourse as the conflict of tragic waste and shattered innocence, many continue to think wistfully of the Second World War as romantic and exciting, as a time when people lived life faster and more fully, as a period symbolized by the heady beat of the big swing bands, the jitterbug, and intense and often fleeting relationships at home and abroad.

In contrast to such pleasant nostalgic notions and the recollections of young men flocking to recruiters, billions of dollars being raised in Victory Bonds, and mountains of salvaged goods, there remains another perspective. Many Canadians agonized over the number of citizens who did not come up to the standards of behaviour expected in wartime, and over the corrosive influence that the conflict seemed to exert on morality. Of course, some grumbling over wartime restrictions should not have come as a shock. Many people were denouncing things they had long opposed, like greater rights for unions, and could now present that opposition in terms of wartime loyalty. Also, the fact that Canadians were for the most part patriotic no doubt intensified and hence exaggerated their reactions to troublesome signs in wartime. Still, in many ways *perception became reality,* that is when considered in terms of the real changes initiated in response to perceived problems – problems that, by garnering such widespread attention, generated strong movements toward both social conservatism and significant and progressive reform.

To many, it was clear that worrying numbers of Canadians chafed against paying heavy taxes or, largely because of steeply progressive tax rates, against putting in extra hours at the workplace. Many other citizens, people complained, were motivated less by patriotism than by their own pecuniary interests, a charge levelled against large segments of rural Canada and an increasingly powerful union movement that because of its growing militancy had to be placated, a move that precipitated a major breakthrough with collective bargaining rights. Lack of patriotism was indeed a failing that appeared rampant among people from every walk of life who were denounced for reaping substantial and illegal gains on extensive black markets. In the context of accommodation, this trend underlined the need for government action to increase the housing supply. Ottawa's responses undoubtedly reinforced a postwar housing boom and far more extensive home ownership, though they were subject to criticism for remaining too firmly wedded to the free market.

People were distressed by quickie marriages, cheating wives, the spread of prostitution, rising illegitimacy, and so-called predatory good-time girls. Men overseas suffered over reports from family, friends, or neighbours about impropriety at home, a number of which were wildly exaggerated but still led to the collapse of relationships. The large-scale presence of servicemen in or near communities not only generated displays of patriotism and enhanced business opportunities but also heavily strained local services and heightened concern over moral and social havoc. Across Canada, sharp increases in VD rates brought crackdowns on brothels and streetwalkers, and many unaccompanied women soon found themselves under increased scrutiny and excluded from certain public places. The appointment of policewomen, a noteworthy and seemingly progressive development, in large part derived from the belief that female constables would be especially effective in identifying and dealing with prostitutes and women considered "loose." Although campaigns initiated by military and civilian authorities to trace female facilitators named by servicemen with VD, and to compel their testing and if necessary treatment, were understandable given the costs of medical care and the need to minimize losses of servicemen and war workers, they were far from perfect and created much unjust suffering. Yet the war years also saw more vigorous and frank public discussion and education on the causes and proper treatment of VD, as well as more medical services, meeting needs that had long gone unmet because VD was a largely taboo topic.

Continuing to fuel the fears of social commentators was the fact that high wartime divorce levels became a permanent feature of the social landscape in the postwar years, never again settling back to even lower than double their prewar rate. But a far more prominent trend of the time was the escalation in marriage and fertility rates. This trend also generated anxiety at first, because of the perception that new couples' hasty and ill-conceived decisions not only showed a lack of respect for matrimony but were certain to bring about even more divorce. Yet after years of uncertainty, loneliness, and turmoil, countless people valued more than ever the potential closeness, security, and predictability of marriage, as well as comfortable, constructed notions of family life. This retrenchment into traditional values was encouraged by employers who handed out countless pink slips to women, by male-dominated unions that supported the process, and by a federal government that, among other measures, discontinued wartime income tax breaks that had encouraged working wives, cut off funding for daycare, and eliminated the three female military auxiliaries.

Numerous women accepted these patterns without complaint. Many had internalized the idea that their new wartime roles had been designed simply to "back the attack" and temporarily release men for active service. They had often been obliged to put off marriage and motherhood for years and at war's end were anxious for both. Many were fatigued after coping for so long with both paid and home-based work – and often with volunteer service as well – and welcomed a retreat into what they deeply hoped would be an easier and more comfortable life. A number felt guilty about having spent time away from their children, or felt pressured to leave paid employment because of widespread assumptions linking allegedly rampant child neglect and juvenile delinquency with working mothers.

Still, returning servicemen seeking a tranquil hearth in which the homemaking woman assumed a dependent role were in many cases keenly disappointed. In the course of the war years, civilian women had acquired greater self-reliance and a stronger sense of independence from undertaking or managing extensive and much-heralded volunteer activities, from running all aspects of the home, from expanding their horizons within universities, and from demonstrating competence in "male" jobs. Women in the military had grown from the comradeship in the services, the obstacles they had overcome in contributing to the war effort, and the new skills they had mastered. Contrasting with reassuring discourse that women would gladly return to the domestic sphere once the shooting stopped, and that whatever task they faced they would always remain feminine, were many other messages heard through the media and government propaganda stressing their accomplishments in unprecedented, physically demanding, and highly skilled domains.

Postwar surveys revealed that many women were unhappy with their housebound lot and large numbers – including those who were married – joined the peacetime workforce. Admittedly, many waited until their children reached school age before making the move and typically found themselves streamlined into low-paying female job ghettos. Nonetheless, it was significant that more wives and mothers opted for the job market and steadily gained societal acceptance in that role after the war. And women's partial success in obtaining legislation mandating equal pay for equal work was, in the context of the time, an important breakthrough. It was also significant that relatively large numbers of women veterans took advantage of DVA retraining programs, although women were usually directed by counsellors toward jobs in traditional female fields – or perhaps naturally gravitated to them or strategically accepted them. The fact that they were technically extended equal access to DVA benefits stood out as one of several signs that women's wartime service, far from being feared and ridiculed, was recognized as significant to the war effort and deserving of a fair reward. Moreover, with thousands of women accessing DVA programs, increasing numbers of women entered non-stereotyped employment, women who undoubtedly provided role models for others to follow. Also noteworthy was the far less controversial, and ultimately permanent, reappearance of women in the military only half a decade after their participation was cut.

As for the young, many found the war years a thrilling time that allowed them to earn great praise for their important patriotic activities. Some children became a source of inspiration, most notably the nearly 6,000 British "war guests" who arrived primarily during the summer of 1940 when people were anxious to hear good news about the war, and who quickly became symbols of British fortitude and Canada's loyalty. By maintaining its focus upon the war guests through the lens of patriotism, the press kept Canadians reading about enthusiastic welcomes, courageous children, and happy experiences. It failed to address the fact that some of these young people were traumatized by being separated from their siblings or mother upon arrival in Canada, did not always adapt well to new families and new schools, were sometimes resented and tossed out of Canadian homes, and in many cases eventually found themselves unable to readapt to life in Britain.

While the propaganda-laden treatment of war guests whitewashed their problems, different conditions and concerns produced a contrasting effect with Canadian children: an emphasis upon the negative. Overcrowded and dilapidated housing, fathers and older siblings in uniform, and especially working mothers were among factors cited as responsible for the large numbers of children perceived to be going astray. Stories abounded about ill-governed youth turning to gangs, truancy, dead-end jobs, and delinquency. Certainly there were cases where parental neglect derived from wartime conditions and where greater direction at home would have helped young people cope better with war-related fears, choose the classroom over earning a fast buck, and stay clear of the law. But conclusions drawn from easily overwhelmed child welfare services, assumptions about declining wartime morality and, particularly, anxieties related to working mothers pushed concerns over Canadian children and youth toward exaggeration, if not panic. Child neglect did not, in fact, rise dramatically in wartime. Furthermore, statistics indicate that the factor largely responsible for high delinquency rates, which continued until 1942 – *before* mothers actually joined the paid workforce in record numbers – was demographics, namely the rising number of adolescents in the general population and the departure of eighteen- to thirty-year-old males for overseas. Still, the perception of a crisis with wartime youth reinforced pressures upon women to prioritize the domestic role as soon as hostilities ended. But the same perception of crisis also led to improved community recreational services, because correcting their deficiencies was seen as a means to more effectively manage the behaviour of youth. Action also intensified to create schools better able to retain, guide, mould, and educate young people and to upgrade a patchwork juvenile justice system.

Without doubt, however, the most disturbing transformations wrought by the war occurred among the men who marched away. The society they left behind was largely kept sheltered from the distressing truths of the circumstances that they faced overseas. Although Second World War news reports were less romanticized and sanitized than those of the Great War, they were subject to much distortion and judicious omission. Most servicemen contributed to this deception by writing letters that, besides being highly influenced by the censor's eye, were typically designed to shield loved ones from worry. Of course, having learned from the First World War, many Canadians understood the deep and often long-lasting physical and psychological scars left by combat. But more than twenty years later, most veterans of that conflict either tacitly underplayed their experiences or, as a coping mechanism, played up the valour of the cause and the positive aspects of military life. Consequently, while some Canadians enlisted to escape the Depression, boring jobs, their wives, or for some other such "practical" reason, most seem to have been motivated by such ideals as patriotism, the defence of democracy, the destruction of totalitarianism, the call of adventure, or the need to prove themselves as men.

Although their behaviour in Canada had caused concern among civilians, the closer they got to action, the more distant servicemen's outlook and comportment grew not only from their idealistic sentiments – by which many were remembered at home – but also from basic moral and social standards governing civil society. By the time Canadian soldiers left Britain to fight in Europe, many British residents had become exasperated with men whose actions too often revolved around scrounging, drinking, brawling, and cavorting, conduct that brought them to the attention of scandal-mongering British tabloids. And by the time the Canadians had fought their way up Sicily and Italy and across northwest Europe, or survived the air war, battles at sea, or life behind barbed wire as POWs, many were primed to provide those who awaited them with a most unsettling shock, often returning with attitudes, ailments, and in some cases physical changes that transformed them into virtual, often disagreeable, strangers.

For the many for whom so much had changed, things could not always be put back together. Some veterans could not cope with more independent women, or with children grown accustomed to their absence who resented their reappearance. Some civilians found the gruffness, restlessness, and belligerence of those they welcomed home too difficult to handle. Some couples who had married in haste during the war came to regret their decision soon after reuniting. Others, including those long married, discovered that letters had not sustained their love during years apart.

But helping matters tremendously was the federal government's realization that it had to assist with the reestablishment and rehabilitation of servicemen far more than it had after the Great War. Most of the key architects of the Veterans Charter had fought in the Great War and recalled well the anger among numerous former comrades over what they considered paltry government support, and recognized the potentially destabilizing force that such disgruntled ex-servicemen could represent. Planning began within weeks of the war starting, and by the end of 1941, the groundwork had been laid to repatriate men expeditiously by a seemingly fair point-based system, and to provide them with an unprecedented array of benefits and opportunities once they arrived home. Of course, DVA programs could not eliminate the difficulties that soon dominated – and sometimes destroyed – postwar unions. However, they could provide men with the money and skills to carve out satisfying and upwardly mobile lives, as well as, in numerous cases, the financial means to run a one-income and "traditional" family unit, which many touted as the most desirable and effective means of re-establishing order and stability after a period of seemingly dangerous social and moral trends.

Apprehensive, and sometimes panicked, reactions to wartime immorality and social instability clearly contributed to many currents of change that flowed in diverse directions. Many Canadians sought to reassert a traditional, conservative, and patriarchal postwar order; but over the six war years, too much had transpired in the lives of too many men, women, and even children for it to be conceivable to reconstruct, or create, such a world. The legacy of wartime black markets, strikes, rising illegitimacy, infidelity, VD, delinquency, divorce, quickie marriages, women in coveralls and khaki, and battle-hardened servicemen endured much longer than the initial anxiety and backlash they caused. These social changes also played a major role in intensifying policy efforts – and considerable action – toward important and typically long-overdue reforms in areas as diverse as housing, schooling, VD treatment, urban police forces, community recreation, labour legislation, juvenile justice, and the management of veterans. At some level, many postwar initiatives were admittedly designed to achieve more effective control over behaviour, and thus had a conservative, perhaps even a reactionary, quality. Yet equally arising from moral and social trends in wartime Canada, and from the fears generated by these patterns, was a legacy of progressive, bold, and often ground-breaking initiatives that provided millions with the means to achieve greater personal growth, social mobility, financial security – and even, it might be said, good reason to speak of a "good war."

Notes

INTRODUCTION

1 Studs Terkel, *The Good War: An Oral History of World War Two* (New York: Pantheon Books, 1984); Michael C.C. Adams, *The Best War Ever: America and World War II* (Baltimore: Johns Hopkins University Press, 1994).

2 J.L. Granatstein and Peter Neary, eds., *The Good Fight: Canadians in the Second World War* (Toronto: Copp Clark Longman, 1995); *Saturday Night*, May 1995, 39-43.

3 *Globe and Mail*, 6 May 1995, D2-D3.

4 See, for example, W. Peter Ward, *White Canada Forever: Popular Attitudes and Public Policies toward Orientals in British Columbia* (Montreal and Kingston: McGill-Queen's University Press, 1978), and Patricia Roy, ed., *Canadians and Japanese during the Second World War* (Toronto: University of Toronto Press, 1990).

5 House of Commons, *Debates*, 1995, 12,186, 12,354; *Canadian Speeches* 8, 4 (1994): Text #1000.

6 *Maclean's*, 1 May 1995, 64; *Ottawa Citizen*, 7 May 1995, D3.

7 J.L. Granatstein and Desmond Morton, *Marching to Armageddon: Canadians and the Great War, 1914-1919* (Toronto: Lester and Orpen Dennys, 1989). Granatstein and Morton's collaboration about the Second World War bears the more inspirational title *A Nation Forged in Fire: Canadians and the Second World War, 1939-1945* (Toronto: Lester and Orpen Dennys, 1989). Bill Gammage, *The Broken Years: Australian Soldiers in the Great War* (Canberra: Australian National University Press, 1974); Denis Winter, *Death's Men: Soldiers of the Great War* (London: Lane, 1978); Joanna Bourke, *Dismembering the Male: Men's Bodies, Britain and the Great War* (Chicago: University of Chicago Press, 1996).

8 See Jonathan F. Vance, *Death So Noble: Meaning, Memory and the First World War* (Vancouver: UBC Press, 1997); Alistair Thomson, *Anzac Memories: Living with the Legend* (Melbourne: Oxford University Press, 1994); and J.M. Winter, *Sites of Memory, Sites of Mourning: The Great War in European Cultural History* (Cambridge: Cambridge University Press, 1995).

9 Historians who challenged this view often faced intense, and sometimes vicious, criticism. The most famous example is Oxford's A.J.P. Taylor, whose *Origins of the Second World War*, rev. ed. (London: Hamilton, 1983) placed most of the blame for the conflict on the Allies for giving Hitler the impression that Germany's expansion prior to the invasion of Poland was not opposed. See Robert Cole, *A.J.P. Taylor: The Traitor within the Gates* (New York: St. Martin's Press, 1993).

10 Certainly this comes across on film. The Great War has become exemplified by dark and grisly movies such as *All Quiet on the Western Front* (1930), *Paths of Glory* (1958), and *Gallipoli* (1980). But it is telling that as recently as 1998, American director Steven Spielberg, in *Saving Private Ryan*, believed it crucial to present an unflinchingly realistic depiction of the D-Day invasion to remind audiences that the liberation of Europe was not gained solely through heroism (which, along with camaraderie and even romance, long remained a staple of Hollywood depictions of the Second World War), but through massive cost, suffering, and less-than-inspiring deaths on the battlefield. For a listing and description of films about the Second World War, see "The War Movie Data Base," <www.geocities.com/

warmoviedatabase>, and Lawrence H. Suid, *Guts and Glory: Great American War Movies* (Reading, MA: Addison-Wesley, 1978).

11 *Ottawa Citizen*, 2 Sept. 1989, 2.

12 Adams, *Best War Ever*, 3.

13 The most powerful expression of the received version is Ruth Pierson, *They're Still Women after All: Canadian Women and the Second World War* (Toronto: McClelland and Stewart, 1986).

14 J.L. Granatstein, *Canada's Army: Waging War and Keeping the Peace* (Toronto: University of Toronto Press, 2002), 203.

15 The most substantial published work on Canada is J.L. Granatstein and Peter Neary, eds., *The Veterans Charter and Post-War Canada* (Montreal and Kingston: McGill-Queen's University Press, 1998). Also see Walter Woods, *Rehabilitation (A Combined Operation); Being a History of the Development and Carrying out of a Plan for the Re-establishment of a Million Young Veterans of World War II by the Department of Veterans Affairs and Its Predecessor the Department of Pensions and National Health* (Ottawa: Queen's Printer, 1953). American literature includes Theodore R. Mosch, *The GI Bill: A Breakthrough in Educational and Social Policy in the United States* (Kicksville, NY: Exposition Press, 1975); and Michael J. Bennett, *When Dreams Come True: The GI Bill and the Making of Modern America* (Chicago: Ivan R. Lee, 1996).

16 See, for example, Pierson, *They're Still Women after All*; C.P. Stacey and Barbara Wilson, *The Half-Million: The Canadians in Britain, 1939-1946* (Toronto: University of Toronto Press, 1987); Michael D. Stevenson, *Canada's Greatest Wartime Muddle: National Selective Service and the Mobilization of Human Resources during World War II* (Montreal and Kingston: McGill-Queen's University Press, 2001); and Peter S. McInnis, *Harnessing Labour Confrontation: Shaping the Postwar Settlement in Canada, 1943-1950* (Toronto: University of Toronto Press, 2002).

17 See, for example, J.L. Granatstein, *Canada's War: The Politics of the Mackenzie King Government, 1939-1945* (Toronto: Oxford University Press, 1975); and J.L. Granatstein and Desmond Morton, *Victory 1945: Canadians from War to Peace* (Toronto: HarperCollins, 1995).

18 See, for example, John Costello, *Love, Sex and War: Changing Values, 1939-1945* (London: Collins, 1985); Costello, *Virtue under Fire: How World War II Changed Our Social and Sexual Attitudes* (Boston: Little Brown, 1985); Richard Lingeman, *Don't You Know There's a War On?* (New York: Putman, 1970); Geoffrey Perrett, *Days of Sadness, Years of Triumph: The American People, 1939-1945* (New York: Coward, McGann & Geoghegan, 1973); and Richard Polenberg, *War and Society: The United States, 1941-1945* (Philadelphia: J.B. Lippincott, 1972).

19 As guides to the generation and use of oral history, this work turned to – among vast literature in the field – Robert Perks and Alistair Thomson, eds., *The Oral History Reader* (New York: Routledge, 1977); Valerie Raleigh Yow, *Recording Oral History: A Practical Guide for Social Scientists* (Thousand Oaks, CA: Sage Publications, 1994); and particularly to Paul Thompson's *A Voice from the Past* (New York: Oxford, 1988). About half the interviews were conducted by the author. Reflecting Canada's geographical distribution, subjects divided roughly equally between an urban background and one in a small town or rural area. Ontario is overrepresented at 51 percent of author-conducted interviews, as is the west at 35 percent. The 8 percent of author-conducted interviews with Quebeckers is compensated by more than twenty that are taped and located at Concordia University and the Eastern Township Research Centre in Lennoxville, Quebec. With the addition of taped interviews housed at the National Archives of Canada, subjects from every province, except Prince Edward Island, are represented.

20 This point is demonstrated in recently completed doctoral dissertations on wartime Halifax and Verdun, as well as on Montreal during the conflict's latter stages and the postwar reconstruction period. See James Frank Edward White, "Conscripted City: Halifax and the Second World War" (PhD diss., McMaster University, 1995); Serge Marc Durflinger, "City at War: The Effects of the Second World War on Verdun, Québec" (PhD diss., McGill University, 1998); and Magda Fahrni, "Under Reconstruction: The Family and the Public in Postwar Montréal, 1944-1949" (PhD diss., York University, 2001).

21 Costello, *Love, Sex and War*, 120; Sandy Cohen, *Norman Mailer's Novels* (Amsterdam: Editions Rodopi, 1979), 42; Joseph J. Waldmeir, *American Novels of the Second World War* (Paris: Martin, 1971), 92-101, 110-17.

22 Dagmar Novak, *Dubious Glory: The Two World Wars and the Canadian Novel* (New York: Peter Lang, 2000), 49; Hugh Garner, *Storm Below* (Toronto: Collins, 1949), 136; Edward Meade, *Remember Me* (Toronto: McClelland and Stewart, 1965).

23 Earle Birney, *Turvey: A Military Picaresque* (Toronto: McClelland and Stewart, 1976), 87; Bruce Nesbitt, ed., *Earle Birney: Critical Views on Canadian Writers* (Toronto: McGraw-Hill Ryerson, 1974), 74, 80-1, 83, 88, 90; Sam Solecki, ed., *Imagining Canadian Literature: The Selected Letters of Jack McClelland* (Toronto: Key Porter, 1998), 4-13.

24 Norman Mailer, *The Naked and the Dead* (New York: Random House, 1948), 184-6; Mary V. Dearborn, *Mailer: A Biography* (Boston: Houghton Mifflin, 1999), 62-3; Michael J. Lennon, ed., *Conversations with Norman Mailer* (Jackson: University Press of Mississippi, 1988), 117. My thanks to Ashton D. Howley of the University of Ottawa English Department who is writing a PhD dissertation on Mailer.

25 See Doug Owram, *Born at the Right Time: A History of the Baby Boom Generation* (Toronto: University of Toronto Press, 1996); Eileen Tyler May, *Homeward Bound: American Families in the Cold War Era* (New York: Basic Books, 1988).

CHAPTER 1: PATRIOTISM

1 *Winnipeg Free Press*, 1 Sept. 1939, 3.

2 *Winnipeg Free Press*, 4 Sept. 1939, 9; *Globe and Mail*, 4 Sept. 1939, 4; *Halifax Chronicle*, 4 Sept. 1939, 12; K.A.H. Buckley and M.C. Urquhart, *Historical Statistics of Canada* (Toronto: Macmillan, 1965), 485.

3 *Globe and Mail*, 4 Sept. 1939, 16; Montreal *Gazette*, 4 Sept. 1939, 11.

4 Margaret Moffatt, interview by author, Dunrobin, ON, 22 Feb. 1999.

5 Thomas Socknat, *Witness against War: Pacifism in Canada, 1900-1945* (Toronto: University of Toronto Press, 1987), 155.

6 Terry Copp, "Ontario 1939: The Decision for War," in *A Country of Limitations: Canada and the World in 1939*, ed. Norman Hillmer et al. (Ottawa: Canadian Council for the History of the Second World War, 1996), 109-119; *Globe and Mail*, 4 Sept. 1939, 1.

7 Terry Copp, *The Brigade: The Fifth Canadian Infantry Brigade, 1939-1945* (Stoney Creek, ON: Fortress Publications, 1992), 3; Ian Miller, "Toronto's Response to the Outbreak of War, 1939," *Canadian Military History* 11, 1 (2002): 7, 9, 21.

8 J.L. Granatstein, *Canada's Army: Waging War and Keeping the Peace* (Toronto: University of Toronto Press, 2002), 187; *Globe and Mail*, 4 Sept. 1939, 1, and 5 Sept. 1939, 5; *Halifax Chronicle*, 4 Sept. 1939, 3; *Winnipeg Free Press*, 5 Sept. 1939, 2; Montreal *Gazette*, 4 Sept. 1939, 21, 5 Sept. 1939, 2, 5, and 6 Sept. 1939, 1.

9 Montreal *Gazette*, 4 Sept. 1939, 4.

10 House of Commons, *Debates*, 7 Sept. 1939, 1; *Ottawa Citizen*, 8 Sept. 1939, 13.

11 *Ottawa Citizen*, 8 Sept. 1939, 12, 14, and 9 Sept. 1939, 19.

12 House of Commons, *Debates*, 8 Sept. 1939, 6.

13 Ibid., 12, 18, 24, 34, 36, 42, 44, 55; Montreal *Gazette*, 9 Sept. 1939, 1; *Globe and Mail*, 9 Sept. 1939, 3; *Vancouver Sun*, 31 Oct. 1939, 4; Granatstein, *Canada's Army*, 177-178, 189.

14 House of Commons, *Debates*, 58-73, 88-89; Montreal *Gazette*, 11 Sept. 1939, 1.

15 See wartime editions of *McKim's Directory of Canadian Publications* (Montreal: A. McKim, 1940-45), and N.W. Ayer and Son's *Directory, Newspapers and Periodicals* (Philadelphia: N.W. Ayer and Son, 1940-45).

16 Buckley and Urquhart, *Historical Statistics*, 485; *Vancouver Sun*, 18 Nov. 1939, 3; National Archives of Canada (NAC), RG36-31, Wartime Information Board records (WIB), vol. 12, file 8-3, pt. 1, Statistical Analysis Based on Elliot-Hayes Monitoring of Four Radio Stations for the Week of Jan. 11 to 17, 1943.

17 By late 1941, under this legislation, the federal government had banned thirty-five organizations. See, for instance, N.F. Dreisziger, "Rallying Canada's Immigrants behind the War Effort," in *Forging a Nation: Perspectives on the Canadian Military Experience*, ed. Bernd Horn (St. Catharines, ON: Vanwell Publishing, 2002), 183-187; and Ramsay Cook, "Canadian Freedom in Wartime, 1939-1945," in *His Own Man: Essays in Honour of Arthur Reginald Marsden Lower*, ed. W.H. Heick and Roger Graham (Montreal and Kingston: McGill-Queen's University Press, 1974), 40. Order-in-Council, PC 882, 13 Oct. 1942.

18 *Globe and Mail*, 6 Sept. 1939, 3; Montreal *Gazette*, 4 Sept. 1939, 6; *Maclean's*, 15 Oct. 1939, 22.

19 These voices included the left-leaning *Canadian Forum* and, from the right of the political spectrum, *Saturday Night's* chief editor, Hector Charlesworth, who expressed concern that the federal government could use censorship as a partisan weapon. J.L. Granatstein and Peter Stevens, eds., *Forum: Canadian Life and Letters, 1920-70* (Toronto: University of Toronto Press, 1972), 178; *Saturday Night*, 13 July 1940, 5.

20 *Globe and Mail* editorial quoted in Cook, "Canadian Freedom," 48; *Toronto Star*, 18 Oct. 1939, 6.

21 S.F. Wise, *Canadian Airmen and the First World War: The Official History of the Royal Canadian Air Force*, vol. 1 (Toronto: University of Toronto Press, 1980), 602, 615-616; Wilfrid Eggleston, "Press Censorship in Canada in World War II," ms, n.d, 5.

22 Individual government departments retained responsibility for different types of censorship. The Department of National Defence directed cable, telegraph, and telephone censorship. The postmaster general was responsible for postal censorship. Press censorship came under the Secretary of State. Broadcasting and radio came under the Department of Transport. Quotation from Eggleston, "Press Censorship," 7.

23 WIB, vol. 22, file 23-14, Press Censorship of American Publications Entering Canada, 11 Nov. 1940.

24 NAC, RG2, Privy Council records (PC), vol. 2, War Cabinet Committee, 10 June 1940.

25 *Ottawa Journal*, 15 April 1942, 1; *Le Droit*, 21 April 1942, 1.

26 On the romanticized nature of war reports received by Canadians during the First World War, see Jeffrey A. Keshen, *Propaganda and Censorship during Canada's Great War* (Edmonton: University of Alberta Press, 1996), chapter 2.

27 Halton quoted in Wallace Reyburn, *Some of It Was Fun* (Toronto: Thomas Nelson and Sons, 1949), 134-136; *Globe and Mail*, 20 Aug. 1942, 1, 3, 20; *Saturday Night*, 12 Sept. 1942, 7.

28 Claude Beauregard, *Guerre et Censure au Canada, 1939-1945* (Sillery: Septentrion, 1998); Emile Montgomery, "'The War Was a Very Vivid Part of My Life': British Columbia School Children and the Second World War" (MA thesis, University of British Columbia, 1991), 12.

29 WIB, vol. 10, file 4-2-2-1, Minutes of Meeting of the Publicity Co-ordinating Committee, 22 Feb. 1944; Directorate of History and Heritage, Department of National Defence (DHH), 112.21009 D209, W. Eggleston, "Background Memorandum on Voluntary Press Censorship," 11 Dec. 1944.

30 WIB, vol. 13, file 8-9-1, Report of the Activities of the Office of the Director of Public Information from April 1, 1941 to February 28, 1942.

31 WIB, vol. 12, file 8-2-2; Daniel Robinson, *The Measure of Democracy: Polling, Market Research and Public Life, 1930-1945* (Toronto: University of Toronto Press, 1999), 109; Gary Evans, *John Grierson and the National Film Board: The Politics of Wartime Propaganda* (Toronto: University of Toronto Press, 1984), 134-141.

32 WIB, file 8-7A, Confidential Report of a Recent Survey of Public Opinion among French-Canadians in the Province of Quebec Conducted by the Canadian Institute of Public Opinion, 6 July 1942.

33 WIB, file 8-5-2, K.H. Olive to Joseph Clark, 9 Sept. 1942; K.H. Olive to A.A. Dunton, 1 Oct. 1942; "Newspapers Now Publishing the Rumour Clinic as of December 15, 1942."

34 NAC, RG19, Department of Finance records (FN), vol. 4031, file 129-W-1-25, WIB Survey No. 33.

35 Jean Pariseau, "La participation des Canadiens français à l'effort des deux guerres mondiales: démarche de ré-interprétation," *Canadian Defence Quarterly* 12, 2 (1983): 48; J.L. Granatstein and J. Murray Hitsman, *Broken Promises: A History of Conscription in Canada* (Toronto: Oxford University Press, 1977), 160.

36 Montreal *Gazette*, 4 Sept. 1939, 4, 5 Sept. 1939, 5, 7 Sept. 1939, 6, and 8 Sept. 1939, 3, 6; *Globe and Mail*, 5 Sept. 1939, 3.

37 The following year, this service was extended to anywhere in the Western Hemisphere. Daniel Byers, "Canada's Zombies: A Portrait of Canadian Conscripts and Their Experiences during the Second World War," in *Forging a Nation: Perspectives on the Canadian Military Experience*, ed. Bernd Horn (St. Catharines, ON: Vanwell Publishing, 2002), 156.

38 Paul Couture, "The Vichy-Free French Propaganda War in Québec, 1940-1942," *Historical Papers/Communications historiques* (1978), 200-210; Éric Amyot, *Le Québec entre Pétain et de Gaulle: Vichy, la France et les Canadiens français, 1940-1945* (Montreal: Fides, 1999), 184-185; WIB, vol. 13, file 8-7A, Confidential Report of a Recent Survey of Public Opinion among French-Canadians in the Province of Quebec Conducted by the Canadian Institute of Public Opinion, 6 July 1942.

39 Granatstein and Hitsman, *Broken Promises,* 160; Byers, "Canada's Zombies," 159.

40 Norm Bowen, interview by author, Ottawa, 27 March 2000; *Ottawa Citizen,* 2 Nov. 1943, 1.

41 For instance, 48.17 percent of New Brunswick males aged eighteen to forty-five donned a uniform despite the province's large francophone population. Pariseau, "Participation," 48. Granatstein, *Canada's Army,* 180-181, 193.

42 Michael D. Behiels, "The Bloc Populaire Canadien and the Origins of French-Canadian Neo-nationalism, 1942-1948," in *Quebec since 1800: Selected Readings,* ed. Michael D. Behiels (Toronto: Irwin Publishing, 2002), 443-455.

43 Granatstein and Hitsman, *Broken Promises,* 231-235; *Ottawa Journal,* 24 Nov. 1944, 1; *Le Droit,* 28 Nov. 1944, 4.

44 Michael D. Stevenson, *Canada's Greatest Wartime Muddle: National Selective Service and the Mobilization of Human Resources during World War II* (Montreal and Kingston: McGill-Queen's University Press, 2001), 38, 52-53, 63; C.P. Stacey, *Arms, Men and Government: The War Policies of Canada, 1939-1945* (Ottawa: Department of National Defence, 1970), 588; Byers, "Canada's Zombies," 159.

45 E.L.M. Burns, *Manpower in the Canadian Army, 1939-1945* (Toronto: Clarke, Irwin, 1956), 22, chapters 3, 4; Granatstein and Hitsman, *Broken Promises,* 152-153, 158.

46 J.L. Granatstein and David J. Bercuson, *The Collins Dictionary of Canadian History* (Toronto: Collins, 1988), 268; J.L. Granatstein and Desmond Morton, *Victory 1945: Canadians from War to Peace* (Toronto: HarperCollins, 1995), 19; David Scott, *The Home Front in the Second World War* (Ottawa: Supply and Services, 1995), 14.

47 During the interwar years, the most well-known Canadian antiwar novels were Peregrine Acland's *All Else Is Folly* (1929), Charles Yale Harrison's *Generals Die in Bed* (1930), and

Philip Child's *God's Sparrows* (1937). None sold well in Canada. Harrison's, the most graphic, was first published in Britain and was heavily criticized in Canada for its "blood-curdling" nature. John Herd Thompson and Allen Seager, *Canada 1922-1939: Decades of Discord* (Toronto: McClelland and Stewart, 1985), 166; Jonathan F. Vance, *Death So Noble: Meaning, Memory and the First World War* (Vancouver: UBC Press, 1997), 193-194.

48 Bowen, interview.

49 DHH, 112.3 M3009(D138), Morale Report, 7 July 1943.

50 Christine Hamelin, "A Sense of Purpose: Ottawa Students and the Second World War," *Canadian Military History* 6, 1 (1997): 35; Donald F. Ripley, *The Home Front: Wartime Life at Camp Aldershot and in Kentville, Nova Scotia* (Hantsport, NS: Lancelot Press, 1991), 30.

51 Granatstein and Hitsman, *Broken Promises*, 207; *Saturday Night*, 23 Sept. 1944, 40; G.W. Hayes, "The Friction of War" (MA thesis, Wilfrid Laurier University, 1983), 3; James Keshen, interview by author, Toronto, 12 July 1994.

52 See, for example, comments in the *Canadian Home Journal*, Oct. 1942, 2-3.

53 *Canada Year Book, 1939*, 136; *Canada Year Book, 1941*, 92-94; *Canada Year Book, 1942*, 134; *Canada Year Book, 1943-44*, 162; *Canada Year Book, 1944*, 154; *Canada Year Book, 1946*, 166-167; *Canada Year Book, 1948-49*, 209.

54 *Ottawa Citizen*, 24 Nov. 1939, 21.

55 *Ottawa Citizen*, 25 Nov. 1939, 4.

56 Michael Dawe, "Community in Transition: Red Deer in the Second World War," in *For King and Country: Alberta in the Second World War*, ed. K.W. Tingley (Edmonton: Provincial Museum of Alberta, 1995), 121; WIB, vol. 14, file "IODE," clipping from *Toronto Star*, 15 July 1940, n.p.

57 *Vancouver Sun*, 24 Oct. 1939, 6.

58 *Saturday Night*, 7 Oct. 1939, 22.

59 Bill McNeil, *Voices of a War Remembered: An Oral History of Canadians in World War Two* (Toronto: Doubleday, 1991), 119.

60 United Church of Canada, *Year Book*, (Toronto: UCC, 1941), 87.

61 NAC, MG28 I17, Imperial Order Daughters of the Empire (IODE) papers, vol. 23, file "WWII – IODE Activity"; IODE, vol. 23, file 6, Warplanes Carrying IODE Insignia, n.d.; IODE, file 4, K.I.G. Drape to Hon. Brooke Claxton, 4 Jan. 1950; *Winnipeg Free Press*, 13 Jan. 1942, 10; Dawe, "Community in Transition," 126.

62 *Ottawa Citizen*, 16 April 1945, 6; *Ottawa Journal*, 31 Oct. 1944, 11.

63 Paul Fussell, *Wartime: Understanding Behaviour in the Second World War* (New York: Oxford University Press, 1989), 145.

64 *Saturday Night*, 13 Nov. 1943, 24.

65 NAC, MG28 I345, Catholic Women's League of Canada papers, vol. 2, *Annual Report, 1946*, 200; WIB, vol. 14, file "IODE," clipping from *Montreal Herald*, 2 June 1943, n.p.; NAC, RG44, National War Services records (NWS), vol. 2, file "Canadian Red Cross," Summary of Some of the Outstanding Activities and Accomplishments in World War II, n.d.

66 NWS, vol. 20, file "Aid for Bomb Victims," The Canadian Red Cross Contributions for the Relief of Bombed Victims, 26 March 1941.

67 *Saturday Night*, 27 Feb. 1943, 4-5; NWS, vol. 2, file "Canadian Red Cross," Summary of Some of the Outstanding Activities and Accomplishments in World War II, n.d.; *Canada Year Book 1946*, 829.

68 NWS, vol. 5, file C-14, Brief General Statement of Financial Condition of Canadian Red Cross, n.d.; *Vancouver Sun*, 15 May 1945, 5.

69 *Ottawa Citizen*, 16 Jan. 1942, 11; *Toronto Star*, 16 Feb. 1942, 23.

70 For example, the United Church of Canada officially declared, "Gambling is like the crooked stick which can never cast a straight shadow. Not even a patriotic appeal can justify this means." United Church of Canada, *Year Book*, 1944, 108; *Toronto Star*, 1 Sept. 1942, 11.

71 Montreal *Gazette*, 6 May 1944, 9; *Toronto Star*, 13 Feb. 1945, 17; *Ottawa Journal*, 20 Oct. 1944, 4.

72 *Toronto Star*, 24 Feb. 1945, 12; NWS, vol. 2, file "Canadian Red Cross," Urquhart to LaFlèche, 29 June 1944.

73 *Industrial Canada*, Jan. 1943, 143; *Ottawa Citizen*, 1 Feb. 1943, 7.

74 The actual figure for Canada was 37.5 percent. The British Red Cross covered 43.75 percent of the costs, the Australian Red Cross 12.5 percent, and the New Zealand Red Cross 6.25 percent. NWS, vol. 5, file C-14, T.C. Davis to J.T. Thorson, 13 March 1942.

75 NWS, vol. 2, file "Canadian Red Cross," Summary of Some of the Outstanding Activities and Accomplishments in World War II, n.d; *Chatelaine*, March 1943, 8-9.

76 NWS, vol. 21, file "War Charities Act," Davis to G.D. Conant, 4 Dec. 1940; NWS, vol. 8, file "Voluntary and Auxiliary Services, part 1," George Pifher to LaFlèche, 24 March 1943, and Pifher to LaFlèche, 10 Dec. 1942.

77 Donna Zwicker, "Volunteer War Services in Alberta, 1939-1945," in *For King and Country: Alberta in the Second World War*, ed. K.W. Tingley (Edmonton: Provincial Museum of Alberta, 1995), 279; James Frank Edward White, "Conscripted City: Halifax and the Second World War" (PhD diss., McMaster University, 1995), 300.

78 DHH, 77/648, "History – Auxiliary Services Overseas," memo prepared by H.N. Crighton, RCAF Wing Commander, 1 Nov. 1944.

79 NAC, MG27 III B5, Ian Mackenzie papers, vol. 58, file 527-17 (2), Report of the Canadian Legion Educational Service, 1942; NWS, vol. 3, file "Canadian Legion of BESL," Address by John Marshall, 1942. The policy was that two auxiliary organizations would service training camps in Canada with a military population from 2,000 to 4,000, and three at places with more than 4,000 personnel. NWS, vol. 9, file "Voluntary & Auxiliary Services, Part 1," LaFlèche to Saunders, 11 Dec. 1942.

80 NAC, MG28 I198, Young Women's Christian Association papers, vol. 34, file "War Services – WWII," Canadian War Services Fund, 1941; James White, "Conscripted City," 302.

81 NAC, MG28 I95, Young Men's Christian Association papers (YMCA), vol. 272, file 3, *Special Canteen Bulletin*, #1, 1 April 1941, n.p.

82 YMCA, vol. 272, file 3, Program Planning List, n.d.; City of Vancouver Archives, 1942-52 (pamphlets), *In This Emergency: The Salvation Army in Canada*, 1942, n.p.; NAC, MG28 I10, Canadian Council on Social Development papers (CCSD), vol. 9, file 68, *YMCA News Bulletin*, March 1945, 4.

83 *Ottawa Citizen*, 15 Nov. 1943, 5, and 23 Oct. 1945, 5.

84 NAC, MG26 J1, William Lyon Mackenzie King papers, vol. 290, Reel C-4571, 280,290.

85 James White, "Conscripted City," 305-307; quotation from Mike Parker, *Running the Gauntlet: An Oral History of Canadian Merchant Seamen in World War II* (Halifax: Nimbus Publishing, 1994), 211; Stephen Kimber, *Sailors, Slackers and Blind Pigs: Halifax at War* (Toronto: Doubleday, 2002), 79-80, 133-135.

86 Federal funding for the Navy League climbed from $100,000 in 1941 to $530,000 for the 1944-45 fiscal year. YMCA, vol. 34, file "War Services – WWII," Canadian War Services Fund, 1941; James White, "Conscripted City," 302.

87 Parker, *Running the Gauntlet*, 21; Alan M. Hurst, T*he Canadian YMCA in World War II* (Toronto: YMCA, 1949), 131-132; quotation from Thomas Randall, *Halifax: Warden of the North* (New York: Doubleday, 1965), 278-279.

88 NAC, MG30 I311, Montreal Soldiers' Wives' League papers, vol. 5, file 13, *War Charities Act*, 1939.

89 NWS, vol. 42, file "Toronto Better Business Bureau," *Newsletter*, 7 Nov. 1940, 3.

90 *Saturday Night*, 17 Oct. 1942, 22.

91 The *Windsor Star* story appears in the *Ottawa Journal*, 24 May 1941, 4.

92 NWS, vol. 9, file "War Charities Co-ordination Board," Pifher to Black, 4 Aug. 1945; NWS, vol. 72, List of Funds, 14 Nov. 1946.

93 NWS, vol. 7, file H-7, Meeting of the War Time Services Coordination Council, Windsor Hotel, 29 Dec. 1941.

94 NWS, vol. 8, file "War Charities," Ian Mackenzie to Ernest Bogard, 28 July 1944.

95 Such a policy was also applied to the annual Red Cross campaign. Starting in 1941, the federal government ordered that most civilian charities consolidate their efforts into a yearly United Appeal during two weeks in November. NWS, vol. 27, file "Community Chest," memo from Thorson, n.d.; Zwicker, "Volunteer War Service," 274-275.

96 Zwicker, "Volunteer War Service," 278; *Halifax Chronicle*, 30 Jan. 1941, 3; Granatstein and Morton, *Victory 1945*, 86; *Vancouver Sun*, 1 May 1941, 8.

97 *Calgary Herald*, 4 Feb. 1941, 9.

98 *Toronto Star*, 20 Feb. 1942, 18; *Saturday Night*, 8 May 1943, 3.

99 WIB, vol. 10, file 4-2-2-1, Minutes of Meeting of the Publicity Co-ordinating Committee, 4 July 1944.

100 *Public Opinion Quarterly*, 1945, 250.

101 Victory Bond purchases made by individual Canadian citizens, at some 50 percent of the total, were nearly double the American figure of 27 percent. Wendy Cuthbertson, "Pocketbooks and Patriotism: The 'Financial Miracle' of Canada's World War II Victory Bond Program," in *Canadian Military History since the 17th Century*, ed. Yves Tremblay, Proceedings of the Canadian Military History Conference, Ottawa, 5-9 May 2000 (Ottawa: Department of National Defence, 2001), 177-178, 181; *Industrial Canada*, March 1940, 100.

102 *Ottawa Journal*, 1 Oct. 1941, 12.

103 Cuthbertson, "Pocketbooks and Patriotism," 181; Moffatt, interview.

104 *Edmonton Journal*, 6 Nov. 1942, 8.

105 Daniel Robinson, *Measure of Democracy*, 143.

106 *Vancouver Sun*, 13 Nov. 1942, 20.

107 *Saturday Night*, 19 April 1943, 19.

108 *Saturday Night*, 30 Oct. 1943, 20.

109 Serge Marc Durflinger, "City at War: The Effects of the Second World War on Verdun, Québec" (PhD diss., McGill University, 1998), 222-223; *Halifax Chronicle*, 22 Oct. 1944, 2.

110 *Ottawa Journal*, 5 June 1941, 5.

111 *Toronto Star*, 25 Feb. 1942, 17.

112 *Vancouver Sun*, 24 Oct. 1942, 1.

113 Richard S. Malone, *A Portrait of War, 1939-1943* (Toronto: Collins, 1983), 80-82.

114 *Edmonton Journal*, 2 Nov. 1942, 15. Reprinted with permission from the *Edmonton Journal*.

115 Spencer Dunmore, *Above and Beyond: The Canadians' War in the Air, 1939-1945* (Toronto: McClelland and Stewart, 1996), 53.

116 PC, vol. 2, Memo from Senior Air Officer covering main parts brought forward by him at a meeting of Defence Committee of Council, 14 Nov. 1938; Jonathan F. Vance, *High Flight: Aviation and the Canadian Imagination* (Toronto: Penguin, 2002), 228-229.

117 *Halifax Chronicle*, 4 Sept. 1939, 3, and 8 Sept. 1939, 3; *Globe and Mail*, 6 Sept. 1939, 3.

118 Starting in early 1941, particularly in coastal, border, and outlying areas, thousands became involved in the Aircraft Detection Corps. Its members were to report by telephone or telegraph any aircraft sighting, or even any sounds they believed might come from an airplane. W.A.B. Douglas, *Official History of the Royal Canadian Air Force*, vol. 2 (Toronto: University of Toronto Press, 1985), 495; NAC, Audiovisual Section, Acc. 1981-100/413, *Comrade in Arms*, 1943; McNeil, *Voices of a War*, 114.

119 Durflinger, "City at War," 193.

120 City of Ottawa Archives, RG20/2, Board of Control records (BOC), vol. 41, file "ARP Matters, 1943," Booklet entitled *Canada ARP*.

121 *Ottawa Journal*, 24 June 1941, 4; BOC, vol. 40, file "Patriotic Activities," Undated memo entitled "Air Raid Precautions."

122 NAC, RG3, Post Office records, vol. 974, file 54-27-10, 7174.

123 *Ottawa Journal,* 27 June 1941, 3, and 18 June 1943, 3. Because contemporary sources in Canada used imperial measurements, this book maintains that system when dealing with Canadian-based matter.

124 Durflinger, "City at War," 203.

125 *Vancouver Sun,* 10 Sept. 1942, 22, and 3 Oct. 1942, 4.

126 *Saturday Night,* 13 March 1943, 9.

127 Kimber, *Sailors, Slackers,* 153; David Bercuson, *Maple Leaf against the Axis: Canada's Second World War* (Toronto: Stoddart, 1995), 95; *Ottawa Citizen,* 5 Nov. 1943, 22; Durflinger, "City at War," 205.

128 Granatstein and Morton, *Victory 1945,* 76.

129 NWS, vol. 8, file "Salvage – Complaints," J.T. Thorson to R.B. Hanson, 14 April 1942.

130 NWS, vol. 8, file "Salvage – Complaints," T.C. Davis to J.T. Thorson, 16 April 1942.

131 NWS, vol. 13, file "Fats, Salvage Advisory Committee," Preliminary Draft Supplementary, Fats and Bones Dominion-Wide Publicity Program, 31 March 1944.

132 *Winnipeg Free Press,* 16 Jan. 1942, 9; Metropolitan Toronto Reference Library, Baldwin Room, Broadside Collection. By the end of 1942, empty tubes had to be returned before new toothpaste or shaving cream could be purchased. Also the salvage of any unusable item containing large amounts of metal and weighing over 500 pounds became mandatory after twenty days of non-use. Those who did not comply could face up to a $500 fine. William Weintraub, *City Unique: Montreal Days and Nights in the 1940s and 1950s* (Toronto: McClelland and Stewart, 1996), 54-55; *Vancouver Sun,* 8 Sept. 1942, 8; *Saturday Night,* 12 Sept. 1942, 39.

133 I am grateful to Jonathan Vance for supplying me with this figure. NWS, vol. 8, file "Salvage – Rubber, Shipping, War Trophies," Ottawa Board of Control to Thorson, 13 July 1942.

134 NWS, vol. 13, file "Salvage Division – Progress Reports," Memo from Acting National Director, J.F. McCallum, 8 Sept. 1945.

135 *Ottawa Citizen,* 13 March 1943, 22.

136 *Toronto Star,* 12 June 1942, 15.

137 Some people took these items themselves to butcher shops, which were authorized to pay four cents a pound for fat drippings and one cent a pound for bones.

138 NWS, vol. 5, file "Press Clippings – Salvage," clipping from *Toronto Star,* 23 March 1942, n.p.; clipping from *Toronto Star,* 8 April 1942, n.p.; clipping from *Globe and Mail,* 20 March 1942, n.p., and clipping from *Globe and Mail,* 28 March 1942, n.p.; *Saturday Night,* 23 Jan. 1943, 26.

139 *Saturday Night,* 24 April 1943, 27.

140 Such was apparently the case in Verdun. Durflinger, "City at War," 212.

141 *Ottawa Journal,* 3 Sept. 1942, 5.

142 On anti-Semitism in Canada see Lita-Rose Betcherman, *The Swastika and the Maple Leaf: Fascist Movements in Canada in the Thirties* (Toronto: Fitzhenry and Whiteside, 1975); Esther Delisle, *The Traitor and the Jew: Anti-Semitism and Extreme Right-Wing Nationalism in Quebec from 1929 to 1939* (Montreal: Davies Publishing, 1993); and Irving Abella and Harold Troper, *None Is Too Many: Canada and the Jews of Europe, 1933-1948* (Toronto: Lester and Orpen Dennys, 1982).

143 See Laurelle Lo, "The Path from Peddling: Jewish Economic Activity in Ottawa Prior to 1939," in *Construire une capitale – Ottawa – Making a Capital,* ed. Jeff Keshen and Nicole St-Onge (Ottawa: University of Ottawa Press, 2001), 239-250.

144 NWS, vol. 8, file "Salvage Complaints," A. Widnall to J.T. Thorson, 21 Jan. 1942; NWS, vol. 8, file "Salvage Committees," Chair of Kitchener-Waterloo Salvage Committee to Thorson, 4 June 1942, and press release by Thorson, 5 June 1942.

145   William R. Young, "Building Citizenship: English Canada and Propaganda during the Second World War," *Journal of Canadian Studies* 16, 3/4 (1981): 124.
146   *Ottawa Journal*, 1 Jan. 1944, 8.
147   *Toronto Star*, 12 June 1942, 15.

CHAPTER 2: GROWTH, OPPORTUNITY, AND STRAIN

1   *Industrial Canada*, Jan. 1943, 144.
2   *Saturday Night*, 13 March 1943, 17.
3   *Saturday Night*, 17 July 1943, 13, 19 Sept. 1942, 19, and 18 Sept. 1943, 9.
4   *Globe and Mail*, 8 Sept. 1939, 26.
5   J.L. Granatstein and Desmond Morton, *A Nation Forged in Fire: Canadians and the Second World War, 1939-1945* (Toronto: Lester and Orpen Dennys, 1989), 7.
6   J.L. Granatstein, *Canada's Army: Waging War and Keeping the Peace* (Toronto: University of Toronto Press, 2002), 178.
7   The guns were delivered on time and for the price specified. C.P. Stacey, *Arms, Men and Government: The War Policies of Canada, 1939-1945* (Ottawa: Department of National Defence, 1970), 100-103.
8   *Industrial Canada*, Jan. 1940, 83; Paul Marsden, "The Costs of No Commitments: Canadian Economic Planning for War, 1939," in *A Country of Limitations: Canada and the World in 1939*, ed. Norman Hillmer et al. (Ottawa: Canadian Council for the History of the Second World War, 1996), 208-209; Michael A. Hennessy, "The Industrial Front: The Scale and Scope of Canadian Industrial Mobilization during the Second World War," in *Forging a Nation: Perspectives on the Canadian Military Experience*, ed. Bernd Horn (St. Catharines, ON: Vanwell Publishing, 2002), 141.
9   Quotation from David Scott, *The Home Front in the Second World War* (Ottawa: Supply and Services, 1995), 14; Robert Bothwell and William Kilbourn, *C.D. Howe: A Biography* (Toronto: McClelland and Stewart, 1979), chapters 6-8.
10   Hennessy, "Industrial Front," 144. For details on the Hyde Park Declaration see J.L. Granatstein, *How Britain's Weakness Forced Canada into the Arms of the United States* (Toronto: University of Toronto Press, 1989).
11   In the Maritimes, there were unproven allegations that Liberal organizers handed out war contracts to party supporters. In Montreal, corruption was alleged over excessive construction costs (three times the norm) for the laying of concrete at Dorval airport by the Dibblee Construction Company, but no criminal charges ensued. National Archives of Canada (NAC), MG26 J4, William Lyon Mackenzie King papers (WLMK), vol. 413, file 3988, Summary of Allegations from Montreal re Alleged Irregularities in War Industry, 28 Sept. 1942.
12   At the war's peak, Crown corporations employed 240,993. Hennessy, "Industrial Front," 147; Peter S. McInnis, *Harnessing Labour Confrontation: Shaping the Postwar Settlement in Canada, 1943-1950* (Toronto: University of Toronto Press, 2002), 33; Stacey, *Arms, Men and Government*, 532-533; E.L.M. Burns, *Manpower in the Canadian Army, 1939-1945* (Toronto: Clarke, Irwin, 1956), 152; *Canada Year Book 1948-49*, 534-535.
13   *Canada Year Book, 1948-49*, 597.
14   Shipbuilding employed nearly 43,000 in Quebec. Paul-André Linteau, *Histoire de Montréal depuis la confédération* (Montreal: Boréal, 1992), 301-303; *Toronto Star*, 27 Feb. 1945, 1.
15   Aircraft production employed 38,500 in Quebec. Because of its status as a centre of aircraft production, its substantial activity linked to the British Commonwealth Air Training Plan, and its more easterly location than Toronto (which employed about the same number of aircraft workers), Montreal became headquarters for Eastern Air Command. Ultimately 9,027 planes left Dorval airport for delivery to Britain, North Africa, and the Mediterranean. John

Irwin Cooper, *Montreal: A Brief History* (Montreal and London: McGill-Queen's University Press, 1969), 172; Leslie Roberts, *Montreal: From Mission Colony to World City* (Toronto: Macmillan, 1969), 337; Hennessy, "Industrial Front," 146; William Weintraub, *City Unique: Montreal Days and Nights in the 1940s and 1950s* (Toronto: McClelland and Stewart, 1996), 35-37.

16 *Canada Year Book 1948-49,* 597.

17 Nearly 44,000 aircraft workers were located in Ontario. Hennessy, "Industrial Front," 146; James T. Lemon, *Toronto: An Illustrated History* (Toronto: James Lorimer, 1985), 84.

18 *Canada Year Book 1948-49,* 597; John C. Weaver, *Hamilton: An Illustrated History* (Toronto: James Lorimer, 1982), 137.

19 J.L. Granatstein and Desmond Morton, *Victory 1945: Canadians from War to Peace* (Toronto: HarperCollins, 1995), 101.

20 As noted earlier, the text maintains the imperial usage of contemporary sources when dealing with Canadian-based matter.

21 Between 1939 and 1944, the number of Canadians employed in the mining sector dropped from 81,000 to 60,000. Comparing 1944 to the 1935-39 average, nickel output increased by 41.5 percent, and aluminum, which was critical to aircraft production, by approximately 1,000 percent. Hennessy, "Industrial Front," 144, 151; Burns, *Manpower in the Canadian Army,* 156; *Ottawa Journal,* 15 May 1941, 25; *Saturday Night,* 15 Aug. 1942, 39; D.M. LeBoudrais, *Sudbury Basin: The Story of Nickel* (Toronto: Ryerson Press, 1953), 169; Matt Bray and Ernie Epp, eds., *A Vast and Magnificent Land: An Illustrated History of Northern Ontario* (Toronto: Ontario Ministry of Northern Affairs, 1984), 139.

22 *Maclean's,* 24 Feb. 1945, 20.

23 Ernest Forbes, "Consolidating Disparity: The Maritimes and the Industrialization of Canada during the Second World War," in *Challenging the Regional Stereotype: Essays on the 20th Century Maritimes,* ed. Ernest Forbes (Fredericton: Acadiensis Press, 1989), 172-199; James Frank Edward White, "Conscripted City: Halifax and the Second World War" (PhD diss., McMaster University, 1995), 240-242.

24 NAC, RG36-31, Wartime Information Board records (WIB), vol. 13, file 8-7D, Ration Book Three As an Indication of Population Shifts, 1 Feb. 1944.

25 Forbes, "Consolidating Disparity," 191-192.

26 NAC, RG19, Ministry of Finance records (FN), vol. 4031, file 129W-1-26, WIB Survey, 11 Sept. 1943.

27 A $1.75 million federal grant to the DOSCO steel plant in Sydney, Nova Scotia, allowed it to reopen a mill that soon was producing "more than one-third of Canada's output of regular ships' plate." Among the "dormant" or underutilized textile plants that "took on new life" were branches of Canadian Cottons in Marysville and Milltown, Nova Scotia. Carmen Miller, "The 1940s: War and Rehabilitation," in *The Atlantic Provinces in Confederation,* ed. E.R. Forbes and D.A. Muise (Toronto: University of Toronto Press, 1993), 314.

28 R.A. Young, "Maritimers Rise to War," in *A Country of Limitations: Canada and the World in 1939,* ed. Norman Hillmer et al. (Ottawa: Canadian Council for the History of the Second World War, 1996), 149-150; James White, "Conscripted City," 211-212; Carmen Miller, "1940s," 339.

29 Thomas Randall, *Halifax: Warden of the North* (New York: Doubleday, 1965), 284; Hennessy, "Industrial Front," 146.

30 J. William Brennan, *Regina: An Illustrated History* (Toronto: James Lorimer, 1989), 150.

31 Mark Hopkins, "Blatchford Field: The War Years, 1939-1945," in *For King and Country: Alberta in the Second World War,* ed. K.W. Tingley (Edmonton: Provincial Museum of Alberta, 1995), 230-232; Catherine Cole, "'Every Kitchen is an Arsenal': Women's War on the Homefront in Northern Alberta," in *For King and Country: Alberta in the Second World*

War, ed. K.W. Tingley (Edmonton: Provincial Museum of Alberta, 1995), 266; Bob Gilmour, "The Homefront in the Second World War," in *Edmonton: The Life of a City,* ed. Bob Hesketh and Frances Sywripa (Edmonton: NeWest Publishers, 1995), 212.

32 *Vancouver Sun,* 9 Sept. 1942, 1; Donna A. Zwicker, "Alberta Women and World War Two" (MA thesis, University of Calgary, 1985), 71.

33 Britain paid $185 million, Australia $40.2 million, and New Zealand $28.8 million. W.A.B. Douglas, *Official History of the Royal Canadian Air Force,* vol. 2 (Toronto: University of Toronto Press, 1985), 222.

34 Douglas, *Official History of the Royal Canadian Air Force,* vol. 2, 262-263; F.J. Hatch, *The Aerodrome of Democracy: Canada and the British Commonwealth Air Training Plan* (Ottawa: Directorate of History, 1983), 2, 200, 206.

35 Hatch, *Aerodrome of Democracy,* 189-190, 207-211; Douglas, *Official History of the Royal Canadian Air Force,* vol. 2, 236; Granatstein and Morton, *Nation Forged in Fire,* 99-100; Spencer Dunmore, *Wings for Victory: The Remarkable Story of the British Commonwealth Air Training Plan in Canada* (Toronto: McClelland and Stewart, 1994), 231.

36 Dunmore, *Wings for Victory,* 207; Brereton Greenhous and Norman Hillmer, "The Impact of the British Commonwealth Air Training Plan on Western Canada: Some Saskatchewan Case Studies," *Journal of Canadian Studies* 16, 3/4 (1981): 134.

37 Making the argument about political favouritism is Peter C. Conrad, *Training for Victory: The British Commonwealth Air Training Plan in the West* (Saskatoon: Western Producer Prairie Books, 1989), 14, 16. Rachel Lea Heade, "The Politics behind BCATP Base Selection at Prince Albert, Saskatchewan," in *Canadian Military History since the 17th Century,* ed. Yves Tremblay, Proceedings of the Canadian Military History Conference, Ottawa, 5-9 May 2000 (Ottawa: Department of National Defence, 2001), 187-194; Douglas, *Official History of the Royal Canadian Air Force,* vol. 2, 225.

38 Although disappointed with the results, British Columbia still received six schools. Dunmore, *Wings for Victory,* 343.

39 Hopkins, "Blatchford Field," 232; Dunmore, *Wings for Victory,* 349-360.

40 Dunmore, *Wings for Victory,* 59, 61; Hatch, *Aerodrome of Democracy,* 66; Hillmer and Greenhous, "British Commonwealth Air Training Plan," 134-135.

41 Douglas, *Official History of the Royal Canadian Air Force,* vol. 2, 222; Patricia Myers, "Watching the War Fly By: The British Commonwealth Air Training Plan in Alberta," in *For King and Country: Alberta in the Second World War,* ed. K.W. Tingley (Edmonton: Provincial Museum of Alberta, 1995), 247; Hatch, *Aerodrome of Democracy,* 118.

42 Directorate of History and Heritage, Department of National Defence (DHH), 77/633, *Slipstream,* June 1941, 2-3.

43 J.G. MacGregor, *Edmonton: A History* (Edmonton: Hurtig Publishers, 1975), 263-264.

44 *Edmonton Journal,* 23 July 1942, 8; *Maclean's,* 1 Nov. 1942, 19.

45 Steven Boddington and Sean Moir, "'The Friendly Invasion': The American Presence in Edmonton," in *For King and Country: Alberta in the Second World War,* ed. K.W. Tingley (Edmonton: Provincial Museum of Alberta, 1995), 182.

46 *Winnipeg Free Press,* 1 March 1944, 9; Hopkins, "Blatchford Field," 238-241; Carl Christie, "The Northwest Staging Route: A Story of Canadian-American Wartime Cooperation," in *For King and Country: Alberta in the Second World War,* ed. K.W. Tingley (Edmonton: Provincial Museum of Alberta, 1995), 220.

47 Some airports, like the ones at Watson Lake and Whitehorse, continued operating after the war with decent air traffic. Others, particularly in the smallest communities, such as Smith River, British Columbia, and Teslin, Yukon Territory, closed down soon after the staging route ended. Christie, "Northwest Staging Route," 213, 222-224; Leslie Roberts, *There Shall Be Wings: A History of the Royal Canadian Air Force* (Toronto: Clarke, Irwin, 1959),

152; NAC, RG2, Privy Council records (PC), vol. 15, Cabinet War Committee, 29 May 1944; Ken Coates and W.R. Morrison, *The Alaska Highway in World War II: The U.S. Army of Occupation in Canada's Northwest* (Toronto: University of Toronto Press, 1992), 221.

48 Far less significant than the Alaska Highway or the Northwest Staging Route was the Canol oil pipeline linking Norman Wells in the Northwest Territories to a refinery in Whitehorse. The $34 million project built by the US Army Corps of Engineers proved ill conceived and had minimal economic impact. Boddington and Moir, "Friendly Invasion," 178.

49 Boddington and Moir, "Friendly Invasion," 183; Gilmour, "Homefront," 216; Coates and Morrison, *Alaska Highway*, 160.

50 Boddington and Moir, "Friendly Invasion," 178; Reginald Roy, "Western Canada during the Second World War," in *For King and Country: Alberta in the Second World War*, ed. K.W. Tingley (Edmonton: Provincial Museum of Alberta, 1995), 116; PC, vol. 16, Cabinet War Committee, 1 Sept. 1944.

51 *Saturday Night*, 13 Nov. 1943, 20; *Edmonton Journal*, 16 Nov. 1942, 11; *Winnipeg Free Press*, 18 Nov. 1942, 1; Boddington and Moir, "Friendly Invasion," 184-185; Bob Oliphant, "Working for the Yankee Dollar during the War," in *For King and Country: Alberta in the Second World War*, ed. K.W. Tingley (Edmonton: Provincial Museum of Alberta, 1995), 193.

52 *Edmonton Journal*, 24 Nov. 1942, 1, 5.

53 In 1942 these Natives suffered epidemics of measles and whooping cough, which often developed into pneumonia, meningitis, and severe influenza. That year, 15 died of such diseases among 150 Teslin band members. NAC, RG85, Northern Affairs records, vol. 1872, part 1, C.K. LeCapelain to R.A. Gibson, 17 July 1943.

54 For example, the 1941 census showed that in the Yukon there were 1.79 males for every female. Coates and Morrison, *Alaska Highway*, 72-77, 81-83, 86-101, 135-136, 144-146.

55 *Edmonton Journal*, 27 Nov. 1942, 12; *Maclean's*, 15 Nov. 1943, 1; *Saturday Night*, 13 Oct. 1945, 3.

56 *Edmonton Journal*, 4 Oct. 1943, 13; Morrison and Coates, *Alaska Highway*, 158-159, 167-169, 178-179.

57 Initial yearly maintenance costs were $700 per mile. Morrison and Coates, *Alaska Highway*, 206-229.

58 Granatstein and Morton, *Victory 1945*, 84; *Canada Year Book 1943-44*, 810; Jane Ursel, *Private Lives, Public Policy: 100 Years of State Intervention in the Family* (Toronto: Women's Press, 1992), 183.

59 *Canada Year Book, 1943-44*, 825; *Canada Year Book, 1948-49*, 96; *Canadian Affairs*, 1 Feb. 1944, 7.

60 *Saturday Night*, 30 Jan. 1943, 38.

61 *Industrial Canada*, Sept. 1944, 90.

62 Royal Canadian Mounted Police, *Annual Report*, 1945, 47.

63 *Canada Year Book, 1948-49*, xxv.

64 *Canada Year Book, 1939*, 888; NAC, RG44, National War Services records, vol. 21, file "Income Tax Exemptions," Memo, 7 Aug. 1940.

65 *Vancouver Sun*, 24 June 1940, 1; *Ottawa Journal*, 25 June 1940, 21.

66 *Canada Year Book, 1943-44*, 810.

67 *Ottawa Journal*, 24 June 1942, 15.

68 FN, vol. 4031, file 126W-1-26, WIB Survey No. 3, 30 Jan. 1943.

69 Metropolitan Toronto Reference Library, Baldwin Room, Broadside Collection.

70 Archives of Ontario (AO), MU2136, #4, Director of Public Information, *Canada's War Effort*, n.p.; *Toronto Star*, 26 June 1942, 6.

71 *CCL Journal*, Aug. 1942, 50.

72 *Saturday Night*, 26 Sept. 1942, 30.

73 Fifteen percent cited "overwork" and the "need for relaxation," 12 percent identified "sickness," 11 percent "laziness," 8 percent "too much pay," and 7 percent "parties [and] frivolity" the previous night. *Public Opinion Quarterly*, 1944, 143.

74 *Ottawa Journal*, 13 June 1944, 20.

75 *Canadian Unionist*, July-Aug. 1944, 28.

76 *Canada Year Book, 1948-49*, 578, 581, 817.

77 *Canadian Congress Journal*, July 1942, 43.

78 Victoria Day and Boxing Day became workdays. *Ottawa Journal*, 24 May 1944, 5.

79 *Canada Year Book, 1948-49*, 569.

80 *Canadian Unionist*, Sept. 1942, 82-83.

81 *Ottawa Citizen*, 31 Aug. 1940, 6; *Canadian Congress Journal*, Nov. 1944, 10; McInnis, *Harnessing Labour Confrontation*, 22.

82 For details on King's early record and ideas regarding social reform and labour relations see, for example, Paul Craven, *An Impartial Umpire: Industrial Relations and the Canadian State, 1900-1911* (Toronto: University of Toronto Press, 1980), and Ramsay Cook, *The Regenerators: Social Criticism in Late Victorian English Canada* (Toronto: University of Toronto Press, 1985).

83 Desmond Morton with Terry Copp, *Working People: An Illustrated History of the Canadian Labour Movement* (Ottawa: Deneau, 1980), 167, 171; Alvin Finkel and Margaret Conrad, *History of the Canadian Peoples*, 3rd ed. (Toronto: Addison-Wesley Longman, 2002), 308; McInnis, *Harnessing Labour Confrontation*, 37-38.

84 McInnis, *Harnessing Labour Confrontation*, 38-39.

85 Fractional bonuses were applied for each one-tenth rise over a full point increase in the CPI. McInnis, *Harnessing Labour Confrontation*, 33; Morton and Copp, *Working People*, 171, 174; Ursel, *Private Lives, Public Policy*, 186.

86 NAC, MG28 I103, Canadian Labour Congress papers, vol. 362, file "Trades and Labour Congress, 1941," Address by Tom Moore, 20 Oct. 1941.

87 *Canadian Congress Journal*, June 1942, 3; McInnis, *Harnessing Labour Confrontation*, 34.

88 Stacey, *Arms, Men and Government*, 403-404.

89 Earlier initiatives were far more timid. In June 1940 Ottawa had created the National Labour Supply Council to advise on maintaining adequate numbers of workers for industry. In October it established an Inter-Departmental Committee on Labour Coordination that brought together representatives from the Departments of National Defence, Munitions and Supply, and Agriculture to plan how to balance the manpower needs of the military and the home front.

90 *Canadian Congress Journal*, Nov. 1943, 9; Michael D. Stevenson, *Canada's Greatest Wartime Muddle: National Selective Service and the Mobilization of Human Resources during World War II* (Montreal and Kingston: McGill-Queen's University Press, 2001), 28-29.

91 *Canada Year Book, 1946*, 762.

92 Stevenson, *Canada's Greatest Wartime Muddle*, 30-31; Stacey, *Arms, Men and Government*, 408-409

93 Stevenson, *Canada's Greatest Wartime Muddle*, 175.

94 Ibid., 32.

95 Peter McInnis, "Teamwork for Harmony: Labour-Management Production Committees and the Postwar Settlement in Canada," *Canadian Historical Review* 77, 3 (1996): 317; Peter McInnis, "Planning Prosperity: Canadians Debate Postwar Reconstruction," in *Uncertain Horizons: Canadians and Their World in 1945*, ed. Greg Donaghy (Ottawa: Canadian Council for the History of the Second World War, 1996), 324-325, 329, 334.

96 McInnis, *Harnessing Labour Confrontation*, 22; WIB, vol. 12, file 8-2-1, John Grierson to Donald Gordon, 30 April 1943, Public Information and Industrial Morale, n.d., Report of

Survey of the Canadian Labour Press, 15 July 1943, and David Petegorsky to A.D. Dunton, 1 Dec. 1943.

97 Wartime Prices and Trade Board, *Annual Report, 1943; Canadian Unionist,* Dec. 1943, 156; *Toronto Telegram,* 7 Dec. 1943, 2; Ernest J. Spence, "Canadian Wartime Price Control, 1941 to 1947" (PhD diss., Northwestern University, 1947), 243-244; Christopher Waddell, "The Wartime Prices and Trade Board: Price Control in Canada during World War Two" (PhD diss., York University, 1981), 297.

98 WIB, vol. 8, file 2-16, Attitudes to Stabilization, Sept. 1943.

99 *Canadian Congress Journal,* May 1942, 19; Finkel and Conrad, *Canadian Peoples,* 308-309.

100 *Canada Year Book, 1945,* 789; *Canadian Unionist,* Sept. 1943, 108.

101 *Canadian Unionist,* Jan. 1943, 191, and April 1943, 270.

102 Brantford *Expositor,* 8 April 1943, 1, and 22 April 1943, 1; *Halifax Chronicle,* 27 July 1944, 1.

103 *Canadian Unionist,* May 1944, 303.

104 *Public Opinion Quarterly,* 1942, 160.

105 The *Column*'s retort read in part: "The town of Arvida was not planned or laid out from the air. Such a statement is absurd ... The streets of Arvida have been named after scientists and others who, through their laborious, painstaking undertakings, have been instrumental in isolating aluminum and making it into the useful and plentiful metal that it is today. Granted that there may be one or two Danish and German names among these scientists ... but the majority ... are French." *Ottawa Citizen,* 16 Jan. 1943, 17; Morton and Copp, *Working People,* 107; Ursel, *Private Lives, Public Policy,* 187.

106 Mitchell quoted in Brantford *Expositor,* 5 April 1943, 4.

107 McInnis, *Harnessing Labour Confrontation,* 41; Morton and Copp, *Working People,* 182-183; Ursel, *Private Lives, Public Policy,* 189. On Cohen's contributions to the labour movement and the development of Canadian labour legislation, see Laurel Sefton MacDowell, *Renegade Lawyer: The Life of J.L. Cohen* (Toronto: University of Toronto Press, 2001).

108 This attitude to Hepburn was largely due to his efforts during the late 1930s to drive the Congress of Industrial Organizations out of Ontario. See John T. Saywell, *Just Call Me Mitch: The Life of Mitchell F. Hepburn* (Toronto: University of Toronto Press, 1991), chapter 14.

109 Irving Abella, *Nationalism, Communism and Canadian Labour: The CIO, the Communist Party and the Canadian Congress of Labour, 1935-1956* (Toronto: University of Toronto Press, 1973), chapter 5; Morton and Copp, *Working People,* 182.

110 James Struthers, *No Fault of their Own: Unemployment and the Canadian Welfare State, 1914-1941* (Toronto: University of Toronto Press, 1983), chapter 6; Spence, "Canadian Wartime Price Control," 27.

111 See J.L. Granatstein, *The Ottawa Men: The Civil Service Mandarins, 1935-1957* (Toronto: University of Toronto Press, 1982), chapter 6, and Granatstein, *Canada's War: The Politics of the Mackenzie King Government, 1939-1945* (Toronto: Oxford University Press, 1975), chapter 7.

112 Michael D. Behiels, "The Bloc Populaire Canadien and the Origins of French-Canadian Neo-nationalism, 1942-1948," in *Quebec since 1800: Selected Readings,* ed. Michael D. Behiels (Toronto: Irwin Publishing, 2002), 455.

113 McInnis, *Harnessing Labour Confrontation,* 41; Laurel Sefton MacDowell, "The Formation of the Canadian Industrial Relations System during World War Two," *Labour/Le travail* 3 (1978): 175-196. Quotations from Granatstein and Morton, *Victory 1945,* 182-183; *Canadian Unionist,* Feb. 1944, 208.

114 *Canada Year Book, 1945,* 752-753.

115 Morton and Copp, *Working People,* 186; McInnis, "Planning Prosperity," 249-254; Abella, *Nationalism, Communism and Canadian Labour,* chapters 5-8.

116 *Canada Year Book, 1948-49,* 354; V.C. Fowke and G.E. Britnell, *Canadian Agriculture in War and Peace* (Palo Alto, CA: Stanford University Press, 1962), 385.

117 In several areas, the drop was more dramatic, such as by 16.5 percent in Deux Montagnes, Quebec, 15.8 percent in Prince Edward County, Ontario, and 17.8 percent in Saltspring and Islands, British Columbia. WIB, vol. 13, file 8-7-D, Ration Book Three as an Indication of Population Shifts, 1 Feb. 1944.

118 *Canada Year Book, 1948-49,* 139, 394-395.

119 In 1939-40, 331 million pounds of pork was exported from Canada to Britain when the contract called for 291 million pounds, and in 1944-45, Canada delivered 1.103 billion pounds when the contract called for 900 million pounds. *Canada Year Book, 1946,* 202-203; *Canada Year Book, 1948-49,* 365; *Family Herald and Weekly Star* (western edition), 17 April 1940, 24; Stevenson, *Canada's Greatest Wartime Muddle,* 136; Fowke and Britnell, *Canadian Agriculture,* 108, 257.

120 Fowke and Britnell, *Canadian Agriculture,* 97.

121 *Family Herald and Weekly Star* (eastern edition), 5 June 1940, 2.

122 Fowke and Britnell, *Canadian Agriculture,* 257; WLMK, vol. 274, Reel H-1493, 188618-9.

123 *Family Herald and Weekly Star* (eastern edition), 30 Sept. 1942, 16.

124 *Country Guide and Northwest Farmer,* Dec. 1940, 12; David C. Smith, "A Period of Waiting Over: The Prairies in 1939," in *A Country of Limitations: Canada and the World in 1939,* ed. Norman Hillmer et al. (Ottawa: Canadian Council for the History of the Second World War, 1996), 95-97; *Country Guide and Northwest Farmer,* June 1941, 31-32; Fowke and Britnell, *Canadian Agriculture,* 90, 108.

125 Fowke and Britnell, *Canadian Agriculture,* 92-95, 390; *Globe and Mail,* 4 Sept. 1939, 20; *Country Guide and Northwest Farmer,* Feb. 1941, 13.

126 *Country Guide and Northwest Farmer,* March 1943, 29; *Canadian Home Journal,* Feb. 1943, 62.

127 In the first year after the war, Canada and the United States exported some 750 million bushels of wheat. Had it not been for over 200 million bushels in storage in Canada at war's end, several items, including bread, might have been rationed. The price of wheat quickly passed the $1 per bushel mark and was stopped by a government ceiling of $1.55. Fowke and Britnell, *Canadian Agriculture,* 157; *Country Guide and Northwest Farmer,* July 1945, 27, Sept. 1945, 35, and Nov. 1945, 33.

128 *Family Herald and Weekly Star* (eastern edition), 3 April 1940, 2; *Country Guide and Northwest Farmer,* March 1941, 9.

129 *Country Guide and Northwest Farmer,* Feb. 1941, 13, April 1941, 5, and Sept. 1941, 12; *Family Herald and Weekly Star* (eastern edition), 31 Jan. 1940, 20.

130 *Calgary Herald,* 22 Nov. 1941, 22; *Country Guide and Northwest Farmer,* Nov. 1941, 12.

131 Fowke and Britnell, *Canadian Agriculture,* 113-115; *Country Guide and Northwest Farmer,* March 1944, 12.

132 *Country Guide and Northwest Farmer,* March 1940, 9; *Vancouver Sun,* 17 May 1940, 27.

133 *Country Guide and Northwest Farmer,* Feb. 1942, 29, March 1942, 7, and Jan. 1943, 18.

134 *Family Herald and Weekly Star* (eastern edition), 14 Oct. 1942, 4; *Industrial Canada,* Nov. 1942, 73; Fowke and Britnell, *Canadian Agriculture,* 186.

135 House of Commons, *Debates,* Address by W.R. Aylesworth, 18 Feb. 1943, 545-546; *Saturday Night,* 2 Dec. 1944, 11.

136 *Country Guide and Northwest Farmer,* July 1943, 3; *Toronto Star,* 2 Oct. 1943, 8.

137 *Family Herald and Weekly Star* (western edition), 16 May 1945, 4; *Country Guide and Northwest Farmer,* July 1942, 3.

138 *Edmonton Journal,* 24 Nov. 1942, 2.

139 Conscientious objectors working on farms were paid as if they were army privates, and POWs were paid fifty cents a day. Agricultural work for POWs was permitted under the Geneva Convention because it was deemed as not directly supporting their enemy's military effort. *Family Herald and Weekly Star* (western edition), 28 July 1943, 4, 11 Aug. 1943, 4, and 6 Sept. 1944, 4; *Country Guide and Northwest Farmer,* July 1942, 10, and Jan. 1943, 12; Brantford *Expositor,* 16 April 1943, 18; Martin Auger, "Prisoners of the Home Front: A Social Study of the German Internment Camps of Southern Quebec, 1940-1946" (MA thesis, University of Ottawa, 2000), 113-121.

140 Quotation from *Khaki* 1, 16: 3; Stacey, *Arms, Men and Government,* 588.

141 *Family Herald and Weekly Star* (western edition), 11 Aug. 1943, 4.

142 Stevenson, *Canada's Greatest Wartime Muddle,* 28.

143 For example, members of the Women's Land Brigade aged sixteen to forty-five undertook, for periods ranging from a few weeks to a few months, farm activities that included milking, feeding, and caring for livestock, stooking grain, picking and packing fruit, and hoeing vegetables. More modest programs included the Holiday Service Brigade, under which citizens gave up a portion of their vacation to earn a few extra dollars on farms. *Maclean's,* 15 Nov. 1942, 16; *Ottawa Journal,* 27 May 1942, 2; *Country Guide and Northwest Farmer,* June 1943, 47; *Family Herald and Weekly Star* (eastern edition), 9 June 1943, 16, 22-26, and 23 June 1943, 16; NAC, MG28 I198, Young Women's Christian Association papers, vol. 34, file "War Services – World War II," memo entitled "Farm Service Women – Women's Work on the Land," n.d.

144 Fowke and Britnell, *Canadian Agriculture,* 189; *Family Herald and Weekly Star* (western edition), 2 Sept. 1942, 4.

145 *Family Herald and Weekly Star* (eastern edition), 20 June 1945, 17.

146 In Quebec, King's delays in implementing conscription for overseas service overshadowed all other issues and produced for the Liberals an overwhelmingly favourable outcome across the province in both wartime federal elections: sixty-three of sixty-five seats in 1940 and fifty-three in 1945.

147 In Prince Edward Island the ridings chosen for the analysis were King's and Prince; in New Brunswick, Charlotte, Gloucester, Kent, Northumberland, and Restigouche-Madawaska; in Nova Scotia, Antigonish-Guysborough, Colchester-Hants, Cumberland, Digby-Annapolis-Kings, Inverness-Richmond, and Pictou; in Ontario, Brant, Bruce, Carleton, Durham, Essex East, Frontenac-Addington, Glengarry, Grey North, Halton, Hastings-Peterborough, Kent, Leeds, Muskoka-Ontario, Oxford, Peel, Prescott, Stormount, and Waterloo South; in Manitoba, Churchill, MacDonald, Neepawa, Provencher, and Selkirk; in Saskatchewan, Assiniboia, Humboldt, Maple Creek, Melville, and Moose Jaw; in Alberta, Athabaska, Bow River, Camrose, Jasper-Edson, and Macleod; and in British Columbia, Cariboo, Fraser Valley, Kootenay East, Kootenay West, Skeena, and Yale. The returns are taken from "History of the Federal Electoral Ridings since 1867," <http://parl.gc.ca/information>.

CHAPTER 3: THE WARTIME PRICES AND TRADE BOARD
AND THE ACCOMMODATION CRISIS

1 Manion quoted in *Ottawa Citizen,* 2 Sept. 1939, 1; King quoted in *Ottawa Citizen,* 9 Sept. 1939, 18.

2 *Saturday Night,* 16 Aug. 1941, 27, and 8 May 1943, 29. On British black markets, see Raynes Minns, *Bombers and Mash: The Domestic Front, 1939-1945* (London: Virago 1980).

3 National Archives of Canada (NAC), RG36-31, Wartime Information Board records (WIB), vol. 13, file 8-7a, Porter to Dunton, 12 Nov. 1943.

4 *Industrial Canada,* Nov. 1939, 47.

5 In Montreal, Steinberg's Wholesale Groceterias reported that during the first week of September 1939, its sugar sales, at 350,000 pounds, were five times the norm. William Weintraub, *City Unique: Montreal Days and Nights in the 1940s and 1950s* (Toronto: McClelland and Stewart, 1996), 29; *Ottawa Citizen,* 5 Sept. 1939, 23, and 9 Sept. 1939, 26; Patricia Roy, "British Columbia in 1939," in *A Country of Limitations: Canada and the World in 1939,* ed. Norman Hillmer et al. (Ottawa: Canadian Council for the History of the Second World War, 1996), 87.

6 *Winnipeg Free Press,* 2 Sept. 1939, 3, and 4 Sept. 1939, 3; *Halifax Chronicle,* 7 Sept. 1939, 3; *Globe and Mail,* 9 Sept. 1939, 13; Montreal *Gazette,* 11 Sept. 1939, 13.

7 Christopher Waddell, "The Wartime Prices and Trade Board: Price Control in Canada during World War Two" (PhD diss., York University, 1981), 50-51.

8 Wartime Prices and Trade Board, *Annual Report, 1943,* 75-76; *Canada Year Book, 1945,* 568.

9 Valerie J. Korinek, "Roughing it in Suburbia: Reading *Chatelaine* Magazine, 1950-1969" (PhD diss., University of Toronto, 1996), 50-51.

10 NAC, RG64, Wartime Prices and Trade Board records (WPTB), vol. 1537, *WPTB March of Time,* 13 Sept. 1943; *Vancouver Sun,* 30 Oct. 1942, 11.

11 Daniel Robinson, *The Measure of Democracy: Polling, Market Research and Public Life, 1930-1945* (Toronto: University of Toronto Press, 1999), 119-120; Pauline Jewitt, "The Wartime Prices and Trade Board" (PhD diss., Harvard University, 1950), 271; Waddell, "Wartime Prices and Trade Board," 541; J.L. Granatstein and Desmond Morton, *Victory 1945: Canadians from War to Peace* (Toronto: HarperCollins, 1995), 79; *Canadian Congress Journal,* Dec. 1942, 9.

12 Gordon quoted in Joseph Schull, *The Great Scot: A Biography of Donald Gordon* (Montreal and Kingston: McGill-Queen's University Press, 1979), 60; Brantford *Expositor,* 16 April 1943, 4; NAC, RG19, Ministry of Finance records (FN), vol. 4031, file 129W-1-26, WIB Survey, 20 Nov. 1943.

13 WIB, vol. 13, file 8-7-B, A.B. Dunton to John Grierson, 21 Sept. 1943.

14 Directorate of History and Heritage, Department of National Defence (DHH), 113.3R 4003, V1 (D1).

15 Magda Fahrni, "Under Reconstruction: The Family and the Public in Postwar Montréal, 1944-1949" (PhD diss., York University, 2001), 205, 360-361.

16 WPTB, vol. 1386, J.M. Goldenberg to Gordon, 26 Jan. 1943; Donald F. Ripley, *The Home Front: Wartime Life at Camp Aldershot and in Kentville, Nova Scotia* (Hantsport, NS: Lancelot Press, 1991), 77-78.

17 Peter Newman, *Flame of Power: The Story of Canada's Greatest Businessmen* (Toronto: McClelland and Stewart, 1959), 216-217.

18 Waddell, "Wartime Prices and Trade Board," 536.

19 Of cases that did proceed to the courts, some 95 percent ended in a guilty verdict. WPTB, *Annual Report, 1946,* 52-53.

20 WPTB, vol. 1386, file "Enforcement Branch," Memo on Enforcement, 9 July 1942.

21 *Canadian Business,* May 1943, 22; Waddell, "Wartime Prices and Trade Board," 728-730.

22 WPTB, vol. 1386, file "Enforcement Branch," F.A. McGregor to André Demers, 15 May 1943, and Memo from F.A. McGregor, 23 June 1943; City of Calgary Archives, RG26, City Clerk records (CCC), file 2295, City Clerk to Gordon, 13 Nov. 1944.

23 WPTB, vol. 1388, Enforcement Administration – Prosecutions, 31 Jan. 1946; WPTB, vol. 888, file 1-20-1, The Black Market Situation, 26 April 1946.

24 WPTB, vol. 690, file 23-30, W.C. Lackey to F.A. McGregor, 6 July 1943; FN, vol. 4031, file 129-W-1-26, WIB Survey, 22 May 1943.

25 WPTB, *Annual Report, 1945,* 55.

26 WPTB, vol. 690, file 23-30, Donald Gordon to Price and Supply Representatives in Brockville, Charlottetown, Edmonton, Halifax, London, Montreal, North Bay, Ottawa, Quebec City,

Regina, Toronto, Vancouver, and Winnipeg, 22 July 1943, and Donald Gordon to Marjorie B. Leslie, 29 July 1943.

27 John Bacher makes this argument in *Keeping to the Marketplace: The Evolution of Canadian Housing Policy* (Montreal and Kingston: McGill-Queen's University Press, 1993).

28 NAC, MG28 I10, Canadian Council on Social Development papers (CCSD), vol. 54, file 1942-46, Panel Discussion on Housing, Eastern Ontario Branch, Canadian Association of Social Workers, 7 May 1943; John T. Saywell, *Housing Canadians: Essays on the History of Residential Construction in Canada* (Ottawa: Economic Council of Canada, 1975), 170-171.

29 John Bacher, "W.C. Clark and the Politics of Canadian Housing Policy, 1935-1952," *Urban History Review/Revue d'histoire urbaine* 17, 1 (1988): 5.

30 Bacher, *Keeping to the Marketplace*, 87, 90, 92, 113; J. David Hulchanski, "The 1935 Dominion Housing Act: Setting the Stage for a Permanent Federal Presence in Canada's Housing Sector," *Urban History Review/Revue d'histoire urbaine* 15, 1 (1986): 20-34.

31 Bacher, *Keeping to the Marketplace*, 163; NAC, MG30 C181, Robert England papers, vol. 3, file 21, *Public Affairs*, winter 1944, 101-102.

32 Between 1939 and 1944, the number of civilian construction workers in Canada – most of whom worked on military projects – dropped from 126,000 to 109,000. E.L.M. Burns, *Manpower in the Canadian Army, 1939-1945* (Toronto: Clarke, Irwin, 1956), 156; Bacher, *Keeping to the Marketplace*, 108; *Saturday Night*, 6 Sept. 1941, 26; *Canada Year Book, 1948-49*, 162.

33 *Canadian Affairs*, 15 Jan. 1944, 2; *Ottawa Journal*, 8 March 1941, 8; James Frank Edward White, "Conscripted City: Halifax and the Second World War" (PhD diss., McMaster University, 1995), 166.

34 NAC, MG28 I198, Young Women's Christian Association papers, vol. 34, file "War Services – Room Registry," *Handbook, 1941,* n.p., and file "War Services – A History."

35 *Ottawa Journal*, 7 Nov. 1942, 1; *Vancouver Sun*, 17 Oct. 1942, 1.

36 Carmen Miller, "The 1940s: War and Rehabilitation," in *The Atlantic Provinces in Confederation,* ed. E.R. Forbes and D.A. Muise (Toronto: University of Toronto Press, 1993), 316; James White, "Conscripted City," 105, 117; *Maclean's*, 1 Sept. 1941, 40.

37 *Maclean's*, 15 July 1943, 42; NAC, RG2, Privy Council records (PC), vol. 16, E.L. Cousins to C.D. Howe, 17 July 1944; James White, "Conscripted City," 108.

38 Barry Broadfoot, *Six War Years: Memories of Canadians at Home and Abroad* (Toronto: Doubleday, 1974), 279; Patricia Roy, "British Columbia," 140; Jill Wade, "'A Palace for the Public': Housing Reform and the 1946 Occupation of the Old Hotel Vancouver," *BC Studies,* 69-70 (1986): 293-294.

39 NAC, MG28 I25, National Council of Women of Canada papers, vol. 84, file "Rehabilitation," Address by Mrs. M. Thacker, Jan. 1944; *Canada Year Book, 1948-49,* 144-145; Glenbow Institute, MG 5841, Calgary Local Council of Women, *Year Book, 1943,* 37.

40 City of Edmonton Archives, City Council records (CCE), file 29, Memorandum in Support of Our Application for Increased Quotas for Goods for Edmonton and Northern Alberta, Submitted by the Wholesale and Retail Divisions, Edmonton Chamber of Commerce, 7 April 1943; Donald Grant Wetherall and Irene R.A. Kmet, *Homes in Alberta: Building, Trends, and Design, 1870-1967* (Edmonton: University of Alberta Press, 1991), 179; Steven Boddington and Sean Moir, "'The Friendly Invasion': The American Presence in Edmonton," in *For King and Country: Alberta in the Second World War,* ed. K.W. Tingley (Edmonton: Provincial Museum of Alberta, 1995), 182.

41 Michael D. Behiels, "The Bloc Populaire Canadien and the Origins of French-Canadian Neo-nationalism, 1942-1948," in *Quebec since 1800: Selected Readings,* ed. Michael D. Behiels (Toronto: Irwin Publishing, 2002), 456; *Maclean's*, 15 Dec. 1940, 37; WIB, vol. 13, file 8-7-D, Ration Book Three as an Indication of Population Shifts, 1 Feb. 1944.

42 NAC, MG28 I64, Canadian Association of Social Workers papers, vol. 17, file 27, Study of the Dwellings of 298 Families Prepared by the Canada Committee of the Montreal Branch of the Canadian Association of Social Workers, March 1947; *Canadian Welfare*, Oct. 1945, 11.

43 James T. Lemon, *Toronto: An Illustrated History* (Toronto: James Lorimer, 1985), 198; *Toronto Star*, 9 Feb. 1941, 5, 1 June 1942, 18, and 24 June 1942, 21.

44 *Canadian Welfare*, May 1941, 29-31.

45 *Ottawa Journal*, 13 June 1942, 2, and 30 July 1942, 10.

46 *Maclean's*, 1 June 1943, 37.

47 *Vancouver Sun*, 19 Sept. 1942, 19; *Chatelaine*, Dec. 1942, 62.

48 NAC, MG26 J4, William Lyon Mackenzie King papers (WLMK), vol. 280, Reel H-1496, 192440.

49 *Globe and Mail*, 15 Sept. 1944, 15.

50 Bacher, *Keeping to the Marketplace*, 129.

51 *Industrial Canada*, May 1942, 82.

52 WIB, vol. 17, file 9-6-2-5, postwar planning information, 15 Sept. 1945; City of Vancouver Archives (CVA), MG28(A)1, City Clerk records (CCV), file "Wartime Housing for Returned Men," Memo, Vancouver Housing, 21 July 1944.

53 CCE, file 6, W.E. Donovan to Mayor Fry, 5 March 1943.

54 Bacher, "W.C. Clark," 9; NAC, MG27 III B5, Ian Mackenzie papers (IM), vol. 21, file 41-18, J.L. Ilsley to Mayor Morrison (Hamilton), 16 Sept. 1941; Jill Wade, "Wartime Housing Limited, 1941-1947: Canadian Housing Policy at the Crossroads," *Urban History Review/Revue d'histoire urbaine* 15, 1 (1986): 43.

55 CCE, file 2, V.T. Goggin to T.M. Bryson, 10 Nov. 1942; CCE, file 4, Report of City Commissioner, 23 Jan. 1943; CCE, file 5, Fry to W.E. Donovan, 25 Jan. 1943; James White, "Conscripted City," 106-107, 114, 117; CCV, file "Housing 1943," Memo re. Housing Accommodation, n.d.

56 *Ottawa Journal*, 3 March 1941, 3; City of Ottawa Archives (COA), RG20/2, Board of Control records (BOC), vol. 40, file "Gasoline Rationing and Rent Control," Joseph Pigott to Secretary of Board of Control, 8 Dec. 1941.

57 After three years of lobbying led by women's groups, organized labour, and the federal Civil Servants' Association – and significant local press coverage in 1942 of the US government's decision to construct twelve dormitories for female civil servants in Washington – Canada's federal government finally agreed in 1943 to build a dormitory capable of housing 360 of its single female employees. Rent with board was $8 a week per person in a shared room, and $9.50 per week for one of the few private rooms, rates that drew considerable criticism for claiming more than half the salary of a Grade 1 clerk. However, given the lack of alternatives, the facility soon had a waiting list more than double its capacity. *Ottawa Journal*, 28 July 1942, 1 and 21 Jan. 1943, 11.

58 *Maclean's*, 15 July 1943, 42; *Ottawa Journal*, 25 Sept. 1942, 1.

59 *Ottawa Citizen*, 27 March 1943, 1; Waddell, "Wartime Prices and Trade Board," 64-65; CCSD, vol. 82, file 594-2, clipping from *Family Life Bulletin*, #1, n.d., n.p.

60 *Montreal Star*, 2 Sept. 1943, 27; CCSD, vol. 135, file 100, "Youth and Family Life," n.d.

61 WLMK, vol. 372, file W-310, J.W. Archer to King, 20 Jan. 1945; *Globe and Mail*, 29 March 1944, 4; CCE, file 35, M. Mills to Mayor Fry, 26 May 1944.

62 See, for example, *Vancouver Sun*, 8 Oct. 1942, 16.

63 WLMK, vol. 372, file W-130-1, Woodery to King, 16 Jan. 1943; *Toronto Star*, 1 Oct. 1943, 32; *Canadian Affairs*, 15 Jan. 1944, 1.

64 *Maclean's*, 1 Nov. 1943, 60, and 15 Nov. 1943, 57; Margaret Moffatt, interview by author, Dunrobin, ON, 22 Feb. 1999; quotation from *Ottawa Citizen*, 29 Oct. 1943, 15.

65 Jewitt, "Wartime Prices and Trade Board," 13.

66 Bacher, *Keeping to the Marketplace,* 127-129; WLMK, vol. 1538, file "Pamphlets," Rental and Housing Report, 31 March 1943.

67 For example, in 1942 the Ottawa government slightly reduced property taxes largely because the virtual disappearance of new infrastructure projects enabled it to run a budget surplus of $192,830. *Ottawa Citizen,* 13 March 1943, 14.

68 WIB, vol. 17, file 9-6-2-5, Income Levels and Low Rental Housing, n.d.

69 *Financial Post,* 2 Nov. 1940, 8; *Canadian Affairs,* 15 Jan. 1944, 2; WLMK, vol. 372, file W-13, Memo from Halifax Board of Trade, 12 May 1943.

70 WLMK, vol. 372, file W-310-1, George Lewis to King, 21 Jan. 1943; WPTB, vol. 29, "Canadian Rental and Eviction Control," n.d.

71 *Canada Year Book, 1947,* 929.

72 CCE, file 30, Mrs. Russell Sheppard to Mayor Fry, 12 May 1943; WLMK, vol. 372, file W-310-1, Gladys Thomas to King, 5 April 1944.

73 *Calgary Herald,* 15 Feb. 1941, 11.

74 WPTB, vol. 29, "Canadian Rental and Eviction Control," n.d.; CCE, file 33, clipping from *Edmonton Journal,* 27 March 1944, n.p.

75 WLMK, vol. 372, file W-310, Albert Urquhart to King, 28 Jan. 1944.

76 CCE, file 12, A.M. Arnold to Mayor Fry, 15 May 1943.

77 *Maclean's,* 15 Dec. 1940, 10.

78 CVA, RG17, Department of Social Services records (DSS), F-1, file 17, Report on Condition of Houses, n.d.

79 CCE, file 33, clipping from *Edmonton Journal,* 27 March 1944, n.p.; Broadfoot, *Six War Years,* 191.

80 Carmen Desbarats, interview by author, Ottawa, 2 March 1999.

81 *Maclean's,* 15 May 1943, 59-60; *Saturday Night,* 15 Dec. 1943, 15; *La Presse,* 14 April 1944, 3.

82 *Saturday Night,* 15 Dec. 1945, 11.

83 WPTB, vol. 29, "Canadian Rental and Eviction Control," n.d.; WPTB, vol. 1538, file "Pamphlets," Rental and Housing Report, 31 Dec. 1943.

84 CCSD, vol. 54, file 1948-49, unsigned and undated article entitled "Private Property Means Personal Freedom."

85 WLMK, vol. 372, file W-310-1, Albert Urquhart to King, 28 Jan. 1944.

86 The districts were St. Lawrence and St. George, Rosemount, Mercier, Notre Dame de Grace, Cartier, Parl Extension, and North End. WLMK, vol. 372, file W-310-1, W.R. Labow to King, 9 and 10 Feb. 1944.

87 WPTB, vol. 29, "Canadian Rental and Eviction Control," n.d.; *New Advance,* Oct. 1944, 21; Bacher, *Keeping to the Marketplace,* 159, 174.

88 Bacher, *Keeping to the Marketplace,* 166-169; Bacher, "W.C. Clark," 9; Saywell, *Housing Canadians,* 188; WIB, vol. 17, file 9-6-2-5, Post-War Planning Information, 15 Sept. 1945; CCE, file 55, Resolution on the Housing Shortage Adopted at a Public Meeting Held in Winnipeg, 25 April 1946.

89 Indeed, though veterans went to the front of the queue at Wartime Housing, more than twice as many opted for subsidized loans to become part-time farmers on one-half to two-acre lots just outside cities under the 1942 Veterans Land Act (VLA). According to Richard Harris and Tricia Shulist, this was largely because under the VLA veterans received priority for building materials and, many thought, a better chance of actually obtaining a place to live. See "Canada's Reluctant Housing Program: The Veterans Land Act, 1942-1975," *Canadian Historical Review* 82, 2 (2001): 253-282; Jill Wade, "Wartime Housing," 47.

90 For example, maximum financing was set at 86 percent for a $5,000 house, and at 83 percent for a $6,000 house. The NHA also stipulated that the "maximum loan ... is $5,000 for

a two-bedroom house, $5,700 for a three-bedroom house, and $6,400 for houses with four or more bedrooms." CCC, file 2390, clipping from *Calgary Albertan,* 3 April 1945, n.p.

91 John Miron, *Housing in Postwar Canada: Demographic Change, Household Formation and Household Demand* (Montreal and Kingston: McGill-Queen's University Press, 1988), 243.

92 IM, vol. 64, file 527-130, Submission by the National House Builders' Association to King, n.d.; Montreal *Gazette,* 8 June 1945, 9; *Industrial Canada,* Oct. 1945, 89.

93 CCE, file 55, Resolution on the Housing Shortage Adopted at a Public Meeting Held in Winnipeg, 25 April 1946.

94 *Public Opinion Quarterly,* 1945, 527.

95 *Public Opinion Quarterly,* 1944, 456; J.L. Granatstein and Peter Neary, eds., *The Veterans Charter and Post-War Canada* (Montreal and Kingston: McGill-Queen's University Press, 1998), 239.

96 *Ottawa Citizen,* 17 Jan. 1945, 1; *Ottawa Citizen,* 13 Nov. 1945, 1; FN, vol. 4031, file 129-W-1-23, *Consumer Facts,* Jan. 1945.

97 A permit system was not applied to Calgary even though its vacancy rate of 0.4 percent was lower than Toronto's, where permits were instituted, largely because this control was not desired by the Calgary or the Alberta government. *Canada Year Book, 1946,* 121.

98 For example, the permit order for Toronto also applied to Long Branch, Mimico, New Toronto, Islington, Lambton Mills, Clairville, Newtonbrook, Weston, Willowdale, Lansing, North York, Forest Hill, Leaside, East York, Scarborough, and Etobicoke. *Toronto Star,* 22 Feb. 1945, 2; CVA, 80-22, shelf 19, box 4, Broadside.

99 *Vancouver Sun,* 31 Aug. 1945, 5; WPTB, vol. 29, "Canadian Rental and Eviction Control," n.d.; WPTB, vol. 1538, file "Pamphlets," Rental and Housing Report, 1 Feb. 1947.

100 Fahrni, "Under Reconstruction," 170; IM, vol. 67, file 527-148, Department of Veterans Affairs, *Bulletin,* No. 5, 28 March 1945.

101 WPTB, vol. 29, "Canadian Rental and Eviction Control," n.d.

102 Respondents were allowed to cite more than one priority. Nationally, 37 percent also identified the need for more rural electrification, 33 percent more roads, 30 percent more parks and community centres, and 25 percent more reforestation. *Canadian Congress Journal,* July 1945, 21; FN, vol. 4031, file 129-W-1-18, WIB Survey, No. 61, 21 April 1945.

103 *Ottawa Citizen,* 12 June 1945, 20; WPTB, vol. 2349, file 22-5-17, G.L. McGee to Sheldon Ross, 28 July 1945; WPTB, vol. 1566, *Weekly Bulletin,* No. 3, 3-10 Dec. 1945.

104 WIB, vol. 17, file 9-6-2-5, Postwar Planning Information, 15 Sept. 1945; *Ottawa Citizen,* 3 Aug. 1945, 17.

105 *Saturday Night,* 4 Aug. 1945, 15; *Canadian Forum,* Feb. 1946, 266-267; FN, vol. 4031, WIB Survey on Re-establishment Trends, n.d.

106 NAC, MG30 I311, Montreal Soldiers' Wives' League papers, vol. 5, file 4, clipping from Montreal *Gazette,* 5 Oct. 1945, n.p.; COA, Proceedings of the Board of Control, 1945, 7.

107 CCC, file 2390, City Commissioner to Chairman of City Housing Committee, 25 May 1945, J. Miller to Wartime Housing Ltd., 26 May 1946.

108 WIB, vol. 14, file 8-14-6, Attitudes of Army Personnel Recently Returned from Overseas, 20 Nov. 1944.

109 IM, vol. 2, file 33, Unidentified 1946 newspaper clipping entitled "Rent Inquiry Promised Here."

110 *Ottawa Citizen,* 16 July 1945, 18.

111 *Calgary Herald,* 4 Feb. 1941, 4; IM, vol. 21, file 41-18, Joint petition from Canadian Corps Association, Canadian Legion, War Amps, and Army and Navy League to King, 9 June 1945; IM, vol. 21, file 41-110, pt. 2, clipping from *Vancouver Sun,* 8 March 1946, n.p.; PC, Cabinet Conclusions, vol. 2367, 13 Feb. 1946; Jill Wade, "Palace for the Public," 308-10.

112 Serge Marc Durflinger, "City at War: The Effects of the Second World War on Verdun, Québec" (PhD diss., McGill University, 1998), 336-338.

113 Fahrni, "Under Reconstruction," 281-283.

114 COA, Mayor Stanley Lewis Scrapbooks, clipping from *Ottawa Citizen,* 18 Oct. 1946, n.p.; BOC, vol. 40, file "Housing – Lansdowne Park," T.A. Lomer to C.E. Pearce, 16 Sept. 1947, C.G. Burnett to Mayor Lewis, 18 Sept. 1947, and A.B. Ullett to C.E. Pearce, 8 Oct. 1947.

115 Passed soon after the Liberals were re-elected in June 1945, the legislation authorized the federal government – ultimately until 15 May 1947 – to "make from time to time such orders and regulations, as may be, by reason of the continued existence of the national emergency arising out of the war against Germany and Japan, deemed necessary or advisable." Ernest J. Spence, "Canadian Wartime Price Control, 1941 to 1947" (PhD diss., Northwestern University, 1947), 13.

116 CCSD, vol. 54, file 1948-49, C.W.B., 28 Oct. 1948, 17-18.

117 The last remnants of federal rent control ended in 1951. Yet that year the national census still defined 22.58 percent of tenant households in Montreal, for example, as "crowded." Fahrni, "Under Reconstruction," 68; *Canada Year Book, 1948-49,* 948; WPTB, vol. 29, "Canadian Rental and Eviction Control," n.d.; WPTB, vol. 1538, file "Pamphlets," Rental Control, n.d.; Wetherall and Kmet, *Homes in Alberta,* 232.

118 Eric Adams, Pearl Ing, Janet Ortved, and Mary Jane Park, *Government Intervention in Housing Markets: An Overview,* Research Study No. 29 (Toronto: Ontario Commission of Inquiry into Residential Tenancies, 1986), 10-11.

119 St. Laurent quoted in Michael McMahon, *Metro's Housing Company: The First 35 Years* (Toronto: Metropolitan Toronto Housing Company, 1990), 11.

120 McMahon, *Metro's Housing Company,* 11, 251; John Bacher, "Canadian Housing Policy in Perspective," *Urban History Review/Revue d'histoire urbaine* 15, 1 (1986): 3-4, 8; Bacher, *Keeping to the Marketplace,* 181, 185; Albert Rose, *Canada's Housing Policies (1935-1980)* (Toronto: Butterworths, 1980), 30-31.

121 Between 1941 and 1951, the population of North York grew from 22,908 to 85,897, Scarborough from 24,303 to 56,292, Burnaby from 30,328 to 58,376 and Coquitlam from 7,949 to 15,697. Lemon, *Toronto,* 194; Patricia Roy, *Vancouver: An Illustrated History* (Toronto: James Lorimer, 1980), 168.

122 *Canada Year Book, 1950,* 638; Central Mortgage and Housing Corporation, *Annual Report, 1948,* 54; *Ottawa Citizen,* 10 Oct. 1999, A9.

123 Cited in NAC, RG38, Department of Veterans Affairs records, vol. 362, file 1946-62, clipping from Brantford *Expositor,* 12 Nov. 1955, n.p.

124 Miron, *Housing in Postwar Canada,* 168-169, 199. See also R. Harris and C.G. Pratt, "The Meaning of Home, Homeownership, and Public Policy," in *The Changing Social Geography of Canadian Cities,* ed. Larry S. Bourne and David F. Ley (Montreal and Kingston: McGill-Queen's University Press, 1993), 293.

125 During this period, all occupational categories in Hamilton demonstrated impressive gains in home ownership. Among professionals and proprietors it rose from 40.9 to 63.0 percent; among white-collar workers from 37.2 to 54.0 percent; and among skilled and semi-skilled labourers from 34.4 to 58.8 percent. Michael Doucet and John Weaver, *Housing the North American City* (Montreal and Kingston: McGill-Queen's University Press, 1991), 329.

126 University of Alberta Data Library, SN 265, CIPO survey no. 253, July 1953.

CHAPTER 4: BLACK MARKET PROFITEERING

1 *Saturday Night,* 11 March 1943, 19; *Ottawa Citizen,* 25 Oct. 1943, 4.

2 *Ottawa Journal,* 5 July 1944, 20.

3 *Canadian Business,* July 1943, 38.

4 *Industrial Canada,* June 1942, 114; July 1942, 239, 283, 291; Sept. 1942, 74; Nov. 1942, 73; and Dec. 1942, 77.

5 Joy Parr, *Domestic Goods: The Material, the Moral and the Economic in the Postwar Years* (Toronto: University of Toronto Press, 1999), 24-25, 66; *Canada Year Book, 1943-44,* 522.

6 *Ottawa Journal,* 13 May 1944, 24; Wartime Prices and Trade Board (WPTB), *Annual Report, 1944,* 41.

7 *Vancouver Sun,* 4 Dec. 1944, 16.

8 *Ottawa Journal,* 17 May 1944, 18.

9 *Ottawa Journal,* 10 Sept. 1942, 2; *Ottawa Citizen,* 17 Aug. 1943, 14, and 14 Dec. 1943, 18; *Industrial Canada,* Sept. 1942, 70.

10 *Industrial Canada,* Oct. 1942, 76; WPTB, *Annual Report, 1943,* 40.

11 The scheme also specified a 20 percent tax on the portion of the purchase price between $700 and $900 and 40 percent on the next $300. *Ottawa Citizen,* 11 Sept. 1940, 15; *Ottawa Journal,* 25 June 1940, 21.

12 *Ottawa Journal,* 5 Sept. 1941, 1; Nancy Gabin, *Feminism in the Labour Movement: Women and the United Auto Workers, 1935-1975* (Ithaca, NY: Cornell University Press, 1990), 41; K.A.H. Buckley and M.C. Urquhart, *Historical Statistics of Canada* (Toronto: Macmillan, 1965), 480.

13 *Ottawa Journal,* 6 Aug. 1941, 20.

14 Buckley and Urquhart, *Historical Statistics of Canada,* 484; *Canada Year Book, 1943-44,* 522.

15 Barry Broadfoot, *Six War Years: Memories of Canadians at Home and Abroad* (Toronto: Doubleday, 1974), 193.

16 *Canada Year Book, 1946,* 1004-1111; *Toronto Star,* 10 Feb. 1945, 20.

17 *Saturday Night,* 10 Oct. 1942, 20; *Ottawa Journal,* 28 Aug. 1944, 7; National Archives of Canada (NAC), MG26 J4, William Lyon Mackenzie King papers (WLMK), vol. 372, file W-10, Ross Slute to King, 6 March 1945.

18 Cited in *Ottawa Journal,* 27 Oct. 1944, 17.

19 *La Presse,* 6 May 1944, 3; quotation from *Maclean's,* 1 Nov. 1944, 7.

20 *Ottawa Citizen,* 29 Aug. 1940, 11; *Edmonton Journal,* 6 Nov. 1942, 4.

21 *Industrial Canada,* May 1942, 69; *Industrial Canada,* June 1942, 115. During the same period the number of tires produced for the military and essential civilian services, such as passenger buses, increased from 250,477 to 1,321,079. Starting in 1942, synthetic rubber became available from the Sarnia-based Crown corporation Polymer. However, it was not designated for civilian use and was ill-suited for tires in any case, since cars using this product were not to travel faster than thirty-five miles per hour. *Commercial Intelligence Journal,* no. 2138, 20 Jan. 1945, 56-57.

22 For example, the only people or vehicles entitled to apply for new tires and inner tubes were physicians, visiting nurses, firefighters, police, ambulances, garbage trucks, ice delivery trucks, postal trucks, armoured cars, public utility vehicles, moving trucks, fuel trucks, school buses, farm tractors and combines, public transportation vehicles, and clergy and rabbis who served two or more parishes at least three miles apart. *Canada Year Book, 1943-44,* 522-523; Mary Jane Lennon and Syd Charendoff, *On the Homefront: A Scrapbook of Canadian World War Two Memorabilia* (Erin, ON: Boston Mills Press, 1981), 46-47.

23 *Edmonton Journal,* 28 July 1942, 18.

24 *Le Droit,* 30 Jan. 1942, 3; *Saturday Night,* 3 Oct. 1942, 9; *Ottawa Citizen,* 20 May 1943, 17.

25 The actual numbers were 292,904 in 1939 and 399,957 in 1942. The next year, the number of traffic tickets issued dropped to 270,021, as people adjusted to the new rules and police eased off somewhat after a strong public outcry. *Canada Year Book, 1948-49,* 284.

26 NAC, RG64, Wartime Prices and Trade Board records (WPTB), vol. 888, file 1-20-1, "The Black Market Situation," 26 April 1946.

27 WPTB, vol. 690, file 23-30, Rev. A. McTaggart to Donald Gordon, 21 Aug. 1944; Montreal *Gazette*, 15 May 1942, 23.

28 City of Vancouver Archives (CVA), RG74, Police Commission records (VPC), D7, Statistical Clerk to D. Mackay, 10 Nov. 1942; *Vancouver Sun*, 1 Dec. 1942, 1.

29 *Toronto Star*, 5 June 1942, 7, and 6 Oct. 1943, 32; *Vancouver Sun*, 10 Sept. 1942, 13.

30 *Ottawa Journal*, 30 June 1944, 1; RCMP, *Annual Report, 1945*, 29.

31 WPTB, vol. 888, file 1-20-1, "The Black Market Situation," 26 April 1946.

32 Michael A. Hennessy, "The Industrial Front: The Scale and Scope of Canadian Industrial Mobilization during the Second World War," in *Forging a Nation: Perspectives on the Canadian Military Experience*, ed. Bernd Horn (St. Catharines, ON: Vanwell Publishing, 2002), 151.

33 *Vancouver Sun*, 17 Jan. 1941, 6, and 1 May 1941, 16; *Ottawa Journal*, 26 July 1941, 2; *Canada Year Book, 1942*, 282.

34 Drivers were asked to halve their consumption. *Ottawa Citizen*, 30 June 1941, 8.

35 *Ottawa Journal*, 6 Aug. 1941, 6, and 3 Oct. 1941, 26.

36 Nonessential drivers were designated Category A. People in Category B, who were entitled to 300 gallons per year, included clergy, rural schoolteachers, undertakers, ARP wardens, and auxiliary firemen. Those in Category C, who were entitled to 1,000 gallons, consisted of doctors, rural veterinarians, taxi drivers, and newspaper reporters. Category D drivers, who received 1,500 gallons, included Red Cross nurses, social workers, and government auditors and inspectors. Category E, the highest at 2,500 gallons, included rural mail carriers, commercial travellers, and diplomats. *Canadian Business*, March 1942, 7, 9; CVA, MS241, Kenneth Caple papers, example of gasoline ration book.

37 *Maclean's*, 15 July 1943, 48.

38 *Ottawa Journal*, 2 Feb. 1942, 22; *Vancouver Sun*, 21 Oct. 1942, 17.

39 *Ottawa Journal*, 18 Sept. 1942, 8, and 5 April 1944, 19.

40 Craig family papers, private collection held by Mary Tasker, Toronto, G. Craig to J. Craig, 2 April 1942.

41 In 1943, the WPTB limited the scope of store delivery service to a thirty-five-mile radius. *Canada Year Book, 1943-44*, 526; *Edmonton Journal*, 25 July 1942, 2; Montreal *Gazette*, 15 May 1942, 21.

42 In the Prairies this ruling reduced intercity bus service by 25 percent overall by July 1942. *Edmonton Journal*, 30 July 1942, 13; Brantford *Expositor*, 21 April 1943, 14.

43 For example, in western Quebec the Provincial Transport Company took some 10,000 people to war jobs daily. *Saturday Night*, 13 Feb. 1943, 18.

44 *Saturday Night*, 1 Aug. 1942, 11; *Canadian Congress Journal*, Aug. 1942, 31; *Edmonton Journal*, 13 Nov. 1942, 4.

45 Between 1939 and 1944 the number of people transported per year by rail nearly tripled from 20,482,296 to 60,335,950. *Canada Year Book, 1948-49*, 689.

46 *Ottawa Journal*, 22 Dec. 1944, 1.

47 Jonathan F. Vance, *High Flight: Aviation and the Canadian Imagination* (Toronto: Penguin, 2002), 253-254; Buckley and Urquhart, *Historical Statistics*, 551.

48 City of Ottawa Archives, RG20/2, Board of Control records, vol. 43, file "OER," Secretary of Board of Control to City Solicitor, 19 Sept. 1946.

49 *Toronto Star*, 9 Sept. 1942, 7; *Edmonton Journal*, 24 Nov. 1942, 4; *Vancouver Sun*, 1 Oct. 1942, 10, and 14 Oct. 1942, 1; *Halifax Chronicle*, 3 Nov. 1942, 1.

50 See Donald Davis and Barbara Lorenzkowski, "A Platform for Gender Tensions: Women Working and Riding on Canadian Urban Public Transit in the 1940s," *Canadian Historical Review* 79, 3 (1998): 431-465.

51 *Ottawa Journal*, 29 March 1944, 6.

52 *Ottawa Journal*, 21 March 1942, 19; WPTB, vol. 690, file 23-30, Young to Gordon, 2 Aug. 1943; NAC, RG36-31, Wartime Information Board records (WIB), vol. 13, file 8-5-2, Current Rumour Clinic, 17 July 1943.

53 *Vancouver Sun*, 6 Nov. 1942, 1; *Winnipeg Free Press*, 16 Nov. 1942, 4.

54 *Ottawa Citizen*, 21 Dec. 1943, 12; *Ottawa Journal*, 13 May 1942, 24, and 16 Dec. 1942, 4; City of Calgary Archives, RG26, City Clerk records, file 2228, Rules on Taxicabs, 17 Nov. 1942; file "Taxicab Matters," Norman Howard to I. Neale, 13 March 1943.

55 *La Presse*, 17 April 1944, 3; *Globe and Mail*, 15 Sept. 1944, 3.

56 Broadfoot, *Six War Years*, 195.

57 Brantford *Expositor*, 21 Sept. 1943, 11.

58 *Maclean's*, 15 Sept. 1943, 15.

59 City of Edmonton Archives (CE), RG11, City Clerk records, Class 66, file 56, F. Orton to Mayor Fry, 11 Feb. 1943.

60 *Maclean's*, 15 Sept. 1943, 15; *Vancouver Sun*, 17 Aug. 1942, 3.

61 *Saturday Night*, 2 Oct. 1942, 6; *Canada Year Book, 1948-49*, 474; WPTB, *Annual Report, 1943*, 54.

62 *Canada Year Book, 1942*, 281.

63 *Canada Year Book, 1948-49*, 508; *Toronto Star*, 10 Sept. 1942, 1; Serge Marc Durflinger, "City at War: The Effects of the Second World War on Verdun, Québec" (PhD diss., McGill University, 1998), 308.

64 In late 1944 Canada's power controller, who was attached to Munitions and Supply, admitted that the daylight saving program had saved little energy. NAC, RG2, Privy Council records (PC), vol. 2636, Cabinet Conclusions, 17 Oct. 1944; *Ottawa Journal*, 19 Sept. 1942, 7; Jean McNiven, interview by author, Ottawa, 15 Oct. 1999.

65 PC, vol. 13, Cabinet War Committee, 5 May 1943; WPTB, *Annual Report, 1943*, 54; Michael Stevenson, "Conscripting Coal: The Regulation of the Coal Labour Force during the Second World War," *Acadiensis* 29, 2 (2000): 60-61; Ernest Forbes, "Consolidating Disparity: The Maritimes and the Industrialization of Canada during the Second World War," in *Challenging the Regional Stereotype: Essays on the 20th Century Maritimes*, ed. Ernest Forbes (Fredericton: Acadiensis Press, 1989), 187.

66 NAC, RG19, Ministry of Finance records (FN), vol. 4031, file 129-W-1-23, *Consumer Facts*, Aug. 1945.

67 *Edmonton Journal*, 19 Nov. 1942, 1; PC, vol. 13, Cabinet War Committee, 24 June 1943.

68 PC, vol. 13, Cabinet War Committee, 5 May 1943; Stevenson, "Conscripting Coal," 70-72; C.P. Stacey, *Arms, Men and Government: The War Policies of Canada, 1939-1945* (Ottawa: Department of National Defence, 1970), 411-412.

69 *Saturday Night*, 25 Sept. 1943, 40, and 30 Oct. 1943, 32.

70 *Saturday Night*, 2 Jan. 1943, 28; Michael Dawe, "Community in Transition: Red Deer in the Second World War," in *For King and Country: Alberta in the Second World War*, ed. K.W. Tingley (Edmonton: Provincial Museum of Alberta, 1995), 131; *Canadian Unionist*, May 1944, 280.

71 *Ottawa Citizen*, 24 Sept. 1943, 12.

72 *Toronto Star*, 7 Oct. 1943, 10.

73 *Saturday Night*, 2 Jan. 1943, 28; *Montreal Star*, 3 Sept. 1943, 17; *Ottawa Citizen*, 21 Sept. 1943, 15.

74 *Ottawa Journal*, 11 March 1943, 16.

75 One Ottawa-based lumber company inundated with job seekers during the Depression, when the standard wage was $2 per cord cut, could not in 1942 find people to work at double that rate. *Ottawa Citizen*, 5 March 1943, 16; *Canada Year Book, 1948-49*, 519-520.

76 *Saturday Night*, 15 Aug. 1942, 40; *Industrial Canada*, Dec. 1942, 114; PC, vol. 13, Cabinet War Committee, 5 March 1943.

77 PC, vol. 14, Cabinet War Committee, 11 Sept. 1943; Stacey, *Arms, Men and Government,* 411; *Ottawa Citizen,* 14 Aug. 1943, 1; *Canadian Unionist,* Dec. 1943, 178.

78 Patricia Galloway, ed., *Too Young to Fight: Memories from Our Youth during World War II* (Toronto: Stoddart, 1999), 155.

79 Brantford *Expositor,* 9 April 1943, 2; *Ottawa Citizen,* 28 Aug. 1943, 25.

80 *Ottawa Citizen,* 3 Sept. 1943, 3; *Saturday Night,* 15 Aug. 1942, 40; *Vancouver Sun,* 16 Oct. 1942, 15.

81 Montreal *Gazette,* 11 Sept. 1939, 3.

82 WPTB, vol. 1538, file "Pamphlets," "Are You a Pre-War Clothing Merchant?" June 1942; *Canadian Business,* Oct. 1945, 45.

83 Michael D. Stevenson, *Canada's Greatest Wartime Muddle: National Selective Service and the Mobilization of Human Resources during World War II* (Montreal and Kingston: McGill-Queen's University Press, 2001), 156.

84 WPTB, vol. 1537, *WPTB March of Time,* 13 Sept. 1944; *Ottawa Journal,* 4 March 1942, 3; J.L. Granatstein and Desmond Morton, *Victory 1945: Canadians from War to Peace* (Toronto: HarperCollins, 1995), 77; *Saturday Night,* 21 April 1945, 33.

85 *Industrial Canada,* Sept. 1942, 74; *Ottawa Journal,* 3 July 1941, 15; Lennon and Charendoff, *On the Homefront,* 42; Elva Skuce, interview by author, Ottawa, 24 Feb. 1999.

86 WPTB, vol. 1538, file "Pamphlets," "Are You a Pre-War Clothing Merchant?" June 1942; *Vancouver Sun,* 17 Aug. 1942, 3.

87 Pauline Jewitt, "The Wartime Prices and Trade Board" (PhD diss., Harvard University, 1950), 81; York University Archives, Jack Lawrence Granatstein papers (JLG), box 4, file 73, Sandra Johnson to Geoff Johnson, 11 Oct. 1943.

88 WPTB, vol. 1386, file "Standards Branch," open letter from Donald Gordon to business leaders in Canada, 23 June 1943; WPTB, *Annual Report, 1943,* 48.

89 WPTB, *Annual Report, 1944,* 17; Lennon and Cherendoff, *On the Homefront,* 42.

90 *Montreal Star,* 13 Dec. 1943, 12, 14; *Ottawa Citizen,* 21 May 1943, 16, and 1 June 1943, 12.

91 RCMP, *Annual Report, 1946,* 34; *Canadian Forum,* Jan. 1945, 232; WPTB, vol. 690, file 23-30, Enforcement Administrator to A.F.W. Plumptre, 11 Oct. 1946.

92 *Public Opinion Quarterly,* 1942, 147.

93 *Vancouver Sun,* 23 Jan. 1941, 3; V.C. Fowke and G.E. Britnell, *Canadian Agriculture in War and Peace* (Palo Alto, CA: Stanford University Press, 1962), 160.

94 *Winnipeg Free Press,* 27 Jan. 1942, 1; *Toronto Star,* 11 Feb. 1942, 3.

95 *Canada Year Book, 1945,* 569; WPTB, vol. 1537, *WPTB March of Time,* 13 Sept. 1944; NAC, RG44, National War Services records (NWS), vol. 20, file "Salvage – Rubber," clipping from *Globe and Mail,* 27 Sept. 1943, n.p.

96 *Canadian Unionist,* April 1943, 272-273; W.H. Heick, *A Propensity to Protect: Butter, Margarine and the Rise of Urban Culture in Canada* (Waterloo, ON: Wilfrid Laurier University Press, 1991), 56-57.

97 There were four categories. For example, when purchasing from Category A (sliced bacon and cooked ham) people received half a pound per coupon, but if opting for Category D (which consisted of blade roast, brisket, beef and pork sausage, and leg of lamb), they received 1.25 pounds per coupon. *Ottawa Citizen,* 25 May 1943, 15.

98 *Ottawa Citizen,* 1 Sept. 1943, 6; WPTB, *Annual Report, 1944,* 18.

99 Fowke and Britnell, *Canadian Agriculture,* 161; Christopher Waddell, "The Wartime Prices and Trade Board: Price Control in Canada during World War Two" (PhD diss., York University, 1981), 61; *Ottawa Citizen,* 1 Nov. 1943, 14.

100 *Canadian Home Journal,* May 1942, 37.

101 JLG, box 6, file 47, clipping from *Calgary Herald,* n.d., n.p.; *Vancouver Sun,* 19 Aug. 1942, 4.

102 Fowke and Britnell, *Canadian Agriculture,* 145; *Canadian Affairs,* 15 Sept. 1943, 2.

103 WIB, vol. 16, file 9-5-9-0, WIB Report on Consumer Income and Purchases, n.d.; *Maclean's,* 5 June 1943, 3.

104 FN, vol. 4031, file 129-W-1-26, WIB Survey, 22 May 1943; J.W. Pickersgill and D.F. Forster, *The Mackenzie King Record,* vol. 1 (Toronto: University of Toronto Press, 1970), 464.

105 Ramona Marie Rose, "'Keepers of Morale': The Vancouver Council of Women, 1939-45" (MA thesis, University of British Columbia, 1990), 62-63; Mary Kehoe, interview by author, Ottawa, 12 March 2001; Brantford *Expositor,* 4 Sept. 1943, 4, and 7 Sept. 1943, 3.

106 Glenbow Institute (GB), M742, Harold W. McGill papers, sample ration book; *Globe and Mail,* 9 Dec. 1943, 2; *Saturday Night,* 17 April 1943, 38.

107 *Canadian Business,* Feb. 1943, 20; *Canada Year Book, 1943-44,* 522.

108 Mary Tucker, interview by author, Toronto, 15 Aug. 1998; WPTB, vol. 690, file 23-30, L. Plamondon to D. Gordon, 30 July 1943.

109 *Vancouver Sun,* 19 Oct. 1942, 3; WPTB, vol. 690, file 23-30, R. Armitage to H.M. Brown, 24 Feb. 1944.

110 WPTB, vol. 690, file 23-30, A.C. Collins to Gordon, 3 Aug. 1943; *Vancouver Sun,* 6 Dec. 1944, 3, and 11 Sept. 1945, 5.

111 *Country Guide and Northwest Farmer,* Oct. 1942, 31-32.

112 Poor pay and unfavourable working conditions partly accounted for some 20 percent of wartime employees leaving this sector by September 1943, when the federal government finally froze meat-packing workers in place. Stevenson, *Canada's Greatest Wartime Muddle,* 137-138; *Canadian Congress Journal,* Nov. 1943, 6.

113 *Country Guide and Northwest Farmer,* May 1942, 31; WLMK, vol. 226, file 1942, Ernest Ackut to Donald Gordon, 26 Sept. 1942; PC, vol. 10, Cabinet War Committee, 2 Sept. 1942; *Saturday Night,* 5 Dec. 1942, 39.

114 *Saturday Night,* 8 Aug. 1942, 28; Waddell, "Wartime Prices and Trade Board," 354-355; Jewitt, "Wartime Prices and Trade Board," 46-47; Joseph Schull, *The Great Scot: A Biography of Donald Gordon* (Montreal and Kingston: McGill-Queen's University Press, 1979), 70; Pickersgill and Forster, *Mackenzie King Record,* vol. 1, 437.

115 *Vancouver Sun,* 31 Aug. 1942, 10; Fowke and Britnell, *Canadian Agriculture,* 261, 265, 377; Ernest J. Spence, "Canadian Wartime Price Control, 1941 to 1947" (PhD diss., Northwestern University, 1947), 215.

116 WLMK, vol. 372, file 310-5, W.M. Abraham to King, 31 Dec. 1942.

117 *Family Herald and Weekly Star* (eastern edition), 21 July 1943, 2; *Ottawa Citizen,* 10 Aug. 1945, 18.

118 House of Commons, *Debates,* Address by W.R. Aylesworth, 18 Feb. 1943, 546-547.

119 WPTB, vol. 690, file 23-30, President of Morantz Beef Company to Gordon, 17 Feb. 1943, W. Lackey to F. A. McGregor, 14 Aug. 1943, H.M. Brown to Gordon, 8 Jan. 1944, and WPTB News Summary, 26 May 1943; *Ottawa Citizen,* 19 May 1943, 1, and 26 May 1943, 1.

120 *Public Opinion Quarterly,* 1943, 312.

121 Supplies of chicken and fish also grew periodically short. The fishery was adversely affected by the U-boat threat off Canada's east coast and in the St. Lawrence. *Saturday Night,* 29 May 1943, 24; Laurie Waller, interview, transcribed, Eastern Townships Research Centre, Lennoxville, Quebec, Special Media Collection, Oral History of Eastern Townships, Anglophone Women during World War II.

122 *Family Herald and Weekly Star* (eastern edition), 16 Aug. 1944, 13; *Saturday Night,* 29 May 1943, 2.

123 As numerous patrons complained, the increase in restaurant revenues also derived from establishments that eliminated "meal deals" in favour of an à la carte menu to augment their profits under the price ceiling. *Saturday Night,* 10 April 1943, 37; WPTB, *Annual Report, 1943,* 18; Spence, "Canadian Wartime Price Control," 290.

124 There was also some recognition that many women in wartime were working harder than ever and required less delicate food. The *Ottawa Citizen* wrote, "Women who previously were employed in office work and found a salad ... quite sufficient for lunch time needs are now in many instances doing manual labour that only steak and other heavy foods will satisfy." 16 Jan. 1943, 18; WIB, vol. 13, file 8-5-2, Current Rumour Clinic, 30 Oct. 1943.

125 Fowke and Britnell, *Canadian Agriculture*, 26; *Ottawa Journal*, 1 March 1944, 18; Waddell, "Wartime Prices and Trade Board," 477.

126 Department of Pensions and National Health, *Annual Report, 1940*, 109-117.

127 RCMP, *Annual Report, 1940*, 30; RCMP, *Annual Report, 1941*, 33; RCMP, *Annual Report, 1943*, 30.

128 *Edmonton Journal*, 14 July 1942, 14; Buckley and Urquhart, *Historical Statistics*, 650.

129 *Saturday Night*, 13 May 1944, 26; VPC, D7, Frederick Fullerton to J. Cornett, 17 April 1944.

130 *Maclean's*, 15 Dec. 1943, 15; Department of National Health and Welfare, *Annual Report, 1945*, 16-18.

131 RCMP, *Annual Report, 1945*, 936.

132 RCMP, *Annual Report, 1943-44*, 822; RCMP, *Annual Report, 1945*, 32-33; *Canadian Affairs*, 15 Jan. 1944, 12.

133 GB, MG1961, DND Collection, file 58, Edmonton Fusiliers, Regimental Orders, 9 Sept. 1940.

134 United Church of Canada, *Year Book, 1944* (Toronto: UCC, 1944), 107; WIB, vol. 16, file 9-5-9-0, WIB Report on Consumer Income and Consumer Purchases, n.d.; *Canada Year Book, 1943-44*, 822; *Canada Year Book, 1946*, 1006.

135 *Halifax Chronicle*, 8 Sept. 1939, 1.

136 *Toronto Star*, 16 Feb. 1942, 6; WLMK, vol. 244, file "Liquor Control 1942," D.M. Perley to King, 21 Nov. 1942.

137 WLMK, vol. 365, file W-303-2, Kramer to King, 18 Feb. 1943, and Army and Navy Veterans in Canada to King, 23 Feb. 1943; *Canadian Unionist*, May 1942, 292.

138 *Canadian Congress Journal*, Feb. 1945, 16; Robert A. Campbell, *Sit Down and Drink Your Beer: Regulating Vancouver's Beer Parlours, 1925-1954* (Toronto: University of Toronto Press, 2001), 42-43.

139 WLMK, vol. 226, file 1942, John Henry Jones to King, 3 June 1942; WLMK, vol. 244, file "Liquor Control 1942," Evangelical and United Church Women's Missionary Society of Langley, SK, to King, n.d.

140 WLMK, vol. 72, file "Liquor," Copy of Radio Broadcast, 16 Dec. 1942, clipping from *Ottawa Journal*, n.d, n.p., and clipping from *Victoria Times*, 17 Dec. 1942, n.p.

141 WLMK, vol. 72, file "Liquor," J. Thomm to King, 12 Sept. 1942, David Sim to J.W. Pickersgill, 14 Nov. 1942, and clipping from *Toronto Telegram*, 17 Dec. 1942, n.p.; *Ottawa Journal*, 17 Dec. 1942, 3.

142 At least in Vancouver, after 1942 a standard beer glass was reduced from 8 to 7.25 ounces. Campbell, *Sit Down*, 44; VPC, D7, Secretary of Women's Christian Temperance Union to Secretary of Police Commission, 22 March 1943; *Toronto Telegram*, 3 April 1944, 6; *Maple Leaf*, 9 Aug. 1945, 3.

143 Campbell, *Sit Down*, 43; *Saturday Night*, 10 June 1944, 1, 3; *Maclean's*, 15 April 1943, 57.

144 NWS, vol. 9, file "Voluntary and Auxiliary Services, pt. 1," Memo to George Pifher, 27 March 1943; *Saturday Night* quoted in Brantford *Expositor*, 16 April 1943, 12; *Maclean's*, 15 May 1943, 59.

145 *Ottawa Journal*, 29 March 1944, 1.

146 *Canada Year Book, 1946*, 1006; WLMK, vol. 365, file W-303-2, Isabel Craig to King, 5 Aug. 1944; *Ottawa Citizen*, 11 Dec. 1944, 22.

147 Katherine Ferguson, interview by author, Ottawa, 23 Feb. 1999; Ella Gilfouy, interview, 1 Oct. 1975, NAC, Audiovisual Division, Tape R-8445.

148 *Globe and Mail,* 10 June 1944, 4; *Ottawa Journal,* 15 April 1944, 1; VPC, D7, Inspector I/C Liquor Detail to Chief Constable, 6 July 1945.

149 Mack Lynch and John David, eds., *Salty Dips,* vol. 1 (Ottawa: Naval Officers' Association of Canada, 1983), 16, 53; *Ottawa Journal,* 9 June 1944, 8; Broadfoot, *Six War Years,* 311-312; WLMK, vol. 244, file N-305-38, Deaths Increase under Government Control of Liquor, n.d.; Granatstein and Morton, *Victory 1945,* 80. My thanks to Dr. Jay White for supplying information on liquor bylaws in Halifax.

150 Such was the case in British Columbia. Campbell, *Sit Down,* 45.

151 *Vancouver Sun,* 28 Aug. 1945, 1; *Public Opinion Quarterly,* 1945, 376.

152 *Maple Leaf,* 24 Dec. 1945, 3.

153 Schull, *Great Scot,* 94; *Canada Year Book, 1947,* 1003.

154 *Public Opinion Quarterly,* 1944, 139.

155 WPTB, *Annual Report, 1945,* 3; WLMK, vol. 377, Reel H-1544, 260,942.

156 Waddell, "Wartime Prices and Trade Board," 684-725; Peter McInnis, "Planning Prosperity: Canadians Debate Postwar Reconstruction," in *Uncertain Horizons: Canadians and Their World in 1945,* ed. Greg Donaghy (Ottawa: Canadian Council for the History of the Second World War, 1996), 242; *Ottawa Citizen,* 25 July 1945, 2; *Public Opinion Quarterly,* 1946, 279.

157 During the first year after VJ day, inflation was 18.6 percent in the United States and 5.4 percent in Canada. WPTB, *Annual Report, 1945,* 61; WPTB, *Annual Report, 1946,* 55; Richard Polenberg, *War and Society: The United States, 1941-1945* (Philadelphia: J.B. Lippincott, 1972), 235.

158 WIB, vol. 10, file 4-2-2, Minutes of Meeting of Publicity Coordinating Committee, 3 April 1945; NAC, MG30 E256, Charlotte Whitton papers, vol. 30, "A Beveridge Plan in Canada"; NAC, MG30 C92, Marion Creelman Savage papers (MCS), vol. 8, file "Press Clippings, 1945-58," unidentified newspaper clipping dated 6 Nov. 1945.

159 Buckley and Urquhart, *Historical Statistics,* 485; Parr, *Domestic Goods,* 32, 66; *Ottawa Citizen,* 18 Oct. 1945, 1; Peter McInnis, "Teamwork for Harmony: Labour-Management Production Committees and the Postwar Settlement in Canada," *Canadian Historical Review* 77, 3 (1996): 339.

160 WPTB, vol. 690, file 23-30, Victoria Automobile Association to Gordon, 25 Feb. 1946; Buckley and Urquhart, *Historical Statistics,* 576-577; Granatstein and Morton, *Victory 1945,* 198.

161 Many servicemen awaiting demobilization were shown a National Film Board production entitled *Goodbye Mr. Gyp,* a "warning in humorous cartoons of some of the ways in which the veteran may be swindled by unscrupulous people." NAC, MG28 I95, Young Men's Christian Association papers, vol. 272, file 8, "Rehabilitation: Learn about It," 1945; NAC, MG31 K13, Olive Russell papers, vol. 2, file 15, Address by Dr. Olive Russell to the Local Council of Women, Ottawa, March 1945.

162 Lennon and Charendoff, *On the Homefront,* 120; *Vancouver Sun,* 21 Aug. 1945, 8; Barry Broadfoot, *The Veterans' Years: Coming Home from the War* (Vancouver: Douglas and McIntyre, 1985), 70-73.

163 WPTB, vol. 1194, file 19-6, "Why We Have Meat Rationing," n.d.; *Industrial Canada,* Oct. 1944, 91; WLMK, vol. 377, Reel H-1544, 260 927-260 936.

164 *Saturday Night,* 6 Oct. 1945, 3.

165 *Public Opinion Quarterly,* 1944, 159.

166 WPTB, *Annual Report, 1946,* 575-576.

167 WPTB, vol. 1388, file 1-20-1, Enforcement Administration Prosecutions, Jan. 1946, and unsigned memo from Enforcement Branch, 18 April 1946.

168 Meat was price-controlled until early 1948. Fowke and Britnell, *Canadian Agriculture,* 167.

169 WPTB, vol. 1194, file 19-6, press release, 11 Aug. 1945; WPTB, vol. 1547, Meat Rationing Guide, Sept. 1945; FN, vol. 4031, file 129-W-1-23, *Consumer Facts,* Aug. 1945; Waddell, "Wartime Prices and Trade Board," 478-488; PC, vol. 2639, Cabinet Conclusions, 19 Dec. 1946.

170 MCS, vol. 8, file "Press Clippings, 1943-1946," clipping from Montreal *Gazette,* 12 June 1946, n.p.

171 *Ottawa Citizen,* 10 Sept. 1945, 1; Schull, *Great Scot,* 102; *Vancouver Sun,* 13 Sept. 1945, 1; WPTB, vol. 1194, file 19-6, John Hill to Gordon, 2 Oct. 1945.

172 WPTB, vol. 1194, file 19-6, clipping from *Vancouver Sun,* 2 Oct. 1945, n.p.; *Vancouver Sun,* 10 Sept. 1945, 1; *Canadian Unionist,* Oct. 1945, 237; PC, vol. 2637, Cabinet Conclusions, 23 Nov. 1945.

173 *Family Herald and Weekly Star* (eastern edition), 22 Aug. 1945, 16; WPTB, vol. 1566, Weekly Prices and Trade Bulletin, 26 Nov.-1 Dec. 1945.

174 Magda Fahrni, "Under Reconstruction: The Family and the Public in Postwar Montréal, 1944-1949" (PhD diss., York University, 2001), 340-341, 346-348; *Vancouver Sun,* 24 Sept. 1945, 1, 25 Sept. 1945, 1, 27 Sept. 1945, 1, and 28 Sept. 1945, 1; Granatstein and Morton, *Victory 1945,* 70.

175 WPTB, vol. 1194, file 19-6, Alfred Savoie to K.W. Taylor, 3 Oct. 1945; WPTB, vol. 1566, Weekly Prices and Trade Bulletin, 3-10 Dec. 1945.

176 WPTB, vol. 690, file 23-30, clipping from Montreal *Gazette,* 27 April 1946, n.p., and Toronto Retail Grocers' Association to J.L. Ilsley, 8 May 1946.

177 WPTB, vol. 888, file 1-20-1, O. Grignon to F.A. Wiggins, 21 May 1946.

CHAPTER 5: (IM)MORAL MATTERS

1 National Archives of Canada (NAC), MG30 E256, Charlotte Whitton papers (CW), vol. 83, "Women's Problems in Post-War Change," *Quotarian,* 1944, 3.

2 James H.S. Bossard, "Family Background of Wartime Adolescents," *Annals of the American Academy of Political and Social Science* 236 (1944): 42.

3 *Ottawa Journal,* 29 May 1944, 1; J.L. Granatstein and Desmond Morton, *Victory 1945: Canadians from War to Peace* (Toronto: HarperCollins, 1995), 206.

4 The only exception in Quebec was if the husband's mistress was maintained in the common domicile. CW, vol. 107, "Report on the Commission on Christian Marriage and Christian Home," by the Board of Evangelism and Social Service, United Church of Canada, 1946.

5 *Globe and Mail,* 6 Sept. 1939, 4; *Winnipeg Free Press,* 5 Sept. 1939, 3.

6 *Canada Year Book, 1948-49,* 220-221; K.A.H. Buckley and M.C. Urquhart, *Historical Statistics of Canada* (Toronto: Macmillan, 1965), series B75-81.

7 For instance, a major's wife with no children received $60 monthly from the government. Legally, spouses received top priority for these payments. Those without a spouse could select a parent or a sibling for their dependants' allowance, although for these recipients the basic government grant was only $20 a month. Parents with more than one child in the military could collect a dependants' allowance from only one. NAC, MG28 I10, Canadian Council on Social Development papers (CCSD), vol. 111, file 1941, The Administration of Dependants' Allowances in Canada, n.d.; NAC, RG36-31, Wartime Information Board records (WIB), vol. 28, file 4-2, Dependants' Allowance Board Rates, 1940; Magda Fahrni, "Under Reconstruction: The Family and the Public in Postwar Montréal, 1944-1949" (PhD diss., York University, 2001), 185.

8 Sidney Ditzion, *Morals and Sex in America: A History of Ideas* (New York: W.W. Norton, 1969), introduction; John Modell and Duane Steffey, "Waging War and Marriage: Military Service and Family Formation, 1940-1950," *Journal of Family History* 13, 2 (1988): 195-200; *Vancouver Sun,* 8 Dec. 1939, 21.

9 *Ottawa Journal,* 23 Dec. 1939, 8, and 1 June 1940, 14; *Halifax Chronicle,* 11 Nov. 1942, 8.
10 *Chatelaine,* Sept. 1941, 9; *Canadian Home Journal,* Jan. 1943, 64.
11 Michael D. Stevenson, *Canada's Greatest Wartime Muddle: National Selective Service and the Mobilization of Human Resources during World War II* (Montreal and Kingston: McGill-Queen's University Press, 2001), 19; *Ottawa Journal,* 15 July 1940, 1.
12 *Vancouver Sun,* 13 Dec. 1944, 15.
13 *Maclean's,* 15 April 1943, 57.
14 *Canada Year Book, 1955,* 224; *Saturday Night,* 6 Sept. 1941, 3.
15 Charges stood at 2,099 in 1943 and 2,442 in 1944. *Canada Year Book, 1942,* 913; *Canada Year Book, 1943,* 984; *Canada Year Book, 1946,* 1113.
16 Carmen Desbarats, interview by author, Ottawa, 2 March 1999.
17 NAC, MG28 I129, Society for the Protection of Women and Children papers, vol. 4, clipping from *Montreal Star,* 22 March 1945, n.p.
18 Margaret Little, *'No Car, No Radio, No Liquor Permit': The Moral Regulation of Single Mothers in Ontario, 1920-1997* (Toronto: University of Toronto Press, 1998), 110-115; *Canadian Welfare,* Jan. 1941, 27-29; *Canada Year Book, 1948-49,* 261-264.
19 *Toronto Star,* 19 June 1942, 12; NAC, Audiovisual Division, *Greetings from the Beaver Club,* Acc# 1981-100/413; *With the Troops in England,* Acc# 1984-0164/0051.
20 Archives of Ontario (AO), MU3542, Maclean-Hunter papers, *Women at War* (Toronto: Maclean-Hunter, 1943), 51; *Edmonton Journal,* 16 Nov. 1942, 4; C.P. Stacey and Barbara Wilson, *The Half-Million: The Canadians in Britain, 1939-1946* (Toronto: University of Toronto Press, 1987), 119; *Vancouver Sun,* 26 Oct. 1942, 3.
21 See, for example, the description of difficulty of trans-Atlantic air mail in *Saturday Night,* 1 March 1944, 3.
22 York University Archives, Jack Lawrence Granatstein papers (JLG), box 4, file 84, Captain C. McDowell to his wife, 1 April 1945.
23 Gloria A. Morrison, "The Voices of Those Who Served: The Early Years and Men of the 1st Battalion, Cameron Highlanders of Ottawa" (MA thesis, University of Ottawa, 2001), 138.
24 Craig family papers (CF), private collection held by Mary Tasker, Toronto, Grace Craig to Jim Craig, 1 March 1943.
25 *Chatelaine,* June 1943, 13; *Toronto Star,* 2 Dec. 1943, 28.
26 *Ottawa Journal,* 16 May 1944, 9.
27 JLG, box 4, file 84, Ruth to Captain C. McDowell, 14 Nov. 1942; CF, Grace Craig to Jim Craig, 5 Sept. 1942.
28 D'Ann Campbell, *Women at War with America: Private Lives in a Patriotic Era* (Cambridge: Harvard University Press, 1984), 191-192.
29 One Canadian chaplain in England noted a letter from "a jealous wife" to her husband stating, "I know you are having a good time. One of the boys who came back injured said all the Canadians were running around." NAC, RG24, Department of National Defence records (DND), vol. 15,633, file "War Diary," Monthly report of the Canadian Chaplain Service (P) Overseas, July 1942.
30 Mary Tasker, interview by author, Toronto, 15 March 1995; CF, Grace Craig to Jim Craig, 12 Aug. 1942.
31 NAC, MG30 I311, Montreal Soldiers' Wives' League papers (MSWL), vol. 2, file 30, President's Report, 1940; MSWL, vol. 5, file 11, Burnett Cited for Service, 19 Aug. 1943; NAC, RG44, National War Services records (NWS), vol. 3, file "Canadian Legion," *War Services Bulletin,* No. 8, 5 June 1943, n.p.
32 Barry Broadfoot, *Six War Years: Memories of Canadians at Home and Abroad* (Toronto: Doubleday, 1974), 243.

33 Norm Bowen, interview by author, Ottawa, 19 April 2000.

34 Barry Broadfoot, *The Veterans' Years: Coming Home from the War* (Vancouver: Douglas and McIntyre, 1985), 128-129.

35 Fahrni, "Under Reconstruction," 134-135.

36 Ibid., 185; WIB, vol. 28, file 4-5, Captain S.A. Sutton to Director of Special Services, 12 Oct. 1942; WIB, vol. 28, file 4-3, J.W. McKee to R.G. Bennett, 10 Nov. 1941.

37 Joyce Hibbert, *Fragments of War: Stories from Survivors of World War II* (Toronto: Dundurn Press, 1985), 12.

38 DND, vol. 15,633, file "War Diary," Monthly report of the Canadian Chaplain Service (P) Overseas, July 1942.

39 Modell and Steffey, "Waging War and Marriage," 210.

40 Fahrni, "Under Reconstruction," 138; WIB, vol. 28, file 4-5, R.G. Bennett to Elizabeth Wallace, 25 Jan. 1944, and George Davidson to R.G. Bennett, 28 June 1944.

41 WIB, vol. 28, file 4-5, R.G. Bennett to Olive Snyder, 28 May 1943; Magda Fahrni, "The Romance of Reunion: Montreal Veterans Return to Family Life, 1944-1949," ms., York University, 1998, 16. (Published version in the *Journal of the Canadian Historical Association*, 9 [1998]: 187-208).

42 MSWL, vol. 111, file 1942-46, J.A. Maines to G. Cameron Parker, 10 Feb. 1942; WIB, vol. 47, file 10, DAB Procedure #10, 11 Dec. 1944; Fahrni, "Under Reconstruction," 137.

43 Fahrni, "Under Reconstruction," 140; WIB, vol. 28, file 4-5, Elizabeth Richardson to R.G. Bennett, 1 Feb. 1943; MSWL, vol. 2, file 33, E.I. Smit to C.H. Young, 5 May 1943.

44 *Canada Year Book, 1943-44*, 145; *Canada Year Book, 1948-49*, 200; Buckley and Urquhart, *Historical Statistics*, series B1-14.

45 NAC, MG26 J4, William Lyon Mackenzie King papers, vol. 336, file S-251, W.E. Clark to King, 19 June 1944.

46 CCSD, vol. 110, file 794-1940, Memo of Dependants' Allowance Board, 13 April 1940; CCSD, vol. 110, file 789A, Nora Lea to Celia Henderson, 23 Jan. 1946; CCSD, vol. 111, file 1941, Memo from Dependants' Allowance Board to Army Commanders, 10 Dec. 1940.

47 Directorate of History and Heritage, Department of National Defence (DHH), 113.3 R4003(D1), Research and Information Section, Trends in the Thinking of Army Units, July 1944.

48 For example, 3,000 civilians in Ottawa quickly scooped up their allotment of tickets and joined 5,000 service personnel to watch the 1944 army boxing finals. *Ottawa Citizen*, 4 May 1944, 20.

49 The best military squads were affiliated with, and came to dominate, senior amateur leagues, twice winning the top prize for this level, the Allan Cup. In 1944 military teams were prohibited from competing for this title after it was concluded that they were recruiting and trading players as if they were professional squads. During the war, military hockey teams were established in Cornwallis, NS, Sydney, Halifax, Dartmouth, Saint John, Moncton, Summerside, Montreal, Quebec City, Lachine, Arnprior, Ottawa, Petawawa, Newmarket, Toronto, Cornwall, Simcoe, Kingston, Brantford, Winnipeg, Regina, Saskatoon, Calgary, Red Deer, Nanaimo, Vernon, Victoria, and Vancouver. See Gabriel Stephen Panunto, "For Club or Country? Hockey in Wartime Canada, 1939-1945" (MA thesis, Carleton University, 2000), and Douglas Hunter, *War Games: Conn Smythe and Hockey's Fighting Men* (Toronto: Viking, 1996).

50 Fatalities began declining significantly after 1942 because of the adoption of a "stricter code of air discipline." Several bases printed numbers on the bottom of aircraft that were visible only at 1,000 feet or below. Civilians able to read them were asked to report such to the "nearest police officer or flying school." F.J. Hatch, *The Aerodrome of Democracy: Canada*

and the British Commonwealth Air Training Plan (Ottawa: Directorate of History, 1983), 115, 150, 154; Spencer Dunmore, *Wings for Victory: The Remarkable Story of the British Commonwealth Air Training Plan in Canada* (Toronto: McClelland and Stewart, 1994), 346; *Edmonton Journal*, 16 July 1942, 1.

51 Glenbow Institute (GB), M1961, DND Collection, file 58, Edmonton Fusiliers, Regimental Orders, 17 July 1941; GB, M8039, DND Collection, file 10, 41st (Reserve) Brigade Group, Regimental Orders, 13 Oct. 1943.

52 At several military bases orders were issued stating, in one manner or another, that "the soliciting of rides ... is undignified and inconsistent with the wearing of the King's uniform." *Ottawa Journal*, 6 June 1940, 12.

53 Graham Metson, *An East Coast Port: Halifax at War, 1939-1945* (Toronto: McGraw-Hill Ryerson, 1981), 31; Patricia Galloway, ed., *Too Young to Fight: Memories from Our Youth during World War II* (Toronto: Stoddart, 1999), 177; DHH, 113.3 R.4003 (D1)V2, General Attitudes, Report 134, 30 June 1944.

54 The VE day riot produced some $5 million in damages, three civilian deaths, 211 arrests, and ultimately a royal commission under Supreme Court of Canada justice Roy Kellock. Although naval personnel led the charge, plenty of civilians joined in, venting their own frustrations over life in wartime Halifax. Overwhelmed and sometimes frightened shore patrols and an undermanned and overaged civilian police force stood by helplessly. Following the riot, Rear-Admiral Leonard Murray defended his men and argued that civilians were equal participants. Haligonians were outraged, and with Mackenzie King readying himself for a federal election, Murray was fired despite an outstanding service record as commander-in-chief of Canadian naval forces in the northwest Atlantic. Kellock's report noted that tensions in Halifax between servicemen and civilians had been building for years, though he also emphasized the "failure" on VE day of "naval authorities to [keep] personnel ... off the streets, and the failure of the same authorities to enforce discipline" for fear that this would precipitate more serious violence. Murray, despite patrolling the streets in a sound truck and pleading for calm, was heavily criticized by Kellock for inherently endorsing this laissez-faire approach toward the rioters. J.L. Granatstein and Desmond Morton, *A Nation Forged in Fire: Canadians and the Second World War, 1939-1945* (Toronto: Lester and Orpen Dennys, 1989), 239; Granatstein and Morton, *Victory 1945*, 22-28; Thomas Randall, *Halifax: Warden of the North* (New York: Doubleday, 1965), 302-303; Roger Sarty, *Canada and the Battle of the Atlantic* (Montreal: Art Global, 1998), 168; Stephen Kimber, *Sailors, Slackers and Blind Pigs: Halifax at War* (Toronto: Doubleday, 2002), 80-81, 211, chapter 6.

55 Urban manning depots were typically established on fairgrounds, where men often slept in buildings that had formerly been occupied by (and might still smell of) farm animals. Camp Borden, near Barrie, one of the country's largest training facilities, was described by many soldiers as isolated and barren. One pilot trainee stationed to the No. 3 Service Flying Training School in Airdrie, Alberta, said that he thought himself in "exile" to the "salt mines of Siberia." Morrison, "Voices of Those Who Served," 47-50, 61; DHH, 77/636, *Foothills' Fliers*, 1 July 1944, 4.

56 Dean F. Oliver, "'My Darling Clementine'? Wooing Zombies for $6.50 a Night: General Service-NRMA Relations in Wartime Calgary," *Canadian Military History* 7, 3 (1998): 46-54; Daniel Byers, "Canada's Zombies: A Portrait of Canadian Conscripts and their Experiences during the Second World War," in *Forging a Nation: Perspectives on the Canadian Military Experience*, ed. Bernd Horn (St. Catharines, ON: Vanwell Publishing, 2002), 162-163.

57 Bowen, interview.

58 Even though the fatal accident rate in the BCATP declined from 1 in 11,516 hours of flying time in 1940-41 to 1 in 20,580 hours in 1943-44, the fact that a pilot trainee typically spent

250 hours in the air before graduating meant that the danger remained quite significant. Quotation from Granatstein and Morton, *Nation Forged in Fire,* 104-105; Hatch, *Aerodrome of Democracy,* 51; W.A.B. Douglas, *Official History of the Royal Canadian Air Force,* vol. 2 (Toronto: University of Toronto Press, 1985), 285.

59 DHH, 113.3R 4003 V1(D1), Unit Morale Report, 30 May 1943; 30 Aug. 1943.

60 Granatstein, *Canada's Army: Waging War and Keeping the Peace* (Toronto: University of Toronto Press, 2002), 204; Frederick Elkin, "The Soldier's Language," *American Journal of Sociology* 51, 5 (1946): 414-422; Anonymous, "Informal Organizations in the Army," *American Journal of Sociology* 51, 5 (1946): 365, 369; Howard Brotz and Everett Wilson, "Characteristics of Military Society," *American Journal of Sociology* 51, 5 (1946): 371.

61 Only when a more serious crime accompanied drunkenness did major penalties result. DND, vol. 10,926, file 239 C3 (D22), Notes on the Preparation of Punishments for Promulgation in Part II Orders, 10 Aug. 1942; Paul Jackson, "Courting Homosexuals in the Military: The Management of Homosexuality in the Canadian Military" (PhD diss., Queen's University, 2002), 466.

62 DHH, 77/636, *Foothills' Fliers,* 15 July 1943, 8; DHH 113.3 R4003 (D1), Unit Morale Report, Sept. 1943.

63 DND, vol. 16,488, 13 Company (Ottawa), Canadian Provost Corps, War Diary, 13-24 Jan. 1942.

64 DHH, 113.3 R4003 V1(D1), Unit Morale Report, Aug. 1943.

65 *Calgary Herald,* 1 Nov. 1941, 13; D. Phyllis Harrison, *Saga of an Airwoman* (Penticton, BC: Sage Press, 1995), 75.

66 Approximately one month after this incident, the Moose Jaw base was shut down, though military authorities insisted this closure had been decided well before the violence occurred. Dunmore, *Wings for Victory,* 225; Hatch, *Aerodrome of Democracy,* 72-74.

67 Indicative of attitudes was the exceptional popularity of pin-ups, pictures of scantily clad women clipped from the pages of magazines such as *Esquire* and *Men Only* that often came to dominate barrack room walls. As a morale booster and despite opposition from padres, military newspapers typically included in each issue not only a pin-up, but also sex-obsessed cartoons such as the American entry *Male Call,* which in each episode illustrated a full-figured woman in a skimpy negligee or in panties and a brassiere. DHH, 77/636, *Foothills' Fliers,* 31 Jan. 1945, 28.

68 James Keshen papers, private collection held by Jeff Keshen, Ottawa, Jim Keshen to Harry Lazarus, 23 June 1943 and 30 Aug. 1943.

69 DND, vol. 16,488, 13 Company (Ottawa), Canadian Provost Corps, War Diary, 15 Feb. 1942, Statement by Bessie Black.

70 Museum of the Regiments (Calgary, Alberta), Lord Strathcona's Horse, Regimental Orders, 3 Jan. 1940; GB, M1961, DND Collection, file 58, Edmonton Fusiliers, Regimental Orders, 10 March 1941.

71 NAC, MG28 I95, Young Men's Christian Association papers, vol. 272, file 3, memo entitled "Dances Held in a Camp or Station," n.d.

72 Harrison, *Saga of an Airwoman,* 24-25; DHH, 77/634, *Pukka Gen,* Aug. 1943, 35.

73 Between 1 January 1940 and 30 June 1943, 35,036 servicemen in Canada contracted VD, requiring 697,259 hospital days at a cost of $7.955 million. DND, vol. 6617, file 8994-6, pt. 1, The Canadian Army Venereal Disease Problem, n.d.; DND, vol. 12,613, file 218-5, Venereal Disease in the Canadian Army in Canada, n.d.

74 CCSD, vol. 74, file 538, "The Regulation of Prostitution." Excerpt taken from *International Women's News* 23, 12 (1942): n.p.

75 Joan Sangster, *Regulating Girls and Women: Sexuality, Family and the Law in Ontario, 1920-1960* (Toronto: Oxford University Press, 2001), 92-95, 102-103, 109, 114-116, 239 n13.

76 Such was apparently the case in Calgary. Shortly after raids on several brothels in the city's red light district, many residents living in the residential neighbourhood near 5th Avenue East complained to police about cars pulling up at all hours in front of a house and servicemen, some of whom were drunk, loudly knocking on the door. Calgary Police Archives, Police Commission Records (CPCR), file 1943-19, Report by Detective J. Strange, 10 June 1943.

77 DND, vol. 134, file 8994, pt. 4, Canadian Army Admissions for Venereal Disease, 1942; William Horrocks, *In Their Own Words* (Ottawa: Rideau Veterans Home Residents Council, 1993), 40; James B. Lamb, *The Corvette Navy: True Stories from Canada's Atlantic War* (Toronto: Stoddart, 2000), 147-148; James Frank Edward White, "Conscripted City: Halifax and the Second World War" (PhD diss., McMaster University, 1995), 306-307, 320-324; Kimber, *Sailors, Slackers*, 118, 152.

78 William Weintraub, *City Unique: Montreal Days and Nights in the 1940s and 1950s* (Toronto: McClelland and Stewart, 1996), 8, 63, 80; DND, vol. 12,612, file 217-31, clipping from *Maclean's*, 15 Feb. 1944, n.p.

79 DND, vol. 6617, file 8994-6, pt. 2, Venereal Disease Control Conference, MD #5, 26 Oct. 1943; DND, vol. 6617, file 8994-6, pt. 4, Inspection Report, Venereal Disease Control, MD #5, n.d.; DND, vol. 6617, file 8994-6, pt. 6, Memo from Major S.L. Williams, RVDCO, 10 Oct. 1944.

80 DND, vol. 12,613, file 218.5, Venereal Disease in the Canadian Army in Canada, n.d.

81 DND, vol. 12,612, file 217-31, Introduction to Training in Protection against VD, n.d., and Talk to Accompany the Showing of the Film *Three Cadets*, n.d.; CCSD, vol. 74, file 538, Unsigned letter to Dr. Donald H. Williams, 10 Aug. 1942.

82 DND, vol. 6617, file 8994-6, pt. 1, Control of Venereal Disease – Responsibility, n.d.; DND, vol. 12,612, file 217-31, An Outline for a Talk on Venereal Disease by a Regimental Officer, n.d.; *Khaki* 2, 9: 6.

83 NAC, MG28 I63, Health League of Canada papers (HLC), Reel C-9815, Report of Meeting, 11-12 Oct. 1939.

84 NAC, RG29, National Health and Welfare records, vol. 1238, file 311-V3-15, Summary of an Investigation of Some Aspects of the V.D. Problem, n.d.

85 DND, vol. 12,612, file 217-31, Introduction to Training in Protection against VD, n.d.

86 J.W. Tice et al., "Some Observations on Venereal Disease Control in the Royal Canadian Air Force," *Canadian Journal of Public Health* 37 (1946): 47.

87 DND, vol. 6617, file 8994-6, pt. 1, Control of Venereal Disease – Responsibility, n.d.

88 DND, vol. 6617, file 8994-6, pt. 6, Memo to Adjutant-General, 12 Dec. 1944; DND, vol. 10,924, file 231 C1.7 (D14), Army Personnel Suffering from Venereal Disease, n.d.

89 DND, vol. 6617, file 8994-6, pt. 4, S.L. Williams to D.H. Williams, 29 Feb. 1944; DND, vol. 134, file 8994-1, pt. 4, Memo from Major Georges Leclerc, 18 June 1945; W.R. Feasby, *Official History of the Canadian Medical Services*, vol. 2 (Ottawa: Queen's Printer, 1956), 109.

90 This wording used in Ontario was essentially the same as that employed in other provinces. Those who ignored this notice in Ontario could be fined $500. DND, vol. 6617, file 8994-6, pt. 3, *Public Health Act*, Form II; DND, vol. 10,924, file 239 C1.7(D19), First Cdn Army, Medical Instructions, 28 July 1945; Feasby, *Canadian Medical Services*, 114; Archives of Alberta, 68.145, Department of Public Health (DPH), *Annual Report, 1945*, 61.

91 Tice et al., "Some Observations," 49.

92 DPH, *Annual Report, 1943*, 97.

93 Paul Jackson, "Courting Homosexuals," 86-87.

94 Tice et al., "Some Observations," 49; DND, vol. 6617, file 8994-6, pt. 2, Brigadier G.B. Chisholm to Command Medical Officer, Pacific Command, and District Medical Officers, All Military Districts, 12 July 1943.

95 DND, vol. 16,488, file "32 Coy, Canadian Provost Corps, pt. 1," Report from Captain W.R. Lake, n.d.

96 On the perceived connection of such places with so-called loose women and earlier attempts to ban women from such establishments, see Carolyn Strange, *Toronto's Girl Problem: The Perils and Pleasures of the City, 1880-1920* (Toronto: University of Toronto Press, 1995), 10-17, and Robert A. Campbell, *Sit Down and Drink Your Beer: Regulating Vancouver's Beer Parlours, 1925-1954* (Toronto: University of Toronto Press, 2001), 52-68.

97 Government of British Columbia, Board of Health, *Annual Report, 1942*, 61-62, 64; Government of Manitoba, Department of Health and Public Welfare, *Annual Report, 1944*, 100-101.

98 For example, in 1944, while the authorized strength of the Winnipeg and Toronto police forces stood at 303 and 1,070 respectively, their actual numbers were 283 and 860. Also to make up for staff deficiencies, several police forces hired older and less experienced male replacements. City of Vancouver Archives, RG75, Board of Police Commission records (VBPC), E1, Strength of Police Departments, 1944.

99 Montreal appointed a police matron in 1914. NAC, MG28 I64, Montreal Council of Women papers, vol. 7, Records of Local Council of Women re: Police Women in Montreal, 1914-1919, n.d; Greg Marquis, "The Police As a Social Service in Early Twentieth-Century Toronto," *Histoire sociale/Social History* 25, 50 (1992): 343.

100 VBPC, D7, D. McKay to Chair and Members, Board of Police Commissioners, 15 Jan. 1943; Donna A. Zwicker, "Alberta Women and World War Two" (MA thesis, University of Calgary, 1985), 93-94; NAC, MG28 I25, National Council of Women of Canada papers (NCWC), Mrs. E.D. Hardy to J.G. Downey, 4 Aug. 1943; CPCR, file 42.11, Secretary of the Board of Police Commission to J. Miller, 9 Feb. 1943; CCSD, vol. 110, clipping from Montreal *Gazette*, 13 Feb. 1946, n.p.

101 CPCR, file 42.11, D.C. Draper to Secretary of Police Commission, 28 Nov. 1941, J.A. McLean to A.D. Aitken, 4 Dec. 1941, Chief of Police, Halifax to A.D. Aitken, 6 Dec. 1941, George Smith to A.D. Aitken, 18 Dec. 1941, Chief Constable to Agnes Ledger, 25 April 1942, and Secretary of Board of Police Commission to J. Miller, 9 Feb. 1943; NCWC, vol. 86, file 1848, Mrs. Robert McQueen to Joseph Laycock, 20 April 1942; VBPC, E1, Secretary of Board to S.H. Sims, 17 Feb. 1944.

102 Jay Cassell, *The Secret Plague: Venereal Diseases in Canada, 1838-1939* (Toronto: University of Toronto Press, 1987), 198-237.

103 Statistics Canada, *Incidence of Notifiable Diseases by Province, Number of Cases and Rates, 1924-1968* (Ottawa: Statistics Canada, 1968), 86-91.

104 Campbell, *Sit Down*, 59.

105 For example, in 1940 Williams successfully pushed this directness on the management of the CBC radio station in Vancouver, who were concerned over public reaction to his use of the term "venereal disease" on the air. CCSD, vol. 74, file 538, Donald H. Williams to Charlotte Whitton, 27 Dec. 1940; British Columbia, Board of Health, *Annual Report, 1940*, 38; British Columbia, Board of Health, *Annual Report, 1941*, 111-114.

106 British Columbia, Board of Health, *Annual Report, 1941*, 59, 113-114; Campbell, *Sit Down*, 57; Donald H. Williams, "The Facilitation Process and Venereal Disease Control," *Canadian Journal of Public Health* 34 (1943): 402.

107 British Columbia, Board of Health, *Annual Report, 1944*, 69-70.

108 DPH, *Annual Report, 1942*, 21; Diane G. Forestell, "The Victorian Legacy: Historical Perspectives on the Canadian Women's Army Corps" (PhD diss., York University, 1985), 105-106.

109 *Chatelaine*, Feb. 1944, 18; *Canadian Home Journal*, Nov. 1944, 27.

110 Department of National Health and Welfare, *Annual Report, 1945*, 55.

111 Polls indicated that nearly 90 percent of Canadians supported prematrimonial VD tests, which were already required in Alberta and British Columbia. CCSD, vol. 74, file 538, leaflet distributed by the National Health Committee of the Junior Chamber of Commerce, 1944.

112 For example, between 1943 and 1946 medical schools at Queen's University and the University of Toronto increased the number of lecture hours devoted to VD from two to nine. HLC, vol. 107, file 123.17, W.T. Brown to Dr. J.T. Phair, 26 Sept. 1946; Major Georges LeClerc, "Requirements for a Good Venereal Disease Program," 13 Dec. 1945; *Canadian Welfare*, Jan. 1944, 32-33.

113 DPH, *Annual Report, 1945*, 57; NWS, vol. 4, file "Health League of Canada," 1945 Report, n.p.

114 Ontario, Department of Health, *Annual Report, 1944*, 157-162, 174-175; DPH, *Annual Report, 1943*, 91-92; Manitoba, Department of Health and Public Welfare, *Annual Report, 1944*, 101.

115 HLC, Reel C-9816, Dominion Council of Health, Minutes of Meeting, 29 Nov.-1 Dec. 1945, Item #10.

CHAPTER 6: CIVILIAN WOMEN

1 N.W. Ayer and Son, *Directory of Newspapers and Periodicals* (Philadelphia: N.W. Ayer and Son, 1944); *Chatelaine*, September 1943, 76.

2 Ruth Pierson, *They're Still Women after All: Canadian Women and the Second World War* (Toronto: McClelland and Stewart, 1986). For example, Jane Ursel, in her survey text on the impact of state welfare policy on women, uncritically adopts Pierson's argument. She writes that during the war, the federal government "achieve[d] maximum utilization of female labour without permitting their integration within the labour market." See *Private Lives, Public Policy: 100 Years of State Intervention in the Family* (Toronto: Women's Press, 1992), 204. Also reflecting Pierson's argument is Ellen Scheinberg's "The Tale of Tessie the Textile Worker: Female Textile Workers in Cornwall during World War II," *Labour/Le Travail* 33 (1994): 153-186. Diane G. Forestell alludes to progressive attitudes developing during the war toward the employment of women, but is very cautious in pursuing this theme, especially when it comes to suggesting any possible longer-term impact. See "The Necessity of Sacrifice for the Nation at War: Women's Labour Force Participation, 1939-1946," *Histoire sociale/Social History* 22, 44 (1989): 323-343.

3 *Canadian Home Journal*, Nov. 1939, 5.

4 National Archives of Canada (NAC), MG26 J4, William Lyon Mackenzie King papers (WLMK), vol. 226, file "National Reg of Women, 1940" undated memo; NAC, RG2, Privy Council records (PC), vol. 4, Cabinet War Committee, 30 April 1941; Alison Prentice et al., *Canadian Women: A History* (Toronto: Harcourt Brace Jovanovich, 1988), 295-297.

5 NAC, RG36-31, Wartime Information Board records (WIB), vol. 11, file "WVS Progress Report," *Annual Report, 1944-45*, Kitchener-Waterloo Centre.

6 One intensive study of wartime Halifax concludes that many women "became more politically or socially conscious as a result of their [voluntary] wartime activities." James Frank Edward White, "Conscripted City: Halifax and the Second World War" (PhD diss., McMaster University, 1995), 261; *Canadian Welfare*, July 1945, 7.

7 Jean Bruce, *Back the Attack! Canadian Women during the Second World War – at Home and Abroad* (Toronto: Macmillan, 1985), 117; *Vancouver Sun*, 9 Oct. 1939, 10; *Mayfair*, July 1943, 85.

8 However, without the motivation generated by the war, and given the disappearance of organizational support from the Wartime Prices and Trade Board, postwar consumer activism declined in intensity. The female-dominated Consumers' Association of Canada aimed for 250,000 members but failed to reach above 2,500. Meanwhile, in the political atmosphere of the Cold War, the membership of several communists in the more militant

Housewives' Consumer Association played a key role in keeping its membership tiny. Joy Parr, *Domestic Goods: The Material, the Moral and the Economic in the Postwar Years* (Toronto: University of Toronto Press, 1999), 85-86, 97, 99; Magda Fahrni, "Under Reconstruction: The Family and the Public in Postwar Montréal, 1944-1949" (PhD diss., York University, 2001), 247-251, 261-262, 270; *Chatelaine,* June 1944, 76.

9 Edward C. McDonagh, "The Discharged Serviceman and His Family," *American Journal of Sociology* 51, 5 (1946): 453; *Chatelaine,* Oct. 1945, 14.

10 NAC, RG27, Department of Labour records (DL), vol. 1523, file X5-12, pt. 1, clipping from *Globe and Mail,* 2 Oct. 1942, n.p.

11 *Saturday Night,* 3 April 1943, 28.

12 *Maclean's,* 15 Nov. 1942, 50; *Chatelaine,* June 1944, 76.

13 *Saturday Night,* 29 May 1943, 28; Mary Turner, interview, 2 March 1983, NAC, Audiovisual Division (AV), Tape R-8550.

14 Many women acquired these skills while preparing under the War Emergency Training Programme to join the workforce, as part of Red Cross or St. John Ambulance driving courses, or from booklets on basic troubleshooting and maintenance provided by several companies no longer able to produce for the civilian market. *Family Herald and Weekly Star* (eastern edition), 9 July 1941, 23; *Calgary Albertan,* 29 May 1942, 8; *Saturday Night,* 13 Feb. 1943, 26; Mary Jane Lennon and Syd Charendoff, *On the Homefront: A Scrapbook of Canadian World War Two Memorabilia* (Erin, ON: Boston Mills Press, 1981), 14.

15 See Catherine Gidney, "Under the President's Gaze: Sexuality and Morality at a Canadian University during the Second World War," *Canadian Historical Review* 82, 1 (2001): 36-43.

16 Nancy Keifer and Ruth Roach Pierson, "The War Effort and Women Students at the University of Toronto, 1939-1945," in *Youth, University and Canadian Society: Essays in the History of Higher Education,* ed. Paul Axelrod and John G. Reid (Montreal and Kingston: McGill-Queen's University Press, 1989), 163-176.

17 Author survey of wartime issues of the *Gateway,* and the edition of 16 Oct. 1942, 1.

18 K.A.H. Buckley and M.C. Urquhart, *Historical Statistics of Canada* (Toronto: Macmillan, 1965), 601; *Canada Year Book, 1940,* 976; *Canada Year Book, 1948-1949,* 320-321; Susan M. Hartmann, *The Home Front and Beyond: American Women in the 1940s* (Boston: Twayne Publishers, 1982), 104-105.

19 *Ottawa Journal,* 6 June 1942, 7.

20 Peter S. McInnis, *Harnessing Labour Confrontation: Shaping the Postwar Settlement in Canada, 1943-1950* (Toronto: University of Toronto Press, 2002), 24; Donna A. Zwicker, "Alberta Women and World War Two" (MA thesis, University of Calgary, 1985), 83.

21 Pierson, *They're Still Women,* 48-49; Ramona Marie Rose, "'Keepers of Morale': The Vancouver Council of Women, 1939-1945" (MA thesis, University of British Columbia, 1990), 70.

22 *Canadian Home Journal,* Aug. 1942, 6-7.

23 *Vancouver Sun,* 10 Sept. 1942, 7; Zwicker, "Alberta Women," 72-73; Pierson, *They're Still Women,* 22-30.

24 In communities where room and board were comparatively high, weekly financial support could be increased to $9 for single and $12 for married participants. Archives of Ontario (AO), MU8108, War Emergency Training Programme, Dec. 1941.

25 Pierson, *They're Still Women,* 63-71; NAC, RG24, Department of National Defence records, vol. 12,278, file 27-1, Bulletin on Vocational Training for Ex-Service Personnel prepared by the Training Branch, Department of Labour, 1944; NAC, MG27 III B5, Ian Mackenzie papers, vol. 58, file 527-17, Walter Woods to Mackenzie, 4 March 1942.

26 *Edmonton Journal,* 9 Nov. 1942, 10; *Canadian Home Journal,* Oct. 1942, 71; *Canadian Home Journal,* Feb. 1943, 23.

27 *Mayfair,* July 1943, 97, 101.
28 Maureen Honey, *Creating Rosie the Riveter: Class, Gender, and Propaganda during World War II* (Boston: University of Massachusetts Press, 1984), 70.
29 *Chatelaine,* Jan. 1941, 4, 6, 20.
30 A similar pattern was evident in US magazine fiction. Indeed, the United States Office of War Information contacted those in charge of major publications like the *Saturday Evening Post* to ask that they provide more fictional accounts revolving around women in war jobs to help break down barriers. Honey, *Creating Rosie the Riveter,* 40; quotation from Phyllis Lassner, "The Quiet Revolution: World War II and the English Domestic Novel," *Mosaic* 23, 3 (1990): 90.
31 *Chatelaine,* April 1944, 5-7.
32 *Chatelaine,* Jan. 1945, 6-7.
33 *Chatelaine,* Nov. 1944, 14-15, 22, 24.
34 *Saturday Night,* 5 Dec. 1942, 28.
35 Jean Brooks, interview, 17 April 1984, Concordia University, Women and War Work in Montreal Collection (WWWM).
36 *Winnipeg Free Press,* 31 July 1943, 18.
37 See, for example, *Canadian Unionist,* Sept. 1943, 87.
38 *Saturday Night,* 17 Oct. 1942, 10; William H. Chafe, *The Paradox of Change: American Women in the 20th Century* (New York: Oxford University Press, 1991), 124.
39 *Chatelaine,* Jan. 1943, 16.
40 *Winnipeg Free Press,* 8 March 1944, 8; *Saturday Night,* 6 Sept. 1941, 19.
41 *Chatelaine,* June 1944, 12.
42 Author survey of the *Canadian Periodical Index.*
43 Stephen Kimber, *Sailors, Slackers and Blind Pigs: Halifax at War* (Toronto: Doubleday, 2002), 159-166.
44 *Maclean's,* 15 June 1942, 10; Zwicker, "Alberta Women," 69.
45 *Mayfair,* Sept. 1943, 88.
46 Valerie J. Korinek, "Roughing It in Suburbia: Reading *Chatelaine* Magazine, 1950-1969" (PhD diss., University of Toronto, 1996), 51; AO, MU3542, *Women at War* (Toronto: Maclean-Hunter, 1943), 10.
47 *Chatelaine,* Feb. 1943, 42.
48 Quoted in Judy Barett Litoff and David C. Smith, "'Since You Went Away': The War Letters of American Women," *History Today,* Dec. 1991, 22.
49 *Saturday Night,* 2 Jan. 1942, 15; *Chatelaine,* Feb. 1943, cover; *Ottawa Journal,* 27 Oct. 1944, 17.
50 AO, MU3542, *Women at War* (Toronto: Maclean-Hunter, 1943), 6-11.
51 Whereas Canadians spent $25,954,200 on movie tickets in 1933, in 1944 that figure reached $53,430,235. One American analysis of wartime movie audiences estimated the female component at 60 percent. *Canada Year Book, 1947,* 833; Hartmann, *Home Front and Beyond,* 191; Marc Renov, "From Fetish to Subject: The Containment of Sexual Difference in Hollywood's Wartime Cinema," *Wide Angle* 1 (1986): 18.
52 John Costello, *Love, Sex and War: Changing Values, 1939-1945* (London: Collins, 1985), 181-182; *New York Times Film Reviews,* vol. 3, 2033.
53 *New York Times Film Reviews,* vol. 3, 1841-1842; Andrea S. Walsh, *Women's Film and Female Experience, 1940-1950* (New York: Praeger, 1984), 37.
54 Renov, "From Fetish to Subject," 34; Hartmann, *Home Front and Beyond,* 192.
55 AO, RG56, Theatre Branch records (TB), series B-2, box 1, Newsreel Cards, 7 July 1943.
56 TB, 20 Jan. 1943; AV, V19001-0022, *Canadian Women Help to Build Great Tanks,* 1942.
57 Gary Evans, *John Grierson and the National Film Board: The Politics of Wartime Propaganda* (Toronto: University of Toronto Press, 1984), 138; M. Teresa Nash, "Images of Women

in National Film Board of Canada Films during World War II and the Post-War Years, 1939-1949" (PhD diss., McGill University, 1982), 262.

58 J.L. Granatstein and Peter Neary, eds., *The Good Fight: Canadians in the Second World War* (Toronto: Copp Clark Longman, 1995), 449; *Public Opinion Quarterly,* 1945, 529.

59 NAC, MG28 I11, Canadian Youth Commission papers (CYC), vol. 42, file 5(3g), Group Interview, General Electric Company, 1944.

60 Brantford *Expositor,* 15 April 1943, 15.

61 For example, as of February 1942, the wife of a Canadian private with one child received $72.60 per month inclusive of her husband's compulsory wage contribution, compared to $62.00 in the United States, $58.80 in Australia, $59.10 in New Zealand, $48.78 in South Africa, and $33.22 in the United Kingdom. WIB, vol. 13, file 8-9-1, Press Release, 23 Jan. 1942.

62 WIB, vol. 29, file 5-5, Statistics of Relief and Service to Families of Enlisted Men (Montreal), June 1941.

63 WIB, vol. 29, file 5-6, R.G. Bennett to Secretary, Imperial Army and Navy Veterans, 28 Feb. 1942.

64 WIB, vol. 28, file 4-5, Margaret H. Spaulding to R.G. Bennett, 21 Nov. 1942.

65 Historian Magda Fahrni estimates that in Montreal some 90 percent of applications for supplemental support related to medical expenses. Applications could also be made for ongoing support when a wife was left with more than six dependent children. Fahrni, "Under Reconstruction," 182; Directorate of History and Heritage, Department of National Defence (DHH), 322.009 (D217), Capt. G.W.H. Medley to Lt.-Col. W.C. Towers, n.d.

66 WIB, vol. 20, file "Ottawa," 1st Meeting, file 2.

67 Michael D. Stevenson, *Canada's Greatest Wartime Muddle: National Selective Service and the Mobilization of Human Resources during World War II* (Montreal and Kingston: McGill-Queen's University Press, 2001), 153; Montreal *Gazette,* 7 May 1942, 1; Nash, "Images of Women," 401-402.

68 *Ottawa Citizen,* 14 Dec. 1943, 11; Clara Clifford, interview, AV, Tape R-8546.

69 NAC, MG28 I10, Canadian Council on Social Development papers (CCSD), vol. 50, file "Daycare 1941-1947," clipping from newspaper article written by Jane Johnstone, n.d., n.p.

70 *Ottawa Citizen,* 25 July 1942, 21.

71 WIB, vol. 13, file 8-5-2, Olive to Dunton, 10 Nov. 1942, and War Information Board Current Rumour Clinic, 17 July 1943.

72 AO, RG29, Department of Public Health records, series I, file I-872, Survey of Dominion-Provincial Wartime Day Nursery Program, Sept. 1942-Sept. 1945; Pierson, *They're Still Women,* 53; *Canadian Unionist,* Feb. 1943, 236; *Le Droit,* 21 July 1942, 3.

73 DL, vol. 1508, file 40-5-6-4, pt. 1, R.A. Sampson to William Lyon Mackenzie King, 6 May 1943; DL, vol. 1508, file 40-5-5-1, Miriam Chapin to Margaret Grier, 26 Nov. 1943.

74 *Chatelaine,* June 1943, 8.

75 *Ottawa Journal,* 16 May 1944, 8; AO, MU5081, Children's Aid Society papers, box 10, file 1939, 1945 Conference Report.

76 NAC, MG28 I129, Society for the Protection of Women and Children papers, vol. 4, Minutes of Board Meeting, 27 April 1942; WLMK, vol. 4, file "Feb. 18, 1942-May 19, 1943," 1942 President's Report, Society for the Protection of Women and Children.

77 *Canadian Home Journal,* Oct. 1944, 96.

78 *New Advance,* Feb. 1944, 20-21.

79 WIB, vol. 28, file 4-5, George Davidson to Ruth Harvey, 27 Aug. 1943.

80 *Canadian Welfare,* Oct. 1942, 15.

81 Ella Gilfouy, interview, AV, Tape R-8445.

82 *Canada Year Book,* 1948-49, 1187.

83 *Ottawa Journal,* 28 May 1942, 8; Ursel, *Private Lives, Public Policy,* 202; Jean McNiven, interview by author, Ottawa, 21 March 2001.
84 Barbara Lorenzkowski, "'Good Morning, Mrs. Motorman' – Women Streetcar Operators
   and Conductors in Wartime Canada, 1943-1945," ms., University of Ottawa, 1996, 1-19; *Saturday Night,* 19 June 1943, 26.
85 Clifford, interview.
86 Irene Wheeler, interview, 3 Nov. 1975, AV, Tape R-8548.
87 NAC, MG28 I25, National Council of Women of Canada papers (NCWC), vol. 84, file 17,
   Highlights of McWilliams Subcommittee Report, 1943; Joan Bailin, interview, 12 April 1984,
   WWWM.
88 Bruce, *Back the Attack,* 70; Ottawa and District Labour Council, *On All Fronts: Made in
   Ottawa* (Ottawa: Workers' Heritage Committee of Ottawa-Carleton and Ground Zero Productions, 1997).
89 The CYC had significant shortcomings in terms of representing the opinions of young
   Canadians. The age range it targeted, fifteen to twenty-four inclusive, missed nearly all
   those legally classified as juveniles. A strong Christian, and particularly Protestant, connection was also evident, as a large proportion of the young people the CYC surveyed
   came from groups such as the Anglican Young People's Association. Nonetheless, the CYC
   remained the most comprehensive effort to that date to examine the views of young Canadians. All told, over 1,000 study groups were formed, each typically containing ten to twelve
   members. See Linda McGuire Ambrose, "The Canadian Youth Commission: Planning for
   Youth and Social Welfare in the Post-War Era" (PhD diss., University of Waterloo, 1992).
90 Brantford *Expositor,* 27 Sept. 1943, 4.
91 Haig quoted in Bruce, *Back the Attack,* 59.
92 *Canadian Unionist,* Feb. 1945, 40.
93 *Saturday Night,* 12 May 1945, 2.
94 DHH, 112.21009 (D209), Memo from Brigadier DCGS(A), 24 Nov. 1942; *Winnipeg Free
   Press,* 25 Nov. 1942, 1.
95 NAC, MG28 I103, Canadian Labour Congress papers (CLC), vol. 362, file "General 1942-
   57," *Your Questions Answered,* 1944, n.p.
96 NAC, RG44, National War Services records, vol. 34, file "Appointment of Director," Margaret Perry to William Lyon Mackenzie King, 12 April 1941; Gail Cuthbert Brandt, "'Pigeon-
   Holed and Forgotten': The Work of the Subcommittee on the Post-War Problems of Women,
   1943," *Histoire sociale/Social History* 15, 29 (1982): 240-241.
97 NCWC, vol. 84, file 15, Mrs. Edgar D. Hardy to M.S. McWilliams, 15 Nov. 1943.
98 Maternity leave was also advocated in order to reduce the incidence of illegal abortions
   among mothers who could not afford to leave paid work. NCWC, vol. 84, file 17, Highlights of McWilliams Subcommittee Report, 1943; *Canadian Welfare,* March 1944, 4-5;
   Prentice et al., *Canadian Women,* 304-305; Brandt, "Pigeon-Holed and Forgotten," 247-251.
99 Brandt, "Pigeon-Holed and Forgotten," 255.
100 *Saturday Night,* 5 Dec. 1942, 28; *Maclean's,* 1 Nov. 1944, 21.
101 Diane G. Forestell, "The Victorian Legacy: Historical Perspectives on the Canadian Women's
   Army Corps" (PhD diss., York University, 1985), 169.
102 Howe quoted in Ramona Rose, "Keepers of Morale," 97.
103 *Canadian Congress Journal,* Dec. 1944, 7; *Chatelaine,* May 1945, 21.
104 *Mayfair,* Dec. 1945, 40-41.
105 NAC, MG30 E256, Charlotte Whitton papers, vol. 83, Problems of Youth, 1944.
106 J.L. Granatstein and Peter Neary, eds., *The Veterans Charter and Post-War Canada* (Montreal
   and Kingston: McGill-Queen's University Press, 1998), 240.
107 *Canada Year Book, 1946,* 751; *Public Opinion Quarterly,* 1945, 375; Ursel, *Private Lives, Public
   Policy,* 210.

108 Ann Porter, "Women and Income Security in the Post-War Period: The Case of Unemployment Insurance, 1945-1962," *Labour/Le Travail* 31 (1993): 114-115.

109 *Canadian Congress Journal*, March 1945, 34; Ursel, *Private Lives, Public Policy*, 224.

110 Porter, "Women and Income Security," 116. Also see Fahrni, "Under Reconstruction," 180, 300.

111 Symbolically, the allowance was mailed to the female head of the household, because as the "natural guardian of the family" she would ensure that the money was used for the benefit of the children. WIB, vol. 8, file 2-22, "What Are Family Allowances?" n.d.

112 Margaret Moffat, interview by author, Dunrobin, ON, 22 Feb. 1999; anonymous source, interview by author, Ottawa, 28 Nov. 2000.

113 Nash, "Images of Women," 428.

114 Wheeler, interview.

115 *Canadian Unionist*, July 1945, 180; Pierson, *They're Still Women*, 115.

116 Brooks, interview; Vivian Bailey, interview, 14 March 1985, WWWM.

117 One woman, describing her wartime routine, said she rose "at 4:30 a.m. to do the housework, prepare breakfast, and bring the baby to the day nursery by 7 a.m." Following work, she "picked up the baby, [went] home, li[t] a fire, prepare[d] a meal and put the baby to bed" before having some time for herself. *Canadian Welfare*, Nov. 1941, 6.

118 By contrast, 5.2 percent said they wanted one child, 38.9 percent wanted two, 24.3 percent wanted three, and 18.1 percent wanted four. Bailin, interview; CYC, vol. 42, file 5(3G), Group Interview, General Electric Company, 1944.

119 *Canada Year Book, 1951*, 166; F.H. Leacey, *Historical Statistics of Canada* (Ottawa: Supply and Services, 1983), series A-5.

120 Mary Louise Adams, *The Trouble with Normal: Postwar Youth and the Making of Heterosexuality* (Toronto: University of Toronto Press, 1997), 20; J.M. Bumsted, "Home Sweet Suburb: The Great Post-War Migration," *The Beaver*, October-November 1992, 30; Veronica Strong-Boag, "'Their Side of the Story': Women's Voices from Ontario Suburbs, 1945-60," in *A Diversity of Women: 1945-1980*, ed. Joy Parr (Toronto: University of Toronto Press, 1996), 59-60. For instance, at Regency Acres, which opened in 1961 just north of Toronto in Aurora, 96 percent of home buyers were between twenty-four and forty-four years old. Doug Owram, *Born at the Right Time: A History of the Baby Boom Generation* (Toronto: University of Toronto Press, 1996), 81.

121 Strong-Boag, "Their Side of the Story," 53; Prentice et al., *Canadian Women*, 320-321; Mélanie Brunet, "English-Canadian Women's Magazines and the Reconstruction of the Family Home during the Post-War Years, 1945-1960" (MA thesis, University of Ottawa, 1999), 26; Eileen Tyler May, *Homeward Bound: American Families in the Cold War Era* (New York: Basic Books, 1988), 137, 170-171.

122 M. Susan Bland, "Henrietta the Homemaker and Rosie the Riveter: Images of Women in Advertising in *Maclean's* Magazine, 1939-1950," *Atlantis* 8, 2 (1983): 72.

123 Joan Sangster, "Doing Two Jobs: The Wage-Earning Mother, 1945-70," in *A Diversity of Women: 1945-1980*, ed. Joy Parr (Toronto: University of Toronto Press, 1996), 104.

124 Hartmann, *Home Front and Beyond*, 203-204.

125 Michael C.C. Adams, *The Best War Ever: America and World War II* (Baltimore: Johns Hopkins University Press, 1994), 144.

126 Tyler May, *Homeward Bound*, 63; Nash, "Images of Women," 599.

127 By 1953 Spock's book had sold 4 million copies in North America. Owram, *Born at the Right Time*, 33; Katherine Arnup, *Education for Motherhood: Advice for Mothers in Twentieth-Century Canada* (Toronto: University of Toronto Press, 1994), 87-88, 124-125; Adams, *Trouble with Normal*, 31; Bumsted, "Home Sweet Suburb," 32-33; Hartmann, *Home Front and Beyond*, 177-178; William Tuttle, *"Daddy's Gone to War": The Second World War in the Lives of America's Children* (New York: Oxford, 1993), 108-109.

128 Farnham and Lundberg quoted in Chafe, *Paradox of Change*, 178-179.
129 Mona Gleason, "Psychology and the Construction of the 'Normal' in Postwar Canada, 1945-1960," *Canadian Historical Review* 78, 3 (1997): 445-447. Also see Mona Gleason, *Normalizing the Ideal: Psychology, Schooling and Family in Postwar Canada* (Toronto: University of Toronto Press, 1999), chapter 3.
130 Granatstein and Neary, *Veterans Charter*, 244.
131 Quotation taken from Joanne Meyerowitz, ed., *Not June Cleaver: Women and Gender in Postwar America, 1945-1960* (Philadelphia: Temple University Press, 1994), 2. Leila Rupp and Verta Taylor, *Surviving in the Doldrums: The American Women's Rights Movement, 1945 to the 1960s* (New York: Oxford University Press, 1987); Veronica Strong-Boag, "Home Dreams: Women and the Suburban Experiment in Canada, 1945-1960," *Canadian Historical Review* 77, 4 (1991): 471-505; Veronica Strong-Boag, "Canada's Wage-earning Wives and the Construction of the Middle-Class, 1945-60," *Journal of Canadian Studies* 29, 3 (1994): 5-25; Valerie J. Korinek, *Roughing It in Suburbia: Reading* Chatelaine *Magazine in the Fifties and Sixties* (Toronto: University of Toronto Press, 2001); Joan Sangster, *Earning Respect: The Lives of Working Women in Small-Town Ontario, 1920-1960* (Toronto: University of Toronto Press, 1995); Franca Iacovetta, *Such Hardworking People: Italian Immigration in Postwar Toronto* (Montreal and Kingston: McGill-Queen's University Press, 1992); and Frances Swyripa, *Wedded to the Cause: Ukrainian Canadian Women and Ethnic Identity* (Toronto: University of Toronto Press, 1993).
132 Patricia Anderson, *Passion Lost: Public Sex, Private Desire in the Twentieth Century* (Toronto: Thomas Allen Publishers, 2001), 130.
133 Moreover, Patricia Anderson writes that given Kinsey's own sexual proclivities – a "bisexual masochist" who "prostituted his wife to colleagues ... seduced his male graduate students" and "participated in group masturbation sessions" – it becomes quite conceivable that he massaged results to demonstrate widespread deviation from "normal" sexual behaviour. Anderson, *Passion Lost*, 132-134; Adams, *Trouble with Normal*, 36-37.
134 Tyler May, *Homeward Bound*, 121, 124-125, 199-201.
135 Strong-Boag, "Home Dreams," 500-503.
136 For even stronger trends in America see Rupp and Taylor, *Surviving in the Doldrums*, 13, and Chafe, *Paradox of Change*, 161, 188.
137 In Quebec, however, where the conservative influence of the Catholic church still loomed large, the figure was just over 17 percent. *Labour Gazette*, 1954, 373; Fahrni, "Under Reconstruction," 77.
138 See, for example, Freda Hawkins, *Canada and Immigration: Public Policy and Public Concern* (Montreal and Kingston: McGill-Queen's University Press, 1988), and Ronald E. Schmalz, "Former Enemies Come to Canada: Ottawa and the Postwar German Immigration Boom, 1951-57" (PhD diss., University of Ottawa, 2000).
139 In 1947, 12.8 percent of men and 32.8 percent of women in the labour force worked less than forty hours a week. *Canada Year Book, 1950*, 678.
140 Women's Bureau, Department of Labour, *Women at Work in Canada* (Ottawa: 1957), 34-35; Nash, "Images of Women," 105.
141 *Gazette* quoted in *Canada Year Book, 1950*, 661; *Labour Gazette*, 1954, 373.
142 *Saturday Night*, 15 Feb. 1947, 32.
143 CLC, vol. 362, file "Ann Francis," radio script entitled "Why Do Women Work?" 2 Dec. 1949.
144 Korinek, "Roughing It in Suburbia," 35. During these years, the only time *Chatelaine* faced worrisome circulation numbers was between 1952 and 1957 when its editorship passed from Lotta Dempsey to John Clare, a "gruff old newspaperman" who moved the magazine in a more conservative direction. *Ottawa Citizen*, 27 March 2001, B1, B4.
145 Monica Boyd, *Canadian Attitudes towards Women: Thirty Years of Change* (Ottawa: Department of Labour, 1984), 45.

146 Shirley Tillotson, "Human Rights Law as Prism: Women's Organizations, Unions, and Ontario's Female Employees Fair Remuneration Act, 1951," *Canadian Historical Review* 72, 4 (1991): 532-557; Joan Sangster, *Dreams of Equality: Women on the Canadian Left, 1920-1950* (Toronto: McClelland and Stewart, 1989), 201-204; Prentice et al., *Canadian Women*, 313; *Labour Gazette*, 1956, 1229.

147 Sangster, "Doing Two Jobs," 109-112; Mariana Valverde, "Building Anti-Delinquent Communities: Morality, Gender, and Generation in the City," in *A Diversity of Women: 1945-1980*, ed. Joy Parr (Toronto: University of Toronto Press, 1996), 37; Owram, *Born at the Right Time*, 130.

148 Laura Harrison, interview by author, Edmonton, 20 May 1993.

Chapter 7: Women Warriors

1 Linda J. Quiney, "'Assistant Angels': Canadian Women As Voluntary Aid Detachment Workers during and after the Great War, 1914-1930" (PhD diss., University of Ottawa, 2001), 154.

2 Ibid., 307; Kathryn McPherson, *Bedside Matters: The Transformation of Canadian Nursing, 1900-1990* (Toronto: Oxford University Press, 1996), 67; Donna Zwicker, "Alberta Women Join Up," in *For King and Country: Alberta in the Second World War*, ed. K.W. Tingley (Edmonton: Provincial Museum of Alberta, 1995), 89; Veterans Affairs Canada, "History of the Nursing Sisters of Canada," 7 Oct. 1998, <www.vac-acc.gc.ca>.

3 Lt.-Col. G.W.L. Nicholson, *Canada's Nursing Sisters* (Toronto: Samuel Stevens Hakkert, 1975), 16, 208; Barbara Dundas, *A History of Women in the Canadian Military* (Montreal: Art Global, 2000), 43; Donna A. Zwicker, "Alberta Women and World War Two" (MA thesis, University of Calgary, 1985), 8; C.P. Stacey, *Arms, Men and Government: The War Policies of Canada, 1939-1945* (Ottawa: Department of National Defence, 1970), 416.

4 McPherson, *Bedside Matters*, 191-192, 199.

5 *Saturday Night*, 3 Oct. 1942, 26; *Chatelaine*, Oct. 1943, 21. Reyburn was affiliated with the *Montreal Standard*.

6 *Montreal Star*, 1 Sept. 1943, 20; *New York Times Film Reviews*, vol. 3, 1969; M. Joyce Baker, *Images of Women in Film: The War Years, 1941-1945* (Ann Arbor: UMI Research Press, 1980), 113.

7 The wartime service of 1,029 military nurses was confined to Canada. Nicholson, *Canada's Nursing Sisters*, 190, 195; Dundas, *Women in the Canadian Military*, 47.

8 Small numbers were assigned to Bermuda, Scotland, and Newfoundland. In mid-1941 some 300 Canadian nurses were made part of the South African Military Nursing Service. In southern and later in northern Africa, they dealt with bleak accommodation, blistering heat, torrential rainstorms, and scorpions. Their camps were often surrounded by barbed wire to guard against bandits. Nicholson, *Canada's Nursing Sisters*, 138.

9 Patricia Moll, interview, 7 May 1985, Concordia University, Women and War Work in Montreal Collection (WWWM).

10 Sub-Lt. Agnes Wilkie died when a German U-boat torpedoed the SS *Caribou* in the Cabot Strait. Veterans Affairs Canada, "Nursing Sisters of Canada."

11 Moll, interview; Margaret Van Scoyoz, interview, WWWM; Nicholson, *Canada's Nursing Sisters*, 160; J.L. Granatstein, *Canada's Army: Waging War and Keeping the Peace* (Toronto: University of Toronto Press, 2002), 230.

12 Granatstein, *Canada's Army*, 96; Kay Christie, interview, National Archives of Canada (NAC), Audiovisual Division (AV), Tape R-8549; Gaetane Kerr, interview, WWWM.

13 Nicholson, *Canada's Nursing Sisters*, 179; Norma Beattie, interview, Eastern Townships Research Centre, Lennoxville, QC, Special Media Collection, Oral History of Eastern Townships, Anglophone Women during World War II (ETRC); Olga Gruhzit-Hoyt, *They Also Served: American Women in World War II* (New York: Birch Lane, 1995), xvii.

14 This description of Kennedy was offered by her long-time friend Phyllis Lee-Wright. Susan Wade, "Joan Kennedy and the British Columbia Service Corps," in *Not Just Pin Money*, ed. Barbara K. Latham and Roberta J. Pazdro (Victoria: Camosun College, 1984), 425.

15 Most were affiliated with either the Women's Voluntary Reserve Corps (which operated in Quebec, Ontario, and the Maritimes), or the Canadian Auxiliary Territorial Service (which operated in western Ontario, the Prairies, and British Columbia), though in Quebec, French-speaking women also joined the Corps de réserve national féminin and the Réserve canadienne féminine. Jean Bruce, *Back the Attack! Canadian Women during the Second World War – at Home and Abroad* (Toronto: Macmillan, 1985), 27-34; Ruth Pierson, *They're Still Women after All: Canadian Women and the Second World War* (Toronto: McClelland and Stewart, 1986), 95; *Ottawa Journal*, 20 Nov. 1940, 6; Dundas, *Women in the Canadian Military*, 38-40.

16 Zwicker, "Alberta Women," 14-18; J.L. Granatstein and Desmond Morton, *Victory 1945: Canadians from War to Peace* (Toronto: HarperCollins, 1995), 53; Diane G. Forestell, "The Victorian Legacy: Historical Perspectives on the Canadian Women's Army Corps" (PhD diss., York University, 1985), 78; Carolyn Gossage, *Great Coats and Glamour Boots: Canadian Women at War (1939-1945)* (Toronto: Dundurn Press, 1990), 24-29.

17 Gossage, *Great Coats and Glamour Boots*, 30-31; *Maclean's*, 1 Aug. 1941, 16.

18 This post lasted until May 1943, when National Defence Headquarters split the directorship of the CWAC. Kennedy became general staff officer while Lt.-Col. Margaret Eaton was named assistant adjutant-general. In April 1944 the command was reunited under Eaton's direction. *Ottawa Journal*, 30 June 1941, 8; Barbara Dundas and Serge Durflinger, *The Canadian Women's Army Corps, 1941-1946* (Ottawa: Canadian War Museum, 1999), 2.

19 Dundas and Durflinger, *Canadian Women's Army Corps*, 3; Bruce, *Back the Attack*, 75; Forestell, "Victorian Legacy," 250; Gossage, *Great Coats and Glamour Boots*, 32-42; Stacey, *Arms, Men and Government*, 416.

20 Granatstein and Morton, *Victory 1945*, 53; Teresa M. Nash, "Images of Women in National Film Board of Canada Films during World War II and the Post-War Years, 1939-1949" (PhD diss., McGill University, 1982), 371.

21 Pierson, *They're Still Women*, 14.

22 The highest rated response, at 26 percent, emphasized women maintaining a stable home life. This was followed at 23 percent by women taking a war job, 13 percent voluntary work, and 11 percent preserving and rationing food. Pierson, *They're Still Women*, 135.

23 Diane G. Forestell, "The Necessity of Sacrifice for the Nation at War: Women's Labour Force Participation, 1939-46," *Histoire sociale/Social History* 22, 44 (1989): 337.

24 Pierson, *They're Still Women*, 159-160.

25 Bruce, *Back the Attack*, 38; Jean Geldart, interview by author, Ottawa, 9 April 2000.

26 Montreal *Gazette*, 22 May 1942, 4.

27 City of Vancouver Archives, Mss 557, Helen Dawe papers, vol. 3, file 1, Unidentified clipping entitled "Wren Is a Lady before She Is in the Navy," 16 Jan. 1943.

28 Gossage, *Great Coats and Glamour Boots*, 121-122.

29 Gruhzit-Hoyt, *They Also Served*, xvi; NAC, MG28 I25, National Council of Women of Canada papers (NCWC), vol. 84, file 18, press release, n.d; Dundas, *Women in the Canadian Military*, 84; Forestell, "Victorian Legacy," 72. Similar problems were experienced by servicewomen elsewhere. RAF personnel were known to call Women's Auxiliary Air Force members "groundsheets," and American sailors often joked that they joined the Navy to "ride the waves." John Costello, *Love, Sex and War: Changing Values, 1939-1945* (London: Collins, 1985), 80.

30 Granatstein and Morton, *Victory 1945*, plate between 64-65.

31 *Canadian Home Journal*, March 1943, 28.

32 *Mayfair,* July 1943, 98.
33 Nash, "Images of Women," 498-501.
34 National Film Board of Canada (NFB), *Proudly She Marches,* 1943; Gary Evans, *John Grierson and the National Film Board: The Politics of Wartime Propaganda* (Toronto: University of Toronto Press, 1984), 137.
35 *Winnipeg Free Press,* 27 March 1944, 8; *Maclean's,* 15 Oct. 1942, 32.
36 *Saturday Night,* 12 May 1942, 2; *Saturday Night,* 23 Jan. 1943, 22.
37 *Family Herald and Weekly Star* (eastern edition), 30 July 1941, 35.
38 *Toronto Star,* 18 Sept. 1942, 21.
39 *Vancouver Sun,* 3 Oct. 1942, 11; Brantford *Expositor,* 10 April 1943.
40 *Halifax Chronicle,* 7 Nov. 1942, 12.
41 *Canadian Affairs,* 1 Oct. 1943, 2-3.
42 Kay Poulton, interview, 29 Oct. 1975, AV, Tape R-8548; Forestell, "Necessity of Sacrifice," 340; Zwicker, "Alberta Women," 59; Gossage, *Great Coats and Glamour Boots,* 52-54.
43 Sara E. Johnson, *To Spread Their Wings* (Spruce Grove, AB: Saraband Productions, 1990), 53.
44 Dundas, *Women in the Canadian Military,* 53-54; Pierson, *They're Still Women,* 110.
45 Directorate of History and Heritage, Department of National Defence (DHH), 113.3 R4003(D1)V2, "Infractions of Discipline – CWAC," Report 26, 20 May 1944.
46 *Ottawa Journal,* 13 Jan. 1942, 10.
47 Geldart, interview.
48 DHH, 113.3 R4003(D1), Research and Information Branch, Trends in Army Thinking, Aug. 1944.
49 *Khaki* 3, 18: 7; *CWAC Newsletter,* Dec. 1944, 1.
50 Zwicker, "Alberta Women," 57-58; Pierson, *They're Still Women,* 113; C.P. Stacey and Barbara Wilson, *The Half-Million: The Canadians in Britain, 1939-1946* (Toronto: University of Toronto Press, 1987), 142.
51 Bruce, *Back the Attack,* 43, 83; Mary Hawkins Buch, *Props on her Sleeve: The Wartime Letters of a Canadian Airwoman* (Toronto: Dundurn Press, 1997), 28.
52 Gossage, *Great Coats and Glamour Boots,* 121.
53 D. Phyllis Harrison, *Saga of an Airwoman* (Penticton, BC: Sage Press, 1995), 80; Bill McNeil, *Voices of a War Remembered: An Oral History of Canadians in World War Two* (Toronto: Doubleday, 1991), 75; DHH, 113.3 R4003(D1)V2, "Infractions of Discipline – CWAC," Report 26, 20 May 1944; W.R. Feasby, *Official History of the Canadian Medical Services, 1939-1945,* vol. 1 (Ottawa: Queen's Printer, 1956), 350-351.
54 NAC, RG24, Department of National Defence records (DND), vol. 12,613, file 218-6, Venereal Disease in the CWAC, n.d.
55 DND, vol. 12,612, file 218-9, Venereal Disease: Unit Practice and Opinion, Jan. 1945, and Outline for VD Lecture to CWAC Personnel, n.d.
56 NFB, *For Your Information,* 1943. This film was made for members of the RCAF(WD). Other anti-VD films made for servicewomen projected similar messages; they included *Feminine Hygiene* and *Fight Syphilis.* DND, vol. 6617, file 8994-6, Captain W.G. Allison to D.D.G.M.S. (B), 24 Oct. 1944.
57 NAC, MG31 K13, Olive Russell papers (OR), vol. 1, file 13, Some Observations and Statistics on CWAC Personnel, 3 Dec. 1943.
58 DHH, 77/652, *Sky-Line,* 1 Jan 1942, 1; Dundas and Durflinger, *Canadian Women's Army Corps,* 3.
59 DND, vol. 6543, file 650-94-28, pt. 4, Job Descriptions – CWAC, n.d.; *Toronto Telegram,* 7 Dec. 1943, 10; *Winnipeg Free Press,* 6 March 1944, 9; Roger Sarty, *Canada and the Battle of the Atlantic* (Montreal: Art Global, 1998), 148.

60 Ben Wicks, *When the Boys Came Marching Home: True Stories of the Men Who Went to War and the Women and Children Who Took Them Back* (Toronto: Stoddart, 1991), 140.

61 This was the case, for example, at the long-range radio navigation station at Lower White-head, New Brunswick. Sarty, *Battle of the Atlantic,* 150; York University Archives, Thunder Bay Navy Interviews, 1984-1986, box 8, file 117, testimony of Mary Armstrong.

62 Bruce, *Back the Attack,* 89.

63 NCWC, *Year Book, 1941,* 44; DHH, 77/632, *Paulson Post,* Nov. 1942, 52; OR, vol. 2, file 14, Russell to Marion, Easter Sunday 1943.

64 NAC, MG26 J4, William Lyon Mackenzie King papers, vol. 255, file "National Council of Women of Canada," Resolutions, 1942; NCWC, vol. 84, file 16, undated memo. Although the federal government balked at implementing completely equal pay for equal work in the military, many Canadians were amenable to the idea. When queried in 1944, women supported the measure by 50 to 30 percent; rather incredibly the results from men were virtually identical at 53 to 34 percent in favour. However, even supporters understandably believed that servicemen had tougher and certainly more dangerous jobs that warranted higher pay. J.L. Granatstein and Peter Neary, eds., *The Veterans Charter and Post-War Canada* (Montreal and Kingston: McGill-Queen's University Press, 1998), 238; Forestell, "Victorian Legacy," 163-164.

65 *Winnipeg Free Press,* 15 March 1944, 10; Dundas, *Women in the Canadian Military,* 52.

66 DHH, 156.2A 34009(D2), Unit Morale Report, CWAC, MD #13, Oct. 1944; DHH, 113 R4003(D1), Some Factors in Maintaining Morale, CWAC Units, 1 Feb. 1945.

67 D'Ann Campbell, "Servicewomen of World War II," *Armed Forces and Society* 16, 2 (1990): 262.

68 Sara Johnson, *To Spread Their Wings,* 8; Barry Broadfoot, *Six War Years: Memories of Canadians at Home and Abroad* (Toronto: Doubleday, 1974), 37.

69 Katherine Ferguson, interview by author, Ottawa, 23 Feb. 1999.

70 Valerie Lowry, interview, 6 Oct. 1975, AV, Tape R-8546.

71 DHH, Naval Board Minutes, vol. 2, Halifax 1942, Minute 52.2; OR, vol. 2, file 14, Olive Russell to Dr. Esther Lloyd-Jones, n.d.

72 DND, vol. 10,767, file C1(D154), Field Censor's Report, 1943.

73 Beverly Drennent, interview, ETRC; *Great Coats and Glamour Boots,* 73, 114-115, 123.

74 OR, vol. 2, file 14, Olive Russell to Miss Royce, 31 Oct. 1944.

75 Drennent, interview; Marguerite McDougall, interview, 6 Oct. 1975, AV, Tape R-8546.

76 *Canadian Home Journal,* Jan. 1943, 5; Ferguson, interview.

77 NAC, MG30 E373, I.S. MacNeil papers (ISM), clipping from *Saturday Night,* 4 March 1944, n.p.; Geldart, interview.

78 Beverly Drummond, interview, ETRC.

79 Buch, *Props on Her Sleeve,* 60.

80 Gossage, *Great Coats and Glamour Boots,* 155; Brantford *Expositor,* 4 Sept. 1943, 4; *CWAC Newsletter,* June 1944, 9.

81 AV, 1981-100-413, *Comrades in Arms,* 1943.

82 Buch, *Props on Her Sleeve,* 10; *Halifax Chronicle,* 29 Aug. 1944, 5.

83 *CWAC Newsletter,* Aug. 1944, 9; Bruce, *Back the Attack,* 51; C.P. Stacey, *Six Years of War: The Army in Canada, Britain and the Pacific* (Ottawa: Department of National Defence, 1966), 211.

84 Initially, only eighty nurses were retained by the military – thirty each in the army and air force, and twenty in the navy – primarily to help with wounded veterans. Veteran Affairs Canada, "History of the Nursing Sisters of Canada."

85 Dundas, *Women in the Canadian Military,* 93.

86 *Ottawa Journal,* 18 Oct. 1944, 10.

87 *Chatelaine,* Dec. 1944, 30, 60; *Canadian Home Journal,* March 1945, 14.
88 Mildren McAfee Horton, "Women in the United States Navy," *American Journal of Sociology* 51, 5 (1946): 448-450; NAC, RG36-31, Wartime Information Board records, vol. 14, file 8-14-E, pt. 1, Research and Information Section, Report #189, 24 May 1945; Magda Fahrni, "Under Reconstruction: The Family and the Public in Postwar Montréal, 1944-1949" (PhD diss., York University, 2001), 177.
89 ISM, clipping from *Halifax Morning Chronicle,* 8 Dec. 1944, n.p.
90 Montreal *Gazette,* 6 June 1945, 6.
91 Gossage, *Great Coats and Glamour Boots,* 204-205; Wicks, *When the Boys,* 160.
92 Geldart, interview.
93 *Canada Year Book, 1948-49,* 1161; Ann Porter, "Women and Income Security in the Post-War Period: The Case of Unemployment Insurance, 1945-1962," *Labour/Le Travail* 31 (1993): 114-115.
94 Walter Woods, *Rehabilitation (A Combined Operation), Being a History of the Development and Carrying out of a Plan for the Re-Establishment of a Million Young Veterans of World War II by the Department of Veterans Affairs and Its Predecessor the Department of Pensions and National Health* (Ottawa: Queen's Printer, 1953), 254-255.
95 Peter Neary and Shaun Brown, "The Veterans Charter and Canadian Women Veterans of World War II," in *The Good Fight: Canadians in the Second World War,* ed. J.L. Granatstein and Peter Neary (Toronto: Copp Clark Longman, 1995), 396-403; NAC, RG38, Department of Veterans Affairs records (DVA), vol. 197, file 65-272-13, Conference on Women's Rehabilitation, Feb. 1946; Fahrni, "Under Reconstruction," 177; *Canada Year Book, 1947,* 1152.
96 *Canada Year Book, 1947,* 1153; *Canada Year Book, 1948-49,* 1161; Neary and Brown, "Veterans Charter," 408.
97 *Saturday Night,* 17 March 1945, 30-31; DVA, vol. 372, News Release No. 168, n.d.
98 DVA, vol. 372, News Release No. 247, 16 Oct. 1946; McNeil, *Voices of a War,* 36-37.
99 Susan Hartmann, *The Home Front and Beyond: American Women in the 1940s* (Boston: Twayne Publishers, 1982), 116.
100 *Canada Year Book, 1948-49,* 320-321; *Canada Year Book, 1955,* 343; Women's Bureau, Department of Labour, *Women at Work in Canada* (Ottawa: 1957), 24-25.
101 Granatstein and Neary, *Veterans Charter,* 244.
102 Dundas, *Women in the Canadian Military,* 95-104; *Saturday Night,* 3 July 1951, 18. Also see Patricia Powers, "With Their Feet on the Ground: Women's Lives and Work in the Royal Canadian Air Force, 1951-1966" (MA thesis, University of Ottawa, 1998).

Chapter 8: The Children's War

1 See Ruth Inglis, *The Children's War: Evacuation, 1939-1945* (London: Collins, 1989), 3, and Carlton Jackson, *Who Will Take Our Children?* (London: Methuen, 1985), 15-16.
2 *Globe and Mail,* 7 Sept. 1939, 1.
3 Geoffrey Bilson, *The Guest Children: The Story of the British Child Evacuees Sent to Canada during World War II* (Saskatoon: Fifth House, 1988), 8, 23.
4 Ibid., 5; National Archives of Canada (NAC), RG76, Immigration Branch records (IB), vol. 438, file 661315, pt. 2, Charles Frederick Blair, Memo for files, 6 June 1940.
5 IB, vol. 439, file 661315, pt. 1, clipping from *Montreal Herald,* 21 June 1940, n.p., and clipping from *Charlottetown Patriot,* 27 Aug. 1940, n.p.
6 Of the 1148 children on the first four boatloads of Children's Overseas Reception Board evacuees, only 12 were Jews. In its defence, Ottawa said it was prioritizing "Allied children," and most of the Jews had escaped from Germany and Czechoslovakia. Some 80 percent of the children were Protestant. IB, vol. 438, file 661315, pt. 3, Memo on the Movement of Evacuated British Children Refugees and Others, 10 June 1940; IB, vol. 439, file 661315, pt. 1,

clipping from Saskatoon *Star-Phoenix*, 26 June 1940, n.p., and clipping from *Toronto Star*, 25 June 1940, n.p.; Bilson, *Guest Children*, 22.

7 Inglis, *Children's War*, 106.

8 IB, vol. 438, file 661315, pt. 2, clipping from Regina *Leader-Post*, 6 June 1940, n.p., and 21 Aug. 1940, n.p.; IB, vol. 438, file 661315, pt. 1, clipping from *Calgary Herald*, 10 July 1940, n.p.

9 IB, vol. 438, file 661315, pt. 1, Voluntary Scheme for the Evacuation of Unaccompanied School-children to the Overseas Dominions for the Period of the War, n.d.

10 Ben Wicks, *The Day They Took the Children* (Toronto: Stoddart, 1989), 155; Bilson, *Guest Children*, 19; NAC, RG44, National War Services records, vol. 21, file "Income Tax Exemptions," *An Act to Amend the War Income Tax Act*, chapter 34, 4 George VI, 7 Aug. 1940; NAC, MG28 I10, Canadian Council on Social Development papers (CCSD), vol. 88, file C1(C), Conditions for Admission of Child to Canada, n.d.

11 Meta Maclean, *The Singing Ship: An Odyssey of Evacuee Children* (Bath, UK: Cedric Books, 1941), 6; Bilson, *Guest Children*, 31, 33.

12 IB, vol. 439, file 661315, pt. 6, Minister of Mines and Resources to Governor General in Council, 9 July 1940.

13 Depots included the Manitoba School for the Deaf, the British Columbia School for the Deaf and Blind, various private schools, and university dormitories. In Alberta, two floors of the provincial legislature were used. IB, vol. 439, file 661315, pt. 1, clipping from *Winnipeg Tribune*, 12 July 1940, n.p., clipping from *Vancouver Sun*, 3 July 1940, n.p., and clipping from *Calgary Herald*, 20 June 1940, n.p.; IB, vol. 438, file 661315, pt. 3, J.B. Dickson to Blair, 3 July 1940.

14 Bilson, *Guest Children*, 90-91.

15 IB, vol. 438, file 661315, pt. 2, Findings of Conference: Dominion Immigration and Provincial Child Caring Authorities re: Possible Movement of Child Refugees and Evacuees to Canada, June 1940; IB, vol. 438, file 661315, pt. 3, Memo on Movement of Evacuated British Children Refugees and Others, 10 June 1940, Charlotte Whitton to F.C. Blair, 21 June 1940, and clipping from Montreal *Gazette*, 24 June 1940, n.p.; Stephen Kimber, *Sailors, Slackers and Blind Pigs: Halifax at War* (Toronto: Doubleday, 2002), 60-69.

16 IB, vol. 439, file 661315, pt. 7, Memorandum for F.C. Blair, 2 June 1941.

17 IB, vol. 439, file 661315, pt. 7, Memo on Movement of Evacuated British Children Refugees and Others by Vincent Massey, n.d., and B.W. Heise to F.C. Blair, 20 June 1940; Bilson, *Guest Children*, 11-12, 14-15.

18 Bilson, *Guest Children*, 78; IB, vol. 438, file 661315, pt. 1, clipping from *Ottawa Journal*, 7 June 1940, n.p., and clipping from Montreal *Gazette*, 21 March 1941, n.p.

19 CORB also sent 836 children to the United States, 576 to Australia, 353 to South Africa, and 203 to New Zealand. Inglis, *Children's War*, 105, 117; IB, vol. 439, file 661315, pt. 7, Memo from F.C. Blair, 17 June 1941.

20 IB, vol. 439, file 661315, pt. 7, clipping from *Ottawa Citizen*, 4 Sept. 1940, n.p.; Wicks, *Day They Took the Children*, 151.

21 IB, vol. 439, file 661315, pt. 6, Massey to Secretary of State for External Affairs, 3 Oct. 1940.

22 IB, vol. 438, file 661315, pt. 1, clipping from *Winnipeg Tribune*, 30 Nov. 1940, n.p., and clipping from *Edmonton Bulletin*, 9 Dec. 1940, n.p.

23 IB, vol. 438, file 661315, pt. 1, clipping from *Edmonton Journal*, 23 Aug. 1940, n.p.; Hardy quoted in George C. Blackburn, *Where the Hell Are the Guns? A Soldier's Eye View of the 'Anxious Years,' 1939-44* (Toronto: McClelland and Stewart, 1997), 72.

24 This message of successful adaptation was also conveyed in a number of special live radio broadcasts starting in mid-1941, in which British children in a CBC studio booth spoke for perhaps a minute each to their parents at a BBC facility in England. The public conversations were often awkward, restrained, and formulaic, though the participants always

insisted that everything was fine. See, for example, NAC, Audiovisual Division, A1 2000-05-028, *Children Calling Home,* 1 June 1941; IB, vol. 438, file 661315, pt. 1, clipping from *Montreal Mail,* 3 Dec. 1940, n.p.

25 Patricia Galloway, ed., *Too Young to Fight: Memories from Our Youth during World War II* (Toronto: Stoddart, 1999), 179; IB, vol. 438, file 661315, pt. 1, clipping from *Winnipeg Free Press,* 15 May 1941, n.p.

26 IB, vol. 438, file 661315, pt. 1, clipping from *Edmonton Journal,* 5 Aug. 1941, n.p.; *The School* 29, 7 (1941): 599-606; Bilson, *Guest Children,* 132.

27 Bilson, *Guest Children,* 152; anonymous source, interview by author, Ottawa, 10 June 2000; Barry Broadfoot, *Six War Years: Memories of Canadians at Home and Abroad* (Toronto: Doubleday, 1974), 125.

28 Anonymous, interview; Bilson, *Guest Children,* 61, 73-74, 164-165.

29 Bilson, *Guest Children,* 119-120, 188-191; IB, vol. 439, file 661315, pt. 7, B.W. Heise to F.C. Blair, 26 Aug. 1941; IB, vol. 438, file 661315, pt. 1, clippings from Montreal *Gazette,* 20 July 1940 and 12 Nov. 1941, n.p.

30 Anonymous, interview.

31 Bilson, *Guest Children,* 120, 137, 180-181; Inglis, *Children's War,* 54; William Tuttle, *"Daddy's Gone to War": The Second World War in the Lives of America's Children* (New York: Oxford, 1993), 13.

32 James Craig Jr., interview by author, Ottawa, 9 Aug. 1997.

33 IB, vol. 439, file 661315, pt. 7, B.W. Heise to F.C. Blair, 26 Aug. 1941; IB, vol. 439, file 661315, pt. 6, Memorandum for file by F.C. Blair, 13 Dec. 1940.

34 Galloway, *Too Young to Fight,* 178-179; anonymous, interview; Bilson, *Guest Children,* 205.

35 Bilson, *Guest Children,* 170, 206, 208-209, 213, 221, 231, 237; Mary Baxter, interview by author, Ottawa, 22 May 2000; anonymous, interview; B.S. Johnson, ed., *The Evacuees* (London: Victor Gollancz, 1968), 97-99; Inglis, *Children's War,* 129, 147-162.

36 Galloway, *Too Young to Fight,* 175.

37 Carrier quoted in ibid., 42, 72, 157; Montreal *Gazette,* 8 May 1942, 2; Serge Marc Durflinger, "City at War: The Effects of the Second World War on Verdun, Québec" (PhD diss., McGill University, 1998), 317-318.

38 Bill McNeil, *Voices of a War Remembered: An Oral History of Canadians in World War Two* (Toronto: Doubleday, 1991), 131; Tuttle, *Daddy's Gone to War,* 148; J.L. Granatstein and Desmond Morton, *Victory 1945: Canadians from War to Peace* (Toronto: HarperCollins, 1995), 87-88.

39 Norah Lewis, "'Isn't This a Terrible War?' The Attitudes of Children to Two World Wars," *Historical Studies in Education* 7, 2 (1995): 207; Charles Johnston, "The Children's War: The Mobilization of Ontario Youth during the Second World War," in *Patterns of the Past: Interpreting Ontario's History,* ed. Roger Hall, William Westfall, and Laurel Sefton MacDowell (Toronto: Dundurn Press, 1988), 373; *Canadian Forum,* Nov. 1940, 241.

40 City of Ottawa Archives (COA), MG32-7-1, Ottawa Public School Board records (OPSB), Chief Inspector's Report, 1943, 3; *The School* 28, 10 (1940): 460.

41 Emilie Montgomery, "'The War Was a Very Vivid Part of My Life': British Columbia School Children and the Second World War" (MA thesis, University of British Columbia, 1991), 67; *Ottawa Citizen,* 20 Nov. 1939, 23.

42 Christine Hamelin, "A Sense of Purpose: Ottawa Students and the Second World War," *Canadian Military History* 6, 1 (1997): 35.

43 *Ottawa Journal,* 7 April 1942, 13.

44 Ontario Department of Education, *Annual Report,* 1944, preface; Edmonton Public School Board Archives (EPSB), *Annual Report,* 1942, 14, and *Annual Report,* 1945, 18.

45 *Halifax Chronicle,* 29 Oct. 1942, 4.

46 *Canada Year Book, 1946,* 828.
47 *Ottawa Journal,* 9 Aug. 1941, 2; OPSB, Chief Inspector's Report, 1943, 3.
48 *Ottawa Citizen,* 11 Oct. 1943, 2; Hamelin, "Sense of Purpose," 37; George Tuttle, *Youth Orga-nizations in Canada: A Reference Manual* (Toronto: Ryerson Press, 1946), 45-46; *Ottawa Journal,* 11 March 1942, 3; *ATA Magazine,* Sept. 1942, 18; *Edmonton Journal,* 21 Nov. 1942, 18; Montgomery, "War Was a Very Vivid Part of My Life," 78-79.
49 CCSD, vol. 82, file 1939-44, Wartime Emergency Service Test for Rangers and Girl Guides, n.d.
50 *Ottawa Citizen,* 9 Sept 1940, 20; *Ottawa Journal,* 7 April 1942, 2; *Saturday Night,* 19 Sept. 1942, 2; *Country Guide and Northwest Farmer,* June 1943, 47.
51 *Ottawa Citizen,* 8 Sept. 1943, 14; *Family Herald and Weekly Star* (eastern edition), 9 June 1943, 16.
52 *Canadian Welfare,* 15 Nov. 1940, 46-47.
53 Archives of Ontario (AO), MU5081, box 10, file 1939-50, 1943 Conference on Delinquency; Carrier quoted in Galloway, *Too Young to Fight,* 65-66.
54 *Montreal Star,* 11 Sept. 1943, 3; *ATA Magazine,* Feb. 1944, 1-2.
55 Kenneth Rogers, *Street Gangs in Toronto: A Study of the Forgotten Boy* (Toronto: Ryerson Press, 1945), 32-33.
56 *Canada Year Book, 1919,* 616-617; AO, RG29, Department of Public Health records (OH), series I-99, Container 3, Work of the Big Brothers Movement, 1939.
57 NAC, MG28 I441, Canadian Association of Social Workers papers, vol. 10, file 10, unidenti-fied newspaper clipping, 6 April 1941, n.p.; *Canadian Welfare,* Nov. 1941, 17-18.
58 John McCarthy, "The Individual Child and His Problems" (bachelor of pedagogy thesis, University of Toronto, 1944), 1; Karen Anderson, *Wartime Women: Sex Roles, Family Rela-tions, and the Status of Women during World War II* (Westport, CT: Greenwood Press, 1981), 95-98.
59 James Gilbert, *A Cycle of Outrage: America's Reaction to the Juvenile Delinquent in the 1950s* (New York: Oxford University Press, 1986), 65.
60 Also of this genre were wartime films like *Teen-Age* and *Are These Our Parents? Ottawa Journal,* 9 Feb. 1944, 16, 16 Feb. 1944, 16, and 16 Sept. 1944, 9.
61 *Canada Year Book, 1945,* 1116; *Saturday Night,* 14 Nov. 1942, 24.
62 *Canadian Periodical Index,* 1930-1948.
63 AO, RG4, Attorney-General records (AG), series 32, file 1217/1942, County Reports on Juve-nile Delinquency, 1942.
64 CCSD, vol. 87, file 1856, Marjorie Bradford to George Davidson, 16 Sept. 1943.
65 Augustine Brannigan, "Mystification of the Innocents: Crime Comics and Delinquency in Canada, 1931-1949," *Criminal Justice History* 7 (1986): 138; *Saturday Night,* 4 Sept. 1943, 1; Tuttle, *Daddy's Gone to War,* 197.
66 Ontario, Department of Education, *Annual Report,* 1943, 18.
67 Metropolitan Toronto Archives (MTA), RG 5.1, Department of Social Services records (DSS), vol. 1, file 73, Report: Juvenile Delinquency, by Brig.-Gen. D.C. Draper, Toronto Police Force, Submitted to the Honourable Board of Police Commissioners, Toronto, 13 April 1944.
68 CCSD, vol. 54, file 1942-46, clipping from *Montreal Herald,* n.d., n.p.; Tuttle, *Daddy's Gone to War,* 201.
69 *Ottawa Journal,* 12 Feb. 1942, 5.
70 NAC, MG30 E256, Charlotte Whitton papers (CW), vol. 82, Address, "Threats to the Home Base," n.d.; CW, vol. 83, Address, "What of this Second Front?" 15 June 1943.
71 This trend appeared evident in at least Moncton, Saint John, Montreal, Verdun, Ottawa, Toronto, Port Arthur, Fort William, Regina, Saskatoon, Moose Jaw, Vancouver, and Victoria. *Toronto Star,* 3 Sept. 1942, 17; *Canadian School Journal,* 20, 10 (1942), 323; DSS, vol. 3, file

73.1, General Manager of Social Problems Committee, Toronto Board of Trade to the Mayor, 23 Nov. 1944; City of Calgary Archives (CA), RG26, City Clerk records, file 2239, Chief Constable J. Downey to J.M. Miller, 24 Oct. 1942; CCSD, vol. 87, file 1856, Agnes Collier to Joseph Laycock, 2 Jan. 1942; AG, series 32, file 740/1942, unidentified newspaper clipping.

72 J. Morton Blum, *V Was for Victory* (New York: Harcourt Brace Jovanovich, 1976), 205-206; Mary Louise Adams, *The Trouble with Normal: Postwar Youth and the Making of Heterosexuality* (Toronto: University of Toronto Press, 1997), 72; William Weintraub, *City Unique: Montreal Days and Nights in the 1940s and 1950s* (Toronto: McClelland and Stewart, 1996), 51.

73 AG, series 32, file 1008/1942, Police Report, #6 Div., 1 June 1943.

74 *Ottawa Journal*, 1 June 1944, 1; Durflinger, "City at War," 348-354.

75 Rogers, *Street Gangs in Toronto*, 5-6, 11-12, 42-53; AO, RG20, Correctional Services records (CS), series C-2, file 3.7, Interim Report for Toronto Big Brothers Regarding Unattached Gangs of Boys in the City of Toronto, Summer 1944.

76 Joan Sangster, *Girl Trouble: Female Delinquency in English Canada* (Toronto: Between the Lines, 2002), 78-82.

77 *Saturday Night*, 4 Nov. 1944, 3; *New Advance*, Feb. 1945, 1-2.

78 Archives of Alberta (AA), 83.129, Department of Public Welfare records (DPW), Jean McDonald to John Wodell, 12 Aug. 1943; *Maclean's*, 15 Aug. 1943, 48.

79 CCSD, vol. 87, file 1856, clipping from *Chatelaine*, June 1943, n.p.

80 City of Vancouver Archives (CVA), RG2, City Clerk records (CCV), series A-1, vol. 292, file "Police Department – 1941," Report of the Juvenile Court and Detention Home, 3 Dec. 1941; CCSD, vol. 86, file 1848, Report of the John Howard Society of Vancouver, 10 March 1942.

81 CCSD, vol. 87, file 1856, Statements by Junior League of Montreal, the Ligue de la Jeunesse Féminine, and Jewish Welfare League for the Delinquency Prevention Week, 12-18 March 1944.

82 *New Advance*, Dec. 1943, 2.

83 *Canada Year Book, 1948-49*, 200; CCSD, vol. 82, file 1944, Canadian Youth as Seen in the Census and Related Statistics, May 1943.

84 *Saturday Night*, 23 Jan. 1943, 5; Neil Sutherland, "'We Always Had Things to Do': The Paid and Unpaid Work of Anglophone Children between the 1920s and 1960s," *Labour/Le Travail* 22 (1990): 135.

85 DSS, vol. 1, file 73, Director of Social Services to City Commissioner, 19 May 1943; Ernest Groves and Gladys Groves, "The Social Background of Wartime Adolescents," *Annals of the American Academy of Political and Social Science* 235 (1944): 28-29; James H.S. Bossard, "Family Background of Wartime Adolescents," *Annals of the American Academy of Political and Social Science*, 236 (1944), 38-39.

86 NAC, RG27, Department of Labour records (DL), vol. 988, file 1-11-4, untitled chart; *Canadian Home Journal*, April 1943, 49; CCSD, vol. 83, file 594-1940-41, Youth Employment Survey, 22 April 1941.

87 Robert Stamp, *The Schools of Ontario, 1876-1976* (Toronto: University of Toronto Press, 1982), 172; Kenneth Rogers, *The Boys Are Worth It* (Toronto: Ryerson Press, 1944), 5-6.

88 CCSD, vol. 83, file 594-1936-51, Report of General Secretary, Big Sisters of Toronto, 7 Feb. 1941.

89 MTA, Toronto Board of Education records, II-I-180-B, Recommendations of Special Committee re Truancy, 1943-44.

90 "Illness" remained the principal cause for school absences, increasing from 61.3 to 65.5 percent of the total, numbers in which some truancy was no doubt buried. Ontario, Department of Education, *Annual Report*, 1943, 62.

91 CW, vol. 80, file "Canadian Youth Commission," clipping from *Chatelaine*, Jan. 1945, n.p.

92 Adams, *Trouble with Normal*, 81; CCV, series A-1, vol. 292, file "Bowling Alleys," George Pearson to George Miller, 24 Feb. 1943; AG, series 2, file 19.23, Report of the London Council of Social Agencies to Leslie Blackwell, 29 Sept. 1944.

93 NAC, MG28 I11, Canadian Youth Commission papers (CYC), vol. 31, file 5(3a), Proposals with Respect to School Attendance, 1944.

94 *Saturday Night*, 16 Sept. 1944, 5; Magda Fahrni, "Under Reconstruction: The Family and the Public in Postwar Montréal, 1944-1949" (PhD diss., York University, 2001), 153.

95 Bossard, "Family Background," 40; *New Advance*, Feb. 1943, 16.

96 CCSD, vol. 87, file 1856, "Children in a World at War," May 1943.

97 *Saturday Night*, 4 Sept. 1943, 1, and 3 June 1944, 22-23.

98 Diane G. Forestell, "The Victorian Legacy: Historical Perspectives on the Canadian Women's Army Corps" (PhD diss., York University, 1986), 164; Doug Owram, "The Cult of the Teenager," ms, University of Alberta, 1993, 12; Eileen Tyler May, *Homeward Bound: American Families in the Cold War Era* (New York: Basic Books, 1988), 74.

99 *Canada Year Book, 1946*, 247.

100 The exact number of teenagers at any precise moment must be inferred, because government statistics break down age categories into ranges of five to nine, ten to fourteen, and fifteen to nineteen. However, over the first four years of the war, 63.3 percent of juvenile arrests in Toronto were of those thirteen to fifteen inclusive. McCarthy, "Individual Child," 3.

101 Throughout the 1920s, births averaged 241,500 annually compared to 229,400 during the 1930s. Between 1932 and 1934, total annual live births were 242,698, 229,791, and 228,296 respectively. Between 1925 and 1929, annual immigration to Canada stood at 84,907, 135,982, 158,886, 166,783, and 164,993 respectively. By comparison, between 1931 and 1935, annual immigration to Canada was only 27,530, 20,591, 14,382, 12,476, and 11,277 respectively. K.A.H. Buckley and M.C. Urquhart, *Historical Statistics of Canada* (Toronto: Macmillan, 1965), series A254-272, B1-14, B100-107, and Y110-118.

102 Juvenile court appearances were 8,707 in 1946, 8,295 in 1947, and 7,878 in 1948. *Canada Year Book, 1946*, 247; F.H. Leacey, *Historical Statistics of Canada* (Ottawa: Supply and Services, 1983), series Z261-269.

103 From 1940 to 1944 inclusive, annual live births stood at 252,577, 263,993, 281,569, 292,943, and 293,967 respectively, and in 1946 hit a record of 343,509. Immigration to Canada enhanced this trend; in 1945 it stood at 22,722, but reached 71,719 the following year, and in 1948 stood at 125,414. Buckley and Urquhart, *Historical Statistics*, series A254-272, B1-14.

104 Over the first four years of the war, annual arrests of juveniles for "theft and receiving stolen goods" rose from 2,916 to 4,023, and for "wilful damage" from 578 to 994. Dominion Bureau of Statistics, *Juvenile Delinquents for the Year Ended September 30, 1943* (Ottawa: Dominion Bureau of Statistics, 1943), 10.

105 Dominion Bureau of Statistics, *Juvenile Delinquents*, 111; CCSD, vol. 87, file 1856, clipping from *Weekly Bulletin*, 13 Nov. 1943, n.p.

106 *Ottawa Journal*, 8 Jan. 1944, 10.

107 In 1940, 54 percent of the 3,772 convicts in Canadian penitentiaries were thirty or younger. With the enlistment and departure overseas of so many young men, "offences against the person," which had increased by 34.2 percent between 1935 and 1939, slowed to a 3.5 percent increase between 1939 and 1943; "offences against property with violence," which had increased by 42.0 percent between 1935 and 1939, dropped by 21.5 percent between 1939 and 1943; and "offences against property without violence," which had increased by 23.3 percent between 1935 and 1939, dropped by 18.7 percent between 1939 and 1943. *Canada Year Book, 1945*, 1073, 1092.

108 OH, series I-99, Container 3, Toronto Big Brothers, "We Dare to Hope," n.d.

109 Adams, *Trouble with Normal*, 175; Sangster, *Girl Trouble*, 52-58, 61.

110 For example, in the twenty years preceding the Second World War, Ottawa's municipal government added just 3.5 percent more parkland to accommodate a population that grew by more than one-third. *Ottawa Journal*, 20 May 1944, 4.

111 Glenbow Institute, M5841, Calgary Local Council of Women (CLCW), *Yearbook*, 1942, 46; *Ottawa Citizen*, 26 June 1943, 26.

112 James Frank Edward White, "Conscripted City: Halifax and the Second World War" (PhD diss., McMaster University, 1995), 340.

113 Rogers, *Boys Are Worth It*, 19-20.

114 NAC, MG27 III B5, Ian Mackenzie papers (IM), vol. 135, file 500, clipping from *Toronto Star*, 10 April 1943, n.p.; *Maclean's*, 15 Aug. 1943, 48.

115 *Canadian Welfare*, April 1945, 12; CYC, vol. 9, file 72, Community Planning for Youth, June 1945.

116 CCSD, vol. 82, file 594-2-1939-44, *YWCA Quarterly*, June 1944, n.p.; Shirley Tillotson, *The Public at Play: Gender and the Politics of Recreation in Post-War Ontario* (Toronto: University of Toronto Press, 2000), 38.

117 CLCW, *Yearbook*, 1942, 45; *New Advance*, Feb. 1945, 10-11.

118 DSS, vol. 1, file 73, "A Plan for the Reduction of Juvenile Delinquency in Toronto," 15 Nov. 1943; DSS, vol. 2, file 73.1, Report of Area Project, Moss Park, 2 Nov. 1944, A.W. Laver to Alderman William Collings, 2 March 1945, and William Turnbull to the Commissioner of Public Welfare, 15 Nov. 1945.

119 Of the 1,816,868 men medically examined for possible service under the National Resources Mobilization Act, only 43 percent met the physical standards for "unrestricted service." However, the increasing rate of rejections over time was inevitable given the declining pool of young recruits. E.L.M. Burns, *Manpower in the Canadian Army, 1939-1945* (Toronto: Clarke, Irwin, 1956), 127-128; *Canadian School Journal* 23, 2 (1945): 46-47; *Canadian Welfare*, April 1943, 16.

120 CYC, vol. 65, file 30(5a), clipping from *Recreation Magazine*, Jan. 1945, n.p.; Tillotson, *Public at Play*, 41-46.

121 *New Advance*, May 1944, 28; Manitoba, Department of Health and Public Welfare, *Annual Report*, 1944, 100; *The School*, Feb. 1944, 485-486.

122 CYC, vol. 38, file 7(3e), Summary of the Interim Report of the Recreation Committee, n.d.

123 *Maclean's*, 1 Jan. 1945, 39; Adams, *Trouble with Normal*, 77; *Canadian Welfare*, 15 April 1946, 8-9.

124 The largest expenditure, $3.7 million, went to the construction or renovation of 115 Legion halls. NAC, RG2, Privy Council records, vol. 2639, Cabinet Conclusions, 19 Dec. 1946; NAC, RG10, Department of Justice records, vol. 20, file 10-3-11, Breakdown of War Memorial Funds, 1 Feb. 1947.

125 DSS, vol. 4, file 73.1, Submission from Department of Buildings, 23 Nov. 1945.

126 COA, City Council Minutes, 9 May 1946, 254-255.

127 Drew quoted in Tillotson, *Public at Play*, 34, 46-47; Shirley Tillotson, "Citizen Participation in the Welfare State: An Experiment, 1945-57," *Canadian Historical Review* 75, 4 (1994): 515.

128 *ATA Magazine*, June 1943, 22.

129 *Ottawa Journal*, 15 Nov. 1944, 8; *Canadian Forum*, Dec. 1944, 197.

130 CCSD, vol. 82, file 594-1944, Beryl Traux, "Training for Citizenship in Canadian Schools," n.d.; AO, MU8106, Ontario Educational Association, Minute Book, 15 April 1941.

131 Ontario, Department of Education, *Annual Report*, 1943, 52.

132 NAC, RG36-31, Wartime Information Board records, vol. 14, file 8-20-3, CCEC, Secretary's Report, Oct. 1945.

133 CYC, vol. 7, file 7(3g), Report on Family Life, Winnipeg Conference, n.d.; CCSD, vol. 82, file 1939-44, Report of the Ontario Youth Conference, 1944.

134 CCSD, vol. 74, file 538, clipping from *National Health,* no. 26, 1941, n.p.; CCSD, vol. 83, file 594-1942-44, clipping from *Health Bulletin* No. 2, n.d., n.p.

135 *Public Opinion Quarterly,* 1943, 487; *New Advance,* Oct. 1944, 19; *The School* 34, 4 (1945): 309-10.

136 NAC, MG28 I63, Dominion Council of Health papers, Reel C-9816, Meeting, 29 Nov.-1 Dec. 1945.

137 CVA, Board of School Trustees records, vol. 58-B-5, file 7, Board of School Trustees, Sub-committee #4 Report, 1 May 1945; Christabelle Sethna, "Wait Till Your Father Gets Home: Absent Fathers, Working Mothers and Delinquent Daughters in Ontario during World War II," in *Family Matters: Papers in Post-Confederation Canadian Family History,* ed. Lori Chambers and Edgar-André Montigny (Toronto: Canadian Scholars' Press, 1998), 24-25, 28-30; Adams, *Trouble with Normal,* 128-134; Saskatchewan, Department of Public Health, *Annual Report,* 1945, 47; *Canadian School Journal* 23, 2 (1945): 55.

138 R.D. Gidney, *From Hope to Harris: The Reshaping of Ontario's Schools* (Toronto: University of Toronto Press, 1999), 30-36; *Saturday Night,* 13 Jan. 1945, 3.

139 *ATA Magazine,* June 1944, 12-14.

140 Quoted in J. Donald Wilson, Robert Stamp, and Louis-Philippe Audet, *Canadian Education: A History* (Toronto: Prentice-Hall, 1970), 382. Stamp, *Schools of Ontario,* 174-178.

141 AO, MU8106, #3, Ontario Educational Association, Minute Book, 3 April 1945.

142 Although many of Hope's recommendations were eventually incorporated into Ontario's education system, his report was shelved when it was submitted in 1950 because it was considered too controversial. For example, it advocated the division of all schools according to elementary, intermediate, and secondary levels, a structure that did not then conform with, and was vigorously opposed by, separate Catholic institutions. R.D. Gidney, *From Hope to Harris,* 23-24; AO, MU8108, #6, Brief from the Ontario Educational Association to the Provincial Royal Commission on Education, 19 May 1945.

143 NAC, MG28 I95, Young Men's Christian Association papers, vol. 290, file 11, Minutes of YMCA Committee to Study Youth Employment Needs, n.d.; IM, vol. 58, file 527-17, Petition to William Lyon Mackenzie King from the Ontario Vocational Guidance Association, 9 Dec. 1940.

144 John Abraham Ross Wilson, "The Counsellor in Canadian Secondary Schools," EdD diss., Oregon State College, 1951, 11-18.

145 CYC, vol. 32, file 9(3a), Booklet printed by *London Free Press, Your Job Is Your Life Pattern,* n.d., n.p.; Ross L. Donald, "The Development of Guidance in the Secondary Schools of the Dominion of Canada," MEd thesis, University of Manitoba, 1951, 25.

146 Also, summer courses in guidance training were established at Nova Scotia's Normal College and at Acadia University. In 1944 Nova Scotia's government hired a provincial director of vocational guidance, as did Saskatchewan and British Columbia. The next year the Calgary and Edmonton school boards hired guidance directors. Donald, "Development of Guidance," 25-26; Wilson, "Counsellor," 13-18, 20-50; Nova Scotia, Department of Education, Superintendent's Report, 31 July 1945, 136-138; Stamp, *Schools of Ontario,* 197; Ontario, Department of Education, *Annual Report,* 1945, 94; EPSB, *Annual Report,* 1945, 17-18; *Canadian Welfare,* 1 Sept. 1946, 27-30.

147 NAC, MG28 I102, Canadian Teachers' Federation papers (CTF), vol. 28, file 331, Brief on the Freezing Order, 3 Aug. 1944; *Canada Year Book, 1947,* 279; *Maclean's,* 15 July 1943, 1.

148 *ATA Magazine,* Jan. 1944, 8.

149 EPSB, Board Minutes, 5 Oct. 1943; Mona Gleason, *Normalizing the Ideal: Psychology, Schooling and Family in Postwar Canada* (Toronto: University of Toronto Press, 1999), 133.

150 DPW, 79.334/86, H.C. Newland to Dr. S.J. Willis, 26 March 1942; CTF, vol. 92, file 1245, Hope to Lieutenant-Governor of Ontario, 2 Dec. 1949.
151 *Saturday Night,* 13 Nov. 1943, 26; CTF, vol. 28, file 331, clipping from *Maclean's,* 15 July 1945, n.p.
152 CYC, vol. 65, file "Canadian Association for Adult Education," *Food for Thought,* vol. 5, n.d., n.p.; R.D. Gidney, *From Hope to Harris,* 12; *Canadian Forum,* Sept. 1941, 168-169.
153 See, for example, CTF, vol. 28, file 331, L.B. Pett to J. Vann, 9 Aug. 1944; Manitoba, Department of Education, *Annual Report,* 1945, 16-18.
154 *Canada Year Book, 1947,* 310; Wilson et al., *Canadian Education,* 387.
155 For the figures see *Canada Year Book, 1950,* 334, and David M. Cameron, *Schools for Ontario: Policy-Making, Administration and Finance in the 1960s* (Toronto: University of Toronto Press, 1972), 48-53.
156 Several school boards complained about the War Assets Corporation selling rather than giving them such items free, since they were originally paid for by taxpayers. CTF, vol. 98, file "War Assets," principal of unnamed technical school to Dr. Charles E. Phillips, 11 July 1946; R.D. Gidney, *From Hope to Harris,* 28.
157 CTF, vol. 92, file 1245, clipping from (Ontario) *Argus,* Sept. 1947, n.p., and CTF memo, Sept. 1949; Jean Dixon Linse, "The Prestige and Professional Growth of Canadian Teachers" (MA thesis, University of Alberta, 1949), 25; *ATA Magazine,* Jan. 1945, 15; L.G. Thomas, *The University of Alberta in the War, 1939-1945* (Edmonton: N.p., 1948), 40-42.
158 Jean Trépanier, "The Origins of the Juvenile Delinquents Act of 1908: Controlling Delinquency Through Seeking Its Causes and Through Youth Protection," in *Dimensions of Childhood: Essays on the History of Children and Youth in Canada,* ed. Russell Smandych, Gordon Dodds, and Alvin Esau (Winnipeg: Legal Research Institute, University of Manitoba, 1990), 206-207; Andrew Jones and Leonard Rutman, *In the Children's Aid: J.J. Kelso and Child Welfare in Ontario* (Toronto: University of Toronto Press, 1981), chapter 5. By 1939 the legal definition of a minor extended to seventeen in British Columbia and Manitoba and eighteen in Alberta.
159 Sangster, *Girl Trouble,* 74.
160 Neil Sutherland, *Children in English-Speaking Society: Framing the Twentieth Century Consensus* (Toronto: University of Toronto Press, 1976), 125-126; AG, series 2, file 24.4, T.W. Laidlaw to Hon. Leslie Blackwell, 26 Sept. 1944.
161 In Western Canada, there were Helen Gregory McGill and Ethel MacLaughlin, and in Ontario Helen Kinnear. Sangster, *Girl Trouble,* 72-73.
162 DPW, 83.192/754, Begg to Miller, 31 Aug. 1943; CCSD, vol. 87, file 1855, Report to Charlotte Whitton, 27 May 1941; CW, vol. 80, file "Montreal Schools," paper entitled "Juvenile Delinquency," n.d.; Dorothy Chunn, *From Punishment to Doing Good: Family Courts and Socialized Justice in Ontario, 1880-1940* (Toronto: University of Toronto Press, 1992), 167-172.
163 CS, series C-2, file 3.7, F.W. Armstrong to Premier G. Drew, 20 Aug. 1943, and Neelands to Dunbar, 14 Feb. 1944, 1 Sept. 1944.
164 CW, vol. 31, file "Memorandum on the Care," 1944 Report on the Care of Delinquent Girls in Ontario; Joan Sangster, *Regulating Girls and Women: Sexuality, Family and the Law in Ontario, 1920-1960* (Toronto: Oxford University Press, 2001), 138-139; Sangster, *Girl Trouble,* 122.
165 *Canadian Welfare,* 15 April 1947, 16-17.
166 DPW, 70.414/2147, Report of the Child Welfare Committee as Appointed by Orders-in-Council Nos. 913/43 and 1256/43, 11 June 1943; DPW, 70.414/2245, *Annual Report,* 1945, 49-50; City of Edmonton Archives, City Clerk records, Class 32, file 9, Mayor Fry to City Council, 12 March 1945.
167 AG, series 2, file 24.14, T.W. Wolfe to C.L. Snyder, 11 Sept. 1945; CCSD, vol. 86, file 1853, clipping from *Globe and Mail,* 26 Feb. 1943, n.p.; DPW, 83.192/754, Report of Magistrate H.S. Wood, appointed by Attorney-General R.L. Maitland, K.C., Sept. 1943.

168 *Maclean's*, 15 Aug. 1943, 48.

169 *Canadian Welfare*, June 1944, 11; Olga Barilko, "A Study of the Incidence of Juvenile Delinquency and Its Treatment in Edmonton, 1944" (MA thesis, University of Alberta, 1956), 40-43; Sangster, *Girl Trouble*, 136-143.

170 See, for example, *Saturday Night*, 26 May 1945, 4; *Canadian Welfare*, Oct. 1945, 32; United Church of Canada, *Year Book*, 1945, 97.

171 CS, series C-2, file 3.7, Eileen Mitchell to G.H. Dunbar, 5 March 1946; AO, MU5081, box 10, file 1939-50, Report from the Children's Aid Society conference, 1944; DPW, 70.414/2147, Report of the Child Welfare Committee as Appointed by Orders-in-Council Nos. 913/43 and 1256/43, 11 June 1943.

Chapter 9: The Men Who Marched Away

1 C.P. Stacey and Barbara Wilson, *The Half-Million: The Canadians in Britain, 1939-1946* (Toronto: University of Toronto Press, 1987), 114-121; National Archives of Canada (NAC), RG36-31, Wartime Information Board records (WIB), vol. 9, file 3-5-2; WIB, vol. 8, file 3-5, pt. 1, Captain F.W. Park to A.D. Dunton, 30 Nov. 1944.

2 The *Maple Leaf* went on to print editions in France, Belgium, and the Netherlands. To get a better handle on morale, many senior officers religiously read its letters to the editor page. Lt.-Col. G.W.L. Nicholson, *The Canadians in Italy, 1943-1945* (Ottawa: Queen's Printer, 1956), 384; Richard S. Malone, *A World in Flames: A Portrait of War, Part Two* (Toronto: Collins, 1985), 82-85; Barry D. Rowland, *Herbie and Friends: Cartoons in Wartime* (Toronto: Natural Heritage/Natural History, 1990).

3 NAC, RG24, Department of National Defence records (DND), vol. 15,633, War Diary, Report of Colonel W.T.R. Flemington, Assistant Principal Chaplain (P), 31 Jan. 1943.

4 C.P. Stacey, *Six Years of War: The Army in Canada, Britain and the Pacific* (Ottawa: Department of National Defence, 1966), 427-431.

5 York University Archives, Jack Lawrence Granatstein papers (JLG), box 4, file 73, Johnston family, Geoff to Sandy, 26 Dec. 1943.

6 Museum of the Regiments (MR; Calgary), Lord Strathcona Regimental Orders, 9 Jan. 1940; DND, vol. 10,706, file 272-73, Brig. A.W. Bennett to Lt.-Col. L.A. Devine, 25 Nov. 1941.

7 Craig Family papers, private collection held by Mary Tasker, Toronto, Grace Craig to Jim Craig, 5 Sept. 1942; Directorate of History and Heritage, Department of National Defence (DHH), 581.023 (D1), Censorship Report, 21 May 1944; Paul Jackson, "Courting Homosexuals in the Military: The Management of Homosexuality in the Canadian Military" (PhD diss., Queen's University, 2002), 60.

8 J.L. Granatstein, *Canada's Army: Waging War and Keeping the Peace* (Toronto: University of Toronto Press, 2002), 185-186; Stacey and Wilson, *Half-Million*, xi, 16.

9 DHH, 312.023 (D1), Field Censor's Report, 31 Oct. 1944.

10 Also, with equipment provided mostly by the YMCA, Canadians in Britain formed seventy-five hockey teams for league play. The Canadian Legion's Educational Service provided men with the opportunity to take correspondence courses in several vocational and professional fields, as well as high school or university classes. By 1942 arrangements had been made with twenty-two British universities, including Oxford, whereby servicemen could take short courses on a variety of "general and cultural subjects." NAC, RG44, National War Services records, vol. 3, file "Canadian Legion of the BESL," Address by John Marshall, 1942; NAC, MG28 I95, Young Men's Christian Association papers (YMCA), vol. 272, file 9, Glen Nixon to Major Webber, 29 Sept. 1943; Stacey and Wilson, *Half-Million*, 96-106, 128; Gabriel Stephen Panunto, "For Club or Country? Hockey in Wartime Canada, 1939-1945" (MA thesis, Carleton University, 2000), 121; E.L.M. Burns, *Manpower in the Canadian Army, 1939-1945* (Toronto: Clarke, Irwin, 1956), 71.

11 Training in Canada provided only the basics. Soldiers arriving in Britain were required to take a six-week refresher course. Many British commanders considered continued preparation for the Canadians to be especially essential because of their dismal performance in several war game exercises. Those relieved of command in England included Generals Pearkes, Potts, Ganong, and Price. Granatstein, *Canada's Army,* 180, 201-205; Burns, *Manpower in the Canadian Army,* 78; DHH, 312.023(D1), Field Censor's Report, 8 Dec. 1943; James Alan Roberts, *The Canadian Summer* (Toronto: University of Toronto Press, 1981), 46; Terry Copp, *The Brigade: The Fifth Canadian Infantry Brigade, 1939-1945* (Stoney Creek, ON: Fortress Publications, 1992), 22.

12 DND, vol. 12,711, file 273/25, Secretary of Polbright and District Rifle Club (Surrey) to General Officer Commanding Canadian Forces in Great Britain, 22 Dec. 1944; Stacey and Wilson, *Half-Million,* 58-62.

13 Spencer Dunmore and William Carter, *Reap the Whirlwind: The Untold Story of 6 Group, Canada's Bomber Force of World War II* (Toronto: McClelland and Stewart, 1991), 157; DHH, CMHQ, Report 119, C.P. Stacey, "Canadian Relations with the People of the United Kingdom and the General Problem of Morale, 1939-44," 30 June 1944.

14 John Costello, *Love, Sex and War: Changing Values, 1939-1945* (London: Collins, 1985), 317; Stacey and Wilson, *Half-Million,* 40, 159-164; DND, vol. 10,725, file 219C1.009 (D52), clipping from Surrey *Mirror,* 7 July 1943, n.p., clipping from Eastbourne *Gazette,* 21 July 1943, n.p., clipping from *Evening Argus,* 16 July 1943, n.p., clipping from West Sussex *Gazette,* 15 July 1943, n.p., clipping from Surrey *Times,* 3 July 1943, n.p., Director of Public Relations for British Army to McNaughton, 5 July 1943, and Lt.-Col. Bean to Ronald, 20 July 1943.

15 DHH, CMHQ, Report 119, C.P. Stacey, "Canadian Relations with the People of the United Kingdom and the General Problem of Morale, 1939-1944," 30 June 1944.

16 DHH, 312.023(D1), Field Censor's Report, 8 Dec. 1943; DND, vol. 10,767, file 222 C1(D14), Field Censor's Report, n.d.

17 In second place to the Canadians were American servicemen, who took home some 17,000 British war brides. "War Bride Statistics," <www.canadawarbrides.com/stats.html> (no longer accessible); Stacey and Wilson, *Half-Million,* 136-140, 148; DHH, CMHQ, Report 119, C.P. Stacey, "Canadian Relations with the People of the United Kingdom and the General Problem of Morale, 1939-1944," 30 June 1944; DND, vol. 10,235, file 345-34, Report of Principal Protestant Chaplain, 18 June 1942.

18 According to an American study, three-quarters of GIs "admitted" to having sex while overseas. Michael C.C. Adams, *The Best War Ever: America and World War II* (Baltimore: Johns Hopkins University Press, 1994), 73.

19 Norm Bowen, interview by author, Ottawa, 19 April 2000; John Modell and Duane Steffey, "Waging War and Marriage: Military Service and Family Formation, 1940-1950," *Journal of Family History* 13, 2 (1988): 211.

20 Jean Bruce, *Back the Attack! Canadian Women during the Second World War – at Home and Abroad* (Toronto: Macmillan, 1985), 131.

21 Incredibly, in 1915 recorded cases of VD amounted to 28.7 percent of the Canadian Expeditionary Force. However, during the Great War, protective measures by the military took some time to appear and were significantly less extensive. Canadian troops in the Second World War could also use British and American EPT stations. Jay Cassel, *The Secret Plague: Venereal Disease in Canada, 1838-1939* (Toronto: University of Toronto Press, 1987), 127; DND, vol. 12,612, file 218-2, Memo re: EPT Centres, 18 July 1944; W.R. Feasby, *Official History of the Canadian Medical Services, 1939-1945,* vol. 2 (Ottawa: Queen's Printer, 1956), 110-111.

22 DND, vol. 12,612, file 217-30, Minutes of Conference held at Home Office, 16 April 1943; NAC, RG29, Department of National Health and Welfare records (NHW), vol. 1238, file

311-V3-15, "General Administration of the VD Control Programme in the Canadian Army Overseas and Progress in the United Kingdom," n.d.

23 Costello, *Love, Sex and War,* 329; Raynes Minns, *Bombers and Mash: The Domestic Front, 1939-45* (London: Virago, 1980), 179.

24 DND, vol. 12,711, file 372-23, Fred Wheler to Officer Commanding Canadian Forces, Manchester, 20 Oct. 1942; DND, vol. 10,725, file 219 C1.009(D52), Director of Public Relations for British Army to McNaughton, 5 July 1943.

25 American soldiers were paid about four times more than the British. Barry Broadfoot, *Six War Years: Memories of Canadians at Home and Abroad* (Toronto: Doubleday, 1974), 287; Wallace Reyburn, *Some of It Was Fun* (Toronto: Thomas Nelson and Sons, 1949), 180-181; DHH, CMHQ, Report 119, C.P. Stacey, "Canadian Relations with the People of the United Kingdom and the General Problem of Morale, 1939-1944," 30 June 1944.

26 Estimates in wartime Britain concluded that about one-third of births were illegitimate and 20 percent of pregnancies were aborted. "Who Are the War Children and What Do They Want?" <www.project-roots.com>; Costello, *Love, Sex and War,* 276-277; Carl Honore, "Canada's Children of Love and War," in *The Good Fight: Canadians in the Second World War,* ed. J.L. Granatstein and Peter Neary (Toronto: Copp Clark Longman, 1995), 431-432.

27 YMCA, vol. 110, file 789A, Nora Lea to Dr. P.G. Price, 20 Sept. 1946, Mary Livesay to Nora Lea, 23 April 1946, and K.M. Jackson to C.A. Patrick, 8 April 1947.

28 DHH, 193.009(D29), Venereal Disease in the RAF and RCAF in the United Kingdom by Command, 1942-43, n.d; Stacey and Wilson, *Half-Million,* 151-152; Brereton Greenhous et al., *The Crucible of War: The Official History of the Royal Canadian Air Force,* vol. 3 (Toronto: University of Toronto Press, 1994), 864.

29 Greenhous et al., *Crucible of War,* 186-187.

30 Also becoming involved were Canada's Army Co-operation Squadrons 110 and 112, which flew slower-moving Lysanders. Ibid., 186-187, 197, 202-203, 210; J.A. Foster, *For Love and Glory: A Pictorial History of Canada's Air Forces* (Toronto: McClelland and Stewart, 1989), 53.

31 Starting in the summer of 1941 RCAF fighter squadrons were assigned to escort British bombers on daytime raids into France and Belgium. Nicknamed "rodeos," these operations produced disappointing results and high losses. Many Allied pilots, particularly the Canadians, were inexperienced, and the Germans were fighting near their airfields and had plenty of petrol for pursuit. Moreover, the Germans had better radar, anti-aircraft equipment, and planes. In 1941 the Allies lost three fighter planes for every one that they shot down. During the last three years of the war, Canadian fighter pilots operated in both the Mediterranean and northwest Europe. Many distinguished themselves, especially George Frederick "Buzz" Beurling who, with more than thirty victories, was nicknamed the "Knight of Malta" before he was pulled out of action in October 1942 with clear signs of combat fatigue. In the Mediterranean, where enemy air strength was less formidable, No. 126 RCAF Fighter Wing claimed 361 victories. In northwest Europe, especially before 1944, things were tougher. Of those flying Typhoons, some 60 percent became casualties before completing a tour of duty. Greenhous et al., *Crucible of War,* 212, 225-226, 328, 648-651; Leslie Roberts, *There Shall Be Wings: A History of the Royal Canadian Air Force* (Toronto: Clarke, Irwin, 1959), 134-135; David J. Bercuson, *Maple Leaf against the Axis: Canada's Second World War* (Toronto: Stoddart, 1995), 80-81; J.L. Granatstein and Desmond Morton, *A Nation Forged in Fire: Canadians and the Second World War, 1939-1945* (Toronto: Lester and Orpen Dennys, 1989), 108, 111.

32 Greenhous et al., *Crucible of War,* 686-687, 864; Dunmore and Carter, *Reap the Whirlwind,* 363-364; Bercuson, *Maple Leaf against the Axis,* 114-115.

33 Most effective was the "window," aluminum strips that were released to show up on and confound German radar, which was adopted in July 1943. Don McCaffery, *Battlefields in the*

Air: Canadians in the Allied Bomber Command (Toronto: James Lorimer, 1995), 120-125; Murray Peden, *A Thousand Shall Fall: A Pilot for 214* (Stittsville: Canada's Wings, 1979), 367; Adams, *Best War Ever,* 109.

34 McCaffery, *Battlefields in the Air,* 74-78; Russell Mackay, *One of the Many* (Burnstown, ON: General Store Publishing House, 1989), 16-20; Greenhous et al., *Crucible of War,* 264, 272.

35 Greenhous et al., *Crucible of War,* 109-110; Peden, *Thousand Shall Fall,* 320; Leslie Roberts, *There Shall Be Wings,* 160-161.

36 By war's end, just six of the fourteen squadrons in No. 6 Group were equipped with the Lancaster X, though others flew British-built Lancasters. The twin-engine Wellington was among the slowest bombers. The four-engine Halifax Mark II and Mark V flown by the Canadians were better, but their exhaust fumes were visible at night and they provided poor downward vision, lacked manoeuvrability, and were exceptionally hard to pull out of the corkscrew turn and dive that was a common evasion technique. Bercuson, *Maple Leaf against the Axis,* 116-119; Dunmore and Carter, *Reap the Whirlwind,* 115-116; Greenhous et al., *Crucible of War,* 641.

37 Greenhous et al., *Crucible of War,* 787; Adams, *Best War Ever,* 110; Peden, *Thousand Shall Fall,* 425-428. Western quoted in McCaffery, *Battlefields in the Air,* 93, 126.

38 Roger Sarty, *Canada and the Battle of the Atlantic* (Montreal: Art Global, 1998), 169-171; Joseph Schull, *The Far Distant Ships: An Official Account of Canadian Naval Operations in the Second World War* (Ottawa: Queen's Printer, 1961), 430.

39 Paul Jackson, "Courting Homosexuals," 190-191.

40 W.A.B. Douglas, *Official History of the Royal Canadian Air Force,* vol. 2 (Toronto: University of Toronto Press, 1985), 470; Marc Milner, *North Atlantic Run: The Royal Canadian Navy and the Battle for the Convoys* (Toronto: University of Toronto Press, 1985), xiii; Bercuson, *Maple Leaf against the Axis,* 96.

41 James B. Lamb, *The Corvette Navy: True Stories from Canada's Atlantic War* (Toronto: Stoddart, 2000), 2, 5; Schull, *Far Distant Ships,* 26-28, 58-59.

42 James Lamb, *Corvette Navy,* 33-37; Sarty, *Battle of the Atlantic,* 94; Mack Lynch and John David, eds., *Salty Dips,* vol. 2 (Ottawa: Naval Officers' Association of Canada, 1985), 102-103; Patricia Giesler, *Valour at Sea: Canada's Merchant Navy* (Ottawa: Veterans Affairs, 1998), 11-15; Paul Jackson, "Courting Homosexuals," 362-363.

43 Paul Jackson, "Courting Homosexuals," 105; Bowen, interview; Greenhous et al., *Crucible of War,* 474; Schull, *Far Distant Ships,* 30-31.

44 Schull, *Far Distant Ships,* 172-173; Bercuson, *Maple Leaf against the Axis,* 138-139, 143, 146; Sarty, *Battle of the Atlantic,* 165-166; Giesler, *Valour at Sea,* 21.

45 William Horrocks, *In Their Own Words* (Ottawa: Rideau Veterans Home Residents Council, 1993), 105-107, 142-143.

46 Jim Egan, *Challenging the Conspiracy of Silence: My Life As a Canadian Gay Activist* (Toronto: Canadian Lesbian and Gay Archives, 1998), 27, 29.

47 Stacey and Wilson, *Half-Million,* 154; James Lamb, *Corvette Navy,* 87.

48 James Lamb, *Corvette Navy,* 89, 92; Schull, *Far Distant Ships,* 88.

49 Granatstein, *Canada's Army,* 195-199.

50 See Brian Loring Villa, *Unauthorized Action: Mountbatten and the Dieppe Raid* (Toronto: Oxford University Press, 1989); Brereton Greenhous, *Dieppe, Dieppe* (Montreal: Art Global, 1992); and Denis Whitaker and Shelagh Whitaker, *Dieppe: Tragedy to Triumph* (Toronto: McGraw-Hill Ryerson, 1992).

51 C.P. Stacey, *Official History of the Canadian Army in the Second World War,* vol. 1, *Six Years of War: The Army in Canada, Britain and the Pacific* (Ottawa: Department of National Defence, 1955), 350-360, 398-399; Bercuson, *Maple Leaf against the Axis,* 65-68; Greenhous

et al., *Crucible of War*, 240-241; Granatstein, *Canada's Army*, 207-211; Bowen (member of Combined Operations and present at the Dieppe raid), interview.

52 During the early part of the Normandy campaign, an estimated 106 mostly Canadian prisoners were systematically murdered by the Waffen SS on orders from their superiors. Howard Margolian, *Conduct Unbecoming: The Story of the Murder of Canadian Prisoners of War in Normandy* (Toronto: University of Toronto Press, 1998).

53 Jonathan F. Vance, *Objects of Concern: Canadian Prisoners of War Through the Twentieth Century* (Vancouver: UBC Press, 1994), 255-256.

54 Granatstein, *Canada's Army*, 211.

55 NAC, RG2, Privy Council records (PC), vol. 14, Cabinet War Committee, 16 Dec. 1943; Lynch and David, *Salty Dips*, vol. 3, 1987, 152-157; Glenbow Institute, M7878, H. Gordon McFarlane papers, file 9, H. Gordon McFarlane, "Conditions in the German Prison Camp of Stalag 344"; Vance, *Objects of Concern*, 112-113, 136, 139.

56 Vance, *Objects of Concern*, 145, 150-151; JLG, box 4, file 76, Private Lynch, Narrative, n.p.; Daniel Dancocks, *In Enemy Hands: Canadian Prisoners of War, 1939-1945* (Edmonton: Hurtig Publishers, 1983), 88, 93; Lynch and David, *Salty Dips*, vol. 3, 154-155.

57 NAC, MG28 I311, Montreal Soldiers' Wives' League papers (MSWL), vol. 2, file 45, *Newsletter*, Canadian Prisoners of War Relatives' Association, Feb. 1942.

58 Vance, *Objects of Concern*, 100, 145, 157, 159; NAC, MG30 C181, Robert England papers, vol. 2, file 1940-3, Report to the War Office on the Psychological Effects of the Rehabilitation of Repatriated Prisoners of War, Feb. 1944; Dancocks, *In Enemy Hands*, 100-107; H.E. Wooley, *No Time off for Good Behaviour* (Burnstown, ON: General Store Publishing House, 1990), 45-50; Greenhous et al., *Crucible of War*, 775; Paul Jackson, "Courting Homosexuals," 318.

59 Lynch and David, *Salty Dips*, vol. 3, 167; Dancocks, *In Enemy Hands*, 188; Vance, *Objects of Concern*, 130, 176.

60 Vance, *Objects of Concern*, 184-185, 188, 196, 205; Granatstein, *Canada's Army*, 199.

61 The one who was executed was Canadian-born. All those sentenced to jail were released by 1957. Dave McIntosh, *Hell on Earth: Aging Faster, Dying Sooner. Canadian Prisoners of the Japanese during World War Two* (Toronto: McGraw-Hill Ryerson, 1997), 124.

62 MSWL, vol. 2, file 45, *Newsletter*, Canadian Prisoners of War Relatives' Association, Feb. 1942; Vance, *Objects of Concern*, 186.

63 Vance, *Objects of Concern*, 194; WIB, vol. 11, file 7-1-4, Canadian Postal Censorship, General Report on Letters from Persons Interned in Japanese Camps, 1942.

64 NAC, MG30 E328, Frank Ebden papers, vol. 1, file 2, List of Rules, n.d.

65 NAC, MG30 E181, Tom Forsyth papers, memoire, 20 Jan. 1944; D.J. Baker, *A History of 413 Squadron* (Burnstown, ON: General Store Publishing House, 1997), 20; McIntosh, *Hell on Earth*, 29, 94, 205.

66 McIntosh, *Hell on Earth*, 18, 24-25, 29; Dancocks, *In Enemy Hands*, 255.

67 McNaughton's final agreement to the invasion was based on the belief that Canadian troops would be sent back to England once Sicily was secured, though this plan was not seriously entertained by most other commanders. DHH, 581.023 (D1), Censorship Report, 23 March 1944; Granatstein, *Canada's Army*, 214, 227; J.W. Pickersgill and D.F. Forster, *The Mackenzie King Record*, vol. 1 (Toronto: University of Toronto Press, 1970), 607.

68 C. Sydney Frost, *Once a Patricia: Memoirs of a Junior Infantry Officer in World War II* (St. Catharines, ON: Vanwell Publishing, 1988), 109; Maj.-Gen. George Kitching, *Mud and Green Fields: The Memoirs of Major General George Kitching* (Langley, BC: Battleline Books, 1996), 145; Maj.-Gen. Chris Vokes, *Vokes: My Story* (Ottawa: Gallery Books, 1985), 93; Bercuson, *Maple Leaf against the Axis*, 158.

69 The most substantial recreational centre for the Canadians was in the seaside community of Catalina, but it was established well into the Sicilian campaign. Granatstein, *Canada's*

Army, 220-221; Daniel Dancocks, *The D-Day Dodgers: The Canadians in Italy, 1943-1945* (Toronto: McClelland and Stewart, 1991), 93, 108; DHH, Sesia War Diary, 17 Aug. 1943; Frost, *Once a Patricia,* 133.

70 Nicholson, *Canadians in Italy,* 174; Kitching, *Mud and Green Fields,* 165.

71 DND, vol. 10,236, file 345-38, Report of the Principal Protestant Chaplain, Sept. 1943.

72 Given the large numbers of men immobilized during the Great War by what was then called "shell shock" or "neurasthenia," Canada's army launched significant efforts before the Mediterranean campaign to minimize battle exhaustion. Psychiatrists were recruited into a new Directorate of Personnel Selection to devise a test to identify those susceptible to this condition. Although unable to predict the likely victims of battle exhaustion, Canada's army, following the lead of the Americans and the British in North Africa – whose facilities the Canadians often used for their troops in Sicily – made some moves toward providing more professional and compassionate treatment. Soon after invading Italy, Canada's Army Medical Corps established "exhaustion units" near battle zones to which the afflicted were sent. However, more than half the patients were returned to action after just two or three days – thus producing much recidivism – following a regimen usually consisting of washing, shaving, changing into clean clothes, resting, receiving decent food, and hearing reassuring words. Many men suffering from battle fatigue did not obtain even this treatment because several senior medical and military officers, like those running Bomber Command, threatened to charge the afflicted as LMF. Terry Copp and Bill McAndrew, *Battle Exhaustion: Soldiers and Psychiatrists in the Canadian Army, 1939-1945* (Montreal and Kingston: McGill-Queen's University Press, 1990), 53, 94-96, 100; Terry Copp, "From Neurasthenia to Post-Traumatic Stress Disorder: Canadian Veterans and the Problem of Emotional Disabilities," in *The Veterans Charter and Post-War Canada,* ed. J.L. Granatstein and Peter Neary (Montreal and Kingston: McGill-Queen's University Press, 1998), 150-151; DND, vol. 12,631, file 224-13, Col. F.H. Van Nostrand, "Neuropsychiatry in the Canadian Army (Overseas)," 9 July 1945.

73 Granatstein, *Canada's Army,* 222; *Khaki* 1, 13: 1; DHH, 581.023 (D1), Censorship Report, 30 Jan. 1944.

74 DHH, Sesia War Diary, 12 July 1943; Frost, *Once a Patricia,* 130.

75 Farley Mowat, *The Regiment* (Toronto: McClelland and Stewart, 1955), 104. This attitude was not unique to the Canadians. One US study done just after the war of soldiers who had fought overseas concluded that about 80 percent had looted to some extent. Malcolm McCallum, "A Study of the Delinquent in the Army," *American Journal of Sociology* 51, 5 (1946): 481.

76 Mowat, *Regiment,* 63; Reyburn, *Some of It Was Fun,* 67; DHH, Sesia War Diary, 6 Aug. 1943.

77 DHH, Sesia War Diary, 19 July 1943.

78 Ibid., 22 July 1943.

79 "War Bride Statistics," <www.canadawarbrides.com/stats.html> (no longer accessible); DHH, Sesia War Diary, 12 and 31 July 1943.

80 DHH, Sesia War Diary, 21 July 1943; Cliff Humford, interview by author, Edmonton, 23 Oct. 1992.

81 DND, vol. 12,560, file 200/23, Report of No. 5 Canadian General Hospital, 10 Dec. 1943; Vokes, *Vokes,* 127-128; Costello, *Love, Sex and War,* 337; Dancocks, *D-Day Dodgers,* 108-109.

82 Dancocks, *D-Day Dodgers,* 434; Granatstein, *Canada's Army,* 218.

83 Dancocks, *D-Day Dodgers,* 113, 124-125; Bercuson, *Maple Leaf against the Axis,* 169.

84 Bercuson, *Maple Leaf against the Axis,* 143, 151; Granatstein, *Canada's Army,* 228, 234; Mowat, *Regiment,* 143; Farley Mowat, *My Father's Son: Memories of War and Peace* (Toronto: Key Porter Books, 1992), 19-20.

85 Farley Mowat, *And No Birds Sang* (Toronto: McClelland and Stewart, 1979), 236-237.

86 Granatstein, *Canada's War,* 239; Copp and McAndrew, *Battle Exhaustion,* 56; Bercuson, *Maple Leaf against the Axis,* 164, 175; Kitching, *Mud and Green Fields,* 186. For the most detailed account of this battle see Mark Zuehlke, *Ortona: Canada's Epic World War II Battle* (Toronto: Stoddart, 1999).

87 Dancocks, *D-Day Dodgers,* 262; Bercuson, *Maple Leaf against the Axis,* 166; Granatstein, *Canada's Army,* 246-252.

88 Such feelings were reinforced by the much-publicized comment from Lady Nancy Astor, the first female member of the British Parliament, referring to those in the Eighth Army as "D-Day Dodgers." Granatstein, *Canada's Army,* 252; Dancocks, *D-Day Dodgers,* 350-351, 381-383.

89 Dancocks, *D-Day Dodgers,* 284, 293, 295, 320-321, 345-350, 370-372, 380-383; Nicholson, *Canadians in Italy,* 147, 452, 562; Copp and McAndrew, *Battle Exhaustion,* 92-94; Granatstein, *Canada's Army,* 282.

90 DND, vol. 16,676, file "1 Det. 1 A.S.," Summary, Aug. 1944.

91 R.G. Moyles, *The Blood and the Fire: A History of the Salvation Army in the Dominion, 1882-1976* (Toronto: Peter Martin Associates, 1977), 200-202; NAC, MG28 I198, Young Women's Christian Association papers (YWCA), vol. 9, file 68, Minutes of the Executive Committee, YMCA National War Services Committee, 26 Oct. 1944; Alan M. Hurst, *The Canadian YMCA in World War II* (Toronto: YMCA, 1949), 177-178.

92 JLG, box 7, file 107, *Handbook for Soldiers Going to Italy,* 1943.

93 Pooch, *Tales of a Forgotten Theatre* (Winnipeg: D-Day Publishers, 1969), 24; DND, vol. 16,640, clippings from *Maple Leaf,* 24 and 30 March 1944, n.p.

94 DHH, Sesia War Diary, 21 Sept. 1943; JLG, box 4, file 65, Father Michael Dalton, Diary, 17 Aug. 1944.

95 Investigations of the Seaforths' conduct were launched by both the British and the Canadian military, but ended abruptly in early 1945 as both forces became consumed with transferring soldiers out of Italy to northwest Europe. Moreover, as J.L. Granatstein states, investigators likely "backed off" after discovering that "virtually all the Seaforth officers were involved and large numbers of men and they simply could not, in effect, eliminate a battalion." *Ottawa Citizen,* 17 March 2001, B1; *Ottawa Citizen,* 18 March 2001, C7; Granatstein, *Canada's Army,* 282.

96 DHH, Sesia War Diary, 4 Oct. 1943; MR, Col. P.G. Griffin papers, Diary, 24 May 1944.

97 DHH, 83/429, *Protection against VD* (Ottawa: King's Printer, 1944), 1-3; Feasby, *Canadian Medical Services,* vol. 2, 112-113; DND, vol. 12,612, file 217-31, PAVD Pamphlet, n.d.; DND, vol. 6,617, file 8994-6, General Disease Control and the Canadian Army Overseas, 22 March 1944.

98 DND, vol. 6,617, file 8994-6, General Disease Control and the Canadian Army Overseas, 22 March 1944; DND, vol. 12,566, file 200-29, Health of Troops, 1st Canadian Corps, Week Ending 29 July 1944, and Health State, Italy, Aug. 1944; Copp and McAndrew, *Battle Exhaustion,* 92; Costello, *Love, Sex and War,* 305.

99 C.P. Stacey, *Official History of the Canadian Army in the Second World War,* vol. 3, *The Victory Campaign: The Operations in Northwest Europe, 1944-1945* (Ottawa: Department of National Defence, 1960), 611.

100 Ibid., 118-120, 161, 163; Granatstein and Morton, *Nation Forged in Fire,* 190-198; Bercuson, *Maple Leaf against the Axis,* 205, 210-213, 221-222.

101 DND, vol. 15,630, file "War Diary," Report of Senior Chaplain (RC) HQ, A Tps Area, 4 Aug. 1944; Granatstein, *Canada's Army,* 266, 269, 278.

102 Stacey, *Official History,* vol. 3, 174-176; Copp and McAndrew, *Battle Exhaustion,* 122-123; Copp, *Brigade,* 198-199.

103 In July and August 1944, Lt.-General G.G. Simonds, one of the country's few outstanding tacticians, though inclined to blame subordinates rather than consider his own plans too complex and ambitious, "sacked a division commander, six of nine brigadiers, and fourteen of twenty-four battalion commanders." Granatstein, *Canada's Army,* 277, 279, 297; J.L. Granatstein, *The Generals: The Canadian Army's Senior Commanders in the Second World War* (Toronto: Stoddart, 1993), 165-167, 169-170; John A. English, *The Canadian Army and the Normandy Campaign: A Study of Failure in High Command* (New York: Praeger, 1991), 256, 307; Bercuson, *Maple Leaf against the Axis,* 216.

104 Bercuson, *Maple Leaf against the Axis,* 241-242; Granatstein, *Canada's Army,* 286-289; Stacey, *Official History,* vol. 3, 329-331, 424-425; Terry Copp and Robert Vogel, *Maple Leaf Route: Scheldt* (Alma, ON: Maple Leaf Route, 1985), 18-20, 58, 80, 116-118; Copp and McAndrew, *Battle Exhaustion,* 141. Also see W. Denis Whitaker and Shelagh Whitaker, *Tug of War: The Canadian Victory that Opened Antwerp* (Toronto: Stoddart, 1984).

105 Copp and McAndrew, *Battle Exhaustion,* 144-145; Granatstein, *Canada's Army,* 291-292, 299.

106 Granatstein, *Canada's Army,* 300, 304-307; Copp, *Brigade,* 177, 180; Bill McNeil, *Voices of a War Remembered: An Oral History of Canadians in World War Two* (Toronto: Doubleday, 1991), 257; Stacey, *Official History,* vol. 3, 460-461, 491, 522, 527, 575-576, 611; Granatstein and Morton, *Nation Forged in Fire,* 70-71.

107 Moyles, *Blood and Fire,* 202; Hurst, *Canadian YMCA,* 105-106; JLG, box 7, file 111, *How to See Paris,* n.d.; YWCA, vol. 9, file 68, Minutes of the Executive Committee, YMCA National War Services Committee, 26 Oct. 1944.

108 DND, vol. 16,643, clipping from *Maple Leaf* entitled "Calvados," n.d., n.p, and clipping from 28 March 1945, n.p.

109 NHW, vol. 1238, file 311-V3-15, VD Control Programme – North-West Europe, First Canadian Army, n.d.

110 DND, vol. 12,613, file 218-7, Venereal Disease, Means of Spread, Dec. 1944; George McMillan, interview by author, Edmonton, 28 Sept. 1992.

111 NHW, vol. 1238, file 311-V3-15, VD Control Programme – North-West Europe, First Canadian Army, n.d.; DND, vol. 12,612, file 217-32, Regulation of Prostitution, Town of Antwerp, n.d.; DND, vol. 12,613, file 218-8, Ghent Area, VDCO Report, March 1945, and Preliminary Report Regarding VD Control and Epidemiology in Brussels, n.d.

112 Stacey, *Official History,* vol. 3, 581-583, 609; Granatstein and Morton, *Nation Forged in Fire,* 235; David Kaufman, *A Liberation Album: Canadians in the Netherlands* (Toronto: McGraw-Hill Ryerson, 1981), 17-19, 33, 53.

113 Kaufman, *Liberation Album,* 70-71, 133; Frost, *Once a Patricia,* 462; DND, vol. 10,926, file 239 C3(D23), Morale Report, 14 Canadian Field Ambulance, July 1945; *Saturday Night,* 17 Nov. 1945, 2; The Foundation Liberation '45, "To All Dutch Friends in Canada," <www.apeldoorn-canada.com/starte.html>.

114 Desmond Morton, "'Kicking and Complaining': Demobilization Riots and the Canadian Expeditionary Force, 1918-19," *Canadian Historical Review* 61, 3 (1980): 334-360; Dave Lamb, *Mutinies, 1917-20* (Leeds: Solidarity Press, 1977), 9-12.

115 DND, vol. 19,547, file 215 A21.023(D1), Report on Morale, July 1945; DND, vol. 10,508, file 215A21.009(D70), Morale Report, 15 Sept. 1945; Kaufman, *Liberation Album,* 141.

116 Kaufman, *Liberation Album,* 131; DND, vol. 10,568, file 215 C1(D40), Memo, 21 Army Group, 12 June 1945.

117 DND, vol. 15,631, file "War Diary," Senior Chaplain (RC), 5th Cdn Armoured Division, 25 and 26 July 1945, and Senior Chaplain (RC), 2nd Cdn Infantry Division, 6 Aug. 1945; Stacey and Wilson, *Half-Million,* 140; Kaufman, *Liberation Album,* 137-138, 141.

118 Kaufman, *Liberation Album,* 138-139; *Maclean's,* 19 April 1999, 20-21.

119   DND, vol. 10,924, file 239 C1.7(D14), Control of VD, Netherlands, 23 April 1945; DND, vol. 12,612, file 217-32, Regulation of Prostitution, Town of Antwerp, n.d.; DND, vol. 12,613, file 218-8, Report by Major W.P. Turner, RCMP, 3 June 1945.

120   DND, vol. 10,924, file 239 C1.7(D19), Memo from Col. W.L. Coke, 1st Cdn Infantry Division, 11 July 1945, and Memo from Brigadier H.M. Elder, DDMS, 1st Cdn Army, 30 June 1945.

121   Stacey, *Official History*, vol. 3, 65, 621-622.

122   J.L. Granatstein and Desmond Morton, *Victory 1945: Canadians from War to Peace* (Toronto: HarperCollins, 1995), 159-160; Hurst, *Canadian YMCA*, 195; DND, vol. 10,568, file 215 C1(D40), Memo from Brigadier J.F.A. Lister, 28 March 1945; DND, vol. 16,643, clipping from *Maple Leaf*, 30 March 1945, n.p.

123   DND, vol. 10,794, file 225 C1.009(D6), Report from Chief of Staff, 25 German Army, 28 May 1945. On the Soviet rampage in postwar Berlin, see Antony Beevor, *Fall of Berlin 1945* (New York: Penguin, 2002).

124   DND, vol. 10,568, file 215 C1(D40), Memo on Rationing in Germany, n.d.; DND, vol. 10,547, file 215 A21.023 (D1), 21 Army Group, Censorship Report, 1-15 Aug. 1945; JLG, box 6, file 96, Brigadier Cameron Murphy to family, 29 July 1944; DHH, 581.023 (D1), Morale Report, 23 Nov. 1945.

125   Barry Broadfoot, *The Veterans' Years: Coming Home from the War* (Vancouver: Douglas and McIntyre, 1985), 236-237.

126   DND, vol. 10,508, file 215 A21.009(D70), Morale Report, 15 Aug. 1945 and 15 Nov. 1945. In fairness, this rate of infection was a product not only of strong demand but also a badly tainted supply. Technically, the Third Reich outlawed prostitution, but to boost the morale of its military it often ignored red light districts where prostitutes, being illegal, were not obliged to take regular medical examinations. Between 1939 and 1942, VD rates soared by 100 percent in Hamburg, 170 percent in Munich, and 200 percent in Frankfurt. DND, vol. 12,612, file 218-4, VDCO's Monthly Report, Jan. 1946; Costello, *Love, Sex and War*, 331.

127   DND, vol. 12,612, file 218-4, Text of ADMS Conference, HQ, 3rd Cdn Infantry Division, 15 Nov. 1945, and VDCO's Monthly Report, Jan. 1946.

128   C.P. Stacey, *Arms, Men and Government: The War Policies of Canada, 1939-1945* (Ottawa: Department of National Defence, 1970), 66.

CHAPTER 10: A NEW BEGINNING

1   National Archives of Canada (NAC), MG30 C181, Robert England papers (RE) vol. 2, file 1940-44, Address by Ian Mackenzie, 6 Dec. 1940. For details on programs for Great War veterans see Desmond Morton and Glenn Wright, *Winning the Second Battle: Canadian Veterans Return to Civilian Life, 1915-1930* (Toronto: University of Toronto Press, 1987). On the roles played by veterans in the Winnipeg strike see D.C. Masters, *The Winnipeg General Strike* (Toronto: University of Toronto Press, 1950), and David J. Bercuson, *Fools and Wise Men: The Rise and Fall of the One Big Union* (Toronto: McGraw-Hill Ryerson, 1978).

2   *Maclean's*, 1 Dec. 1939, 2.

3   Also on the committee were the ministers of public works, national defence, agriculture, and labour. NAC, MG27 III B5, Ian Mackenzie papers (IM), vol. 60, file 527-61(4), PC 4068.5, 8 Dec. 1939.

4   Dean Oliver, "Canadian Demobilization in World War II," in *The Good Fight: Canadians in the Second World War,* ed. J.L. Granatstein and Peter Neary (Toronto: Copp Clark Longman, 1995), 370.

5   RE, vol. 2, file 1940-43, "New Veterans and Old Fictions," 1942.

6   Woods went on to become the first deputy minister of veterans affairs. Walter Woods, *Rehabilitation (A Combined Operation), Being a History of the Development and Carrying*

out of a Plan for the Re-Establishment of a Million Young Veterans of World War II by the Department of Veterans Affairs and its Predecessor the Department of Pensions and National Health (Ottawa: Queen's Printer, 1953), vi.

7 The Western Hemisphere was defined as "the continents of North and South America, the islands adjacent thereto and the territorial waters thereof including Newfoundland, Bermuda and the West Indies." J.L. Granatstein and Peter Neary, eds., *The Veterans Charter and Post-War Canada* (Montreal and Kingston: McGill-Queen's University Press, 1998), 259.

8 NAC, RG38, Department of Veterans Affairs records (DVA), vol. 364, file "General Clippings, 1943-52," clipping from *Saturday Night,* 22 April 1944, n.p.

9 A veteran had to reapply to his former boss within three months of being honourably discharged and could be denied his old job only if he had originally held it after another and longer-serving veteran who also reapplied. RE, vol. 2, file 1938-44, *Reinstatement in Civil Employment Act, 1942; Canadian Unionist,* July 1941, 27.

10 Morton and Wright, *Winning the Second Battle,* 94, 134; *Veteran,* Feb. 1919, 2; NAC, RG24, Department of National Defence records (DND), vol. 12,278, file 26-37, Routine Order 2080, n.d.; RE, vol. 2, file 1940-43, Report on General Advisory Committee on Demobilization and Rehabilitation, Nov. 1941.

11 *Ottawa Citizen,* 30 Aug. 1945, 2; Jane Ursel, *Private Lives, Public Policy: 100 Years of State Intervention in the Family* (Toronto: Women's Press, 1992), 224.

12 *Public Opinion Quarterly,* 1942, 665.

13 See J.L. Granatstein, *The Ottawa Men: The Civil Service Mandarins, 1935-1957* (Toronto: University of Toronto Press, 1982), chapter 6; J.L. Granatstein, *Canada's War: The Politics of the Mackenzie King Government, 1939-1945* (Toronto: Oxford University Press, 1975), chapter 7; and Doug Owram, *The Government Generation: Canadian Intellectuals and the State, 1900-1945* (Toronto: University of Toronto Press, 1986), chapters 9-11.

14 Directorate of History and Heritage, Department of National Defence (DHH), 113.3 R4003 V1(D1), Unit Survey, May 1943.

15 *Canadian Forum,* Aug. 1944, 100.

16 DVA, vol. 272, Press Release No. 54, 28 Nov. 1944.

17 Dean F. Oliver, "Public Opinion and Public Policy in Canada: Federal Legislation on War Veterans, 1939-46," in *The Welfare State in Canada: Past, Present and Future,* ed. Raymond B. Blake, Penny E. Bryden, and J. Frank Strain (Toronto: Irwin Publishing, 1997), 198.

18 *Khaki* 1, 20: 3; DVA, vol. 183, file 31-8-44, Memo to Governor General, 17 March 1944.

19 NAC, RG36-31, Wartime Information Board records (WIB), vol. 11, file 6-3-5, Rehabilitation Information Committee, Film Sub-Committee, Report, 19 March 1945; National Film Board (NFB), *Welcome Soldier,* 1944.

20 More popular was the satirical *Johnny Home Show,* which started broadcasting weekly soon after D-Day. Starring Johnny Wayne and Frank Shuster of the No. 1 Canadian Entertainment Unit, it presented a humorous take on the trials and tribulations servicemen might face after returning home, including with the DVA bureaucracy. Some officials criticized the show for "celebrating two shiftless smart-alecs," but most military and government authorities accepted it as a morale booster. WIB, vol. 9, file 6-3-5-8-1, Canadian Broadcasting Corporation, Rehabilitation Programs Committee, Report 3, 11 Dec. 1944, and file "Johnny Home Show."

21 Dean F. Oliver, "Awaiting Return: Life in the Canadian Army's Repatriation Depots, 1945-1946," in *The Veterans Charter and Post-War Canada,* ed. J.L. Granatstein and Peter Neary (Montreal and Kingston: McGill-Queen's University Press, 1998), 41.

22 DHH, 113.3 R4003(D1), Rehabilitation: A Survey of Opinions Among Army Personnel Awaiting Discharge, Dec. 1944.

23 IM, vol. 64, file 527-132, OR Feelings Concerning their Post-War Welfare, Nov. 1944.

24 *Canadian Forum,* July 1945, 80.

25 C.P. Stacey, *Six Years of War: The Army in Canada, Britain and the Pacific* (Ottawa: Department of National Defence, 1966), 432; Oliver, "Canadian Demobilization," 367-386.

26 C.P. Stacey, *Official History of the Canadian Army in the Second World War,* vol. 3, *The Victory Campaign: The Operations in Northwest Europe, 1944-1945* (Ottawa: Department of National Defence, 1960), 617; Stacey, *Six Years of War,* 433-434; Oliver, "Awaiting Return," 36, 51-52; WIB, vol. 17, file 9-6-2-1, Department of National Defence (Army), Public Relations Future Release, 4 July 1945.

27 NAC, RG19, Department of Finance records (FN), vol. 4031, file 129-W-1-23, clipping from *Consumer Facts,* Sept. 1945, n.p.; DND, vol. 10,508, file 15 A21.009(D68), "After Victory in Europe," May 1945, n.p.; J.L. Granatstein and Desmond Morton, *Victory 1945: Canadians from War to Peace* (Toronto: HarperCollins, 1995), 141-142; Michael Stevenson, "The Industrial Selection and Release Plan and the Premature Release of Personnel from the Armed Forces, 1945-1946," in *Uncertain Horizons: Canadians and Their World in 1945,* ed. Greg Donaghy (Ottawa: Canadian Council for the History of the Second World War, 1996), 115-132.

28 DHH, 312.023(D1), Field Censor's Report, 6 June 1945; Oliver, "Canadian Demobilization," 379.

29 DND, vol. 12,705, file 272/7; Oliver, "Awaiting Return," 44-45.

30 NAC, RG2, Privy Council records (PC), Cabinet Conclusions, 6 Jan. 1946.

31 IM, vol. 64, file 527-132, OR Feelings Concerning Their Post-War Welfare, Nov. 1944; J.L. Granatstein, *Canada's Army: Waging War and Keeping the Peace* (Toronto: University of Toronto Press, 2002), 309.

32 York University Archives, Jack Lawrence Granatstein papers, box 4, file 67, Rev. J.A. Falconbridge to Laura and James, 19 Sept. 1945.

33 WIB, vol. 17, file 9-6-2-1, Postwar Planning Information, n.d.; WIB, vol. 14, file 8-14b, WIB Lecture Sheets, n.d.; IM, vol. 57, file 527-14(b), Speech by Mackenzie, 31 Dec. 1945; DND, vol. 12,279, file 27/45, Memo from General H.D.G. Crerar, n.d.; Oliver, "Awaiting Return," 41, 46-47.

34 DND, vol. 10,513, file 215 A21.009, Address entitled "Going Home," Aug. 1945; Glenbow Institute (GB), MU6222, file 3, *Report Centre,* 11 Jan. 1945.

35 *Chatelaine,* May 1944, 9.

36 Susan M. Hartmann, "Prescriptions for Penelope: Literature on Women's Obligations to Returning World War II Veterans," *Women's Studies* 5, 3 (1978): 223-239; *Canadian Home Journal,* May 1944, 8-9, and Aug. 1945, 2-3.

37 Edward C. McDonagh, "The Discharged Serviceman and His Family," *American Journal of Sociology* 51, 5 (1946): 452.

38 NAC, MG30 I311, Montreal Soldiers' Wives' League papers (MSWL), vol. 3, file 64, Brigadier G.B. Chisholm, "Women's Responsibility for Mental Reestablishment of Soldiers," 13 Nov. 1944; DVA, vol. 372, News Release No. 77, 24 March 1945, News Release No. 85, 23 May 1945, and News Release No. 243, n.d.

39 WIB, vol. 18, file "Edmonton," Minutes of Monthly General Meeting of the Citizen's Rehabilitation Council of the City of Edmonton, 18 Dec. 1944; DVA, vol. 372, News Release No. 172, n.d.

40 Granatstein and Morton, *Victory 1945,* 160.

41 Barry Broadfoot, *The Veterans' Years: Coming Home from the War* (Vancouver: Douglas and McIntyre, 1985), 14.

42 Bill Irvine, interview by author, Edmonton, 20 Nov. 1992; Magda Fahrni, "Under Reconstruction: The Family and the Public in Postwar Montréal, 1944-1949" (PhD diss., York University, 2001), 188.

43 DHH, 322.009(D217), Morale Report, Pacific Command, 20 July 1945.

44 WIB, vol. 14, file 8-14-6, pt. 2, Attitudes of Army Personnel Recently Returned from Overseas, 20 Nov. 1944.

45 Bill McNeil, *Voices of a War Remembered: An Oral History of Canadians in World War Two* (Toronto: Doubleday, 1991), 241-242; Donald F. Ripley, *The Home Front: Wartime Life at Camp Aldershot and in Kentville, Nova Scotia* (Hantsport, NS: Lancelot Press, 1991), 188.

46 *Canadian Forum*, May 1945, 38-39, and Aug. 1945, 105.

47 *Khaki* 3, 23: 3; *Khaki* 3, 25: 3.

48 NFB, "Getting the Most out of a Film," a filmed discussion appended to the NFB's movie, *Welcome Soldier*; Fahrni, "Under Reconstruction," 172-173.

49 WIB, vol. 14, file 8-14-E, OR Feelings Concerning their Post-War Discharge, n.d.; Broadfoot, *Veterans' Years*, 212.

50 Instructive in this regard is an American study that tracked representative samples of veteran and civilian males between 1945 and 1950. It discovered that in every age cohort, veterans married far more quickly. John Modell and Duane Steffey, "Waging War and Marriage: Military Service and Family Formation, 1940-1950," *Journal of Family History* 13, 2 (1988): 212; FN, vol. 4031, file 129-W-1-23, Rehabilitation Trends, Montreal, Nov. 1945.

51 Eleanor Taylor, interview, Eastern Townships Research Centre, Lennoxville, QC, Special Media Collection, Oral History of Eastern Townships, Anglophone Women during World War II.

52 *Canada Year Book, 1946*, 1113; *Canada Year Book, 1947*, 283; Fahrni, "Under Reconstruction," 147.

53 *Saturday Night,* 23 Feb. 1946, 29.

54 Mona Gleason, "Psychology and the Construction of the 'Normal' in Postwar Canada, 1945-1960," *Canadian Historical Review* 78, 3 (1997): 456; NAC, MG28 I95, Young Men's Christian Association papers (YMCA), vol. 50, file "Divorce in Canada 1936-49," unidentified clipping entitled "Social Welfare Groups Consider Action to Combat Divorce," n.d., n.p.

55 YMCA, vol. 50, file "Divorce in Canada 1936-49," clipping from *Ottawa Citizen*, 7 Feb. 1946, n.p.; Archives of Ontario, RG4, Attorney-General records, 615/1946; Wendy Owen and J.M. Bumsted, "Divorce in a Small Province: A History of Divorce on Prince Edward Island from 1833," *Acadiensis* 20, 2 (1991): 98-101.

56 *Canada Year Book, 1955*, 224.

57 Broadfoot, *Veterans' Years*, 121, 141, 144-145; McDonagh, "Discharged Serviceman," 452.

58 Joyce Hibbert, *The War Brides* (Toronto: Peter Martin Associates, 1978), 103; Broadfoot, *Veterans' Years*, 133.

59 Some charged that the war brides were like prostitutes, having "hung around ... [military] camps" to lure Canadian servicemen so they could leave behind the misery of war-ravaged Britain or Europe. *Vancouver Sun,* 25 Aug. 1945, 4; Ben Wicks, *When the Boys Came Marching Home: True Stories of the Men Who Went to War and the Women and Children Who Took Them Back* (Toronto: Stoddart, 1991), 118-119; *Canadian Home Journal*, May 1945, 68.

60 MSWL, vol. 3, File 54, Press Release, 15 Dec. 1945; WIB, vol. 8, File 2-26, L.B. Connery to W.S. Durdin, 13 Jan. 1947.

61 McDonagh, "Discharged Serviceman," 454.

62 Broadfoot, *Veterans' Years,* 412.

63 Sheila Waengler, interview by author, Toronto, 12 Aug. 1999.

64 WIB, vol. 14, File 8-14-E, OR Feelings Regarding their Post-War Welfare, 7 Feb. 1945.

65 Mary Turner, interview, 2 March 1983, NAC, Audiovisual Division, Tape R-8550; Diane G. Forestell, "The Victorian Legacy: Historical Perspectives on the Canadian Women's Army Corps" (PhD diss., York University, 1985), 171.

66 Jean Bruce, *Back the Attack! Canadian Women during the Second World War – at Home and Abroad* (Toronto: Macmillan, 1985), 161; Broadfoot, *Veterans' Years*, 140.

67 *Vancouver Sun,* 23 Aug. 1945, 19.

68 DND, vol. 10,924, File 239 C1.7(D19), First Cdn Army, Medical Instructions, 28 July 1945; W.R. Feasby, *Official History of the Canadian Medical Services, 1939-1945,* vol. 2 (Ottawa: Queen's Printer, 1956), 114; Archives of Alberta, 68.145, Department of Public Health, *Annual Report, 1945,* 61.

69 Statistics Canada, *Incidence of Notifiable Diseases by Province, Number of Cases and Rates, 1924-1968* (Ottawa: Statistics Canada, 1968), 86-91.

70 William Horrocks, *In Their Own Words* (Ottawa: Rideau Veterans Home Residents Council, 1993), 226; Wicks, *When the Boys Came Marching Home,* 91.

71 *Canadian Home Journal,* July 1945, 5-7, 22; Patricia Galloway, ed., *Too Young to Fight: Memories from Our Youth during World War II* (Toronto: Stoddart, 1999), 91.

72 During the war the army discharged 8,018 men for various "mental, nervous and psychotic" disorders, though these were only the most serious cases. E.L.M. Burns, *Manpower in the Canadian Army, 1939-1945* (Toronto: Clarke, Irwin, 1956), 113.

73 Turner, interview.

74 DND, vol. 2093, File 54-27-7-391, "Psychoneurotics Discharged from the Canadian Army," excerpt reprinted from the *Canadian Medical Association Journal,* vol. 52, 1945, n.p.; Terry Copp, "From Neurasthenia to Post-Traumatic Stress Disorder: Canadian Veterans and the Problem of Emotional Disabilities," in *The Veterans Charter and Post-War Canada,* ed. J.L. Granatstein and Peter Neary (Montreal and Kingston: McGill-Queen's University Press, 1998), 153-154.

75 In 1952, from the sale of Japanese assets in Canada authorized under the formal peace treaty between Japan and the Allies, these Canadian POWs were provided with a lump sum payment of one dollar per day of captivity, on average $1,360. In 1958 they received another fifty cents per day. In 1964 the Canadian Pension Commission undertook an analysis of the "Hong Kong veterans" that revealed abnormally high rates of "optic atrophy, neurological, muscular and minor circulatory defects of the feet and legs ... and coronary artery disease." In 1969 all those held by the Japanese were given a minimum pension of 50 percent of the maximum pension award. In 1987 the War Amps of Canada argued before the United Nations Human Rights Commission to have the Japanese pay these men restitution, but were "stonewalled" by Tokyo. Finally, in December 1998 Canada's federal government provided another $24,000 in compensation to each of the 350 surviving POWs held by the Japanese, and to the widows of former prisoners. Dave McIntosh, *Hell on Earth: Aging Faster, Dying Sooner. Canadian Prisoners of the Japanese during World War Two* (Toronto: McGraw-Hill Ryerson, 1997), 250-255, 258; War Amps of Canada, "Government Pays Hong Kong Claims on Humanitarian Basis," 11 Dec. 1998, <www.waramps.ca>; Jonathan F. Vance, *Objects of Concern: Canadian Prisoners of War through the Twentieth Century* (Vancouver: UBC Press, 1994), 221-225.

76 Daniel Dancocks, *In Enemy Hands: Canadian Prisoners of War, 1939-1945* (Edmonton: Hurtig Publishers, 1983), 281; Joyce Hibbert, *Fragments of War: Stories from Survivors of World War II* (Toronto: Dundurn Press, 1985), 111; DND, vol. 12,631, File 224/18, Lt.-Col. A.T.M. Wilson, RAMC, "Report to the War Office on the Psychological Aspects of the Rehabilitation of Repatriated Prisoners of War," Feb. 1944.

77 Cliff Humford, interview by author, Edmonton, 24 Oct. 1992.

78 Metropolitan Toronto Library, Baldwin Room, untitled pamphlet distributed by Rehabilitation Wing, No. 2 District Depot, n.d.; DVA, vol. 372, News Release No. 138, 18 Oct. 1945 and News Release No. 147, n.d.

79 Many other DVA employees were seconded from the Department of Labour or had a background in adult education or personnel service. DVA, vol. 272, Memo entitled "Training of Rehabilitation Counsellors," n.d.; DVA, vol. 372, News Release No. 63, 27 Nov. 1944.

80 DVA, vol. 272, News Release No. 200, n.d.; Granatstein and Morton, *Victory 1945*, 161-162.

81 DVA, vol. 183, File 61-28, clipping from *Rehabilitation News*, 30 April 1945, n.p.

82 Walter Woods, *Rehabilitation*, 63-64, 70-71; RE, vol. 2, File 1938-44, Notes on *War Service Grants Act*, n.d.; NAC, RG27, Ministry of Labour records, vol. 2349, File 22-5-14, Memorandum on Progress of Veteran Rehabilitation, 1947.

83 DVA, vol. 272, News Release No. 147, n.d.

84 Eighteen months after the war, that figure rose to over 95 percent. DVA, vol. 272, News Release No. 255, 21 Nov. 1946, and News Release No. 259, 3 Jan. 1947; Robert Bothwell and William Kilbourn, *C.D. Howe: A Biography* (Toronto: McClelland and Stewart, 1979), chapter 12; Granatstein and Neary, *Good Fight*, 452.

85 Said Ian Mackenzie on this point, "We don't want our ex-servicemen and women spending their gratuities for a purpose for which the out-of-work benefit was designed." DVA, vol. 272, News Release No. 162A, n.d.

86 Woods, *Rehabilitation*, 107; DND, vol. 12,278, File 27-1, Bulletin on Vocational Training for Ex-Service Personnel, 1944.

87 IM, vol. 58, File 527-41(3), "Vocational Training on Civvy Street."

88 DVA, vol. 272, News Release No. 261, 16 Jan. 1947; Walter Woods, *Rehabilitation*, 87.

89 Woods, *Rehabilitation*, 109.

90 DVA, vol. 272, News Release No. 259, 3 Jan. 1947, and News Release No. 260, 15 Jan. 1947.

91 DVA, vol. 272, News Release No. 80, 13 April 1945; DND, vol. 12,278, File 26-37, pamphlet entitled "The Veterans Land Act," March 1944.

92 Some men qualified overseas while awaiting their repatriation to Canada, as the army ran an agricultural school in Dordrecht, Netherlands, between 29 July and 15 December 1945. Oliver, "Awaiting Return," 53; DND, vol. 12,278, File 27-1, Bulletin on Vocational Training for Ex-Service Personnel, 1944; IM, vol. 60, File 527-61(4), Second Report of the *Veterans Land Act* for the Fiscal Year Ended 31 March 1944; Morton and Wright, *Winning the Second Battle*, 148, 204.

93 *Canada Year Book, 1947*, 1147; DVA, vol. 272, News Release No. 252, n.d.; DVA, vol. 364, File "General Clippings," clipping from *Winnipeg Tribune*, 13 Nov. 1947, n.p.

94 DVA, vol. 364, File "General Clippings," clipping from *Red Deer Advocate*, 17 Nov. 1954, n.p.

95 DVA, vol. 364, File "General Clippings," clipping from *Financial Post*, 5 Oct. 1946, n.p.; Woods, *Rehabilitation*, 107-109.

96 As of February 1951, of the 9,000 veterans who started university without enough credited military service to cover the time necessary to complete their degree, 6,068, or 67.4 percent, had been granted an extension of funding. P.B. Waite, *The Lives of Dalhousie University: The Old College Transformed, 1925-1980* (Montreal and Kingston: McGill-Queen's University Press, 1998), 148; DVA, vol. 272, News Release No. 256, n.d.; Peter Neary, "Canadian Universities and Canadian Veterans of World War II," in *The Veterans Charter and Post-War Canada*, ed. J.L. Granatstein and Peter Neary (Montreal and Kingston: McGill-Queen's University Press, 1998), 122, 124, 128-129.

97 For example, during the 1947-48 academic year, just 48 veterans enrolled at Bishop's University compared to 6,858 at the University of Toronto. Neary, "Canadian Universities," 139-141.

98 *Saturday Night*, 14 April 1945, 14; *Vancouver Sun*, 31 Aug. 1945, 11, and 15 Sept. 1945, 5.

99 *Canada Year Book, 1948-49*, 322-323.

100 Neary, "Canadian Universities," 119, 127-128; DVA, vol. 364, File "General Clippings," unidentified and undated clipping; PC, vol. 2637, Cabinet Conclusions, 2 Aug. 1945; L.G. Thomas, *The University of Alberta in the War, 1939-1945* (Edmonton: n.p., 1948), 58; Martin Friedland, *The University of Toronto: A History* (Toronto: University of Toronto Press, 2002), 373.

101 The maximum total that could be borrowed was $2,000. Each loan was interest-free for the first year and calculated at 5 percent per annum thereafter. Walter Woods, *Rehabilitation*, 95; DVA, vol. 364, File "General Clippings," undated and unattributed article entitled "Mackenzie Replies to Student Vets' Brief"; Broadfoot, *Veterans' Years*, 143-144.

102 For details on this dispute and militancy among several veterans, especially those from McGill University, see Neary, "Canadian Universities," 135-137.

103 Also, the government allowance could be reduced if a veteran skipped classes. However, this rule was hard to enforce given the large number of students in many courses. DVA, vol. 364, File "General Clippings," clipping from *Varsity Magazine*, 8 Nov. 1949, n.p.

104 DVA, vol. 364, File "General Clippings," clipping from *Financial Post*, 5 Oct. 1946, n.p.

105 WIB, vol. 14, File 8-14-E, Report of a Survey of Thirty-Two Ex-Service Personnel Attending the University of Toronto, 20 Feb. 1945.

106 Waite, *Lives of Dalhousie University*, 148; DVA, vol. 364, File "General Clippings," unidentified and undated clipping, and clipping from *Financial Post*, 5 Oct. 1946, n.p.; Friedland, *University of Toronto*, 372.

107 Neary, "Canadian Universities," 128-129.

108 Granatstein, *Canada's Army*, 204; DHH, 113.3 R4003(D1), "Rehabilitation: A Survey of Opinions among Army Personnel Awaiting Discharge," prepared by Coord 2, Adjutant-General Branch, Oct. 1945.

109 Broadfoot, *Veterans' Years*, 56, 184, 192.

110 Woods, *Rehabilitation*, 109.

111 Morton and Wright, *Winning the Second Battle*, 153, 220; Desmond Morton, "'Noblest and Best': Retraining Canada's War Disabled, 1915-1923," *Journal of Canadian Studies* 16, 3/4 (1981): 77; *Canada Year Book, 1920*, 688.

112 *New Advance*, July 1941, 20-21.

113 Within these ranges, officers above the rank of lieutenant received higher rates. DVA, vol. 183, File 31-8-44, Memo to the Governor in Council, 17 March 1945.

114 For example, just weeks after VJ day, the pension rate for total deafness went from 50 to 80 percent of the maximum award. DVA, vol. 272, News Release No. 30, n.d., and News Release No. 153, 22 Nov. 1945; IM, vol. 11, File 3-125, Speech by Mackenzie, 11 Dec. 1945.

115 For any pensionable injury, veterans had the right to free medical treatment in perpetuity. All veterans received free medical care for one year following their discharge, during which at least some initially overlooked war-related and pensionable injuries were discovered. For veterans with an annual income below $1,200, free treatment at DVA facilities continued past the one-year point for a number of ailments. In 1953, after many complaints, the DVA introduced a sliding scale of medical coverage for those earning between $1,200 and $2,500 per annum. DVA, vol. 364, File "General Clippings, part 2, 1953-55," clipping from *Blyth Standard*, 20 Oct. 1954, n.p.; DVA, vol. 272, News Release No. 205, n.d.; DND, vol. 12,278, File 26-37, Department of Pensions and National Health News Release, 1 Jan. 1944.

116 DVA, vol. 272, News Release No. 139, n.d., and News Release No. 193, 23 March 1946; DVA, vol. 362, File 1946-62, clipping from *DEE-VEE-AYE*, vol. 2, No. 9, Oct. 1947, 1.

117 DVA, vol. 372, File "DVA New-Rel," Casualty Rehabilitation, n.d.; YMCA, vol. 272, File 8, *Rehabilitation: Read All about It*, 1945, n.p.

118 *Industrial Canada*, July 1945, 318-319; RE, vol. 2, File 1940-44, Employment of Canada's Disabled, pt. 1.

119 *Canada Year Book, 1948-49*, 1160; Woods, *Rehabilitation*, 370.

120 See Senate of Canada, *The Aboriginal Soldier after the Wars: Report of the Senate Standing Committee on Aboriginal Peoples* (Ottawa: Queen's Printer, 1995). Another dispute concerned veterans who were mentally unable to care for themselves and housed long-term in DVA institutions. On their behalf, a class action suit was launched in 1999 claiming that

the DVA, in the administration of their pensions, failed to fulfill its fiduciary responsibilities as trustee because it did not secure any interest on these funds. In July 2003 the Supreme Court of Canada ruled in favour of the federal government. *Joseph Patrick Authorson v. the Attorney General of Canada,* Ontario Superior Court, File No. 99-GD-45963; *National Post,* 18 July 2003, A6; DVA, vol. 364, File "General Clippings," clipping from *New Glasgow News,* 24 Feb. 1954, n.p., clipping from *Prince Rupert Examiner,* 11 March 1955, n.p., and clipping from *Lethbridge Herald,* 19 July 1955, n.p.

Index

Note: "f" after a number indicates a figure.

abortions, 128
absenteeism, 55, 112, 134, 135f, 158
accommodation, 75
  crisis, 77-81
  landlords, 82-83, 85
  permit system, 87
  surveys of homeowners, 81
  tenants, 81, 82, 83-84
  for veterans, 87, 89-90
  for war workers, 29, 77
  See also housing; rent
Action libérale nationale, 19
Adams, Michael, *The Best War Ever,* 3
Adjutant-General's Office, 178
adolescent girls, 208-210
  facilities for delinquent, 224
  illegitimate births, 209-210
  and servicemen, 134, 209
  sexual behaviour, 208-209
  VD rates among, 209
adolescents. *See* adolescent girls; children; youth
Advisory Committee on Demobilization and Rehabilitation, 190, 262
Advisory Committee on Postwar Reconstruction, 85, 162
Ahearn, Thomas, 34
Air Board, 15
Air Cadets, 203
air force. *See* Royal Canadian Air Force (RCAF)
Air Raid Protection (ARP) program, 35-37, 203

air support, for convoys, 237
air traffic controllers, 185
air training
  casualty rates, 131
  construction for, 48
  See also British Commonwealth Air Training Plan (BCATP)
air transportation, 99
aircraft, 234-236. *See also names of individual aircraft*
Aircraft Repair Limited, 48, 78, 84
airgraphs, 124
airmail service, 124
airmen, 131, 234-236
  in Bomber Command, 234-236
  losses among, 234, 235-236
  morale of, 235-236
  strike in Odiham, 264
  See also servicemen
airwomen
  in information-handling trades, 185
  Women's Auxiliary Air Force (WAAF), 176
  See also servicewomen
Ajax (ON), 78
Alaska Highway, 50, 51-53, 79, 88
Alberta
  air training in, 49
  anti-VD campaign in, 142
  Borstal system in, 226
  Child Welfare Act, 224
  coal miners in, 61, 102-103
  committee on treatment of juvenile offenders, 224